JOURNEY

OF A LIFETIME

To Alan and Mair,
from a fellow Rhondda product.
Kindest Regards,
John.
18.xi.08.

FROM THE DIARIES OF JOHN MORGANS

COMMENTS BY JOHN AND NORAH MORGANS

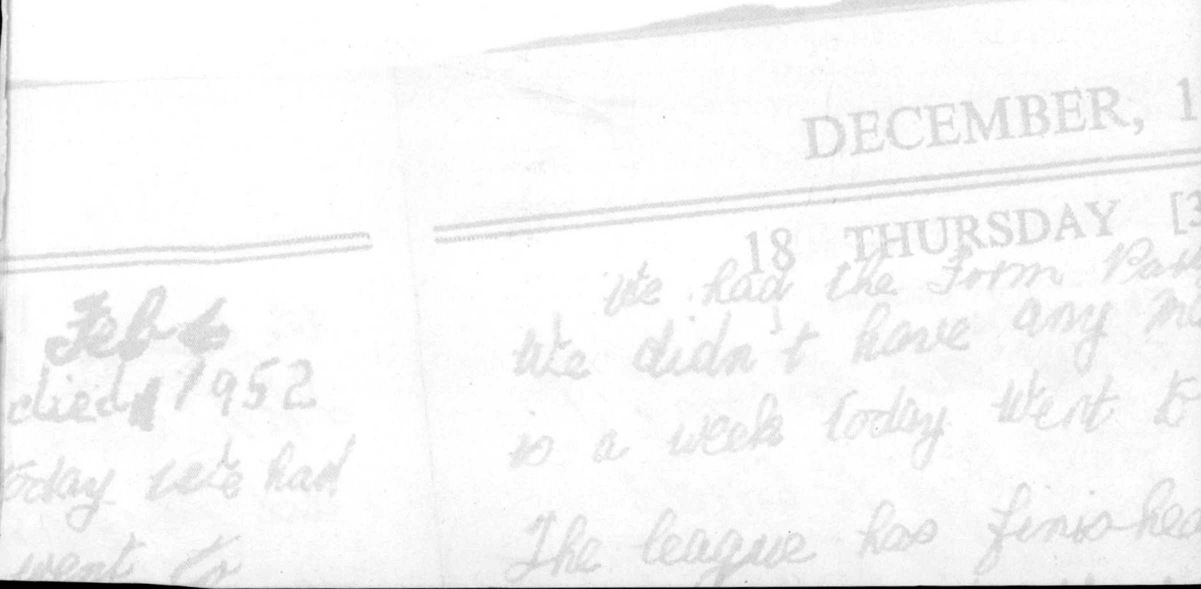

ISBN 978-0-9560689-0-3

The publishers and authors wish to thank Faber and Faber Ltd
for granting permission to use extracts from T.S. Eliot's Four Quartets.

Cover Photographs:

Ordination of Kevin Watson at Manselton, May 16th, 1987.

Father Robert, Abbot of Caldey, Norah and John on Caldey.

Gathering of 30 Penrhys people with the Ecumenical Pilgrims at the Black Bridge, Pontypridd, preparing to walk the nine miles to Penrhys, May 27th 1995.

Published by John and Norah Morgans

Printed in Wales by Cambrian Printers, Aberystwyth

TO OUR CHILDREN,

HUGH, DYLAN AND CATHERINE

AND TO SHARON,

OUR FRIEND AND CO-WORKER ON PENRHYS

In gratitude to friends over many years who have urged me to publish extracts from my diaries,

and special thanks to our son Hugh, and our friends Mary and John Breeze for their advice after patiently reading through the final text.

We wish to express our gratitude to Jenksdesign
Liz Jenkins, Dai Jones and the staff of Cambrian Printers
for their advice, patience and skill

DECEMBER, 1952

14 SUNDAY [349—17] Feb 6 died 1952

3rd in Advent. Ember Week
King George VI born, 1895

David went back to Ealing today we had

CONTENTS

A WORD OF EXPLANATION

INTRODUCTION

PRELUDE

1.	COUNTY SCHOOL BOY	1952 - 1957	1
2.	STUDENT	1957 - 1967	55
3.	LLANIDLOES	1967 - 1974	175
4.	MANSELTON	1974 - 1977	246
5.	A MODERATOR	1977 - 1989	284
6.	PENRHYS	1989 - 2004	434

POSTLUDE

A WORD OF EXPLANATION

Amongst my gifts for Christmas 1951 was a Letts School-Boys Diary. Dutifully, on the first day of January 1952, I wrote my thoughts for the day that was passing. Little did I imagine that 56 years later, every evening before I sleep, I still pick up the diary and Parker pen I received for my 21st birthday and continue to write. In 1952 I wrote a dozen words each night; since 1955 when I gradulated from Letts to a 'page a day diary,' I write between 250 and 300 words each evening. This has happened every day throughout the years and the total number of words amount to more than 5 million.

When we retired from Penrhys in 2004, I began to read through the diaries for the first time. I soon realized I was describing a world that had passed. I was no longer the boy of twelve (weighing 6 stones, and 4 feet 10 inches in height), or the young man in his twenties, or & .! As I approach my seventieth birthday, I know I am the same person as the twelve year old, but it would be difficult to recognize the effects of the journey, had it not been that 'my life has been recorded in the diaries.'

As I have been changing unconsciously and imperceptibly, so has the world in which we all live. The Tylorstown of 2008 is physically very different from the village in which I was born, just before the outbreak of War in 1939. Most of the terraced streets remain, but the basic infrastructure of pits, chapels, schools and shops has disappeared or been replaced. Alongside the physical changes, the life of the community is also very different. Would my reflections of a 'day and a world that has past' be of interest to anyone other than myself ?

During the three years of reading and recording from the diaries, I also discovered that so much has changed in every aspect of my life journey. The educational establishments, the churches and communities in which I have served are often barely recognisable.

As I read, it is as if I am watching a recording of my life and the life of my times unfolding before my eyes. Although it is a record of a story that has passed, I am also aware that the present is constructed from its foundation. 'A community without a history is like a person without a memory.'

Three quarters of 'The Journey of a Lifetime' is composed of extracts from every diary, and from almost every month from January 1952 to the end of February 2004. It has been an almost impossible task to be concise, but I have managed to extract 160,000 words (less than 3% of the original) which I trust will be of some interest to those who have urged me to put it into print. The content and style of course vary from those of a young schoolboy, to one who has lived through most of the 'seven ages of man.'

In addition to the original diary text, I found it necessary to add explanatory notes about people, places and events within the text (they are in italicised print). I have also included introductions to each 'chapter' or period into which I have divided the main text. For example there is a relatively short introduction to Chapter 1 (County School Boy) but lengthy attempts at explaining the complexities of Chapter 5 (A Moderator) and Chapter 6 (Penrhys).

As I recorded and reflected upon the diaries, I noted the themes of a journey - from childhood to one celebrating his sixty-fifth birthday; from a mining village to a housing estate half a mile away; towards discovering roots and community; and towards seeking to live in the light of the Gospel.

Words cannot express my good fortune/the act of providence that the journey has been made with Norah and our three children, Hugh, Dylan and Catherine. We are grateful that the journey has been in the nature of a common pilgrimage.

INTRODUCTION

Thirty years ago when the Family Bible was entrusted to me, I found within its pages, a newspaper cutting reporting the death of my great-grandmother on July 14th 1908. Her funeral 'took place on Saturday last. Deceased, who was 74 years of age, had resided at Tylorstown for the last 32 years, and was highly respected by all who knew her. A large concourse of people attended the funeral, especially the old inhabitants of the place.'

Elizabeth had come to Pendyrus in 1876 with her husband John Davies and their children. New pits were being opened by Alfred Tylor who gave his name to the new community of Tylorstown. John Davies had been a lodger in 'Pendyrus' before bringing his family across the mountain from Aberdare. The coal seams were reached in 1876 and the first coal was sent to Cardiff in January 1877. John was killed in a pit accident in May 1883, leaving his widow and children destitute, including my grandmother, Miriam who was born in 1872. Miriam was amongst the first pupils to attend the new Tylorstown school which opened in 1881, and when she died in 1953, she was described as the oldest serving member at Ebenezer Welsh Congregational Chapel which began its life in 1877.

This was the beginning of the Tylorstown connection with the Davies/ Morgans (my father's families from Carmarthenshire), and the Williams/Davies (my mother's families from Cardiganshire and Pembrokeshire). All were drawn to the new mining communities of the Upper Rhondda Fach. This connection continued until my father's death in 1983 and the sale of the family home. My father, David Trevor was the son of David and Miriam Morgans of Brynheulog Terrace, and my mother, Elizabeth Morwen, the daughter of Hugh and Elizabeth Davies of Church Terrace. Both grandfathers were coal-miners and chapel deacons, David a Congregationalist, and Hugh a Baptist. Hugh's life however turned towards 'the Sea' during the Depression of the 1920s and 30s, when his life was spent on coal ships steaming from Cardiff to South America.

My father was the first in his family to have higher education. When the family could afford to send one of its sons to further education, they gave Trevor the opportunity. He went to the South Wales Training College, Carmarthen (Trinity College) between 1921 and 1923 where he pursued a Teacher's Training Course. He taught for 44 years in the Rhondda Fach before retiring as Head-teacher of Tylorstown Primary School in 1967. Like his father, he was a deacon at Ebenezer and played a prominent part in community life. My parents (Trevor Morgans and Morwen Davies) married in 1929 and I, their second son, (brother to David who was born 9 years earlier) was born in 1939 in Brynbedw Road where my parents lived the rest of their lives.

Tylorstown, like all South Wales Valley communities owed its existence to coal. It did not exist as a community before the sinking of the first pit in 1876, and its raison d'etre ceased when the last pit closed in 1960. However, when I was growing up in the 1940s and 1950s, Tylorstown was a flourishing community, and I was formed by the presence of an extended family, and the communities of street, school and chapel. It was only after the closure of the colliery that Tylorstown began its rapid decline. Within 40 years it lost its chapels and shops and many of the traditional meeting-places which help create a flourishing community.

As a child Penrhys was synonymous with Penrhys Uchaf farm from which we fetched eggs on Saturday mornings. Although there were also a ruined wall and a derelict well, we were unaware of the long heritage of Penrhys. It did not enter our minds that it was at the crossing point between an ancient ridge road and a cross-valley track between the fords of Pont Rhondda and Pontygwaith. Even when the Statue of Our Lady was erected in 1953, most Nonconformists had more sympathy with the reforms of Latimer and Cromwell than with Medieval Christianity.

Most Valley people did not welcome the creation of the vast housing estate in the late 1960s. 'The Council would be putting all its problems in one place - and why should it be our place? In our back yard?' There was the added danger of losing the open space of the mountains to a housing estate. And of course no more eggs from the farm!

Little did I think that my journey, beginning in Tylorstown would many years later, lead me up the very steep hill to Penrhys.

PRELUDE

July 7th1966

'A high point. Norah and I went to the top of Tylorstown tip, the huge monster looking over the valley. It is 400 feet above the mountain and provides one of the best views in the valleys. I have always wanted to reach the top but it was inaccessible when the pits were operating. The view is spectacular as we looked almost vertically down. A panoramic view of 60 miles.'

We looked south to the Bristol Channel and the hills of Somerset; north to the Brecon Beacons; east to the succession of ridges of the Cynon, Tâf, Rhymni, Sirhowy and Ebbw. To the west, at my very feet was the Rhondda Fach and the village of Tylorstown. I could almost stoop down and cradle it in my arms:

> home of my parents and grandparents since 1876;
> redundant pits,
> 5 and 6, closed since 1936, where two of my great-grandfathers,
> John Davies and David Davies had been killed;
> where my grandfathers Hugh Davies and Dafydd Morgans had
> worked;
> 8 (closed 1936) and 9 (closed 1960);
> Co-op (Cop) and the dozens of shops;
> Welfare Hall for 'the pictures,' snooker and the library;
> Chapels for worship, Sunday Schools, discussions;
> Schools: Tylorstown and Hendrefadog, and the Youth Club;
> Pendyrus Choir and the Silver Band.

At the age of 27 I discovered a sense of community. I could not define the word community, but I sensed I belonged to one. Twenty-one years later ....

December 22nd 1987

I have watched the sun set on the longest day, and rise on the shortest day this year. It was a calculated decision and awesome on both occasions: a kind of death and birth of light and life; a form of death and resurrection. I stood in our bedroom and looked at the sun coming up behind the half dozen trees above Wattstown; I watched it climb and in my imagination I saw it light up Mary and child, while when I looked through the back window, the windows had turned to gold and the whole estate was alight. It was Magnificat Now! In the bleak midwinter we witness the triumph of the light.'

In October 1986, Norah and I and our three children, Hugh (aged 20), Dylan (aged 18) and Catherine (aged 16), moved to Penrhys. As a child 'Penrhys' was Penrhys Uchaf Farm, farmed by Morgan Williams and his family. Although Penrhys had once been famous for its Medieval and Reformation history, it achieved notoriety because of the estate of 951 properties opened on Friday, September 13th 1968. There, as a family we discovered a new kind of community.

> 'We shall not cease from exploration
> And the end of all our exploring
> Will be to arrive where we started
> And know the place for the first time.'
>
> T. S. Eliot, 'Little Gidding.'

COUNTY SCHOOL BOY

1952 - 1957

INTRODUCTION

January 1st 1952 was the day when as a 12 year old, I started keeping a diary. My recording was necessarily brief because from 1952 to 1954, I used a Letts School-Boys Diary which had 7 days on two small pages! As the years passed, the pages grew larger as did my world.

The Letts Diary encouraged me to be methodical. For example, in the 1952 Diary, there were lists of Latin and French verbs, Logarithmic Tables, Books to Read, Sporting Records, a World Atlas; other pages were for school timetables, examination results each term, books and articles borrowed and lent, a book list (51 read), letters written and received, addresses, birthdays, presents, autographs (all the boys in my Form), films (26) seen during the year, sports fixtures and results (Wales rugby, and Cardiff and Swansea soccer), athletics results, pocket money and pages for notes - on one of these I 'competed against myself' in the number of hours of homework I did each week. On another page I recorded lists of cricket players from England, South Africa, India and the West Indies.

As I reflect on this period of six years, I note how unconsciously life was focussed on the nuclear and extended family, most of whom lived within walking distance of home in Brynbedw Road. This was just as well because few people had cars, and although public transport was regular and reliable, people walked a great deal. I note my Saturday evening visits to my father's mother (Mamgu Brynheulog Terrace) until she died in September 1953, and visiting several times each week my mother's parents (Mam and Dac, Church Terrace who died in 1955 and 1964) until I left for University in 1957. Innumerable aunts, uncles and cousins also lived in Tylorstown. [In their turn, my parents became 'Mam' and 'Dac' when they became grandparents.]

The Street was important. Brynbedw was a terrace of 52 houses rising very steeply from the 'main road' (East Road) and, because there were no houses opposite, it offered sunshine, wind, rain and superb views of the Valley below and the mountain and village of Stanleytown opposite. Boys played together in the street and on 'our mountain' which was on the same side as the street and rose to Penrhys and Bristol Tump. We also sometimes ventured across the river and behind Stanleytown to where the 'other mountain' stretched towards mysterious places like Llanwynno and Ynysybwl. To the north was Maerdy and the two reservoirs which we reached by walking along the mountain ridges.

Childhood was lived in Tylorstown. Most shopping was at the local Cooperative on Queen's Square, and all one's needs were catered for along the main street. A few hundred yards from Queen's Square was the Welfare Hall for the cinema, snooker hall, library, reading room and other entertainment. Even when I went three miles away to the County Grammar School at Porth, most of our time was spent in Tylorstown. As I entered mid-teens we ventured as far as Ferndale, our larger neighbour a mile to the north. There we enjoyed the Saturday pictures, the Sunday evening after-chapel 'monkey-parade' when boys walked on one side of the road and girls on the other side (for most of the evening), and had coffee at the Italian Bracchi (as all Italian cafes in Rhondda were called) on the Strand in Ferndale. Just before Christmas came the annual visit for shopping in Cardiff. As I grew into late-teens, Cardiff became a place for occasionally watching sport and visiting the opera.

School dominated a great deal of life with its demands of homework in preparation for O and A levels. When I reached Form VI, I played in the School Cricket XI for two years and enjoyed the weekly match against local schools.

Chapel was the key to our social and religious life and there are innumerable references to Sunday services, Sunday School and the Friday Young People's Guild. Annually there was the Easter Singing Festival (the Gymanfa Ganu) and as years passed under the leadership of our minister, Alwyn Charles, the introduction to an ecumenical world and a wider experience of Wales.

There are many references to sport. At first, games were played in the street - cricket against the telegraph pole, soccer with tins for goal-posts. From the street we ventured to the mountain - the Graig, Moggs Field and the Rose Bowl which we shaped out of the hillside. The first time I played on a level grass wicket was for the school at the age of 17. When on holidays, I began watching Glamorgan cricket and supported them throughout my school years. In the early diaries, I noted the soccer results of the three South Wales professional soccer teams (Newport, Cardiff and Swansea) while International Rugby dominated the end of Winter. As a family, we gathered around the wireless and later the television to follow the Welsh rugby team. My parents did not buy a television until 1957, after I had left for University. That was a deliberate decision.

A great deal of entertainment came through the wireless through which I was introduced to drama, comedy and music, both classical and jazz.

During my early years, holidays were spent with my parents, but from Form V onwards, I also enjoyed holidays with friends from the street, hitch-hiking and youth hostelling in Breconshire in 1955, West Wales in 1956 and Scotland in 1957. I also had two weekends with my brother and his wife Beryl, in London. The world was beginning to widen.

DECEMBER, 1952

14 SUNDAY [349—17] *Feb 6 died 1952*

3rd in Advent. Ember Week
King George VI born, 1895

David went back to Ealing today we had
[illegible] today Uncle [illegible] went to

1952

JANUARY

1st

Party at Uncle Noel's and home at 12 o'clock in time to hear the hooter.

The Colliery Siren greeted the New Year. Noel was my mother's youngest brother, living with his family in Tylorstown. He taught locally and his wife, Mair was a pharmacist. They lived above the shop. People who earned their living in Tylorstown lived in the community: miners, teachers, shop-keepers, all the professions. This provided a balanced community.

2nd

Bristol Tump yesterday.

I climbed the local high mountain, 'Twyn Disgwylfa' on many special occasions. It was called Bristol Tump either because it gave a view of the Bristol Channel, or because the 'Bristol boys' in times past had their fights there with the 'Welsh boys' after drinking on Saturday evenings.

4th

Guild with Dadda for Young People's Prayer Meeting.

The Guild was held every Friday evening in Ebenezer, our local chapel.

Sunday 13th

Chapel all day. In the afternoon there were 85 children. In the night 18 new members were made.

19th

Wales beat England by 8pts to 6 at Twickenham. England were winning 6-0.

26th

Welfare to see 'Lost Stage Valley.' A good cowboy film. Went to Mamgu's.

Sunday 27th

Mam's for tea.

FEBRUARY

6th

The King died in his sleep this morning. My birthday and I had 17/6, a knife and a propelling pencil.

I met the Queen Mother in November 1998 and shared with her the fact that I had recorded the death of George VI on my thirteenth birthday.

Sunday 10th

Chapel this morning and read out a hymn.

MARCH

6th

Mamma went to N.S.P.C.C. meeting in Chapel.

N.S.P.C.C. = The National Society for the Prevention of Cruelty to Children.

8th

Wales beat Ireland 14 -3. They have won the Triple Crown.

17th

I have £2 in savings stamps.

Sunday 23rd

Chapel in morning and evening. Ysgol Gân. Listened to Oliver Twist.

APRIL

1st

Uncle Frank said he saw a 'flying saucer.'

Note the date. Frank was brother to my mother's father, and lived in Brynbedw Road, Tylorstown.

4th

Saw the concert 'Princess of Poppyland' in chapel.

The operetta was conducted by my father.

12th

Watched Patty Campbell's wedding. 40 cars. Listened to the Archers.

Patty Campbell was the daughter of the local doctor. Her brother Norman was capped for playing rugby for Scotland. 'The Archers' had started broadcasting on January 1st 1951.

Sunday 13th

Gymanfa Ganu in afternoon and night.

The Gymanfa (the annual singing festival) was the highlight of the Chapel's Year. Five services were held on the Easter Sunday and Tuesday; rehearsals (Ysgol Gân) had been held on Sundays from the autumn onwards. It was the opportunity for families 'ar wasgar - in exile' to return home. My father was the Codwr Canu (conductor) during most of my life.

15th

Gymanfa in morning, afternoon and night. A great success. Dadda was in charge of conducting. Our party under Hywel's mother sang and we were very good. Mam's birthday.

Hywel was one of my close friends.

16th

Farm for eggs.

The first reference to Penrhys.

21st

Swotted for three hours and listened to Carol Levis' Discoveries. I must swot 100 hours this term.

22nd

Stafford Cripps is dead. Mamma is in the Welfare with the N.S.P.C.C.

The Welfare Hall allowed an annual collection for the NSPCC. Stafford Cripps had been Chancellor of the Exchequer in the Attlee government.

MAY

Sunday 4th

Children's Service and recited a hymn. No 116. 100 children in Sunday School. We have the 10/6 for Mrs Davies and John S bought the present.

Mrs Davies had been our Sunday School teacher throughout our Junior School age. This was the end of our period in the vestry.

6th

Dadda has a job of Headmaster at either Pontygwaith or Treherbert.

My father chose to be Head-teacher at Pontygwaith where he remained two years before transferring to Tylorstown.

9th

Sunday School party, and had ice-cream and jelly.

Sunday 11th

Our class went upstairs and our S.S. teacher is Mr Thomas (Geog). John Sadler gave Mrs Davies the present.

Mr Thomas was Geography teacher at Porth County.

14th

Listened to the London Philharmonic Orchestra.

24th

Opened a Post Office Savings Bank account.

JUNE

7th

Walked to the reservoir with Mr Charles and the Sunday School.

Our minister, Alwyn Charles had been ordained in Ebenezer in 1951.

11th

Dadda's concert of Messiah is today and tomorrow.

This was a concert given by Hendrefadog Secondary Modern School at the Welfare Hall.

21st

Barry with the Sunday School. It wasn't raining and we had a lovely day.

JULY

5th

Cricket up the Graig. I broke Keedwell's wicket in half. Went on the boats on Darran in the evening.
The Graig was a clearing in a local wood. John Keedwell was a friend from the street - even after I snapped his wicket with the ball. The Darran was a lake in Ferndale.

Sunday 6th

Sang with a party in Cwrdd Cwarter. We finished at 8 o'clock.
Cwrdd Cwarter = Quarterly Meetings in the chapel when members participated.

8th

Finished my Biggles book.
Biggles was written by Captain W.E. Johns. I read a dozen of these in 1952. They replaced for me the 'Adventure' series by Enid Blyton.

11th

My result today. I came 6th out of 33. Broke up for August holidays for 7 weeks. Dadda has finished in Hendrefadog.

Sunday 13th

Chapel in the night and had two missionary books.
Missionary books were presented to those who had collected for the London Missionary Society.

19th

Rhoose today. It's a smashing place. Listened to a lecture by Jack Jones. Enjoyed Square Dancing.
An Annual Residential Conference held at the YMCA Rhoose for Rhondda Secondary Modern School children. I attended because my father was an organizer. Jack Jones was a Welsh novelist. He did not lecture on square dancing!

Sunday 20th

Church in the morning and afternoon. Gymanfa and records in the evening. I am in the Yellow team.

21st

Late for chapel this morning. A lecture by Mansel Thomas. Porthkerry Bay this afternoon. Twenty Questions tonight.

Mansel Thomas, the eminent Tylorstown musician, was born in Pontygwaith. He became Head of BBC Music in Wales.

22nd

Chapel this morning. Listened to a lecture by the Rev. R. Williams. Cricket on the lawn in the afternoon. Community Singing in the evening.

23rd

Two lectures in the morning by Haydn Davies and Daniel Jones. Trip around Vale in the afternoon. Supper before dancing.

John Haydn Davies was the conductor of Treorchy Male Choir; Daniel Jones, the Swansea composer was a close friend of Dylan Thomas.

24th

Lecture by Mr Steligman on Art. Dancing after the lecture.

25th

Lecture by Mrs Rachel Thomas. Sports. We won the cup.

Rachel Thomas was a Welsh actress.

AUGUST

4th

Saw Indians play Glamorgan. Glamorgan were 204 for 9 dec and India 306 for 9 dec. Ramchand scored 78 and Sen scored 75 not out.

Holidays in Swansea.

6th

Carmarthen to see Aunty Kay. I had a book off her called 'Through the Bible' and 7/6. On the way home we caught the Fishguard Express.

8th

Porth Choir won the mixed choral. Saw Mr Ivor Owen in the Brangwyn Hall.

Porth won the Eisteddfod. Results were eagerly awaited on radio. Ivor Owen was the Organist at the Brangwyn Hall and the 'Organizer for Music' in

Swansea. He was a close friend of my father. His brother was Dickie Owen, Welsh scrum-half. I put on his Welsh cap that day!

9th
Treorchy won the Male Voice.

15th
I have been swimming 25 times. Forte's for a shilling ice.

25th
Lost my knife. Walked over to Bristol Tump, Treorchy, back to Maerdy and the same way home. Walked ten miles. I walked with Byron, Alan and Graham.
Friends from the street who also attended Ebenezer.

28th
Farm this evening. Beat Alan Powell at chess. Errands this morning and played catty and doggy.
'Catty and doggy' was a game played with two sticks: the large one 'doggy' was used to hit the smaller, 'catty.' Alan Powell was a neighbour from our street.

SEPTEMBER

13th
Our trip to the homes of William Williams and John Penry. We went over the Rhigos to Brecon, Llandovery, Builth and Llandrindod.
Ebenezer organized its first 'pilgrimage,' to the homes of William Williams, Pantycelyn, the Methodist hymn writer and John Penry of Cefn Brith, the Congregationalist martyr.

Sunday 14th
Started Sunday School.
For the first time I read the Scriptural passage and a hymn to begin Sunday School.

OCTOBER

Sunday 5th

Big Meetings in Chapel all day. Dac's for dinner because Mamma went to chapel this morning.

Cwrdde Mawr (Big Meetings) were another highlight of the year with 'special preachers.' They were held twice each year with services on Saturday evening and all day Sunday.

7th

Finished 'Through the Bible.' I took 8 weeks 6 days to read it.

When I had completed the book, I shared it with my grandmother (my mother's mother.) I asked her what was her favourite story from the Bible Her reply was 'the Story of Joseph.' I remember reading it to her. Was this the seed for my choice of Joseph for my first sermon in the summer of 1960?

9th

A quartet from La Scala Opera House. They were Disma de Cecco, Anna Maria Canelli, Isodore Antoniole and Guiseppe Modesti. I collected £4 for programmes.

A Welfare Hall concert with Italian soloists.

13th

Welsh Class in Ebenezer. Mamma and Dad saw television with Uncle Ivor.

Ivor, my mother's brother was a sea captain with British Petroleum. He and his family lived in Tonteg, and were the first in our family to own a television.

18th

Eisteddfod in the Welfare. Sold 19s in programmes. I didn't win with my essay. Started at 1 and finished at 11.

29th

The boys cut trees for the bonfire this morning but I went to see Howard. Took broth to Mamgu's.

Our family were unhappy about the cutting of trees.

31st

Cardiff at 10 and home by 3. I bought chess and long trousers. Guild.

NOVEMBER

Sunday 2nd
Listened to the last part of 'Mansfield Park'.

4th
Mamma went to L.M.S. meeting over the other valley.
L.M.S. = The London Missionary Society. The 'other valley' was the Rhondda Fawr. As children we knew nothing of any other valleys.

7th
Guild had a meeting with Soar Pontygwaith. I won Musical Chairs and had to speak on 'Monkeys' in One Minute Please.

19th
Swotted Act 1 of 'Twelfth Night.' Listened to 'The Wandering Jew' with Donald Wolfitt.

21st
Guild with a lecture by Mr Charles on 'Religion and Healing.'

26th
English imposition for the whole class. Listened to Constance Cummings in 'Hedda Gabler'.
The whole class was told to write an essay as a result of unruly behaviour.

DECEMBER

6th
Cardiff with Mamma. Bought a Diary and a Knowledge Book for Christmas. New Suit.

13th
Moggs for ½ hour and Daily Worker Jumble Sale. Watched Tylorstown beat Treorchy 8-1.
Morgan's Field on Penrhys Farm was a favourite venue for sport. The 'Daily Worker' was the Communist newspaper.

15th

My result: came 11th. Welsh class this evening. Not many there. I learnt 2 verses of my poem.

16th

Drunkards on the bus.

Sunday 21st

I didn't go to chapel this morning. Sunday School. Cwrdd Cwarter this evening and I forgot part of *'Ble mae'r Iesu?'* I also read a chapter from the Bible.

Cwrdd Cwarter were Quarterly Meetings in which members of the congregation participated.

22nd

Cardiff today. Bought presents.

23rd

Bought a book in Lewis. Bought lipstick (7/6) for Mamma and a brush, 2 shaving soaps and talcum powder for Dadda. Won 18-9 this afternoon on the Flat. Went to Mamgu's.

Lewis the Bookseller was a Tylorstown shop. 'The Flat' was a flattened tip near the river.

25th

Woke at four. I had 19 books and a Xmas stocking. Parcel from Anne this morning. Saw the Youth Club beat the Albions 8-1. Bed at 10. Turkey for dinner.

Anne was my London cousin who was soon to emigrate with her family to Australia. Tylorstown Albions had been a good local team but had wound up a few years previously. This was a 'special fixture.'

31st

Party in the Vestry this evening and then watch-night service. I wasn't home until 1 o'clock. Bed in 1953.

The first attempt for Ebenezer to organize a party and worship for New Year's Eve.

1953

JANUARY

Sunday 11th

Children's Service this morning. Had Album off Mr Charles. Sunday School. I became a member this evening along with 17 others.

The Stamp Album was to encourage good attendance at Sunday morning worship. We received a stamp each Sunday to stick in the book. Theoretically, young people were received into membership by confession of faith. In fact it was more part of a growing into adulthood, and was a ceremony which took place when you reached early teens. Almost all of the new members that day had to move away from Rhondda to find employment.

27th

Youth Club to see Cardiff Soccer players.

The players were Alan Harrington, Jack Mansell and Charlie Rutter.

FEBRUARY

Sunday 1st

Chapel this morning. I had my stamp. This afternoon I saw Alan Hughes in Church Village. He is in Ward 10. Swotted this evening. Mamgu's after supper.

Alan Hughes was a chapel friend.

2nd

Wales beat Northern Ireland in Top of the Form. There are 250 killed in floods in England and 400 in Holland. Mamgu is not very well.

4th

Saw 'The Girl who Couldn't Quite' in the Welfare with the Jocelyn Players.

6th

My birthday. I had 4 cards, £4, a box of chocolates and sweets. Sweets came off the ration yesterday. Heard Mr T. I. Ellis in the chapel. Played table-tennis.
T.I. Ellis was a well-known Welsh writer and story-teller.

9th

Wales beat England in Top of the Form by 1 mark.

21st

Cardiff on 10.45 train to see the Matinee performance of 'La Boheme.' Terribly tragic. Lunch in The New Continental.
My first visit to the Opera, although Opera singers came each year to Tylorstown.

MARCH

6th

Guild this evening for Open Night. Joe Stalin is dead. Played weak-horses, strong-donkeys up the field.
An 'Open Night' was one in which parents and friends were invited. The team game, played by boys involved jumping on the backs of the other team.

Sunday 8th

Communion this evening.

9th

Tommy Farr lost his fight against Don Cockell.
Tommy Farr, the Tonypandy boxer had tried to make a 'come-back.' This effectively ended his career.

11th

Half-day today because Ken Linton had a scholarship to Oxford.
Such a rare event for the County School. Ken Linton became a Congregationalist minister.

27th

Annual meeting of the Guild. I was made a committee-member.

APRIL

Good Friday April 3rd

David and I walked 10 miles. I saw a tumulus and the old cart road. Went to Chapel.

My brother David, a school-teacher, was home from London for his holidays.

Easter Sunday 5th

Chapel this morning at 10. Communion. Had 3 eggs. Gymanfa this afternoon and evening.

6th

I went to the pictures this evening to collect for the N. S. P. C. C.

7th

Gymanfa this morning, afternoon and evening. Read the Psalm this morning. Gymanfa finished at 8 o'clock. It was very good.

8th

A walk on the other mountain. Collected for N.S.P.C.C. this evening. Total collection was £23, 1s, 3d.

9th

In the car to Brecon at 1 and were back at 8. Mamma came. Salad for tea there.

My mother's brother Ivor, home from sea, hired a car for the family.

MAY

2nd

Cup Final on T.V. this afternoon. Blackpool beat Bolton 4-3. A great game. Had a game soccer this evening. Mam came to tea. Saw Newsreel and Saturday Special.

I watched the match with many others, in a neighbour's house. Mam, my mother's mother was a semi-invalid, having suffered a stroke in the 1930s when she was about 50 years old. She lived in Church Terrace, the street in front of our house.

21st

Sports in Tonypandy. Walked there and back. We won Senior Boys and came second in Junior Boys. We went back to the school and had a row off Boss.

The Inter-School Sports were an occasion of great rivalry.

23rd

Visited Leicester Square, Piccadilly Circus, Trafalgar Square, St Martin's in the Fields, the Mall, Buckingham Palace, St James' Palace, Tower of London and Hyde Park.

My first visit to London, to stay with my brother.

24th

Heard Skewen in the Royal Festival Hall and had tea there. St Martin's this evening and Festival Hall for dinner. Piccadilly.

25th

Chessington Zoo this morning. David and I went on a boat from Richmond to Westminster Bridge. Bought a Souvenir of the Coronation.

JUNE

2nd

Mt Everest has been climbed. Her Majesty Queen Elizabeth II was crowned Queen of England. Saw the coronation on television. Our street tea in the Coliseum. Had my crown money-box. Bed at 11.30. Fireworks in the street.

The Coliseum was a disused cinema at the bottom of Brynbedw Road. My father informed me that it had been once owned as a cinema by Jimmy Wilde, the boxer.

15th

Mr Vaughan Rees, the missionary left today. Entered £3 in the bank. I have £16.11s.

Mr Rees had stopped in our house for the weekend when leading worship at Ebenezer.

25th

Drobny beat Patty 8-6, 16-18, 3-6, 8-6, 12-10. It lasted 93 games and 4½ hours.

Was this the longest match in Wimbledon history? It was in the third round.

Sunday 28th

Chapel this morning, afternoon and evening. We celebrated our 75th anniversary. I read Psalm 96 in Chapel this evening. We had a type of Gymanfa.

30th

Elfed was in Chapel.

Howell Elvet Lewis, 'Elfed' (1860-1953), Congregationalist minister, hymn writer and prominent Free Churchman. Archdruid of Wales 1923-7.

JULY

1st

Heard H.T. Jacob Abergwaun in Ebenezer.

H. T Jacob was Congregationalist minister in Fishguard.

Sunday 4th

Supper in Mam's. Listened to 'Jane Eyre.' Started reading 'Northanger Abbey.'

9th

The Queen passed through Tylorstown with the Duke. I saw them. I stood by the Post-Office.

15th

Played tennis up Penrhys. Elwyn and I beat Hywel and Alun 5-7, 6-2, 6-2. Went to Mam's.

The first time to play tennis, playing with friends from the same street.

30th

Saw Pakistan Eaglets beat Swansea. Ivor was hit in eye.

This was before there was a Pakistan national side. Ivor, a new friend and my future brother-in-law, was struck by a 'six' from Gilbert Parkhouse, a great Glamorgan batsman. He had free tickets for the Australians match!

AUGUST

1st

Bathed this morning before I saw the cricket. Glamorgan batted first and scored 201 (Watkins 73) and Australia 93 for 1 (Morris 48). 9 autographs: 5 Australian and 4 Glamorgan.

3rd

Bathed this morning in Swansea Bay. Watched cricket all day. The Australians were all out for 383 (Harvey 180, McDonald 58, Craig 50. McConnon 7 for 167). Glam scored 61 for 6. Fireworks in Singleton Park.

4th

Autographs today: nine Australians, 3 Pakistan, Dai Davies and eight Glamorgan plus two reserves. Watched cricket this afternoon. Glam scored 183 for 7 (Wooller 71 not out, Muncer 56). Bowls with Dadda this evening.

8th

Had Eagle. Saw the Welsh Youth Orchestra at Brangwyn Hall. The conductor was Clarence Raybould.

The 'Eagle' comic was an enjoyable and influential comic. The Welsh National Youth Orchestra was founded in 1945 and Clarence Raybould was its first conductor.

13th

A walk as far as Blackpill and saw the sunken forest and Roman Bridge. Fishing this evening. Walked to docks.

22nd

Went down to the butchers and up the farm this morning. Howard smashed Miss Howell's window. Over Ynys-y-bwl to fish. Saw Quatermass Experiment.

The Quatermass Experiment was broadcast by BBC Television in the summer of 1953. Originally comprising six half-hour episodes, it was the first science-fiction production to be written especially for an adult television audience. Howard was my young cousin.

SEPTEMBER

Sunday 6th

Mamgu died this morning at a quarter to eleven. She has been in bed for nearly a year. Mamma was up till six this morning. Dadda was up just too late. Dadda went up all day. Sunday School.

Mamgu was my father's mother and lived in Brynheulog Terrace. She had come to Tylorstown in 1876 and had the privilege of being the longest serving member of Ebenezer.

10th

Mamgu was buried today. Mam's for tea and supper. Aunty Maggie and Aunty Bess came over.

Two of my father's sisters, one living in Lowestoft and the other in London.

19th

Blew my soccer ball up. Saw Proms on TV. Worked in Mam's this evening.

Watched the Proms on Uncle Noel's TV.

21st

Read 'Around the World in Eighty Days' by Jules Verne. Listened to second part of 'As You Like It.'

22nd

Banked 10/-. I have £19, 7s, 0d. Worked on a time chart. Finished a half. Mr. Elwyn Thomas came up this evening.

Elwyn Thomas, a local Art teacher was to become a well-known local artist.

23rd

Finished my Date-Chart of English History.

OCTOBER

Sunday 4th

Harvest thanksgiving this evening.

The first harvest service in Ebenezer.

17th

Eisteddfod. Borrowed 'Macbeth' and a Poetry Book from Dac's. Acted as a messenger between Libanus and Welfare. Tylorstown won Children's Choir.

The Eisteddfod competitions took place in the local chapels as well as in the Welfare Hall.

27th

I am reading 'Kidnapped.' Uncle Noel talked to me about poetry. Listened to 'The Name's the Same.'

NOVEMBER

5th

An operatic concert in the Welfare Hall. The singers were Silvana Zanalli, Sandra Baruffi, Isidore Antoniolli and Otello Borgonovo. I had their autographs. The pianist was Jeanne Reddin. Had £3 3s 6d for programmes.

Sunday 8th

Listened to the last part of 'Phineas Finn.'

25th

Hungary beat England 6-3.

A very famous match. Little did I dream how important Hungary would be in the life of our family.

DECEMBER

1st

Called in Mam's. Helped her down to the Chemist. She is going to have a television.

My grandmother was visiting her son Noel who with his wife Mair and children lived above the Chemist Shop.

5th

Mam had a television today. She has a Philips Consul.

17th
Cardiff with Uncle Noel, Aunty Mair and Howard this afternoon. I bought The Pocket Atlas (4/6), Wales (21/-) and The Oxford Shakespeare (17/6). Tea in David Morgan's.

Sunday 20th
Chapel this morning, afternoon and evening. Had a stamp. Rehearsal for the play. We had the Nativity Play this evening. It was very good. I read all right.
The first Nativity Play in Ebenezer. An example of Alwyn Charles' introducing the Church Year.

21st
Listened to 'A Midsummer Night's Dream.'

22nd
Cardiff with David and Dadda. I had Great Events of 1953 (5/-) 100 Famous Lives (15/-), a Crystal set and accessories (43/-).

25th
Saw my presents at seven o'clock: a camera off David and 'Stockbroker' off Howard. I made the crystal set work. Walked up Bristol Tump. Saw the play on T.V.

31st
Helped to put up trimmings. Party in chapel this evening. Returned home in 1954. We had a service.

1954

JANUARY

2nd
David and I saw Cardiff City lose 3-1 to Wolverhampton Wanderers.
My first visit to Ninian Park, Cardiff.

14th

My new Geography Book 'The World' came. It was 12/6 and is very good. I bought a Postal Order. Looked at my new book this evening. I didn't do much work.

15th

Listened to Children's Hour and the Goon Show.

Sunday 24th

Guild Meeting this afternoon and it was decided that Guild should finish. After Ysgol Gân Mr Charles told us we would have a 'Debating Society' on week Friday.

27th

Latin Translation and Welsh History essay on the Agrarian Revolution. Listened to Ann Todd in 'Rebecca.' Very good.

FEBRUARY

12th

Cylch Myfyr this evening. Two debates and a One Minute Please.
Cylch Myfyr (Meditation Circle) was a new name to replace the old Guild. The name did not catch on.

20th

Cardiff Arms Park with Dadda to see New Zealand beat the Barbarians 19-5. A wonderful game. We were in the ground by 1.

26th

Ferndale to the Laundry; a haircut, Coop and home.
Ferndale had a Chinese laundry where collars would be starched.

MARCH

13th

Dadda and Mamma and I saw the afternoon performance of 'La Traviata' in Cardiff. Excellent.

20th

Started Boy's Own Paper and finished with the Eagle.

'Boys' Own' began in 1879 and ended in 1967. The first version of 'The Eagle' ran from 1950 to 1969.

27th

Ceiriog won the shield in the Eisteddfod with Elfed second and Pantycelyn third. We won the Action song and Cydadrodd. I came second in my essay.

This was the first Chapel Eisteddfod for many years. It was an attempt to widen the social aspects of chapel life.

28th

Listened to 'The Kraken Wakes'.

'The Kraken Wakes' was an apocalyptic science fiction novel written by John Wyndham in 1953. John Wyndham also wrote 'The Day of the Triffids.' He lived for a while at the Quaker Penn Club - some of us as Moderators of the United Reformed Church (URC) were later to use the same Club.

MAY

6th

Roger Bannister did the mile in 3.59.4 in Oxford today.

8th

Mam went to New Quay. Mamma and I went to Cardiff and I bought a new suit, 'Mr Midshipman Easy', a map of South Wales and News Chronicle Cricket Annual.

My mother's family originated from New Quay. My mother and grandmother (and their ancestors at least as far back as the Seventeenth Century) were born there.

13th

I went down the Flat this evening. 'Lord George Sanger's Circus' was there. I didn't go in.

15th

A hike with Graham Daniels, Graham and Austin Jones, Ralph Thomas, Peter Curtis, Dewi Griffiths and John Parcel. We started at 10.30. We reached

Llanwonno at 11.15, had food on the mountain above Cwmaman at 12.30. Reached the top reservoir at 2.45 and the Rhigos at 4.30. Graham Daniels, Graham and Austin Jones went home but the rest of us went to Craig y Llyn (1969 feet high) but only Ralph and I reached it. Came back to the Rhigos from where we had a lift to Pentre. Walked to Ystrad and bused up the hill, met rest of the boys. Home by 7.30.
All the boys were about the same age and belonged to Ebenezer. Craig y Llyn was the highest point in the 'old county' of Glamorgan.

17th
I had 'The Ascent of Everest.'

JUNE

5th
Aberystwyth on the Western Welsh. Arrived at Uncle Phil's house and looked round the house with Keith. Played with Keith's electric train. Sleep at 12.
A holiday with my father's brother Philip, his wife Ann and their son Keith. Philip Morgan had become 'Master' of the Bronglais Poor Law Institution in 1934 which became the Bronglais Hospital of which he was the first secretary and Ann the first Matron. It was there we spent our holiday. The buildings were later demolished and replaced by Bronglais Hospital.

8th
Butlin's Holiday camp with Keith's church. Started at 10.10 and arrived at 12.30. Cricket in the nets.
My first visit to North Wales, if Butlin's in Pwllheli can be termed North Wales.

19th
Bowls at Penrhys with Hywel and Graham.

Sunday 20th
Chapel this morning, Sunday School this afternoon and Missionary Meeting this evening. Miss Mair Griffiths from Madagascar spoke
Little did I think of the future relationship with Madagascar. Mair Griffiths was a well-known Welsh missionary.

21st
John Landy ran the mile in 3 min 58.1 sec.
John Landy was an Australian.

24th
Michael Davies is in the last 16 in Wimbledon.
Michael Davies was a tennis player from Swansea.

26th
Barry at 10 on our Sunday School outing. Lunch on the beach and then played cricket. Saw cricket for half-an-hour. Played golf twice. Did it in 44 each time. Went to the Fair.

JULY

16th
Aunty Olive, Aunty Mair, Uncle Ivor and Uncle Noel came to supper. I didn't go to bed till midnight.
A typical family gathering to coincide with Uncle Ivor's holiday from sea. Ivor and Noel were two of my mother's brothers.

19th
Helped Mamma in the house this morning. Cut sticks and cleaned windows. Played badminton outside John Jones' this afternoon. Played bowls with Graham Daniels this evening. I am reading 'Satan Island.'
'Satan Island' by Julian Watson was one of my favourite books.

SEPTEMBER

1st
School started. Dadda started as headmaster in Tylorstown Junior Boys' School. I am in Form VA.

2nd
Finished 'Scott's Last Expedition,' a set book for C.W.B. Read the introduction of Caesar's Gallic Wars Book III and translated a chapter.
C.W.B. = Central Welsh Board. It was an Examination Board.

17th

Workmen's Hall this afternoon to see Shaw's 'Pygmalion' presented by the Arts Council of Great Britain. Guild meeting this evening. We planned a programme. A dozen there.

Workmen's Hall was in Ferndale. It has since been demolished.

18th

Saw 'The Last Night of the Proms' and Harold Lloyd in 'Crazy' in Mam's. It was very good.

Harold Lloyd was famous for his silent movies. He was a great favourite of my grandfather.

Sunday 26th

Sunday School and Guild Meeting afterwards. Officers were chosen. I am Chairman.

OCTOBER

Sunday 3rd

Big Meetings this morning and evening. I received my stamp. Listened to 'Martin Chuzzlewit.'

19th

Dai Dower beat Jake Tuli to win the British Empire fly-weight championship. Heard it on the wireless.

Dai Dower, from Abercynon became British, Empire and European flyweight champion.

NOVEMBER

Sunday 14th

Communion this evening and Discussion Group where a Nigerian was speaking.

This was my first conscious meeting with a black person: Samuel Akbo from the Student Christian Movement at Cardiff.

DECEMBER

18th

Cardiff with Michael and Peter and bought 'The Robe', 'Expedition Fawcett', a diary, a history book and a record.

21st

Read the Prologue in the Nativity Play.

31st

Finished 'The Robe.' I went down Mam's at 9.30 and to the Watch Night Service at 10.30. Home by 12.30.

1955

JANUARY

Sunday 2nd

Three of us had full albums. Sunday School this afternoon. Mam's before chapel; Dac and I chatted about South America.

My grandfather had been 'on sea' during the Depression in the coal industry. His journeys were usually taking coal to various parts of South America. The World map in the kitchen was constantly referred to, and the arrivals and departures of ships to Cardiff checked in the Western Mail. From an early age I was familiar with places like Rio de Janeiro, the River Plate, and Montevideo.

3rd

Walked to Bristol Tump. It was very cold and there was a strong biting wind. We were nearly blown off our feet. Walked across the mountain to Penrhys road and then home.

13th

Received our CWB book 'The Importance of being Earnest' by Oscar Wilde. Read it this evening. Excellent comedy.

Sunday 23rd

Mr David Davies B.A, gave the sermon. Sunday School this afternoon. I started it by reading a hymn and a chapter from the Bible.

25th

Mamma went to Maes-yr-haf to hear a music recital by Yfrah Neaman (violin) and Howard Ferguson (piano).

Maes yr Haf was the Quaker Settlement established in Trealaw in the 1930s.

FEBRUARY

1st

Listened to 'The Goon Show,' and 'Treble Chance' on Radio Luxembourg.

5th

Walked up to Ferndale. I bought 'I Love Paris' and 'I Still Believe' by Ronnie Harris in Ferndale, and 'Little Brown Jug' and 'String of Pearls' (Glenn Miller) in Tylorstown.

19th

Letter from the Y.H.A. today. I received my Membership Card, Handbook and Metal badge. Wrote the notes I have done on my Poems in one book. It was over 36 pages.

YHA = The Youth Hostel Association. The poems for O Level were: Goldsmith's 'The Deserted Village'; Keats' 'The Eve of St Agnes'; Tennyson's 'The Lotos Eaters'; Matthew Arnold's 'The Scholar Gypsy' and 'The Death of Cuchulan' by W.B. Yeats.

MARCH

3rd

Mamma went to Mam's to help her come downstairs. Mam is to sleep in the front room downstairs from now on.

12th

Went to the Coop to pay 'Pen Cwarter.'

Bills had to be settled and Dividend paid out at the end of each quarter.

Sunday 13th

'Cwrdde Mawr' this morning. Mr Glyndwr Jones gave the sermon. His text was 'God - Power.' Took dinner down to Mam and trifle for her tea. Chapel this evening. Mr Jones' text was 'Do not build your nest among the stars.' Ysgol Gân afterwards.

I was baptised by Glyndwr Jones in 1939 when he was minister at Ebenezer. By this time he was minister in Rhyl.

19th

Saw Mam immediately after breakfast. Polished the kitchen floor. Translated Latin. Took dinner to Dac. Eisteddfod at 4.45. I won first prizes for hand-made article (15-19) and with my essay on 'A Description of Wales.' Our house 'Tŷ Ceiriog' beat 'Tŷ Elfed' by 57 points to 49.

APRIL

9th

Mam's relatives from New Quay came today.

12th

Saw Mam after breakfast. Gymanfa. Took collection this afternoon and this evening.

16th

Mam died this morning at a quarter past eight.

20th

A beautiful day. Mam's funeral took place this afternoon. There were nine cars. Took Howard near Cynllwyn Du while the funeral was on.

28th

Rhondda was made a Municipal Borough this morning. The Duke of Edinburgh presented the Charter. Dac came to dinner. Saw Edmundo Ros on Dac's T.V.

MAY

14th

A trip with the chapel to a meeting in Bethania, Neath. Lectures at 3.30 and 7. The lecturer was Shaun Herron, the editor of the 'British Weekly'. He was very good.

These meetings were organised by a group of younger ecumenical ministers inspired by the Blaendulais Centre under the leadership of Erastus Jones. 'The British Weekly' was a very influential Nonconformist weekly newspaper.

17th

I rose at 4 o'clock this morning and heard the Heavyweight Championship fight from San Francisco. Rocky Marciano (U.S.A.) beat Don Cockell (England) by a technical knockout in the 9th round.

26th

Dadda didn't have school because of the Election. I stayed up to hear the Election results coming in, until 12.45. When I went to bed, Labour had 86 seats and the Conservatives had 80.

Anthony Eden's Conservatives defeated Labour under Clement Attlee.

JUNE

6th

Dr Harman, the missionary from China and Northern Rhodesia spoke in chapel. Rained torrentially. Water and mud flowed into Nos 20 and 21.

8th

Our Geography paper this morning. We had to answer six questions in 3 hours.

The beginning of O levels which lasted until July 5th. Examinations continued throughout the month of June, ending with the Spanish papers in July.

25th

Bought sandals and paid for the papers. I bought a Louis Armstrong record in Griffiths. It is 'I'm not rough' and 'Put 'em down Blues.'

My first 'real' jazz record, bought from the shelf in my local shop.

JULY

5th

2 hour Spanish Unseen paper this morning and 2 hour Spanish grammar this afternoon. Dictation after that.

8th

Collected envelopes for the Blind, from Church Street.

16th

Barry with the Sunday School Trip. We left on the last bus. I was in charge of the bus with Alun and Brian. Played golf with Alan Hughes and Byron. I lost the ball. Lunch and tea in the Café Royale. Cold Knap in the afternoon. We went on the boats. The fair with Peter, June, Robert Weekes and Patricia. Scenic Railway and dodgems. I had 6½d coming home.

20th

Most of the boys cleared the field at Cynllwyn Du of stones and played cricket.
Cynllwyn Du was a ruined farmhouse and the field was by the side of the ruined house. The new pitch was dubbed 'the Rose Bowl.'

Sunday 24th

Helped count the collection for the Blind: £16.6s.6d.

26th

Byron and I caught the 8.45 bus to Aberdare. We walked to Hirwaun where we had a lift in a lorry as far as the turning for Ystradfellte. Walked to Ystradfellte and arrived at 11.30. We booked in and walked to the caves and along the dry river bed to the village. Wrote and sent letters to Mamma and Dadda, Dac and Peter. Bed at 9.45.
My first hitch-hiking holiday. A night at Ystradfellte and another in Storey Arms.

AUGUST

10th

Received £5 off Mamma and Dadda last night because I have saved £50. They promised to do so when I started saving. Went to the butcher's. Painted the posts of the garden gate before dinner and the gate after dinner.

13th

Bought a Penguin book on 'Jazz.' Empire Theatre to see the Old Vic Company presenting 'Julius Caesar.' Excellent.

Annual family holiday in Swansea. The Jazz book was by Rex Harris

Sunday 14th

We all walked to Mount Pleasant Baptist Chapel. The preacher was Dr Gwyn Walters. This evening we heard an Open-Air service near the Brangwyn Hall.

20th

Empire Theatre to see Lita Roza and Jimmy James. Most enjoyable.

Lita Roza had sung with Ted Heath and was well-known for 'How much is that doggie in the window?' Jimmy James was a popular comedian. The Empire Theatre closed in 1957 and was demolished in 1959.

23rd

Left at 9.30, Carmarthen by 11 and Cardigan by 1. Sandwiches there. Then St David's through Fishguard, and looked around the cathedral. Our next stop was Haverfordwest where we had sandwiches.

24th

Rose at 7.30 to fetch the papers. Our results have come out. I passed in all subjects - ea, el, w3*, l, sp*, h, g, m.

O and A Level results were published in the 'Western Mail.' Candidates were not informed personally. English language and literature; Welsh for learners with oral proficiency; Latin; Spanish with oral proficiency; History; Geography, Mathematics.

27th

Church Army meeting this afternoon. Walter gave me Daily Bible Notes.

The Church Army was holding 'missions' on the beach. I had stopped to listen, became acquainted with Walter Watkins and received Bible Notes from him for several years.

Sunday 28th

Ebenezer Welsh Congregational Church this morning; Unitarian church in High Street this evening. It was very good. Discussion Group outside Guildhall after returning. Walked from High Street to the Guildhall. I have bathed 17 times since I came to Swansea.

29th

Bought two records: 'Sweet Georgia Brown - Way Down Yonder in New Orleans' - Jimmy Noone, and 'Canal Street Blues - Dippermouth Blues' - King Oliver.

SEPTEMBER

5th

School started. I am in 6b. I take History, Geography and English for Higher.

6th

We had some English books - Milton's Areopagitica; Chaucer's Prologue and Nun's Priest's Tale; Shaw's St Joan; Sheridan's The School for Scandal; Goldsmith's She Stoops to Conquer; and Shakespeare's Much Ado about Nothing.

7th

We had nine History books. I brought the British history books home. Bought new shoes. Read history for an hour. Our period is 1484-1763 for British history and 1494-1789 for European history.

15th

Read the poems of Keats, Shelley and Wordsworth in Book 4 of Palgrave's Golden Treasury. It took 3 hours.

17th

Trip with the Guild to Brecon, Llandrindod Wells, Rhayader and the Elan valleys. I rowed on the boats in Llandrindod for one hour. We all had a walk in the Elan valley.

22nd

In preps I wrote a geography essay on 'You cannot study the British Isles without a knowledge of N.W. Europe.' Took records to school for the school Gramophone Society meeting. Four of my records were played, including the first ever played for the Society. We had the meeting after school and I wasn't home until 5.30.

Sunday 25th

Wrote a talk for Children's service in seven weeks time. It is on William Wilberforce.

OCTOBER

18th

The recording of 'Top of the Form' took place this morning. We were opposed to Newtown Grammar School. We lost by 54 points to 44. Mr Robert Mc'Dermot was in charge with us. Received a new English book - 'A Short History of English Literature' by B. Ivor Evans. Read 70 pages this evening.

29th

We are stopping at the Old Malt House in Wick. A walk before breakfast. After breakfast a lecture from Huw Wyn Griffith followed by discussion. After a break, a talk from T.J. Davies followed by discussion. A free afternoon and a walk to the beach. A talk by Erastus Jones and discussion. Noson lawen.
A young people's Ecumenical Conference was held at this Centre belonging to the Society of Friends. The ministers were all leading ecumenists in Wales. In later years I knew them all very well.

31st

There is a new junior history master and Mr Jones takes us. I started Fisher's 'History of Europe.'
Mr O Vernon Jones later became Head-teacher of the County School. Mr Lewis Thomas, Senior History master retired at the end of October.

NOVEMBER

4th

Read over my lecture before Guild. We had a discussion on Wick. I had to give the address. After tea I gave my lecture on jazz.

Sunday 6th

Lecture by Mr John Williams, vice-secretary of the United Churches Aid for Refugees.

The introduction of Christian Aid concerns.

8th

Mr Burnell our English master gave me seven novels. I started 'Wuthering Heights' by Emily Bronte.

9th

Finished 'Wuthering Heights.' It is an excellent novel but very tragic. It brought a lump to my throat in parts. I also summarized two more pages of Trevelyan and I have reached Queen Mary. Started 'Pride and Prejudice' by Jane Austen.

Trevelyan 'History of England' was a standard text alongside H A L Fisher's 'History of Europe.'

10th

Stayed in during dinner hour and argued with Stranks about Communism. He is standing as Communist candidate in the school election tomorrow.

11th

Received the names of Overtures from Norman Cooper.

The beginning of a 'serious' interest in classical music.

12th

Finished 'Pride and Prejudice' and read the chapter on Maximilian in Tanner. Helped clear a spare room in the vestry in which to keep paper.

Recycling newspapers for Christian Aid.

23rd
Listened to Holst's 'The Planets' by the B.B.C. Symphony Orchestra under Sir Malcolm Sargent.

DECEMBER

7th
Listened to the B.B.C. Symphony Orchestra conducted by Otto Klemperer playing Brahms' 'Symphony No 4, in E Minor.'
A symphony which 'returns' at many important events in life.

12th
Terminals. We had our examination on English set books. 3 hour paper. I should get a decent mark. European history this afternoon. Pretty decent but no choice. I wrote 15 sides of a page on each examination. Took the Christmas puddings to Dac for him to boil

14th
English criticism examination. The hardest so far and I wrote only 7 sides. I went down the Chemist and weighed: 9 stone exactly and my height is 5 feet 9½ inches. My pocket money is raised to 7/6 a week.

19th
Polished the upstairs' floors. Caught the 6.30 bus to the Maes-yr-haf hall in Trealaw for our form party. 20 girls from the Girls' school there. Caught last bus home.

23rd
Cleared the School hall for the Youth Club party. I danced almost all the dances and can now dance (some shape) the tango and quick step.

Sunday 25th
Byron and I fetched hymn books from chapel at 10 and took them to Libanus where we had a united service. I sat by Dad, Dac and David. Dac came to dinner. Wrote letters to Aunty Kay, and Walter thanking him for the Bible notes. Aunty May and Uncle Caleb came to tea. Nine Lessons and Carols Service in our chapel this evening. I read a lesson. Ysgol Gân afterwards. Gave Peter a diary and received three handkerchiefs.

The morning service at Libanus was the first ecumenical service in Tylorstown: for the 4 Welsh speaking chapels.

26th

David and Beryl got married today at Seven Sisters and we had the reception in the Boys' Club. All the family went to Neath to see David and Beryl off on the 5.40 train to London.

The officiating minister was Erastus Jones, the inspired ecumenist. Beryl and David have always been most supportive of our family, and although they have spent most of their lives in Northumberland, we always meet for important family occasions.

1956

JANUARY

Sunday, 1st

Our service was on the wireless from 11 to 12. Sunday School this afternoon. Collected money for the Guild party. Chapel this evening and afterwards a concert by the Children's Choir. I sold programmes.

11th

Listened to Mozart's 'Symphony No 31 in D.'

13th

Guild party this evening: food first, games and dances from 7.45 until 10.45. A great success. 70 there excluding servers.

17th

Finished 'David Copperfield:' the best book I have read.

18th

Bought a new record of Joan Cross singing 'One Fine Day' and 'They Call me Mimi.' Listened to 'Symphony 88 in G' by Haydn. Read Trevelyan all evening.

19th

Wrote Geography essay on 'The Rhondda has been influenced socially and economically by geography.'

28th

Trip to Neath. A sermon from Mr John Williams (secretary of British Council of Churches), tea, discussion groups and another sermon. I read the Bible passage in Welsh in the evening service.

FEBRUARY

3rd

Finished 'The Heart of Midlothian.' A very good story once I got into it. Very difficult language. We had a Mock-Trial on breach of promise. I was counsel for the Prosecution. The Defence won.

8th

A young man named Haydn Fine called. He had been told I had jazz records and came to hear them.
Haydn Fine had travelled three miles from Maerdy to meet another jazz fan. We were few and far between.

9th

Funeral of our Gym master Mr William Morris in Penrhys Cemetery.

25th

Gaumont Theatre to see 'The Marriage of Figaro' by Mozart. Excellent.
The Gaumont in Cardiff was the name given it in 1954 for the Empire Theatre. It was demolished in 1962.

Sunday 26th

Children's service. I read the passage.

27th
Listened to 'Othello.' I followed the text. The play lasted 2½ hours. Superb.

28th
Read two lectures by Carlyle. They are very difficult. I went through European history notes. Started 'Hamlet.' Listened to 'World of Jazz.'

MARCH

2nd
Finished 'Hamlet' and started 'Macbeth' on the train. David met me at Paddington. Saw 'The Benny Goodman Story.'
My second visit to London to stop with my brother David and his wife Beryl.

3rd
Tube into London and saw the matinee performance of 'The Rivals' starring John Clements and Laurence Harvey at the Saville Theatre. Enjoyed 'The Strong are Lonely' starring Donald Wolfit at the Theatre Royal, Haymarket.

Sunday 4th
Haven Green Chapel to hear Ithel Jones. Richmond this afternoon; The Royal Festival Hall this evening to hear the Royal Philharmonic Orchestra conducted by Stanley Pope. They played Tchaikovsky, Rachmaninov and Wagner.
Ithel Jones was minister at Haven Green Baptist Church in Ealing from 1950 to 1957 before becoming Principal of the South Wales Baptist College in Cardiff.

5th
'Richard III' at Leicester Square Theatre. Oxford Street this evening to see Terry Lightfoot's Jazzmen at Humph's club.
Terry Lightfoot made his professional debut as a bandleader in 1956, and established an international reputation as a clarinettist, saxophonist and vocalist of the highest calibre. He was prominent in the traditional jazz revival in Britain in the 1950's.

22nd

School Distribution at Salem Porth. Mamma and Dadda went too. The guest speaker was J.C.J. Metford M.A.

Professor Metford, an old boy of Porth County, was the first professor of the Department of Hispanic Studies at Bristol in 1955. This was School Prize Day.

30th (Good Friday)

I went to the vestry at 10.30 and moved scenery to the Welfare Hall. Home by 11.30 and polished floors until dinner time. Welfare at 5.15. The play 'Caesar's Friend' started at 7.15 and finished at 10.

The play was directed by Alwyn Charles, our minister and was produced in the local Miners' Hall.

APRIL

1st

Communion at 10; Gymanfa this afternoon. I read to start Gymanfa this evening. I visited Brynheulog. Aunty Bessie and all the family were there. They returned at 10.30. We went to the bus with them.

My father's sister Bessie and family were soon to emigrate from London to Australia.

3rd

Gymanfa all day: a terrific success.

Sunday 29th

Dac came to dinner. Horeb Big Meetings this afternoon. The preacher was Mr John from Cwmbwrla. Horeb with Dac this evening. The sermon was wonderful.

MAY

5th

Caught the 10 bus to Ystrad. Our school beat Ferndale. We scored 147 for 6 declared (I scored 12) and got them out for 44. My bowling average was 6.3: 2: 18: 1 wicket.

My first cricket match for the School XI. I played regularly for two years.

9th
Caught up with Bible Reading.

JUNE

2nd
Holton Road Chapel, Barry to hear Dr Martin Niemöller. He preached 95 minutes.
Martin Niemöller was the prominent German anti-Nazi theologian. I met him years later in the more intimate surroundings of Coleg Coffa.

8th
Roy Paul came to school with the F.A. Cup. I riddled small coal for an hour. Listened to Adrian Rollini in 'World of Jazz.'
Roy Paul (born in Pentre played for Manchester City. He also represented the Welsh team over 30 times and is regarded as one of Wales' best ever players. In 1955 he captained Manchester City to the Cup Final and vowed to take his team to Wembley again, and the following year he lifted the FA Cup trophy. Adrian Rollini, an American band leader had died in 1954. 'World of Jazz' was broadcast by the Voice of America. To 'riddle' coal was to save larger pieces of coal by shaking them through a sieve.

Sunday 24th
Children's service. I gave a talk on William Tyndale. It lasted 20 minutes.

JULY

6th
Terminals: a 3 hour English literature paper and a 2½ European history paper.

16th
I bought tin-soups, beans, and spaghetti (12 small tins) for my hike.
And carried the tins a hundred miles!

23rd
Graham and I caught the 8.45 bus to Aberdare and from there to Hirwaun. Arrived in Swansea by 3 lifts, tram to Blackpill and walked 7 miles to Parkmill and bus to Port Eynon. A bathe in the sea, and supper .

A hitch-hiking holiday with a school friend from Ebenezer to Youth Hostels in West Wales.

28th

Lifts to Synod Inn and Llandyssul. Bought a loaf of bread and ate it all. Visited the Church. Reached Pentre Cwrt and talked to two German boys all evening and played chess with one.

AUGUST

6th

Caught a bus to Swansea. The Australians took their score to 408 for 4 dec, and Glamorgan scored 116 and 79 for 0 when we left the ground. Mackay 163 not out, Archer 148, W.E.Jones 47, Parkhouse 53 not out.

7th

The Royal Welsh National Eisteddfod in Aberdare. Travelled on the Choir bus. Pavilion from 10 until 1 before looking around the exhibitions. Tylorstown Choir came 4th out of 9.

14th

Caught 3 mackerel. Out as far as Pen Anglas Head where we fished and back to Needle Rock.

Family holiday in Fishguard, birth-place of my mother's father.

17th

Mamma, Dadda and I walked to Drim Mill. Out in the boat (CA4 - Pat) almost as far as Strumble Head. Caught 13 out of 43 fish. In the house by 10.15. Rough out in the boat tonight but it was terrific. I am looking forward to go out fishing again.

My grandfather had lived with his uncle at the Drim Mill in the 1890s. He often talked about delivering flour on a donkey to Strumble Head. He had been born in Parc y Llyn, Llanstinan.

SEPTEMBER

6th

Youth Club at 9. Dai Benjamin gave me autographs of Sid and Humph. The boys in Youth Club are going crazy about Rock and Roll - I am not keen.
Autographs of Sidney Bechet and Humphrey Lyttelton who had been playing in Cardiff.

12th

Wrote to 4 universities for their prospectuses. Continued 'The Puritan Revolution' by Gardiner.

15th

Reached Llanddowror and after looking around the Church we set off for Llanybri where we looked at the old Church. Visited Blaenycoed before a meal at Llandovery. Reached Rhandirmwyn and I climbed Mwyn.
Ebenezer Pilgrimage in the search for roots. Llanddowror was the centre of Griffith Jones' Circulating Schools; Blaenycoed was the birthplace of Dr Elfed Lewis.

Sunday 23rd

Took a class in the vestry.
This was the first time for me to teach in Sunday School.

OCTOBER

Sunday 7th

Big Meetings three times. The preacher was Eurig Davies. His sermon was 'The Cross as a stumbling block'.
Dewi Eurig Davies was a friend of Alwyn Charles and later was Professor of Christian Doctrine at Coleg Coffa when Norah was a student there.

12th

Guild where we had a debate for or against Anthony Eden's policy over Suez. I was against. Application Forms from Swansea.
An awakening of political consciousness?

17th

A break-in at school early this morning but nothing stolen. The school assembled at 12 to listen to the opening of the Calder Hall Power Station.

On 17 October 1956, Her Majesty the Queen opened Reactor number 1 at Calder Hall, bringing into service the world's first industrial scale nuclear power station.

23rd

Danny and I were on Junior Assembly. I read Psalm 8.

Danny Simmonds and I went on to become fellow students at Swansea University College.

27th

Went to the God's in the Empire and saw 'Rigoletto' with Vic Oliver.

The Empire Theatre was in Tonypandy. Vic Oliver was a comedian and musician. He was the first castaway on Desert Island Discs.

NOVEMBER

3rd

The position is very serious in the Middle East.

Sunday 4th

The Hungarian situation has worsened. It is very grave.

I was to hear first-hand accounts of the situation from close friends and in-laws in years to come.

5th

Sent for Application Forms for Aberystwyth and Cardiff. Resistance seems to be being crushed in Hungary while in Egypt the situation is vague.

6th

Wrote a note to Form VI in the Girls' School concerning Eden's policy in the Middle East. Our form has split into two, roughly equal antagonistic camps. Much bitter discussion intensified by the Hungarian situation.

8th

The girls reply: 'The majority believe Sir Anthony Eden did the wrong thing …Our hearts go out to the Hungarian refugees.'

12th

Listened to Muggsy Spanier on Voice of America at 11. I have been right through the work we have done since the beginning of 6B. It took 66 hours.
Muggsy Spanier was a prominent white cornet player. He died in 1967.

DECEMBER

6th

A performance of 'St Joan' by the Girls' School. Very good.

14th

City Radio where I bought 9 jazz records. Guild at 8 and played my records. They are Sidney Bechet, Duke Ellington, Stan Kenton, Dizzy Gillespie, Gerry Mulligan, Milton Jackson, J.C.Heard, Miles Davis, Serge Chaloff. I have a fairly good representation of Jazz on record.
A well-known record shop in Churchill Way, Cardiff. It has been closed many years.

17th

Supper with Mr and Mrs Charles with Alun, Peter and Michael. Home by 1.

18th

An excellent dance in school. I danced every time. Caught a bus to 'The Star' and walked home.

19th

A terrific fuss about boys who had been drinking before coming to the party yesterday. 17 had been drinking out of 29. I had 56 (3rd) and 58 (1st) in English: Lit and Crit.

29th

Bought a diary in Boots. The Gaumont at 5 to see the Italian Opera Company in 'La Boheme'. Tea in David Morgan's.

1957

JANUARY

4th

St John's for my first proper dance, with a band; it will not be the last.
St John's Hall was in Cymmer, Porth.

7th

Listened to 'Lord of the Flies' by William Golding. It was about school-boys cast away on a desert island and the type of society into which they organized themselves.

9th

Sir Anthony Eden has resigned as Prime Minister because of ill health. Is that the real reason? Who will be the new Prime Minister? Will there be a General Election? The country is in a terrible state and if something isn't done soon, we shall be in a shocking mess.

14th

'Richard III' in the Tudor Hall. Excellent.
I had seen the film in Leicester Square on my London holiday.

16th

A letter from the University College of Swansea accepting my application. I am very pleased. I wrote saying I wanted to go to Swansea and asking for an application form for the Hall of Residence. Welfare at 6.30 where I was an usher for the play which was Josiah's Well. Very enjoyable.

26th

The Gaumont for 'Peter Pan' with Janette Scott, John McCallum and Frances Guthrie.

FEBRUARY

16th

Received my Bank Book. With the interest I now have £100.0s.5d.

MARCH

1st

Concert in the hall to celebrate St David's Day, but 4 of us played cricket on the field. I hooked a ball 50 yards right through a glasshouse. We went to the concert at 11.15.

4th

Saw the London Symphony Orchestra conducted by Norman del Mar. Very disappointing because they didn't start until 3.45 (1½ hours late) and it was a rehearsal.
The rehearsal took place in the Park and Dare Theatre, Treorchy.

15th

Norman and I caught a train to the Gaumont and saw 'Otello' (Verdi) by Covent Garden. It was packed. The opera was magnificent, particularly Ramón Vinay as Otello, Otaker Kraus as Iago and Cesy Broggini as Desdemona. Vinay was wonderful. He had to use a walking stick as he had injured his leg. The best opera I have seen. We caught the 10.28 from the station and I was home by 12. A thrilling experience and I am very glad I did not miss it. Carmen tomorrow.
Born in Chile, Vinay is often regarded as the finest singer of Otello.

16th

Coffee at the New Continental before 'Carmen.' It was rather disappointing. Muriel Smith looked Carmen but her voice was not strong enough. James Johnson as Don Jose neither looked nor sang the part. The Chorus and Orchestra were however wonderful and Muriel Smith was worth looking at.
Muriel Smith became the first black opera singer to take the lead in Carmen at Covent Garden. She later devoted her life to the furtherance of reconciliation through Moral Re-armament.

APRIL

13th

An excursion train to Stratford on Avon and walked to Anne Hathaway's cottage. Reached the Memorial Theatre and saw Peggy Ashcroft as Rosalind in 'As You Like It.' The performance was excellent. A memorable experience and I should very much like to go again.

Easter Sunday 21st

Gymanfa was very successful. The boys sang this evening. We were so good we are to sing it again on Tuesday evening.

23rd

The Children's Gymanfa finished at 3.45 and practice for our hymn afterwards. Gymanfa at 6 and it did not finish until 8.15. The Gymanfa was a great success again this year. Dadda conducted excellently. A great crowd particularly this evening which is always the most popular. Mamma was in a party reciting the psalm this evening.

27th

Went to the Fair and saw the comet discovered by the Belgian astronomers last year. It was very faint but could be seen distinctly.
Comet Arend-Roland was discovered on November 8 1956, by Arend and Roland. It appeared brightest in 1957 and became very bright as it passed through the inner solar system. The Fair was on the Flat in Tylorstown.

MAY

3rd

A Geography hike to the mountain opposite school. When we were coming down the mountain, I discovered I had lost my wallet. Five of us went back but were unsuccessful.

4th

Played Pontypridd on Ynysyngharad field. We scored 90 all out (I scored 6) and they were all out for 58. Their last man was out on the last ball of the match. A policeman called to report my wallet had been found by a boy in Cymmer.

20th

Higher Geography Practical this afternoon. We had a 2½" map, Conic with 2 Standard Parallels and a Graph in Statistics.

This was the first A Level (Higher) exam. They continued during the next few weeks.

JUNE

10th

West Indies continued from 87 for 9 to 119 all out. Glamorgan were all out for 77 (Ramadhin 6 wickets). West Indies won by 5 wickets. Kanhai scored 52.

The touring team always played Glamorgan on the Bank Holidays: Cardiff in June and Swansea in August. Here were some of the greatest West Indian cricketers.

18th

Higher started. Geography A1 this morning.

JULY

2nd

English A2 this morning. I ought to pass. Santos gave me 3 books to read for State Scholarship. I shall read them if I have time. A great relief to have finished Higher. It feels great that what I have been working at for months is over. Terrific to have nothing to do.

Santos was the affectionate nickname for Mr Jones, history master.

8th

History State Scholarship. Not as bad as I thought. Returned 42 English books.

15th

Arthur took us as far as Bromsgrove, near Birmingham. We called at Garringtons for tea. Arthur had a call there. Our next lift took us to Middlewich … Manchester by-pass … Preston … Kendal via Morecambe. Byron and I and a German boy named Hertz walked along the bank of the river and returned through the village. We saw the church.

Hitch-hiking holiday with Byron, a friend from the street, to Scotland began with a lift from Arthur Hughes, a close relative. Garrington's, United Engineering Forgings (UEF) Birmingham, was at one time one of the largest employers in Bromsgrove with over 3500 workers. It closed in 2002.

16th

Reached Carlisle and had pie and chips in a café. Visited the castle, museum, art gallery and cathedral. Walked along the River Eden and through the village of Etherby. I am very glad I went through the Lakes. The weather was beautiful and the scenery magnificent. I've never see anything like it. Indescribable.

20th

A lift (after 2 miles walking) to Inverness. Decided to chance my luck north. A lift with a gentleman from Nigeria all the way to John o' Groats via Dingwall, Invergordon, Dornoch and Wick. Arrived at 5.30 and left Wick for Inverness. It poured all day. 4 very short lifts but was able to get only as far as Berriedale by 8.30, a village 7 miles from Helmsdale. Stopped at a Bed and Breakfast. A very nice place and I had supper there. I trusted to luck too much today and I felt fed up before reaching this place. It is wild here. Hope Byron is alright. I'll try and catch up tomorrow.

22nd

Byron and I climbed Ben Nevis (4,406'). A long climb but not difficult. The path was very wide. We arrived at the top at 12.40 and stayed for 10 minutes. The view was beautiful. We were back outside the hostel by 3.15, before walking to Fort William for a meal. Most enjoyable. Fetched milk with a Dane afterwards. An achievement to climb The Ben. Not easy and the weather was very warm. You could see for miles from the top. Really thrilling.

23rd

A lift to the top of the Pass of Glencoe from where I walked 3 miles; lorry lift to Crianlarich. The Pass of Glencoe is magnificently rugged, the cliffs are oppressive. The mist covering the cliff tops seemed about to pour out the blood of the MacDonald's. Loch Lomond was peaceful, blue and a complete contrast, but beautiful.

29th

Caught the 7.40 bus to Pontypridd. I worked with Sid from 8.15 to 5.15 with an hour break for lunch. Various jobs, chiefly sealing, labelling and stacking the extinguishers, although I made seals and pins as well.

Began work filling fire-extinguishers in a small factory owned by Arthur Hughes.

AUGUST

2nd

Cleaned out two foam-extinguishers and painted a CO2 cylinder. Received my pay of £4 less 3/11 insurance. Fred was sacked.

5th

Caught the bus from Aberdare to Swansea and walked to St Helens. West Indies were all out for 253 (Smith 46, and Ganteaume 92). Glamorgan scored 99 for 4 by 5 (Parkhouse 48*) when it started to rain.

15th

I went down to Lewis's and bought a 'Western Mail.' I passed in all 3 subjects. Posted a form for university.

31st

I have worked for 5 weeks and earned nearly £20. I shall work next week when I shall finish. I am satisfied. I may buy a portable radio out of what I have earned.

From 6 weeks' earnings I was able to buy my first radio.

SEPTEMBER

6th

Finished working. It has been very enjoyable and I have learnt a lot. I have gained in experience, been one of the workers and although pleasing for a time, encourages me to work hard in university.

9th

Had my grades: B in Geog, B in History, B in English, E in Scholarship. I was top Arts boy with Woosnam and Donald Morgan. Bought a Vidor Lady Anne Portable (Mains and Battery) in Porth. It cost £20. I am very pleased with my grades. I didn't expect to do so well. The new radio is very good. I am listening to V.O.A. at this moment and the reception is exceptionally fine.
V.O.A. = Voice of America.

12th

Started to read 'A History of Europe' by H. A. L. Fisher. Dad went to my old school and saw Boss and my teachers. All said I have a future if I work for it.

16th

Howard Lloyd and family took me to Aberdare to the Convention at Carmel where the Rev Omri Jenkins was preaching. I am probing into Fundamentalism. I don't know whether to accept it or Modernism. There seem to be good points on both sides. It is a very difficult question but neither answer questions which puzzle me. I suppose it will come through experience. I hope I have time to think about them in future.
Omri Jenkins became the leader of the European Missionary Fellowship.

19th

Aberdare where the Rev Omri Jenkins preached for 65 minutes. Supper in Dac's. The sermon was inspiring and the atmosphere electric. A wonderful experience. Mr Jenkins is a downright Fundamentalist but I have moved towards the same views this week.

21st

I have flu.
A very serious outbreak of influenza throughout South Wales. All our family were ill. The so-called Asian Flu pandemic had already killed thousands of people around the globe - many of them in the United States. The virus is believed to have originated in North China before spreading worldwide. By December 3,550 people had died from influenza in England and Wales - three times as many flu fatalities as in the corresponding period of 1956.

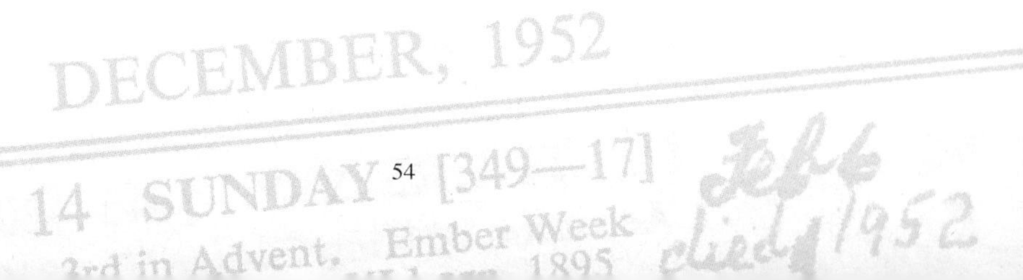

STUDENT

1957 - 1967

INTRODUCTION

School Days were left behind in July, and College life began on September 30th 1957. My intention was to study for a BA Degree in Arts at the University College Swansea and eventually follow family tradition to become a school-teacher. Although University meant leaving family, close friends and the street, I left Tylorstown feeling secure because of reasonably good grades at A level, a religious life shaped by Ebenezer, and I had travelled as far as John o Groats with the help of a 'hitching thumb.' In retrospect, I left Tylorstown as a very raw student, and although Swansea was only 35 miles from Tylorstown, I was entering a new world.

1. UNIVERSITY COLLEGE OF SWANSEA 1957-1960

Life in Swansea was very different from home. In the first year I lived in Neuadd Gilbertson in Blackpill, and the following two years were in 'digs' in Oystermouth and Brynmill. Neuadd Gilbertson was a hostel for about 90 male students, each with his own room, and having meals in the dining room. I found the adjustment very difficult from being tutored in classes of half a dozen students in school, to lectures for 100 students. At school, essays meant putting into one's own words the notes of the teacher. It took me more than a year to grasp that University education was very different. This explains my perplexity in receiving low marks for essays, and exams which resulted in a re-sit in English at the end of the First Year and the disappointment of not entering the Honours Class in History.

In the English class I had a love-hate relationship with John Donne and T S Eliot, not grasping what they were offering, but somehow feeling they were important. In retrospect failure might have benefited me as it afforded a wider education of three subjects in the Second Year (History, Geography and English) and two Finals (History and Geography).

I remember particularly the privilege of lectures on the Sixteenth Century by Glanmor Williams, on the novel by Kingsley Amis and tutorials in Geography by Gerald Manners; and who could forget 'field trips' to Dublin in 1959 and Exeter in 1960?

Of particular interest were the Freshers' Lectures on themes like 'fascism,' 'atheism' and 'nationalism,' which demanded essays written for a tutor (Mr Smyth of the Classics department) and reading one's essay individually to Principal Fulton. I believe every first-year student had a personal tutorial with the Principal.

Extra-curricular interests slowly developed as I grew in confidence. I learned a great deal from discussions with fellow students at Hall in my first year, and afterwards with Gareth Jones of Blaenau Ffestiniog with whom I shared digs from 1958 to 1962. After an outstanding profession in education, Gareth became Assembly Member for Conwy in the Welsh Assembly. During the three years I continued to enjoy Classical Music and Jazz, and experienced the rich cultural life of Swansea, especially the Swansea Festival. In College I joined the Mixed Choir in my second and third years, and at home I became a member of the Pendyrus Male Voice from 1958 to 1960. I continued my interest in sport, especially rugby and cricket at St Helens and the Arms Park.

My religious life was intriguing. When I returned home, it was centred on Ebenezer and I 'knew where I was.' In Swansea it was very different. Like many students I found it a period of searching, visiting several chapels and churches of very different traditions without settling in any one in particular. I struggled with my certainty that Jesus was a key figure in the life of humankind and should be for me personally.

1957

SEPTEMBER

30th

Noel, Dad and Brian took me to Swansea. We reached the hostel and they helped me unload. They then left. My room number is No 9. It is very smart and I should be happy here.

The men members of the family deliver me safely to Neuadd Gilbertson, Swansea.

OCTOBER

2nd

My interview with Professor Kerferd was followed by visits to the Professors of History (Glanmor Williams), English (James Kinsley) and Geography (W.G.V. Balchin). Lunch in refectory and registration this afternoon. Bought Joyce's 'Dubliners,' Shaw's 'Androcles and the Lion,' Donne's 'Poetry,' all Penguins. They cost 7/6. Spent the evening alone in my room, listening to the wireless.

Glanmor Williams became one of Wales' most eminent historians; William Balchin headed the new Swansea Geography department in 1954; James Kinsley's work on Dryden was published in 1958.

Sunday 6th

Walked as far as the Kingsway and bused to Ebenezer for a Children's service.

This proved to be one of the few times I worshipped at the Welsh speaking Congregational Chapel in the centre of Swansea. I had expected another Ebenezer like Tylorstown. Despite the warm welcome of the minister, the Revd Glyn Richards, it was quite a different experience from home.

8th

Jazz Society in the Padded Cell. A lecture for New Students with Professor J.C.Rees lecturing on 'The Idea of Progress.' Walked into town for the Mass Radiography Unit.

J. C. Rees was professor of Political Theory and Government. His was the first of the Principal's lectures for first year students. They were compulsory but not assessed. The Mass radiography was designed to tackle the scourge of TB.

10th

The boys came and heard The Goon Show.
Very few of the students had their own radio.

22nd

Jazz Club (Buck Clayton) and a lecture on Fascism. Listened to the Richardson v Pastrano fight. Received my grant (£42. 13s. 4d) and paid my hostel fees of £42.

29th

Lecture on 'Marxism.'

30th

I had only 6/20 for my essay for Walker. I shall have to take more care. Essays appear to be more important than I thought.
Dr Walker lectured in the History Department.

NOVEMBER

2nd

Dance in Coll at 9 and we came out at 9.30. It was hopeless. The boys came in at 11.30. We talked until 1, chiefly about Christianity and Atheism. We didn't seem to get anywhere by the end.

Sunday 3rd

Clyne Chapel for Communion. I didn't like it at all. Too formal and conventional. I doubt if I'll go again to a Church Service. The Russians have sent up another satellite - Sputnik 2. I am not satisfied with the way things are looking. Yanks and Russians are competing against each other tooth and nail, and goodness knows where it will end. All we can do is hope for the best.
Clyne Chapel was almost in the grounds of Neuadd Gilbertson. It was my first encounter with Anglican worship.

5th

A lecture on 'Communism and Democracy.' If it wasn't for terminals, life would be terrific. University life is the best life possible.

8th

Saw 'Nabucco' at the Grand, performed by the Welsh National Opera company. The star was the chorus who were superb.

9th

Geog trip with Mr Cousens to the docks and around the town of Morriston.
Mr Cousens lectured in the Geography Department.

16th

Saw 'War and Peace' in the Carlton. Tea in my room and the boys came and argued until 1.45. The film was excellent. We started arguing about the superiority of the English race, Nationalization and Christianity. No decisions.

Sunday 17th

In the arguments this term, I have not changed from Christianity and Socialism. My views have been strengthened and I have gained much. I hope I am not too optimistic but I believe I have made the other boys think a little more about Christianity. I am thankful to God I am certain of his existence and the truth of Jesus.

25th

Read my Fresher's essay with Mr Smyth. He thought my essay on 'The Role of Organized Religion in Politics' was very good, well planned, precise and well emphasized. I was very pleased.
Mr Smyth lectured in the Classics department.

26th

Fresher's lecture on 'Evolution.' Manners, the Geog tutor, is getting on my nerves. He is the only chap I dislike in University. Perhaps I'll get used to him before long.
Gerald Manners had only recently been appointed to the Geography Department. The tutorial group comprised 4 first year students. I found 'growing up' from school very uncomfortable. As the year progressed, I began to understand his approach.

28th

A debate on 'Pacifism is impractical.'

DECEMBER

17th

Four of us went with Mr Charles in the car to Ferndale to see 'House of Dracula' and 'Godzilla, King of the Monsters.'

It was almost unthinkable for a minister to watch a 'horror film' with young people from the church. Such was the man who helped break down barriers.

18th

Caught the 7.10 to Ferndale and bused back to Tylorstown for my Post Office round from 8 until 11. It is Brynbedw, Parry, Vivian, Brondeg, Brynhyfryd and Penrhys. The same round this afternoon.

I worked as a temporary postman from the Ferndale Office for the next seven years.

Sunday 22nd

Read Isaiah 53 in the Refugee Service, and Ysgol Gân afterwards.

1958

JANUARY

4th

Watched Wales beat the Wallabies 9-3 at the Arms Park. Very enjoyable.

7th

Wrote my paper for Sisterhood and gave my talk this evening. Although I say it myself, it went down very well. Came home with Mamma. My paper lasted longer than I thought. I was very pleased, particularly as I hardly used my notes. 25 ladies there and I think they enjoyed it.

I spoke about the holiday in Scotland. It was the first 'formal' talk I had given.

14th

Passed in Geog: 45%. Only 7 had more than 50% and 30 failed.

18th

Registered for National Service.

I was among the last 'years' eligible for National Service. Failure in the University First Year examinations meant the end of deferment and 'entering the forces.' This happened to some of my friends at Swansea. I can remember one boy looking at the results on the notice-board and saying, 'It's the Army for me. Cheerio everyone.'

22nd

History marks. Although I passed with 43%, I was disappointed, considering the work I had done.

23rd

English results: 34%. I was very surprised and disappointed. I expected to pass and cannot imagine what went wrong. However, I have passed 2 subjects out of 3 and that is a lot to be thankful for. The result of these exams is an incentive to work harder. The pace is hotter than I imagined.

FEBRUARY

4th

Manners and I don't get on very well. Freshers Lecture on 'Science and Religion' was excellent.

13th

I am beginning to appreciate Donne. He is very witty and much deeper than I thought, and I enjoyed writing the essay this evening.

26th

12/20 for my last history essay. Heard Gwynfor Evans speaking on 'Unemployment in Wales.' Very interesting. Tea in Tony's. We discussed the hydrogen bomb.

MARCH

Sunday 2nd

Gareth, Danny and I went to Mount Pleasant Baptist Chapel to hear Emrys Davies. He was very good. I have been invited to speak to Crwys in the Meeting Room tomorrow. This is an honour but I shall have to watch my step as far as Welsh is concerned for although I can understand it fairly well, I am slow in speaking.

Gareth Jones became Professor of History at Aberystwyth, and Danny Simmonds was a school friend who became a teacher. Mount Pleasant was a well-known 'evangelical centre.'

3rd

The Rev Crwys Williams - Arch-druid of Wales - was the guest with penillion singers. Enjoyed meeting Crwys. Not a word of English spoken and I understood nearly everything.

4th

Read my Fresher's essay to the Principal from 4 to 5.45. It was a pleasant interview. I wrote my Geography essay and an English appreciation of T. S. Eliot's 'Journey of the Magi.' I enjoyed writing about Eliot. It is the first poem of his I have ever read, let alone criticized. I am interested in mysticism. When I have time I would like to learn more about it.

6th

Three of us saw 'Witness for the Prosecution' in the Albert Hall. The film was excellent, one of the best. The twist at the end was most ingenious and beautifully worked out.

This is the great Billy Wilder film starring Charles Laughton, Marlene Dietrich and Tyrone Power.

Sunday 9th

Heard Leon Aitkin. His sermon was good but I didn't think much of the ceremonial. He is a kind of High Congregationalist. I have begun to realize my great need for Christianity. I have read the Bible more searchingly than I used to and find a lot of comfort.

Leon Aitkin exercised a radical ministry, especially reaching out to the unemployed, in St Paul's Brynmill, Swansea.

11th

Geography Tutorial was the best we have had. Manners was quite decent.

14th

Socialist Society to hear the presidential address of the Rt Hon James Griffiths, M.P. for Llanelly and Deputy Leader of Labour. He spoke very well on foreign affairs. Tea in Tony's where we had a big argument about Christianity. I know what I believe but I cannot convince the other boys. I pray one day I shall have help from God to convince the boys that it is only through Christ that we find eternal life and solve the problems of the world.

17th

Read my Fresher's essay on 'The Welsh Sunday' to Mr Smyth. The peculiar thing about the discussion was that all believed it should be maintained. I thought the majority would have wished it to become more modern. I fit into it at home. It has become a part of me which if it disappeared, I would lose something very important. It is gradually changing, not by direct attacks by cinema and pubs, but underground by television. Sunday should be retained but it seems very difficult to maintain.

27th

Distribution at school. I had a certificate and prize as Top Arts boy in 2nd Year VI.

At County, School Prize Day was also know as 'School Distribution.'

APRIL

6th Easter Day

Gymanfa at Ebenezer this afternoon and evening. The boys sang 'Go Down Moses' and 'Balm in Gilead.'

Here were the dozen 'boys' who had been taught by Mrs Davies in the Sunday School and were all now about 19 years of age.

15th

I think I have an interpretation of 'The Waste Land.' Although it was hard work, I thoroughly enjoyed it. It was most satisfying to think I understand. I shall find out next term.

26th

Plaza to see 'Pal Joey.' The film was excellent. Kim Novak looked wonderful and was gorgeous.

'Pal Joey' starred Frank Sinatra, Rita Hayworth and Kim Novak.

MAY

10th

A stroll in the Park. Wonderful walking through the park this evening. The flowers and trees were transformed into an ethereal quality by the sombre colours of light and shade from the sky playing on the brilliant reds. Thrilling.

14th

Formal dinner with Kingsley Amis as guest.

Kingsley Amis lectured at Swansea from 1948 to 1961.

JUNE

3rd

I have been working hard at English and even if I fail, I have learnt a lot about literature. My views on poetry have widened - particularly about poets like Donne, Dryden, Browning and Eliot. If I fail, this year has certainly not been a waste of time, and I have enjoyed discovering poetry. I think I am beginning to understand, although maybe too late for exams. We shall see!

8th

In 90 hours, I shall have finished exams and my fate will be sealed. What will be the results of my labours? Nothing is more certain than that as we have sown, so shall we reap - except those lucky in spotting questions!

11th

Bought 4 LPs at 6/- each. They are 'Turk Murphy and George Lewis at Newport,' 'Dennis Wilson Entertains,' 'Rampart and Vine,' and 'Morgana King Sings the Blues.' They are all terrific especially the first and third. After Early Dinner Dan, Gerry and I had the greatest session of all time (from 7 to 9.45) with the George Lewis and Turk Murphy L.P. We went wild particularly when all the boys came in. I think we were all exhausted. I finish exams tomorrow.

The records were bought through a student who acted as an intermediary from Kingsley Amis who had reviewed them for the Observer.

12th

Geography Practical in the Geology Lab. Exams are over. I have nothing to do. I am free; tomorrow I can get up and there is no book I have to read, no notes I have to swot and nothing I have to write. There is a little thing called results.

20th

Met Dac at the bus station. We had hake and chips in a café.

27th

Passed History and Geography and a re-sit in English - as have most of the boys. I had 36 in English. The end of first year University, and if I pass English in September, I shall be doing Finals.

JULY

7th

Met the van outside the Tylors and was in Pontypridd by 7.30. Reached the factory and after being introduced to the workmen I did odd-jobs.
I was working in the same fire-extinguisher factory as the previous year.

18th

Didn't have much to do and was told I wouldn't be needed next week. I am not going to work tomorrow because I have had the sack without the slightest warning.

AUGUST

Sunday 3rd

Communion this evening and the Pendyrus Annual Concert in the Workmen's afterwards. The artistes were Geraint Evans and Patricia Johnson. Sat by Mamma. The concert was very moving and at times I was completely carried away. A particular instance was when the choir sang 'Myfanwy.'
Two great opera stars sang with the choir.

Sunday 17th

Sunday school. Joined Pendyrus afterwards.

The Pendyrus Choir had been formed in 1924. The first formal meeting was held in Ebenezer Vestry when my uncle, John Morgan was appointed Secretary, and my father Contributions Secretary. My father later served as Chairman during the War Years and became a Life Member in 1980.

Sunday 31st

Took a class of 10 in Sunday school. Pendyrus practice.

SEPTEMBER

Sunday 7th

On stage at the Patti pavilion from 8 until 9.45, singing the old favourites - 'The Charge,' 'Nidaros,' and 'Myfanwy.' Thrilling.

This was my first concert with the Pendyrus. It was held in Swansea and coincided with my re-sits the following days. The Charge is 'The Charge of the Light Brigade.' All three pieces were favourites with the choir - and the audiences.

8th

A tram to college for the English exam. It was neither difficult nor easy, but as in previous English exams I found it impossible to know how I did. North Wales on Thursday. I am looking forward to it very much as I have never been further north than Pwllheli and then only for a day from Aberystwyth.

The tram was the Mumbles Railway which opened in 1807 and closed in 1960.

9th

Second English exam. Exactly the same feeling as yesterday. Bought Frank Sinatra's 'Songs for Swingin' Lovers' in the Coop.

11th

A lift in a cement lorry as far as Pontryhdfendigaid and a lift to Ponterwyd on the back of a lorry. Arrived at Blaenau Ffestiniog by 5.15.

The first real visit to North Wales, for a holiday with the parents of Gareth Jones, fellow student. Blaenau Ffestiniog proved to be similar to the Rhondda except for the Welsh language. Gareth and I shared digs for four years from 1958 to 1962.

16th

Hitched to Conway, Penmaenmawr, Bangor, Caernarvon, Waunfawr - the mountains were very beautiful. Arrived home in a Bentley.

19th

Gareth and I visited Mr and Mrs Garlick and had coffee there.
Raymond Garlick, the poet, was Gareth's English master in the local school.

25th

I have passed English re-sit. What a relief! I have finished Part 1.

27th

Mr Davies B.A. called and asked if I would speak in chapel tomorrow morning. I have been looking up something on Justice.
David Davies was know as David Davies B.A. because he was the only member in chapel who had a degree. He taught Welsh and Religious Education at Tonypandy Grammar School and stood as a Plaid Cymru candidate for Rhondda East in 1950.

Sunday 28th

Wrote my paper on 'Justice' and gave my paper in chapel. Took Dadda's Sunday School class this afternoon. Pendyrus bus to Nantymoel where we gave a concert in the cinema.

OCTOBER

4th

Gareth and I met the Pendyrus boys and had a rehearsal in a chapel vestry. We were at the Pavilion at 7, but didn't sing until 9. Treorchy sang some piece from Cherubini while we sang 'Sons of the Desert.' Lost by 3 marks.
This was the Miners' Eisteddfod in Porthcawl. It had started there in 1948, inspired by men like Dai Francis who became General Secretary of the National Union of Miners.

Sunday 12th

Worshipped at Tabernacle Independent Chapel this morning and evening. Sat with the Choir in the front. Attended Sunday school.

I was a student living in Oystermouth. Tabernacle was in walking distance of digs.

22nd
Bought a duffle coat for £5-19-6. It will come in very handy because I don't want to wear my best coat to college.

NOVEMBER

1st
Joined the choir at Bancyfelin where a new hall was opened.
Pendyrus sang at this village, west of Carmarthen. The soloist was the young tenor, Stuart Burroughs.

12th
The buses left for Aberystwyth. We won 3-0. A wonderful experience! A tremendous surprise to beat Aber particularly as the ground was heavy and they have a stronger pack. All the boys played magnificently. At last the University of Wales Championship is within reach after winning 3 games out of 3. If Coll beat Bangor next week, we will be the new champions.
They did beat Bangor and were Champions.

Sunday 23rd
An excellent sermon from a student from Brecon - Peter Williams.
Peter Williams became a Congregational and later a United Reformed Church minister.

DECEMBER

17th
In the Post Office by 6 and after sorting the round, Evan and I did the Penrhys walk between us. Back in the office by 9 and took parcels along the Strand before sorting the round and delivering the whole Penrhys walk.
The Penrhys walk constituted streets running into Penrhys Road. There was of course no housing estate. Evan was a senior postman.

Sunday 21st

I rose at 4.45 and after breakfast I had a lift to Pleasant Hill in a Post Office van. I finished by 10.30, came home and slept until 4.30. Chapel at 6, followed by the Youth Club Carol service in Libanus. I read John 1.1-14.

27th

I bought 'Ella and Louis' in Barrett's. Caught the bus to Treorchy for the party in St Matthew's hall. I have never seen such a shambles. A drunken orgy. Most of the boys were under 16 and nearly all were drunk. The new L.P. is fabulous.

Barrett's shop was in Ferndale.

Sunday 28th

I was asked to read Mamma's paper in chapel this evening: on the Quakers.

30th

Helped trim the vestry for the Sunday School party and organize games for the children.

31st

Collected my pay: £7-6s-3d, making a total of £12-15s-9d.

1959

JANUARY

13th

Geography results: 42% and third of Final Arts. Gareth came 1st with 50. There are 8 of us studying Mains Geography. Started to read the Gospel according to St Matthew. I shall read a portion each evening before I sleep.

17th

Gareth and I were in the Arms Park (Enclosure) and had quite a good position although it emptied down throughout. Wales beat England 5-0. Train to Porth and a bus home. We had a frame in the Welfare before catching the 9 to Treorchy. We were in the Library by 9.15 and danced all evening.

19th

My history mark is 50%. Very respectable.

23rd

Passed English with 45%. Heard J. B. G. Thomas speaking on Welsh Sport.
J B G Thomas was a well known commentator on Welsh rugby.

30th

Bought in the Coop, Beethoven 'Symphonies No 5 and 4' by Arturo Toscanini and the N.B.C. Orchestra. Chapel to Young Peoples meeting and collected 5/- for my Missionary Card.

FEBRUARY

3rd

A Departmental Lecture on 'Economic Problems in Central Africa' by Prof Steel of Liverpool. I am taking 'The Times' regularly. I think it is worth it from a cultural standpoint.
Professor Robert Steel became Principal of the University College of Swansea from 1974 - 82. He and Mrs Eileen Steel both served as elders at Manselton during my ministry there.

10th

The college choir sang in a school-hall in Llanelli for the Old Age Pensioners.

12th

Twenty of us went to Margam to look around the Steel works. Fantastic.
The Abbey Works had been completed in 1952 and became the largest Steel Works in Europe.

Sunday 15th

Chapel this evening and a very good sermon. Gareth and I had a discussion until 12 particularly about Christianity. I do not think enough about religion - it is a Sunday and 'ten minutes before I go to bed' affair. I dont live as I should. Christianity is so vital, while with me it is secondary or tertiary.

27th

Philip Noel Baker spoke excellently on the Arms race.
At the time he was Labour MP for Derby, and had been an architect of both the League of Nations and the United Nations.

MARCH

25th

Walked to Bristol Tump. A wonderful view from the Beacons to the Channel and even the other side. It was very clear. Saw the chapel production of 'Hansel and Gretel' in Maerdy. Dad conducted. It was very good.

27th (Good Friday)

Read and prayed in chapel for half an hour.
This was the first time the chapel had been opened for meditative prayers.

APRIL

11th

The boat, 'St David' docked in Rosslare. The Dublin train left at 10.45. We were taken to Trinity College Hostel. A party of ten led by Mr Board had a walking tour of Dublin in pouring rain. It was very interesting. Coffee in O' Connell Street before dispersing. A lecture by Prof (Balchin) on the background to Dublin. Ireland seems very poor.
The Geography Field-Trip to the Dublin area.

Sunday 12th

I found Grosvenor Rd Baptist Church and talked to an old man on a seat until 11.30 when it was time for service: conducted by Dr Orr, a missionary from Brazil. The service was good - 150 in the congregation in a predominantly

R.C. country. Bus tour to the Howth peninsula, Dublin Airport and Phoenix Park. A lecture by Dr Cousens.
Little did I realise I was listening to Dr Edwin Orr, an Irish evangelist who travelled the world and had been in Brazil in the 1950s.

MAY

2nd
We have a new L.P. - Schubert's 'Unfinished Symphony' and Brahm's 'Theme on Haydn Variations.' They are brilliant.

Sunday 17th
I swotted in the quarry and later on the beach in front of the house. Methodist Chapel at 6 before a walk along the Pier. The chapel was very important during the Evan Roberts 1904 Diwygiad. [Revival]
I joined my parents for a week's 'holiday' in New Quay. This was the birthplace of my mother. The quarry was at the end of Rock Street and the beach, Traeth y ddolau.

JULY

Sunday 5th
Communion and presentation to Mr Charles. I had to speak on behalf of the Young People tonight. It was very emotional, lasting 2 hours. I was scared stiff when I had to speak.
Alwyn Charles' final service at Ebenezer. He moved to Alltwen, Pontardawe. I did not realise that our relationship would continue throughout his life.

6th
Went to Treforest to look around the factories. We couldn't find a job anywhere.
Looking for summer employment in the two Trading Estates of Treforest and Hirwaun.

7th
Hitched to Hirwaun where we looked for work but were unsuccessful.

9th

Mr Charles' induction service in Alltwen.

AUGUST

7th

A lift to work in the Gas van. After work, I walked home over the mountain. My pay today was £3- 18s-1d, not too bad but nothing to gloat over.

I found employment for two weeks in the Gas Offices in Pentre in the Rhondda Fawr.

8th

I got up at 4.15 and caught the Pendyrus bus at the Queens. Breakfast in Llanidloes by 8 and lunch at 1.30 in Caernarfon. Rehearsal at Moriah and on stage at 4.30. We came 3rd - Treorchy, Rhos, us and Rhos Orpheus. We sang with Treorchy from 7.30 to 9.45. We were on the air from 8.15 until 9. A disappointment today but a great experience. Treorchy were definitely preferred today but there you are!

The National Eisteddfod at Caernarfon. The Queens Hotel in Tylorstown has been demolished.

SEPTEMBER

1st

I applied to 4 universities for entrance to Teachers' Training.

11th

Cory Hall for rehearsal. We sang on 'Friday Night is Music Night' with Welsh Orchestra and Ray Jenkins, Park and Dare Band and Laurie Payne. We sang 'Martyrs' and 'Matona.'

Cory Hall Cardiff was the venue for a concert in which Pendyrus sang .

12th

Caught the Pendyrus bus to Llanidloes where we sang in a chapel schoolroom. Beryl and Emlyn were the artistes. A meal before leaving at 11.15. Bed as soon as we were home - 2.45. The concert was the best I have sung in. It was marvellous. Everything seemed to click. In 'Iesu o Nazareth',

it was as if the whole of the party were moved by the Spirit, and Duggan said it was the best he had heard it for years. A truly unforgettable experience. The audience were in raptures, really appreciative.
The artistes were Beryl Jones (Watts) from Brynbedw, Tylorstown and a member of Ebenezer, and Emlyn Lewis of Ynysybwl.

OCTOBER

5th
If I had the vote, it would be for Labour - their policy seems humane and modern while the Tories don't have any social policy. The election will be close with Labour just having the majority.

9th
Conservatives won the Election by 100 seats. A disgrace! It makes one think of Home Rule to kick the Tories out. It makes you sick. People don't know what's best for them.
The Election in which Macmillan defeated Gaitskell.

13th
Brangwyn to see the Hallé under Barbirolli - Wagner, Handel and Haydn.

16th
Hallé under George Weldon with William Kemff in a concert devoted to Beethoven. Superb. 'The Pastoral' was beautifully soothing, the product of a great mind. Even better than Tuesday.

22nd
St Mary's to hear the Philamusica of London. The concert this evening was great. I enjoyed it more than the Hallé. I particularly liked 'Four Poems' by Lennox Berkeley. It was top class. The conductor, Granville Jones, is a real eccentric, long hair, black suede shoes.

23rd
'Peer Gynt' with Oliver Neville at the Palace was brilliant. I had no idea it was possible to portray so much on so small a stage. I was deeply moved, particularly with Peer's salvation by love of his wife, after all his materialism and intellectual musings had resulted in despair. He found his true self by the revelation of himself in the love of Solveig.

Oliver Neville became Principal of RADA. The Palace Theatre was built as a Music Hall in 1888 but became a night club in the 1970s.

29th

Piano recital by Phyllis Sellick.
Phyllis Sellick was one of the most influential pianists of the second half of the Twentieth Century. Her husband was the pianist Cyril Smith.

31st

Brangwyn to see 'Stabat Mater' and 'Sixth Chandos Anthem' by a choir of 450.

NOVEMBER

7th

Wrote to Mr Charles and filled in Teacher Training forms before going to St Helens to see Swansea beat Blackheath 13-0. Saw 'I'm Alright, Jack.'
The Boulting brothers film, starring Peter Sellers.

10th

Played traditional records in Jazz Club. I think it was quite successful.

12th

Two buses were in Tylorstown for the concert at Ebenezer. 80 of us in choir today.
The University Choir sang at Ebenezer.

27th

Heard Edward Heath, Minister of Labour, in Conservative Society.

30th

I have been considering studying for a B.D. in the Annibynwyr College, but I dont know whether I am worthy enough. I shall have to pray and think hard.

DECEMBER

2nd

Geography trip to Felindre.

The Felindre Works were commissioned in 1956.

3rd

Brangwyn for 'The Messiah.'

11th

Had an interview in Swansea for Teachers' Training and it seemed alright.

18th

Up at 4, breakfast and bused to Ferndale to be on duty at 4.30. Sorted until 8.30 when home for second breakfast. Worked again from 9 to 12.30.

A postman - again.

22nd

Saw Fred Astaire in 'Swing Time.'

I never thought I would be enjoying Fred Astaire 50 years later.

25th

Finished work at 9.15. Robert and I watched 'High Noon.'

Robert was one of the friends from Ebenezer. Robert was tragically killed in a car crash in December 1962. 'High Noon' stars Gary Cooper and Grace Kelly.

29th

Received £8-2s-9d today which makes a total of over £10. Not too bad considering that overtime has been reduced since last year.

1960

JANUARY

1st

Helped organise games in Sunday School party. Excellent news that I have been accepted for Teacher Training in Swansea.

5th

Spoke to the Sisterhood about 'Problems of the 1960s.' Again I felt the calling of the Ministry. I have to think hard.

28th

We went to the Brangwyn to see the Warsaw Philharmonic conducted by Witold Rowicki, with Wanda Wilkomirska (Violin). Tchaikovsky '5th Symphony' was fab.

In 1958 Witold Rowicki was appointed artistic director and principal conductor of the Philharmonic, a post he held until 1977. Wanda Wilkomirska was a famous Polish violinist.

29th

History marks confirmed and I am very pleased with 57, particularly as I came top - never before in a Coll exam. I still have never failed a History or Geog exam. Hope I shall not start now.

Sunday 28th

Frank Lee preached on 'Og and his big bed.'

Frank Lee was minister of Pantygwydr Baptist Church. Why are some sermons remembered - and most forgotten?

FEBRUARY

8th

3 LPs from Doug today - Sibelius 2, Haydn 100 & 104 and Dvorak 5. I have a good selection of Classical music, particularly Symphonies.

Bought from a second hand record club. Doug was a fellow student.

22nd

Ferndale Sec for practice - Pendyrus, Imps and Morlais under Mansel Thomas for a broadcast on Sunday.

The rehearsal took place on neutral ground in the local Grammar school. The three male voice choirs were all local: Pendyrus from Tylorstown; Morlais which began in Ebenezer Vestry as 'The Mustard Singers' in 1928, and Ferndale Imperial Singers which began in 1949.

APRIL

12th

Noel was up this evening and we had a long chat about the decline of chapels, socialism, Trade Unions and the disruption of family life. Interesting although impossible to draw conclusions except that we are in an age of transition, cynicism and disintegration.

19th

Gymanfa was a great success. Excellent this evening - one of the Welsh traditions which must be kept alive.

MAY

9th

Gareth and I had a long chat on Welsh nationalism. I'm not sure there is great political need, but it is essential that economic, social and religious changes take place: in economics we need better communications to bring large scale industry, and a reform of agriculture to prevent rural depopulation. Socially and religiously there is even greater need because we have a culture which is neither English nor Welsh - we have lost our culture and there is nothing in its place. Religion is gone.

It is clear that I had not been introduced to 'Anglo-Welsh' culture, despite the fact that I had studied English in School and for two years at University.

16th

My last lecture as undergraduate. These three years have been wonderful. Lectures have been interesting and I have enjoyed most of the 1000 lectures.

24th

I read in the Gazette that a Welsh Nationalist had been returned on the Council for the first time, defeating Labour. Is this significant or an isolated example? Does it mean the beginning of a new era in Welsh politics which could end in Home Rule? I am undecided on whether this is good for Wales, but changes are needed in Welsh economic and cultural life.
The Gazette was 'The Rhondda Leader.'

31st

Tomorrow I start my exams. This is my ultimate exam, the end for which I have been working since entering Grammar school - or really all my life. The last and hardest hurdle, and I pray to God I shall succeed. I feel nervous but I have worked hard. If I keep my head and the questions are OK, I should do it.

JUNE

Sunday 12th

Rev Emrys Davies of Llanelly preached excellently on the Ascension at Walter Road Congregational Church.
I later became a close friend of Emrys Davies when he was minister at Tenby United Reformed Church.

23rd

I passed history and have my degree. I am a Bachelor of Arts, after 3 years in University. God has been very good to me and I thank Him from the bottom of my heart.

24th

Met Dac at 2. We went to the Brangwyn and had tea in the Milkmaid. He left on the 6. I phoned Mr Charles and will see him on Sunday to find out the possibilities of studying for a B.D. Nothing definite.

2. THE BRIDGE

After nearly 50 years, I still find it difficult to put into words what happened during the Summer of 1960. On June 24th 1960, the day I learned I had passed Finals, my grandfather spent the afternoon with me in Swansea, and that evening I phoned Alwyn Charles, minister in Alltwen, near Swansea. We met a few days later and we discussed issues of 'training for ministry' and studying theology. Apparently he was not surprised by my dilemma but had been waiting for me to make an approach. The consequence was that throughout the summer I wrestled with these issues until I decided to follow Christ and 'allow the church to make the decision.' If the church thought I was suitable, I would walk in this new direction. Ebenezer, my home chapel recommended me in August for the Ministry of the Undeb yr Annibynwyr and in October I entered theological college in Swansea.

JUNE

Sunday 26th

Mr Charles and I had a very serious talk and he advised me to think very carefully about entering the College next year and sitting for my B.D. I am very uncertain and although I think I could cope with the work, I'm not sure whether I am fit for it. However I must pray hard and think hard about it.

JULY

Sunday 3rd

I joined the Pendyrus bottom bass because I found first bass too high. After tea Communion before going to the café in Ferndale with the gang. Yesterday I bought 'The Symphony' by Ralph Hill. I have started 'Essays in Orthodox Dissent' by Bernard Lord Manning.
Bernard Manning was a formidable Congregational thinker.

4th

Caught the 6.30 bus to Porth yard. I worked on the scavenging lorry in the Porth and Trehafod areas. Tea in the morning and an hour for lunch. I made 2/9 on the side; they collect rags and metal from the bins and also do 'favours' for people. We finished at 3.30. The work today was hard but is excellent for humility, although the workmen have great pride in their work.
My first day on a holiday job for Rhondda Borough Council.

5th

Same lorry in the Ynyshir area. It was the nearest I could imagine to hell because it was pouring and I could hardly lift or bend because my back was terribly stiff. The end of a hard manual day's work. This is soul destroying. I hope I shall get used to it.

19th

Saw the Glamorgan Youth Orchestra in Ferndale with Mam and Dad. Their chief works were Beethoven's 'Fourth Piano Concerto' and 1st and 2nd movements of Brahms's '1st Symphony.' The conductor was Russell Shepherd. The concert was good, particularly the Beethoven.

Sunday 24th

Dad was preaching in chapel.

This was the first time for me to hear Dad lead worship. He led worship very rarely. It was only after he retired that he preached more frequently.

27th

Dad, Mamma, Dac and I caught the 6.40 to Aberdare and Swansea. I went to the Brangwyn Hall by 9.45, signed the roll and went to graduation from 11 to 12.45. I am finally and completely a Bachelor of Arts. I am pleased it is all over. The ceremony impressed upon me that I had passed my final exam. I probably won't see many friends again, after being together for three years. An awful feeling to be saying goodbye to such great chaps. A lot of sentiment today.

28th

I bought the 'Faber Book of Modern Verse' and the 'Penguin Book of Contemporary Verse.' I will try to read through both and brush up my knowledge of literature. I haven't read much English for quite a time but I hope to get back into it quickly.

Sunday 31st

After chapel, I took the student, Aeron Davies to Mrs Griffiths' house. Had tea with him before chapel this evening. I have almost decided to enter the ministry. I talked with Aeron today and my mind becomes clearer and is pointing towards my entering the church. I still haven't made up my mind. Material factors are important because I realise that I shall give up a lot I have planned. I shall come to some decision soon. It will be a great step.

Aeron Davies was a student at Swansea, soon to become minister of the Congregational Church in Ferndale. He had hospitality for the day with 'Mrs Griffiths No 1'- she lived in No 1 East Road, Tylorstown.

AUGUST

4th

I am certain of a few basic facts. There is a great need for ministers and I would try my best to spread the word of God. I do not know if I would be a 'success' but I would give it all my efforts. If only I could be sure I would not be a failure and let God down.

5th

Dr Pennar wrote me a very nice letter and gave me instructions for entering the college. I think I shall do it. I have prayed and feel it is the right thing. Time will tell if I am making the right decision.
Dr Pennar Davies was Principal of the Congregational Memorial College Swansea.

9th

I stacked bricks all day - 2500, very monotonous but ideal for contemplation. I finished the excellent 'Essays on Orthodox Dissent' by Bernard Lord Manning and I read the first 20 chapters of Genesis.

11th

I am to see Pennar on Saturday about entering the ministry. It is now definite that I shall do it. I realise it will be hard work but I won't mind that. I pray I shall do the work God wants me to do.

13th

I was up as usual and out scavenging. I was home by 10.30, bathed, had dinner and Dac and I caught the 1.40 to Aberdare. I saw Pennar Davies from 3.50 to 5.30. I had my interview and shall be entering the Congregational Memorial College on the 4th of Oct. I have an entrance exam on Sept 6th. I feel very happy now I have at last settled things. I am more contented. I hope I shall live up to my calling.

17th

I am almost prepared for my first service. I will preach on famine relating to the life of Joseph. The material isn't too bad but my method of expression and the way I handle the service remains to be seen.

Why my choice of Joseph? I assumed it was because my text was 'And Pharaoh said unto his servants, Can we find such a one as this is, a man in whom the spirit of God is?' (Genesis 41. 38. Authorized Version.) My theme was that economic problems would not be solved by Capitalism nor by Communism, but only by leaders who were obedient to the Way of God. Or, was my choice some subliminal awareness that I had read the story many years before to my grandmother? (see October 7th 1952.)

19th

I wrote a prayer and the Order of Service for Sunday. I feel nervous but shall pray for power to speak so that the congregation will not consider it a waste of time to listen to me.

20th

Visited Cledan and Enid at St Michael's. The hostel has single rooms, they have ample opportunity to study but the regulation is forbidding.

Cledan Mears was a lecturer at the Anglican college of St Michaels's Llandaff. He was later to become Bishop of Bangor. His wife Enid was a cousin of Uncle Noel's wife Mair.

Sunday 21st

Tea in Dac's. I looked over my sermon. I took the service in Libanus. I have taken my first service and am quite pleased although I hope to do much better. I preached for half an hour. I received 12/6, the proudest money I have ever received.

I preached my first sermon at Libanus Welsh Presbyterian Chapel Tylorstown. Dr D. M. Phillips had been its most famous minister. Sadly the chapel has been long demolished.

22nd

Received J.B. Phillips' New Testament from Mamma and Dad and I read St Mark this evening. I read Psalm 22 for the first time and saw the remarkable parallel with the Crucifixion.

27th

I have finished two months of work and feel a free man. I can now get up at a reasonable hour and do the reading I want. It was an excellent experience and has taught me how to live with working men. All have basic goodness and kindness and are willing to give a helping hand. I have had a lot of fun, learnt a lot and earned money for my holidays. I wrote my second sermon - on Mark 5.36.

'As soon as Jesus heard the word that was spoken, he saith unto the ruler of the synagogue, Be not afraid, only believe.' (Authorized Version).

31st

Took the service in Ebenezer and preached on Mark 5.36. After speeches, we came out at 9.45. A relief to have this first and very difficult service over. I found a hwyl this evening which banished my nerves. Everyone thought I was good but of course they couldn't very well say otherwise. What they said privately may be different. Mr Charles told me my faults but said he was very pleased.

This was the first 'Pregeth prawf:' preaching before one's home congregation. Ebenezer then recommended that I should train for ministry for the Undeb yr Annibynwyr Cymraeg. (the Union of Welsh Independents)

SEPTEMBER

6th

The exam was reasonable enough and I ought to pass. I am looking forward to the beginning of term.

Sunday 25th

Preached in Trerhondda in my second 'Pregeth Prawf.' I am glad this second sermon is over because my parents and family were there. I wasn't as nervous as in Ebenezer but I had too much in the sermon and could have made more emphases. I realize I am a beginner and have a lot to learn.

Trerhondda chapel was in Ferndale. It is now used as a Community Arts Centre.

26th

Noel criticized my sermon very thoroughly and after he finished I didn't know where I stood. He was right in many respects. I must try to be simpler and less of a lecturer. This is a natural fault after university for 3 years. I am satisfied with the content in my sermon although there was too much in it. I hope I will develop and readjust the elementary ideas I hold now.

3. CONGREGATIONAL MEMORIAL COLLEGE, SWANSEA 1960-3.

The small theological college in a leafy side street in Ffynnone, Swansea was a different world from the University looking over Swansea Bay and the Mumbles. The College had established itself in Swansea in 1959 and was the union of the old Dissenting Academies of the Presbyterian College at Carmarthen and the Memorial College at Brecon. Trevor Evans and D P Roberts, lecturing in Old and New Testaments came from Carmarthen, and D J Davies and Principal Pennar Davies from Brecon. It was a College of 40 students from all over Wales, half Welsh speakers from West Wales. Their world was rural, often literary and reflected a church life which had long died in the Central and Eastern Valleys from which many of us came. A very vociferous minority belonged to the 'fundamentalist camp.' They were waiting anxiously to leave College unscarred by scholarship so that they could effectively preach the 'Word.' Others of us, less certain of our theological positions, had also been called into ministry by a love for Jesus, but were eager to learn the art and skill of theological and ministerial training.

The Welsh BD was a rigorous discipline and in the Second and Third Years, examinations were held in the University. I found the Course exciting, struggling with Hebrew in the first year but enjoying Greek and Latin throughout the three years. The languages were necessary for studies in the Bible, Christian Doctrine and Church History. My special subjects were the two latter subjects and in retrospect, they provided an ideal foundation for my later work in the exploration in theology with congregations. Scripture was compulsory throughout the three years and introduced us to modern scholarship, much to the disgust of some of the more conservative students who never forgave their lecturers or the Curriculum.

As important as study in the classroom were discussions amongst the students which often took place formally in the College Forum called 'Ad Rem' but more often informally and in very heated conversations between 'fundamentalist' and 'liberal,' and 'Welsh' and 'English' students. A variety of cultural and theological positions were expressed, and I learned a great deal from both measured discussion and heated argument.

During the three years, students were expected to preach on most Sundays and this meant long journeys to and from chapels throughout South Wales. Often it meant catching the early morning 'preachers' bus' as the Swansea to Cheltenham bus was called, which made its way up the Vale of Neath and along the Heads of the Valleys. This was a salutary experience as many Valley churches had very small congregations and were struggling to survive. It was a wonderful training ground for ministry during the continuing decline which has taken place throughout the second half of the last century. I was fortunate to spend two 'summer pastorates' at Bethany, Godreaman and Tabernacle, Abertillery. The former small congregation in Aberdare had been without ministry for many years, but Tabernacle was one of the strongest churches in Monmouthshire. I received far more than I gave through both experiences, especially in the ministry of visiting.

During the three years I struggled with the relationship between religion and politics, particularly with issues of peace during the nuclear crisis and the 'Hands off Cuba' campaign, and the crisis of the future of Wales and its culture as experienced with the flooding of Tryweryn, listening to Gwynfor Evans and Waldo Williams, and my friendship with John Gwilym Jones.

Although a small College, Coleg Coffa introduced us to the ecumenical dimension. Highlights were lectures on Scripture by Suzanne de Dietrich, Church History by Kenneth Latourette and a landmark meeting with Martin Niemöller, all organized by the Blaendulais Ecumenical Centre with its visionary leader, Erastus Jones.

Within the field of Church History, I was particularly enthralled by lectures by Pennar on 'Puritanism in England and Wales,' and during the Christmas term, he suggested I should study in that field for a B Litt in Mansfield College, Oxford. Although this meant a delay in ordination and entering the ministry, this was an opportunity too good to miss. After being interviewed by Stanley Greenslade and George Caird in December 1962, I was accepted as a probationer B Litt student.

At this time, towards the end of studies at Swansea came the most important meeting in my life on the evening three theology students met three trainee teachers from Swansea Training College, the College on the hill. I met Norah Evans of Craigcefnparc in December 1962 and that story continues to be lived and told. Norah had also been involved in the Hands off Cuba protest and later was to spend a year studying her First Year B. D. in Coleg Coffa.

SEPTEMBER

28th

Met the 10 other students and had my medical at 12. We appeared before a committee of 20, each in turn and then together, to be accepted into the College. I have been re-convinced of the significance of a tradition in Ministry. I shall do my best. I know my task is to spread the word of the Gospel and strengthen the Church.

OCTOBER

12th

Broadmead Annibynwyr Church for the quarterly meeting of East Glamorgan. A very exciting day, particularly discussion led by Alban Davies. I am officially a student at Coleg Coffa and a recognised member of the East Glamorgan Union.
The Welsh Congregational church in Bristol met at Broadmead Baptist Chapel. Alban Davies was the radical, long-serving minister at Bethesda, Ton Pentre.

14th

Sermon class with Peter Williams. He was excellent - II Chronicles 2.2. I bought 'Vocabulary of the Bible' (27/6) edited by Von Allmen. The new book is excellent for sermon making, theology and scriptural information.
I had first heard Peter preach when I was at university.

Sunday 16th

Preached in Pentrechwith (40 there and also gave a children's story). 100 this evening and the whole atmosphere was exhilarating. It seemed everyone cared. I shall have to be more careful with the prayer. It was however the best service I have taken. I enjoyed it.
Pentrechwith Congregational Church was on the east side of Swansea.

17th

CND meeting was very effective.
This was held at the University.

18th

Prayers, Pastoralia and lectures from 11 to 12.30 on Church History and OT. Fellowship in which R. E. Edwards spoke on Missionary work. Trouble is brewing between fundamentalists and others. They are quite powerful and some want to be baptised by complete immersion officially by the College. Pennar has given permission but there is a lot of discontent. A bad example for Congregationalists.

R. E. Edwards was the London Missionary Society Secretary for the Undeb yr Annibynwyr Cymraeg.

20th

Cardiff University to hear Prof H. D. Lewis on 'Our Knowledge of God.' The lecture was excellent, encouraging us to keep the *via media* in theology. On the way home on the bus, from talking to other boys, it struck me that my task is to be a minister of the gospel and not a social reformer or youth leader. The Church is to be interested in these things, but our task is to preach Christ crucified.

Hywel Lewis was the Professor of the History and the Philosophy of Religion at King's College in the University of London.

NOVEMBER

Sunday 6th

I am happy in my new life. I am determined to learn as much as I can because I want to combat the apathy and opposition to Jesus Christ today. Christianity must be shown to be practical and essential, even to the most well-educated. Young people want a rational explanation of religion and I shall try to show its relevance in a modern world.

7th

Old Testament study is stimulating and exciting, because there is so much to learn. It must be awful to be afraid of criticizing this wonderful book. The significance of the OT increases when it is approached critically.

16th

I led College prayers, reading the 5th chapter of Romans. I felt nervous about taking prayers and am glad it is over.

30th

In Ad Rem we discussed the behaviour of students, quality of lecturers, fellowship; then I proposed a statement to the Press concerning 'Sunday Opening.' Of the 30, only 4 were against making a statement.

DECEMBER

1st

Life is wonderful. I am thrilled by my work. I love it all. I even find the JDEPH sources fascinating. Marvellous that I shall spend my life studying the Bible, learning about Christ and greatest of all, with God's blessing, I shall win souls for Him.

JDEPH were studied as the historic and linguistic sources of the Pentateuch.

2nd

Six of us had tea in Dr Pennar's. He is a wonderful man: a Christian, a representative of Jesus Christ, humble, sincere and a brilliant scholar.

Sunday 11th

Preached in Trinity Calvinistic Methodist and went to Sunday School. They are fundamentalists but of course grand people and very sincere. 40 in the morning and 80 in the evening. Prayer Meeting at 5.30. Impossible to argue with them. If you are not a fundamentalist, you are not saved and do not know Jesus as Saviour.

Trinity was in Tonypandy and was known as the 'graveyard of students'- presumably by those of a more liberal approach.

12th

Walked behind Hendrefadog School and along to Penrhys. Quiet on the mountain; up there is peace, spiritual communion. I love the valley - I was a boy there.

14th

Preached in sermon class. No criticisms. They must have felt in good moods to let me off lightly.

Each year every student preached before the whole College.

15th

Bought Beethoven's 'Choral.' I received the 'Revised Standard Version' of the Bible from Aunty Kay. A beautiful volume.

16th

The 'Choral' is magnificent, probably the best symphony I have with Brahms '4th Symphony.' The new edition of the Bible is much easier to read and can be understood with little difficulty.

17th

I called to see Dac. He gave me £25 to buy books. I didn't know what to say.

19th

Walked to Pleasant Hill by 12 midnight and worked until 7.30. One of the strangest things, working all night and sleeping all day.
Holiday work with the Post Office.

21st

I reckoned we sorted 25,000 letters last night, because we manage 1400 each every hour.

23rd

I am living in a dream-like world with one's whole existence tied up with Christmas cards to be sorted, primarily and secondarily. Three of us have personally sorted 150,000 and the others another 50,000. This is only inward sorting.

1961

JANUARY

2nd

I spent the last three nights in Dac's. He is great, wonderful for his age, intelligent, a pillar of strength and young at heart, although he misses Mam very much. I love him a tremendous amount. He is a good friend.

6th

We have been discussing Sunday Opening. There are more important problems but that doesn't mean we must ignore this. Drunkenness is a social evil, a personal sin and it is our duty as Christians to fight against more opportunities for vice. We have to put our own house in order.
The Welsh Sunday Closing Act 1881 required all public houses in Wales to close on Sunday; in 1921, it was extended to cover Monmouthshire. The Licensing Act 1961 gave Welsh districts the right to vote on whether they desired the Sunday opening of public houses, with subsequent polls to be taken in 'dry' areas every seven years.

10th

Bought books on art, literature, architecture to widen my education which is tending to become narrow.

11th

The Christian faith must be presented as vital and urgent, needing adventurous people. The Bible is essential to discover this faith.

12th

Tragic to see how small a role the Church plays in modern society. It seems afraid to commit itself on important issues of the day. As Congregationalists, we have become leaders of conformity, afraid of disapproval or to offend.

24th

At Fellowship I read II Cor 4. The speaker was Gwynfor Evans, President of Plaid Cymru. He spoke very well. He is perhaps a romantic rather than a realist, but one must admire his conviction, enthusiasm and sincerity. Only history can judge whether his movement will be a success. Culturally and on religious grounds, his views are admirable but possibly he may be economically unsound.
In later years I spoke with Gwynfor Evans in Swansea, and he also accepted an invitation to speak on Penrhys.

FEBRUARY

11th

The Synoptic Gospels are inspired and inspiring. Behold the man! Whoever reads them must come to the conclusion that Jesus was wonderful, and be almost convinced he was the Son of God.

21st

A thrill to have a letter from Bethany, Godreaman, asking me to be their pastor this summer.
Congregations without a minister often contacted the College to suggest a student who would care for the church during the Summer. Bethany was such a congregation near Aberdare.

23rd

The 'Literalist' and 'Modernist' schools have been at each other in Coll again. No-one is convinced by the argument. We all must be fundamentalist but not literalist.

MARCH

1st

I have been reading Oman's 'Grace and Personality.' Christ came not as a sacrifice to a just God, for God is love. The incarnation is to show man the nature of God, the lengths to which God is prepared to descend, that man might be reconciled to His nature. To follow Christ is to live His life, do as he would; and despite our failures and sins, have faith we shall be saved. Eternal life begins when we have faith in Christ.
Many theological books were being published in paperback and were introducing a new audience to theological issues.

2nd

'Our Faith' by Emil Brunner is an excellent theology written in understandable style, different from Oman. Christianity is real life, not to be trifled with. Without faith, living is monotonous, fearful and leads to a dead end. With faith in God through Christ, life takes on a new meaning. Man finds reality, purpose and knows trust in Christ will lead to eternal life, because his - my - sins - have been forgiven.

3rd

The St David's Day Dinner was first class, but has resulted in the split in College becoming wider. Four boys refused to attend. They are English and literalist, while two are not Congregationalists but have come to College by the back-door from Presbyterians. They have a down on the Welsh boys for what they describe as frivolity and dishonesty. We all lack humility and the love that would reconcile our divisions.

7th

We were addressed on the new Commissions for Congregationalists. There is a strong movement for unity amongst independent churches which are organized very loosely in an outdated, ramshackle system. But does centralization cut across the original ideals of Congregationalism? A Statement of Faith has been prepared. I need prayer and thought before I come to a decision.

These were the years when the Congregational Union was developing into the Congregational Church of England and Wales which ultimately united with the Presbyterian Church of England to form the United Reformed Church.

9th

There will be no Revival until we are steeped in Scripture. We must do the preparation. We mustn't always look for the spectacular. Time is on God's side and we all play our parts, however small.

16th

Peter Williams preached in a Pentecostalist Church in Tumble. Plenty of enthusiasm but at times misguided, particularly during the prayer. Some of the enthusiasm sounded forced.

The student body had been invited to lead worship in Tumble. Not all students were prepared to participate.

27th

Walked to Penrhys, Bristol Tump, above Maerdy and back (8 or 9 miles). It was glorious, possible to see for miles, particularly towards the Beacons although it was hazier to the coast. Not a soul there. Rhondda people don't seem to appreciate the beauty of their own valley. You can see for 30 or 40 miles. Even the valley looked great - bathed in afternoon sunshine.

APRIL

14th

A Russian went into Space yesterday and was welcomed into Moscow today. A fabulous achievement creating a new period of history.

Yuri Gagarin was the first human in Space. It was on the 12th April.

MAY

16th

I have been reading about the Virgin Birth and Resurrection. To be 'part' of the resurrection of Christ should affect the way we eat, dress, behave to our neighbours. It must transform and make us new, to be resurrected now, and go forward into reality and unity with Christ.

20th

We assembled for the CND march in the Castle grounds in Aberystwyth. Most speeches were excellent and the march was most impressive, 3-4000 people from all parts of Wales, walking silently around the town. The H Bomb is deadly, not a deterrent and who would use it to retaliate? A Christian could not.

24th

Gymanfa Bwnc at Nanternis is a Bible class when a visiting minister questions children and grown ups on passages from the Bible. It could be tried in the South. It is an important social occasion for this small country village. Surprising to see so many men. Very different from home where few working men attend churches.
Nanternis is a small village near New Quay. I was on holiday with my parents.

JULY

6th

It was good visiting people in their own homes. It would have results if it was done consistently. I had a fine welcome in every home.
The Student pastorate at Godreaman.

26th

Hywel spoke on 'Evolution and Christianity.' 15 young people present.
Hywel Jenkins and Graham Daniel were Ebenezer friends and were happy to share their experience with the young people in Godreaman.

AUGUST

2nd

Graham spoke on 'Poetry and Religion.'

Sunday 6th

Christened Pamela and Robert after Sunday School. My final service with 50 present. The last hymn was repeated. It was very emotional and the young people were particularly moved.

9th

A farewell party. They presented me with 2 LPs. The young people were very kind. The 30 present form the basis of a strong church if they stick it. All spoke sincerely. I am sorry to leave and they seemed sorry too.
Later in the month, the congregation shared a farewell evening when I was presented with a brief case.

16th

At Ballinskelligs the water is only 300 yards away from the hostel. At an Irish dance, we watched the 'College,' children learning Gaelic who come for a month to this Gaelic speaking village. Talked with Irish boys who are very poor and have grand ideas of emigrating to England or America where they think there is plenty of money.
A hitch-hiking holiday in Ireland during the next few weeks. Some of the experiences created a permanent image. Ballinskelligs is in the Gaeltacht (Irish-speaking) region of County Kerry.

17th

At the dance yesterday, the priest finished with prayers and went through them at a fantastic rate. Impossible to distinguish between the words. However, the listeners, all on their knees, made responses at the right time.

19th

Glin is quaint. It does not have summer time because the priest does not allow it because of the cows. The time in town is 9.45 while in the hostel, ¼ mile away, it is an hour later. There is no Protestant church at present because the family is on holiday.
Glin is in County Limerick. To alter the clocks would affect the time of milking.

26th

Black Saturday with Ulstermen and all towns packed. There have been grand parades with different coloured banners. Most wore bowler or hard hats with white gloves and seemed to be having a good time. It must arouse the hostility of the Roman Catholics and the South. I'm told I speak like a Cork man.

Sunday 27th

The Presbyterian Church was packed, although it was a second service. A good sermon. The Baptist service was in the Public Library. The preacher was a very hot gospeller and extremely repetitive. What a difference between two services, one intellectual and the other very emotional. Both seemed sincere.

SEPTEMBER

12th

I spoke in Tylorstown Youth Club, inviting them to the Youth Service. There is a grave situation in this district. Were there 200 in church last Sunday out of a population of 10,000? Most young people are apathetic. Why has this Christian community declined so rapidly in 30 years?

I was inviting the young people to a service organised by Memorial College for the 18th of September.

16th

All one reads is wars, threats of wars, strikes, quarrels, disasters. People seem insulated, either not caring, or feeling they can do nothing about it, particularly to the threat of a H bomb War and total destruction. Individuals seem incapable of fighting the swift stream racing to the open sea.

Sunday 17th

9 and 20 in Hermon Pontygwaith. They are still a strong spiritual church although numerically very weak. Evan Roberts preached there during the Revival. An honour to be in the same pulpit.

This was the Baptist Chapel in which my mother's parents were members (my grandfather Hugh Davies had been a deacon) and where their 4 children were baptized. It has long been converted into flats.

18th

A wonderful service at Ebenezer! We four students did our part well; Mr Charles presided and Pennar preached excellently; 250 present, of which 100 were teenagers. 42 came from Godreaman. Many of the youngsters have never been inside a chapel and they talked with Pennar afterwards.

21st

Most of my friends are away teaching and this makes Tylorstown quiet. It is a tragedy for Rhondda life to lose the better educated who leave to find jobs. Once they are away, it is rare to return. The loss of its 'braver spirits' results in a less adventurous community.

22nd

Capitalism seems as alive today as ever. It has created the 'never had it so good society' or the 'economic man.' Leadership is measured by the money motive which results in a corrupting individualism.

In 1957 the British Prime Minister, Harold Macmillan, made an optimistic speech telling fellow Conservatives that 'most of our people have never had it so good.'

OCTOBER

9th

Brangwyn for the Halle with Sir John Barbirolli. The highlight was the magnificent Brahms 'Fourth Symphony.' I am reading Kierkegaard. The more a man understands himself, the more he is misunderstood in the world - the essence of tragedy. Is man incapable of communicating his deepest feelings to anyone? Man is an island in himself.

Kierkegaard was the Danish Nineteenth Century theologian.

14th

Brangwyn for the ethereal '9th Symphony' of Beethoven. It must prove even to the most bigoted atheist the existence of a glorious Creator.

27th

50-60 young people in Guild. 50% have no connection with any place of worship. However, they are interested in Christianity and the challenge is open. They would like to have Bible study during the hour of free activities.

Who is to take them?
I spoke at Ebenezer Young Peoples Guild.

NOVEMBER

2nd
Finished 'The British Churches Today' by Kenneth Slack. Congregationalism has lost 50% of its adherents since the beginning of the century, largely because it was associated with a declining political Liberalism.

6th
'The Distinctive Ideas of the Old Testament' by Snaith is excellent, giving the essential nature of the Old Testament which we disregard or interpret literally. Preach Biblically not textually.
I was beginning to discover the sense of the 'sweep of the Bible' rather than coaxing meaning from individual texts out of context. Norman Snaith was an Old Testament scholar.

8th
Voting for Sunday Opening seems a foregone conclusion. It should be a day of rest and worship. The drink problem results in moral breakdown.

9th
8 counties decided to remain dry. Both sides claim victory but as only 40% voted and 394,000 voted for closing, there could not have been such a demand in Wales. 91,000 voted against in Glamorgan which was a great surprise. There are still people with Nonconformist leanings.
The first National Vote for the opening of public houses in Wales on Sunday.

10th
Dynevor School for a CND meeting where Gwynfor Evans, Pennar and Michael Foot all spoke. 400 attended a meeting to provoke thought and action. This is a crucial point in history. The world is in God's hands, but this does not mean we should retire from the world and ignore its problems.

14th
Rev Erastus Jones spoke on the Ecumenical Movement.

Erastus Jones, a Welsh Congregational minister, exercised pioneering ministries at Blaendulais (Seven Sisters) and at Tŷ Toronto at Aberfan, following the Aberfan disaster.

Sunday 19th

New Trinity, Cardiff. 350 there, about 2/3 children. The service was stimulating and encouraging. 200 present this evening. A wonderful experience and raises one's hopes because not only were there large numbers, but the congregation was attentive.

23rd

A major discussion on Civil Disobedience and the Committee of 100. There is a 'sit-down' arranged for Dec 9 in Cardiff. Non-violence is justified over such an extreme and urgent case.

24th

We met Pennar and Trevor Evans and discussed Civil Disobedience. In emergency Ad Rem, it was agreed there should be an official delegation for the Cardiff demonstration and if there were any arrests they would be bailed out from Ad Rem funds. The moral law of God is transgressed by reliance on nuclear weapons. Because it is impossible to change public opinion because of the control of mass media by the authorities who are in favour of nuclear defence, the democratic system has broken down. The only alternative is non violent resistance to the civil authorities.

28th

Two LMS missionaries, one from Madagascar and the other from North India. The former was very radical and declared the nationalist dreams of the African. He condemned the West, particularly the Church, for hypocrisy. The Rev Raymond Abba spoke this afternoon and emphasized the centrality of the Word and the importance of the liturgy. An important day: the ecumenical movement has been praised and the importance of liturgy has been stressed. *Raymond Abba, a Congregational minister was a lecturer at Swansea College of Education.*

29th

Five of us went to the Neath Forward Movement to hear Dr Martyn Lloyd Jones. After hearing so much about him, I found him very disappointing. There was little in his message and he seemed more keen on attacking the

ecumenical movement and the non-literalist approach to scripture than on preaching the Gospel.
David Martyn Lloyd-Jones was minister of Westminster Chapel in London for almost thirty years. He was strongly opposed to what he regarded as the liberal theology of many denominations.

DECEMBER

9th
We joined the banner, marched along St Mary St and sat outside the castle throughout the afternoon. 300 took part, the majority Christians and ministers. Mr Charles was there. No violence of any sort and no one arrested. We were a little island of 50. Thousands watched and an impression made. This is a start in Wales! It must be followed up.
A CND protest in Cardiff. Norah was also at the protest, although at the time we did not know each other.

11th
A literalist in College justifies war: there is nothing we can do about it, and it is none of our concern. This is a negation of the life of Christ, who demands humility, self-denial and a refusal to execute revenge. Christ is the Prince of Peace, the Suffering Servant.

1962

JANUARY

1st
Students visit declining chapels which face insurmountable obstacles. The struggle and sacrifice of a small faithful number keep the doors open. The days of the churches seem numbered in many parts of Wales, but because it is the Church of Christ, there is hope it will continue to proclaim the Gospel and again become central to society.

3rd

Uncle Noel and I had an important discussion on Pacifism. If the Germans and Japanese had become masters of the world, what would have been our fate? The majority would have been thrown in concentration camps or indiscriminately slaughtered? Since the Christian has responsibility to the State, is he to take part in a defensive war? However the H bomb has such destructive power that there can never again be a defensive war. If H bombs are used, friend and foe will suffer and be destroyed. There would be no victor, no vanquished, no terrestrial world for the children of ashes.
Noel rarely shared the tragic and courageous account of his 3½ years as a prisoner in Japanese concentration camps in Thailand. Eventually he published his story in 'The Red Dragon and the Rising Sun - Captivity' John Penry Press, 1988.

5th

Young people seem to have lost hope. Why plan if at any moment a H Bomb War could begin and the world be eliminated? The consequence is the ancient one of 'Eat, drink and be merry, for tomorrow we die.' 'Tomorrow' in the saying has been understood as applying to the individual, but now for the first time in history, it applies to mankind. Many feel 'Lets have a good time and forget it,' or 'What can I do in such a situation?' or 'There are people who know better than I do.'

6th

Bed at 11.15. There is a terrible row and an awful fight in the street behind the house. Most of the people are normally pleasant, but when they have been drinking, there is no holding them. Women are screaming, men are howling and murder could take place. People soon lose the veneer of civilization. The night is filled with their cries.

Sunday 7th

What is the relation between the Christian and the Church? Many believe it possible to be a good Christian without attending a place of worship. God can be worshipped on top of a mountain - the church is corrupted by the hypocrisy of Church members. What a dangerous heresy! The Church is ordained by Christ to fulfil His purposes. The Church is God in action.

8th

I am enjoying the way our strong views are tempered in the melting pot of discussion. Outlooks are broadened daily and new horizons opened ceaselessly.

Sunday 21st

Arrived at Brynmawr at 10.55 where I preached at Rehoboth to a vast congregation of 3. It was still a privilege to be preaching the Gospel of Our Lord Jesus Christ. Sunday School with 1 teacher and 12 children, ranging in age from 5 to 14. How could one teacher cope? Service at 6 with 20. There seemed little interest. Perhaps this is teaching me humility.

I had left Swansea on the 'preachers' bus' at 8 am and had walked the two miles from Tŷ Coch to catch the bus in town. Returning was even more difficult because there was no direct service from Brynmawr to Swansea.

22nd

We identify God and the State, to the Russian it is totalitarian; to the British it is democracy. What does one do when one's conscience is opposed to the government? Most of us sublimate conscience with questions like 'What can I do about it? Give unto Caesar the things that are Caesar's! The government knows best; why make trouble?'

25th

The US will put a man in orbit soon. This is the beginning of the exploration of space. What will happen in the next 10 years? Much could be achieved but there is the hideous possibility of nuclear war resulting in our self-destruction. Thank God for the Gospel: Jesus Christ is the Son of God, Creator of this wonderful universe and each individual. Jesus shows the depth of God's love by going to the cross for us. It should make us leap for joy and cry out in happiness.

27th

At Ebenezer, Elfed ap Nefydd Roberts spoke very effectively on the three conversions to Christ, Church and World. The second meeting took the form of slides of New Delhi. After the meeting, the young people went to Bethany for a social evening, led by David Bowen of Tredegar. There were 150 from different local churches. I hope something constructive will emerge: will they worship and act together?

Another ecumenical conference for young people. This was held at Ebenezer. Elfed ap Nefydd became Principal of the United Theological College in Aberystwyth. David Bowen served with the Council for World Mission before entering the field of lecturing.

30th

Professor Rhodes of the Geology Department spoke on 'Christianity and Evolution.' The problems Evolution poses include how to interpret the Bible, haphazardness, insignificance, the doctrine of God and Man, but none of these problems disprove the Christian faith.
Professor Rhodes had a glittering academic career and became President of Cornell University in New York State.

FEBRUARY

7th

Six of us walked to St Helen's Church where we split into pairs and went around this huge housing estate. It poured and we had a good soaking. We found it worth-while because although no one committed themselves, there was no outright animosity. Lionel Walker is doing a fine job of work but is afraid the damage the hard-liners could do because they have neither tact nor charity.
St Helen's Memorial Church was established in 1957 on a new housing estate at Port Mead, Swansea. After the departure of the minister in 1969 the church encountered problems maintaining effective leadership and closed in 1970. The experience affected me deeply. How can one develop effective ministry in similar communities? It was many years before we served on Penrhys. Years later I inducted Lionel Walker to the United Reformed Churches in Cwmbrân, and we became close friends of Lionel and his wife Bette.

8th

Dr Suzanne de Dietrich addressed us as a College on the nature of Bible Study and how it could be made relevant to the laity. She stressed seeing the Bible as a whole, and the re-discovery of the great themes of theology, pictorial images and the contemporary relevance of Scripture. She opened our minds and made us realise the vast store in the Word of God. She was a loveable lady and was strong and agile in mind although she walked with two sticks. The Bible was at her finger-tips and she saw it in its wholeness. She

warned us not to pick out verses and do what we liked with them. See the New Testament as the fulfilment and sometimes correction of the Old Testament, and be triply converted to Christ, the Church and the world. Feed my sheep and don't desert them.
A seminal experience. Suzanne de Dietrich, pioneer in the field of ecumenical Bible studies and one of the first professors at the ecumenical institute at Bossey in Switzerland.

9th
Three of us led worship at St Helen's Congregational Church. The attendance was disappointing with 10 grown ups (beside our 7) and 4 young people. No one came from the houses we canvassed. Is it that people cannot be convinced (from our standpoint) or forced (from the conservative angle)? Is the way ahead through personal contact between Christians and non-Christians? This alone can win people's confidence. There are no short-cuts to revival.

10th
The march began in Wind St. Barry carried the cross. 20 were affiliated to Coll, of whom 11 were students. We were 100 altogether. We marched to the Brangwyn where Dr Pennar spoke. We then left for the Ecumenical meeting at Blaendulais. Dr Suzanne de Dietrich spoke in the afternoon, and led a Bible Study of I Peter 2.9 in the evening. 400 present. Dr Suzanne stimulated discussion with her forthright remarks. She appealed for Bible study in which all participate and discover for themselves, rather than being told everything. She favoured the cell system, preferably in people's own homes before gathering together for discussion and recapping how it should apply in our lives.
A good combination of social action and Bible study. Barry Jenkins was a fellow student.

13th
More visiting on the Portmead estate. We visited 400 houses and again the response was apathetic. 3 or 4 energetic men need to work together full-time in such an area. The task is too vast for an individual.

Sunday 18th
My first time to lead worship at Ebenezer, my home chapel. I preached in English and read in Welsh. A very responsive atmosphere. 50 in the morning and 150 this evening. The regulars feel depressed because numbers are

dwindling rapidly. Yet many families are connected to the chapel. It is rare for young people to understand a sermon because they do not speak Welsh.

28th

Y Gymdeithas Gymraeg held its annual St David's Day Dinner at Ammanford. Mr Waldo Williams spoke excellently on Wales and although I couldn't understand it all, what I did, moved me. We should be proud of our nation. There seems no hope for Wales without Home-Rule. I received a great compliment from Dr Pennar. He asked if Ad Rem had chosen its President and stated it was a pity he could not vote. The dinner finished with 'Cofia'n Gwlad, Benllywydd Tirion' with great hwyl and we all left on our separate ways, thinking of God and our beloved land. I have been reminded I am Welsh and should be proud of it. It would be a moral outrage if the language disappeared because of apathy.

Waldo Williams has been described as 'the poet of a humane Christianity, and a civilized nationalism and pacifism run like a silver thread through his poems.' (Encyclopaedia of Wales)

MARCH

2nd

30 present at Ebenezer Guild for 'What's my line?' I took the Epilogue on immortality in I Cor 15. All remained for a tremendous discussion. They were a mixed group of chapel and non-chapel people. They asked about Hell, Christian, Spirit. Young people need a relevant challenge.

Sunday 4th

Took services at Siloa, Maerdy (8 and 18). They have been worried about the small-pox scare, as Maerdy is the centre of the epidemic. The outlook for religious life is grim. Of the four large chapels, not one has a Young People's meeting. There is bitterness between the chapels. A United Hymn singing was held last Sunday at Ebenezer Calvinistic Methodist and only 40 attended, not one from Bethania CM. They are prepared to talk about unity, as long as they all meet in their 'building.' Very common in South Wales.

'The last outbreaks (of smallpox) in Wales occurred in 1962 after a Pakistani man who had travelled to Cardiff was diagnosed with the disease. 25 cases occurred in the Rhondda, and 6 people died. Later that year, a second outbreak occurred at Glan-Rhyd Psychiatric Hospital, Bridgend. In 20 cases,

the diagnosis was confirmed and 12 died. Approximately, 880,000 Welsh people were vaccinated.' (Encyclopaedia of Wales.) Siloa has since closed. Its communion set was taken to a congregation in Madagascar. The Thomas family who had lived in 30 Brynbedw Road originated from Siloa, and I have a copy of the New Testament presented to David Thomas in 1888.

7th

Our College Pilgrimage to Brecon and Radnor. At Llanfillo Church we saw a magnificent 15th century rood screen, symbolizing the conquest of death by Jesus Christ and the progress of the Church militant (nave) into the Church spiritual. From there through very desolate country to Maesyronnen Congregational chapel near Bronllys, which was very old and steeped in the tradition of early Nonconformity. The shape of the chapel was peculiar but effective. Here was the simplicity of the beauty of holiness and one could feel awe of the self-sacrifice and struggle for freedom of worship. Finally to Trefecca college, the home of Howell Harris. A very lonely spot for a college and the students feel right out in the wilds. It seems a wilderness.
The first of many visits to Maesyronnen, the oldest nonconformist building in Wales.

APRIL

18th

Hywel and I walked to Bristol Tump. We watched a skylark in its spiral ascent, singing its way with artistry. The air was pure and our conversation soon got round from the joys of nature, and thankfulness for being alive to gratitude to the Creator and Sustainer of it all.
Young people from Ebenezer were still committed to the Church, its faith and witness.

20th, Good Friday

Thirteen young people read and the service lasted from 2.45 until 3.20. Graham announced the hymns and pronounced the benediction. 40 present from various chapels - Horeb, Bethany and Ebenezer.
Hywel, Graham, Byron and I had organised a united service in Tylorstown, led by young people. Byron was another of the Ebenezer young people.

22nd Easter Sunday

The most important day in the Christian Year. Mr Davies officiated this morning and I helped serve Communion. I have never done it before. The Gymanfa went very well, children in the afternoon and the whole church in the evening. Many new hymns. The youngest was a boy of 3 who sang a solo. He raised the atmosphere a number of degrees. Byron was in the chair this afternoon.

24th

Dad conducted well and the singing was with feeling. It would be a tragedy if the Gymanfa died out. There were 4-500 present today. Dad worked hard all winter with children and adults.

26th

At the Missionary Conference at Coleg y Fro, a young lady gave herself for missionary work. We all felt proud of her and I felt the call to be a missionary. Is this the work to which the Lord has called me? The London Missionary Society and other societies are crying out for help. Am I to answer it? Or is my work within Wales?

The United Missionary Council was formed in 1921 and its annual conference had a considerable impact.

JUNE

13th

I have been elected President of the College: there are 16 leaving students this year.

15th

Hywel and I walked on the mountain behind the new housing estate. The estate has taken two fields in which we used to play but which we regarded as marshy.

This is the Hendrefadog Estate, now long demolished.

29th

Played cricket in the Rose Bowl. We had to be almost carried off by the time it got dark. Although we are fortunate to have a place to play, it is an atrocious cricket field. It is in a little bowl and the flat part is 10 yards wide and 40 yards long, with thick reeds at one end and a water channel running alongside. *As teenagers we had created the Rose Bowl, by the side of the demolished Cynllwyndu farm.*

JULY

4th

The opening Ceremony of the International Congregational Council was at the Church of the Remonstrant Brethren in Rotterdam. The retiring Moderator spoke excellently, although many accused him of speaking clichés - I hadn't heard them before! He stressed freedom and toleration. I spoke with Americans, Swedes and Dutch. The Americans have a wider education; the Swedes learn more languages and the Dutch theological students study 6 to 8 years before entering the ministry. All have to learn Hebrew to read the Old Testament.
My first journey outside the British Isles and my first International Conference. The Moderator was Dr Russell Henry Stafford. The Associate Secretary was the Revd Glynmor John who had been minister of Ebenezer Tylorstown when my father was a young man, and had married my parents in 1929.

7th

After devotions by Dr Pennar, a lecture by Cunliffe-Jones on 'The Word of God:' as Christ, then in the Bible, Church and World. Reports from the new churches of Africa and Samoa. I was appointed Welsh representative on the Youth Committee. Roger Pilkington's lecture on 'Science, Faith and the Church' was amusing and very interesting.
Dr Cunliffe-Jones was Principal of Northern Congregational college, Manchester. Roger Pilkington (a member of the Pilkington Glass family) was a geneticist, an author and in 1962 was President of the London Missionary Society.

9th

Paul Minear's lecture on 'The Meeting Place' was a fine exposition of existentialism.
Paul Minear was a key translator of the Revised Standard and New Revised Standard versions of the Bible. He died in 2007 at the age of 101.

10th

I spoke concerning the petition against nuclear tests. The response has been good and a number of US delegates have signed.

12th

The induction of Norman Goodall as Moderator was followed by Communion led by Dr Duthie of Edinburgh.
Norman Goodall was Secretary of the Joint Committee of the International Missionary Council and World Council of Churches. Charles Duthie was Principal of the Scottish Congregational College.

20th

A public lecture at Ebenezer Swansea by Professor Latourette of Yale on 'The significance of the Post Christian Era.' Although Christianity seems to be a declining force in this century, the Twentieth Century has in fact seen the first world-wide expansion of our faith. There is no reason to be disillusioned.
Kenneth Latourette was one of the foremost historians of Christian mission.

31st

Watched a programme about the Common Market. We must cooperate in this rapidly shrinking world. The sooner age-old barriers are eliminated, the nearer we shall be to a peaceful world. Economic unity will cause hardship for Commonwealth countries and European political unity is hazardous because of extreme nationalists like De Gaulle and Adenauer.

AUGUST

2nd

Dac is still keeping exceptionally well for his age, which is I believe 83 - he never talks about his age. He remains very aware of current affairs and draws upon his very rich experience. He has been a great influence on me, with his fund of delightful stories from his days in the mill in the late 19th Century, his coming to the Rhondda in its days of prosperity and his many years on sea when unable to find work at home. He then travelled the world.

17th

A play on television about the Levellers showed their insight in common ownership. Their religious motivation was that all men have equal rights.
The Levellers were a group within English Seventeenth Century Puritanism.

20th

Dr Tudor Jones of Bangor lectured in Tabernacle, Cardiff on 'The Significance of 1662.' He stressed that the motives for the Ejection should apply to Nonconformists today. Are we too eager to give them up, or are we are more tolerant? What does ecumenicity mean?

Tudur Jones was amongst the foremost historians of Welsh Christianity and Congregationalism. Two of his classic works were 'Congregationalism in England 1662-1962' and 'Hanes Annibynwyr Cymru.' The Ejection of Nonconformist ministers from the Church of England took place in 1662.

24th

The walk to Bristol Tump is always delightful, but I am apprehensive about the new houses rising very rapidly and a road being constructed from Penrhys Uchaf farm to the stile and along the bottom of the whinberry field to the top of Park Rd. This will spoil one of the best walks.

Sunday 30th

Led worship at Horeb Welsh Baptist (Dac's chapel) with its responsive congregation. The family came to tea and to the evening service when there were 60 present. I felt conscious of my grandmother's presence.

OCTOBER

12th

I asked Dr Pennar about studying at Mansfield. He stated I should do research - I wondered if I was capable. I told him of my interest in 17th Century period Welsh Puritanism, and he suggested I work on William Erbery. Mr Charles was very pleased with the idea of Mansfield.

13th

I looked at books on 17th Century Puritanism. Erbery is hardly mentioned and is regarded as eccentric and not of the calibre of Powell, Craddock and Llwyd. Is this fair? He did not recant in 1638 (although Wroth of Llanfaches did) and his theological views have not been explored. Apparently he tolerated Papists and Turks. Cwrdde Mawr at Ebenezer with Rev R J Jones, Barry. He preached from Romans 5 - the first time I have heard the term 'supralapsarianism' from the pulpit! Mr Jones is stopping the night with us. He is an inspiration to us.

Supralapsarianism and infralapsarianism are differing views of God's decrees regarding the nature of sin: a technical and abstruse element of theology. However, such abstractions have been instrumental in dividing the Church, to the detriment of its mission.

23rd

The possibility of war. The Americans are blockading Cuba and preventing the shipment of weapons to the island. Russia has stated that if Cuba is attacked, they will come to their defence. We live from day to day. The Annual Lecture at Cardiff was given by Prof E O James on 'The Sky God in the Old Testament.' The difference between Hebrew and other Semitic religions lies in the Covenant-relationship between a God who is transcendent (like other Semitic sky-Gods) and personal and who met and talked with His people in His revelation, particularly to Moses and the prophets. He explained the basis of OT theology profoundly and concisely. I proposed the vote of thanks to Prof Johnson and his staff for their hospitality.
A lecture by Edwin Oliver James who was an anthropologist in the field of comparative religion. He was Professor of the History and Philosophy of Religion in the University of London.

24th

An ironic day: United Nations Day. While the UN flag was raised above the Guildhall, the Americans, flouting international law, began blockading the island of Cuba. A false move by one human being could result in terrible devastation. Irving Fuchs and other Training College CND supporters asked if we would take part in a demonstration outside the Guildhall. We were joined by 300 from the University, and totalling 600, we marched from the Guildhall around the town. It stretched from the YMCA to the Albert Hall along Kingsway: the largest protest I have seen in Swansea.
Norah was also on this demonstration. We were to meet a few weeks later.

Sunday 28th

I preached at Salem Tresalem today. We wait expectantly for news. Khrushchev will withdraw the missiles and Russians technicians from Cuba with UN supervision. This seems courageous and sensible, and the hope is that Americans will not feel that Russia is itching for a H bomb war. With our defence depending upon nuclear weapons, it is like living in an earthquake zone.

Salem Tresalem is a Welsh Congregational chapel in Aberdare. Later, in exploring the family tree, I discovered that my great-grandparents Thomas Morgans and Sarah Davies were married there in 1863.

NOVEMBER

1st

I bought 'Teach Yourself Chess' in the Uplands Bookshop. Who should I see there but Gerald Manners, my geography tutor at Swansea! He seemed pleased to see me. I developed under his careful eye and lashing tongue.

6th

The Rev Elfed ap Nefydd Roberts of Llanelly spoke inspiringly on the Ecumenical movement. His exposition was the best I have heard.

Sunday 18th

Preached at Hermon Welsh Baptist, Pontygwaith. Although we were only 8 in a dilapidated, huge, old, ramshackle icy cold building, God's Spirit was there. They are a warm, human group of God's people.

22nd

The Moderator saw the leaving students. He agreed it would be better for me to receive extra education and then he would be pleased to help me on my return to my native country.

DECEMBER

10th

At my prompting we phoned Norah Evans at the Training College and arranged to meet outside the BBC building. Six of us ate at the Beaufort, Kittle. We had chicken and chips, and coffee, reasonably priced at 42/6. Despite a damp evening we paddled at Caswell Bay, had a 'Gymanfa Ganu' at Rotherslade Bay and walked on Mumbles pier.

The key meeting of life! Our relationship developed quickly, we were engaged the following summer and married in August 1964. Norah was from Craigcefnparc. Her parents, William and Alice Evans, and mine had very similar interests and soon became close friends. All were Welsh speaking chapel-goers of mining background.

13th

I was interviewed by Professor Greenslade at Christ Church College. We sat in his study by the fire and although he was extremely friendly, he questioned shrewdly, particularly about Erbery. He told me he would speak favourably to the committee in January. I saw Dr Caird who stated that officially he could not tell me I was accepted, but unofficially he was sure I would be accepted as a Probationer B. Litt student.

Stanley Greenslade was Canon of Christchurch and Regius Professor of Ecclesiastical History in the University of Oxford. His main works were 'Schism in the Early Church'(1953), and editing the 'Cambridge History of the Bible' and 'Early Latin Theology.' George Caird was Senior Tutor at Mansfield and one of the foremost New Testament scholars of his day.

17th

A terrible day. Awful news. Robert was killed with four other boys near Hirwaun yesterday evening. All Tylorstown is shocked. I went to see his parents. His mother kept remembering all the time that Robert would not be coming home. He was not quite 18, still at school and had his whole life before him. What is the answer to this tragedy? The only security is that God remains with us in sickness and health, life and death.

Robert was an Ebenezer boy and a pupil at Porth County. It was a devastating tragedy.

18th

Day becomes night; night becomes day. Only Robert Morgan and one postman can understand Welsh. We sort the mail alphabetically into special pigeon holes for very large streets, before breaking down the letters into streets: primary and secondary sorting. They are then ready for the postmen to put into correct order numerically for delivery. They come in at 4.30. We began work at 10 pm and finished at 6 am.

Holiday work with the Post Office.

19th

Only one postman has any overt religious feeling and he speaks Welsh. This raises questions. Why have these men no apparent desire for religion? Not long ago, most men in these districts were religious. What happened? Why doesn't religion appeal - they are the same men as those twenty or thirty years ago? Why is the Welsh speaker the only one religiously-minded. Is there a contact between culture and religion?

20th

Byron and I went to Penrhys Cemetery for the funeral of Robert. The weather echoed the dereliction. It was cold, windy, wet. Mr Charles and W G Thomas took the service and asked me to read 'The Lord's My Shepherd' - what else is there on such an occasion?
W G Thomas was the minister of Trerhondda Welsh Congregational Chapel, Ferndale.

1963

JANUARY

1st

Bristol Tump in snow and ice with drifts 3 or 4ft deep, with a piercing wind. An hour to climb but slid back down in 15 minutes.

Sunday 6th

Hermon again. Although there were only 10 this evening, there is a wonderful spirit in the chapel. I was shown the marks on the linoleum in the Sêt Fawr where deacons had gone upon their knees to pray. The remnant in the Rhondda is left, showing wonderful patience. I thank God for the strength they are instilling in me. I am proud to serve and be inspired by them.

10th

A programme on people who keep diaries. Remarkable that some become works of art and are treasured for posterity. In my diary I give vent to my feelings, it helps me think clearly and evaluate life. It is of no use to posterity because it is purely personal.

FEBRUARY

9th

Brunner's 'The Mediator' is an experience rather than a text-book.
Brunner was the highly influential Swiss theologian.

18th

Calvin is logical, thinking very clearly and yet he has a lyrical style. I have been stimulated by 'The better a man is, the more he feels his guilt.' This is the first time this has sunk home. Why does God forgive sin? This is a mystery but I praise God for his forgiveness and ordaining that I should declare His glory.

19th

At Bible Class we discussed 'unity in the spirit,' particularly the document published yesterday on 'Towards Unity' in Wales. I could raise no serious objection and hope it will be acceptable to the four denominations. Unity is important for Wales; it would enable the Churches to pool resources and preach the Gospel more effectively.

The document was an attempt to draw together the four major Nonconformist denominations in Wales: Baptist, Congregational, Methodist and Presbyterian.

26th

John Gwilym and I discussed the arrest of the young man who set off an explosion in Tryweryn. I sympathize but cannot condone violence. John posited that because all democratic methods to save the valley have failed, there is no alternative to violence.

John and I were the only two BD students of our year and had many classes together. John exercised a long and faithful ministry in Bangor and is one of Wales' most significant contemporary poets, as are his two brothers James Jones and Aled Gwyn. The village of Capel Celyn and the Tryweryn valley near Bala were drowned in 1965 in order to supply water for the City of Liverpool. Eight hundred acres of land was drowned, as well as the school, the post office, the chapel and the cemetery, in order to create the Llyn Celyn (Celyn lake) reservoir. On three occasions between 1962 and 1963 there were attempts to sabotage the building of the reservoir. On 10 February 1963 a transmitter exploded on the site and an Aberystwyth student, Emyr Llew, was sentenced to prison for twelve months for his part in the act. The flooding of Tryweryn proved to be one of the turning-points in the history of Wales. John and his wife Avril were later to take Norah and me on pilgrimage to Tryweryn.

MARCH

5th

The Moderator spoke about the churches. I was disturbed by his answer to my question about the dilemma facing Congregationalism in Wales. There is the alternate possibility of a United Church of Wales, and the probability of the formation of the Congregational Church of England and Wales. What would be the decision of the English speaking churches of Wales? His reply was that 'North Wales and Monmouthshire would definitely go east, while Glamorgan would split in half.' What a prospect? I felt very disappointed but hope this will not happen.

8th

Trevor Evans responded to my question on Tryweryn. Because legal attempts had been foiled, democracy had broken down and therefore destruction of property was justifiable. Ought Wales to be able to make these decisions for herself? Although 30 out of 36 Welsh MPs voted against Liverpool flooding the valley, this had no effect on the decision.

13th

The book of Job expresses the greatest of problems. Is the Almighty righteous? Why should we think that because God is all powerful, He is necessarily good? The answer comes not through reason but through Job's experience of God, accepting God as God, knowing we are 'but dust and ashes' and yet God has deigned to meet us. God would not have created or continue to sustain us is if He were not righteous.

14th

Dr Pennar sympathizes with Emyr Llew over the use of explosives but he cannot condone violence.

26th

Dr Pennar called me to see the staff. They have received a request from Tabernacle Abertillery for a student to serve as summer pastor. They are an excellent church with 250 members, and as Pennar said, it was one of the best organized churches in South Wales. I could learn so much.

29th

Norah phoned during break and asked if I was going to Carmarthen to hear the result of the trial of Emyr Llew. We were soon outside the Assize Court and the atmosphere was tense although the verdict of 1 year's imprisonment had just been announced.

APRIL

16th

The singing at the Gymanfa was excellent although each year fewer attend. Despite this, there were 400 in chapel this evening. I chaired the Children's Gymanfa. Most moving to see a little girl and a little boy of 5 both singing solo from the pulpit. Dad is a very sympathetic conductor.

MAY

10th

The lecture with Dr Pennar on Puritanism was gruelling but superb. He dealt with Baxter, Milton and Erbery. His remarkable scholarship has made the period alive.

15th

Job tackles classical problems - the righteousness of God, the meaning of faith, the discovery of what we mean by the self, God's transcendence and immanence. The problem of suffering is only the sparking-off point. I have had a great experience. Suffering stimulated Job's self-examination and in the process, his relationship with God.

16th

With Dr Pennar, we studied the nature of the Church as understood by Congregationalists - the local company of believers in Christ. This is the church: not an edifice or superstructure and not even 'The Congregational Church of England and Wales' or 'The United Free Church of Wales.' Pennar said that George Caird was one of the foremost leaders of the idea of a Congregational Church - Paul to the Church at Galatia. Pennar pointed out that there is a difference: Congregationalism is a denomination and not the whole Church.

17th

Last day at Memorial College. It has provided a far greater fellowship than the University. We are a small college and are all dedicated to the same task.

Sunday 26th

Watched Monitor with a profile of an Anglo-Welsh poet - Thomas, a vicar in North Wales. It was very interesting and he expressed the hardness of life there. It made me want to visit the area.

My introduction to the character and poetry of R S Thomas, one of the foremost religious poets of the second half of the Twentieth century.

JUNE

13th

I have left Swansea for the last time as a student, after spending six years at that delightful town. Dr Martin Niemöller addressed the College magnificently concerning pacifism. He was wonderfully explicit and showed the meaning of faith as a personal relationship with Christ. Heard Niemöller again at the Training College where his address on 'The Relevance of the Gospel' was first class. He stressed the re-creation of humanity into what we should be.

As a teenager I had heard Niemöller preaching in Barry. Now to hear him speak in College to an audience of 30 was a rare privilege. Norah and I both heard Niemöller at the Training College.

25th

I have passed the B.D.

30th

Worship for the first time at Tabernacle: 60 this morning - the best morning congregation I have had for a very long time. Sunday School at 2.30 and after addressing the Intermediate Class on the 1st Commandment I went around the whole S S, the five departments - 103 present. This evening was excellent with the choir and congregation singing well; 140 there, excellent. I was very pleased with my first services.

The beginning of the Student Pastorate at Abertillery. I received so much from the experience during the summers of 1963 and 1964. Tabernacle was a lively, compassionate and well organized church. It was serving its community.

JULY

1st

Mr Lloyd took me visiting all afternoon. In three hours we visited 5 homes. All helped me appreciate the essential nature of pastoral work. I met a couple married 66 years; an old nurse of 88; a man in his late 50s who had Parkinson's disease as a result of seeing his friend killed by his side in the pit ten years previously. They all appreciated my visit very much. A dozen small children in Band of Hope. It was admirable. Afterwards Intermediate Fellowship, with 20 young people.
Bert Lloyd was a senior deacon who loved Tabernacle and Abertillery. I was so fortunate to have his company.

3rd

We drove with John and Avril across the moors to Tryweryn, down to Bala and then to Bryneglwys where we are stopping with Avril parents.
This was John's (John Gwilym Jones) way of reinforcing his argument of the validity of protest against Liverpool's desecration of the valley.

4th

Too late for the service at Llanidloes. At tea in the Church hall, I had to sit on the top table because I recommended Alan on behalf of the College. This evening Dr Pennar preached on 'At Antioch they were first called Christians.'
Norah and I were late arriving at the ordination of Alan Willcocks, a college friend. I had problems throughout the summer with my car.

Sunday 11th

I preached a 'missionary sermon' and who should be in the congregation but Miss Myfanwy Wood who has been 40 years a missionary in China. As she is stopping with Miss Waters, I was privileged to join her for tea. A very enlightened lady.
Myfanwy Wood had served through the London Missionary Society in China from 1908 until 1951. She served as Headmistress of the Girls Boarding School in Beijing and lectured at the University. She was a close friend of Amy Waters, a remarkable deacon at Tabernacle.

10th

Talked with David Davies BA, our Chapel Secretary about his chances as a Plaid Candidate at the local County Council election. He'll be pleased to get a couple of hundred votes. One will be mine because although I'm not sure whether I'm a nationalist, he is the only 'chapel' person standing.

David Davies had stood for the Parliamentary seat of Rhondda East in 1950. He had a great influence on the survival of Welsh culture in Rhondda.

12th

Labour had 900+ and David Davies (Plaid) had 491 and came second. I went back to the house afterwards and talked to the electioneering agent and supporters. Although Glamorgan people, most were Welsh speaking. I am ambivalent because of my Socialist convictions.

Sunday 29th

80 in chapel this morning and the 10 children gave verses for the first time. Children's Harvest this afternoon with 120 present. Good to see them bringing their gifts to Jesus - it was as simple as that to them. How wonderful is the faith of a child. Evening service was wonderful with a congregation of 160 with excellent singing. The physical harvest was transformed to thanksgiving to God for all his gifts, secular and spiritual.

AUGUST

14th

Norah and I were engaged in the most beautiful place either of us have visited. We reached the top of the road from Torridon before it descends to Diabaig. We climbed a rock giving a magnificent panorama of the mountains and the glorious loch. There Norah accepted to marry me and we were engaged. It is wonderful.

Torridon is on the North-West coast of Scotland.

25th

We went out to Penhill to see Norah's school where she begins teaching tomorrow. At the moment it is housed in temporary buildings.

Norah began her teaching career in Swindon, alongside two friends from the Training College in Swansea. Because Oxford was only 28 miles from Swindon, it meant we saw each other very regularly.

OCTOBER

1st
Called in Mrs Butler's today and Mary (aged 5) gave me 2 sixpences as a present. She had kept them in her moneybox since my first Sunday at Tabernacle.

2nd
A short intimate communion service with Nurse Mason because we were only 5 in an ordinary room. Is not this similar to the Early Church and our Puritan forefathers? All our house-bound members should be able to partake in this way.

Sunday 6th
The experience at Tabernacle will serve in good stead when I enter full-time ministry. I have had a free hand with willing workers in every department. It is one of the few churches with a cross-section of society from manual workers to professionals, all working well together. My final service included receiving David Harding and Robert Winstone as members, followed by Communion. One of the finest experiences of my life. God has been gracious to me - I don't deserve this.

4. MANSFIELD COLLEGE OXFORD 1963-1965

This was to enter another world, a more precious, specialised world with more scholars per square mile than anywhere else in the country. Mansfield presented two most fulfilling years. The College was very different from Coleg Coffa. Although still a Permanent Private Hall within the University, the buildings had all the hall-mark of other Colleges. Mansfield is a product of a triumphant Victorian Nonconformity eager to reveal that it had arrived at the ancient University. The Chapel, Library and Dining Room were different from anything I had previously experienced in Swansea, although my tiny room in the Principal's buildings was cosy, small and shabby. The College Staff included the eminent theologian, Principal John Marsh, the Biblical Scholar George Caird and the kind and approachable Church Historian Donald Sykes. I enjoyed everything about College life, particularly fellow students like Bill Rusch the American Lutheran ecumenist, Brian Wren the eminent hymn-writer and Colin Gunton, who became Professor of Theology at King's London. Norah and I became close friends of the Guntons and Wrens after our marriage in 1964. At first, worship at Mansfield seemed strange and cold after Swansea, but as the two years passed, I began to appreciate the Mansfield liturgy and lectionary.

I had the unsurpassed privilege of my research being supervised by Stanley Greenslade, Canon of Christchurch and Regius Professor of Ecclesiastical History. Every fortnight for one hour, I made my way from my room in Mansfield across the city to Christchurch. After passing under Big Tom (the great clock tower in Christchurch) I turned right to knock at Dr Greenslade's door. The next hour was spent in his study, sitting by his fire and discussing 'how to do research.' He was gentle, firm and incisive, and I benefited so much from his guidance. There was one problem. Dr Greenslade was a specialist in Early Church and Reformation History, but had little knowledge of Puritanism. It resulted in my reading indiscriminately in my early terms, but perhaps in the long run I was the beneficiary. I enjoyed studying William Erbery, one of the early Welsh Puritans, especially at the Bodleian Library which became a second home. Eventually I completed the thesis 'The Life and Work of William Erbery 1604-1654' and received my B Litt in 1968, but it was after a long, arduous struggle.

Norah and I married in the summer of 1964 and spent our first year together in Summertown. On our honeymoon we climbed to 'The Table' on Quiraing on Skye - a place which became important in later years. Norah taught in Kidlington and we enjoyed the friendship of fellow students, including the Benedictine Jonathan from Ampleforth, and the Americans Rusch, Hornbecks and Powers. We explored the riches of Oxford cultural life, including New College Evensong and not forgetting the Scala Cinema. The only sadness had been the death of my grandfather in April 1964. His influence had been most significant. Sport again played an important part of life, watching Oxford at rugby and cricket in the Parks, and playing cricket, tennis and table-tennis for Mansfield.

As the two years drew to a close and I was once more preparing for ordination and returning to serve in Wales, there came a meeting which altered life. While having lunch in College in September before term had begun, I was joined by Horton Davies who was on sabbatical from Princeton. He opened our eyes to the relationship between 'religion and culture' (he was researching his magisterial 'Worship and Theology in England') but he also introduced us to Robert Paul, Waldo Professor of Church History at the Hartford Seminary Foundation. A consequence of the persuasion of these two great scholars was that Norah and I left for Hartford in September 1965 and ordination was delayed for a further two years.

OCTOBER

8th

Mansfield College, Oxford and my life has begun as a research student. My room, No 6 in the top Floor of the Principals Building is old fashioned and small. Dinner at 7 with a long Latin benediction was in an old panelled room surrounded by pictures on the walls. On my table was an Australian, an American and a chap from Yorkshire. After the meal, the Principal and President of Union spoke.

During my first year at Mansfield, Norah was teaching in Swindon. I often visited Swindon and Norah entered fully into Oxford life. She was able to stay on weekends with Tylorstown friends, Glan and Phyllis Evans. Glan Evans was a 'scout' at Oriel and sadly died in November of that year.

9th

Different from any other university. There is every facility if one wants to work, and yet if one doesn't want to work, there is every opportunity to escape. I was awakened at 8 by my scout with a 'Good Morning Sir, it's 8 and breakfast is served at 8.30.'

12th

Communion at the College chapel led by Dr Marsh: 2 dozen present. Despite external differences, it was not very different from Swansea except that John Marsh wore robes, knelt for prayers (others also did this) and a cup of wine (alcoholic?) was used for communion. A spirit of devotion.

14th

I found it strange that John Marsh's reading was the whole of Matthew 1. Registered in the Bodleian, looked at the Catalogue of Printed Books and had the thrill of seeing Erbery's name.

I later appreciated Marsh's emphasis on the whole of Scripture as being the Word of God. We are not to 'pick and choose' the pieces we enjoy, and ignore the rest.

Sunday 20th

Norah, Dad and I walked down the steps together, steps along which I have gone to chapel for many years. Service this evening was most moving because, after the reading I noticed Mrs Davies, my old Sunday School teacher in chapel. She hasn't been well for years, and she is so important to me. My first communion at Ebenezer. I gave Dad communion and asked him to serve me.

22nd

I matriculated into the University of Oxford through Mansfield College. I dressed in dark suit, white shirt, white bow tie, Commoner's gown, and carrying my mortar board, I met the other freshers and the Dean outside the College main entrance. After our instructions, we marched academically with some of our boys singing 'Beatles' music. After queuing in Bodleian Square, we entered the Divinity School where we were addressed by the Vice Chancellor. We sat in rows, the same words were spoken to each College and we returned to College - all for 10 guineas!

31st

I owe my being to the glory of God. Here I am, a little chap in a small room in a vast world and an even vaster universe with multitudinous souls, and God cares for me and has a task for me to perform.

NOVEMBER

6th

God will never reject us. How do I know? God's love in Christ has been revealed to us, seen clearly in His crucifixion. We are forgiven and accepted.

11th

Chapel Prayers have not been as inspiring as some services at Coleg Coffa. Hymn- and psalm-singing is atrocious, morning readings have all been from I Samuel and responses are so hesitant. My first tutorial with Greenslade at Christchurch. He is a very pleasant person and expects hard work.

15th

Communion at 7.45. Two dozen of us and helpful, although John Marsh reads as if from a railway timetable.

19th

I am specialising in 17th Century Puritanism. I could devote my life to this obscure aspect of Church history, and realise I am touching a fraction of knowledge. We are so insignificant compared with the splendours of the universe, and we are limited by three score and ten years. Despite our pretentiousness and pride, the God of creation is love. He manifests Himself in one murdered by our pride.

22nd

A terribly disturbing day. President Kennedy has been assassinated. A great man has been killed too young. The horror of it is overwhelming. We heard this evening as we fetched fish & chips before going to the vestry to hear Mr Budd's choir. This morning was equally tragic and more personal because Glan Evans died. A gentle man has passed away after great suffering.

29th

Communion at 7.45. How eerie it was walking up the steps outside the Principal's Lodgings and feeling the cold, clear air, seeing the dawn creeping into existence, hearing a solitary bird welcoming the day, noticing fellow students, almost invisible in their gowns, walking slowly around the quad towards chapel; then to enter the dimly lit chapel, sit in the front and thank God for the privilege of worship.

DECEMBER

6th

Dr Greenslade questioned me on the theology of separatism and the authority of Puritanism. Is it caused by their emphasis on the immediacy of the Spirit? How can you measure the validity of the claim that one has the Spirit? Where does authority lie? In the Bible or Church? Do they help to 'measure the Spirit'? I was being examined by a man of formidable intellect.

I was 'taxed' by all these questions. 'Separatism' is the tendency within Calvinism to seek a more and more holy way of life, with the result that denominations keep on splintering, often as the result of 'charismatic leadership.' The tendency is not unknown today!

17th

My seventh year as Temporary Postman. The big removal van arrived, we met the train in Porth, collected parcels in Pleasant Hill and delivered in Pontygwaith, Stanleytown and Tylorstown. We delivered in Maerdy this afternoon. There is an awful state on some of the new houses. They are dirty.

My final year as postman.

18th

The mountains are placid in soft sunshine. This must have been a glorious valley before industrialization. Even so the haphazard building has its charm and there is beauty in the starkness of derelict pits and frozen tips. The terraced houses huddle to keep warm, but the new houses have an impersonal formality. Many are already dreadfully neglected. How can people live in such squalor? Little Moscow this afternoon has lost the political fervour which justified that name, but the name is deserved because of its bleakness.

Sunday 22nd

Siloa Maerdy. 6 this morning and 12 this evening. How do they keep going? I enjoyed myself despite the extremely cold chapel.

25th

Ebenezer before Christmas dinner. Dac pulled out his annual cigar and sat by the fire.

1964

JANUARY

Sunday 5th

Libanus Calvinistic Methodist where I preached my first sermon 3½ years ago. 20 were sitting together in the top left-hand side of the chapel around the fires, because it is so cold elsewhere. I preached from the big seat and was surprised with the delightful atmosphere and spirit of reverence. This afternoon I walked down to Ebenezer for the Christening of Hywel's baby - Simon James behaved excellently. Finally down to Hermon Welsh Baptist for the evening service. Although only 17 on their books, 15 were present and all extremely attentive. An Ecumenical Sunday with Presbyterian, Congregational, Baptist. Why couldnt we worship together? Small groups struggling to worship the same Lord.

7th

Mamma and I walked down the steps to Ebenezer - rarely have we done this because I am always in a hurry on the way down. This evening we walked together to Sisterhood. 27 present. I spoke on TS Eliot's 'The Journey of the Magi.'

24th

Evensong at New College was beautifully devotional.
Norah and I often joined the congregation at New College. It was only a short walk from Mansfield and introduced a new world of Anglican spirituality.

26th

Heard George Caird at St Mary's preaching on 'The Truth of the Gospels;' fine intellectual preaching of the Word.

27th

I am reading Thomas Richards' compendious but prosaic 'Puritanism in Wales.' Fact is piled on fact, with lists of persons and events. Bill Rusch took me to the Bodleian and showed me the procedure. I sat patiently at T8 but the librarian went to T10 because I had put the wrong number. This was the first time for me to see and then hold in my hands 'The Testimony of William Erbery,' the first and only publication of 1658. A white cord held the cover to the book which seemed very fragile. I opened the book, was too excited to do anything for a while and then copied the titles and checked them in Wing, the British Museum Catalogue and DNB. I read 20 pages - it is obscure but not terribly difficult.
Bill Rusch was studying early Christian doctrine for a D Phil and later became a most accomplished ecumenical theologian. He became Director of the Faith and Order Commission of the National Council of Churches in the USA. Donald Wing created the catalogue of printed books in English between 1641 and 1700. DNB = The Dictionary of National Biography was edited by Leslie Stephen and Sidney Lee in 63 volumes, being completed in 1900.

28th

How many have read this book since its publication? I am on a sea of discovery. I collected 'The Testimony' from the Tower and sat down for three hours, reading 40 pages or three tracts.

29th

To the Bodleian with my briefcase under my arm. Away I walked on to Holywell, down to the corner of the Broad, up the well-worn steps and through the arch into the Clarendon building before enjoying the calmness of the Bodleian courtyard.

FEBRUARY

13th

The freedom of research work demands discipline. It is a voyage of discovery, having to think for yourself, being a detective or an explorer but what an achievement when pieces begin to fit.

MARCH

1st

Bishop Neill spoke at the University Church on the Church's mission of communicating the Biblical revelation to the Grecian and Roman world of the Early Church. He hardly used notes.

Stephen Neill, Associate Secretary of the World Council of Churches gave the Bampton Lectures. They were published as 'The Church and Christian Union' in 1968.

7th

Bergman's 'The Seventh Seal' at the Scala. It captures the atmosphere of medieval life with the horror of the plague and charm of the troupe of players, but there was also the mysterious elemental battle in a miracle play with the eternal questions and responses to death, God, Christ, disease; the rationalism of the squire, the mystical simplicity of the juggler and the inexplicable searching of the knight. It created intense self-involvement and left me struggling. A magnificent work of art.

A film of this kind would always be followed by intense, probing discussions at dinner the following day.

Sunday 8th

Bishop Neill's fourth Bampton Lecture was on the need for 'conversation' between Christianity and world religions. Since the Reformation the Church has failed in this respect, and has also been producing Christians on a Western pattern rather than allowing them retain their cultural identities.

9th

At Keble I was thrilled by Schutz's 'St Matthew Passion' with Peter Pears as Evangelist. He was magnificent, what feeling and control. I have lived another day - thanks to God. I would be an old man in some countries.

12th

Two years at one of the finest universities in the world. I am very happy at Oxford and at Mansfield with its warm community spirit. There are less than 70 students who know each other intimately. The strangeness of the first weeks has disappeared. I am learning from those with theological and non-theological backgrounds.

18th

Dac is still keeping remarkably well and we had a good chat. He went back to the Fishguard when he was a boy. I am fortunate to have a grandfather with whom I have such close contact. He is so interested in contemporary affairs as well as what happens in the family. He follows my career most closely. He is very alert in mind and body.

19th

It is 12.45 just after midnight. As I reached the top of Brynbedw it was very quiet except for the gurgling of melting snow and the sound of the river down below in the valley-bottom. A sheep called into the night. Mist reached down to the bottom of the Tip while lines of white snow streaked across the mountain. The orange glow of the main road showed up prominently, while the back streets were in semi-darkness. It seemed so mysterious.

25th

Dac is looking exceptionally well, chatting about the garden (he will plant potatoes and onions this evening) and the sea, where he went because he couldn't find work during the depression.

30th

Walked up to Bristol Tump, leaving at 11.07 and back in the house before 12. Out of the house by the back door, up Donald St, past the school and then I struck up the mountain, past the old levels by which time it was fairly easy going, up the whinberry field, past the Third Baltic (no idea where the name came from) across the flat, marshy stretch, climbed over the broken-down wall, up a slight gradient, and then the Tump with the pylon behind it. Lovely at the top, the valleys merging into one another - not a soul in sight and not a sound.

31st

Gymanfa day at Ebenezer, the annual singing Festival. The choir this morning has shrunk to 40: the faithful ones who attend Ysgol Gân throughout the year. They knew their work and the singing was quiet and dignified. A choir of 100 this evening with Dad exercising good control. I took Dac to our house for supper. We were a merry crowd with Dac king of the family. Poor old Dac is breaking a little now. His eyesight is failing. We all love him so much. I slept at Dac's.

APRIL

13th

My dear Grandfather died this morning, so suddenly that we cannot get to grips with what has happened. I was with Dac yesterday and now he is dead. Thank God he went peacefully, and thank God for his rich life, character and the effect he had on us all.

30th

John Marsh has been stressing the resurrection of the dead - this helped so much. If God loved the world so much that Christ was crucified and raised, then eternal life includes personhood.

MAY

Sunday 3rd

The fifth Bampton lecture by Bishop Neill was on 'The Sacraments and Mission:' although the sacraments have a commemorative element, their main emphasis is looking to the Last Things when there will be the fulfilment of the Church's mission.

26th

We were out for 124 for 9 by tea. After tea Wadham batted and were out for 33. I had the opener lbw first ball, bowled three others and two were caught behind the stumps. My analysis was 9.4. 2.17.6. I was presented with the ball.
I played cricket for the Mansfield XI for two seasons. They were very competitive but also great social occasions.

JUNE

2nd

Stratford on Avon on the annual college outing. Sat in the balcony for a Theatre Club performance of Henry V which was thrilling. The play came to life and the change of scenery remarkable. Three hours of drama for 4/-. We are proud of Shakespeare.

5th

At Communion I realised my insignificance within the vastness of creation, and my amazement that God has called me to share the news that the power of creation is no brute force but is personal love

Sunday 7th

My father has done great service to Ebenezer. He is a sensitive, conscientious precentor, and leader of the Sunday School. How many headmasters in our valleys are prepared to serve the cause of God? This has not prevented Dad playing his part in society with the Pendyrus Male Voice (chairman for years), Welfare Hall vice-chairman and he is always prepared to help anyone (he is also a strong socialist). Mamma in a less conspicuous way has also always served the church faithfully. Mamma has been London Missionary Society secretary and a Sunday School teacher. David Davies preached today - on MD - Mab Dafydd, Duw a Dyn.
MD = Son of David, Son of God, Son of Man.

23rd

Mamma and I looked at the 90 new houses behind Brynbedw in what we called the 'first field.' I used to run home across it from the Infants' School and played in the pond.
This was the creation of the Hendrefadog Housing Estate, demolished in the 1990s.

26th

I am sitting in the front bedroom and from my chair I can see down the valley as far as the sharp bend at Wattstown. Although the windows are open because of the warm weather, for an industrial area it is remarkably quiet. We are now a dormitory town; the men are away during the day because the pits are closed and the railway has stopped. I can hear the buses groaning up the Police Station hill. I can see the mountains green with ferns, a few grey sheep, boulders, gaping quarries which betray the source of the cottages huddling together in long winding terraces. Down in the valley I see Dad's school and children playing cricket on the tarmac yard. The river glints in the sunlight. It is a good place to be, this window. Yet I also see Dac's house and I look expectantly at the back wall to see if his grey head shows he is at work in the garden. But all is still there, weeds grow and no smoke rises from the chimney. We had stewed rhubarb from Dac's garden for lunch.

Sunday 28th

Evening service at Ebenezer. The 50 listened intently. I mentioned that a new township of 600 houses is to be built at Penrhys with no place for a church. What would our forefathers have done? What did they do?

AUGUST

3rd

The most important day of my life, because I was married to Norah. A wonderful day. I feel proud Norah has taken me as her husband. We are now fully husband and wife, and I pray to God we shall have a long and happy life. We are now together for always. On the Blaengwynfi side of the Bwlch, a very unfortunate incident when I ran into a stone on the road. I had to leave the car and went on in Hywel's car. I shall never forget my first glimpse of Norah when I fetched her into the big seat.
Norah and I spent our honey-moon in the Hebrides: Mull, Skye, North Uist and Lewis. It was on Skye that we reached 'The Table' on Quiraing.

29th

We arranged a joint account at Barclays in Summertown. The Chief Clerk was very amused when Norah signed herself 'Evans' three times.
Our first home was in South Parade, Summertown, a house which was owned by Elizabeth Lindsey, a secretary at Mansfield. It had been inhabited by her

two elderly maiden aunts and was full of their furniture. It was quaint but very cold in winter. Norah taught at Kidlington Infants' School during our first year of marriage.

SEPTEMBER

10th

The half dozen of us sat down to lunch and an unassuming chap sat opposite me. He introduced himself but I didn't catch the name. Imagine my surprise when 5 minutes later I realised that it was Horton Davies! He took me to the Senior Common Room afterwards and we chatted until 2.30. He has such diverse interests, and shared good ideas for reforming worship. I thoroughly enjoyed his company.
Horton Davies was Putnam Professor of Religion at Princeton and was researching his magisterial series 'Worship and Theology in England'(a 5 Volume series). Previously he had researched in the area of Puritan theology and worship.

17th

Horton Davies talked about the relationship between art and religion. He believes that the puritan neglect of the arts is because of the emphasis on the atonement, burial in Christ and negation of self; compared with the Roman Catholic and Anglican stress on Incarnation, God coming into the world and redeeming all things.

23rd

Horton and I had tea in Kemp's. His study of the cultural side of theology makes him most fluent. He talked about architecture, art, poetry, his life, the crisis in the Church. Later he came to supper. Norah catered very well with grapefruit, lemon sole, boiled potatoes, green beans and parsley sauce, rhubarb tart and cream, cheese and biscuits and coffee. Horton is so stimulating

26th

I visited the Moderator - William Samuel. The opportunities in my native land are limited. Because I wish to serve in the country, an opportunity has arisen at Longstone and Lanteague, two very small churches in rural Pembrokeshire. It is in the hands of the Moderator.

OCTOBER

1st

A most satisfying day because of two men, one dead for 300 years; the other very much alive. The former is William Erbery. I have been exploring his theology of the Church as the body of Christ, Spirit-filled saints, those recognizing Christ in them giving new life and purpose. The other is Paul Tillich who emphasizes that theology must no longer be preoccupied with the Greek or Reformation periods, but seek to give meaning to a society which sees life as conflict, apartness, separation, frustration and meaninglessness. The message of the Gospel is about the New Age and the New Being.

Tillich was one of the great theologians of the Twentieth Century.

9th

I read the fourth chapter of the thesis to Horton Davies. I went to Horton's room by 1.45 and slogged at my chapter until 5.45. It was gruelling and worth while. He was critical, careful about the exact choice of word, generalizations. I thought I was going to be torn apart. Despite the criticism of detail, he said the thesis easily merited a BLitt and I had the ability to write a D.Phil. My classification was accurate and I have a clear mind and a good clear style. I was pleased because I feared the material and approach were not good enough. I am thrilled by Horton's judgment, because I trust his honesty.

Sunday 18th

Mr Charles took Norah and me to London airport, the Terminal and Roof Garden where we watched the planes landing and taking-off. Watched TV - Lynn Davies of Nantymoel won an Olympics gold medal for the long jump in Tokyo.

Because of my uncertainty on whether to seek Ordination during 1965, Alwyn Charles insisted on taking us to Heathrow, pointing out a plane leaving for New York and telling us that 'It's New York for you. Longstone and Lanteague can wait.' As it happened, there was no choice. I never heard from the Pembrokeshire churches nor the Moderator.

27th

A letter from Horton Davies: 'This evening (26th Oct. 1964) in the SCR after dinner I asked the Principal for his judgment of you. It was extremely favourable & so I followed it up by indicating that I thought well enough of you to admit you to our doctoral programme at Princeton University, but said that I hoped you'd first go to Union Seminary ... I'm quite sure he'll back you strongly with complete conviction (as I should).'

NOVEMBER

1st

Joost de Blank, once Archbishop of Cape Town spoke at St Mary's of the necessity of cooperation and the interchange of ideas because the 'newer' churches could have a great influence upon the older - their enthusiasm, their Christocentric lives. Later at Mansfield, Dr Norman Goodall led one of the finest services in my experience with superb readings, devout prayers and a magnificent sermon on the Wedding Feast. His control of language was so remarkable that it was like poetry.
Two remarkable sermons by two remarkable Christian leaders. Joost de Blank was Archbishop of Cape Town from 1957 to 1963 and was known as the 'scourge of apartheid.' Norman Goodall, a Congregationalist minister was a moving force in the development of the Ecumenical Movement.

5th

Horton is enthusiastic about our going to the USA. He would like us to spend a year at Union before Princeton to work for a PhD. We still haven't heard from a church in Wales and it is 7 weeks since I wrote to the Moderator. Are we wanted at home?

6th

Norah and I had a meal with Brian and Brenda Wren in Kidlington. They are going to a church in Essex at the end of the year and he hopes to stop a few years before University teaching. He feels this is his calling. In Wales this is viewed as an escape from 'the real work of ministry.' My work is in the pastoral and preaching ministry.
Brian Wren entered the Congregational ministry and proceeded to work most effectively on the sharp edge where issues of faith and justice interact and sometimes collide. Brian has created many sensitive and poetic hymns.

9th

Horton Davies and I arrived at the other place, the University in the Fens. I immediately felt a prejudice at visiting the only serious rival to Oxford. It was cold, clammy, misty. I went to the not-of-this-world, incomparably ethereal King's College Chapel with its superb vaulting and mysterious mingling of the organ pipes with the roof. However, should Rubens' 'Adoration of the Magi' be the centrality of worship? I walked to our sister college, miniature Cheshunt, had lunch in hall with Rev Jack Newport and coffee in his house. His wife is from Skye.

The Non-conformist College (1768-1969), moved to Cheshunt in 1792 from Trefeca, and to Cambridge in 1905. It is now incorporated within Westminster College.

10th

Horton made it clear that I could go to Princeton this coming September and start a PhD, work entailing two years but the drawback is I would be expected to pursue University teaching. I am not prepared to do this. That is therefore out. I cannot go back on my word.

11th

The Annual Evening at Regent's Park where we had a superb chicken dinner followed by a magnificent talk by David Jenkins of Queens speaking on the necessity of God for a real humanism.

Regent's Park was a sister Baptist theological college at Oxford. David Jenkins was Fellow of Queens and later became Bishop of Durham.

16th

David and Becky are graduates of Austin, Texas and David has completed his first year at Union. He is doing second year BD (Union degree) at Mansfield. He spent last year at the Harlem Mission, the Church of the Resurrection. What a formidable and fruitful task! They face the most gruelling problems with zeal and patience. The Church will encounter urbanisation all over the world before the end of the century - Port Talbot, Swansea and other Welsh towns and estates.

Dave and Becky Hornbeck spent their lives in education, particularly struggling for the disadvantaged. Dave became Superintendent of Schools in Philadelphia. They had come for a meal at our home.

17th

Horton Davies introduced me to Robert Paul, Professor of Church History at Hartford and author of 'The Lord Protector.' The next hour was a thrilling appraisal of the political effects of the Puritan revolution. He invited me to

Hartford to work on the connection between Anglo American Puritanism under his supervision. I was thrilled. Norah and I went to the Schweitzer Society to hear Christopher Hill lecture on 'Puritanism.' I spoke to him afterwards. He thought Erbery most exciting.
Robert Paul, Waldo Professor of Church History at the Hartford Seminary Foundation was a world-authority on English Puritanism. The Schweitzer Society met at Manchester College, a Dissenting Academy, founded in 1786, which came to Oxford in 1889. Christopher Hill was elected Master of Balliol in 1965. He was a Marxist historian specializing in Seventeenth Century History. He resigned from the Communist party during the Hungarian revolution.

26th

Without God there is non-existence. All we have is from God's creative power; God provides for us day by day with His sustaining care; we shall be perfectly His on the Day of the Lord.

30th

Bought a map of 'Wales and the Marches' and put it on the wall.

DECEMBER

3rd

Just before Uncle Haydn died he sang two Welsh hymns - 'Yn y dyfroedd mawr a'r tonnau' and 'Iesu, Iesu, rwy't ti'n ddigon' and then said 'God bless all the family - God bless you all - Amen' - and he died in peace.
Haydn Morgan was one of my father's brothers. He had been station master in Maerdy. He would have learned the Welsh hymns as a child in Ebenezer.

6th

I would like to live again in the Rhondda. It is home - Mamma and Dad, Dac, family, friends; Ebenezer; schools - Hendrefadog, Tylorstown and Porth; places in which I played as a child - the Graig, the rocks, the 'other mountain', Moggs field, the 'flat' which is anything but!; the Cwm and the Rose Bowl, and of course Bristol Tump, a real mountain. How will my attitude change as I grow older? parents pass on, the church deteriorates, my friends leave the district, the places on which I played get turned into building sites? I can't forecast. Now, it remains the foremost influence on my life. The name

Rhondda is itself emotive. I rush to its defence because I love Tylorstown and Brynbedw.

7th

I am accepted as a Teaching Fellow at Hartford Seminary Foundation. I shall work for two years in the United States for a PhD; I shall learn about the flourishing American church. Collected 14 of the Library of Christian Classics. Colin and Jen came for a meal. They are such a nice couple.
The Student Christian Movement were offering 17 volumes of the Library of Christian Classics for £12 in total. Colin and Jen Gunton became close friends. Colin trained for the Congregational ministry and eventually became Professor of Christian Doctrine at King's College London and a well-known author.

11th

Spoke with Dr Pennar, the man I admire most. He was extremely pleased to hear about Hartford because it would benefit my ministry in Wales.

25th Christmas Day

Libanus for the united service. I felt grateful to preach to the People of God in Tylorstown.
The congregation was composed of most of the remaining loyal worshippers in Tylorstown. This of course did not include the majority of women who would have been at home preparing the Christmas meal!

28th

The sun streamed through the window and I looked out on a brilliantly blue sky and dazzling white snow. The mountain opposite, the mysterious 'other mountain' was gloriously covered in this new purity.

1965

JANUARY

7th

The first Theological Leavers' Conference has provided a useful introduction to Memorial Hall and Livingstone House. I feel more confident in the future of the denomination. In a lecture on 'The Ministers Finance' by John Evason, we learned that the minimum stipend is £670 per annum and a free house. At the 'Open Forum' scores of questions were asked, particularly about equality of stipends.

Ministerial stipends varied greatly and probably were a major factor in the movement of ministers - usually from the 'poorer' rural congregations to the 'grand' City congregations. That inequality was largely removed by the formation of the United Reformed Church and the Scheme for Ministerial Remuneration.

8th

Another 'final year.' I had a similar feeling when I left Coleg Coffa, and my friends entered ministry. I must be patient and be grateful for the opportunities provided by the grace of God. I hope to serve His kingdom in Wales and I must continue training for work there.

13th

Studying at Swansea provided an understanding of the world in the light of the Gospel. The study of History, Geography and English were ideal.

Sunday 31st

John Robinson, Bishop of Woolwich preached at St Mary's on the need for a new reformation of liturgy, church organization and theology. Is the Church answering questions which trouble our contemporaries, or questions in which society is no longer interested? We should replace the question of how to find a gracious God (Reformation) by the question of how to find a gracious neighbour.

FEBRUARY

9th

John Robinson's radio lecture on 'Atheism' showed God as intellectually superfluous, emotionally dispensable and morally intolerable.
Naturally he wished us to dispense with the picture of the 'God with the white beard in the sky,' but found it difficult to provide an adequate substitute.

24th

An ordeal. I arrived at Mansfield, put my sermon on the preaching desk and entered the vestry by 6. I preached for 20 minutes, started nervously but don't think it went too badly.
It certainly was an ordeal to preach at the Wednesday service at Mansfield. The Staff and theological students were all present, including John Marsh, George Caird and C. H. Dodd. I asked the Principal whether I needed to wear a gown and his swift response was 'in Rome, do as the Romans do.'

MARCH

1st

As schoolboys, we wore leeks which grew progressively shorter throughout the day. During the morning came the School Eisteddfod or concert. In Porth we had the concert with dozens of recitations and boys from Form I singing soprano. We were let out at 12 and joyfully went home. It always seemed a fine afternoon and we played soccer on Moggs field or walked to Bristol Tump. In the evening, the pictures (or twice to a chapel eisteddfod). In Coleg Coffa we had a couple of days off, and there was the Welsh Society's St David's Dinner. Oxford has a very different atmosphere and no afternoon off. Welsh Service at Jesus College where Canon Harry Williams of St Mary's, Swansea preached in English. He was honest and sincere about the problems facing Welsh religious life

6th

Thrilled to see Cromwell's portrait and his memorial at Sidney Sussex. We visited Kings, Queens, Peterhouse, Pembroke and the other great Puritan College, the Emmanuel of Peter Sterry and others, before returning to Kings Chapel for Evensong. We sat in the ante-chapel. The superb texture of voice,

organ, mingling with the light and shade of the fan vaulting, candles flickering.
A second visit to Cambridge.

7th
A fine service at Mansfield. John Marsh read, prayed well, preached forcibly on making decisions and received Peter Poulter as a member of the Church. My eyes filled with tears as John Marsh met Poulter half-way down the aisle, shook his hand and offered the blessing.
Peter Poulter entered the ministry and became Moderator of the Northern Province of the United Reformed Church.

APRIL

7th
My meeting of 2¼ hours with Dr Greenslade proved agonizing. He pointed out many mistakes which I had no wish to deny. I felt sick. He does not think I can submit by the end of Trinity.

26th
Bristol Tump or Twyn Disgwylfa holds magic memories. It is Everest, South Pole, our annual pilgrimage on the first day of each new year, Shangri-La. The wind was powerful and I felt like a boy soaring to the top, propelled by the wind. I gazed around in triumph to our valley and 'the other valley,' mountains towards the Bwlch, Beacons to the north, the Sea to the South and our own Cefn y Rhondda.

MAY

3rd
Coffee with Visser 't Hooft, the secretary of the World Council. He is a humble, witty, dedicated man, answering every question without evasion.
Visser 't Hooft was the first general secretary of the World Council of Churches

4th

Is the resurrection of Christ a historical event? What is the relationship between faith and the event? What is the significance of the empty tomb and the appearances? At the Graduate Colloquium, Al Churchill spoke on 'The Resurrection and History.' He, like me, favours the reality of the historical events.

Allen Churchill was a pastor and teacher in The United Church of Canada for forty years.

8th

'Lawrence of Arabia' astounded, captivated, repelled and mystified. The film was brilliant, the scenery staggering, especially the desert - the arrival of Sherif Ali. But, what of the man? A romantic figure, responsible for uniting the Arabs and the capture of Damascus. But, himself? I am exhausted by a very strange man, a schizophrenic (?) who hated and loved killing; burning with an ideal but glorifying in his hero-worship.

The David Lean epic.

21st

Brasenose Seconds were all out for 76. I bowled right through, although against the wind:10.5; 2; 30; 5. My best bowling of the season. We won by 6 wickets.

Mansfield Cricket XI.

26th

I have won the Fulbright Travel scholarship. We travel on the United States Line on September 2nd.

JUNE

1st

An extremely important day. Norah is pregnant and the baby due on December 10. What wonderful news. God has blessed us. We are responsible for new life.

Sunday 13th

St Benet's where Jonathan showed us how to follow the service, handed us a Missal and took us to our seat. The monks sat opposite each other. A strange,

moving experience with the monks intoning beautifully. Throughout there was a sense of holiness. After the service Jonathan changed and we went to Mansfield for Communion. John Marsh preached for those going down this term - this included me. A shame I could not share Mass with Jonathan nor he in our Communion. Perhaps the day will come in our lifetime.
I met Jonathan Cotton when playing on the same interdenominational cricket team (The Mongrels). I had never met a monk before: I was 'first slip' and he was 'second slip.' Norah and I later visited him at Ampleforth.

19th

No longer an Oxford student. I have fallen in love with the finest city in England. Mansfield has been a real joy. I feel enriched personally and as a prospective minister. At the Annual Commemoration Service, JM led devotions and Dr Norman Goodall preached on 'a cloud of witnesses.' A gloriously inspiring service and magnificent sermon which was a joy and a challenge. The glory of the Gospel. How privileged we are as people and responsible citizens of God's Kingdom.

24th

'The Puritans' is an excellent introduction to American Puritanism. There is nothing like it for England where the best introduction are the two books by Haller. He also is an American. Nuttall over-emphasizes the spiritualist side of the Puritan movement; perhaps he is not as interested in the Calvinist emphasis, which is the backbone for the majority.
'The Puritans' was edited by Perry Miller and Thomas H Johnson. William Haller wrote 'The Rise of Puritanism' and 'Liberty and Reformation in the Puritan Revolution.' All three were American scholars. Nuttall's key works were 'The Holy Spirit in Puritan Faith and Experience,' 'Visible Saints' and 'The Welsh Saints: Walter Craddock, Vavasor Powell and Morgan Llwyd.'

JULY

1st

Norah, Bill Rusch and I went to the first performance of 'Timon of Athens' with Paul Schofield. Magnificent: the production and setting were of course first class, but we did not expect the play to be so stimulating. The violent change in Timon's character was perfectly credible. What a strange naive existence he had, and what degradation he experienced. Which was worse?

His inability to be aware of sycophancy or his later humiliation?
The Stratford performance has lived with us to this day.

10th

I was awakened by the clamour of an electric generator. They were laying the drainage for the new housing estate to be built on Penrhys mountain - 1000 houses. I saw the workmen at the top of the street, and guessing some would be Irish, I went to chat. Four Irishmen, one from Donegal and three from Killorglin in Kerry which I visited a few years ago. They were pleased I showed interest. They were strong men, working hard, living in lodgings and living life hard. Straightforward, honest, and a long way from home.

15th

Norman Cohn's 'The Pursuit of the Millennium' provides a fascinating account of extreme chiliasm in the Middle Ages.
Chiliasm is that fervent expectancy that the world is about to come to an End, and that 'God's Chosen People' have a political role to play - often in violent and intolerant forms. It is not confined to Christianity! Tragically it continues in contemporary fanaticism, both religious and secular.

16th

A remarkable, foreboding book. It is frightening to see how 'common people' can be captivated by psychological escapism. The allurement of the Millennium and apocalyptic, revolutionary Messianism led thousands to complete hysteria, uncontrollable hatred, perversion of all that is good.

Sunday 18th

I led worship at Zion English Congregational Church. It was most stimulating, 50 to 60 present, including children who left for Sunday School during the service. This afternoon I preached at Glanhafren, a small church connected with the main church at Llanidloes. It is in a gloriously wooded valley, near the source of the Severn. The church is on the banks of the river; an old, squat building with a high pulpit. A delightful group of 15. Evening service at 6 with 50 present.
Norah and I were stopping with Alan and Catherine Willcocks. Alan was a College friend and minister at Llanidloes and Glanhafren. We had no idea how momentous the visit proved.

19th

Cohn shows a rare combination of psychological and historical insight. He carefully builds up the picture until he leaves the horror stare out. It is devastatingly possible to draw modern parallels of these medieval wielders of popular ferment.

Sunday 25th

My last Sunday in Ebenezer before we sail for America. Dad and I walked down the steps to Ebenezer - 2 dozen there and warm attentiveness, particularly from the big seat. At Sunday School I took the whole of the upstairs, 16 from the age of 13 to 65, a good honest discussion of a passage from Luke. 50 tonight, including Hywel and his father, and Ivor, Olive and Huw. I spoke to many outside, including Mrs J G Davies (SS teacher, great influence on my life).

AUGUST

10th

We arrived at Dolgellau and found Andrew Montague's studio empty but went to his house and bought 'Crucifixion,' a 1961 painting. An emotional study commanding response. If we hadn't bought it, it would have haunted us. Paid £9 -9s.

Andrew Montague was leaving for Ireland. We never heard anything of him again, but we still have the painting.

18th

Jonathan was waiting for us at Ampleforth to take us to lunch in the Abbey guest room (first married visitors for 3 months). Jonathan introduced us to Aelred who is responsible for guests. Jeremy (also Oxford) came for coffee. The five of us toured the Abbey: relics of the Cross and St Lawrence, and heard the glorious organ. Saw the theatre and the school with its Library, Common Room and Dorms. The woodwork of Thompson is superb. He is known as the mouse-man because he carves a mouse on his work. The three brothers pushed the car until it started, and waved until we were out of sight.

28th

I slept well in the bed in which I slept for many years. It was drizzling as I walked up the street, turned at the corner of the steps, waved goodbye and made my way down the steps. To leave Brynbedw and parents was the greatest pain. As I waited at the bus stop at Queens Square, Dad arrived with my pen. He had come down in the rain. I waved goodbye and looked through the misted glass as we went up the valley, across Maerdy and out of my beloved Rhondda. I purposely watched the Rhigos climb out of sight in the mist. I have left.

31st

It is 5 years since I first met Dr Pennar about entering College. He is so interesting and generous in spirit.

5. HARTFORD SEMINARY FOUNDATION 1965-7

In the 1960s, Hartford was one of the finest places to study Puritanism. This New England town had been founded by the Congregational divine Thomas Hooker in 1636, three years before the formation of Llanfaches, the first Congregational Church in Wales. The Seminary had a Calvin Scholar and a Puritan scholar working in tandem. Robert Paul had already written 'The Lord Protector,' a biography of Cromwell and 'An Apologetical Narration' and Ford Lewis Battles, Philip Schaff Professor of Church History had translated and indexed Calvin's 'The Institutes of the Christian Religion' in the Library of Christian Classics series. During the first semester, I was Battles' only student, translating Calvin from the original Latin, and in the second semester, part of a small class reading and commenting on the whole of 'The Institutes.' That experience provided a theological platform which has remained with me for a lifetime. Ford Battles encouraged us to be freed from a Calvinism which was dependent on cliches, and enabled us to seek the 'spirit of Calvin,' understanding him in his context and recognizing Calvin's love for Christ and the Church. Reading Calvin created the foundation of the theological series developed in Manselton and later on Penrhys. With Robert Paul I thoroughly enjoyed Courses in Ecumenics (in which I specialized in the Orthodox Tradition) and English and American Puritanism as well as his serving as supervisor in my research in Puritanism.

The intention was in the first year to complete the Comprehensive Examinations which were part of the PhD degree and submit the Erbery thesis to Oxford in the summer. Things did not work out as planned. Although I successfully completed the examinations and submitted the thesis, I was unsuccessful in my 'defence' in June

1966. I presented the thesis before Dr Geoffrey Nuttall and Dr Barry White but did not have the result until the following December, by which time I was working in Hartford on the second thesis. I learned then that the thesis had been 'referred' (given another chance) and I planned to resubmit when the thesis had been revised. One consolation of spending the summer in Wales was the day Norah and I climbed to the top of Tylorstown tip. There I experienced that sense of belonging to a community which has proved influential for the rest of my life.

In the meantime, work on the second thesis progressed well. I chose as a theme 'The National and International Aspects of Puritan Eschatology.' I was intrigued by the effect a sense of the imminent 'End of History' had upon politics. For research purposes, the seminary had a superb Puritan Library which included (on microfilm) all the Sermons preached before Parliament between 1640 and 1660. As I compared this theme in England, Wales, Scotland and New England, most of the essential and rare material was found either in the College Library or at the Connecticut Historical Society Library.

I was fortunate to have two Youth Advisor posts, in the first year at Broadview Community Church in Hartford (United Church of Christ) and in the second year at The First Baptist Church in Waterbury (American Baptist Church) under the excellent leadership of the Revd Paul Humphreys. Both pastorates introduced me to American Church life but at Broadview I learned a salutary lesson of how an arrogant minister destroyed the equilibrium of a happy church. It was a lesson well learned.

We benefited greatly from living with fellow students in Tyler Hall on campus. They came from all over the world: India, South Africa, Lebanon, South America and of course Americans.

Just as in Swansea and at Oxford, we benefited greatly from 'special lectures.' Amongst many others, we heard George McLeod of Iona, Otto Weber the Calvinist scholar, Oscar Cullman on the New Testament, John Marsh and Stanley Greenslade. A highlight was the debate between J J Altizer and Daniel Day Williams on the 'God is Dead Movement.'

Although most of our time was spent at Hartford, we enjoyed a Christmas with the Comstock family in Ohio, and a visit to Expo 67 in Montreal with the Schoonmakers. A highlight was a weekend at Union Seminary New York when Easter morning was spent at the East Harlem Protestant Mission. Later Norah heard George Webber speaking in Hartford and the encounter had a major effect upon us both. I visited an Urban Project in the North End of Hartford, and the run-down State Hospital and both visits helped confirm the scandal of inequality in a prosperous city.

The greatest joy of the two years was undoubtedly the birth of Hugh in December 1965. He gave happiness to us as a family and also to the seminary.

At the beginning of January 1967, we turned our thoughts once more to returning to Wales and at last to ordination. Although I processed through the Moderator system of the Congregational Church, it was in fact through reading a cutting from a newspaper sent to us by Norah's sister, that my attention was drawn to the fact that there was a vacancy at the Congregational Church in Llanidloes. Through a succession of letters, 'the call' to serve at Llanidloes and Glanhafren came across the Atlantic. Norah and I had of course visited the churches in July 1965 and that was apparently enough to convince them to invite us.

When we returned to Wales at the beginning of September 1967, Norah and Hugh spent the next few months in Swansea with Norah's parents, while I lived in Oxford to complete research for the submission of the Erbery thesis. This was a difficult period for us both, particularly as Dylan, our second son was born in October. There were many journeys between Oxford and Swansea and vice versa, long before the creation of the M4! We were glad to be reunited as a family and begin the first ministry in Llanidloes in December 1967.

SEPTEMBER

8th

I am writing in our apartment in Hartford, Connecticut, USA, listening to the sound of crickets chirping. Our steward called us at 5.15 with a 'rise and shine with the US Line.' We passed beneath the new suspension bridge while it was still dark. Breakfast before rushing to the top deck to see the first skyscrapers rising majestically from early morning mist, the sun rise over New York and docking at Pier 86 at 8.20. The stewards asked me to pray for the ship. We started the medical and immigration examination at 8.45 and went ashore onto American soil at 10.05. A great experience, a new continent. Then the hectic rush for luggage, a call for a Hartford student and there were Libby, Chuck & Dave. After customs we met Paul and Judy Schoonmaker from Hartford. Hartford by 3. Tyler Hall and fetched the key from Dr Paul's.

We had crossed the Atlantic on 'The United States' and when we arrived at New York we were greeted by American friends we had met in Mansfield, and the Schoonmakers, Hartford students who supported us during our two years in Connecticut.

9th

Woke at 5.45 to a superb dawn chorus. Tyler Hall is surrounded by trees. A grand flat with a small hall, good kitchen with fridge, fine electric cooker, modern washing unit and plenty of storage; the lounge has new three piece furniture, solid desk and bookcase; bedroom also has new furniture; a well appointed bathroom and two large cupboards for clothes; all centrally heated. We are so very fortunate. Lunch with the Schoonmakers and afterwards to the supermarket - First National. It seemed incredible but we were there for 2 hours and spent $24.60. It seems a terrific amount.

13th

Robert Paul suggested I should aim for a PhD and spend two years at Hartford. 'This might be the last chance of you getting the degree which matters.' I should return to England next summer to be vivad for the BLitt. He would read the thesis and suggest improvements (he has been informed by Greenslade that it is a matter of style). I asked Ford Battles for a course on Calvinism (he is a world authority) although he hasn't a course this semester. He was delighted and we start next week in Latin.

17th

The new minister of Broadview Community Church took me to church to meet his secretary and the Christian Education Chairman. They offered me the job of Youth Adviser and Sunday School teacher. I take a class of 15 year olds, Junior High and Senior High. The church has every amenity. It is a congregation of the United Church of Christ, and uses the excellent curriculum. The pay is $18 a week for 39 weeks.
The secretary was Millie Egan, who was still Church secretary 40 years later.

Sunday 19th

My first day as youth adviser at Broadview Community Church. I shall learn a great deal to take back to Wales. I went down to my classroom and was introduced to my class of 10th grade (aged 15). Seven present (out of 10). A nice group, intelligent and all ambitious of going to College. All from good family backgrounds. The lesson today was on maturity and responsibility. At

7.30 we had Senior High - 17 of us. A good introductory meeting. They range from 15 to 18 and are not as mature as English people of that age. A fine group.

21st

European history with Dr Paul in his room before my seminar on Calvinism with Dr Battles also in his house. I led Prayers - at 11 - the first student this academic year. A seminar on Research Method with Leser and Battles. Leser is entertaining, perpetually on the move, physically and mentally.

The excellent course was led by Battles and Paul Leser. Leser was professor of Anthropology at the Seminary. His research on the usage of the agricultural plough made him a world expert in the field. He had left Germany during the rise of Hitler and eventually taught at Hartford. The Course proved of great value for all embarking on research work.

23rd

Dr Battles and I sat in the garden on a lovely morning, with the sound of insects. A grey squirrel scampered along the ridge of the wooden roof (lots of squirrels about - a reminder of Christchurch meadow). I enjoyed the 75 minutes seminar and we read a dozen verses with exact thoroughness. Extremely stimulating particularly as he is kindly in his criticism.

Sunday 26th

The minister helped me on with the gown - I've only worn one once before, at Mansfield. We walked up the central aisle in processional and divided at the front of the church. I took the responsive reading, the lesson and children's address. Norah and I shook hands with everyone as they left. Chapel was packed until the children left - even the small gallery in the back. At 5.30 I met Junior High. 20 present and a nice set of kids. A sack meal. At 7 I met Senior High. The minister was there and told them off about the coming Retreat. He should have been more tactful.

OCTOBER

14th

Norah had her medical examination with Dr Emmel - the best she has had since she became pregnant. He examined her for a full hour and told her that he would not charge. Apparently he is an extremely kind person who prays for his patients. People at home make lots of jokes about Americans and their superficial religion. I have never met such generosity or lack of snobbery as in the Seminary where students and tutors rub shoulders naturally - rather different from Mansfield.

Norah was working part-time on the College switch-board, 'the nerve-centre of the Seminary.'

20th

The Hartford Symphony Orchestra played Haydn 98, a Gloria by Poulenc and Brahms 4th at the Bushnell.

The Horace Bushnell Theatre was named after the Hartford pioneer in religious education.

NOVEMBER

2nd

Calvin is seeping into my bones. He has been sorely maligned by my generation.

9th

One of the worst electric cuts in the history of the North East: from Chicago through New York to Boston. It started at 5.30 and we have just had our electricity back at 9.15. A strange experience, realising it wasn't simply Tyler Hall, then Hartford but this vast area. Two disappointing reactions - was it caused by sabotage and probably Russians? reports of looting. Two weak spots of US life.

On November 9, 1965 the north-eastern region of the United States and Canada was abruptly plunged into blackness. The worst blackout on record came to be known as the 'Big Blackout'. At 5:16 pm, at the height of the evening rush hour, electrical power to one-sixth of the continent's population was suddenly cut off, trapping millions of people on expressways, in elevators and in office buildings. Thirty million people in eight U.S. states and in the province of Ontario were affected by the disruption.

13th

Completed the first book of 'The Institutes.' It is superb, combining a beautiful theological construction with deep piety and gratitude for the grace and power of God.

17th

Trinity this afternoon and evening for talks by George McLeod. He didn't say much that was new, but he touched the grandeur and overwhelming comprehensiveness of the Gospel. The earth is the Lord's and every aspect is to be lifted up. Beautiful and stirring.
Norah and I were deeply impressed by McLeod's personality. It was a privilege to be in conversation with the founder of the Iona Community.

18th

Dr Battles is pleased with my progress in Latin and he told me I read our passage as well as it could be read. Shopped in gigantic Foxe's. Bitterly cold with a biting wind sweeping around the blocks. Norah and I heard Dr McLeod at Trinity on Christian attitudes to money and war. He spoke in the chapel. Afterwards a dozen of us went to the cave (student coffee house) and entered discussion. He has a deep conviction in the Gospel's significance for the whole of existence; a mystical Calvinism? Nothing should be apart from the love of God - all is a part of Him. Stimulating and searching; thank God for his witness.

Sunday 28th

An important day for Broadview and I hope they made a wise choice. My fear is they have not. At his examination, the new minister gave a paper on the meaning of the church and was then questioned. (Bob Edwards of Emmanuel sat by us, and I introduced myself to him. He told us we can have a church bed at the hospital. Wonderful news.) Incompetence and evasion by the minister who could not answer any theological questions: he was asked about the 'God is Dead' theology, hadn't heard of it and tried to bluff. I feel sorry for him and the church. Dr English preached well at the Installation Service.

30th

Paul's Letter to the Romans is an inspiration. He has such an awareness of the Gospel. Paul gets to grips with what Christ did for him and for all.

DECEMBER

2nd

Praise God. The baby has been born and both he and Norah are excellent. Hardly credible as it happened so quickly. A wonderful experience. At 6.20

I was called over intercom to the 5th floor and saw Norah and baby boy (fair, 7lb 12oz, beautiful - Hugh). Norah looked wonderful, had a natural birth, and was so happy. A wonderful day. Praise God. Baby born at 9 minutes to 6. Beautiful sunny day.

3rd

I know how Joseph must have felt - and my father. Praise the Lord for life and all it entails, and for life in His Kingdom. Happy day that fixed my choice.

7th

Norah and Hugh came home today. Wonderful. Hugh is now safely tucked up in bed. Here are the three of us under one roof, having eaten, and dependent on the Lord for all things. A great day.

17th

This semester has been so worthwhile because of studying Puritanism and Calvinism/Latin. Nowhere else, probably in the world, could I have had such a fine partnership as Battles and Paul. I have also had the fine critical training of the Research Method Class.

1966

JANUARY

10th

It took 4 months for a happy and united church to become desperately unhappy. I have learned a great deal about high-handed ministers. I see no imminent solution but it will come, by God's grace. Save us from those within the church rather than those outside - they are much more dangerous. I bought T S Eliot's 'Collected Poems'

13th
The Latin/Calvin seminar has improved my Latin enormously. I can translate reasonably easily and have begun to enter into the spirit of the master, Calvin. His subtlety of expression, controlled style and magnificent choice and structure of language communicate his grasp of the fundamentals of the Gospel and makes them live. What a great privilege to study under Dr Ford Battles who has a penetratingly classical and evangelical insight into Calvin's thought alongside kindly humility. This seminar will be of lasting significance for the development of my expression of the Gospel. I am becoming closer to Calvin's forceful and humble declaration of God's Word: it recognises the sin and dignity of man, and the power and grace of God.

28th
Five of us met Dr Battles for the seminar on 'The Institutes' at 8am until 10. Puritan class with Dr Paul at 2 to 4.

FEBRUARY

4th
I no longer strive to reach the impossible goal of rational faith. An old weather beaten cross starkly bisects time. This is all we know and need to know - no beauty or form that we should desire it.

18th
Research work is developing my intellectual expression of the faith. There is a need for continuity with the historic church, and a demand to reinterpret for each generation and cultural background. Wales has lost so much so quickly. Chapels close each year; no new ones are built; less men are entering the ministry and those entering soon feel the frustration and loneliness of their calling. The residuum of Welsh Nonconformity with its Independency, anti-liturgical prejudice and insipid cultural liberalism will need to disappear before there can be progress.

19th
The Cleveland Symphony Orchestra, conducted superbly by George Szell played Wagner's 'Lohengrin', Mozart's '29th Symphony' and the magnificent Bruckner's '3rd Symphony'.
A concert at the Bushnell Theatre.

21st

Dr Otto Weber spoke on 'Calvin and Church Unity.' Although his English was difficult to follow, it was a great honour to meet such a major theologian. *Otto Weber succeeded Barth as Professor of Reformed Theology at Gottingen. He was supervisor to Jurgen Moltmann. He died during 1966.*

25th

It is a travesty that Calvin is depicted as intellectual, unfeeling and uncharitable; Calvin breathes through the Institutes as a vibrant, stirring saint endeavouring to express his Biblical experience of the living Christ.

Sunday 27th

My first opportunity to preach in the United States. 200 people listened intently and no one passed at the porch without thanking for the sermon.
A privilege to lead worship at Broadview Community Church.

28th

The Boston Symphony Orchestra with Eric Leinsdorf played Vivaldi's 'Concerto Grosso,' Strauss' 'Till Eulenspiegel,' Debussy's 'Prelude to the Afternoon of a Faun' and Tchaikovsky 'Pathetique.'
Another concert at the Bushnell.

MARCH

5th

I listened (on record) to Eliot reading 'Alfred Prufrock' and 'Ash Wednesday.' I have been reading Eliot every night since January and have read 'The Collected Poems' twice.

7th

Dr Gerhard Ebeling of Tübingen spoke on 'The Meaning of the Gospel in the Secular Era.' Although man believes he can plan his own salvation, the Word of God declares this impossible. In Europe the violent battle between Christianity and secularism is raging but it is also taking place beneath the surface in the US.
Gerhard Ebeling was a student of Bultmann at Zurich. He was a prominent participant in the movement known as 'the New Quest for the Historical Jesus.' He was a member of the Confessing Church in its protest against Hitler.

19th

A damp English day - this is the way Americans describe such a day. I visited an inner-city experiment where a coloured minister has opened a social centre for youth in the slum district of the North End of the city. It has a TV room cum lounge (smaller than our living room), an office and a room with coffee tables. 30 kids each night. The atmosphere is informal and the kids run the place themselves. They are doing an excellent job. There is a completely different atmosphere between the North End and our end of the city. The majority are black; I saw one white man; lots of men and kids standing about; poorer and dirtier. The church needs to witness there, and this project makes contact.

Sunday 20th

Full attendance and first-rate discussion in Church School. The kids are asking the right questions. The Bushnell was packed with 3000 young people between 15 and 18 (the same last week, all United Church in Connecticut). The first half of the programme had singers and worship. Sandwiches in the State Armoury before returning to the Bushnell for the film 'Lust for Life,' the story of van Gogh. Tremendously poignant, the genius who commits suicide, loving and hating life at the same time.
Lust for Life starred Kirk Douglas.

28th

My Ecumenics paper is on 'the influence of the Orthodox Church on the ecumenical movement.' This is all new to me as I know little about either the Eastern Church or the Ecumenical movement.

APRIL

9th

New York, one of the greatest cities in the world. Fascinating faces, especially on the subway. A great adventure. We parked opposite the main gate of Union Seminary, found Van Dusen Hall and were greeted by Becky, Libby, Dave, Chuck and his sister, Jeanie. They took us to the Empire State and the 86th floor to the main platform. The view was very clear and was one of the great moments of our lives. Looked in Macys (biggest shop in the world). This evening we visited the superb Lincoln Centre and Greenwich Village. The place was swarming, police, beatniks or artificial ones everywhere. Coffee at the Figaro, what atmosphere. Returned by Washington Square and subway. A great day.

Founded in 1836, Union forged a new vision for theological education: to establish ministerial training in an urban context so that academic excellence and personal faith might respond to the needs of the city. It continues to play a key role in theological education. Our Mansfield friends provided us with hospitality at Union Seminary.

Sunday 10th (Easter Sunday)

The greatest day of the Christian Year has been spent in such joyous manner at East Harlem Protestant Mission, the Church of the Ascension. The church began in 1948 in empty shop-fronts and has gradually built up to have two churches and a group ministry in one of the toughest parts of the city, or any city. We were in by 11 to an absolutely packed church of more than 300 worshippers. The service was joyous, informal and yet beautifully and simply ordered. Prayers for members (asked for at service); we introduced ourselves; a period when we all walked around shaking hands; a good sermon, tremendously lively singing, meaningful liturgy and communion in which all in turn, stood around the Table and sang 'Let us break bread together.' Tour of the United Nations, the Security Council and the General Assembly where the world's problems are decided. It needs our prayers.

In 1948, J. Archie Hargraves, George (Bill) Webber, and Donald Benedict set up a 'store-front parish system' in East Harlem, where over 300,000 people lived jammed together in a little over a square mile from 96th to 125th Street. According to an early 1950s Parish pamphlet, the atmosphere was 'tense with hatred, fear, discrimination, and conflict; people were separated by race, religion, language, and culture.' By 1953, the East Harlem Protestant Parish (EHPP) had set up four storefront churches and offered practical and spiritual help to people of all ages. Bruce Kenrick, in his 1962 book, 'Come Out the Wilderness: the Story of East Harlem Protestant Parish,' wrote that mainly through Bill Webber, 'more than 500 students were to do field work in East Harlem, and over twenty were to commit themselves to a long-term ministry there.' Webber divided his time between duties as Union's Dean of Students and duties of the Parish from 1950 to 1957.

N.B. Dave Hornbeck writes 'For two of my years at Union, I lived and worked in East Harlem with clergy and lay people, while I learned from so many great teachers. This hands-on, practical work was invaluable. But it was because my field experience was grounded in specific theological reflection that I was able to develop the principles that have guided me since.' [From Union Seminary website.]

Norah listened to Bill Webber in Immanuel, Hartford and this confirmed her conviction about the need for urban ministry. Norah distinctly remembers the words: 'You must live in the place.' She sees a direct connection between Easter 1966 and our move to Penrhys thirty years later.

MAY

17th

The final of my five Comprehensives was a 24 hour project. I collected the paper Battles had set for me. It was a very amusing letter from F. Ludovic Pugnax, editor of the Oxbridge UP, Camford. He asked me to draw up an approach to a dual problem: (1) the New Israel concept as developed through Constantine, Theodosius, Justinian, Augustine and through the Middle Ages with Caesaro-Papism. (2) The outburst of eschatological and apocalyptic thought with Joachim of Flora, Franciscan spirituals and the Crusades. A fascinating problem. I was in the Library at 9 and collected bibliographical data until 10.30. I worked in one of the camels in the stacks.

A key element in the study for a Hartford PhD was the passing of Comprehensive examinations. My five papers were set by Ford Battles, Robert Paul on 'English Church History' and 'Puritanism;' Harvey McArthur on 'The Kingdom of God in the New Testament,' and Richard Weingart on 'The Kingdom of God in Christian theology.' I sat the examinations in a week in May. Almost immediately afterwards we flew back to Heathrow and returned to Wales to prepare for the viva at Oxford.

JUNE

Sunday 26th

Hugh has been baptized at Ebenezer into the Christian Church and Norah and I have made our vows to lead him in the Christian life.

Both Norah's and my family were present for this most significant occasion. The service was taken by the minister Dewi Myrddin Hughes and Alwyn Charles. Dewi became General Secretary of the Union of Welsh Independents and served on the Penrhys Sponsoring Body.

JULY

7th

A high point. Norah and I went to the top of Tylorstown tip, the huge monster looking over the valley. It is 400 feet above the mountain and provides one of the best views in the valleys. I have always wanted to reach the top but it was inaccessible when the pits were operating. The view is spectacular as we looked almost vertically down. A panoramic view of 60 miles.
This experience proved seminal in my understanding of community.

14th

Today will dominate years to come. I sense I have failed my viva and that my thesis will be sent back. At 1.30 I dressed in sub fusc and Norah and Hugh walked with me to the Examination Schools by 2.10. I waited outside the room where I was to be interviewed by Dr Nuttall and Dr White. The latter acted as chairman and asked questions for the first half, and then Nuttall questioned during the second half. I felt terribly disappointed when I left at 3.25, convinced of failure. They asked questions about details of the thesis and pointed out mistakes. I wasn't questioned about the main aspects of the thesis.
In 1945, Geoffrey Nuttall became only the second nonconformist theologian to become Doctor of Divinity at Oxford. That year, he became a lecturer in church history at New College, University of London, where he remained until his retirement in 1977. Barry R White was Principal at Regent's Park College, Oxford (1972-1989) and then Senior Research Fellow in Ecclesiastical History, also at Regent's Park (1989-1999).

28th

A letter from Dr Nuttall: 'You will understand that examiners are not permitted to inform examinees what they recommend, either during a viva or afterwards, because it is formally only a recommendation. Examiners are never told, however, whether, or when, their recommendation has been adopted and the candidate informed. Consequently I dont know whether you yet know the outcome of your recent submission for BLitt. If you do, or when you do, would you please let me know? And I will then send some advice which Dr White and I agreed I should send when the time arrived.' It seems clear they have referred the thesis.

AUGUST

2nd

Hywel and I walked to Bristol Tump, past the quarry and returned towards Penrhys (the site of the new estate - abomination of desolation at the moment). The mountain is miraculous.

6th

I left the house at 9.50, with camera and lunch. I took photographs throughout the day. I walked up Donald St, along Park Rd and struck onto the mountain near the school and from there past the quarry to reach Bristol Tump by 10.25. Windy and sunny but it looked as if it might rain. From the top, down the ridge to the old parish road, across the rocks and up to the tumulus above Maerdy Cemetery. I descended to the new school, down Oxford Street, crossed the bridge and climbed the mountain on the other side. Ate my lunch just before Blaenllechau at 12.30, from where I walked by the side of the forestry, crossed the road and climbed to the top of the tip - the view in every direction was staggering. Along the road to Llanwynno, through the plantation to the farm, down to the bridge and home at 2.55.

7th

Uncle Frank took us to Penrhys to see an erratic which might have come from Oban; it is in an exposed position near the 2nd tee. Returned to where they are excavating for the new housing estate - we saw a medieval millstone, found 4' 9" below the surface.

SEPTEMBER

23rd

Norah will be spending 10 hours a week in the Post Office, earning in total $1250. Met Rev Paul Humphreys and Miss Eckard, the Christian Education Director of First Baptist Church, Waterbury. A Sunday job, Church, SS with 8 and 9th grades from 11.45 to 12.25, visiting in the afternoon with the minister and Senior High at 6.30.

We returned to Hartford on September 12th. Norah was able to work at the Switch Board in the Seminary (where she had worked the previous year) and I served in Waterbury, an industrial town 30 miles south of Hartford.

Sunday 25th

First Baptist Church of Waterbury. Service began at 10.30 and I gave the readings for Christian Education Sunday (we were on radio). Mr Humphreys preached a good sensible sermon. Sunday school class - 8th and 9th grade. Only 6 of them but they are interesting and attentive. Home with Mr Mrs Humphreys who have a fine split-level home on Bunker's hill. He has been in the ministry 35 years and has had only three churches. He is a fine person and I shall enjoy working with him and Miss Eckhard (Mimi). A short tour of the city - industrialized, 100,000, hilly.

OCTOBER

Sunday 9th

This 9th grade group are much more Bibliocentric than last year's group. Mr and Mrs Foote took us to their home 5 miles out of Waterbury. Delightful 85 acres, including a lake. He is a retired vice President of Waterbury Savings Bank. Mr Foote showed us casts of dinosaur's tracks, 5000 Christmas trees and the barn full for the Church Auction next Saturday. I took my 5 Senior Highs in a discussion of social problems of the town.

We visited the Foote family at Christmas Tree Farm when I defended the thesis in 1970, and later they stopped with us in Cardiff.

12th

I have passed Comprehensives. The letter stated 'At the meeting of the Council for Advanced Studies, held on October 5, 1966, it was announced: "Certified in Welsh language; Committee reports that Mr Morgans has sustained Comprehensive Examinations; Mr Morgans reports that he will know the results of his Oxford B Litt examinations in November. Please accept my congratulations and best wishes for your continuing academic success." Last year was hectic, what with GRE, two languages (Latin and French), Course work and Comprehensives, as well as two months rewriting the Erbery thesis.

The GRE was a Graduate Record Examination which was a compulsory test for all proceeding to higher degrees.

20th

I completed reading on microfilm the Sermons before Parliament: 249 sermons, written between 1640 and 1662. The final one proved one of the most important - a sermon by Hugh Peters in 1646.

The key resource for my Puritan studies were the sermons preached before Parliament during the two decades beginning in 1640. They were of great variety, and they commented on and reflected the radical political and military changes of the period. Preachers included Anglicans, Presbyterians and Independents.

21st

Horror. A terrible tragedy in Aberfan, near Merthyr. A coal tip moved into two schools just after Assembly and it is feared that 200, almost all children, have been killed. We have just (at 6.30pm) seen the TV report and the position seems hopeless I have never seen anything as dreadful as the surging mass of mud and slag. To think I stood proudly on our tip two months ago without recognizing it as a killer. The first news I heard was at 9 but it appeared inconsequential. Gradually the full horror came through. The sight of those poor mothers was terrible. It is now night and the search continues for, what now seems like bodies. 55 bodies have been found.
The event that marked the 1960s in Wales.

22nd

The whole horror of yesterday's tragedy has hit home. This is where I was born, these are people like ones I know, the school is like Dad's, the pit like No 9, the houses like ours and that monstrous tip like the one I thought towered strangely and beautifully over the whole valley. Now its dominance has changed into an awful menacing. Another hazard to Welsh mining life, on top of all our people have suffered for a hundred years. A final torment.

24th

The lecture by Oscar Cullman was a judicious, honest assessment of the Vatican Council. There can be no unity of Protestant and Catholic because of Catholic dogmatic inflexibility. This great Biblical scholar spoke insistently on salvation history.
Oscar Cullmann is best known for his work in the ecumenical movement, being in part responsible for the establishment of dialogue between the Lutheran and Roman Catholic traditions. He was invited to be an observer at the Second Vatican Council. I was particularly influenced by his New Testament essay on the need to hold together the Lord's Supper and the Resurrection Breakfasts for our understanding and celebration of the Eucharist.

NOVEMBER

21st

Heard from Oxford. The Board of the Faculty of Theology, after careful consideration of the report of your examiners, finds itself unable at present to grant you leave to supplicate for the degree of Bachelor of Letters.

DECEMBER

5th

The letter from Nuttall was an awful shock: 'I think I had better tell you that your examiners were gravely dissatisfied with your thesis. On balance, we feared that it was unlikely that you would be able to improve it sufficiently to meet our requirements [However] you also made a far better impression upon us in the viva voce than the thesis had done, which led us to hope that there might be some possibility of improvement with further supervision.' His criticisms were vague, including the particularly hurtful one, 'You seemed to have a rather incurious and uncritical mind.' He states he is not prepared to help in any way while I am in America.

16th

A letter from Dr White was pleasant, helpful and made reasonable suggestions. What a difference from the curt letter of Dr Nuttall. 'I was glad to hear from you and to gather from your letter that you plan to re-submit your thesis on William Erbery. I hope these suggestions, made on the basis of notes taken before and at your viva will be useful to you and that you will press on with your work.' Nuttall's letter made me feel like giving up the work completely. White did not suggest re-writing the thesis but a re-examination of certain portions. He suggested that 'all links posited with 20th century thought' should be omitted. I showed the letter to Dr Paul. He was much happier.

1967

JANUARY

14th

I wrote to Bill Samuel, Moderator for Wales, asking to be introduced to a pastorate.

The beginning of the process of seeking a pastorate for ministry. I had been interviewed by the Moderator while we were at home during the summer, and had been one of 'his students' since 1960.

16th

The Introduction to 'Puritanism and Liberty' is a brilliant piece of work, serving as a preamble to the Putney Debates which deal with the problems of democracy. Should everyone be allowed to vote (natural rights: Rainsborough)? Should it depend on their permanent 'interest' (illustrated by land ownership or finance: Ireton)? or by being on the right side (saints: Peter)? The Whitehall Debates discuss the issues of religious liberty.

19th

Mrs Gettemy took me to the Austin School (Private) where I was interviewed by the Headmaster and offered the position of teaching European History (1789-1914) to 10 girls. It will be 50 minutes a day for $500.

Mrs Gettemy was the wife of the President of the Seminary, James Gettemy.

FEBRUARY

20th

A letter from home. Mamma had phoned the Moderator: he hadn't answered my letter because 'there is nothing available.' I decided to write to English Moderators. I posted to Moderators of Lancashire, North West, West Midlands, South and South West.

28th

A letter from the Moderator with the name of only one semi-rural church which already has a candidate. He would put my name before the Moderators. It seems my first ministry will be in England.

MARCH

21st

The Seminary has organised a debate between Daniel Day Williams and Thomas J J Altizer. Altizer drew most attention and the larger crowd. Williams spoke this afternoon on 'The Meaning of Grace' and Altizer this evening on 'Self-annihilation in Man and God.' Williams spoke with clarity and scholarship; Altizer was haphazard. Both were involved in a dialogue after their lectures. Williams demolished Altizer's thesis and I felt sorry for Altizer because he could not answer questions from the floor and used banal generalizations. This leader of the 'God is Dead' movement has achieved a reputation he does not deserve.

Altizer is famous/notorious for inventing the 'God is Dead' statement. While teaching at Emory, Georgia, Altizer's religious views were featured in two Time magazine articles in 1965 and 1966. The latter issue was published at Easter time, and its cover asked in bold red letters on a plain black background, 'Is God Dead?' Daniel Day Williams was a lecturer in theology at Union Seminary New York.

22nd

The conclusion of the Williams/Altizer dialogue. Altizer was unable to answer questions and passed them on to Williams who appears to be deeply sensitive and thoughtful with a fine combination of intellect (Whiteheadian), piety and poetry (GM Hopkins).

A N Whitehead was a mathematician, philosopher and theologian. Gerald Manley Hopkins was a Jesuit and a poet.

26th Easter Sunday

The ecumenical service was at the beautiful Plaza with the sun rising, a choir, Salvation Army, procession of clergy, 5000 congregation. A Jesuit preached excellently.

31st

Dr Greenslade gives the Carew lectures. I admire him so much. Should I spend Michaelmas term at Oxford and work under Dr Greenslade for the BLitt? I would then start in a church in December. I took Greenslade to meet Norah. He told me the Erbery thesis had been good enough for the BLitt.

APRIL

1st

The Connecticut Historical Society Library is delightful; the librarian knew her work and obscure material arrived quickly. A little like Oxford with its quaint efficiency.

3rd

Dr Greenslade was succinct, clear, fair with a superb sense of humour. Such laughter in a formal lecture.

4th

The second Carew lecture was on the Reformers' scholarship in their use of the Patristics. [Early Church Fathers] Dr Greenslade's visit this evening was hilarious. We were watching 'Secret Agent,' and just before the end there was a knock on the door, I hallooed 'come in;' Greenslade popped his head around the door and we were all gaping at TV - Ed on floor, Norah curled on the settee and I with my feet on a chair. Ed beat a hasty retreat and we chatted until 10.15.

Ed Mays was a fellow student who became a minister in the United Church of Christ.

5th

The third lecture on the Reformers and the Councils was both erudite and personal; Dr Greenslade dealt with their responses to Roman Catholics and Puritans.

8th

The difficulties of the Seminary become more complex. Many research students are dissatisfied with the changes in the new BD curriculum which asks for (1) only two introductory courses to Bible, History or Theology and (2) the two semesters should be replaced by three terms. The purpose is to allow students more electives. This means a student could get his BD with the minimum 'traditional' courses. I chatted to Battles and fellow research students who are all disappointed with the new curriculum. Dr Paul talked about the faculty split.

The College Staff was divided on the issue of replacing 'traditional' subjects by more contemporary and contextual themes. Probably this was the reason Robert Paul and Ford Battles left for Pittsburgh Seminary. Is it possible that the Hartford Declaration of 1975 was a reaction to this trend? 'An Appeal For Theological Affirmation: The renewal of Christian witness and mission requires constant examination of the assumptions shaping the Church's life. Today an apparent loss of a sense of the transcendent is undermining the Church's ability to address with clarity and courage the urgent tasks to which God calls it in the world. This loss is manifest in a number of pervasive themes. Many are superficially attractive, but upon closer examination we find these themes false and debilitating to the Church's life and work.' James Gettemy, President of Hartford signed the Declaration.

15th

A letter from Bill Samuel. I have been accepted by the South Wales Association and he suggests Albany Haverfordwest, or Risca and Cross Keys.

MAY

3rd

A new Nuttall collection of essays includes a very critical review of 'The Lord Protector.'

'The Puritan Spirit: Essays and Addresses' by Geoffrey F Nuttall. Dr Paul had written 'The Lord Protector' which was first published in 1955.

15th

Could this be an important day? We received a letter from Doreen [Norah's sister] with a cutting saying that Alan Willcocks was moving from Llanidloes to Newport. Why haven't I heard from the Moderator as this is the kind of church I described to him? I wrote to Mr Watson (the Secretary whom we know well), to Alan and the Moderator. It is fortunate we have heard nothing from Risca.

18th

I bought theology books including Macquarrie's 'Principles of Christian Theology.'

John Macquarrie's book published in 1966 became seminal when I approached the issues of education and mission in Llanidloes in 1969. Macquarrie was Professor of Systematic Theology at Union Theological Seminary New York.

25th

Mr Watson writes: 'The contents of your letter gave me quite a thrill... As I expected they (the deacons) were all very delighted and were anxious that I should do everything possible to bring the matter before our Church... the very thought of the possibility of your coming here will spur me on to try to produce a good show (of roses) to mark your arrival.'

26th

The Moderator's writes 'Since you are interested in Zion I think it might be as well if we follow this up... In view of this I think Zion Llanidloes would be the right place for you.' Strange that I turned down an introduction to Llanidloes four years ago.

JUNE

Sunday 4th

My last Sunday in Waterbury. I preached and the service was broadcast. After service we watched a film about a very sad West Virginian family. Many in the congregation could not understand how people could be so bogged down by environment.

15th

Mr Watson, secretary of Zion, Llanidloes communicated the decision of the church: 'At a well attended Church Meeting held last night, and presided over by myself, it was unanimously decided to invite you to become Minister of our Church and Glanhafren.' £720 and £50 from Glanhafren, £25 expenses and 6 free Sundays (with 6 also if I find supplies). There is also a children's allowance. I hope I shall serve the two churches faithfully. We start on the 1st of December.

The church's decision was the consequence of my preaching there two years previously. God works in a mysterious way.

JULY

3rd

I completed the first draft of my thesis. The 400 pages will need considerable revision, but I believe I have expressed the main arguments. What will Dr Paul think?

24th

We received a photograph in the Western Mail of Dad's retirement. The title of the report was 'the end of an 80 year link.' Mamgu had been one of the first pupils when the school opened in 1882 when she was 10.

AUGUST

25th

The rioting in Detroit is the climax of years of under-privilege and is a tragedy with no quick solution. The United States must recognize this as their major domestic problem.

27th

Is the United States in the middle of a revolution? The nation's cities are in turmoil. Will they all erupt into the bloody warfare which has taken place at Newark and Detroit? Stokely Carmichael of 'Black Power' has referred to the battles as similar to Vietnam. This nation has intolerable ranges in wealth. In Hartford we have two classes - very rich and very poor. The range between West Hartford and the North End is scandalous and something is bound to happen. The nation has a choice: solve the problem of Vietnam or the problem of the black poor. The administration has chosen Vietnam.

SEPTEMBER

9th

Hugh and I walked to Bristol Tump. A glorious morning, warm and calm. A struggle to get Hugh there as he gets no lighter.

Norah, Hugh and I returned to Wales by the Queen Elizabeth II in early September. The following months were spent with my finishing research at Oxford, and Norah and Hugh spending the autumn with Norah's parents in Clydach, Swansea. It was a particularly busy time completing research, awaiting the arrival of Dylan our second son, and preparing for Ordination.

14th

The deacons recognize the difficulties of the church and are eager for change. I have great hopes and feel we can do something.

My first meeting with the deacons at Llanidloes.

OCTOBER

4th
Zion entertained the Autumn Assembly of North Wales Congregational Churches. After I led with devotions (from Eliot), the business meeting was dominated by Congregational/Presbyterian talks. This afternoon Dr Aubrey Vine spoke on 'What is essential Congregationalism?' In the evening I took devotions and Dr Vine preached excellently on Paul's free-born citizenship.
Aubrey Vine was a Congregational minister, Tutor at Bradford Theological College and Secretary of the Free Church Federal Council.

10th
Our second son has arrived. What a surprise. He (we haven't decided the name yet) was born at 9pm on the 9th in the Oxford Room, Mount Pleasant Hospital, Swansea. He is a delightful little chap with dark hair, blue eyes and open, good skin.

11th
Our second son and dear Norah are both alive and healthy. How different it could be. We rejoice and thank God we have been blessed. The baby looks very handsome and very intelligent!

12th
A third day of basking in the joy of having our second son. We have decided on the name - Dylan John. Norah has been reading 'October' by Dylan Thomas - the month he was born.

14th
Oxford is a strange city with an atmosphere all its own. At its best it produces the finest scholarship, at its worst the most pointless pedantry; at its best generosity of character, at its worst flamboyant effrontery.

20th
My two hour session with Dr Greenslade was very fruitful, and although he had various suggestions, none were crucial. I must be more careful in my language. We worked through the first half of the thesis and will continue when he returns from East Germany for the 450th anniversary of Luther's Theses.

23rd

Uncle Ivor died this morning. His agony is over. He has suffered dreadfully during the past six months. I pray he is now at peace. I have no conception of what happens after death but trusting in Christ, my hope is that Uncle Ivor lives in a fuller, richer existence. I remember the superb yarns he told in our middle room, the exotic presents, carpets, tables, Turkish delight, his uniform and braid, and waiting impatiently for his holidays. When is Uncle Ivor coming home? Where is he now? Persian Gulf, Australia, the US, Sweden. No more. The hero is dead, the last of our sailors.

25th

Uncle Frank told me I was going to have a hard life but I must at all times pray to Almighty God for guidance. He has little patience with the church, but today he revealed himself as deeply religious. He prayed for me in Welsh, and I for him. He has prepared himself to die.
Uncle Frank was brother to my grandfather Hugh Davies.

NOVEMBER

13th

Bryce and I heard F R Leavis speaking on Eliot in the Union. The place was packed; a small, brown-faced man spoke quietly and authoritatively. His reading light flickered a great deal. He read from 'Marina,' 'Ash Wednesday' and a few others. He felt Eliot's poetry was 'a whole' and led to the climax of 'The Four Quartets,' which could be appreciated despite their Anglo-Catholic leanings.
Bryce Morrison is considered among the world's leading authorities on piano performance. A music scholar of the Kings School Canterbury, he later read English at Oxford University before teaching in Canada and America. He is a professor of keyboard literature and performance at The Royal Academy of Music. Leavis was one of the foremost literary critics of the last century.

14th

Bryce and I saw Peter Hall's 'Macbeth' which was stirring, symbolic and convincing. Lady Macbeth hid the horror until it made her mind crack, wither and die; Macbeth, with his vaulting ambition became subhuman; Malcolm's innocence triumphed; the witches' horrible power. The incredible setting was drenched in red; the acting of Paul Schofield and Vivien Merchant

marvellous. One can never forget the dream scene of Lady Macbeth. Her cruel strong character had been destroyed and like us she was a petty, small being needing forgiveness.
A visit to Stratford.

17th
I arrived at Christchurch a little early but enjoyed standing in the sun watching the stones mellow in the winter sun and waiting for sonorous Old Tom. Dr Greenslade and I managed 32 pages. He has been marvellous. I gave him £10 for tutorial fees but he refused to take it. 'You will need it starting in a new parish.' What a gentleman. I feel privileged to have worked under him.

23rd
Christchurch by 10 and the next hour and a quarter was spent with Greenslade. He had little to add. He gave me Temple's 'Readings in John's Gospel.' As I left his words were 'God Bless you in your work.' I have such respect for him. I left Oxford at 3.

Sunday 26th
Dad and I walked to Ebenezer and although we were only a few, I was with friends who have known me since childhood. I took three ladies, including Mamma in Sunday School. 50 this evening. I preached on my major theme as a preacher - 'Christ and him crucified.' [The Grace of God revealed in the Death of Christ]. We all went to the Ferndale Workmen's Hall for the Pendyrus Annual Concert. The choir sang new pieces including work by Mansel Thomas.

DECEMBER

December 1st
We have arrived in Llanidloes and our new life here has begun. Arrived at Llanidloes by 2.
Norah, Hugh who was to celebrate his second birthday the following day, Dylan and I arrived at our first proper home. It was so good to be together after the separation of the previous two months - the longest time we were to be separated as a family until university days arrived for the children.

5th

I have been preparing since 1960 for next Thursday, and still I am still not sure what is involved. What is the essence of calling and the fundamental task? I am to witness to Christ, but the implications of ordination remain uncertain. Will life be qualitatively different after ordination, or is it about function and service? Time will tell. I pray for grace to work faithfully.

6th

I am being set apart by the church and for the church to shepherd the congregation and lead by example and teaching.

LLANIDLOES

1967 - 1974

INTRODUCTION

It was fitting that my final Sunday as a student should be in leading worship at Ebenezer. The chapel had helped in my nurture to the point of Ordination on the 7th of December 1967. Now, as a young family, we were to settle for the first time in a community and a pastorate. This was our first 'real home.' Although Norah and I had prepared long and carefully for this day, there was the sense of embarking upon an adventurous and unknown journey. The seven years at the joint pastorate of Zion Congregational Church Llanidloes and Glanhafren Welsh Independent Church were to shape much of what followed in the next 40 years. Many of the patterns created in Llanidloes served as a foundation for all which was to come.

Our life at Llanidloes was marked by the birth of Catherine in November 1969. Later she joined the boys at the new Welsh Medium Primary School at Trefeglwys. The children have benefited from their introduction to the bilingual heritage which is Wales. They all look back with affection on their Llanidloes days.

1. PASTORAL CARE

For a minister to arrive at the beginning of December means the frenetic preparation for Christmas. One of the first tasks was to visit the 'elderly' (the over 70s!) to extend Christmas greetings and take gifts from the church. I had already discovered from my experience as a student pastor in Godreaman and Abertillery that visiting people in their own homes is a key element of ministry. Visiting that group of elderly people every month throughout my ministry proved a most enriching element of ministry. I also created a programme of visiting church families every six months and this proved invaluable when the inevitable crises came.

2. YOUNG PEOPLE

On the second Sunday of my ministry we invited teenagers to our home after Sunday evening service, and on the last Sunday of December, the deacons agreed that a youth meeting should be held on Sunday evenings on the church premises.

The work developed rapidly. Informal discussion began almost immediately and the first Youth Services were held on the first Sunday of each month (beginning in February 1968), and were followed that year by Easter and Nativity Festivals. Links were encouraged and exchanges organized with Abertillery and Tylorstown; we took young people camping in 1969 and 1970, and after 1971 our link was established with the Cistercians on Caldey, and young people participated in mixed age group visits several times each year until we left Llanidloes in 1974. As early as September 1969 it was necessary to have two youth meetings, one continuing on a Sunday and the second for older teenagers on a Friday evening meeting in the home of each young person. That involved discussion and 'a spread.' It is difficult to assess which was the stronger attraction for young hungry men aged 17 or 18! This was however the beginning of the experiment in house groups (without 'spreads.')

In September 1970 the 'Glanhafren Project' was initiated. The chapel in the Hafren Valley owned three small cottages (the original place of worship, and home for the caretaker) next to the chapel, and when the second cottage became vacant, the youth group rented it at 5/- (25p) each week, and met there every Sunday evening. It helped the smaller church feel it had a valuable contribution to make, and encouraged young people from both churches and from no church background. It was also used for 'weekends' by the young people. It was 'their place.' By September 1972, 17 teenagers met in two different groups, and the number had increased to 27 by September 1974. One of these youth groups met at home under Norah's guidance.

An important consequence of working with young people and introducing them to the discussion of issues of faith was that eight decided to study theology at University level. Four of these entered and remain in Christian ministry.

Discussion Groups were for young people who had reached the age of 16, or were at First Year VI in the High School. At the same time an Under 14s Club (later under 13s) met on Friday evenings. Highlights were the famous (or infamous) two football matches against the Baptist Church held at Victoria Park, the Town football pitch. It is uncertain whether ecumenical relations improved, especially as 'the Congs' won both matches! It is rumoured that the Congs cheated because 'a Baptist from the country' played for them!

3. WORSHIP AND NURTURE

Glanhafren had services on a Sunday afternoon. Worship there proved reassuring and stable. Like many small congregations (there were rarely a dozen present), everyone knew who would be there and if they were absent, there was a good reason. Worship was partly in Welsh and somehow this reminded us of a tradition which once existed throughout most of Wales. The small 'homely' building was on the banks of the upper Severn and often the only sounds in the chapel would be those of the friendly clock and the river passing outside. The worshippers were always good listeners and provided encouraging support. The members were delighted to encourage young people to use the 'middle cottage' and this brought a new sense of purpose to Glanhafren.

The high-point (literally because the organ is built on the front gallery, as well as spiritually) of Zion's worship was the music of the organist, Mr Erfyl Evans. He was always able to create the right atmosphere for worship and was eager to respond to the challenge of new hymns and music. I never knew a more accommodating and competent musician. Zion's morning Sunday School averaged 7 small children although it became apparent that the wider church family included nearer 40 children. In September 1968, the Church of Adventure was launched with adequate teachers, following the United Church of Christ Curriculum which Norah and I had brought back from Hartford. This programme of education had recently been completely revised by the UCC and included teacher's and pupil's materials. This was all quite new at the time as far as Welsh churches were concerned but was received by the church with great enthusiasm. The time of morning worship was brought forward half an hour so that teachers and children could complete their work in a morning session. Once each month the service was led by the children who matured rapidly and fully participated in worship. Throughout the years the average number of children increased from the original 7 to 30.

Although I had been leading worship for seven years, nothing prepares a young minister for the challenge of creating two acts of worship every Sunday and a 'mid-week service' which also demanded fresh material. Without the benefit of an authorized Congregationalist lectionary, I created sermon material from several series on Biblical books like Genesis and Matthew, and themes like one based on the Apostles Creed. In my second year I discovered 'The Peterhead Lectionary,' an experiment created by Allan Macarthur of the Church of Scotland. It had the advantage of following a revised form of the Church Year combined with a balanced and thoughtful choice of Old and New Testament lessons.

Although the first youth group had begun in September 1969, the first 'adult house group' came into existence in October 1969 and the second group a month later, on the birth day of our daughter Catherine. All groups met fortnightly. The first group of 'older ladies' met on an afternoon and opted to study the Bible. I prepared a course on Mark's Gospel based on the commentary by Dennis Nineham. The second group, meeting in the evening was a healthy mix of worshippers from different congregations in town and those who came to enquire 'what's it all about.' We began with a general conversation about the nature of community, and as the sessions progressed, each session picked up where the previous one had left off. After six months we were looking at the 'nature of resurrection.'

This programme was workable when there were only two groups, but by the autumn of 1970 it was clear that soon there would be 8 house groups and two youth groups. It was clearly impossible to develop such a variety of programmes. This was when I decided to introduce a missiological approach to theology which would present the substance of what Christians believe and be suitable for both those exploring for the first time, and those established in the life of the church but wanting to press more deeply. This led me to John Macquarrie's recently published 'Principles of Christian Theology.' The programme eventually developed into a series of 130 sermons used for preaching on Sunday evenings and discussion in the house groups. Each week I produced a two page paper of 1000 words, and 100 copies were distributed and discussed by more than a hundred people during the next four years. These were paid for by a local garage owner who attended one of the house groups. During each discussion session (10 each fortnight) I took careful notes of what I was hearing from the members of each group. As I was in conversation with more than a hundred people every two weeks, from the ages of 16 to over 80, I had the privilege of learning the theology of the people. It proved an unparalleled experience, and I wish all ministers could enjoy the same excitement and fulfilment.

Macquarrie began with 'Philosophical Theology' as he attempted to relate the religious quest with the human adventure; 'Symbolic Theology' as the heart of the Biblical and Christian faith; and finally 'Applied Theology' with its interpretation of the life of the church and Christian ethics. It proved a splendid ecumenical theology for groups which included Catholics, Anglicans, people from all the other local denominations and a large number of participants not related to any church. All were inquisitive and caring searchers for truth. We were learning and discovering together.

4. CALDEY

The Abbot of Caldey, the Very Revd James Wicksteed had been a regular speaker at annual talks organized by Father Kenneth Gillespie and held in the Friary at Llanidloes. Normally the meeting was attended by a dozen Catholics, but in the summer of 1971 he found there were also 30 enquiring 'house group' people in his regular audience. The result was an invitation to bring a group to Caldey. Without any high expectation, eighteen of us sailed from Tenby to the island for a weekend in November 1971. It proved a transforming experience for all of us and proved to be the first of nearly a hundred visits that continued throughout my ministries until retirement in 2004. The Cistercian community of prayer and work proved to be an inspiration throughout my ministry.

5. THE WIDER CHURCH

Even in 1967, Congregationalism in Montgomeryshire was in a parlous state. There were three 'town' churches and seven rural churches with three ministers and about 200 worshippers in total. I learned a great deal from meeting the two older and more experienced ministers and the faithful lay representatives in the District Meetings. We all knew we were struggling against the odds. Because of the death of the District Secretary, I succeeded him in the position and for one year this meant that I also attended the Executive Meeting of the Congregational Churches of Wales. This met six times a year in Cardiff, and it was through attending these 'national meetings' that I soon discovered how decisions were made by the very few people who 'controlled the information.' The experience convinced me that democracy may not be as efficient as an oligarchy, but at least it creates a sense of ownership of decisions, without which there can be no fruitful action. I remain fearful of centralization shaped in the name of greater efficiency - I always ask 'efficiency for whom?' The Church constantly falls into the trap of creating a decision making process by those who are not in pastoral charge.

My experience of the Church at its widest was much more productive. Without fail, the Congregational May Meetings held in London were inspiring. I had confidence in a radical church seeking to reflect the Gospel in rapidly changing circumstances. The period included the optimism engendered by the creation of a 'new church' born out of the Congregational and Presbyterian traditions. It was seen as a stage in the coming together of God's people. Translating Assembly decisions to the local level could however be discouraging, particularly when it touched the raw points where church and society meet.

6. ISSUES OF MISSION

On several occasions I addressed Rhondda and Breconshire young people at Local Education Authority Conferences at Coleg y Fro in Barry. There I met totally secularised young people and found their questioning invigorating. Similar experiences took place in Tylorstown in 1969. On the first occasion our Llanidloes young group led a service for 200 young people in Ebenezer. On the second occasion, also in 1969, I addressed the annual Tylorstown Youth Club Service in Libanus Chapel. It proved a salutary experience. During the service 20 young people intimated they would enjoy regularly this kind of 'open service' and many local adults present agreed to support them. However it soon dawned on us that trained leadership did not exist to take advantage of this mission opportunity. The church was unprepared for renewal. It would not know what to do if there was a movement of the Spirit. Is it more prepared forty years later? This sharp encounter has affected my attitude ever since.

Another fascinating experience was the short relationship with the Ecumenical Institute, formed in Chicago and having an English base in Thornaby on Tees. I had met them through a Student Christian Movement Conference in Llandinam and was so impressed that we organized two weekends for the church and house groups in Llanidloes. The first occasion was most stimulating but on the second occasion I realised that their theology was not only completely secular but that the leaders were almost 'programmed' by a curriculum emerging from Chicago. The contact ended regretfully and swiftly.

7. CRITICISM? MISUNDERSTANDING?

I arrived in Llanidloes as a young minister in a first pastorate. I had ideas and energy, but not all felt the church should move in the directions forged by the work with young people and house groups. A few positively disliked 'theology.' For some, the way forward was the way back to a half remembered period when the church had a recognised role within society. I did not find it easy to see young people criticized, and of my being accused of pandering to young people by turning worship into concerts - 'worship is not to be enjoyed!' The young people grasped they were not welcomed and were happier in discussion groups in their own place at Glanhafren Cottage. It is never easy to draw different generations together, particularly if the younger emerge from an unchurched background. The same unfortunately was true with some attitudes towards house groups which were sometimes accused of being secret societies, and of 'taking religion into the pubs.' Of course this criticism was from a very small minority, and was minimal compared with the learning and adventurous experience which was Llanidloes.

8. THE THESIS AT OXFORD

When we arrived at Llanidloes, there were two pieces of unfinished academic business. I had originally submitted the thesis on 'The Life and Work of William Erbery, 1604-1654' in July 1966 but the consequence of the viva was that the work was 'referred.' During the Spring of 1968 I redrafted the original thesis under the supervision of Dr Greenslade and made a new submission. I was examined in May 1968 by Dr Barry White, lecturer at Regent's Park Oxford, while the external examiner was Dr Ernest Payne who had just retired as General Secretary of the Baptist Union. This time I was successful at the viva and was granted the degree that autumn.

Pennar Davies had suggested in 1962 that I might like to work on Erbery because he was the most neglected of the early Welsh Puritan leaders. During his lifetime he had been accused of holding 'many grosse Errours' and preaching 'blasphemous errours in this City (Oxford)' because he had even regarded 'that Univeral redemption is nearest the Gospel indeed.' Those charges should have intrigued Twentieth Century historians but even Geoffrey Nuttall who had been my examiner in 1966 had written that 'He was not of the same calibre, mentally or spiritually, as the other three men' (Craddock, Powell and Llwyd).

I was glad to show that Erbery's contribution to Welsh Puritan life was of considerable significance. He had been Vicar of St Mary's in Cardiff, been dismissed from his office for his Puritanical views and created the first Congregational Church in Cardiff. He influenced the Congregationalists Walter Craddock and Morgan Llwyd, and the Presbyterian Christopher Love. Erbery is of particular interest in his exploration of theology which saw him move away from orthodox Calvinism and be influenced by the radical thinking of Unitarians and Quakers; his ecclesiology moved from being a Vicar of the Church of England to founding a Congregational cause, and to becoming a 'seeker' who worshipped with the 'scattered saints.' He was not prepared to receive a state stipend for his church work and suggested that the money would be better used by giving it to the poor in Cardiff. After spending time as an army chaplain with Cromwellian forces, he became a pacifist. He advocated a tolerant attitude towards Jews and Muslims. His shifting towards 'an inclusive position' and his radical questioning of orthodoxy won him few friends. His exploration of theology, ecclesiology and the relationship between religion and politics should make him surprisingly relevant.

9. THE THESIS AT HARTFORD

When the work on Erbery was completed in May 1968, there remained one final hurdle. I had completed the original research and finished a first draft under Robert Paul's supervision at Hartford. In September 1968 I renewed the re-writing and eventually submitted the thesis for a 'defence' at Hartford in May 1970. By this time Robert Paul and Ford Battles had both left for Pittsburgh and my advisor was LeRoy Moore, although Robert Paul remained on the supervisory committee at Hartford. The external examiner was Winthrop Hudson of Colgate Rochester, who weeks before my defence had published 'Nationalism and Religion in America,' the first section of which paralleled the period and theme of my research. I was grateful for his encouragement in and after the defence, but of course my deepest gratitude lay with Robert Paul, my adviser during the two years at Hartford.

The thesis was much broader in scope than the work on Erbery. It attempted to examine the eschatological thought common to Seventeenth Century Puritanism and to interpret that within the different national and geographical settings of England, Wales, Scotland and New England. It suggested that although the original focus of the Puritan movement was the reform of the church, it led to a Puritan concept of society and a deep sense of vocation in the 'British nations.' Ultimately this had an undoubted effect upon the creation of more democratic structures both in Church and State, although its development is long and devious. It suggested that 'the growth of a British Puritan nationalism with its sense of calling gave all these people a curious blend of nationalism and internationalism that characterizes them even today and finds its focus in a sense of vocation for the world. For all its dangers, this calling was deeply affected by a strong ethic characteristic of Puritanism.'

'The Puritan nations'were convinced that this period of political crisis which witnessed the execution of a 'divinely ordained monarch' and various experiments in the government of church and state would end with the ushering in of God's Kingdom. The Puritan people were to precipitate its inauguration. The combination of a belief that 'we are living in the Last Days' with the sense of holy vocation has ominous parallels with the Evangelical role in United States politics at the beginning of the Twenty First Century. Similarly the sense of the imminent end is reflected in the popularity of Adventist and Pentecostalist churches in the United Kingdom. A study of history could make us wiser.

AN AFTERTHOUGHT

Despite the encouragement to pursue academic research and to seek publication of the theses by the examiners both at Oxford and Hartford, by September 1970 my concern had already turned away from the 'academic world' to the world of 'the pastoral care, nurture and mission of the church' However, little did I think that reading Macquarrie and forming house groups would prove a turning point in life. I never returned to the world of academic scholarship and instead my life has been spent in pastoral ministry. At Llanidloes an unconscious decision was made.

I was introduced to the church at Manselton in June 1974 and in October we left our satisfying ministry and life in Llanidloes. We would be surprised by what took place in three short years in Swansea.

1967

DECEMBER

7th

The great day has arrived. What a thrill! I am ordained to Christian Ministry and in particular to the churches of the Congregational Order. I hope to work faithfully, energetically and charitably. At 12, Mr Charles phoned to tell us he, Gareth and John Gwilym had failed to get through because of snow in the Llanberis Pass. I found the service deeply moving and had difficulty in getting through my statement - how I came to faith, what I believed and hoped for the future. The ordination took place at 3. Pennar gave the Charge instead of Alwyn. Rhondda and Graig buses returned immediately afterwards. Donald Sykes preached very well at the evening service.
Alwyn Charles, Gareth Watts (a student friend and minister in Llanberis) and John Gwilym Jones were all unable to attend because of the snow. Buses had come from Tylorstown and from Norah's home chapel (Pantycrwys, Craigcefnparc). In the evening the sermon was preached by Donald Sykes, a Church Historian and later Principal of Mansfield College, Oxford.

Sunday 10th

My first Sunday as a minister at Zion, Llanidloes. The congregations seemed interested in what was said, and I felt happy with their response. Because of snow, there was no service in Glanhafren. This morning there were a dozen children in a congregation of 40. Many expressed their appreciation. Evening service included the celebration of the Lord's Supper. 40 present.

Sunday 17th

Met the deacons to discuss the Presbyterian/Congregational talks. Drove to Glanhafren for a service which was relaxed and devout. After supper, 6 young people came to the house. I felt very happy about them, real potential. Something can be done.

19th

I visited the elderly people who appear grateful to meet me. As minister I constitute an important link with the outside world. We had prayer in each house and all seemed glad. I found it completely natural although some were surprised. The young people read well in the Carol Service.

Sunday 31st

Met the deacons to discuss a Young People's Meeting on Sunday evenings from 8 until 10. They were very supportive.

1968

JANUARY

1st

A New Year. What is in store? I hope to be accepted as friend and pastor, and work honestly and lovingly. I trust the churches will strengthen and be renewed. I am grateful to be with a church looking eagerly to the future. We can work well as long as we are conscious of God's grace and power.

5th

The local fraternal of seven ministers looks interesting and refreshing. We are discussing D M Baillie's 'God was in Christ.' A significant fact is that the RC priest and Anglican vicar attend.

We were the ministers of the Anglican, Baptist, Congregational, Methodist, Welsh and English Presbyterian, and Roman Catholic churches. Often, at that time, there were Nonconformist fraternals from which the Anglican and Roman Catholic were excluded or excluded themselves. They were called fraternals because there were very few women ministers. D. M. Baillie was professor of systematic theology at the University of St. Andrews from 1934 to 1954 and brother of Professor John Baillie of New College, Edinburgh. 'God was in Christ' was his most famous work.

Sunday 7th

The first Children's service with 9 children. A good start as we had only 4 children last week. 50 in church. Communion in Glanhafren with the normal number of 9. An attentive group. A beautiful afternoon with the stream and clock providing the only sounds. I would be sorry to see that little church close. I was received into membership at evening Communion. Five came to Youth Meeting and we met in the vestry. Chatted and drank coffee. Good potential.

8th

Communion for Mrs Ellis and her daughter. She is hard of hearing and has poor sight. It was very moving to be with an old lady of nearly 90 who hasn't been out for years, and a daughter who has given up so much to care for her mother. The first of our services in the World Week of Prayer: 20 attended.
I celebrated Communion with Mrs Ellis almost every month during my seven years in Llanidloes. I offered it to others, but they felt uneasy with receiving Communion at home. The World Week of Prayer was a Nonconformist series of prayers at the beginning of each year. They were held for three evenings in the separate chapels and together on the final Thursday evening.

11th

United Prayer Meeting in Bethel St with over 100 present.
Bethel St was the Presbyterian Church (English speaking) which united with Zion United Reformed Church in 2004 to become Trinity Llanidloes.

12th

Writing sermons takes the whole day. The most difficult aspect is finding the idea from which to start. From today I shall have less problems because I will use the Peterhead Lectionary which provides a constructive programme for preaching based on the Christian Year, and combines the major aspects of the Christian faith with a selection of readings from every Biblical book.
Allan Macarthur's 'The Christian Year and Lectionary Reform,' published in 1958 provided a most important vehicle for combining teaching and worship in a consistent fashion.

18th

I was privileged to visit the Minhafren Ward with Mr Watson. Very few communicate with words and many are lying vacantly. How can one help? Quite a contrast this evening when I visited a member with two teenage sons, intelligent young men who see no sense in Christianity. Here were young, healthy, enquiring minds - so different from this afternoon, but both part of God's Kingdom.

FEBRUARY

Sunday 4th

I didn't sleep well, feeling apprehensive about the service. The first Youth Service was enjoyed by the congregation who were prepared to make constructive criticism. 70 present, double our normal congregation. Took Hugh to Glanhafren; his first time in the chapel. He behaved excellently, only once shouting 'Bwrw glaw' when wind and rain swept at the window. Six of us in Youth Meeting and all enthusiastic.

9th

Sermon-writing day is a test of devout ingenuity. What has this episode, this 'word' to say for our situation in Llanidloes? The interpretation must be honest to Scripture and speak to our situation. The more I read the Bible, the more I recognise its authenticity. There is no pretence or sham and I am overwhelmed by the honesty of the writers. They seek to communicate what they have seen and heard.

12th

I went along the 'back road' to Glanhafren and turned up the mountain to Caenfedw to see William Davies who hasn't been in church for months and didn't seem at all well. He has his meals next door with his son and family and is well looked after, but it seemed sad to see this once vigorous young man who had been years in South Wales and London, sitting there by the fire. We chatted for an hour in Welsh before I returned down the hill to the almost hectic Old Hall. I saw John Davies before talking with Mr and Mrs Evans at Minhafren. I learnt a good deal about the old days in the valley when life was humming and culturally alive. It has changed so much, the chapels are closing and it is a struggle to keep the few going.
William Davies is reported to have brought the first tractor to the Hafren Valley, and John Davies had once been 'the champion ploughman in the world' and had a shield to prove it.

28th

Nine turned up for the under 14 Club: our best number yet. It was such a lovely evening that I took them to Llawryglyn, a beautiful village with a ruined church.

MARCH

Sunday 7th

Signs of progress. There is a better spirit in the church and we have a youth group of 17 young people, ten in an under 14s Club, and we have had imaginative Youth and Children's Services. A few older people have returned to church. This is very encouraging.

APRIL

5th

An awful tragedy. Dr Martin Luther King has been murdered in Memphis, Tennessee. The repercussions could be and already are devastating. The powers of evil are so strong. The most moderate of the Civil Rights leaders has been killed. We must pray for peace within as well as outside the States.

12th, Good Friday.

United Free Church Communion. Although I presided, it felt strange to have Communion today. 105 communicants from the 5 churches. Mr Grey gave the address, Meredith Powell the reading and Mr Griffiths the prayer. Mrs Jarman sang 'He was despised.'

The ministers were of the Presbyterian, Baptist and Methodist Churches. The soloist was a Baptist.

14th, Easter Sunday

God answered our prayers with our Youth Service. It was the breakthrough the young people needed. They have worked hard and tonight felt it was worth it. Now eager to start the next! Arrived at church by 8 this evening with people already arriving! Prelude began at 8.15 and service lasted from 8.28 to 9.35. Voices were clearer and passages read intelligently; music was good; no hitches technically except end of Messiah record skipped a little. Congregation of 150 - 4x average.

16th

Gymanfa day, a pinnacle in the chapel calendar. I chaired at the Children's Gymanfa and told a Tolstoy story. Chapel at 6 with a choir of 60 and congregation of 150. I remember the church packed. Dad led the choir well. *I had been invited to preside at Ebenezer, my home chapel. The story was 'How much land does a man need?'*

20th

I was disappointed by such a negative response to the Youth service. It is depressing and explains why young ministers leave the church or accept the status quo. I am only too aware that the Youth Group has started from scratch and that the majority are as unchurched as any in Llanidloes.
After the hard work of creating a youth group and persuading the young people to participate in worship, it was not easy to receive criticism of the form and detail of the service.

25th

I am sitting in the study by an open window. A marvellous evening, the night is still and sounds are carrying a vast distance; sheep and lambs are bleating; birds have just ceased singing; a car chugs up the hill towards Pantydwr and a boy whistles in the distance. We can be thankful we live in peaceful natural surroundings and have much to do. God has a task for us in Llanidloes; the 'call' becomes clearer as time moves along.

MAY

7th

Could this be a major turning point? The diaconate supports the Christian Education programme. They could have rejected the proposals as too ambitious. We pray for the future of Zion.

22nd

Have I passed? The viva was pleasant and there were no nasty moments. Payne and White were very complimentary. I base my optimism on (a) you have 'proved' your thesis that Erbery was not mad (b) you have made the revisions necessary from the last viva (c) would you, if encouraged, publish sections of your thesis? (d) when in US, I ought to study at the Huntingdon Library because no 'accomplished English scholar' has worked there since Albert Peel (e) we hope you will continue working in this field (f) take thesis to the Bodleian - necessary if I am to receive the degree (g) proved G.F Nuttall wrong in his claim that Erbery was a 'popular preacher.' Viva lasted from 2.15 to 3.45. Both were courteous, friendly and just. What a difference from last time.

My examiners were Dr Barry White (as in my earlier viva in 1966) and Dr Ernest Payne, who had been a Church Historian at Regents Park Oxford, General Secretary of the Baptist Union from 1951 to 1967, and was about to be elected as President of the World Council of Churches from 1968 to 1975. Albert Peel had been a great Congregational historian.

JUNE

6th

A great and good man is dead. What is happening to our civilization? The dockers marching against our coloured immigrants reflect the shots that destroyed Robert Kennedy. In a tribute tonight Macmillan emphasized the Kennedy's' faith that 'we are all God's children and we must all do His will,' and Mayor Lindsey stated 'Of course we will go out into our streets and walk through our slums.' We must go on.

17th

I spoke to 75 young people in Rhoose, most with no idea of the Gospel. They listened intently.

This was the Conference for Rhondda young people which I had attended as a boy in 1952! What a change in attitudes in sixteen years.

Sunday 30th

Mr Grey christened Dylan. Norah, Hugh and I sat in the front seat and the two boys behaved excellently.

Mr Grey was the local Presbyterian minister. Norah and I made our promises as parents.

JULY

2nd

Bible study by Prof Edgar Jones had the theme 'renewal in the Old Testament.' He gave a new incentive to tackle Bible study. I am impressed by Glanville Jones and Emrys Davies. Miss Gwyneth Evans spoke on 'Religious

Education' with special reference to the Gittins report. She spoke with authority and verve.

The Summer School for Congregational Ministers was held in Aberystwyth. Edgar Jones was professor of Old Testament in Northern College Manchester. Glanville Jones and Emrys Davies were both Congregational ministers. All three originated from the Valleys. In August 1963, the then Minister of Education, Sir Edward Boyle, asked the Central Advisory Council for Education (England) 'to consider primary education in all its aspects and the transition to secondary education.' The Council, under the Chairmanship of Bridget Plowden, presented its report to the Secretary of State for Education and Science, Rt. Hon Anthony Crosland, in October 1966. The Central Advisory Council for Education (Wales), under the leadership of Professor C. E. Gittins, produced a similar report for Wales which included a valuable chapter on bilingualism.

9th

My first funeral since coming to Llanidloes - the funeral of William Davies, Caenfedw, secretary of Glanhafren and aged 89. Over 200 present, mostly men. All walked to the cemetery (Dolhafren) led by Kenneth Jones, Mr Watson and myself. We sang 'O fryniau Caersalem' at the grave.

Kenneth Jones was a past minister of Llanidloes and Glanhafren.

Sunday 14th

Perhaps the worst floods for Llanidloes in living memory. We had just finished at Glanhafren when it started to pour (thunder). A harrowing drive back; wherever gates touched the road there was a turbulent yellow stream. As we came up Smithfield St, there pouring down Llangurig road was a raging torrent. I struggled into our drive. We could not cross to the school, cars strewn all over the road. Helped in Garden Suburb where houses were flooded out; then to town where Smithfield St was a river 3 feet deep in places. Had a 20 minute service in chapel before going home to change. Returned to Glanhafren and Nantyrhebog - water through. Visited many houses in town.

18th

The 150th Anniversary of Zion. I talked on the history of the cause this afternoon, and this evening Emlyn Jenkins preached well in the old Welsh style.

Emlyn Jenkins was minister of Ebenezer Welsh Congregational Chapel, Cardiff.

SEPTEMBER

6th

I enjoy the newspaper: it is almost as important as the Bible. The Bible interprets the present but if there is no concern for and knowledge of today's world, the Bible can be scholastic and irrelevant.

Sunday 22nd

The new Church School programme began with a Dedication Service which went beyond expectation. Instead of the 18 in church last Sunday, there were over 70, including 55 in the Dedication Service, those babysitting and those arriving at 10.45. We had 31 'scholars' including my class of 10 on the gallery. The church seemed a different place; everyone was excited by the numbers and sense of newness: 'The Church of Adventure.' We have started well: the job lies firmly with the teachers.

OCTOBER

17th

I have graduated with the B.Litt. The Oxford thesis and episode is over. It is six years next December since I first went to Oxford for my interview with Dr Greenslade. It has been a hard, long slog but today's colourful ceremony provided a fitting climax. I borrowed an advanced student's gown. Then to Castells for a B. Litt gown. Back to Mansfield Senior Common Room: the family came to lunch and were thrilled. John Marsh had come to SCR to congratulate. Walked to the Sheldonian with Caird. I was the only B. Litt.
Brian and Brenda Wren looked after Hugh and Dylan while we were in the Sheldonian.

NOVEMBER

10th

Two remarkable services were aided by the devotional singing of Martin's choir. Morning congregation with 40 young people and 30 adults. My sermon

was an approach to faith with Tertullian, Aquinas and Calvin. Glanhafren had a delightful service. Uncle Jack thought it was a very good sermon. Church at 6 where I preached the second approach to faith, referring to Tillich, Bultmann and Bonhoeffer. Great atmosphere, congregation of 100. Thrilling. Sadness all round as the choir returned to Abertillery. Our youngsters ran to the end of the Gro to wave goodbye. A weekend far beyond expectation.
Martin Budd was Music Teacher in Nantyglo, and Church Secretary and organist at Tabernacle Abertillery. His youth choir spent the weekend with young people in Zion.

Sunday 17th

Thrilling services led by our Llanidloes young people at Ebenezer: God was praised and his people challenged to live with vigour and responsibility. Service at 10.30. Imagine our amazement to find 100 people there, 75% under 21. This evening we looked breathlessly as people kept on coming until 300 were in worship and the ground floor was packed. The best service we have ever done: readings crisply relevant, music of great spirit. Everyone was lifted. All seemed overjoyed, people kept on thanking us and congratulating. Wonderful. Thank God for our young people.
A remarkable act of worship at Ebenezer Tylorstown. Our young people had spent the weekend there and taken their 'Easter service' to Tylorstown.

18th

This sort of thing could make you give up the ministry. What a return to Llanidloes and church life here. I received a catalogue of complaints about last week: the disgraceful state of the church on Saturday with sweet papers (unspecified number), footmarks on the carpet (unspecified), Bible and water-jug on the floor of pulpit; schoolroom in a disgraceful state (after our concert a week last Saturday). The church must not to be used after Thursday. Amazing idolatry of a building. My response was to speak of the barns of our ancestors, the Meeting House of the Pilgrims, the new community hall type of church. After wonderful yesterday! The church is an amazing institution. Yesterday shows potential; today does not.

DECEMBER

1st

In Youth Group a few of us read my play (completely unrehearsed) and the effect was staggering because of the race issue. A few are vehemently racist.

I was pleased the issue came into the open and perhaps we can now do something about it.

5th

Llanwnog for the Quarterly Meeting of Montgomeryshire Welsh Independents. The business meeting was dominated by 4 men, and the other 18 of us, silent partners, lifted our hands to vote. What can we achieve if our Church organization and policy is dominated by four men? We talk vehemently of Independency! This is prelacy.
I was invited to preach at this meeting of the Undeb yr Annibynwyr.

Sunday 8th

I gave a balanced, hopeful impression of the year. Those present are good workers in the church and community. Those not present and loosely attached need to be brought deeper into the life of the Church as a worshipping and serving community.

10th

In Guild, two local educationalists spoke on 'The Purpose of Education.' Referring to the stimulating remarks about changes in primary teaching, I asked whether Sunday Schools could learn from the new techniques. Concrete suggestions were made by one of the speakers, but the other attacked vehemently the attempt 'to entertain young people in the church - they are there to worship and not to be entertained' referring of course to our experiments in Zion. I was disappointed by this lack of courtesy in making the point in our church.

Sunday 22nd

I felt pleased with our two nativity service: Children's Nativity at 10 when 22 took part. Service at 7.30 with a congregation of 100 and 24 taking part. Miss Bärbel Edwards sang magnificently.
Bärbel Edwards, a local woman was a soloist with the Welsh National Opera Company. Our young people had never heard such singing and literally jumped in their seats which were immediately below the pulpit from which Bärbel sang. Later in my ministry, I officiated at the wedding at Zion of Bärbel and Peter Meredith.

31st
The year ended in the parish church at Tylorstown and perhaps this is where we ought to be. A lay-preacher, David Livings took the service and preached. It was timely and devout because the Prayer Book carries itself. At the stroke of 12 when the single bell called out, the two clubs opposite opened their doors and out poured hundreds of intoxicated revellers into the street. The hope must be that those outside will one day see the significance of what we are trying to do inside.

1969

FEBRUARY

Sunday 16th
I preached on Christ sitting at the right hand of God, and it struck me that if Christ is not alive today, his bones are lying in an unknown tomb in Jerusalem; that is preposterous. The life of Jesus denies this.

17th
Because I have been occupied with the thesis and preparing worship, I have had little time for general reading or such theological disciplines as the Bible, Theology, Ethics, Church History and Philosophy. It is critical to understand both the text and context if the Gospel is to be communicated effectively.

18th
I will begin my wider reading with the Old Testament, then turn to the New Testament and on to Theology. I began Gottwald's 'A Light to the Nations.' I am travelling along almost completely new ground.
Norman Gottwald's introduction to the Old Testament proved most stimulating.

20th
Hetty and Adam suddenly sprang from the pages of George Eliot 'to live' in Llanidloes. I had been immersed in a novel which suddenly burst into life and I was no longer reading an idyllic account of late 18th Century pastoral England. It became stern and bitter. The meeting of Hetty and Arthur in the wood electrified the situation. The seeds of tragedy had been present from the

beginning but now they were writ large. The weakness of Hetty; the obdurate firm, unsympathetic Adam; the conceited Arthur and none realizing the tragic consequences of indiscretion.
Adam Bede came to life. Wider reading included English literature.

Sunday 23rd
'A low' point in ministry and frustrations came to the surface. I must walk patiently with God and not lose the vision, become lethargic and allow the calling to slide into a sinecure because of the lack of progress. Church-life must not continue its inevitable decline.

MARCH

1st
Hardly our National Saint's Day. The most fervent nationalists live abroad. When in Oxford and Hartford we were Welsh on March 1st. Today, I forgot all about it.

Sunday 2nd
The gift of Glanhafren is the building's intimacy, the friendship of the people, the clock and the river.

11th
I hope soon to complete the half-yearly visitation.
I attempted to visit all members of the church every six months.

22nd
I started reading William Barclay's translation of the New Testament (Volume 1.) I read aloud the first three chapters of John and was thrilled. This is John's account of the Good News; this is what he believed about Jesus. I was impressed by the detail and grandeur of thought. It was like reading the New Testament for the first time because the Biblical message jumped out of the printed page.
Barclay's New Testament (Volume 1) was published in 1968, and Volume 2 in 1969.

26th
My first meeting of the Welsh Executive Committee (The Provincial Committee) at Wood St, Cardiff. There are 16 representatives - 4 from North Wales, 4 from Monmouth, 8 from South Wales and the Moderator. 10 were

present and the agenda included Presbyterian/Congregational talks and Memorial College, Swansea. I shall soon get used to discussion and policy making. So few determine the policy of a denomination. The meeting lasted only two hours.
The centralized structure of the meeting raised questions for me. They remain unanswered. Centralization, efficiency, agenda setting, control of information are issues for every generation.

27th
The new housing estate will include 1000 houses with a further 750 to be built the other side of Penrhys Road and stretching to the Isolation Hospital.
The planners intended that Penrhys should be doubled in size. The intention never became reality.

MAY

15th
The soccer match between our under 13s and the Baptist under 13s was exciting and the standard higher than expected. Not only did the boys enjoy themselves but a crowd of 150 turned up to watch and enjoy an open, clean, hard fought and skilful game. Our team won 7-5. Photographs before the match.

20th
The important Assembly debate took place with charity and intelligence. The church was packed for the two sessions. The day was devoted to discussion of Presbyterian - Congregational Unification. The Report of the Committee was recommended by an overwhelming majority to the churches for detailed discussion. There were few dissidents. I also attended the Caxton Hall meeting organized by the Congregational Association who oppose unity. It was a drab affair, attended by 100 and addressed by Tudur Jones. It made me realize the dreadful alternative.
The Annual May Meetings of Congregationalists took place in Westminster Chapel London. They were inspiring occasions.

21st
It is gratifying to belong to a denomination restructuring to witness to the modern world. An excellent debate on encouraging individuals/churches to give 1% of annual income to Christian Aid.

22nd
I return to the local church encouraged, indeed enthused. Our leaders have a vision of Christ's church and they work hard and patiently. Lunch with Brian Wren. He is ministering in Hockley, has a doctorate and two children. The issue of 1% was passed with only 1 in dissent.

JUNE

11th
A deacons' meeting to discuss giving 1% of our income to Christian Aid. It was turfed out unanimously. We can watch photographs of Biafran children. After the London meeting, this is down to earth with a crash.
This was a personal disappointment but I needed to remember that I was the only one who had been present at the debate in London. Nigeria was torn apart by Civil War.

28th
We were relieved to wake to blue sky and the sun shining. With great excitement, 26 of us started walking at 12.30 (8 others left at 2), we walked to the railway line and then strode or plodded the 5 miles to Llandinam. It was very hot. Pop at the pub, then through Oakley Park to Morfodion where Mari Chapman had prepared plenty to eat and drink. Great enthusiasm when I announced an estimate of £107. What an achievement.
It is always important to remember that the Church is capable of renewal especially when it is challenged to look outside itself. The Walk was organised by Church people and proved an alternate way of raising funds and stimulating concern for mission. Morfodion is the name of a farm between Oakley Park and Llanidloes.

JULY

4th
The Moderator forecast rapid decline during the next 30 years. Young men are not entering the ministry.
The Moderator was sharing his 'state of the cause' to the ministers at the Annual Summer School. This view was repeated and grew more gloomy as the years passed. Note March 15th 1971.

20th

The last Children's Service to complete 10 months of the new system. It has been worthwhile: numbers have increased 200%. We must now aim for consistency. The 17 in youth group listened to the Americans reaching the moon - 9.18 our time. The first walk takes place at 2.15.

21st

Men have walked on the moon. An American, Neal Armstrong is the first man to put his foot on the moon. An incredible achievement and what potential. What will my life-time produce? Certainly the exploration of the solar system! What of others? We got up at 2 to see the Moon-walk with Harry, Margaret and their children on their television. Remarkable to see Armstrong climbing down the ladder, setting foot on the moon and walking.

28th

Our 'idyllic sojourn' in the Gower began disastrously. It has been torrential all day, starting before we got up and continuing until gone 11 tonight. Because of the dreadful weather, some young people have appeared at less than their best with bad tempers and slight hysteria. A slice of life. We will learn more during these few days than we have during 18 months of Sunday evening meetings. It poured and poured: we waited until 4.45 and then just had to set up camp. And the rain it raineth every day.
The first 'holiday' with young people was near Rhossili on Gower.

30th

Alwyn came this evening and led discussion excellently.
Alwyn Charles came and spoke to the young people about the first chapters of Genesis.

AUGUST

1st

Seventeen of us went to the Carlton and 5 of the younger boys bought pipes and smoked in the cinema. All had to leave and were sick before bed. We saw 'Where Eagles Dare' with Richard Burton. Blood and bombs for 3 hours.

SEPTEMBER

12th

We have been puzzling how to accommodate all the young people in the same meeting - those wanting discussion and those who want to 'play.' Conversation has often descended to the lowest common denominator or it has been beyond the reach of others. We decided to have two groups: one on Sundays, and another for older young people (18-20s) meeting on Fridays in different homes. It will also serve as a bridge with non-churchgoers.

14th

The church has a built-in mechanism against change. To be a Christian means to accept the structure of the local church (shaped on a Victorian pattern) while we must create new patterns to present the Gospel. Possibly our youth groups and house groups might point in the right direction.

15th

One of our older members died this morning. Although well in his 80s, he was always fresh and clean, had a delightful twinkle in his bright blue eyes and was always courteous and appreciative. I can see him wheeling his little barrow with his window cleaning ladders. Recently I saw him on the roof of the bay-windows of Green Villa.

OCTOBER

1st

David has been accepted at Memorial College, Swansea. Thrilling for the family after the problems of the last few years. It has been a transformation. *The first of our young people to study theology. He had been stimulated by the Sunday evening discussions.*

2nd

D R Thomas, a lecturer at the Education Dept at Aberystwyth preached 'the social gospel.' The church has heard nothing like this deeply compassionate, fluent expression of our concern for our brothers throughout the world. He urged the church to take risks, back young people and not be afraid of getting into debt. He made a strenuous appeal for overseas aid.
D R Thomas was a minister of the Presbyterian Church of Wales.

3rd

What a start to under 13s. One of the boys set off two bangers in the church. Fortunately we were able to clear up the tatters.

14th

The first House Group was held at Miss Ellis' house at 2.30: 6 ladies (average of 70+); 4 our own people. I discussed the function of house groups and why I thought them necessary. We will meet fortnightly for Bible Study and will start with Mark.
This was the first 'proper meeting' of a house group in Llanidloes. It met regularly for many years, long after I left in 1974. All the eight adult groups met twenty times a year, and the programme continued for the next five years. The two youth groups met almost every week. I enjoyed such a fulfilling teaching ministry. Of course in each group the members also 'nurtured' each other.

Sunday 19th

An electrifying moment at Libanus Tylorstown. The potential of the Gospel is beyond our wildest dreams. A service had been organized by the local Youth Club and 50 young people came to Libanus. At one point when I was speaking, I knew they had been reached and challenged them to keep together and attend any church of their choice. To my amazement, about a half of them put their hands up and said they would try. I then asked the adults how many would be prepared to accept these young people into their church, and the same number raised their hands. If only they had a leader! If only there was a follow through. The Church would be frightened if 25 young people walked in next Sunday night. What can be done? The church needs retraining.
A seminal experience. How is the Church to live with renewal or revival? A similar experience took place at the Harvest Festival in Builth a few days later.

22nd

How can the church be restructured and retrained? Are there blueprints for this work, or must we create them? Can we discover new techniques in Llanidloes? Tylorstown showed how unprepared we are.

23rd

The day has been inspired by reading about Thomas Bevan and David Jones of Neuaddlwyd, the first missionaries to Madagascar. They had been challenged by the sermon of their minister in a village church in Cardiganshire. It gave me hope. Can this happen the other side of

Plynlimmon? How dare we limit the Spirit? If God is God, his Spirit can move men and women today. The reserves of divine energy are waiting to be tapped.

I never thought I would learn so much about Madagascar and develop such a close relationship.

NOVEMBER

6th

Catherine (Elizabeth or Miriam) has joined our family. We are thankful to God that once more our child has been safely delivered and Norah is well. We have a little daughter. It seems incredible after having two good, strong sons. I hope they will look after their little sister. I saw Norah and Cath this evening and both looked fine. She has clear skin, brown hair and looks a lot older than one hour. One hour old and absolutely perfect. The wonder of creation / Heaven and earth cry aloud in their beauty / But for real beauty in perfection / I must see little Catherine. Thanks be to God. Matron phoned at 7. I walked to hospital by 7.30 and stopped 1½ hours. Then to a new house group at Moss Villa for an excellent discussion.

7th

The life kicking within Norah is living in the open air of our world. What a transformation in her little life, to be snugly secure in the warmth of the womb and then suddenly to be an independent creature, or an independent creation. This happened to me and everyone alive. Miracle and providence? Yes. Luck and accident? No.

20th

This evening's house group began discussing secularisation and the breakdown of the Corpus Christianum. The diversity of views coalesced with the need for us to ask questions. We must beware of rigidity created by Biblical or ecclesiastical literalism. Faith grows through doubt. The group decided that in the next session we turn to the crucial question of 'belief in God.' The questions so readily expressed by young people are identical to those of the adults, but the latter are reluctant to articulate their questioning. Today barriers were broken and the future is full of possibilities. It has taken only two sessions of a couple of hours.

The group presented such exciting possibilities and growth was tangible.

22nd

All home again. The big boys returned to see their baby sister Catherine Elizabeth. The excitement was intense when they dashed into the front room and saw her lying in the carry cot. They couldn't believe she would be so small. Both wanted to touch her and to share sweets. It was awfully difficult to convince them she was too young for that delicacy.

The boys had been staying with their grandparents, Nan and Tadcu (Norah's parents) who had retired to Clydach.

DECEMBER

15th

House Group started with two sessions on the decline of the Church in the 20th century. We began to understand what has gone wrong, and this led to the major reason for the church's decline - the crisis of faith. Why do Christians believe in God? I gave a session on Biblical faith, based on God's acts in history, centred on the Exodus. The fourth session centred on the Resurrection. Now we go back to the New Testament and start with Mark. We begin at the beginning.

31st

Youth Work, Church School and House Groups have been most encouraging but another year is necessary before we can make an analysis.

These new signs were all taking place within the life of the local congregation. Most members of the Llanidloes congregation were members of groups and almost everyone was most supportive of the new developments.

1970

JANUARY

15th

It would be easy to pop into houses, stop for 10 minutes and walk on to the next. This might keep people happy because the minister has called, but there will have been no ministry. I try to make my calls worthwhile. It takes time to create trust, but then people open up with their problems or talk significantly about the Church.

20th

A strength of pastoral ministry is caring for people to whom you are responsible for leading worship. In this ministry the vertical meets the horizontal, where theology and ethics cross. It is an indissoluble connection. The specialized ministry is impoverished because it divorces the various ministerial disciplines. I spent time with a 70 year old widow with married children who live several hundred miles away. She is so kind-hearted. We chatted and helped each other because I was her minister who preaches and administers sacraments.

21st

The Missionary Committee in its inaugural meeting decided to order and distribute periodicals to the church, have a mission table and collect by boxes rather than by subscription.

FEBRUARY

Sunday 8th

'What is the purpose of preaching in todays church?' To deepen faith and develop skills for evangelism, but these are often met more adequately through house groups. Yet there is an esoteric side of worship, a peculiar inspiration especially within preaching when ideas jump into consciousness, often coupled with fertility of expression.
I suppose this was an attempt to express those 'moments of transcendence' often experienced in public worship; the music, the stillness, the preaching 'catching fire' as R S Thomas once wrote.

MARCH

9th

Two house groups met to 'study' the faith. We need both worship and study, which together should lead to service. All are vitally important for God's people.

10th

An important suggestion in house group. How do we develop appropriate forms of Sunday worship? Could we provide the house group with material which would be the basis of worship the following Sunday. There are now 33 in house groups, 21 from our own church. We will start this experiment next autumn.

I was eager to relate the 'teaching/mission' taking place in house groups, with the worship life of the congregation. I was still seeking a method by which this could be done. I wished to avoid the house groups becoming alternate churches, and to help public worship become more accessible to newcomers to the life of faith. I was not the first nor last to struggle with this dilemma.

17th

The event of the week and perhaps of the century has been the publication of the New English Bible. I received the Library edition, including the Apocrypha. This translation will prove authoritative in England for the next half century because it has been done ecumenically and is the work of the finest scholarship. In all probability the Roman Catholics will use it in time as they have been observers during the last couple of years.

Although the Roman Catholic Church joined the other Churches in the British Isles to sponsor the Revised English Bible, no one could have imagined the innumerable translations which have appeared during the past forty years. It is difficult now to talk of an 'authorized version.'

23rd

Two excellent house-groups. We finished for Easter and are 2/3s of the way through this first year of experimentation. The older ladies' group becomes extremely devotional at times, akin to prayerful meditation. The young people's group probes intellectually, and there are times when it stretches beyond reason and recognises mystery. This evening we continued with the problem of Resurrection and I deliberately led them along the difficult path of portions of Paul. Some had begun to think the writers of the NT were naive but this made them think again. They were amazed at the profundity of the Pauline vision of Romans 8, I Cor 15 and 2 Cor 4 and 5, and were forced to recognize we must struggle with the Biblical revelation.

MAY

14th

My most important academic day. The Faculty proposes I shall graduate with the PhD at Commencement in two weeks. Charles Ranson, one of my Committee stated this morning that he was thrilled by the thesis. Norah, Catherine and I walked across to Hartfrant by 3.55 and I was asked in by 4.05. Present around the table were Bijlefeld (Dean), Moore, Winthrop Hudson (external), Ranson and Paul; Grislis, Macarthur, Hohlfeld, McCutcheon and Underwood. The Specialist Committee questioned for an hour; Grislis and McCutcheon asked a question each; it returned to the 'table' for Moore to make the final queries. I went out at 5.50, was fetched by Robert Paul and the magic words and congratulations given at 6. It was so exciting. The committee described the thesis as exciting, well-written, scholarly, urged me to publish. It is an excellent piece of work and defence. I could not be more thrilled.

Charles Ranson was a professor at Hartford and had been general secretary of the International Missionary Council. Le Roy Moore was my Hartford supervisor (although most of my research had been under the wing of Robert Paul) and Winthrop Hudson was James B. Colgate Professor of the History of Christianity, Colgate Rochester Divinity School, Rochester, New York, 1948-77. Professor of History, University of Rochester, 1970-77. He was author of 'Religion in America.' The others were also members of the Seminary Faculty. It was a very different experience from the Oxford viva before two specialists.

15th

Le Roy Moore told me that when Winthrop Hudson was asked to serve as external examiner, he accepted on condition that he would be unable to attend. However as soon as he read the thesis, he decided to come! He gave me a copy of Hudson report. It contained the following: 'It is a remarkable fine piece of work. You can be proud of it as a Hartford dissertation. My comments are incidental. They are of the type that Morgans may wish to take into account if he revises it for publication. They raise no question of its acceptability for the degree.' Moore's report is also something I shall treasure.

Sunday 17th

A symbol of solidarity and hope. We left Broadview Community Church 4 years ago and yet our meeting today was as if we had been away for only weeks. It was the longest and most serious discussion about the social / political problems of this sad nation. Our conversation with these College students lasted 6 hours and revealed a concern I have not seen in Wales. These young people love their country and want it delivered from its tortuous dilemma. They have burning convictions but feel torn because of loyalty to the older generation and their ideals. The 30 young people present had all been members of the Sunday school or Youth Groups when I was Youth Adviser (very few now go to church).

19th

The American confidence of 'Climb every mountain has gone.' The older generation realizes to its horror that the American dream of materialistic and educational success has been rejected by their children. Their values are no longer the values of young people. For the first time in a hundred years of American history this idealism is vociferous and aggressive. Its voice is heard from coast to coast and seems capable of organizing itself. The more conservative blame it on 'communism and drugs,' an outside group polluting the youth of America. In reality America is splitting from within and the bogey-men are symptoms and not culprits.

20th

Our friends at Waterbury confirmed our view that the generation gap has widened alarmingly, and that radicalism is seen as inherently evil. The allurement of the natural wilderness is over and the young American realizes, perhaps for the fist time, that the problems to be solved are here and now. They are not over the horizon and he cannot pack his wagon and leave behind the corruptions of iniquitous civilization. He cannot start again. This could result in a healthy regeneration but older people are fearful and suspicious, and the youth's advocacy of violence is self-destructive. The church is conservative and divorced from young people. The Church could be the reconciling agent but there is a widening gulf between the laity and the so called radical leadership.

JUNE

1st

Only 7 present in the Council of Churches. I am President for the coming year and suggested a programme of ecumenical house groups which might lead towards unity. It was opposed as too risky.

My wish was to integrate ecumenical house groups into the more formal ecumenical life of Llanidloes. It was not to be. Fortunately, five years later it happened in Manselton.

JULY

Sunday 5th

For the first time we had extempore prayers in Children's Service: a ten, six and five year old came on to the platform and offered prayer.

11th

I visited the Penrhys estate, a new Council Project of 1000 houses nearing completion. It has been well-planned with fascinating shapes, centring on an almost completed Community Centre. It is difficult to make an assessment because so much rubbish is lying about because of the contractors. The question is what treatment will the place have during the next five years? I chatted with residents who said that sections had already been vandalized. They feared for the future of their community. Here is a new community starting from the very beginning!

Sunday 19th

Catherine was baptized by Mr Grey and I baptised Sarah, aged 4.
John Grey, the local Presbyterian minister baptized both Dylan and Catherine.

SEPTEMBER

Sunday 6th

After evening worship I met 14 young people and took them to the cottage at Glanhafren to use as a 'centre.' We shall try for a year and see what happens. The young people now have their own place.
The beginning of the Glanhafren Centre. The middle cottage (once part of the original chapel) was used by the young people for many years. It became their place. They paid the rent, all bills and maintained the upkeep of the building. It gave them a sense of responsibility.

7th

The first time to return from summer holiday and not have the thesis waiting. There is instead the exciting prospect of beginning the 'theology' sermons. I will study Macquarrie's 'Principles of Christian Theology' which will

provide an excellent basis for a balanced theology. I also have the challenge of 'recreating theology' into preaching material.
The beginning of a more formalized theological search which has continued to the present!

9th
I received a letter from Winthrop Hudson in which he writes: 'I do hope that you can secure publication of your dissertation for it contains so much new and fascinating material that is of interest on both sides of the Atlantic.' He suggested Oxford University Press.

10th
Macquarrie provides a thrilling foundation for the new series of sermons. I will duplicate the Sunday evening sermon for discussion in house groups. This will create the link between groups and worship.

17th
By reading Macquarrie I am evaluating new ideas and forced to use new language. This is my first serious work since the thesis.

22nd
It is a difficult to prepare material which is theological, radical and can be read and preached. It is a challenge to preach radical theology to a church generation brought up on Biblical literalism. How does one relate the theology of the study with the sermon of worship?

OCTOBER

6th
County Meetings at Newtown. This county is facing a bleak future denominationally. 30 years ago there were 11 Congregational ministers; today there are 2, one retiring at the end of the year. Yet when we talked of Congregational/Presbyterian unity, these little churches were in favour. Henry Williams of Cefnfaenor said the only way we gain something is by giving up something; a Sarnau deacon said we ought to pay the Home Churches Fund to help weaker churches. Their membership is 20! They reflect the essentials of the Gospel.

Meetings of the Montgomeryshire Congregational Meetings. I served as its last secretary until the inauguration of the United Reformed Church. Cefnfaenor, near Berriew, closed many years ago. Sarnau, near Welshpool is still open.

19th

How is the rural church to continue its ministry? Dwindling, ageing congregations and shortage of ministry are signs of impending crisis. The most far-reaching proposals advocate local unity, but unless there is renewal, this would only perpetuate the system a little longer. Could there be an experiment in creating 30 groups within a radius of say 10 miles? They could meet weekly, and come together for 'traditional' worship monthly in a central location. Only one centre need be maintained, and if adults contributed 5/- a week, it would pay two full-time ministers. Is this one direction into the future?

A dream?

NOVEMBER

9th

A good discussion on the atonement. One lady was Abelardian, (without having heard of him), while another was Anselmian. Our expectations are much too low. People have resources which ought to be cultivated.

The discussion was on 'what is the effect of the death of Jesus' on the relationship between God and humankind. The Abelardian view sees Christ's death as creating a loving response in the faithful; Anselm emphasized the death of Jesus as 'satisfying the justice of God.' This discussion took place amongst the oldest ladies' group.

17th

The steering committee of 5 met this afternoon in Wood St, Cardiff to discuss our approach as a Welsh Province to the proposed union between the Congregational Church of England and Wales and the Presbyterian Church of England. The proposals create no enthusiasm with the committee or with most Welsh churches. I am enthusiastic. There is a meeting in London next month to discuss the matter with headquarters. Even more significant than these talks is the personal view of the Moderator that 'organized religion as we know it in this country is finished and some far more radical churchmanship is necessary to continue ministry in the future I told him about our developments in Llanidloes and he felt they were in the right direction.

19th

The showing of 'Between Two Worlds,' a film of mission work in Zambia, had been organized by the Sunday School. John Higgs showed this film and comic and sport features; the girls served coffee and cakes. A decent crowd of 50 children and young people, and 30 adults.

John Higgs, a local electrician, was the father of one of our young people in the Under 13 Club.

1971

JANUARY

5th

Heather and Susan are eager to study theology and play their part in the creation of a more effective church life. They are interested in applying to the College in Swansea.

Both young women had been attending the Sunday evening youth group for a considerable time and their enquiring minds were being focussed on the relationship between faith and social action. They wished to proceed to the Congregational Memorial College, Swansea.

6th

Our convictions are unrealistically bound up with a pre 1850 interpretation of the Bible. We have begun to break down the seemingly indissoluble link between religion and Nineteenth Century church buildings. Now we have to replace the naive, fairy-tale view of the Bible. In this evening's group one member was agnostic, reasonable and prepared to change if convinced; another, a scholar in his field but traditional, literalistic and with an anxiety that what he holds sacred could be shaken.

Discussion in each group was honest and searching, and also provided lots of fun.

7th

Llunos is also enquiring about Memorial College. She is keen, academically capable and has a strong chapel background (Llawryglyn Calvinistic Methodist). It would be ideal if the three studied together.

8th

The Training and Mission Department at Church House suggests that 'your young ladies enter a Teacher's Training College and become schoolteachers. We don't have any openings for people trained in Religious Education within the church structure.'
I wrote to the normal channels within the Church, seeking advice. I had of course lived in Connecticut for two years where it was common for women to be employed professionally in church activities, particularly in education and social work but increasingly so in the ministry of Word and Sacrament. Neither Church House nor the Welsh province knew what to do with these young people. I suppose they were before their time. How much change there has been in forty years.

12th

Our Moderator writes in similar vein: 'I would strongly advise against going into a theological college... a diploma in theology is not sufficient qualification for teaching or much else than actual ministry... women ministers are not entirely welcomed in our churches and until such time as we have worked out team ministries, I do not see much future for them... get her trained for earning her bread and butter... their husbands might well not be sympathetic to their calling.'

21st

A delightfully liberal family listened and commented thoughtfully about house groups and the development of young people: 'What kind of people will house groups produce compared with traditional church? This is what counts. Where is religious experience being developed most?' Holy Pragmatism.
It was good to have such encouragement from members of one's own congregation.

FEBRUARY

1st

A new house group met for the first time. The seven women are young, alert, open, eager to understand religious experience and have few preconceptions. Most left the church in their early teens, but are open-minded and wish to explore religious concepts.

Often a group would be formed because there was a contact with the congregation. In this case I approached the mother of children coming to Sunday School. Would she be interested in exploring issues of faith? Would she approach some of her friends to attend a 'taster group' which could meet at her home? Within a year there were eight such groups and 100 participants. The majority attended regularly during the next four years - and long after we had left for Manselton.

4th

I spoke on 'Revolutionary Puritanism' to the Labour Party group at Llanidloes. Thirty there including half a dozen of our young people who came especially to hear my talk. They asked the right questions - references to Diggers and Levellers, Vavasor Powell, relation between religion and politics. They had hope that young people were enquiring and compassionate, searching for the better life and needed guidance and not coercion. What a refreshing contrast with the Conservatives (with large or small 'c' in church affairs.) Their basic drive is close to Christ compared with Tory acquisitiveness. I felt at home.

MARCH

8th

House Group 6 started. Each group is quite distinctive. The six young women raised questions of free will and predestination, life after death, suffering, who and where is God? the purpose of life, how do the Bible and science, especially evolution, fit?

How much I received from being in group. I took voluminous notes from the contributions to the discussions while I was in Llanidloes, and felt it was there that I learned how to understand and communicate theological issues.

15th

The Provincial Committee meeting at Newtown accepted the decisions of our sub-committee. It wholeheartedly recommends the Scheme for Union with the Presbyterian Church of England and rejects any attempt to form an Independent Welsh Church. The Moderator gave a very dismal report on our denomination: 255 churches (200 by 1980; 100 by 1990); 74 ministers (50 by 1980; 20 by 1990), and no prospect of lay leadership.

APRIL

1st

I received more severe criticism of my new preaching style. I need to assure myself of certain facts: (1) 'Theology sermons' are preached once out of three weekly services (2) my 'traditional preaching' had little response. No-one had talked positively of sermons and no-one came to church because the minister preached well. New House Group (VII) in Hillfield went extremely well.

Not everyone responded well to the attempt to relate mission, worship, theology, preaching and discussion. At first I found it a considerable challenge - how to 'translate theological issues' into worship material. Eventually the answers came with the connection between the Bible, theology and the Christian Year.

Sunday 4th

The youngest classes led the service - Hugh and Dylan sang in the cherub's choir. Dylan and Timothy had a little fight. After lunch Catherine, Linda, Dylan and I went to Glanhafren for Communion. The girls (12-13) were so attentive that I invited them to take Communion. They are not members but they certainly love the Lord. Was a 'rule broken?'

11th (Easter Sunday)

Five young people joined the Church. Three responded as a result of Youth Group, and two from House Group. All asked to join the church and used a Declaration of Faith they had prepared themselves. I hope the church felt a sense of solidarity.

13th

Heather, Llunos and Susan tried their Entrance Examinations, were interviewed by the staff at Coleg Coffa and did splendidly. Pennar, Trevor and Dewi Eurig regard this as a most exciting adventure for Coleg Coffa and are amazed by the girls who have all impressed them greatly.

Dr Pennar Davies, Trevor Evans, Professor of the Old Testament and Dewi Eurig Davies, the Professor of Christian Doctrine

26th

The girls were interviewed individually by the Executive Committee of Coleg Coffa and then officially received by Alban Davies. Prayer was offered by D E Williams. The meeting rejoiced.

Alban Davies, the Chairman of the College had spoken fluently the day I was received by the Cyfundeb (East Glamorgan District) in Bristol in 1960. The Revd D E Williams was minister in Pontyberem.

28th

So many new ideas and actions are emerging from house groups. Many are regular church-people but they are now growing rapidly because of (1) a supportive context (2) being challenged by theological ideas and by people outside the church.

Regular worshippers who had been 'silent in church' throughout their lives were now enjoying the opportunity to ask questions in a supportive situation. They enjoyed the adventure of searching to put their faith into words.

29th

Now that half a dozen house groups exist, the first stage is coming to a close. The second stage is to see if the work can be sustained? If a hundred people continue with theological discussion for a few years, something wonderful will emerge. Alongside the house groups are the exciting links with Coleg Coffa, the Glanhafren project, Church School, and Mission work. What will unfold?

MAY

Sunday 2nd

Our Communion at Glanhafren (by the side of the Severn) this afternoon was as near heaven as possible this side of Jordan river. This evening during a deacons' meeting to discuss the School on World Poverty at Llanidloes next Saturday (arranged by Christian Aid and Workers Educational Association) one of our deacons blew his top and said the money (30new pence to attend) would be sent to guerrilla groups, and that the British Council of Churches did not reflect or represent church opinion.

Although it was only one deacon who spoke so vociferously, the others understandably, did not wish to 'make a fuss.' Sadly the church often 'keeps the peace' when it ought to be more courageous.

11th

We Congregationalists in London and the Presbyterians in Newcastle have decided that the United Reformed Church should come into existence. It will now be sent to the local churches to make their decision. This will prove more difficult but this important stage has been reached. At Newcastle 539 voted - 79.3% in favour, and in London 2121 voted (1888 for and 233 against) - 89%.

At the May Meetings at Westminster Chapel, we Congregationalists voted in favour of the Union. It is worth noting the size of the different assemblies.

12th

I am grateful for Congregational heritage and the prophetic attitudes expressed today. The Spirit's charisma to God's People were reflected in liberalism, tolerance, charity and a concern for justice. Although 2000 people met in Westminster Chapel, it was possible to feel an intimacy because of the sense of belonging. We do not wish to be Independents; we oppose the Immigration Bill, Sale of Arms to South Africa and we agree to join with the Presbyterians.

13th

Our 'radicalism' at Llanidloes is in the mainstream of the Church's life. The new Church is in the vanguard of an advance into an uncharted future, rather than a retreat into the wistful, secure but anachronistic past.

The Annual Congregationalist meetings were always encouraging. They were not only decision making bodies, but were meetings to inspire the local to fare forward.

JUNE

11th

Pastors and deacons should be supportive, tolerant, attentive listeners, discreet and trustworthy. Through house groups it is possible to recognize many with the potential for these roles.

14th

I spoke at the annual conference at Coleg y Fro to 70 school leavers from Rhondda and Breconshire Secondary schools. Of the 55 Rhondda fifteen year

olds, only 2 attend worship (both girls: one RC, the other Anglican). Of the 14 from Brecon, 4 attend church (all girls, three Anglican and one Methodist). Bill Evans, the organizer of the conference and a teacher at Hendrefadog told me that only a half dozen of 350 in the school go to church.
Another visit to the conference centre at Rhoose.

15th

Should we expect the people I met yesterday to become like us? Or do we need to change so that together we become one people? Many of yesterday's people could become convinced Christians, but only if the people of God are flexible and tolerant enough to engage with this generation. We protect ourselves in our tabernacles while the storms rage outside, unaware that the cracks in our structures are ominously large and soon the walls will come crashing down.

JULY

2nd

Norah and I were walking at the top of town when Father Kenneth stopped his car and introduced the Abbot of Caldey who invited us to bring our groups to the island.
Father James Wicksteed, the first Abbot of Caldey spoke each year at the lectures organised by Father Kenneth Gillespie in Llanidloes Friary. This year the audience had included a large number of people nurtured through house groups. He was intrigued by the development. Father Kenneth, a Franciscan and the Revd. D.J Owen, a Presbyterian both regularly attended the same house group and were most encouraging participants.

30th

As I wrote Theology 35 on the Imago Dei, I was thrilled by the miraculous vision of mans destiny: to be sons of the living God, assured we shall be in the image of the Christ. A miracle that God in his creative, loving imagination sees us transformed into who He wants us to be.

AUGUST

23rd

We travelled to the tip of Lleyn and looked at Bardsey across the straits. How mysterious it looked shrouded in mist, with a cloud capping it like Sinai. A joy to climb the little hill with all the family and have this superb view of the end of Wales. It was far more conducive to an experience of God than yesterday's formal worship. Many tell me they prefer a church when it is empty. Visited the church at Aberdaron where R S Thomas is vicar.
Our summer holiday as a family was spent in a Dormobile and a tent. We spent it alternately on the West coast of Scotland or nearer at hand.

SEPTEMBER

16th

The end of the first fortnightly cycle of house groups. Each group has restarted and is rediscovering its shape for the year ahead. No one was absent and there was no need to persuade regulars that groups were worthwhile. During last year I contacted 70 people to find the 50 who joined.
This was the first 'full year' for house groups. Soon there were to be eight adult groups and two youth groups meeting regularly. The average attendance for each cycle of two weeks was 100 people.

OCTOBER

12th

Stimulating and exhilarating days at the Ministers' Reading Party in the Lake District. We are grappling with a theology which is intellectually honest and devotionally fulfilling. I hope I am communicating a similar comforting challenge to the 90 people in groups at home. I have been delighted to discover that my approach is shared by the other 10 members of this reading party and that I am seen as a main-line moderate evangelical Christian, and I hope human being. We have been most adequately led by John Marsh who has revealed himself as a Barthian, passionately evangelical and profoundly compassionate. He has worked us hard today. I led two of today's three sessions, on 'God and the world' (providence, miracle, evil and sin) and 'Revelation and God as Being.' I was comfortable leading because of my training in groups at home.

I was attending a United Reformed Church ministers' reading party. It was held at Buttermere and was guided by John Marsh, Principal of Mansfield when I was a student. The experience was most affirming of my approach to nurture.

14th

I feel confirmed in faith and ministry. Our approach in house groups and the theological enterprise is a most fruitful approach. My fellow ministers have been greatly encouraged by the work and urge perseverance.

Sunday 24th

The congregation decided unanimously to join the United Reformed Church. *All congregations were invited to decide individually on whether to join the new Church. In Montgomeryshire, two out of nine opted not to enter the URC. Similar divisions took place throughout Wales.*

NOVEMBER

12th

We have arrived at our destination. A fellowship forming during the last few years is proving to be genuine and sustaining. Fifteen, all 'Llanidloes people' [some were students in Swansea and Cardiff] have arrived from different parts of South Wales to share meaningful relationships, centred on prayer and study. We would discover the mind of Christ for us. The place to which we have come is of great significance - Caldey Island, the home at this time of the Cistercians. We feel one with them. As yet we have met only Father Abbot and Brother Robert who is responsible for hospitality. Their generous and simple welcome helped us find that Christ-centred relationships provide the key for our own personal and communal salvation. Marvellous to cross the stretch of water. We were warmly greeted and taken to the Guest House for tea and biscuits. Most of us went to Monastery Chapel to listen to (partake in) service at 6.

One of the pivotal experiences for Llanidloes young and not so young people. For Norah and me, it was the first of two or three visits each year until 2003. Each occasion was life-transforming. Father Robert was guest master and later became Abbot after the resignation of Father James.

13th

The Youth Group is discovering koinonia (relationships centred on Christ). The Abbot's views are fresh, original, honest and radical. We felt we belonged to each other. Father Robert took us on a guide of the island: the Abbot's chapel in the monastery, the 11th century St Illtud's church, down a cliff to one of the bays (Drinkim) and along a cliff to prehistoric caves. Tea accompanied by questions and answers with some of the brothers - the Abbot, Robert, David, Aelred and Joseph. A fascinating encounter.

14th

A day of intellectual and spiritual struggle, but we are all nearer faith than when we started a couple of days ago. We have all been impressed by the calibre of living and character of our brothers in Christ who live in this place. They have shared with us, showed themselves to be men of great variety, and manifested that what divides us is minimal compared with what we share. We walked to the 11th century St Illtud's church, (the ancient Benedictine chapel and probably the foundation of the 6th century Celtic settlement under St Samson.) Tremendous privilege to worship there. A simple service of readings, unison prayers and psalms, as well as communion (cup and bread passed from hand to hand). We were so near its significance (it gave strength and comfort).

15th

We have been in the company of godly men. It has been a privilege to be with Christians of such quality of faith and living. Here is the nearest example in my experience, of Christian living in community. To say they have escaped from being in the world would be just not true. They are providing to the world a living testimony to the love Christ has for his people. I have matured as a result of their being. At discussion we were joined by the Abbot and four monks. Frank, charitable discussion. The Abbot is a great radical, evangelical catholic. 'The new reformation is with us; we need prophets and prophetesses of the Word; how sadly we confuse the Church with an institution. We are one family in Christ - his brothers and our group. Protestants and Catholics are one people of God.' The boys were shown around the Abbey - hard living, good library (Protestant books in plenty).

17th

A sad but inevitable chapter in the history of Zion Congregational Church, Llanidloes. The deacons voted 5-1 to stop the under 13s meeting in the

Schoolroom. The tragic fact is that now the Youth Group (who left 15 months ago) and the under 13s have left, the Schoolroom is used only once a week (Church School on Sunday). The traditional church is destroying its very roots and will have no hope of development in the future. No ball (foot, table or shuttlecock) can be used there. It will become a fossil of the 1930s (when it was built - really it is Victoriana).

The straw that broke the camel's back was in fact the breaking of one of the small panes of glass in a window by a ball. Attempts had been made to play games where the ball must not rise above knee level, but accidents happen. The sadness is that many of our buildings are inappropriate for today's church. As the years have passed, and as I have grown older, I can see the dilemma. However the consequence was that the church building became associated with negativism by the young people.

DECEMBER

14th

Creation/ reconciliation/ consummation represent different facets of the continuing and eternal process and purposes of God (the letting-be of God for Macquarrie); the person of Christ represents a distinctive and crucial stage in the process (revelation of the mystery once hidden, but now manifest).

Macquarrie was struggling to translate 'faith' into contemporary philosophical language. It was not an easy process.

21st

An excellent house group with a superb confrontation between Miss George and Mrs Dance re Marlowe's and Goethe's interpretations of Faustus. What a fine movement of minds over significant issues and at such depth. I felt so privileged.

The former was arguing from the standpoint of an English teacher in the local High School, and the latter as a teacher of German literature in Newtown. Denise George often commented on how house groups added another dimension to relationships with some of her students in the High School.

1972

JANUARY

10th
Seventeen young people in their late teens are all working hard at theology. When we began in Zion, not one young person was interested, and the younger pupils in the High School were anti-chapel and anti-religious.

FEBRUARY

2nd
I listened to Eliot reading his 'Four Quartets' on an LP we bought in Hartford. I followed the text, and although not understanding everything, it was a fine experience.
Another attempt to get to grips with Eliot. I had been unsuccessful as a student in Swansea, again in Hartford and did not get much further this time. My time still lay ahead!

3rd
Insights continue to develop in the area of 'time and eternity' because of 'The Four Quartets.' Here is creative theology, a magnificently contemporary expression of the faith once delivered to the saints. Is it similar to what I have been reading in Tillich?

24th
Bill Samuel advises me to candidate for our church at Newport. 'It appears to me that you might consider moving out of your very comfortable and useful pastorate at Llanidloes into something bigger and more demanding.'

28th
The Moderator phoned: 'I need future denominational leaders at strategic points (you are out of touch in Llanidloes) and if you are to reach your potential, you must leave this rural area. You will be challenged more and forced to grow more quickly in Newport.'

29th

We stop in Llanidloes. Our experiment must be seen to succeed or fail. The attempt must be made and several years are necessary before there can be adequate evaluation. Our people are struggling hard with a theological system of 100 sermons. They are on their way, have burnt their bridges but need more time before coming to a faith which has conviction.

MARCH

18th

My first encounter with the Ecumenical Institute centred on Chicago but having a 'community' in Tees-side. A Student Christian Movement conference held in Broneirion Llandinam was led by an American couple with a first class approach and technique. They explored the questions of Christ and the Holy Spirit, using Tillich and Bonhoeffer. Their leadership was dynamic and sympathetic.

The Ecumenical Institute was formed in Chicago in 1962 and developed courses for what seemed Christian Development. Has it developed into The 'Institute for Cultural Affairs?' Its mission statement is 'to advocate for and actualize the fundamental right of all peoples to define and shape their own futures, toward the goal of realizing sustainable, just solutions to human challenges.' Laudable as this seems, it is a long way from the Course that day at Llandinam.

Sunday 26th

I preached at Ebenezer for the first time since ordination and the response pleased me so much. Dad and I chatted to David Davies after morning service. He was so interested in the sermon and mentioned C S Lewis, Dr Orchard, Professor Joad and Charles Moule. He is a remarkable scholar. Eighty this evening: my theme began and ended on the theme of time, space and existence. First class atmosphere.

27th

The Rosedene group were all present and these older people talked about anxiety, void, meaninglessness from their own experience.

These older women were articulating their life experience, encouraging each other's sense of honesty and strengthening each other's faith.

APRIL

6th

What is todays significance? The County meeting for 'Covenanting in Wales' was held at the Church Hall in Newtown, attended by 50 delegates from the major denominations except Baptists and Roman Catholics who sent observers. Anglicans are treating the scheme with great seriousness. We were addressed by Ungoed Jacob and Huw Wynne Griffiths, a Welsh Presbyterian from Aberystwyth. We live in hope.

The Covenanting Scheme was to play a significant role in the ecumenical history of the Churches in Wales for the next forty years. Ungoed Jacob a priest in the Church in Wales played a leading role in developing ecumenical life in Wales. I was to work with him when I moved to Manselton. I had first heard Huw Wynne Griffiths when I was a young person at Ebenezer. Huw Wynne was a leading Presbyterian ecumenist and I was to learn from and work with him during many years on the Covenant Commission

MAY

12th

Norah, Catherine and I heard the plaintive cry of a curlew in flight beyond Marsh's Pool. It is a strange, sad sound echoing a poignant hollowness. The first cuckoo of Spring offers a grand optimism which is just as real as the curlew. Both present two facts of reality. We also need the superb flight of newly returned swifts and the glorious sound of the skylark.

26th

Norah and I enjoyed a sophisticated, civilizing privilege when we attended a concert given by Benjamin Britten, Peter Pears and Osian Ellis at Gregynog. Strange poignancy and rare beauty with one of the greatest English composers accompanying his best friend. At times I felt Pears realized he was ageing: he expressed superb control in very beautiful sad songs. The programme included Schubert's 'Songs of the Harper;' Pears and Ellis; Hugo Wolf's 'Six Songs and a Suite for Harp' by Britten. In the second half were Shakespearean songs by Thomas Arne, Roger Quilter and Britten's 'Who are these children?' on poems by Soutar. Shirley Hooson introduced us to Hywel D Lewis - he is drawn more and more towards Christology and especially the Christological hymns; also selfhood and eternity. We also met Lord Morris, Lord Chalfont, Ben Bowen Thomas, Pennar Davies, Stephen J Williams.

Gregynog Hall, the home of Gwendoline and Margaret Davies was donated to the University of Wales in 1960. It is an important cultural centre. Shirley Hooson had become a family friend by attending a house group.

JUNE

15th

The Abbot of Caldey spoke on 'The Eucharist in an Ecumenical Age' in the Friary. 35 present, either Roman Catholic or House groups. Our groups are breaking barriers - no Protestant there except from group members. His talk was radical - the need to pressure the hierarchy for intercommunion, but not to jump the gun.

JULY

1st

A solid workmanlike day at Old Hall with room for hope and joy. During the day the Ecumenical Institute introduced the Christ event, the life of the Spirit, Picasso's 'Guernica' and 'Requiem for a Heavyweight' with Anthony Quinn.

Sunday 2nd

Children's Service at 10 with 40 children and 50 adults. Lunch at Old Hall and a session on the Church by Charles and a discussion on Richard Niebuhr led by Desmond.

Charles and Desmond (no surnames recorded) were members of the Ecumenical Institute. The weekend had been a great success and many were inspired by the new approach. Many were introduced to Tillich, Bonhoeffer, Bultmann and Niebuhr for the first time and in a most accessible way. In the process they were discovering that 'faith' made sense and invoked commitment. It was certainly worth following-up with a second weekend.

SEPTEMBER

5th

Hugh and Dylan started in the Welsh class of Trefeglwys school. This has been a major decision because the boys have already settled well in Llanidloes school opposite the house and now they have a 4 mile journey. For many, the school is identified with Plaid Cymru and this causes us discomfort in church

and town. However we do what we feel best for the children and a bilingual education will prove an advantage.
Although Llanidloes is very conscious of its local history and has played a significant role in the history of Wales politically (especially Chartism and Liberalism) and culturally (especially in music and publishing), the creation of Welsh Language schools during the past fifty years has proved controversial in many localities

OCTOBER

Sunday 8th

Our first Sunday in the United Reformed Church. The hope is we will not be this new church for very long because it will serve as a temporary stage in the reunification of Christ's Church.
The United Reformed Church had come into being legally on the 5th of October 1972. Part of the vision was that the new Church would prove to be a pioneer, encouraging and leading the way towards the formation of a United Church in England ? England and Wales? United Kingdom? Wales? It seemed straightforward in those halcyon days. Covenanting in Wales was seen as part of that wider process.

16th

A strange, proud, sad day. I have seen the glory of being human. Just before getting to bed, I looked at Catherine, not yet 3, beautiful, peaceful and my mind flashed back an hour to what might have been my last visit to one of our older members (84) who seems to be slipping out of this life. She was as near a child as an adult could be, straining to sit up in bed, asking her daughter to cwtch her because she felt cold, asking for her sister and brother, long dead; and there was I privileged, allowed to offer prayer for us all before Jesus our Shepherd. Where are we without Thee, O my Jesus, my dear Lord? To see this lady feebly determined, strongly dignified with her daughters as they cared for their dying mother.

18th

Another of God's saints is reaching the culmination of her earthly pilgrimage and reaching into an existence translated into the heavenly. One of our oldest, most faithful and active members, moved onwards. I knew her well because every month we spent a couple of hours together. We had become close friends and I loved her dearly.

26th

Each group is concerned about the others, and a structure is being shaped to reflect the mutual concerns of the groups. One hundred individuals belonging to nine groups now have a central forum of 25 people. They are reflecting to the local churches that they should be emphasizing our common faith rather than our historic denominational differences.

27th

I met a young leader of the L'Abri Fellowship, founded 20 years ago by Francis Schaeffer. This very conservative (theologically) organization, centred in Switzerland has a 'house' in Hampshire. It sympathizes with the 'charismatic movement' which according to this young man, is sweeping through the more conservative groups throughout the world. It centres on speaking with tongues (which prove the presence of the Spirit) and the expectancy of the return of Christ before 1987 (a generation after the shrivelling of the fig tree in Matthew 25). This young man has been in touch with the Jesus people who are deeply eschatological (anticipating the imminent Return of Christ) and literalist in their Biblicism. Moderate radicals could be squeezed between conservatives in the church who will not change and the new 'enthusiasts.'

Francis August Schaeffer was an American Evangelical theologian who established the L'Abri Fellowship. A number of scholars credit Schaeffer's ideas with helping spark the rise of the Christian Right in the United States. The Community in England is in the village of Greatham, Hampshire. I suspect that my 'prophecy' of the 'squeezing of moderate radicals' was not far wrong.

NOVEMBER

Sunday 5th

Sunday helps create the rhythm of life: being alive is a gift of God, we have fallen from our God-given potential, but God promises to restore and consummate. The Lord's Day, the Sabbath, is God's gift to enable us grasp these heavenly themes which surpass all thought, word and action.

18th

A theological struggle with our friends of the Ecumenical Institute. Their philosophy is 'secular' with no ontology or transcendence; they reject resurrection and eternal life. They avoid crucial questions for the sake of

general impact. Yet they are disciplined and dedicated people, motivated by what they know in Jesus. They have much to give the world, but I cannot throw in my hand with them.
In reality the Ecumenical Institute were trying to create a 'God-less Christianity.'

Sunday 19th
What is the new charismatic movement saying? It is not dissimilar to the 1904 revival, but it needs a sound theology and a flexible ecclesiology and liturgy. The new movement is literalistic and emphasizes the end of the world, tongues and primitive communalism.
I was becoming convinced of the urgency for careful and caring nurture in each local congregation. This would help give confidence and wholeness to the local church, and would avoid both the drift towards secularism on the one hand, and fundamentalism on the other.

DECEMBER

Sunday 26th
Sunday is an integral part of the week's rhythm. The life of our people will not deepen until the year is shaped by the Christian year, the week by the Lord's Day, and the day by a period of private reading and prayer. The whole of life, from cradle to grave should be marked by the signs of God's presence and grace.
It was not until the Penrhys ministry that this pattern became actuality in the community of Llanfair.

Sunday 31st
Our family and six others worshipped at Holy Trinity, Tylorstown. Mr Livings read the liturgy and I preached. It felt a part of history.

1973

JANUARY

18th

A One Day School had been organized by the Extra Mural Department at Swansea and the Blaendulais Ecumenical Centre, and to everyone's amazement the room in the Students' Union was packed, chairs had to be brought in and 70 attended. Most were ministers or students for ministry from Coleg Coffa - the majority were Annibynwyr including the College staff, Trebor Lloyd Evans (Sec of UWI), Iorwerth Jones (Tyst editor) and Ieuan Jones (CCWM). I spoke and answered questions, feeling free and relaxed.
I had been invited to speak at the University in Swansea about our Llanidloes experiment in 'ecumenical theological house groups.' I felt I was at my home University but I was not aware of how much I had owed the Blaendulais Centre during my teenage years.

24th

Richard slipped away in his sleep this morning. Here is the end of a brief but bright life. He lived it well and his reward is great. There are many images springing to mind and most of them are so happy.
Richard had always lived 'Life to the full.' He seemed to enjoy everything and always communicated his sense of fun. He showed immense courage in hospital, cheering his parents and brothers by asking for an Elvis Suit and a punch-ball. Richard had been faithful in Sunday School and his mother formed one of the house groups. In latter years, Pat has devoted much of her energy to bereavement counselling through CRUSE. Richard parents, Andy and Pat were, and are very close friends. I treasure a most sensitive letter from Andy, written soon after the funeral.

27th

A gruelling but enriching day. I doubt if I shall experience anything in my life as intense as this morning, or a day in which I could be of more service. The depths of life were laid bare today and we were placed face to face with ultimate questions and answers. Richard's funeral was at 11, the largest funeral in our chapel in my experience. I could hardly get through the 35 minutes but thanks to God's grace, I managed. The men walked to the cemetery where we joined the women at the graveside

FEBRUARY

22nd

The afternoon was spent with 8 year olds at a Llanidloes Primary class. After rooting Palestine into its historical and geographical background, and showing the difference between history, poetry and myth, many questions followed: How did Jesus get out of the tomb? (we then acted Easter); where have the dead gone? how is Jesus with us all the time? (transcendent love in relationships); how did God create the world?
Such a significant experience. I had been invited to the class because Richard was one of their classmates. The teacher was Penry Roberts, later Crowned Bard at the National Eisteddfod of 2001, who married Susan Vaughan, one of our theological students - also close friends.

MARCH

7th

Two Jehovah's Witness arrived at home to discuss the Trinity, but drifted into spiritual arithmetic. When I showed them the theses, they were taken aback to see their arguments presented centuries ago. That such faith and courage should be directed towards misguided beliefs.
There was some value in academic research. 'Spiritual arithmetic' is a term coined to respond to the attempt to calculate the timing of the End of the World by referring to Biblical texts. This had been an element of my research in Seventeenth Century Puritanism. One of the visitors later joined a House Group and 'converted' to Christianity.

16th

How privileged to be on Caldey once more, to acknowledge the power of God's presence and know Christ is the source of life. 'Men stand or fall by the attitude they take to Jesus; the great question is - Will they risk their lives, if need be, for what he lived and died and rose again for?' (Alan Dale) This weekend our thoughts and prayers will be centred on Christ from the moment we wake to the moment we sleep; with the knowledge that awake or asleep, He centres himself on us.

The work of Alan T Dale had a major effect upon my understanding of scripture in his presentation of 'New World - The Heart of the New Testament' (1967), and 'Winding Quest - The Heart of the Old Testament.' (1972).

22nd

There have been 400 group sessions since 1968 and over 150 this year. There have been 12 sessions in 6 days.

House Groups had now become a part of Llanidloes Christian life. Was there anywhere else in Britain where this was happening? I treasure the full notes which I took recording each discussion.

APRIL

5th

I decided not to serve on the Board of CCWM. It was a difficult decision because of my commitment to the Church's mission. Probably I had a contribution to make and certainly I would have learned a great deal, but the work here demands thorough commitment.

CCWM = Congregational Council for World Mission. The London Missionary Society, founded in 1797 became the CCWM in 1966. Later it became the Council for World Mission. I found throughout my life that there were many times when I would have liked to say 'yes' but said 'no' when I considered what were my priorities. I'm sure I did not always make the right decision.

11th

Every member of the Rosedene Group believes in universal salvation because it reflects the ultimate victory of grace.

12th

56 out of a total of 67 attended groups this week.

MAY

3rd

Why is the Mother of Christ, who ought to be the focus of unity for all Christians, the subject of division and animosity? Will a common understanding be reached through ecumenical relationships?

Later in my ministry and particularly through the World Council of Churches, the Taize movement, our visits to Caldey and our life on Penrhys, the Mary of the Magnificat became an inspiration for Llanfair - Mary's Church.

JUNE

Sunday 3rd

Cath took collection for the first time this morning and afternoon; Dylan came out to say a prayer this morning: 'Thank you God for Jesus;' Hugh said prayers from his seat. How lucky Norah and I are.

5th

The first conference for me to lead: the Annual Women's Conference of the United Reformed Church for Wales at the Montpelier Christian Centre at Llandrindod. Our theme is 'God' and the first two sessions have been 'The ? of God (mystery, incomparable),' and 'God as creative Spirit.'

6th

The Women's Conference has been so encouraging because although the majority are elderly, they have excellent spirit, deep concern for life's problems and a sharp, enquiring vitality. They are salt.

10th Whit Sunday

How sadly we neglect the Holy Spirit. The Puritans focussed on the Work of the Spirit by emphasizing justification, sanctification and the centrality of the Word, Sacraments and Service of the Church. Now the Spirit is abandoned to 'charismatic' elements in the life of the church. Another disappointing deacons' meeting. I mentioned church membership and was attacked vehemently. One deacon said: 'We shall accept them on our terms' and another 'What do these people sec in groups?' Others deacons were as disappointed as I was.

Sunday 17th

New Quay at 9 this morning saw the car parks empty and only the milkman on the streets. As I walked to chapel this evening I felt so conspicuous walking up the hill in my dark suit while hundreds were on their way to and from the beach. Lovely to enjoy the family today and to preach at my grandmother's chapel which was a centre of the 1904 Revival.

Tabernacle Calvinistic Methodist Church, Cei Newydd had been the spiritual home of my mother's family since my great great great grandfather Jenkin Phillips and his wife Sarah (Jones) had their children baptized there from 1825 onwards. My parents and many other members of the family were present at Tabernacle to hear me lead worship.

18th

The Word of God must be preached in season and out of season. By trusting God, the seed will fall, and some will fall on fertile soil. The need is for patience and courage to keep on and on.

Sunday 24th

It was astonishing to find four elderly visitors sitting in the front of the church, asking for Bibles, following the readings and worshipping with eagerness. They lifted the whole tone of worship. Half a dozen with eager, expressive faces helps to transform worship. They were members of the Dutch Reformed Church and all in their 70s.

The four Dutch friends joined us on Caldey and made it a most memorable experience.

28th

Once more on Caldey we have searched and been searched by the creative and sustaining Word of power. In Christ we have felt the power of the Almighty. We have been held powerfully and tenderly by redeeming love and sustaining grace. Our 11 from Llanidloes, the 4 friends from Holland, the Abbot, Father David and Father Robert have provided penetrating discussion and Christian fellowship. We concluded with words of thanks from Ploos van Amstel and Dr Roos whose quiet, simple and sincere words moved us to tears. He asked us to say 'Our Father.' What a privilege.

JULY

Sunday 1st

28 new members have been received into the Church of Jesus Christ, and 130 took Communion. No histrionics, but the Word broke through the words of Scripture. We were confronted by the words of eternal life. Afterwards the majority came to the schoolroom for tea and speeches from Mr Watson, our Dutch friends and responses from Heulwen, Nigel, Anthony and Ceridwen.
This was a major experience in the history of Zion. Most of the new members

had entered into the life of the Church through belonging to house groups for several years.

AUGUST

13th

David Fowles was interviewed at Bangor by Dr Tudur and Gwilym H Jones and has been given a virtual acceptance. He is a capable, likeable young man and could be a great servant of Christ. He has been looking for 'meaning and purpose' for several years but a combination of attending house groups, visiting Caldey and the making of the new members brought everything into focus. Five young people are studying theology full-time - Susan, Llunos and David at Swansea; Robert Bebb at Cambridge and David at Bangor.
David was to study under Alwyn Charles who was now Professor of Christian Doctrine at Bala Bangor. Robert Bebb, a member of Oakley Park Presbyterian Church had been a member of a youth group during his late teens. Robert is a minister in the Presbyterian Church of Wales.

SEPTEMBER

5th

Peter Trow called on the way home from school. He returned Church History books, and said next year he wanted to take a degree in theology. He is trying A levels. He is a fine, intelligent young man and his decision has been well thought-through. He will be our 6th student of theology.
Peter was the son of Ernie and Gwenda Trow. Gwenda was a teacher in the Welsh speaking stream at Trefeglwys School and was a member of house groups, as was her brother Geraint Jones. They were the daughter and son of the Revd Llewelyn Jones, an eminent Welsh Methodist minister and scholar. Peter became a minister of the United Reformed Church.

6th

At 9.30 am [it was a Thursday morning] we enjoyed one of the quietest and most delightful weddings. It felt perfectly natural to have it like that.

15th

Hugh, Dylan and I walked through what used to be Brown Town (now grassed), crossed the new Parfitt estate and climbed up to the Penrhys estate. Already it is a good deal the worse for wear. I felt saddened and helpless. Is this where we should be living?

Brown Town (four terraced streets built at the turn of the Twentieth Century) had all been demolished and was replaced by a Council Housing Estate (named after a local Labour Councillor Mrs Parfitt). I asked ourselves an ominous rhetorical question. One should never test God in that way!

20th

Susan has decided to apply for the ministry. A great decision. Now the administrative wheels.

27th

Susan has talent and conviction, and as she matures will serve the church well. Having studied theology for 2 years she knows what it is about - much more than I knew when I made my decision 13 years ago.

Sunday 30th

The first night of the experiment with two youth groups. Llunos took 7 in Group I with Theology 33, and I went upstairs and had 8 young people in Group II and Theology 1.
So many young people now belonged to the Sunday evening discussion groups that they had to be divided into an 'older' and 'younger' section. Fortunately there was now leadership amongst the theological students.

OCTOBER

9th

Eric Ryan led group and I listened, thoroughly enjoyed it and felt they coped so well. It is a delight to be dispensable.
This was the first house group to be led by one of its own members. It was the beginning of a new stage in the developing maturity of house groups. Wing Commander Eric Ryan was a member of the Roman Catholic Church and had recently retired to Llanidloes. It shows how locals and incomers integrated well.

10th

Another group was led by Geraint Jones. The time is coming when groups will carry on without me.
Geraint was the son of Llewelyn Jones, a Welsh scholar and Methodist minister.

Sunday 14th

Glyndwr Jones, Rhiwbina phoned (from home where he was preaching at Ebenezer) and in the briefest of conversations, said I ought to be in the city where the front line of the battle is being fought. This is my weakest, or strongest point. Am I shirking responsibility by remaining in a small rural charge?

Glyndwr Jones had baptized me in 1939 and was minister of Beulah Rhiwbina, a suburban Cardiff church.

25th

The Annual Sale of Work was opened by Mamma. Good crowd present, all went smoothly and by the end of the day, over £140 had been raised - with other efforts, women have given £250 this year. A tremendous achievement.

Each year the balancing of the church budget depended upon the unstinting effort of the fund raising of the women of the church. Their working together also served to give a sense of common achievement. The combination of the October Harvest Services and the Sale of Work contributed a very large proportion of the church's annual income.

31st

Each visit to Caldey creates the miracle of deeper, happier, more sensitive and committed people. People belong together because they first belong to Christ. Paul's Christology emerges from (1) his desire that people should live in peace and with courage (2) God in Christ makes this possible through his reconciling work (3) The one who reconciles is the Christ, the image of the invisible God.

NOVEMBER

1st

Mass for All Saints. Father Dominic celebrated his 50th anniversary as a monk by officiating at the Mass. Bro James took us to caves he has excavated on the cliffs. He has unearthed remains 22,000 years old and has removed tons of soil in the process. Fr Robert gave us his paper to the Biblical Institute, on 'Jesus giving sight to the blind man.'

A remarkable occasion. Father Dominic was one of the original Cistercian community; Brother James, on loan from Scourmont was an amateur archaeologist. Father Robert was guest master. He later became Abbot.

20th

An elder referred to last Sunday as a 'terrible day in the life of the church' because the Trewythen had been announced as a location for house group. 'To think of all the struggles of the past... the pubs will be rejoicing tonight!' *The Gospel was being discussed in a pub. How dreadful! How wonderful!*

23rd

Ministry is to enjoy being with your community. It is easy to dissipate time and energy in committees, conferences, special mission exercises. The slow continued local effort is essential but of course is a hard slog. Do the one thing, and do it well.

DECEMBER

1st

The Revd Llewelyn Jones was buried on a bitterly cold day. He was a man of great faith and lived out his trust in the eternal presence of God. The funeral was confident and hopeful, and I was refreshed from attending, and privileged to participate.

7th

The Church and Society Department of the Council of Churches of Wales met at Aberystwyth. It was my first meeting. We were a dozen, chaired most intelligently by Bishop Vaughan. An impressive bilingual Presbyterian minister from Pwllheli, Meirion Lloyd Davies spoke about the problems caused by holiday homes.
I served on this committee for several years until the Church asked me to concentrate on Doctrine and Worship issues. Benjamin (Binny) Vaughan was Bishop of Swansea and Brecon.

24th

Midnight service was held in the vestry by candlelight: John 1 for the heart of the Good News; John 14 for its effects; John 17 for Christ's prayers for us - all from Alan Dale's New World.

31st

I was privileged to lead worship at 11.30 in Tylorstown Parish Church. God is with us and we are constantly surrounded by his presence.

1974

FEBRUARY

6th

Newchapel for a film on Russian Baptists by Peter Jupp of Thame (URC and a Mansfield student while I was there). Father Barnabas answered questions. Chapel was packed.

My first visit to Newchapel Baptist Church. Peter was a Mansfield colleague. Father Barnabas, a monk of the Orthodox Church was living temporarily in the house opposite the chapel - the house we bought for £5000 in 1976, and to which we retired in 2004. Father Barnabas took part in the service celebrating the formation of Llanfair in 1992.

13th

A letter from one of our University students thanking me for 'introducing him to the Lord.' He has grown in the 6 years we have known each other.

MARCH

14th

An important URC Synod at Llanidloes. 140 came from all parts of Wales: here was a family church, meeting at the central spot in Wales. The highlight was the unanimous acceptance of the Scheme for Covenanting with only one speaking against and one abstention

This was my feeling of the importance of Synod. I retained that conviction when I was appointed as Moderator.

26th

I have been listening for three months to the six Early Beethoven Quartets. I am not yet ready for the Middle and Later Quartets.

One of our students, David Fowles had recently introduced us to the Quartets. It has been a passion ever since.

28th

While Susan and Llunos took Professor Trevor Evans and four students to Rosedene, I took Pennar and another four students to Cae Gwyn. Our ladies soon lost their shyness and spoke about the theme lucidly, intelligently and with solid experience. Peter Trow and I went this evening to Group VI where a student spoke on his conversion. Norah's group was at the Friary and David's in Pengeulan.

The three day residential visit of Coleg Coffa staff and students to Llanidloes was of mutual benefit. The groups were now led by their own leaders. We had all come a long way since 1969 and each member had attended, on average 80 such discussion groups.

29th

Christ was present in this evening's meeting. 80 arrived, Trevor and Pennar spoke superbly on Christology. The students served and read aloud at supper. It was simple, direct and most effective.

30th

Heulwen and Susan led the two youth groups before we all met staff and students to share our common experience and hope in Christ.

APRIL

20th

Hugh, Dylan and I visited Mrs J G Davies who is over 80, almost blind, never goes out, but is contented and looks well. She taught me in Sunday School for many years and is a great soul.

MAY

14th

I spoke twice today at the 'Sasiwn Genhadol Merched y De' at Castell Newydd Emlyn. It was amazing to see buses rolling up, and I was grateful to sit quietly in the Roman Catholic church and walk by the castle. At 2, T J Davies and I spoke at Bethel to 700 women. Because of his wife's death, T J spoke for only 15 minutes and consequently I was given 40 minutes. After tea I spoke at Ebenezer to 300. Tea with John Gwilym's parents.

This was an awe-inspiring experience. The annual meetings of the women of the Presbyterian Church of Wales were so well organized, well attended and the congregation very responsive. The Revd T J Davies was the General Secretary of the United Council against Alcohol and Drugs. John Gwilym, my colleague from College was from Parc Nest, a farm on the edge of Castell Newydd Emlyn. While we were advocating support for Penrhys, Norah spoke to the Presbyterian Women's meetings in both North and South Wales.

23rd

Clydfan for Group IV. A great joy to see them being strengthened by the theme of redemption. Lives are being helped by theological discussion. Gareth Watts and a young Baptist student, Densil Morgan came to group at Mwynfynydd. It went exceptionally well.

Gareth a fellow student from College became Professor of Old Testament at Coleg Coffa. Densil Morgan has written an authoritative history of Twentieth Century Christianity in Wales: 'The Span of the Cross.'

30th

The Moderator phoned to ask if I would be introduced to Manselton URC because Fred Noden leaves in September. I allowed my name to be considered, but made no commitment.

JUNE

6th

The Abbot feels it might be a call from God to share house groups in an industrial setting. There are important issues: (1) Is Manselton prepared to experiment? (2) Will groups continue in Llanidloes?

14th

Miss Smale took devotions and introduced me to the elders. I spoke on (1) my conception of Christian ministry; (2) how I tried to embody this in Llanidloes; (3) what I would seek from and for Manselton. Seventeen elders were present and asked perceptive questions about the church's role in the local and world community, my theological approach, attitudes towards church unity, world development, the place of prayer and worship. I spoke about my commitment to theology and groups.

Vera Smale was chairperson of the Elders' meeting. She became a most loyal advisor and friend for Norah and me.

21st

Susan and Llunos have passed the Diploma in Theology at Swansea. Such an achievement for two 20 year olds who 4 years ago were struggling with the Certificate of Secondary Education. Both worked hard and will do great things.

Sunday 30th

I have never preached 'with a view to the pastorate' because at Llanidloes, I came from America and the call was given while I was there. We faced today with apprehension. This morning over 200 plus children were present. I preached Theology 77. I felt nervous, especially at the beginning. Norah and I went to Sunday School at 2.30 and went round the various departments - 100 altogether, including two adult classes. This evening, chapel was packed with 330. I preached Theology 92 and it seemed to go well. A social gathering in the hall was enjoyable with no fuss but a genuine friendliness.

The material I used for my sermons was what I used at Llanidloes in the 'theology series.' Theology 77 was on the theme of hope with the text, 'God could not possibly play us false, to give powerful encouragement to us, who have claimed his protection by grasping the hope set before us. That hope we hold. It is like an anchor for our lives, an anchor safe and sure.' (Hebrews 6. 18-19). Theology 92 was on 'The Apostolic Church' with the text, 'Full authority in heaven and on earth has been committed to me. Go forth therefore and make all nations my disciples; baptize them everywhere in the name of the Father and the Son and the Holy Spirit, and teach them to observe all that I have commanded you. And be assured, I am with you always, to the end of time.' (Matthew 28. 18-20).

JULY

6th

One of our young people asked to become a church member. He feels ready and eager. I first asked him 6 years ago, but now he asks! Marvellous at the age of 22.

Sunday 7th

God is working his purposes out as year succeedeth year. There is a direction, a source, guide and goal to history, and at times we witness it in our own lives. This evening John James phoned from Manselton to offer the call. In their church meeting, the church had voted 187 to 2 (and then unanimously) to ask me to serve as minister.

John James was secretary of the church at Manselton.

9th

The letter from Jack James included: 'We feel we have been guided in our choice and I look forward to hearing in due course that you, too, under the same guidance of the Holy Spirit, have been led to accept this invitation to the pastorate at Manselton.'

11th

Heulwen Evans has been accepted to study theology at Birmingham.
Heulwen graduated in theology before pursuing a degree in medicine. She is now in General Practice.

25th

Hilary Jones has decided to study theology at Bangor: the 8th of our young people to make this decision. Christ calls today; people answer the call and the future is exciting.
Hilary graduated with a first class honours in theology at Bangor.

SEPTEMBER

2nd

I am reading Calvin, digesting his theological approach and allowing myself to be penetrated by the Word of God. Returning from holiday I am refreshed in body, mind and spirit, ready to embark afresh upon the great adventure in faith, trusting in Christ. He alone can speak a word to today. Let us listen and obey. There are many things of which I am uncertain, but I am certain that Christ is life
Having spent four years on developing a series of 'theological material' based on the work of John Macquarrie, I was now beginning the search for another attempt at creating accessible material.

13th

I again looked at my Calvin notes, the order of theological themes in the series, glanced at other systems like Melancthon, the 17th Century Reformers, Brunner, Tillich, Barth, and then returned to Calvin. I am moving firmly towards Calvin's 'Institutes' as the source of the next series.

16th

One of the members of group put her finger on our growth: 'We now basically understand what Christianity is, but how do we get to feel it?' - and 'allow it to shape our living?'

20th

Can we ensure that the solid foundations will continue with a strong, flexible structure. I prepared lists of group members and discovered 130 people were loyal members with 100 very faithful.

Sunday 22nd

27 young people came to the cottage to discuss Theology 2.

Sunday 29th

A sister and brother were received into church membership: the last I shall receive at Llanidloes and they could not be a finer young couple. Today marked the end of the theology series. I started preaching this series 4 years ago, with the intention there would be 50 sermons. Today I preached Th 130 and it provided great satisfaction. Twenty young people came to the cottage.

OCTOBER

9th

Another group has created its own leadership. I am amazed by people's potential if they are encouraged and given basic training.

13th

Glanhafren for the final Youth Group (18 present) after 7 years since the first youth meeting and 4 years of theological discussions with young people.

25th

The completion of the most valid aspect of our Llanidloes ministry. The last house group met in Dolgwenith. They have been a grand faithful group and I have gained so much from them.

Sunday 27th

The close of ministry at Llanidloes. We all retired to the Schoolroom for a Children's service and the presentation by Jane. Glanhafren for our last Communion. This evening saw an excellent congregation before the presentation in chapel. Tea in schoolroom. Marvellous friends.

29th

We have left Llanidloes, crossed the Rubicon, left joy and challenge, and now face a great unknown. I must rise to the new challenge and serve God whose grace saves, serves and inspires.

It was a trauma to leave Llanidloes after seven years. There was the thought of starting all over again with the fears and challenges of a new beginning. The children were to leave a small excellent school at Trefeglwys and were to live in the city for the first time. How would they settle? Norah had been able to develop a full life because of caring and responsible baby-sitters. She was fully occupied in the church, especially in teaching Sunday school, leading a youth group, presiding at women's meetings and attending house groups. She also enjoyed a weekly painting class with a group of local women who were also in house groups. Life would be very different.

MANSELTON

1974 -1977

DECEMBER, 1952

18 THURSDAY [353—13]

INTRODUCTION

Llanidloes had been our first family home, Trefeglwys the children's small and happy school, Zion and Glanhafren our first ministry and we were saying goodbye to a small town in which we had lived most happily. What would it be like to live in a large town and minister with one of the largest congregations in Wales? We were soon put at ease. We were ministered to by a mature and maturing congregation. The children settled well and continued their education through the medium of Welsh, our house was comfortable and we soon found ourselves part both of a church and 'village' community. We enjoyed the benefits of a large town, Norah studied her First Year BD at Coleg Coffa, and the children took music lessons and enjoyed the fulfilling church life.

What we hadn't realised was that we had not come to live in Swansea, but in a suburb of Swansea. Swansea is a collection of 'villages' and our village was Manselton with its straight streets. The village was clearly defined and was quite distinct from Landore, Brynhyfryd, Gendros or other neighbouring Swansea villages. Although Manselton had members scattered throughout Swansea, the majority lived within walking distance from the chapel. That was our patch. The 'Congre' was on a corner and was very much a 'parish church' although there were also strong Anglican and Baptist Churches, as well as a Presbyterian and Methodist presence. We soon discovered new depths to Christian life in this community.

We were blessed with an enriched inheritance. Fred Noden had exercised a remarkable ministry at Manselton. Ordained as a young student in 1963, Fred had built up the church through a combination of gifts: a rare combination of a winning personality, a persuasive manner and a remarkable gift of pastoral care and visitation. He and his wife Christine became close friends during their ministry in Wilmslow and encouraged the development of the Penrhys-Wilmslow relationship in the Partners Group. The ministry at Manselton included nineteen elders which included a rich variety of gifts and experience, including young people who had been away for further education, and had returned to work in Swansea. Another group of elders had been deepened and challenged by serving as elders in the church on the Portmead/Blaenymaes housing estate. Now that the church had closed, they were eager to contribute from their experience. The congregation itself was a nurturing people, prepared to lead, serve and care in many aspects of church life: Men's and Women's meetings, Sunday School, the Band of Hope, youth work and serving alongside others in more 'secular' organisations. Coming to Manselton at this particular moment in our ministry was, and is still a gift we treasure.

The Induction on November 2nd was a remarkable occasion. It gave the opportunity for the people of Ebenezer, Pantycrwys, Llanidloes and Manselton to join representatives of the wider Church to celebrate this new ministry. It was a particular delight that James Wicksteed, Abbot of Caldey read the Bible, Pennar Davies offered prayer and Alwyn Charles preached the sermon. It could not have been a more fitting beginning. What would it be like the following morning? After the night before?

1. A WORSHIPPING COMMUNITY

The heart of the church was its worship. It enjoyed a remarkable music tradition (a previous organist had been Emrys Jones, the conductor of Manselton/ Swansea Male Voice Choir), a rich prayer life and meetings for all ages. Every Sunday there was an expectancy that the Word of God would break through the prayers, singing, reading the Bible, preaching and Holy Communion. Worship nurtured the community. I sense this deepened as the years passed and I learned to know the congregation at a deeper level. I knew the majority well through teaching an Adult Sunday School Class, discussions in House Groups, developing Morning Family Worship, enjoying their company on Caldey and above all through pastoral work.

2. A SERVING COMMUNITY

The Church's service of the community came as a revelation. Norah and I were both involved in pastoral visitation. I was supported by the Church Secretary, Jack James and Norah by Vera Smale, a senior elder. During the first year we visited several hundred families and began to discover the intimate patterns which made a creative community. There were also baptisms, marriages and sadly many funerals, but the consequence was we were soon an integral part of Manselton.

We were blessed by close relationships with many 'extraordinary ordinary people.' We met some during ordinary pastoral visitation, through discussion in groups but particularly during the moments of crisis in which the minister offers a particular service. Other remarkable people were visitors like the missionary Dr David Landsborough, and Dr Kao the General Secretary of the Presbyterian Church in Taiwan. However the experience which touched me most deeply was the relatively brief but sensitive relationship between members of the young mother's Sunday School class and a vulnerable single man threatened with eviction from his Council property.

Because the church was large, lively and caring, it related to many other organisations. Next door to the church was the Swansea Multiple Sclerosis Centre where the Manselton minister served as chaplain. There were strong links with Rose Cross, a Home for the elderly and Maes Glas, a residential home for the vulnerable. The young people created a special relationship with Maes Glas and two of its residents came to play a key role in the life of the congregation. These relationships made the church sensitive to the needs of others and in turn the church was served by compassionate and courageous people.

For many years Manselton had combined the celebration of Harvest with an awareness of Christian Aid and the World Development Movement. This resulted in an Annual Project which began in October and was completed at Christmas. It not only raised large sums of money but sensitised the congregation to issues of development. During our period we supported and received from partners in India, Bolivia and Rhodesia/Zimbabwe.

3. PERSONAL THEOLOGICAL DEVELOPMENT

It was only when I had completed the work in Puritan studies that I embarked upon the 'theological journey' of attempting to interpret the faith of the Church in our contemporary context. This had begun when I focussed on the development of house groups in Llanidloes and shared studies of 'Principles of Christian Theology' by John Macquarrie. As the four years passed, I extended my reading into historic and modern theologians but when I arrived at Manselton, I was ready for a new theological challenge. I began at the beginning by re-studying Scripture and through studying 'The Library of Christian Classics,' a collection in 26 volumes of the thinking of the Church from the 'Early Christian Fathers' to 'English Reformers.' The series included 'Early Latin Theology' translated and edited by Dr Greenslade, and Calvin's 'The Institutes of the Christian Religion' translated by Dr Battles. After a year of study I found myself focussing on Augustine, Luther and Calvin. The heart of my theological approach from this point on was to be 'All is grace.'

At the same time I was determined to spend time with the poetry of T S Eliot. I first struggled unsuccessfully with 'The Waste Land' as a young first year student at Swansea. I had a second attempt during spare time reading in Hartford. I was haunted by the wish to know what Eliot was saying to his and our generation. While in Manselton I studied with care his poetry from 'Prufrock' to the 'Four Quartets,' began to discover Eliot's journey into faith and found it speaking to my pilgrimage. Another element in the search was the discovery of the Biblical research and interpretation of Alan T Dale. His work which was often dismissed as books for children, opened up ways of enjoying and interpreting the heart of the Biblical message. I studied his 'New World' and 'Winding Quest,' and his Bible Study notes in 'Making Sense of our World' and 'Living in Our World.' This material made the Bible accessible to ordinary people.

The final member of my quartet involved the wider reading of great liberal thinkers like Kenneth Clark, Jacob Bronowski, David Attenborough, Ronald Eyre and J K Galbraith. I hope this helped prevent me from narrow theological exclusivity.

4. HOUSE GROUPS

The experiment of developing house groups focussing on theological issues was discussed and accepted by the elders and church meetings. As local ministers, we presented the programme to the Manselton Council of Churches and my Baptist colleague, Malcolm Hopkins and I enjoyed two happy years of leading ecumenical groups. The theological material was presented in the Church magazine, used in adult Sunday school classes, ecumenical house groups, the youth group, on Caldey and above all was appreciated in worship.

5. THE WIDER CHURCH

There was no 'aloneness' in Manselton. I had a particularly creative relationship with Malcolm Hopkins, and together we worked well with the three other ministers who served in the vicinity. At the Council of Churches in Manselton, we were engaged in developing a Local Covenanted relationship and this exploration was endorsed by Bishop Vaughan of Swansea and Brecon.

This was also the period of the inauguration of the Covenanted Churches at a special service in Aberystwyth in 1975, and the establishment of the Covenanted Commission. I was fortunate to be a URC representative on this body and remained so throughout the next 15 years. One of our specific tasks was to serve on the 'Worship Group' which met in our manse and developed a contemporary eucharistic liturgy. At the same time I served on the Doctrine and Worship Committee of the URC and the Theological Advisory Group of the Council of Churches for Wales.

One of the highlights of our ecumenical experience was when Eileen Steel, one of our elders served as a URC representative at the Assembly of the World Council of Churches at Nairobi. This brought the thinking and action of the WCC right into the heart of Manselton worship.

6. THE CALL TO SERVE AS MODERATOR

There could be no preparation for the phone conversation which took place late one evening in February 1977. Arthur Macarthur, the General Secretary of the United Reformed Church was only 'a name' to me and 'a figure on the platform at the General Assembly.' A year previously I had turned down the invitation to apply for the post of a lecturer in theology at Northern College, Manchester. I made my decision to remain in the pastoral ministry when I stored my theses on Puritanism on the shelf and began exploring theology in house groups. That was my vocation.

I knew that William Samuel, the URC Moderator for Wales was to retire at the end of August 1977, and that a committee had been established to look for a successor. But the request from Macarthur came as a complete shock. I was 37, had been in ministry only 10 years and had recently come to Manselton. However when I discussed the issue with family, close friends and senior elders at Manselton, I realized I had little choice. The Church had made a decision and I could either accept or reject. I felt I had no choice but to accept.

It was with sadness that we left Manselton at the end of August 1977, but at the same time we were excited and apprehensive of the challenge waiting us. What was the work of a Moderator? How was I to serve the churches of Wales?

1974

NOVEMBER

2nd
The Induction was thrilling, comforting, overwhelming, reassuring. The Abbot read, Pennar prayed, I gave my statement of faith and Alwyn preached from Ephesians 5 on 'the Church and Christ as lover.' The singing was overwhelming.

Sunday 3rd
Ministry at Manselton began yesterday evening, but today work began, almost seven years since the ordination at Llanidloes. Leading worship will be a much greater challenge here. Evening Communion had a congregation of 300.

4th
My first funeral is of a 69 year old man living on the council estate and who had dedicated his body for medical research. A young couple called about a baptism for Sunday. Mens Fellowship of 70 to whom Miss Smale spoke on 'Iona.'

6th
Prayer Meeting at 7.30 with 40 present, a marvellous spirit and three led in extempore prayer.

Sunday 10th
Leading worship with large receptive congregations is both a challenge and comfort. I should learn rapidly from this experience.

12th
The slow interesting task of meeting the members of the church will go on for months. The scheme for worship will take the form of a year's cycle based upon a theological system centred on 'The Institutes.' The material will be duplicated and linked with discussion groups.

DECEMBER

13th

The first visit to the Multiple-Sclerosis Day Centre has been intriguing and enriching. I have accepted the position of Chaplain and see how much I will learn and receive from their courage and cheerfulness.
The Mary Cave MS Day Centre had been recently opened just behind the church.

22nd

I am grateful to be strengthened, comforted and challenged by the Gospel setting of Manselton. We rejoiced in the Children's 'Christmas around the world:' Dylan was a cowboy; Cath a little Welsh girl, and Hugh a king. Plenty of good new carols. After an evening of carols, Koinonia and Second House went Carol Singing in the centre of Manselton. 40 of us sang and collected £98.
Koinonia was a group of 'older young people' who were now in their 20s. Second House was a gathering of older teenagers. Both groups met on a Sunday evening.

Christmas Day

I would not have linked today's lectionary readings from Song of Songs 2 and John 1 but in fact I saw them as the expression of the emotional and intellectual in the Person of Christ. My theology has leaned towards 'conceptualism' but must be balanced by the glorious love song of Solomon.

30th

130 from the MS enjoyed the pantomime, 'Mother Goose' at the Grand with Ryan Davies who dominated the Show and met the MS afterwards.
Ryan Davies was a very popular entertainer of the 1960s and 1970s. His series with Ronnie Williams 'Fo a Fe' has become a Welsh comedy classic.

1975

JANUARY

2nd

I completed Luther's 'Romans.' Since July I have read the two greatest works of the Reformation: this commentary by the early Luther, and Calvin's 'Institutes.' I have taken careful notes which will provide insight and information for the next series of sermons. The basic standpoint which I reached during the Llanidloes series has been deepened and consolidated by the rediscovery of the emphasis on the grace of God as the sole criterion for salvation. What other hope is there? How can I appear before God unless God is the one who comes in Christ? My knowledge of God and self can only be through Christ, and he is the centre of Scripture. I must search the Scriptures, the Reformation and Augustine.

7th

While we were at Westminster College, Colin Gunton introduced me to John Macquarrie and we had lunch together. He was most interested in the work at Llanidloes, especially as we used his approach to theology. Martin Cressey and David Thompson (Churches of Christ) led a debate on re-baptism. John Huxtable presided at Communion.

I had been appointed as a member of the Doctrine and Worship Committee of the United Reformed Church. I remained on this group until my appointment as Moderator. An annual residential meeting was held at Westminster College, Cambridge. On this occasion, Colin Gunton, fellow Mansfield student introduced me to Macquarrie. This was also a period leading towards the union with the Churches of Christ. One of the major issues for discussion arose because of the Churches of Christ emphasis on believer's baptism. I was to meet this issue again and again during the discussions within the Covenant and the Council of Churches.

18th

A lovely journey to Aberystwyth with snow on the hills, blue sky, lovely crisp air and a sense of this being an exhilarating part of winter. Siloh for the Service of Thanksgiving for the Covenant. Worship was exciting, well constructed, encouraging in its bilingualism, sense of adventure and

thankfulness that great traditions were growing together. The Archbishop preached very well.
Siloh was one of three Welsh speaking chapels belonging to the Presbyterian Church of Wales in Aberystwyth. Huw Wynne Griffith was minister. Gwilym Williams (G.O.), Bishop of Bangor was Archbishop from 1972 to 1981.

20th
Started Augustine's 'Enchiridion,' reading 30 pages and taking notes.

FEBRUARY

Sunday 16th
The liturgical rhythm of Preparation, Word and Response/ Eucharist is now our pattern for every service. This evening I preached on suffering and pain and many made a point of thanking me for expressing their problems and meeting a real need.
The three-fold pattern now seems a matter of form even in nonconformist worship, but the service with which most of us grew up reached its climax with the preaching of the Word, and if there was Communion, it was usually seen as a 'second service.' There was often a marked division between the 'two services' when non-communicants would leave the chapel.

21st
My first 'church' funeral at Manselton was a 'good' occasion. The 'end' was marked by dignity and compassion, sadness and hope as befits the passing of the human being.

28th
We celebrated St David. Most schools had a half day and children were dressed in national costume.

MARCH

7th
All is grace and there is nothing else to say. Theology is founded on the grace of God; worship is praising God for his grace; ethics is reflecting the grace of God in our lives. Grace is God in Christ. Christ reveals that God is grace; Christ shows what grace can and will do for man. I have now completed the four works by Luther in the Library of Christian Classics. Throughout this

year I have kept reading 30 pages a day (5 days a week). After completing Luther, I wonder where to go next - either forward to Melancthon or back to the Early Fathers. I decided to go back with a distinct sense of excitement.

10th

The MS 'patients' have so much to teach because they are grateful for their lives, thankful for friendships and happy for each day as it comes. Ryan came to MS and entertained us all for half an hour. What a great entertainer. Our children arrived and received autographs. I shall remember him singing 'Ar Hyd y Nos' for Mam who celebrated her 92nd Birthday

13th

The first CEM conference in West Glamorgan for 5 years. I drove to Sandfields Comprehensive. Excellent beginning with the Prologue taken by 2 young people. Their reading Dale and Quoist set the hallmark for the day. I gave a 25 minute talk on man/ sin/ falling apart and the kids audibly responded. This afternoon we watched the excellent Czech film 'Homo Homini.' 60 young people from 4 or 5 schools had their first taste of a religious conference and responded excellently.
CEM = Christian Education Movement. It is supported by the British churches and the local education authorities to support religious education in the schools of Britain. The new secretary for Wales was Ann Bonner Evans who was enthusiastic to promote the work throughout Wales. Michel Quoist's 'Prayers for Life' had a considerable impact on styles of prayer in the 1960s and 70s.

24th

Attended my first Theological Advisory Committee of the Council of Churches in Wales which met in the vestry at Seilo Aberystwyth. Chaired by Dr Yarnold (Anglican), the secretary was Owen Evans (Methodist) and the others were the Bishop of St Asaph, Eurwyn Morgan (Baptist), Cynwil Williams (Presbyterian). We discussed Yarnold's paper on theology behind world development.
There was considerable over-stretching of limited resources, and sometimes overlapping of agendas between the Council of Churches for Wales and the newly emerging Covenanted Churches' Commission. The search for visible unity was exciting but painful.

30th, Easter Day.

One of the greatest of Easters, from Palm Sunday through the crisis of Holy Week to the great climax. Our Christian experience has been strengthened and enriched. At Easter morning communion, on the spur of the moment, or an impulse of the Spirit, I felt it should be a family service and everyone had communion (150 of us). It was joyous and meaningful. Evening communion, included the MS, was so full that some had to sit upstairs. 230 took communion.

APRIL

12th

Mrs J. T. Morgan told me she was looking forward with great excitement to what comes after death.

Mrs Olwen Morgan was a formidable and compassionate Nonconformist leader, especially in the Swansea area. She originated from Ferndale.

18th

Mrs Mem Williams remembered Evan Roberts preaching at Capel y Gât. When he climbed the pulpit, there was a sense of awe; lots of people were changed permanently.

Here was a personal memory of the 1904 Revival. Capel y Gât, a Swansea chapel has long been demolished.

28th

I started 'Early Latin Fathers', edited by Greenslade, my supervisor at Oxford. How kind he was to me as a very raw research student. I would benefit even more now from his great insight.

MAY

1st

Most Swansea schools were represented in the Form VI Conference at Bishop Gore. A dogmatic and critical group from Dynevor were vociferous and dominated the morning, but as the day progressed, the more liberal spoke up and resented the others' aggression. A fascinating encounter but sad to see enclosed minds and attitudes.

Another Christian Education Movement Conference, held at the Roman Catholic High School.

21st

I read the remarkable Melancthon. How exhilarating to read this powerful and determined piece of theology after the medievalism which has dominated my last few months. I could feel the exhilaration and relief of those who heard the message of the Early Reformers. It was a new world - more accurately the old world of the Gospel was here again.

JUNE

7th

Malcolm and I shaped 20 theological themes for worship and discussion groups. Elders' Meeting set up a steering committee to help organize ecumenical and URC groups to begin this autumn.
The Baptist minister, Malcolm Hopkins and I agreed together on the themes. The fact that we could work ecumenically, and that it was endorsed formally by the Council of Churches and the deacons/elders of our churches made all the difference to the establishment of house groups. They were seen as an extension of the nurture and mission of the Church.

22nd

Visited an elderly member who spoke of her love for her husband who died 13 years ago, and of the romance of their meeting. She went on to talk of deaths (a) her husband whose last words were of his love for her; (b) her brother in law who told her that her husband would be fetching him at 1.30 - the time he died; (c) her sister in law who also expected the husband to come for her; (d) her mother who heard a heavenly choir and said she would die at 7, and did. She spoke in very lucid fashion and each incident was verifiable. Not surprising that she is ready to die. When I entered her room, she was reading the psalms.

23rd

I gave the induction prayer for the new minister at Llanidloes. My work in Llanidloes is completed.
I was succeeded at Llanidloes by the Revd Meirion Thomas.

AUGUST

Sunday 10th

We crossed the hill to Ty'n y Cornel, walked the old track, a pilgrim road across the mountain to Soar y Mynydd. We were on the back of Wales before coming down to the chapel and watching the dozen arrive for service. We were introduced before receiving so much from a great, simple, flexible, Spirit inspired service led by the Rev Bryn Roberts of Llanrmon yn Ial. He preached on prayer. Beautiful Welsh with fluency, power and tenderness. Hymns sung with meaning. We were in the heart of wildest Wales, in the most remote chapel in Wales, on a holy day and it was great to be alive and thank God.

As a family we spent a holiday camping in the Pysgotwr Valley, east of Llanddewibrefi. On this particular Sunday we walked to this most remote of chapels which has a natural 'holiness.'

Sunday 17th

A beautiful day in the centre of this wilderness of Wales. I was sleeping 'upstairs' in the Dormobile and when I first woke, I saw the breaking of light and mist filling the river. The next time I woke, the sun's rays were stealing over the hill lower down the valley; gradually the heat and light crept closer until at last the sun itself came over the mountain and streamed with power onto the bed. I felt warm in 5 minutes and settled to an hour's reading of Calvin. We walked the 2 miles to Soar y Mynydd and were delighted to join the children of Llangeitho and an almost full chapel for enthusiastic singing and excellent sermon by Penry Roberts' (Dr Barnardo's organizer) father. He preached from the last chapter of Philippians. When he went into the hwyl, there was an electric feeling.

22nd

I have completed Calvin's Institutes for the second time within a year, and the third time in my life. To read 'The Library of Christian Classics' has been an ambition during the last 12 years but I never thought I would do it. Having read the 4½ million words (11,000 pages) and taken 300 pages of typed notes from the Early Fathers to the English Reformers, I feel more in control of Christian theology. This will be especially true when I have filed and 'systematized' the notes in September.

Sunday 31st

The chapel was almost full but we managed to sit together. There was an air of great expectancy, as we waited quietly for the preacher (from Cydweli), John Williams (Brynambor) and the Codwr Canu to enter. They came at 2.25 and there was perfect silence until the service began - great singing, excellent reading, prayers and sermon on the authority of the Scriptures. Tea outside - chatted to Cyril Williams, the minister and locals who know us by this time. Evening service at 6. Great sermon on the poverty of man and the wealth of God. Saw three ravens - one of the Nant Llwyd brothers pointed them out.
John Williams was our neighbour at Pysgotwr. He passed every day and we often chatted, especially about chapel life. He was murdered in his own home in 1983 by Anthony Gambrell. The brothers of Nant Llwyd were well-known members of the chapel. Cyril Williams taught theology at Aberystwyth.

SEPTEMBER

26th

Beck Hall for the Annual Day School of the Swansea Free Church Federation Women. I spoke on the roots of theology: Bible, Church History, Doctrine, personal background and experience. Chatted with Sir Archie Lush (Nye Bevan's political agent) and Lady Lush. During lunch we sat by young National Union of Mineworkers leaders having a 2 week training course at the Extra Mural department. I felt there was hope of contact and conversation.
Mrs J T Morgan was the President of this important organization in Swansea life. Archie Lush spoke on 'Aneurin Bevan as a human being.' It was recorded by Hywel Francis for the South Wales Miners' library.

Sunday 28th

Our first Harvest and Project is on the theme of Bolivia. The play on Bolivia was a most telling parable. The Steels brought a new family - Professor of Electrical Engineering. In the evening service we were introduced to the South American situation with Helder Camara, the Bolivian Manifesto and the childrens play where they ate bread and milk. I used the 'elements' as a lead into the Institution and the offertory.
Principal Robert and Eileen Steel were members and future elders at Manselton and they brought Professor John and Julienne Oldfield.

OCTOBER

Sunday 12th

I took my new Sunday School class and introduced theological questioning. *This was a class of young mothers who came with their children to Sunday school.*

22nd

The Annual Synod of URC met at St Andrews/ Walter Road. The church is ready to move outwards if we train ourselves for ministry and mission. With the potential of Covenanting, local renewal could spark new life. But, there is the feeling that decline is inevitable and as long as our Moderator does not take up the challenge of the evangel, I see little hope.

28th

As a result of being immersed in 'The Institutes,' I sense that nothing valid can be said of God or man without reference to Christ's redemptive work.

NOVEMBER

7th

I am determined to write on Redemptive Christology before tackling creation and sin. The next themes will be Redemptive Christology: Christ as Prophet, Priest and King; God the Father; the Holy Spirit; the Trinity; only <u>then</u> shall I move on to creation, sin, man.
My reading, studying and discussing theology since 1969, and particularly since I immersed myself in 'The Library of Christian Classics', was 'forcing' me into the recognition of God's saving action in Christ as the centre of all thinking about God and humankind.

Sunday 9th

I took my class of 10 mothers who started being more open today. In Second House we discussed the first theological paper where they were introduced to Luther, Calvin, Suso, Athanasius. It was most exciting: 23 present.

13th

In the last series of theological sermons, I followed Macquarrie's structure but now I have my own approach and structure.

Sunday 16th

During the week we have been privileged and challenged by being taken across the world. Last Sunday we remembered Nairobi and Bolivia; on Monday we were in Bihar; yesterday in South East Asia and today in Taiwan with Dr David Landsborough. Here is the catholic and apostolic church. A privilege to meet a Christian of such humility, dedication and compassion.
On the previous Sunday we had been exploring the new project of Bolivia, and the World Council Assembly in Nairobi (to which Eileen Steel was a delegate); on Monday the Men's Fellowship had been addressed on a project in Rahini, Bihar; on Saturday The Revd George Hood of the Council for World Mission spoke on South East Asia, and on this Sunday we had the company of Dr David Landsborough, who spent the weekend in our home and made a powerful impression on all our children. His father, also David Landsborough established the Changhua Christian Hospital in 1896 and 'our David' served as a missionary doctor throughout his life, including 28 years as Superintendent of the same hospital as his father. He retired in 1980. Our children still remember his generosity when he stopped at our home for several days.

25th

Fourteen of us met in the second Ecumenical group, searching for deeper commitment without fencing or hedging. The potential of the Gospel and the people of God continue to amaze.

27th

After listening once more to Beethoven's Quartet 132, the Grosse Fugue and 135, I return to 132, the one with which I started 2½ years ago, and especially to the plaintive, tender slow movement.

DECEMBER

Sunday 7th

The nine in class discussed 'religious experience': they had not thought since childhood about Moses and the burning bush, and did not know the Isaiah experience. There are great possibilities in this afternoon group.
The Sunday School discussion group.

19th

Seilo for the first meeting of the new Committee for Covenanting in Wales. We were 6 representatives from each of the 4 covenanting churches, plus 2 from the Baptist churches who have covenanted (10 of them). Ungoed Jacob and Meirion Lloyd Davies acted as temporary chairman and secretary.
I had met these leaders previously when I was minister in Llanidloes. It was only a few years but a giant step for me from the days of Llanidloes and listening to these senior leaders.

Sunday 21st

I sensed the great excitement in the hall when I arrived as all the children were changing into angels, kings, shepherds, people from Taiwan, Nigeria etc. A large congregation for a service which balanced the traditional and modern, and held together the incarnation, atonement and the responsibility of the people of God. Donald Anderson and family present for the first time. After I had read the Bolivian letter, we discovered that Mrs Anderson had been born in Bolivia of missionary parents.
Donald Anderson was a fellow student at Swansea University. He became Labour MP for Swansea East from 1966 to 1970, and 1974 to 2005. He is now Baron Anderson of Swansea.

31st

Worship comes alive when the congregation is determined, compassionate and open. During the year our people have deepened in conviction and witness, and because of Caldey and house groups next year should see further maturing and mission.

1976

JANUARY

Sunday 4th

The first of a new series based on Dale's 'Making Sense of our World'. Hugh read the passage (My Own Experience) and Dylan read the hymn (638 - Great God we sing that mighty hand). This evening I preached on 'Resolve to Evangelise' based on Mortimer Arias' speech at Nairobi.

This was the beginning of a series of services based on a newly published booklet of Bible readings. Alan T. Dale attempted to introduce people completely unfamiliar with Scripture to the heart of the Bible. His approach is based on two deaths: the deaths of the cities of Samaria and Jerusalem in the Old Testament, and the death of a young man on a hill in the New Testament. The evening series was based on material from the Nairobi Assembly of the World Council of Churches. Mortimer Arias was a Methodist Bishop in the Bolivian Church. He was a delegate at Nairobi and Eileen Steel brought a personal letter from him to Manselton.

7th

Brian Wren, John Huxtable and I caught the 8.53 from Cambridge to Liverpool St. A most interesting conversation about how the URC's standing had risen since Union; a 'setting the pace' church.

Returning from the annual Doctrine and Worship meeting at Westminster College. John Huxtable the Joint General Secretary (with Arthur Macarthur) of the URC.

30th

Dale's material is a great discovery and I am combining a realistic approach to the Bible in morning worship, with the work in theology in the evening service. Christ is central to both approaches.

FEBRUARY

3rd

I led the Christian Education Movement Conference for Form VI students from Mynyddbach, Penlan and Cwmtawe at Mynyddbach School. The theme

I was given was 'Freedom' and I tackled it Biblically by expressing communal and personal responses to the Exile/ Death of Jesus. It was a deliberate step back from 1970 issues which are naturally blurred and difficult to assess. The reaction to using Biblical material was startling: 'It has nothing to say to us; we don't want religion imposed on us'. By keeping my nerve, as the day progressed we acknowledged the validity of exploring the Bible to discover man's response to life issues. By doing so, we held the conservative biblicists in the fold. They appreciated that the Bible was treated responsibly, and the great 'freedom' issues were all raised. Our best conference so far because of a genuine conversation.
I was using material from Alan Dale's recently published book.

19th

The new Covenanting Committee is holding its first meeting in St Illtud's in Cardiff. Bill Samuel was elected chairman and we had reports on national and regional levels. A preliminary draft of the Scheme of Union is to be brought to the Committee by Easter 1977 and presented to the churches before Easter 1980. There should be a full time secretary shared with the Council of Churches for Wales.
St Illtud's, almost in the grounds of St Margaret's in Roath was a community of Anglican sisters. Sadly it closed many years ago.

MARCH

Sunday 7th

We started Morning School with 3 teachers and 15 children.
Manselton's nurture programme was based on two worship services and an afternoon Sunday School which was highly successful, well organized and with dedicated teachers. It even had two adult classes, led by two elders. Probably the number in afternoon School would number close to a hundred. However there was need to develop a form of Family Worship and this was the beginning of this approach.

25th

The Covenanting sub-committee on worship arrived, and because I was responsible for convening, I discovered I was chairman. We read Dean Jacob's paper and by reading in turn, we went through it carefully, drawing comments and conclusions. The discussion was lively, informed, practical and concerned. We were struggling towards consensus and although we couldn't come to full agreement (especially on 'eucharistic presence'), we agreed that our next task was to approve an order of worship. Today we accepted the essential ingredients and move on to examine the Church of South India Liturgy and our own liturgies.

Ungoed Jacob had produced an excellent approach to an ecumenical celebration of Holy Communion. The committee represented the four Covenanted denominations and Malcolm Hopkins on behalf of Covenanted Baptists.

APRIL

5th

Multiple Sclerosis Centre for our first Communion. Nearly all, helpers and patients took communion.

6th

Three significant Christian 'experiences' by young women in our afternoon class: a young mother who becomes a church member at Easter, received her first Communion and found it exhilarating. A second who has been struggling with faith, recognised on Sunday evening that God's Spirit was everywhere and was with her. The third who has been growing for many years saw everything fall into place this weekend. These are remarkable testimonies to the way God works amongst us. Here are three mature, intelligent women, all of whom have started to arrive together, without conferring with each other

9th

The Covenanting Liturgical Group looked at the Church of South India liturgy. We found the framework acceptable: Preparation, Word and the Breaking of Bread. However dissatisfaction increased because of its language until ultimately only one of the Anglicans defended the service because it would be acceptable to Anglicans. For the rest, the language was too antiquated for contemporary Wales, and if Covenanting is to be speaking to today, its worship must be relevant.

18th, Easter Day

What a day; what a Sunday; what an Easter Day. The floor was packed and some had to sit in the side pews. The atmosphere was incredible; the singing remarkable. The whole congregation read the conclusion of I Cor 15. The receiving of a family by transfer; 7 members by profession of faith; 2 infant baptisms and 3 believer's baptisms. Communion for 300, including children. Coffee in hall. Everyone on top of the world.

27th

On Caldey we enjoyed a healthy confrontation between the extremes of a young 'Marxist' and a 'Jehovah's Witness' at which we were joined by the Abbot, Fr Robert, Br James and Fr Aelred.

MAY

5th

'This College [The Congregational College Manchester] is considering the appointment of a full time lecturer whose main responsibility will be in Theology... would you be interested?.. The post is not being advertised'. The interview is on June 1st. I would enjoy teaching theology and help train for ministry.

By deciding not to apply for the teaching post, I was in a sense saying goodbye to an academic ministry. I knew from my experience at Llanidloes that my full-time energies needed to be focused on the life of the local congregation. I would not be able to pursue research work while in a pastorate. I had been blessed to complete my theses in my first two years at Llanidloes because the basic research had all been completed before ordination. I have always felt the need to be single-minded and to focus on priorities.

6th

The Worship Committee looked at Series III of the Church of England and felt much happier with its language than with the Church of South India liturgy. In the afternoon we began constructing an act of worship until the Anglican representative burst out with 'you can't go on like this.' We were all disappointed, and do not know how to be more constructive.

In a sense the rest of us were all naïve to the 'political' aspects of ecumenicity. The Church in Wales was independent of the Church of England, and a group of 'amateurs' like ourselves could not begin to create a liturgy, however temporary it might prove to be. Most of us were coming from the call to reach out in worship to those inside and those outside the church. We were seeking a liturgy for mission.

14th

I drew up lists of Bible readings, texts, hymns, quotations and outlines of the 20 sermons. Interesting facts: 177 quotations from 49 writers: 84 Early Church; 20 Medieval; 73 Reformation; major ones Calvin 29, Luther 23; Augustine 22; Nyssa 10; Irenaeus and Athanasius 7 each. My second attempt at a theological series is almost accomplished. It is much shorter than the previous series and provides a solid introduction to the Faith.
I was laying a foundation for my theological journey.

17th

The third meeting of the Covenant Committee at Trefecca. I reported on the Swansea worship group and while having tea I sat by Huw Jones who told me of the Church of South India (Modern Language) version. He had a copy with him. We made new recommendations which included the endorsement of CSI (new version).
Huw Jones was to become Bishop of St David's from 1995 to 2002.

JUNE

25th

David, Llunos and Susan all have graduated with the BD (2a).
The three Llanidloes young people had graduated, David at Bangor, and Susan and Llunos at Swansea.

JULY

15th

The final session of groups for the summer. Malcolm has led a Baptist Group and an ecumenical group (which Norah attends) and I have an ecumenical and four URC groups which all started last November. Many have deepened substantially and relationships have developed. People are looking forward to resuming in the autumn.

17th

We were on Caldey when a bus load of Manselton friends arrived. We all went to the Abbot's guestroom for milk and biscuits and to our surprise were joined by John Huxtable who was making his first visit to Caldey.

26th

We looked at St Helen's Memorial Church on Portmead. This congregational church opened 19 years ago and closed 6 years ago. There is no church on this estate of 3000 houses. It represents our greatest failure in Swansea. Many think it is too late for such an area, or is it that we need a new strategy? House groups? Should there be a trained core before the church organizes large Sunday Schools, buildings, full-time ministry?

My first visits to St Helen's had been as a student at Coleg Coffa. Little did I think then that my final ministry would be in a very similar community.

30th

A meeting at Tŷ John Penri with Dr Kao, the General Secretary of the Presbyterian Church of Taiwan and his wife Ruth. He and the church are making a courageous stand against the government. We were in the presence of a potential martyr. This afternoon the local Catholic priest and I conducted the marriage of a URC woman and a Roman Catholic man. We presented the couple with the 'Common Bible.' This was the first occasion for a Roman Catholic priest to take part at a wedding in our church

The Reverend Dr Chun-Ming Kao was the General Secretary of the PCT from 1970 to 1989, during which period he became a political prisoner for assisting participants in the Kaoshing incident (1979). For this he was sentenced for 7 years in prison, and served his sentence from 1980 to 1984. While he was in prison, his wife Ruth Kao organized groups to help him and raised awareness in the worldwide Church about the human rights situation. When a new president was elected in 2000, Dr Kao was appointed a senior advisor to the Office of the President. At Manselton a piece of history was also being made with the wedding.

AUGUST

Sunday, 1st

Dr Kao of Taiwan took part in worship. His presence was remarkable. He is a devout, courageous Christian gentleman.

18th

Susan Roberts (Vaughan) was ordained to the Christian ministry at Bwlchyffridd. An exceptional act of worship presided by Dewi Eurig; ordination by Pennar, and I preached the charge to the minister.

I felt deeply privileged to be participating in the ordination of a young woman

who had entered ministry through Llanidloes, especially through theological discussion groups. That the ordination prayer was conducted by Dr Pennar made it all that more special. Susan had married Penri Roberts.

SEPTEMBER

9th

I read 'Prufrock' and feel I got to grips with it.
Another attempt to allow the poetry of T S Eliot to speak to me. The adventure had begun when I was a 19 year old student at Swansea.

13th

'Gerontion' is remarkable. Reading Eliot combines with Calvin and listening to classical music as formative areas in my theology.

15th

Good news from Llanidloes. There are 28 members of the youth group with two leaders.
Two of the main leaders were Pat Swallow and Gwenda Trow, still members of a Llanidloes house group in 2008. Other leaders of adult groups were Mary and John Breeze. All four remain good friends and members of the same house group, which we are privileged to attend in our retirement.

16th

I turn theologically to Calvin; Biblically to Alan Dale; poetically to Eliot and musically to Beethoven

17th

A privilege to spend the morning with 'The Waste Land'. I am beginning to enter a poem which has eluded me for 20 years. It was decided at the Council of Churches to accept the Executive's recommendation that a Commission should investigate the possibilities of a United Church in Manselton.
The Manselton Council of Churches wished to explore the Covenant Commission's recommendation to seek local covenants. Manselton was in an ideal position because of its natural geographical shape and its history of cooperation amongst the churches.

18th

Every time I read this masterpiece ('The Waste Land') I receive something new. I began the struggle when I was 19 and must now persevere and not allow this opportunity to slip away again. I am learning a language of poetry I had forgotten, or perhaps I am learning for the first time.

21st

A day with 'The Hollow Men'. As I follow Eliot's development, I am moving along with him. As well as noting his changing view of society and humanity, Eliot is helping me value words with their precision, associations, sounds, rhythms. I have been forgetting the value of poetry.

23rd

'Ash Wednesday' is so different in style and approach. We are on pilgrimage.

OCTOBER

Sunday 3rd

A great day: powerful, compassionate, reassuring. Our Harvest/ Project Service is to support the Honde Technical College in Zimbabwe/Rhodesia.
The church had embarked upon an adventurous project because the political divisions within the United Kingdom were also reflected in the churches. Was it 'Rhodesia' or Zimbabwe'? Who were the heroes and villains: white, black, 'democrats,' 'Marxists'? It provided a rigorous period of growing up.

5th

The day has been spent with the marvellous Ariel poems, especially 'Marina'. Something real was being grasped, especially when I remembered the long road from Prufrock through The Waste Land and Ash Wednesday.

14th

Norah had her first lectures. She enjoyed doctrine with Dewi Eurig, and Greek with Elwyn Davies. The magnificent 'Burnt Norton' has pushed my approach to language, and my attitude towards religious experience and life. The way Eliot says things and what he says are illuminating.
Norah embarked on her studies for a Bachelor of Divinity at Coleg Coffa. The year was to prove enjoyable and exciting. One of our regrets on leaving Manselton was that although Norah successfully completed her First Year BD, moving to Cardiff meant she was unable to complete her studies. She

was however able to continue studying Hebrew by attending classes led by Rabbi Rachel Montague in the Reform Synagogue in Cardiff.

18th

The five ministers in Manselton have agreed on a way forward. We could be creating an ecumenical experiment which will be a sign in Wales.
The five of us were ministers of the Anglican, Baptist, Methodist, Presbyterian and United Reformed Churches in the community.

21st

I finished 'The Dry Salvages' and went to the magnificent 'Little Gidding'. What a treasure.

29th

The overnight 'Read In' for Christian Aid raised £100 but also did something for us. Christ is the centre of the Bible and he opens up the most hidden corners. Three trestle tables were placed in the choir vestry, and 30 started to read 'New World'. There was continuous reading until 7.45 am.

NOVEMBER

3rd

I gave the Report on worship. The Archbishop asked that we use the traditional liturgy, as the modern one would create friction with some of his people. We agreed to set up a specialist committee to draft a new liturgy.
A meeting of the Covenanted Commission. After all the work of the Swansea group, we were asked to wait. One of the reasons of the Archbishop was that if we used any 'careless or inappropriate or less than exact words', priests like R S Thomas would be, to say the least, very unhappy. However our work helped pave the way for 'The Holy Communion' produced in 1981 for joint Communion services of the Covenanted Churches.

4th

The Executive of the Manselton Council of Churches was summoned to meet the Diocesan Church Unity Commission: Bishop Vaughan, Ungoed Jacob and the Rural Dean. We explained our views and hopes and by the end won their commendation, but it was hard earned. The job had to be done.

10th

Spoke to Sisterhood about my Desert Island programme: Beethoven's 9th (4th movement), Ellington's 'A Train;' Beethoven 'Opus 132 (slow movement);' Modern Jazz Quartet 'Round about midnight'; Bach 'Cello Sonata No 6 (gigue);' Streisand 'The Nearness of You;' Anthony Bloom's 'conversion;' conclusion to 'Little Gidding'.

15th

Christ's ambassadors are to relate to persons as persons. We are dealing with people. A representative from SASH called because he was worried about a man from Penlan who is to be evicted on Wednesday. I called in Penlan (no answer); returned (no answer); called again at 7 and this time 'he' came to the door and after a 20 minute conversation, promised to let me come tomorrow with others to clean. I called on several women to help.
SASH = Swansea Single Homeless Project. The story is one of a modern miracle, based on the graciousness of half a dozen Manselton women working with those responsible within the statutory authorities.

16th

After breakfast I went to Penlan to see 'the man' but got no answer. Chatted with the woman next door: 'he is a harmless man living in appalling circumstances.' I took a group of women but again he wasn't in. The social worker arrived; the neighbour pointed that he had taken his ladder. We eventually found him wandering on the estate carrying his ladder. He gave me his key and we returned. An incredible sight as we climbed the stairs and entered his flat: litter, tins in the sink; no furniture; a bed of filth. The women were great and by 4, the rubbish was outside in sacks. When he returned, we chatted. Can we win his confidence?

17th

A breakthrough. Is a miracle of compassion taking place? This afternoon I knocked only once, and he answered; we talked in his kitchen until 3. What a nice man. There is very little wrong with him that friendship and concern could not cure. He would have been evicted today. He was grateful for what had been done, but we all know the job is just beginning. He has hope at last.

19th

The organizer for home-help in Swansea, called and we went to see our friend in Penlan. As usual he was waiting. He is to have a home-help twice a week, and the lady's responsibility will be to cook his meals. Since she starts the week after next, we have to shape the house first. I met an official at the housing department - along with the social worker. A reprieve has been granted for two weeks.

20th

An amazing difference. One of our church members repaired a fuse and for the first time for 4 years, he has electricity. He has light at last after living in darkness all these years; it will transform his life. He has bought plastic sacks for his rubbish; his clock was working; he had poured himself tea; he had a marmalade pot and a bottle of pop (not cider or alcohol). He is beginning to grow.

24th

The morning was spent in putting up and making his bed; cleaning, hanging curtains.

25th

A phone message that an elderly member was dying and wished to take communion. I went at once. The lady asked for Psalm 23, we had prayers, Communion and I stayed several hours until she was ready to sleep. She spoke a 'Puritan sermon on her deathbed'. Here was courage, assurance, humility, forgiveness, gratitude and humour. This is what human life is about.

29th

Moved furniture to our friend in Penlan. His home help starts tomorrow.

DECEMBER

Sunday 26th

The Manselton churches, except the Parish Church, worshipped together this morning. We all walked to Bethel. A great sensation to see all the people making their way to the one place. The service was held in the hall and to our amazed delight it was crammed full; chairs had to be fetched from the chapel. Malcolm took devotions and the children's address; I preached the sermon on Magnificat which included singing Fred Kaan's hymn to the 'Red Flag;' Gwynfor gave the intercessions. Exhilarating worship; we belonged together as a community. It seemed crazy for Malcolm to announce that next week we would be meeting in our usual places.

Bethel was a small church belonging to the Presbyterian Church of Wales with a keen young minister, Gwynfor Evans, in his first ministry. The community responded to the hymn, both words and tune. That says a great deal about the community. Fred Kaan's hymn was inspired by the Magnificat: 'Sing we a song of high revolt'.

1977

JANUARY

Sunday 2nd

The beginning of the new theology series, extended from the 20 of last year to 40 this year. Those in house groups will use the same theme for worship and discussion. This series is shaped by the Church Year as well as being an introduction to Christian theology. Our first theme was Theology 1 on 'Who am I?' In the evening I resorted to the Dale series from 'Making Sense of Our World'. I am pleased with this combination for Nurture of 'theology themes' and 'understanding the Bible'.

This Sunday marks the beginning of a nurture programme which regrettably was to last only 7 months because of the unforeseen circumstance of my being appointed Moderator. It reflected a combination of a theological and a Biblical approach which found their focus in Jesus Christ. There was also the beginning of an attempt to shape the material according to the Church Year. The result was the publication of 'Discovering Together' in the summer of 1977, and a completely revised Second Edition the following year. Although I developed this material during the next dozen or so years, it was not until the opening of Llanfair that I was able to return to a systematic development of the nurture programme. At Llanfair I had the opportunity to refine it many times.

FEBRUARY

Sunday 20th

We sang a new hymn, 'Jesus the Lord said I am the bread' immediately before partaking in communion. 119 present including children. Our normal morning attendance has doubled within a year. The Project was completed with a grant of £760 to Christian Aid for the Honde school in Umtali.

25th

A phone-call this evening from Arthur Macarthur asking me to become Moderator of the Province of Wales of the URC. Three hours later I remain overwhelmed. I do not know what to say. Apparently the 10 Welsh delegates were unanimous in their decision, but on talking to the 10 from the whole church, it was felt that because of my youth, Howard Williams, Moderator of the North East should be offered the position. He turned it down because he has been Moderator only five years. I have been chosen because of my (1) work in the local church (2) ecumenical concern (3) concern for Wales. I am humbled by the challenge and confidence of our struggling churches in Wales. Should I take it to sound a new note of hope? Am I equipped for the work? Does God want this of me, and now?

26th

I have accepted the position of Moderator for Wales. I felt so sure this is what God wants that my decision has been made within 24 hours.
During those hours I had the opportunity to share my dilemma with of course Norah and the children, our families and respected leaders in the church. In a sense the decision was made for us.

MARCH

Sunday 6th

I have shared the decision with our people at Manselton. I'm not sure whether I made the decision, but I know I freely respond to this call. I shall seek to work vigorously and compassionately. The Elders supported with understanding, recognizing with joy and sadness I had no choice.

9th

A letter from John Huxtable, 'It was my business to preside at the meeting which had to consider this nomination; and therefore I feel I may write to assure you of the confidence with which the members of that group centred on your name. I hope that I may say that there is real need for you to put your own stamp on what you do... a new style is now necessary; and you are young

TYLORSTOWN FROM THE TIP, AUGUST 6TH 1966

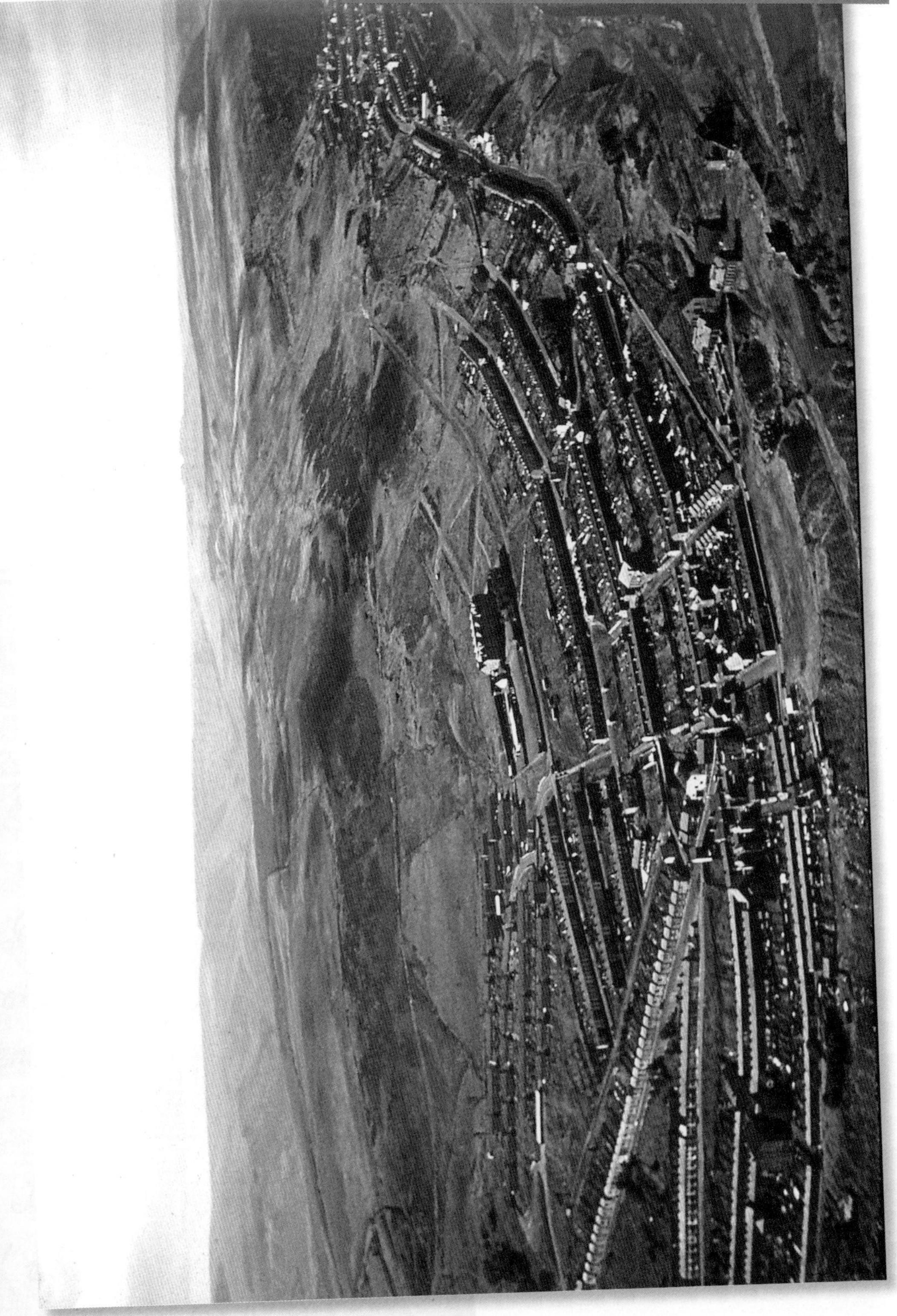

Outside Ebenezer, after a performance of 'Cissie in Toyland' by the Band of Hope in the Vestry. I am the page boy on the front left, aged about 4. (1943?)

Ebenezer Chapel, Tylorstown. Built in 1882 and demolished in 1989

With my grandfather (Dac, Church Terrace) in Porthcawl. c 1948, aged about 9

Tylorstown Junior Boys' School, 1947. I am back row, second from left. Our teacher throughout the Junior School was Mr David Rees.

The Rhondda County Grammar School for Boys (Porth County) Cricket XI. I am first left in front row. 1956.

First year University. A walk in Clyne Gardens after dinner at Neuadd Gilbertson. May 10th 1958.

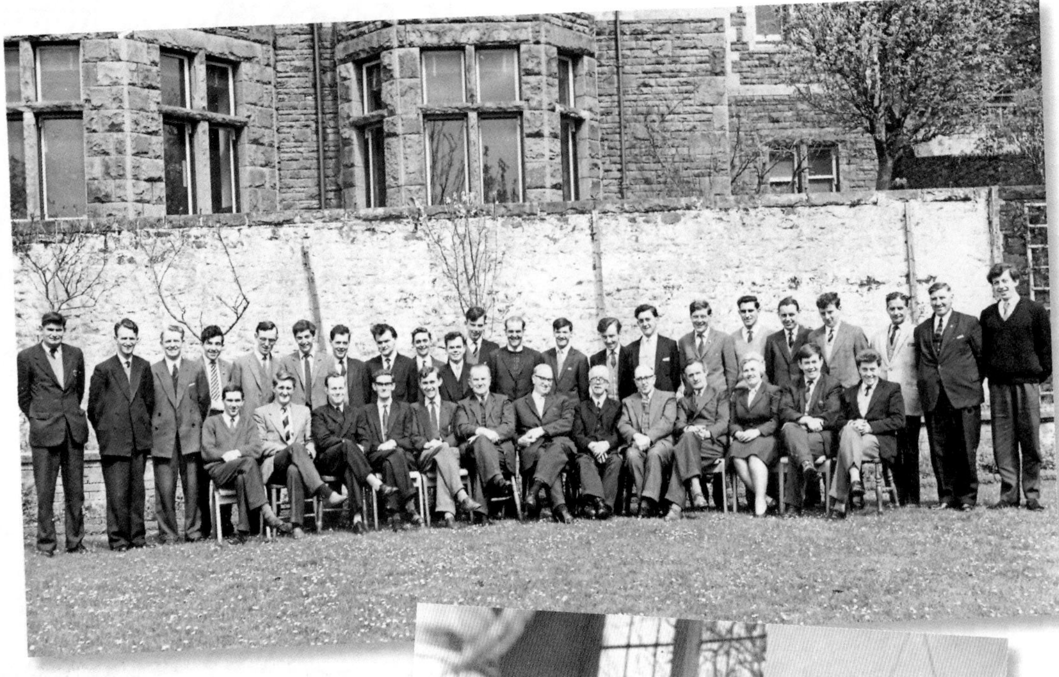

Coleg Coffa'r Annibynwyr, Abertawe 1963 with Principal Pennar Davies, members of staff and students. I am front row 5th from the left.

In the pulpit at Maesyronnen Congregational Chapel with fellow student, Emyr Evans, March 7th 1962.

Signing the marriage register at Pantycrwys, Craigcefnparc, August 3rd 1964.

Norah on our honeymoon on Skye, August 13th 1964.

Mansfield College, Oxford, 1965.

Mansfield College Cricket XI, 1965.

Hartford Seminary Foundation, Connecticut, 1965

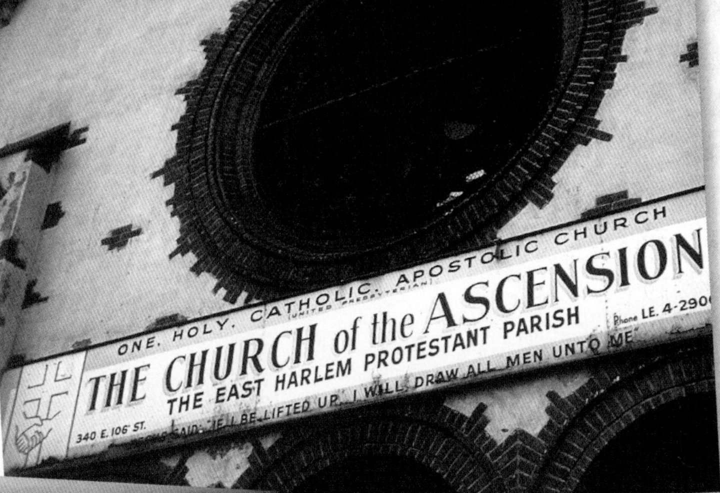

The Church of the Ascension, East Harlem Protestant Parish, New York, Easter Sunday 1966.

Broadview United Church of Christ, Hartford, Youth Group Reunion, May 17th 1970.

Zion Congregational Church Football team at Victoria Park, Llanidloes, May 15th 1969.

Preparing for the Christian Aid Walk, outside Zion Llanidloes, June 28th 1969.

Annual Sale of Work at Zion: Catherine presents my mother with a cake after 'opening' the Sale, October 25th 1973.

Sunday School outside Hall at Manselton United Reformed Church, c 1976.

The first Protestant - Roman Catholic marriage at Manselton of Ann and Zbiszek, by Father Morrisey and me, July 30th, 1976.

Ryan Davies with Hugh, Dylan and Catherine when he visited the Multiple Sclerosis Day Centre (the Mary Cave Centre) on March 10th 1975.

The first Manselton Church Family Day on Sunday July 10th 1977 at Talyllychau (Talley Abbey).

A Llanidloes and Manselton Group on Caldey in the lounge of St Philomena's with Z and Jo.

Closing worship at St Illtud's on Caldey.

The first Hungary/ Wales exchange group on Caldey, July 12th 1987.

Moderators' meeting in Tavistock Place: Peter Chesney as Chairman and Howard Williams as Secretary.

At the Reformation Wall in Geneva on Moderators and wives' visit to Geneva, April 3rd, 1982.

Outside the Synod Office, shared with Minster Road URC, !989.

Ordination of Pamela Lewis at Carmarthen Road, May 17th 1984. Malcolm Page, Synod Clerk (on left) and Glyndwr Harris, Chairman of Ministries Committee (on right) of Pam Lewis.

Ordination and Induction of Julian Thomas at Gilwern, January 30th 1988.

Beulah Rhiwbina weekend at Trefeca.

The Welsh group outside the Reformed Theological University at Debrecen, Easter Sunday, March 30th 1986.

Visit to Maerdy Colliery, March 11th 1986 with Revd Andrew Morton, Vicar of Maerdy, Eric Price, Lodge Secretary and Norman Hadfield.

Kántus sing in St Andrew's URC, Roath, Cardiff July 18th 1984.

Norah and Sithembeso from Zimbabwe
outside the Worship Tent at the World Council
Assembly at Vancouver, July 1983

Norah with some of her 'small group' at Vancouver.

Meeting John Paul II in Cardiff Castle, June 2nd 1982

Presenting *Y Beibl Cymraeg Newydd* to Metropolitan Philaret of Minsk at the Danilov Monastery, October 4th 1988.

enough to be able to give that new departure which is now necessary in my view not only for the URC but also for Wales at this juncture of history.'

APRIL

2nd

My minister died last night. Alwyn Charles, one of my greatest friends and a man who has influenced me as much as anyone, died in Bangor where he had lectured in Christian Doctrine for ten years. My memories go back to 1951 when he came as minister to Ebenezer. He was fresh from college and he presented me and my chapel friends with a new spirit to the Christian life. He was one of us, a real human being. I remember going with him and others from chapel to the Tudor Hall Cinema, Ferndale; bringing students from the university at Cardiff (probably The Student Christian Movement) to speak after chapel; his producing Passion plays in the chapel and in the Welfare; taking us to hear Niemöller; teaching us week by week in Sunday School; then in 1960 when I decided to enter the ministry, his kindness with me at Alltwen; going to the Cyfundeb at Bristol; while at Oxford, meeting him at Windsor (where he and Pegi took Norah and me to Heathrow to see the jets flying to the United States - his insistence I should study there); while I was at Llanidloes, his visit to our youth group at Rhossili, joining us at Caldey; his great sermon at my Induction at Manselton (he could not come to my Ordination at Llanidloes because of snow;) our walks on the prom during Summer School at Aberystwyth. What a loss to Wales and the Church of Christ! What a gain in the eternal kingdom to have such flair! I read I Timothy 1.1-2 - just opened Bible - and Alwyn speaks again.
'Paul, an apostle of Christ Jesus by the command of God our Saviour and of Christ Jesus our hope, To Timothy, my loyal child in the faith: Grace, mercy, and peace from God the Father and Christ Jesus our Lord'.

Sunday 3rd

I asked that the Tanzanian hymn 'He has arisen, Hallelujah' be offered as a thanksgiving to the life of Alwyn Charles, and it was sung with great joy.

10th, Easter Sunday

The Resurrection was celebrated with joy. The floor was packed and we stood to thunder the Eastern Orthodox greeting; infant baptism and new members before communion for 250.

Sunday 17th

Manselton has presented us with new strength through its worshipping life: the church family worships.

21st

Is it possible for Wales to discover the power we experience on Caldey?

28th

The Commission recognized that a tough challenge lies ahead but there is also an earnestness, a sense of responsibility, humour and a willingness to criticize and be criticized. We discussed ministry in Yarnold's paper and noticed that Anglican and Presbyterian/ URC use the same words of deacon/ elder, but the words have different meanings. God has entrusted his treasures to the churches and we need to learn how to share them with each other and the world.

We were discussing 'Covenanting for Union in Wales' and were in the process of producing 'Principles of Visible Unity in Wales' which was published in September 1980. The Revd Dr Grenville Yarnold, a Canon of St Asaph, had been a representative of the Church in Wales on the Joint Covenant Committee since 1967. He had been a physicist before ordination.

29th

Unless the work is developed locally and regionally, the Scheme of Union will only be a paper scheme.

I was already aware that 'A Scheme' would be of little value unless ecumenism was rooted locally. However much 'principles' were discussed and even accepted by the 'hierarchy' of the church, it would count for little until the local Christian community cried 'this is the reality of Gods presence, ministry and mission here in this place'. The recognition that the local vision needed to be rooted in community was one of the many factors which led us to Penrhys.

30th

I believe my life will be spent serving Christ in this nation. The URC is ecumenical, new and open; we have historic roots with theological and evangelical toughness; we live in a nation which can respond to the love of Christ; we need theological and liturgical forms which will be appropriate for the people of our nation. I believe my own work has been in the right direction, but we need methods of reaching the wider community. What of house groups? retreats on Caldey and at Trefeca? How can we encourage people to take on positions of leadership? There are opportunities for growth and renewal.

MAY

3rd

Michael Hubbard and I were received as new Moderators by the vote of Assembly. We shook hands with John Young, the Moderator of Assembly. I then realized I had been accepted.
Although Michael and I had both studied at Mansfield, we met for the first time on the platform of the Assembly at Birmingham. We became close friends and as Moderators stopped together at the Quaker Penn Club when we came to Moderators' Meetings in London.

7th

St David's Roman Catholic Church (at the instigation of Ron Howells) had a day of recollection at Stella Maris, a convent in Eaton Crescent. My theme was 'A Christian Progress': the sense of the absence of God; Discovery; the Sense of the Presence of God. I used Eliot's poetry in three 25 minute talks. An Anglican Eucharist this morning and a Folk Mass to close. The sisters are trained in seeking God's presence. Extempore prayers - like a Nonconformist prayer meeting. The church is drawing closer together.
Ron Howells was a faithful and visionary ecumenist. At last I was able to use my work on Eliot. It had been a long time coming.

13th

I enjoy the good ordinary straight streets of Manselton, with shops on corners, people shopping, old and young people chatting on doorsteps in the warm Spring sunshine. I felt I belonged and wanted to continue to share its life.
I had walked onto the hill called the Racecourse (greyhound racing at one time?) behind Manselton and had that experience of community I had known on the great tip above Tylorstown in 1966 and on the Gorn Hill in Llanidloes.

Sunday 22nd

We worshipped in the hall, with tables forming a square. Adults sat around the table and children sat on the floor inside, safe in the fold. The theme was the

Fatherhood of God and we acted the parable of the Lost Sheep. I found the lost sheep hiding behind the piano and carried him back on my shoulder. Then an infant baptism. Children in Communion and 130 received.

Sunday 29th

All baptized during my ministry were invited to the Cradle Roll service. Sixteen little ones turned up - out of 22. We also celebrated the church's birthday; two were baptized as believers; and a baby baptized. The baptized received an account of the resurrection from the Good News Bible. 200 present.

JUNE

1st

Nigel Goodfellow preached his 'trial' sermon with sincerity and careful preparation. He preached the Gospel. His theme was 'trusting God' in which he used Dale's account of the Good News, Psalm 91 used at Compline on Caldey, and referred to our visitors from Taiwan last year.

Nigel was to enter the ministry of the United Reformed Church through Manselton. He has served as a hospital chaplain since 1992.

9th

'The Ascent of Man' has such penetrating human insight. It reminded me of the catholicity of knowledge and urged me to beware of dogmatism which only sees truth in one's own thought and life. I am apprehensive of the new perilous fundamentalism slowly permeating Welsh church life. What future lies ahead for our churches? Whatever the failure of the 'old style liberalism' it created openness of mind and spirit.

'The Ascent of Man' was the book based on his television series by Jacob Bronowski.

Sunday 19th

The Christian community at Manselton combines stability of fellowship with a sense of adventure. Why? Because the church is centred on Christ.

30th

At Summer School I chatted with John Humphreys. He is a first class student and I would be delighted to see him coming to minister in Wales.

John Humphreys was ordained and inducted to the ministry of Bridgend and

Pontycymmer in 1978. Later he was to serve in the Reformed Church of Hungary and to be the only person to serve as a Moderator twice in Wales from 1989 to 2001 and in Scotland from 2005.

JULY

Sunday 10th

Our first Church Day went beautifully. We boarded buses and drove to Talley/Talyllychau: 180 of us had lunch on the grass in the ruins of the abbey; games to get to know each other; communion in the abbey with a table in the nave. I had my back to the high wall, the people sat on the grass and we shared bread from a large loaf, and wine from large jugs, distributed by the Sunday School teachers.

The abbey at Talley is unique in Wales in being founded for the monastic order of the Premonstratensians, or White Canons. Their constitution and way of life was based on Cistercian lines, even adopting the same white habit, but followed the Augustinians in their undertaking of duties within the parish.

Sunday 17th

Our joy was shared. The hall was packed with 200; children sitting on the floor. Our theme was on the changes in the Council for World Mission which became operative this week. The children went North, South, East, West; fine baptism and an excellent communion. Evening worship with 120. Morning services have doubled, averaged 130 this year and the age has halved.

We worshipped in the hall because of refurbishment in the chapel. CWM is a worldwide community of Christian churches. The 31 member churches are committed to sharing their resources of money, people, skills and insights globally to carry out God's mission locally. CWM was created in 1977 and incorporates the London Missionary Society (1795), the Commonwealth Missionary Society (1836) and the (English) Presbyterian Board of Missions (1847).

Sunday 24th

300 different worshippers and our membership is 300. These have been wonderful 3 years. This morning Principal Steel read the lesson and Mrs Steel spoke on the CWM service of thanksgiving.

25th

We have learned so much from one of our number who has been described as 'disabled.' Chatted with the Abbot, Fr Joseph, Fr Robert, Z and Jo whose grand-daughter drowned at Sandtop last week. Our 'disabled' friend spoke of how he learnt to walk by the age of 10; he understood Ecclesiastes because he had been a patient at Hensol castle. This man is a thinker.

Caldey never failed to surprise with joy, but also this time with tragedy. Z (Polish) and his wife Jo looked after the Guesthouse. We had become close friends over the years. One of our members of Manselton who was a resident at the Maes Glas care-home shared his experience and taught us the heart of the Good News.

Sunday 31st

No sadness because my emphasis is that I will be continuing to serve Manselton through the wider ministry. 200 this morning in a superb act of family worship, based on the priesthood of the People of God. Hugh and Dylan read the Bible; Cath read a hymn; Alexia and Raymond offered prayers. What singing! What worship! This evening the floor of the chapel was very full, close on 300, for a remarkable service based on the People of God as Servant/King. A great final act of communion. Hopeful and not in the least tearful. We were moving on together. 500 worshippers today - 400 different people. A great day and a wonderful three years.

Leaving Manselton did not seem like the end, but it marked a profound change for the family. For Norah and the children, the church was the nurturing community. For Norah it meant leaving her studies at Coleg Coffa. This was a wrench but she was compensated theologically by immersing herself into the life of the Synod.

AUGUST

15th

I finished Küng and found little which was not familiar. At first this disappointed me, but on second thoughts I am pleased. It shows my material in 'Discovering Together' is mainline theology and agrees with the best ecumenical thinking; it shows the barriers between the churches' theology are breaking down; it shows how I have grown since reading Macquarrie 'Principles of Christian Theology' in 1970. Until 1970, my field was church history, and theology was a great unknown.

'On Being a Christian' by Hans Küng was published in German in 1974 and in English in 1977. I had bought it as a tribute to the friends at the Day of Recollection at Stella Maris. Although the Vatican rescinded its permission to Küng to teach Catholic theology, he remains an emeritus professor of ecumenical theology at Tübingen.

31st

The end of my ministry at Manselton. Three very happy years. The discoveries made during my first seven years of ministry bore great fruit in the receptive Christian people of Manselton. I have renewed hopes for 'the Llanidloes experiment' because house groups are continuing to deepen under their own lay leadership, and are ready for positive ecumenical cooperation. Manselton is safe with fine lay leadership and solid groups, vibrant morning worship and a concern for mission. I am grateful for 10 years in both local communities and tomorrow I begin a new ministry. I am apprehensive but God will enable me fulfil the challenges. The work will be done not by me but through me. I wish to continue to be Christ's instrument

A MODERATOR

1977 - 1989

INTRODUCTION

Gerard Hughes wrote The God of Surprises. There could also be a book called 'The God who Takes Risks'. The Assembly Appointments Committee looking for a new Moderator for Wales was chaired by John Huxtable, the Associate General Secretary of the United Reformed Church. The Committee was composed of 10 from Wales and 10 representing the Assembly. Their first choice was the experienced Howard Williams who was already serving as Moderator of the Northern Synod. The Assembly Committee felt he would have been ideal to introduce the United Reformed Church to Wales. However, Howard was convinced he should continue to serve in the North to introduce the role of Moderator to a largely ex-Presbyterian Synod. The lot therefore fell on me. Apparently I had been the choice of the Welsh representatives from the beginning. They were taking a great risk. If it had been a post inviting applicants, I would never have asked for application forms! But because the Church had made the decision and offered an invitation, I responded to the Call.

I had no idea of the role of a Moderator. Both my ministries had focussed on the local and I was ignorant of Synod structures. I had met Bill Samuel, our Moderator, several times, particularly at the annual Ministers' Summer School at Aberystwyth and Trefeca, but I had no understanding of his ministry. The one fact I remembered was that the URC in Wales was in such a decline that the Moderator believed it to be terminal:

'At the Provincial Committee meeting at Newtown, the Moderator gave a very dismal report on our denomination: 255 churches in 1971 (200 by 1980; 100 by 1990); 74 ministers (50 by 1980; 20 by 1990), and no prospect of lay leadership'. (March 15th 1971) This had in fact not taken into account the schism which took place within Congregationalism in Wales with the formation of the United Reformed Church in 1972. 156 local congregations in Wales entered the United Reformed Church and constituted the first Synod which met at Charles Street Church Cardiff, on 18th October, 1972.

1. MODERATORS

In 1919 the Congregational Union of England and Wales adopted a scheme for Provincial Moderators. It is not until there was a more acute awareness of national consciousness that the name 'province' has been replaced by synods, and in Wales and Scotland 'national synods'. England and Wales was divided into nine provinces and the Moderator was appointed 'to stimulate and encourage the work of the denomination' and 'to assist churches and ministers in all matters connected with ministerial settlements and removals'. For Congregationalists the heart of decision making lay with the Church Meeting. The Moderator was in a sense a direct advisor to the local congregation. For the Presbyterian Church of England, the heart of oversight and discipline was conciliar and lay with Presbytery and General Assembly.

When the United Reformed Church came into existence in 1972, it attempted to combine the Congregational personal oversight of the Provincial Moderator (responsible to the local church meeting) with the Presbyterian conciliar oversight of the Presbytery. It was accepted that there would be a period of learning and readjustment as ex Presbyterians began to grasp the role of Moderators, Synods and Church Meetings, and ex Congregationalists learned to work in presbytery (District Council). However not much learning went on in Wales partly because there had been only three Presbyterian churches (two in Cardiff and one in Swansea). The Moderator had also convinced many of the churches to enter the URC because 'there won't be any difference... we are the same people wearing different hats'. The Scheme of Union which had been passed by Act of Parliament, was not introduced to Wales.

I was not the only person in Wales to be uncertain of the role of the Moderator. I had a lot of learning ahead. On my first visit to Church House in London I was presented with a copy of 'The Manual' of the United Reformed Church which defines the role of the Moderator:

'There shall be a Moderator for each provincial synod, being a minister appointed from time to time by the General Assembly to which he shall be responsible. The Moderator shall be appointed for such term not exceeding seven years as the General Assembly shall in each case think fit... the Moderator shall be separated from any local pastoral charge; he shall stimulate and encourage the work of the United Reformed Church within the Province; he shall preside over the meetings of the Synod and exercise a pastoral office towards the ministers and Churches within the province; in consultation with interim moderators of local churches he shall suggest names of ministers to vacant pastorates; he, or his deputy, shall preside at all ordinations and/or inductions of ministers within the Province; he, being a member of each District Council in the Province, shall participate with each such Council in the discharge of its responsibilities and in particular in the oversight of local churches and ministers. The Moderators of the Provincial Synods shall meet together at regular intervals for the better discharge of their duties'.

One of the functions of the Moderator was to 'suggest names of ministers to vacant pastorates'. No Moderator could do this on his own and the result was the strange institution known as the 'Moderators Meeting' held each month at Church House in Tavistock Place, London. The twelve men (they were all men in my time) soon became close friends and colleagues because of their common function. At first I was greatly supported by the older men but the time passed only too quickly for me to become (with Michael Hubbard of Western Province) the senior Moderator, although still the youngest in age. Moderators share a range of experience at the disposal of the whole church. During my time in office, our fellowship was strengthened and our experience enriched by study visits (with our wives) to Geneva, Hungary and Ireland.

There was no period of working alongside, no interim period, no learning programme. On the first of September 1977, I walked to the office in St Mary Street and started. What? I had no idea what the first phone call or letter would bring. At least there could be no e-mails! However, I was most fortunate to inherit the friendship and expert services of a part-time personal assistant in Gwyneth Lawrence who had served under my predecessor and with whom I worked throughout my twelve years as Moderator. I began where I started in my previous ministries in Llanidloes and Manselton. I was eager to know the churches and the people. I began with the local because I felt that the centre existed to serve the local.

2. THE LOCAL CHURCHES

I respected the small local church, particularly when it was struggling in its mission. Was it because of my upbringing in Ebenezer? Was it my experience as a student in Coleg Coffa where I empathized particularly with the declining churches of the Valleys? Was it because I had received so much from the small but stable Glanhafren? On our first Sunday I looked at the United Reformed Church (URC) Year Book, found the smallest church in Cardiff and that evening, as a family we worshipped in tiny Hannah Street, off Bute Street in the Docks. I was fortunate that, during the early years in particular, Norah and the children accompanied me on my Sunday visits to churches. Often we were the only family in worship. Some churches had not welcomed a family for many years. Throughout the twelve years I made every effort to lead worship and serve all the churches, whatever their size and wherever they were in Wales. I fulfilled that ambition and had the greatest satisfaction in presiding at Communion at Maesmynis high up in Epynt on July 23rd 1989, just five weeks before I completed my second term as Moderator. Throughout the years, on almost every Sunday and on a multitude of other occasions, I was visiting the churches for worship. That proved the greatest satisfaction of the Moderator's ministry. From Llanfaches to Penmaenmawr, from Maes Pennant to Milford Haven, I - and often our family, received the same welcome and koinonia. I came to have the feeling that we were One Church within One, Holy, Catholic and Apostolic Church. The heart of the mission of the Church is local. The congregation needs at times to be supported, challenged and encouraged in its life of worship and service. The local usually, but not invariably knows what is best for its community.

One of my difficulties on arriving at the Synod office was the absence of information about local churches. All I had to help were the names of churches and their officers found in the General Assembly Annual Year Book. No records existed. My predecessor felt no need for a filing system because of the combination of a good memory and his experience of the churches of South Wales which had continued since the 1930s. But this did not help his successor! In retrospect it was perhaps as well to begin with a clean sheet. I had no preconceptions and the only way to learn was through meeting people face to face.

3. DISTRICT COUNCILS

The Moderator is a member of District Council in the discharge of its responsibilities. Unfortunately the majority of congregations in Wales had no connection with a District Council or the Synod. The only relationship between the local and the centre was the Moderator and the Finance / Executive Committee of a dozen people, mostly male ministers (meeting six times a year). The only communication between this central committee, (always meeting in Cardiff on a weekday), and the churches took place in the annual Synod. This was held on a Thursday and was attended largely by ordained ministers and retired lay people. Channels of communication between Synod and the local churches needed to be created.

Local congregations were suspicious of Cardiff because they felt isolated and vulnerable. 'Cardiff wants to close us down and take our property away from us'. In fact congregations were isolated. As I visited the churches throughout Wales, the predictions of decline seemed ominously true. In 1974 the 39 ministers of the Wales province served 68 churches. 104 were outside pastoral care. How could they be shaped into pastorates and given ministry? Not without District Councils and District Pastoral committees. In 1977 only the South Wales District was functioning effectively. It had a Pastoral group and had begun five yearly visitations. It was a long and arduous struggle to create six District Councils with pastoral committees, but the effect of their industry and patience was that by 1988 there were 47 ministers serving 112 congregations. That still left 42 churches outside pastoral care, but at least there now existed a structure and process through which all congregations could be offered ministry.

Many of the new pastorates were ecumenical. The URC worked hard in developing close relationships at local level with the other churches in Wales. One remarkable statistic for 1988 was that of the 5000 churches in Wales, 55 were in ecumenical pastorates (1%); of the 154 URC churches, 31 were in ecumenical projects (20%). This reflected the time and effort put into creating pastorates and providing local ministry. This process has accentuated throughout subsequent years and shows the Welsh commitment to the ecumenical vision which created the United Reformed Church in 1972.

4. SYNOD COMMITTEES

In 1977 there was one Synod Committee: the Finance / Executive Committee agenda was almost totally composed of property matters. Moderator and Synod Clerk also served as Chairman and Secretary of the Trust Bodies. Very few people knew 'how the system worked'. It all took place in an office in Cardiff. The Synod met annually to approve/rubber stamp decisions.

The next twelve years saw a deliberate attempt to encourage people from all over Wales to participate and initiate work previously not done at any level outside the local congregation. Synod gradually developed groups concerned with Faith and Life, World Church and Mission, Church and Society, Ministries, Youth, Property, and Finance, and was coordinated through a General Purposes Committee. A hundred people, most of whom had never been used by the wider church, helped further the mission of the church at Synod level and there was new life, new programmes and new relationships. The taking of risks helped the church grow.

5. MINISTERS OF WORD AND SACRAMENT

The Moderator's report in 1971 forecast a shortage of ministers. The decline in the number of congregations would be accentuated by the unavailability of ministers.

Candidates for ministry from Wales became increasingly rare. It was also difficult to attract ministers to Wales, partly because 'they won't want us across the border'. Between 1967 and 1977 there had been seven ordinations in Wales, all of whom had been trained in Wales.

My first ordination was on September 3rd 1977 at New Trinity Cardiff and my final engagement as Moderator was an ordination on 31st August 1989 at Cwmbran. Between those two dates, 37 students from Wales were trained for ministry (an average of three each year) and there were 30 ordinations, 27 of whom were for stipendiary ministry. Of those 15 emerged from Wales and 12 came from other Synods. Amongst those ordained were John Humphreys, Peter Noble, Kevin Watson and Howard Sharp, all now serving as Synod Moderators. Wales was able to attract experienced ministers into Wales and this helped provide a varied, competent and dedicated ministry. Many of these senior ministers had been trained and had served in the Presbyterian Church of England and they brought a much needed new insight into Welsh church life. It would have been an abortive exercise for Districts and Synod to create viable pastorates if they had not been able to attract able ministers. Wales was greatly blessed.

6. TRAINING FOR MISSION

The creation of local pastorates resulted in the arrival of new ministers. The development of Synod and District structures encouraged participation by a large number of people, some of whom were new to wider church activity. Their meetings resulted in both formal and informal training. Self-training took place informally by creating committees of people who shared a variety of experience. People trained themselves by shaping agendas appropriate for the local, district and national contexts. In a more formal context, the ordained minister could take advantage of the School of Ministry, weekends for young ministers and their spouses at venues like Llanthony, the annual Summer School and the opportunity of sabbatical leave. The women of the Province continued to meet at Llandrindod every year; the Church Life Committee organised weekends at Trefeca and there were District and Synod youth activities. The training of elders became a priority and I enjoyed numerous elders' training days in all the Districts. And of course there was the opportunity to visit Caldey. Throughout the twelve years, three times each year, 20 people were able, on each occasion, to find the island not a place of 'retreat' but a place of advance. Reading the Bible, breaking the bread, and sharing fellowship were focussed in innumerable memorable experiences.

As the church grew in confidence, Synod organized more daring and elaborate activities. The first Provincial Day at Llanidloes in 1982 attracted 2000 people and the second occasion, also in Llanidloes in 1984 brought together 1500, again from all over Wales. 1986 witnessed the remarkable ecumenical Teulu Duw when 20,000 people converged on Llanelwedd and enjoyed Bishop Tutu's inspiring presence. In 1987 the General Assembly met in Wales for the first time, and Saint David's Hall, Cardiff was packed for a memorable act of Celebration. The people of the Welsh Synod confidently shared their style of worship and mission. My final Synod Day included my fare-well as Moderator in September 1989.

7. ECUMENICAL ACTIVITY

The Moderator was regarded by other denominations as the representative of the URC. Ecumenical responsibilities and representing the URC in official functions became a most significant element in the work. The Moderator attended the Covenanted Church Leaders meetings, locally in Llandaff and Newport, and nationally in Shrewsbury. I continued to serve on the Covenant Commission throughout my period as Moderator. I noted the tension between those pressing for 'immediate joint recognition of ministry' and those who wished to encourage local ecumenical projects and therefore provide a local groundswell which would make joint recognition inevitable.

The URC had entered into the Covenant for Visible Unity with the other Covenanted Churches (The Church in Wales, the Methodist Church, the Presbyterian Church and a dozen Baptist churches in the Baptist Union of Great Britain) and also was a member of the Council of Churches for Wales. I became President of the Council of Churches in 1986 for two years, and was then asked to continue for a further two years. This resulted in my having a 'presiding' responsibility during the 'Not Strangers but Pilgrims Process'. The decisions to proceed towards 'Churches Together in Britain and Ireland' and 'Cytun' were made at the Welsh national conference at Bangor and the British consultation at Swanwick. During those years I also served as a member of the Assembly of the BCC, one of whose memorable meetings was in Cork.

On the wider ecumenical front, Wales enjoyed the visits of John Paul II in 1982, the first delegations from China and the USSR, Jim Wallis the American social activist, Bishop Desmond Tutu preaching at Teulu Duw, and Emilio Castro, the Secretary of the World Council of Churches.

8. CHURCH AND SOCIETY

The main focus of my work was always to strengthen the life of the churches. In my earlier years this meant helping the United Reformed Church to arrive in Wales in reality, as well as in name. It involved the creation of a Synod framework, developing District Councils, shaping pastorates, encouraging ministry, and helping the Church initiate new programmes of worship, education, mission and with young people. At the same time there came the imperceptible development of ecumenical relationships locally and nationally.

As a student and during my previous ministries, I was concerned about the interface between church and society, but while serving as Moderator, several pivotal experiences demanded a more focussed response. I was invited by the URC to lead its first official delegation to Hungary since the Hungarian Revolution of 1956. Relationships between the Presbyterian Church of England and the Reformed Church of Hungary had become very tenuous during the darkest days of the Cold War, but in the early 1980s steps were taken to renew traditional relationships. A small delegation spent two weeks in Hungary and a few days in Prague during Easter 1983. Because the British religious and political media focussed on the underground church in Eastern Europe, the prevalent British impression was that all other Christian bodies were time-servers. The Hungarian journey became a personal pilgrimage and the consequences proved far reaching. I went to Hungary fearful of what I might discover. I returned aware of the life of a great sister church in the Reformed faith, and with the obvious recognition that the majority of people were yearning for a more peaceful, stable society. One of our recommendations to the appropriate Assembly Committee was the twinning of a URC Province with the Hungarian Church. If you suggest, you get landed with the job! During the next 6 years, young people left Wales to work at diaconal homes in Hungary; others taught English at the seminaries at Budapest and Debrecen; John Humphreys, our minister in Bridgend and Pontycymmer spent 4 years as assistant to Bishop Tóth in Kálvin Tér, Budapest; groups of young people from Wales and Hungary made several interchanges, and Norah and I led a group of 53 from Wales to spend Easter in Hungary in 1986.

The Christian Church crosses political and economic boundaries but the policy of the British government demanded that we needed ultimate weapons to defend ourselves against an ultimate enemy. I returned from Hungary determined to ally myself with those seeking to break down barriers between West and East, and to oppose the continued reliance on nuclear weapons. I was already deeply suspicious of our government's foreign policy because of the jingoistic propaganda reflected in the tragic Falklands War. Those who demanded that as a nation, we embark on a crusade to defend islands in the South Atlantic were in control of our nuclear arsenal. I spoke in favour of the Synod's resolution for nuclear disarmament and seconded the resolution at the General Assembly at Brighton in May 1983 which resulted in the URC adopting the policy of being a 'nuclear disarmament church'.

During the following years the Synod supported the Anti-Apartheid Movement and advocated disengagement from South Africa. In Wales this was particularly controversial because of the Welsh Rugby Union's connections with South Africa.

The United Reformed Church was recognized as a Church prepared to speak and act on issues of social and political justice. It became part of its *raison d'etre.* However the church was to be tested by an issue which divided the whole of Britain in 1984-5. Where did we stand during the Miners' Strike? It was impossible not to take sides. My personal history and environment, and the contacts I had already developed with the National Union of Mineworkers convinced me that there could be reconciliation between the Union and the National Coal Board. Four Welsh Nonconformist ministers committed ourselves to attempt to cross the chasm between the two parties. We achieved this in spectacular fashion within Wales, and if it had been solely a Welsh issue, there would have been an amicable and just settlement. On the wider British front it was doomed to failure, and the consequences? The suffering of the miners, their families and communities. All Welsh pits were soon to be closed and only Tower Colliery experienced renewal to survive for a further decade. The struggle proved a steep learning curve and confronted many of us with the twin issues of 'the nature of community' and 'national energy policy'. The failure of successive governments to grasp the seriousness of both these issues continues to haunt contemporary Britain. For Wales, the reason for the existence of the coal mining valleys was destroyed. History was erased and no future promised.

9. PERSONAL AND FAMILY GROWTH

When we moved to Cardiff, I was no longer nurtured by a local congregation. This was not true for Norah and the children who worshipped and participated in the life of Roath Park with its fine minister Jeffrey Plowman. For our children, Cardiff was the city in which they grew up as teenagers. They continued with their Welsh medium education in Ysgol Gynradd Bryntâf, Ysgol Gyfun Llanhari for Hugh, and Ysgol Gyfun Glantâf for Dylan and Catherine. To this day, Cardiff is their home, and they are comfortable in the city and enjoy its opportunities and challenges.

The decade of the 1980s proved seminal in our experience as a family. It was a period when both Norah and I lost our parents, and when our brother-in-law and close friend, John also died. We had both been nurtured by loving families, and we were grateful that we lived near enough to Rhondda (my parents) and Clydach (Norah's parents) to be receiving so much from them even during their final years. It is not melodramatic to say that 'as they taught us how to live, they also showed us how to face death'. However, as often happens through grief, all our family received strength and comfort, and grew closer together.

For Norah it proved an exceptional period of personal growth. As well as being a member of the local congregation, she also became the first secretary of the Synod Church Life committee. In time this resulted in her being a member of the Assembly Church Life, and World Church and Mission Committees, and to being a URC representative at the Vancouver Assembly of the World Council of Churches (WCC). Norah's complete involvement in a preparatory conference for women in the Bahamas and her commitment to the work of the Assembly resulted in her speaking of her experience more than a hundred times throughout and beyond Wales. Just as Nairobi touched Manselton through Eileen Steel, Vancouver was lived by many through Norah's ministry. The children and I grew through Norah's experience.

Other factors deepened my personal growth. In the months before we left Manselton, I produced 'Discovering Together', a small book which combined the theological exploration which had taken place in Llanidloes and Manselton. The book went into a second edition which included theological extracts from the 'Library of Christian Classics', the Dutch Roman Catholic 'New Catechism' of 1970, the ecumenical 'Common Catechism' of 1975 and the Congregational 'Declaration of Faith' of 1964.

I spent several years reading Alan Dale's 'Winding Quest' and 'New World', checking the translation with the Revised Standard Version and all Dale's interpretation with 'The Interpreters Bible', 'The New Interpreters' Bible and 'Peake's Commentary'.

Alongside the gifts I received through theological and Biblical study came a prayer life deepened by Taizé, Iona and the World Council of Churches Prayer Cycle. John Paul, Brother Roger and Philip Potter all emphasised spirituality and social justice as the two hands of the Christian. Finally came the remarkable period in our sabbatical of 1988 in Eastern Europe, when Norah and I made the journey to Russia to present a copy of the New Welsh Bible to Metropolitan Philaret. In the glory of worship in Moscow, Leningrad and Zagorsk we experienced the living together of spirituality and faithfulness.

10. PENRHYS

As a boy I collected eggs from Penrhys Uchaf farm and played soccer and cricket on Moggs Field. As a teenager I walked with friends after Sunday evening worship at Ebenezer to Penrhys. As a young man I saw the creation of the new town and wondered what could be the role of the church.

In 1971 the Rhondda Churches of the Council of Churches of Wales agreed to work together to create a Christian Fellowship on Penrhys. By 1977 the programme ran out of money and it seemed the experiment would end. As Moderator I suggested that a URC salaried minister could be seconded to the Penrhys Sponsoring Body and minister to the Penrhys Fellowship. The new appointment would be funded as one of the thirty special ministries adopted by the General Assembly in mission situations which could not 'afford' ministry. Malcolm Hill began his ministry in 1980 and was succeeded by Pat Parrish in 1983. It was in 1986, while Penrhys was experiencing a particularly distressing time that Norah, the children and I agreed we should move to live on Penrhys.

There is no doubt that the whole family felt the 'call' to Penrhys. Norah in particular had felt for many years that this was a place in which she could live. She felt an empathy with the congregation and community. This had been deepened by her experiences in the wider church. The children had visited the area many times because of their grandparents' home in Tylorstown, and all of them had been affected by the harrowing experience of the Miners' Strike.

We moved to 12 Heol Dyfed in October 1986. Norah and the children worshipped in the little chapel and Norah was deeply committed to the church and to community life. I continued my ministry as Moderator with the 'only difference being a change of address'. However at the end of 1988, Pat Parrish had moved to Paignton, there was no minister on Penrhys and I was completing my second term as Moderator. I felt the call of God to serve as their next minister. Many reasons had drawn me to this point of decision: the emphasis on spirituality and justice, the experience of the Miners' Dispute, the conviction that mission and unity were two sides of the same coin, and of course living on Penrhys for two years. This seemed to be the right place for us to be at this point in time. Norah and I had gained a wide experience during the past 12 years and many wondered whether it should be spent with a congregation of ten on a marginalized housing estate? Only time would tell.

1977

SEPTEMBER

1st

When I woke, I felt so apprehensive and wondered how I would cope. I turned to Discovering Together and read the theme for the week. It began ‘A new day; a new start; a new world. We greet them’. I felt a good deal better, took a deep breath and Norah and the children walked with me as far as the office. *It is a walk of several miles from Llwynygrant Road in Penylan to the Provincial Office in St Mary's Street. I was particularly grateful for the reassuring welcome of Gwyneth Lawrence.*

3rd

My first Ordination. What format would I use? What would I wear? How would I feel? The ordination and induction of Michael Gudgeon at New Trinity was such a creative experience and I was with good, friendly people. *Was it a coincidence that the first ordination should be of the new minister to New Trinity Cardiff, the church which traced its origins to the ministry of William Erbery? I could not have been granted a greater gift. It seems even more strange that our son Hugh and daughter-in-law Mónika (Dylan's wife) should now be deacons/ elders there, and that our three children and families should be worshippers at Canton Uniting (New Trinity and Llandaff Road Baptist united in 1995).*

Sunday 4th

I looked for the smallest Cardiff church - Hannah St (off Bute St). Excellent service led by a lay preacher; the place was full; a first class sermon on ‘memory’; good communion at which we had to share glasses; marvellous atmosphere; members delighted to see us there.

The lay preacher was Arthur Porter who became a good friend.

7th

My first Moderators' Meeting. On the train I sat opposite two elderly women going on holiday with Saga to the Costa Brava - they played cards at 1p a time. Most serious enterprise. Douglas Stewart and I went to the Wigmore Hall to a recital by Georgetta Psaros, mezzo soprano, accompanied by Robert Sutherland. Lovely voice - awed by control of four languages.
Douglas was Moderator of the North Western Province and proved a helpful friend and mentor. Georgetta Psaros, critically-acclaimed mezzo-soprano and recording artist performed with The Royal Opera House, Covent Garden, The English National Opera, and many other prestigious companies.

10th

A useful encounter at Holywell. They had no idea which way to turn, and felt they had no support or advice in their struggles. If the local church, the District and I can work together, something can be done.
The beginning of my meeting local churches. In the early years it was usually a meeting to deal with a crisis. This changed as the years passed, and churches felt they could turn to District Council or / and Moderator for support and guidance.

16th

The desk is full of letters which have been answered but have no system. In the filing cabinet at home there are files for churches and ministers, but nothing has been added for 10 years. I shall have to find out for myself and confer with people 'on the ground'. There is no system for different aspects of church work - mission, education, social issues, youth.

20th

I have spent days clearing the desk with its jumble of letters and reports. How am I to discover the needs of churches and ministers and unlock the gifts in our churches? The infinite resources amongst our 10,000 members cannot be tapped until we know what they are. This will be one of my many jobs.

28th

I met the church meeting (10 people) at Llandrindod Wells. They have not used the main building for 4 years, and worship in the vestry. They have had a Council Order that the building is unsafe. They did not know which way to turn. After a long discussion, they decided to leave the premises, ask to form a United URC/ Presbyterian church and also develop Caebach.

After many years the building was demolished and a sheltered accommodation scheme built on the site. It includes a place of worship which is the home of the continuing congregation. Unfortunately the possible union with Ithon Road Presbyterian Church did not take place. Caebach was the Eighteenth Century building which had existed since before the expansion of Llandrindod as a Spa in the Nineteenth Century. It contains a memorial to Thomas Jones, Pencerrig, the Welsh artist. There exists a flourishing faithful congregation.

OCTOBER

6th

St Teilo's for the first concelebration of the Eucharist in Wales: the setting was the clean, bright chapel; the celebrants included the Archbishop and Windsor Hicks.

A memorable occasion. A concelebration within the Covenanted Churches in Wales took place for the first time, when a minister of the 'Nonconformist tradition' and a priest of the Church in Wales presided together at the Communion. It allowed all of the congregation to participate in the Communion and respect each other's traditions and views of ministry. Windsor was minister at Minster Road, Cardiff and Synod Clerk and regarded this experience as one of the most significant in his life. He had been ordained in 1946 and had never dreamt such an occasion would ever take place.

7th

I spoke (preached) at the Inaugural Service at the University College Swansea. I contrasted the bewilderment of a First Year student with the sense of mystery which comes from an acceptance of self, relationships and the universe. I used personal references from my first weeks as a fresher 20 years ago. It sounded bells for many on the staff as well as speaking to the students.

An experience to be 'home' at Swansea. In my sermon I quoted from my early days as fresher student from my diary from 1957. Principal Robert Steel had invited me to preach.

10th

I sat with the Pontycymmer elders around a lovely fire in the vestry. They were very dispirited and had little hope. However they bucked up with the possibility of a minister.

12th

Did it mark a new day? It certainly was a day of celebration and commitment. As I approached the church I was greeted by a huge poster 'Welcome to the Synod'. John Young presided and Arthur McArthur preached at the Induction; lessons by Mr Watson and Windsor Hicks; the 'Statement of Faith' led by Eileen Steel. Church packed (600). What singing.
My induction as Moderator took place at Synod at Manselton.

Sunday 13th

Yesterday was my first Synod. Laymen and ministers participated; the Synod was not a rubber stamp for the Executive, nor was it dominated by 'business and administration'. The URC is seeking the mind of Christ.

NOVEMBER

7th

The URC/Presbyterian Eastern Association met at St Davids in Shrewsbury. As we examined a document leading towards union, several Presbyterians stated their fears of the office of Moderator and its danger of prelacy. Bill did not help when he said that a 'Moderator was a kind of bishop; in fact a benevolent dictator'. What if he chose not to be benevolent? Are there checks and balances? I introduced the URC slant on the office and the atmosphere improved.
The English speaking Eastern Association churches of the Presbyterian Church of Wales had been involved for several years in a conversation with the Welsh Province. Could there be a 'United Presbyterian / Reformed Church' in Wales? More feasible were the possibilities of cooperation locally and regionally. However there were many 'unilateral' talks going on: with Methodists, Welsh Congregationalists (sharing a traditional heritage). Interdenominational negotiation and cooperation was and remains complex.

8th

A free concert at the Reardon Smith by the Gabrieli String Quartet. All the family sat in the front middle row, just feet from these artists who played Haydn and Shostakovitch quartets in the first half; and Debussy in the second. Music ranged from gay and precise, fierce and uncompromising to sensuous tender beauty.
These concerts were arranged by the Music Department at the University of Cardiff. The Gabrieli is one of the most well-known British string quartets.

9th
Districts Councils are essential to enable the Moderator make responsible decisions, and prevent the Moderator doing as he pleases.

19th
Our churches have many good, conscientious people, eager to find a way forward for the church they serve faithfully. We need a vision and ways to implement that vision. We have people with conviction and ability; we need models for today.

DECEMBER

Sunday 4th
A masterly performance of Dvorak's 'Cello Concerto' by Paul Tortelier and the Welsh BBC at the New Theatre.
Paul Tortelier died in December of 1990, at the age of 76. His musical legacy is carried forward by his son, Yan-Pascal Tortelier, the internationally famous conductor of the BBC Philharmonic.

9th
Ministry is Christ's gift and we enter ministry through baptism. All ministry is full-time, but within the ministry of the church, some are called and trained to the ministry of Word and Sacrament.

1978

JANUARY

10th
Nigel Goodfellow has been accepted as a candidate for URC ministry.
Nigel was a young man from Manselton. He is now a Hospital Chaplain in Newcastle upon Tyne.

Sunday 22nd
Penrhys for service at 6. After some difficulty, we found the room near one of the entrances to the Community Centre. When we arrived there were 5

ladies (4 over 70), 1 man and the preacher. Later a youngish couple arrived. The sermon was rigid and judgmental.
Our first visit as a family to the Penrhys Christian fellowship, supported and recognised by the United Reformed Church and seven other denominations who were members of the Council of Churches of Wales.

31st
The Synod structure exists to rubber-stamp decisions made by the Officers of Synod.
This is an inevitable consequence of a centralized structure where the Congregational tradition of local decisions were made by church meetings, and 'Welsh regional / national' decisions made by the Moderator and his advisory group. No decision making body existed between the local church and the Moderator and his advisors. This was a totally different system from Presbyterianism where decision making lay with presbytery and elders. The intention of the creation of Synods and District Councils within the URC was to bring together the best of the two worlds. In fact in Wales it strengthened the centre at the expense of the local - and there was no regional District structure. Checks and balances had become unbalanced and tipped towards the centre. Of course the General Assembly had become the over-arching decision making body for the new Church, but its influence depended upon all the other elements of the Church functioning effectively.

FEBRUARY

22nd
Bruce Kendrick's 'Come Out The Wilderness' is a classic of urban theology. Reading it has been a salutary experience and has confronted me with Christian courage and conviction. The ministry in Harlem combines the miracle of compassion with intelligence, determination and infinite patience. An original leap of faith resulted in fourteen years of an increasingly encouraging ministry in which the Gospel was lived. I felt humbled when I consider my puny efforts and comfortable existence. I started Daniel Jenkins' 'The British', a comfortable and urbane book. I shouldn't read it immediately after the Harlem experience.
Norah and I had visited East Harlem and the Church of the Ascension at Easter 1966 and been profoundly affected by the experience. She suggested that I read the book.

MARCH

6th
I met the elders of the West Wales District at Mumbles. This is the first gathering of elders since URC came into being - 80 present from most churches. I spoke about the opportunities presented by Caldey, the District structure, candidates for ministry. There was applause at the end.
The office of the elder was a cardinal gift from the Presbyterian Church of England. In Wales all that had happened was that deacons were now called elders but needed to become aware of their wider responsibilities.

13th
Provincial administration should be built on the foundation that the 'church is mission'. How is the church to fulfil its work? Structure is for mission and not preservation.

18th
Sixty elders at Salisbury Park Wrexham for the first meeting of North Wales Elders. The District needs reinvigorating and a new administrative model.

20th
The initial stage of enthusiasm and expectancy has been created; now comes the creation of the right 'structures' for mission throughout the Districts. In a meeting of North Wales ministers, we introduced each other; I talked about District and Synod expectations and the necessity of a mission strategy. There is considerable experience of mission amongst the North Wales ministers: Meirion Lloyd of Lushai; Alan Seager of Botswana; Percy Thomas from Indonesia and the Bible Society.
There was a range of Christian gifts within every District, and North Wales reflected this in abundance. The three ministers had retired to North Wales: Meirion Lloyd had served with the Presbyterian Church of Wales in North India; Alan Seager with the London Missionary Society in Botswana, and Percy Thomas with the British and Foreign Bible Society. None had been asked to serve the wider church, and were delighted to serve within the District and Synod.

APRIL

4th

Since 1971 I have taken seventeen groups to Caldey. How is that enriched experience to influence the churches? How can that 'vision' help the 'reality' of the local church? How can the style of worship, discussion and love become a normal experience?

7th

The Moderators are so different: the wisdom of Dick Hall; kindness and humaneness of Ron Taylor; careful ordered thinking of Alistair Walker; adroit language of Hugh Jones; warmth and friendliness of Howard Williams; agility of mind of Michael Hubbard; gentility of Douglas Stewart; spirituality and kindness of Cyril Franks; the ordered discipline and firmness of John White; the flair of John Williamson; the solid, careful Peter Chesney - good friends and colleagues. I trust them all, and will miss the three retiring this summer.

Those retiring were Richard Hall of Thames North, Ron Taylor of Eastern and Hugh Jones of West Midlands. They were replaced by Michael Davies, Colin Evans and Fred Kaan.

10th

Are ministers being trained to share theology and encourage family worship and house groups? Are they supporting the training of teachers and house group leaders? How does a local church re-train? The District must help. Can the District fulfil that ministry? Not in its present state. Can the Synod fulfil that ministry? Not in its present state!

15th

170 turned up for the South Wales District Day at Coleg y Fro. Their theme, 'celebration of the resurrection' should be experienced by all church members. How can it be introduced to them all?

25th

The first meeting of the Property Advisory Committee: Chris Webb, Graham Browning, John Reason, William Graham, Bill Samuel (Trusts), Alan Trinder, Selwyn Roberts and Malcolm, Windsor and me. An excellent start. This help is long overdue.

This was a new key development in the life of the Synod. Ministers are not trained to deal with property issues, and yet constantly the local church faces challenges with its property. This was the first time that the Synod had searched for professional support within the Church. The Committee was to prove a boon to the Church in every sphere. William Graham serves as Assembly Member for South East Wales.

27th

Malcolm Page has a marvellous grasp of many areas of church life, including the Scheme of Union, Trust matters and property. He has an incisive mind, sees problems clearly and has total integrity. His election as Synod Clerk has been critical.

Malcolm was minister of Star Street in Cardiff and served the wider church faithfully and wisely for many years.

MAY

16th

The Covenanting Commission meeting at Hawarden recognised that ecumenism must be manifested at local level and that church bodies are the enablers for this to happen. We must work locally and swiftly or our witness will be irrevocably impaired. The right questions are being asked.

20th

Thirty attended the structure review day at Windsor Place. In the morning, four groups explored Mission, Church and Society, Ministry and Worship, and Christian Education. This afternoon three groups discussed Administration, Property and Finance. In the reporting back, the emphases were on 'the Districts relationship with the local church', and the need for Synod Resource People.

The Synod had charged the Executive to establish a working group and report back within a year. It proved successful because there was a goal to be met. It was not a talking shop.

JUNE

17th

Fifty Pembrokeshire elders met at Haverfordwest. Each church introduced themselves with their potential and problems. We began to explore 'how can the churches grow?'

23rd

A meeting with Peter Noble of Brynmawr and David Fox of Newbridge. Both should make fine ministers.

Peter and David are Synod Moderator and Synod Clerk respectively. Tragically, David, a much loved and faithful minister 'disappeared' while on an adventure holiday in Slovenia in June 2008.

28th

Pennar spoke on Howell Harris. Pennar is a joy. How much we owe him. Eifion Thomas spoke with such sincerity: it was a beautiful expression of the faithfulness of the preacher of the Good News. We were humbled.

At the Ministers' Summer School, two senior ministers led us. Pennar was of course Principal of Coleg Coffa, and Eifion had served in local ministry in Breconshire since 1938. In URC circles he was known as the Bishop of Breconshire.'

JULY

25th

If ministers and congregations developed family worship, house groups, concern for theology, Caldey-like experiences, our situation in Wales would be transformed in a few years. For generations we have seen continued, accelerating decline and have not grasped that the power of the Gospel is always the same. What is wrong is our response. God is always at work in our land.

Reflection after another four days on Caldey.

SEPTEMBER

8th

Could we shape 56 pastorates by December 1981? We had dropped to 40 ministers by January 1977 and despite retirements we have now reached 46. The three issues are (1) shaping vacancies; (2) attracting ministers; (3) attracting the right ministers is the toughest but most important issue.

The whole of the United Reformed Church was looking at the issue of a fair sharing of ministry throughout the twelve synods. The oversight of this process lay with the Assembly Deployment Committee. The principle lay with the URC's vision of sharing ministry justly according to need. It helped transform our number of pastorates and ministers in Wales.

Sunday 17th

As a family we drove to Gwenddwr, turned towards Eppynt and ended up in the farmyard of the Gyrnos. We joined others walking through lush green fields to Beilheulog Chapel, dating to the 1690s, and in superb condition because of the hard work and care of half a dozen people. It is in a magnificently secluded spot. To my amazement people kept on arriving so that when the service started at 2, the chapel was full - gallery and floor - with 80 people, including many young people and children. Lovely day, great atmosphere, a lady led the singing by pitching. After a lovely tea, we returned to chapel by 6. Dusked beautifully - no light or heat in chapel.
The heart of Christian ministry.

19th

The Property Advisory Group was chaired for the first time by Chris Webb, a job he did gently and firmly. Many issues: Llandrindod looks increasingly hopeful; good signs for Tabernacle Ebbw Vale. Many property issues were dealt with expertly. What a relief compared with a year ago.

30th

A Christian Celebration - the ordination and 27th birthday of Dafydd; the inauguration of the United Reformed Church of Ely and the induction of Mary and Dafydd as ministers in a team, the first of its kind in Wales for the URC. It was held at a packed Saintwell - good hymns, clarity of language, fine sermon from Tony Burnham; I presided at communion which included passing the peace. George Thomas, Donald Anderson and Lord Mayor present. Fine meal at Grand Avenue, presided by George Vincent, chairman of District.
Another memorable occasion, especially as Dafydd was another Manselton boy, who had grown up during the ministry of Fred Noden. Mary Evans had been a faithful servant at Grand Avenue Ely since 1966 and rejoiced in the colleagueship and new shape to the pastorate. George Thomas was of course 'Mr Speaker' and Donald Anderson the MP for Swansea East - Dafydd's local MP and an occasional worshipper at Manselton. George Vincent was secretary of New Trinity Cardiff.

OCTOBER

2nd

Mary Evans arrived with a prospective candidate for the ministry: Kevin Watson, a young man of 25 from County Durham. He graduated in geography and is trained as a probation officer. He was a member of Grand Avenue for 2 years, is pleasant, has conviction and is articulate without being domineering. How marvellously God is working in the call of candidates for ministry!

Kevin studied at Mansfield, served in two ministries in Wales, the Rhyl Group, and Manselton where he helped the congregation move from the old premises to 'Christ Well'. Note the account of the move from Manselton to Christ Well in 'These Hundred Years' by Robert Pope, 2006. He is now Moderator of the Yorkshire Synod.

14th

Synod met on Saturday for the first time, and in the East Wales District (Victoria Road, Newport) for the first time. Because Synod dealt with the restructuring report, some were distinctly unhappy. It would have been fascinating to watch from the sidelines but being at the centre was exhilarating, dangerous and hopeful. Structures Report took an hour and was superbly introduced by Malcolm. All recommendations and nominations passed, plus two Synods a year. Lesslie Newbigin preached with his usual brilliance, and I presided at Communion.

A historic Synod because of its endorsement of the new recommendations. Lesslie Newbigin was a Bishop of the Church of South India from 1936 to 1974, and was the current Moderator of the General Assembly.

19th

Ebenezer celebrated its centenary. The church was founded in 1878 at about the same time as the sinking of the pits and the formation of the community of Pendyrus/ Tylorstown. Our family has been associated with the chapel, probably from the foundation - my grandmother belonged to the Sunday School; my grandfather was a deacon from 1911, and Dad from 1936 (both serving together for a while). Tonight I wore Dadcu's cuff-links, and Norah and our children sat with Mam in the family pew. There was a sense of community and trust that our future is in the hands of God. Great privilege to preach: what we owe our forefathers.

21st

A joy to meet Alan Dale at Manselton. This delightful, dedicated Christian described with verve how the work came into being. I sense he has experienced a good deal of criticism because he answered many questions defensively, often noting how he had been inspired by great British scholars. What was clear was his passion to communicate the Good News. He has succeeded in a way which will in time be recognized. I read Tom Torrance's introduction to 'The School of Faith', a collection of Catechisms. 'Discovering Together' has the same drive and style as the Reformed Tradition.

A privilege to meet one of the great and most humble teachers of the Bible.

Sunday 22nd

A perfect day with a great Christian gentleman. This morning Alan Dale's theme was the Last Supper and the words of Jesus. We chatted this afternoon and he spoke of the care he had taken with his work and how it had been read by some of the greatest scholars. He showed how he had used scholarship - Mark (Bultmann), Q (Jeremias, Manson). Excellent service at 6. Floor packed. He preached on Pentecost - hearing the Word of God. Simply and clearly put.

NOVEMBER

14th

In those early days of starting house groups at Llanidloes there was a young, shy girl called Llunos Jones who came, listened and rarely participated. Today I was her guest at Glynarthen to help set up groups in her community.

Llunos was now minister of the Welsh Congregational church at Glynarthen.

15th

Prayer Meeting at Hill URC, Swansea. Frank Trollope got on his knees in the vestry, praying that we might experience the risen Christ.

Frank Trollope was the church secretary. Of such is the greatness of the church.

25th

Another excellent young man has been ordained and began his ministry in Wales. John Humphreys is capable and compassionate, and will be a great leader. It felt like the start of a new day for the two churches.

John was ordained and inducted to the joint pastorate of Bridgend and Pontycymmer. As a result of the connection between the Welsh Synod and the Reformed Church of Hungary, John served for four years in Hungary. He followed me as Moderator of the Welsh Synod, and is now Moderator of the Scottish Synod of the United Reformed Church.

Sunday 26th

A day rooted in the Gospel. What could have been a day of ending a long tradition, happy associations and a century of continuity in a small tightly-knit community, in fact provided a gleam of light and hope. I led worship for the last time at Tabernacle, Ebbw Vale. The final hymn was 'Blest be the tie that binds.' A poignant but proud moment.

27th

John Humphreys was welcomed to Pontycymmer which has not had ministry for 28 years. I was delighted by the different atmosphere compared with my visit a year ago when they seemed down and out. Their only thought then was of survival. Doris Leyshon's sermon was as always, well considered, excellently delivered and full of the courage and joy that is Doris.
Doris Leyshon, a close personal friend of both Norah and me, served as an LMS missionary in Calcutta before becoming a minister in Ogmore Vale. Doris was an inspiration to generations of younger ministers. I was privileged to officiate at Doris' funeral in 2004.

DECEMBER

5th

At Penrhys I met David Reece, Archdeacon of Margam, Handel Bowen the secretary of the Rhondda Mains committee and Mr Cox, Vicar of Tylorstown. I put to them my suggestions and they responded graciously and enthusiastically: (1) we seek a URC minister for Penrhys (with Ferndale and Tonypandy) (2) URC meets the salary but expenses come from the other churches (3) the minister is to serve the community (celebrating sacraments for all Christians of good standing). That is the first hurdle and many lie ahead. Hope for Penrhys.
This was the tentative suggestion to the Penrhys leaders that the United Reformed Church might accept the ministry of Penrhys as one of its 'special ministries' under the deployment quota. There had been several crisis meetings during the past months because the denominations were either

unwilling or unable to meet the salary and expenses of ministry during this period of high financial inflation.

11th

The completion of the Yearbook. Our membership dropped by 100, but the number of children increased by 300 last year. We must watch trends.

1979

JANUARY

Sunday 14th

I presided at the service of recognition of Bethesda'r Fro as a church within the URC. A dozen members were received as well as adult and child baptisms.

Bethesda'r Fro is a historic Congregationalist cause. There is an irony about the fact that it is on the edge of the St Athan military site because Bethesdas most famous minister was Thomas William whose hymn 'Adenydd colomen pe cawn' is a hymn to peace.

20th

The first meeting of the Synod Church Life Committee: the first time for the Synod to have a forum for these crucial areas. The chairperson is the energetic and dedicated Alun Jones, and Norah is the secretary of this committee of ten. We started with Communion before all shared their concerns about the life of the church. It was decided to focus on ministry (especially auxiliary ministry) and membership (stewardship).

Alun Jones was an elder and organist at Beulah, Rhiwbina. It is not possible to over-estimate the significance of the creation of these Synod Committees. They brought potential leadership together and they helped nurture and envigorate life throughout the URC churches in Wales. This was true for the other committees coming into existence.

Sunday 21st

I preached at Llandaff Cathedral at the annual service of the Council of Churches for Whitchurch and Rhiwbina.

31st

The South Wales Pastoral Committee has developed into an effective group. They considered Beulah and Llanishen; Penrhys; the Merthyr Valley. The tragedy is that in no other District is this continuous work going on. I have encouraged the other Districts to have pastoral committees.

FEBRUARY

Sunday 4th

Alan Dale has died. It came as a complete shock as we heard the news on Sunday. I am grateful we met last October. He opens the sweep of the Bible in a remarkable way.

'Sunday' is a weekly programme on Radio 4 dealing with the religious scene.

6th

Cyril Franks, Tony Burnham and I drove to Penrhys to meet Handel Bowen and David Reece of the Mains Committee, and Brian Head and Jeanne Jones of the District. We had a tour of the Community Centre and visited the manse. Cyril and Tony are recommending that Penrhys be one of the special ministries for the URC. Marvellous news when it is official - and then to find a minister!

Cyril was Moderator of the Southern Synod and Tony the Secretary of the Deployment Committee of the URC. Tony was to become a Synod Moderator before becoming General Secretary of the URC. Brian was minister at the URC/Presbyterian Church of Wales united pastorate in Merthyr and Jeanne, District Secretary. Brian and I had been friends for many years, sharing the same lodgings while at Coleg Coffa. Sadly he died later in 1979. His widow, the Revd Nanette Lewis Head, was also minister of the URC and a friend from Coleg Coffa days. Nanette courageously was later inducted to the same pastorate as her late husband. She was an inspiration to the whole Church. Handel Bowen was Baptist minister in Ferndale and secretary of the Mains Committee; David Reece was Assistant Bishop of Llandaff and the committee's Chairperson.

8th

Moderators are aware of problems and potential: the decline in the number of viable pastorates; the shortage of ministers; the dwindling influence of the church within society. But there is a determination to fulfil the purpose of God in Christ, and Moderators can encourage morale and help the church to grow.

18th

How much tougher is life in Tylorstown compared with Cardiff. The climate and geography are harder; the houses smaller and more difficult to live in; it is more of a struggle to maintain the social and religious life. This is my background and the area I love and respect. I was reminded of the suffering and struggle my people faced when Dad mentioned that Dadcu had to be helped to climb the steeper banks underground by holding on to the horses tail. We have no idea of that way of life, but it has shaped me and I wish to discover more.

19th

The first meeting of the World Church and Mission Committee: Eileen Steel as Chair and Brian Head as Secretary.
This was the second of the Synod Committees to come into being. Eileen Steel was an elder at Manselton and had attended on behalf of the URC, the Nairobi Assembly of the World Council of Churches.

MARCH

1st

St David's Day evokes the past but says little about the future. This has been a special First of March because Wales and Scotland have voted on the government's devolution proposals. I voted in favour for several reasons: the accountability of standing committees; we are over-centralized; the Welsh issue.

2nd

D for the demolition of the government's proposals for devolution in Wales. No one could have expected the complete and devastating rejection by the majority of people living in Wales. Only 11.9% of the total electorate voted in favour. What is it saying about nationalism and attitudes towards the government? It is a most perplexing result.

7th

Daniel Jenkins invited me to the Athenaeum for a meal and a chat by the fire. He questioned me about latest developments in Wales. Although he appeared to be listening, I'm not sure. He is out of touch with what is going on in Wales. *'The Athenaeum Club is a gentlemen's club standing at 107 Pall Mall'. Dr Daniel Jenkins was serving as minister at Regent Square URC after a long academic and ecumenical career. He was a well-known writer.*

8th

I did not feel comfortable at the Athenaeum. How can the existence of such a club be justified? and how a minister can belong is beyond my comprehension! It must be pleasantly and conservatively reassuring, but how different from Jesus and his way of life. The Church dares not question life-style!

24th

At the Synod meeting at Portland Street, Aberystwyth, our only URC minister in Rhondda spoke against the Penrhys commitment. He was supported by the ex-Moderator who proposed we withdraw from Penrhys. When their amendment was put to the vote only 3 supported them. The resolution was then passed almost unanimously.

APRIL

21st

The Church Life committee has a deep concern for the individual Christian and the church, local and nationally: it discussed ministry, membership renewal, youth and children's work. This committee is composed of men and women with deep Christian conviction and expertise in their fields.

26th

The South Wales District Women's Meeting met at the United Church at Pontypridd, the first time it has been held outside Cardiff.
There was an assumption that Cardiff people would not attend meetings in the Valleys. Valleys people were of course expected to travel to Cardiff. Strangely it is the same distance from Cardiff to Pontypridd as it is from Pontypridd to Cardiff.

MAY

7th

It seemed blasphemous celebrating Workers' Day after an overwhelming Tory victory. I experienced two of the worlds of contemporary Britain and felt most uneasy. My background is in one and we live in the other. We visited a member of the family living in Blaenllechau: a widow in her mid 60s living in a small two up, two down with outdoor toilet.

8th

Archbishop Hume's presence and speech at the General Assembly was a historic moment. He reflects a profound sense of God's presence.
The first time for the Catholic Primate to address the General Assembly. He served as Archbishop of Westminster from 1976 and President of the Catholic Bishops' Conference of England and Wales from 1979 until his death. Hume was created cardinal in 1976. Cardinal Hume's time in office saw Catholicism become more accepted in British society than it had been for 400 years, culminating in the first visit of the Queen to Westminster Cathedral in 1995. He had previously read the Epistle at the installation of Arehbishop Robert Runcie in 1980. It was also during his tenure in Westminster that Pope John Paul II made a groundbreaking visit to England, Wales and Scotland. He was a central figure resulting in the creation of Churches Together.

11th

The Finance Report of the Assembly should drive the Church to make radical changes. The answers are to be found in the New Testament church. I am reminded of Stephen's sermon. Why did we replace a tent with a building? What of Paul's itinerant ministry! We have become an establishment and it will take a revolution to liberate us from our static patterns. We are not far from the end and a beginning.
'Our ancestors had the tent of testimony in the wilderness, as God directed when he spoke to Moses... But it was Solomon who built a house for him. Yet the Most High does not dwell in houses made with human hands'. (Acts 7. 44-48 passim.)

Sunday 24th

Worship is the core of life. The life of the church is to celebrate the creative love and power of God, Father of Christ. People, buildings, money, structures must all be seen in the light of worship.

JULY

27th

A wonderful celebration on Caldey of Mam and Dac's 50th wedding anniversary. As we walked to the table for breakfast, we were greeted by 'Happy Jubilee to you' and a red rose on the table. Prayers from Frs Joseph and Robert. Later the cutting of the cake with all the guests present plus Frs. Aelred, Joseph and Robert. This very special day could not have been celebrated in a happier, more meaningful way.
Since the birth of our children, my parents had inherited the names of their parents.

28th

Each day on Caldey becomes a sabbath, a foretaste of the glory to come. Worship becomes the offering of the greatest things to the Father of Christ by the inspiration of the Spirit. Today has been the still point of the turning world, where the dance is. A merry day indeed. Today is the feast of St Samson, patron of Caldey. A lovely and lively act of worship, including the peace and the presentation of a holy relic of Samson. Strange that nothing caused offence but all fell into place. Saw Br James and the excavations of his prodigious digs. He sang in French to a tape of his home abbey at Scourmont.
Scourmont Abbey is in Belgium. Br James later returned to Scourmont.

AUGUST

13th

Kenneth Clark's 'Civilization' reflects his major interest in painting, sculpture and architecture. However his views of Christian conviction, basic to an understanding of the 'culture' of Western Europe, leaves much to be desired. He also approves of an elitist society and I find his approach quite different from my evangelical, rather puritanical approach. Not that I fail to enjoy the fruits of artistic creation!
Kenneth Clark, author, museum director, broadcaster, and one of the most famous art historians of his generation. In 1969, he was catapulted to international fame as the writer, producer and presenter of the BBC Television series, 'Civilization: A Personal View'.

14th

Clark's approach to the 19th century breathed a liberal, genteel, humanitarian air. He reflects tolerant and open virtues.

24th

Paul Crossley played Messiaen at the Proms. When he was at Mansfield, I remember his practising, driving Bill Rusch up the wall, because Bill's room was above the Junior Common Room.

While a student at Mansfield, Paul Crossley was discovered by Olivier Messiaen and his wife Yvonne Loriod, who invited him to come to Paris to study with them. Crossley is particularly associated with the music of Messiaen. Bill Rusch was an American Lutheran studying for his PhD in Early Church theology.

25th

'The Ascent of Man' reflects the author's tolerant and zealous spirit. Christians often become dogmatic and fall into a dangerous sub-human approach. The books I have read from television programmes are by enquiring, humanistic and cultured men: Kenneth Clark, Bamber Gascoine, Ronald Eyre and Jacob Bronowski. Although I am convinced of the validity of the Gospel for all people everywhere, I hope never to fall into the trap of zealous intolerance.

Bronowski's 'The Ascent of Man' was a ground-breaking series made in 1973 for television. It was written specifically to complement Kenneth Clark's 'Civilization' (1969) in which Clark argued that art was a major driving force in cultural evolution. Bamber Gascoine and Ronald Eyre also presented for television, two series on Christianity and the search for religion. Books were produced from their series.

SEPTEMBER

24th

The Harvest festival at Pontycymmer presented such a contrast to my first visit two years ago. Then they were totally dispirited but now they were full of hope with 5 teenagers and 16 younger children taking part in worship. Why the change? A good energetic minister. That is the strategy - and it works.

OCTOBER

1st

My first time to lead worship in the historic congregation of Llanfaches. I was preaching to a congregation first ministered to by William Wroth.

Llanfaches was founded as a conventicle (a house church?) in November 1639. Wroth and Erbery had both refused to conform to reading the Book of Sports and appeared before the High Commission Court in London in 1635. The Book of Sports advocated sports on the sabbath, and Puritans found this distasteful.

NOVEMBER

13th

I read the Bible because of inner compulsion. It brings joy, reassurance, strength, patience, determination, vision. I wish I reflected these gifts but they are there for the receiving.

14th

Lord, deliver us from being over-subjective in our interpretation of Scripture, and thus twisting the words into a message which suits us. Let us hear the Word of God.

27th

Although I hope to witness a renewal of God's people in Wales, I must be content with being faithful. Enable us, Lord, to persevere and seek every opportunity to share the Good News of Jesus.

DECEMBER

Sunday 16th

The first view of Berea, Blaina is awesome. It is a large stark chapel on the edge of tip clearance. There are a few trees to the side, a graveyard behind and the only houses are a short terrace.

Berea was built in 1842 by men bringing stone to the site before they went to work in coal mines and iron works. It was opened for worship in 1850 as a Welsh Church. Berea closed in February 2002.

29th

As we drove through Trehafod we were moved to tears because of the after effects of the floods. People's possessions were stacked on the pavements, ready to be carted away. There were feet of black ugly silt. We had nothing to say to each other as we moved up the valley to Tylorstown.

31st

What have I learned this year? The need for stamina, grit, how to cope with disappointment as well as rejoice in signs of hope; the need to combine flexibility, open-ness and tolerance with the search for principle and the need to stand firm for what one believes to be right

1980

JANUARY

3rd

Kenneth Galbraith is incisive, balanced and radical. There are universes to explore, I am only touching the tip of the iceberg and half my life has gone.
Galbraith, the Canadian economist, wrote 'The Age of Uncertainty' which was published simultaneously with the release of the television series of the same name.

16th

The Bible is always contemporary because of its honest depiction of human nature. In its realism the Bible is the vehicle for the hope of the world. Julian Thomas mentioned his uncertainty about ministry. The key issue behind vocation must be the wish to share the Good News of Jesus
Julian was a student of history at the University of Cardiff. I met him when speaking to the Methodist / URC Student Society. Julian has been a faithful URC minister since 1988.

17th

Ministers ordained in the last 2½ years share the common problems of loneliness (for single ministers) and preparing two services every week. None were particularly concerned about finance.

I invited recently ordained ministers to spend a day together to share their common experience.

30th

I am reading three good commentaries ('Peake,' 'The Interpreter's Bible' and the 'One Volume Interpreter's'), the Revised Standard Version of the Bible and checking every word in Winding Quest and New World. I am discovering how Alan Dale worked both in broad principle and in his detailed handling of the text.

This was a task which occupied me for two years. I wrote all the notes into my personal copy of 'Winding Quest' and 'New World'. I now need a magnifying glass to read them!

FEBRUARY

2nd

The Synod is now asking the right questions and answers will come.

13th

Sometimes I fear our tenuous churchmanship will cause the structure of the Synod to crumble. The resources of the churches are being dissipated: should ageing congregations maintain ageing buildings? The costs of providing ministry are accelerating. Some of our churches are threatening to secede. Yet I have faith that if we have stamina, provide dedicated ministry and create the framework and personnel for mission and service, there will be a harvest.

21st

Malcolm Hill was inducted at Penrhys. The Assistant Bishop, David Reece presided; Malcolm spoke well and I preached on Elijah at Horeb. The hall was packed with 350 people for a historic event.

This was the wonderful consequence of the District and Synod's application to the General Assembly that Penrhys should be depicted a special ministry.

MARCH

Sunday 2nd

New Trinity, Cardiff is a lively church, based in its community. This church could easily become a 'gathered congregation' and, like many churches, made up of a few dwindling families. However it is discovering its community roots and serving the area.

Sunday 16th

Watching 'Cromwell' whetted my appetite to re-read in the field of Puritanism. I wish I could deepen my knowledge of the Puritans, but once I decided to become a pastor-minister rather than a scholar-minister, I had burned my boats. I made the right decision but at times the strenuous struggle with 'live people' makes me think wistfully of historic figures.
The film Cromwell directed by Ken Hughes starred Richard Harris and Alec Guinness.

25th

The day has been spent in a local church. In a few days I have been working with the Synod, District and local church. Tomorrow at Moderators, we work at Assembly level, while next weekend on Caldey I shall be with individuals and groups in teaching, praying and living together. All these circles are inextricably linked and must not be separated. If they separate, the health of the church suffers.

26th

My first visit to Mansfield for ten years. The College is identical except for new gates and a tall tree in the centre of the Quad. It is the location for a film set for an 1870s Western. Mansfield Quad is Harvard Yard. The cost of the tree? £15,000!
The film was Michael Cimino's 'Heavens Gate'. It helped Mansfield's funds but it bankrupted United Artists.

29th

The Abbot has resigned. I have felt for years that he has been tired. Will he return? I hope so for he has been such a friend.
Another visit to Caldey. We learned the sad news that Dom James Wicksteed had resigned. He had been as great ecumenist and was so encouraging from our days at Llanidloes. Sadly he never returned to Caldey.

31st

On Caldey we experienced searching, struggling and growing and a few made leaps into the future; some articulated doubts and fears; above all there has been honest loving endeavour. The highlight was Julian's commitment to offer himself for ministry. We are grateful to God for a calling and a response. *Julian was the Julian Thomas mentioned in January.*

APRIL

11th

The Commission of Covenanted Churches meeting at Llandinam Hall, Aberystwyth endorsed the 'Scheme of Union' and the 'modern eucharistic service for special occasions'. We had a splendid lecture by Martin Conway on the background to unity. It reminded us of God's reconciling purposes for the universe, and the place of the church in God's work. How can the Church be effective in its splintered form? His talk was followed by Bible Study by Lesslie Newbigin, on I Corinthians 1. The Commission needed inspiration. *Martin Conway served as President of the Selly Oak Colleges, Birmingham from 1986 to 1997.*

12th

Lesslie Newbigin continued his Bible study and also led worship. I found myself agreeing with his approach: he spoke within the powerful Calvinist/ Augustinian/ Pauline tradition.

21st

A unique experience. I visited a coal mine, including the face. Maitland Evans, a minister from Jamaica and Lee Ching Chee from Hong Kong are visiting the URC on behalf of the Council for World Mission. We met at the Lady Windsor Colliery, were introduced to the manager, had tea, were fitted with protective clothing and boots, and received lamps and safety equipment. Then the descent of nearly 700 yards in the cage. When we reached bottom, we walked a mile and a half to the actual face where they are working the 4ft seam. A great privilege to walk alongside the machinery with its cutting edge, moving line and hydraulic jacks to hold up the roof. I cut a small piece of coal and received a plug of tobacco from a young miner. I felt part of 150 years' tradition in my own family. After walking from the face, we rode back and came up the shaft out into the light and the sun.

Maitland Evans and Lee Ching Chee were part of a visitation which produced a Report entitled 'Speaking the truth in love'. Part of the itinerary included this visit to Lady Windsor colliery in Ynysybwl. Maitland described it as the scariest experience in his life!

23rd

Maitland Evans and Lee Ching Chee feel the Churches are afraid 'to be the church'. They note a fatalistic acceptance of decline, and an inability to communicate the faith because the faith is not understood, and because it is unseemly to share the Gospel.

30th

Arthur Macarthur met the Moderators for the last time and spoke in a graciously responsive, humble way. He was grateful to have done what the church had asked him; his obedience, discipline and integrity serve as an example to us all. I could say very little.

Arthur Macarthur was ordained in 1937 and served as General Secretary of the Presbyterian Church of England, Joint Secretary of the URC from 1972 to 1974 and General Secretary from 1975 to 1980. Arthur Macarthur died in 2008.

MAY

9th

At the key debate on union with the Churches of Christ, Norman Goodall, who is going blind and has been sick, spoke persuasively. We were hearing the Word of God. I sensed he would have given his life for the unity of Christ's People.

I had first heard Norman Goodall preach when I was a student at Mansfield.

22nd

At the Women's Conference, when there was sharing in small groups, most women were asking, sharing, receiving, giving and growing. At an open session only the more vocal spoke.

I was leading the URC Women's Conference at the Montpelier Centre in Llandrindod Wells. Norah led several of their conferences in the 1980s: on the Vancouver theme, and on the 'community of women and men in the church.'

JUNE

24th

Edgar Jones' Bible Study on Second Isaiah was, as always, sound and most helpful. Bishop Lesslie Newbigin led on 'The Mission of God', a magnificent expression of Old Testament faith. He especially emphasized the covenant with Noah. In his second session he spoke on 'The Mission of Jesus, the Kingdom and the Holy Spirit'. He handled the Scriptures in a masterly way.
The annual Ministers Summer School.

25th

Lesslie Newbigin's final lecture on ministry reflected a splendid radicalism, based firmly on the Gospel. He used Jesus' call of the disciples and John 15 as texts.

27th

The 'church leaders' in South Glamorgan met at Llandaff. None of us knew why we were there. I felt we should discuss shared ministries; the Bishop preferred to discuss cooperation in social action.
This was the first gathering of 'church leaders'. It was without an agenda. It developed into a meeting where the 'leaders' found mutual support, and learned to understand that although their titles were different, much of what they did was very similar. The Bishop was John Poole Hughes who was a Bishop in Tanzania before becoming Bishop of Llandaff.

SEPTEMBER

1st

My fourth year as Moderator. I must keep before me the portrait of Jesus. He is Lord of the church and Lord in God's world. My work is to enable his Lordship to be manifested in church and society.

6th

North Wales District enjoyed its best Council meetings. There was shape to its business and a well-founded optimism. The hard work of the last few years and the new people serving in the District means we are turning a corner.

8th

Cefn Mawr has recently had a traumatic life. The 4 worshippers considered closure but now they worship fortnightly and have grown to 20. The District Council is growing in experience and winning respect from the churches. Three years ago, South Wales was the only District with a Pastoral group. Gaining the trust of the churches is a slow process and is the task of District Councils. Once there is mutual respect, pastorates can be shaped.

Cefn Mawr was a church near Wrexham.

23rd

Malcolm and Kathleen Hill talked about their first 8 months on Penrhys. They described it as a difficult and volatile community with a high proportion of families with problems. Malcolm loves people and seeks to serve them; he has a good sense of churchmanship and is nurturing a young church; he is developing contacts and relationships between the church and society. The problem of churchmanship will present thorny issues. They are fine workers, deeply committed and open to the needs of people.

The problem of churchmanship refers to the recognition of minister and church by all eight denominations. All could accept the presence of 'a Christian fellowship' but 'fellowship' could not be identified with a 'church'. This meant that an Anglican priest needed to come to Penrhys to celebrate Holy Communion.

OCTOBER

21st

Father Martin, the temporary guest master is on loan from the Cistercian house at Ballymena. He is a most gracious Christian; if the whole of 20th century monasticism created one man like him, it has proved its worth. His kindness, generosity and open-ness were remarkable and he made a lasting impression on us all. Communion was at St Illtud's and all took part, including Fr Martin. It was totally reassuring and a great assertion of the wondrous love of Christ, our Saviour.

'Our Lady of Bethlehem' is 9 miles west of Ballymena.

27th

One day at a time. I do not think about tomorrow until today's work is completed. I do not spend time thinking of yesterday. I try to live each day as it comes, taking advantage of the present opportunity. Learn from the past and prepare for the future, but do not be obsessed or mesmerised by either.

DECEMBER

12th

How can we instil confidence in the 'small' church? How are they to cope with large, crumbling buildings? Often isolated from the wider church, they can become introverted. The easy solution of allowing the church to close is not the answer. It is easier to close a church than encourage a new church to come into being.

13th

I am reading about Shoki Coe's important contribution to contextualization. My discovery of the need to relate the Text of the Gospel with the Context of the Community is a result of my experience of the need for training of the whole People of God. What started at Llanidloes was in line with these discoveries. My methodology of forming house groups, listening to the questions of individuals and the community (the context?) opened up the way for a re-discovery of the Gospel (the text?) In an isolated small-town like Llanidloes, I discovered some of the things the Theological Education Fund also discovered at about the same time! Early 1970s.

Shoki Coe,1914-1988 was a pioneer Taiwanese theologian recognized worldwide as a scholar, ecumenical leader, and theological educator. One of his most significant contributions in theological education was his proposition on the methodology of contextualization for Third World theologies. He advocated an interaction between the text and the context. He stated that the task of theological education is threefold: Christian formation, theological formation, and ministerial formation.

16th

The Ministerial Review group looked at 'contextualization'. In the group was Shoki Coe who conjured up the term 10 years ago; Jack McKelvey with his fascinating African experience, Tony Burnham and me. Shoki's experience in this field is invaluable because of his seminal thinking with the WCC.

Jack McKelvey served as tutor and Director of Internship Training in the United Congregational Church, South Africa from 1959 to 1978 and had recently been appointed Principal of Northern College. Tony Burnham was exercising a pioneering ministry in Manchester and become Moderator for the North West Synod in 1981.

1981

JANUARY

21st
Fr Thomas welcomed us to Mt St Bernard where I spoke on the 'Ministry of the People of God'. Supper with the Superior (John) and Thomas. This community felt alert and very human.
Father Thomas, guest master at Mt St Bernard, had served on Caldey as temporary guest Master during our last visit. He had invited Norah and me to Mt St Bernard, a Cistercian monastery near Coalville in Leicestershire, so that I could speak at their Chapter Meeting.

22nd
We woke at 3 to the sound of the great bell at Mount St Bernard. The community were preparing for prayer and work. The next bell was at 6, followed by another at 7.30. Fr Thomas brought tea and took us to Mass at 8. We were glad to be at Mass for Christian Unity, listen to the antiphonal singing, hear Norah's, my name and the URC being prayed for, and recognize the glory of communion.

23rd
Llandaff for the Church Leaders' meeting: the Bishop, George Evans, Norman Fairbairn, David Reece, Wyndham Bold and me. I introduced 'Principles of Visible Unity' as I would for lay people. I did it by beginning with the Mosaic Covenant. I encouraged all to participate and they did with frankness and freshness. We were delighted and the Bishop suggested I did another one when we next meet. Most encouraging to note this deepening relationship and mutual respect.
The Bishop was John Poole Hughes. George Evans was superintendent of the Baptist Union of Wales; Norman Fairbairn minister at Penarth represented the Covenanted Baptist Churches; David Reece was Assistant Bishop of Llandaff, and Wyndham Bold was Methodist Chairman of the South Wales District. 'Principles of Christian Unity' had been produced in September 1980 by the Commission of Covenanted Churches.

FEBRUARY

11th

The first time for the church 'leaders' of the Covenanted Churches in Wales to meet to share common interests. Bishops and Methodist chairmen have been meeting for two years, but today a Presbyterian Church of Wales leader and I joined them. We met at the Prince Rupert Hotel in Shrewsbury. The major concerns were 'Principles of Visible Unity' and the relationship between the Welsh and English Covenants. The discussion was amicable, honest and helpful. We are beginning to trust each another. Poole-Hughes spoke warmly of our Bible discussion at Llandaff. Despite a potentially explosive subject, there was courtesy and a willingness to listen, receive and respect each other.

APRIL

23rd

God has blessed and we have been strengthened and comforted as the day has grown. I praise God, the Father of Jesus for having shared the life of a wonderful mother. Despite its harrowing nature, this has been a wonderful day. I slept badly, felt that frightening heaviness of loss - I had lost my mother who has loved all my 42 years and more. She was no longer there. We shall miss her so much but I am reconciled to her quiet, safe crossing and her arrival in the land of Promise. She had several Nebos during the last few weeks, all preparing her for the dignity of her dying. The staff at the hospital and we as a family witnessed her lack of fear and total trust in the Lord - 'The Lord's my shepherd' she would say so often to us, and add 'I'm not afraid to die, you know'.
My mother had died on the previous day at Llwynypia Hospital. It was from Nebo that Moses viewed the Promised Land. Norah and I and the children had driven through Nebo in Gwynedd a few days previously.

30th

We need to pick up the old threads and create new ones. But it must be done quietly, patiently and with that great gift of time. Each day will help with its medicine: it will be that much further from the shock, numbness and searing pain, and that much nearer the glorious reunion with all God's people. Now I have seen my mother make that journey in peace, confidence and love, I know we walk the same path and she will be waiting at journey's end.

MAY

13th

Francis Hughes, the second Irish hunger striker died yesterday. I posted a letter to him from Fr Martin when we were last on Caldey.
Francis Hughes died in the H block, Northern Ireland, two weeks after Bobby Sands, the first Republican hunger striker.

29th

I was sitting in front of the cottage, in the middle of our grass, enjoying the warm sunshine, the sound of the birds and I was looking down the road towards Cwm Mawr and the Dingle. I felt Mam was part of me and was looking down the same road, enjoying the same sunshine and hearing the same birds. It was not a 'mystical feeling' and I 'know' Mam is not 'here' but 'there' in heaven. What is this all about? Perhaps a moment of happiness when I realized Mam is with God, the Father of Jesus, and that she, as my mother, is part of me and would 'want' me to enjoy that lovely moment. That experience must help.
We had bought the cottage at Newchapel near Llanidloes in 1986. It served as an excellent base as I travelled throughout Wales, and for all our family holidays.

JUNE

Sunday, 7th

Pentecost A re-birth of the church at Cefn Mawr with six new elders (none before) and thirty new members. A great story.
The congregation had 'come to life again' when the few worshippers decided that a fresh approach was necessary: they decided to worship once a fortnight, have tea after each service and invited all past members and neighbours to come to church. Very straightforward and it worked.

Sunday 21st

Treforest is a church showing new life. The congregation is committed, responsive and has good leadership with its elders.
Another congregation showing signs of life. I felt that part of my work was to share these good-news stories around the Districts and Synod.

JULY

11th

The ordination of Peter Trow at Ogmore Vale was a fine, well ordered service with an excellent sermon from Buick Knox. Remarkable to think of Peter as the 15 year old at Llawryglyn.

Buick Knox was professor of Church History at Westminster College, Cambridge.

AUGUST

12th

The first time for our family to climb a mountain. Norah and I had climbed Ben More and Liathach, and we have had fine walks on holidays at Sandwood Bay and Pysgotwr. Today recaptured those memories and was the start of a new phase? We went through the Idris Gates, through the steep wood and into the magnificent corrie surrounding Llyn Cau. We climbed the steep south edge and skirted Cwm Amaeth (1617ft) to the top of Penygadair (2928ft). Ate apples in the mist.

Ben More and Liathach are in the Torridon range; Sandwood Bay is near Kinlochbervie in Sutherland, and Pysgotwr is near Llanddewibrefi. Today's mountain was Cadair Idris. During the holiday we also climbed Snowdon, Plynlimmon and Pen-y-fan in the Brecon Beacons.

27th

It has taken two years to complete my ambition of reading and adding notes to the thousand pages of 'Winding Quest' and 'New World' with three commentaries and the 'New Revised Standard Version'.

SEPTEMBER

9th

Representatives of the English and Welsh Commissions met at Birmingham Central Hall. Bernard Thorogood chaired and we discussed consequences of the two forms of approach.

This was the period when the United Reformed Church (and the Methodist Church) was involved in two conversations: 'Covenanting in England', and the 'Covenanted programme in Wales'. What would happen if both schemes were accepted? Would Wales be a part of a United Church of Wales? Or, remain part of the United Church of England? Halcyon days. Both schemes seemed perfectly feasible. Bernard Thorogood was the newly appointed General Secretary of the United Reformed Church. He had been General Secretary of the Council for World Mission.

10th

Our meeting of Pentwyn 'leaders' is proving to be a time of sharing, as well as the place to discuss Pentwyn. Derek Childs, Bishop of Monmouth brought an Indian visitor who is a bishop in the Church of North India. He spoke on Indian church life and church unity. During the last 4 years I have been concentrating on the life of this URC Province and have not been as challenged ecumenically as I should. I am now being led to make a more positive ecumenical stance.

Derek Childs served as archbishop of Wales from 1983 to 1986.

12th

A day of great contrast: this morning we had quiet, prosaic business; this afternoon polemic, slogans, arrogance, invective; this evening a hopeful act of worship. All in one day! This morning's District, chaired by Fred Jones, went well. This afternoon was a special session to discuss the English Covenant; introduced by Ronald Williams of Rhayader (for) and the minister of Port Sunlight (against). To my astonishment there was a group (whom I had never seen before and who had never attended a District Council) who applauded every anti statement. The atmosphere became tense and discussion impossible. The old slogans were shouted: back to Rome, prelacy, betrayal of our heritage, priest-ridden church. I spoke briefly towards the end, asking for speaking the truth in love. After tea the opening of Salisbury Park's renovated schoolroom as the new church. I preached on Eph 2. It included a plea for unity.

The discussion on 'The English Covenant' was angry and polemical. Old battles were being fought. A formidable anti-lobby had been organised. Port Sunlight was in the Mersey Synod of the URC. This was not the experience of the discussions within Wales on the Welsh Covenant. It would be interesting to compare the impossibility of compromise in England over the Covenant and during the Miners Strike, with the more temperate and measured attitudes within Wales. Is there something different within the Welsh temperament? Are the Welsh more pragmatic?

OCTOBER

7th

All Moderators are concerned about the opposition to the proposals for Covenanting. The violent unthinking opposition I have noted in District Councils is experienced throughout the country. The anti Covenant lobby has plenty of ammunition and is well organized. I feel Bernard Thorogood is worried and unhappy about the effects of the debate on the life of the church.

10th

A resolution to support the 'English Covenant' was passed by 51 votes to 20 at Synod at Rhaeadr. I have experienced so much unthinking invective in District Councils that I did not expect the light of today's debate. It was of the highest quality and 20 people participated in questions and comments. We were fortunate to have Martin Cressey present as Assembly Moderator to speak before lunch and answer questions. There were 160 for tea. I presided at the Covenant debate: excellent spirit, good questions. Doug Bale moved an amendment which was defeated; the resolution was then carried; Synod decided not to vote on advocating a 75% Assembly majority.

Martin Cressey was Moderator of General Assembly and in his Moderatorial Address decided to speak on the English Covenant. Later I was accused of priming him to speak in favour of the Covenant. In fact, I had no idea what would be the substance of his address.

21st

I received a letter from one of our ministers alleging that I had acted in an underhand manner and had fixed the approach of Synod towards the Covenant. Copies of the letter were sent to the Synod Clerk and to Bernard and Donald Hilton. I found the allegation very hurtful.

Donald Hilton was one of the organizers of the anti-covenant lobby. He later became Moderator for the Yorkshire Synod.

Sunday 25th

Surprised to find six 6 young people at Fleur de Lys. Just as I began my sermon, there was a noise outside; Ieuan (the church secretary) went out and returned with 5 teenage boys. I encouraged them to participate; we had communion; the congregation welcomed them and gave them fruit; tea to finish. Genuine mission.

An experience of mission which can happen when there is a relationship between a local congregation and its community. Ieuan Evans was church secretary.

29th

Peter Chesney and I interviewed Mansfield Ordinands and I noted Kim Fabricius and Kevin Watson, both of whom could come to Wales

Peter Chesney was Moderator for Wessex Synod. Both Ordinands came to Wales: Kim to Sketty, Swansea and the University Chaplaincy; Kevin to the Rhyl group of churches. Both exercised excellent ministries.

NOVEMBER

14th

Our final induction of the year. We began with Daphne Jones at Fairwater; the Recognition service of Mary and Dafydd at Ely; the Ordinations of Richard Helmn, Peter Trow and Roger Jones; the Inductions of Ron Williams, Peter Scotland and Peter Mark; today Lionel Walker began at Elim, Penywaun and Bethel, Cwmbran. These new ministries serve 14 churches and represent a crucial element of the work this year. The journey continues but it is good to be placing signposts of hope for our fellow pilgrims. I presided and Pennar preached on Luke 4.

I knew Lionel Walker from student days when he was minister at Portmead, Swansea.

26th

The URC 'visitors' have begun our Welsh journey. John Rhys, Michael Dunford, Robert Way and I joined the students at Coleg Coffa for prayers; met Elfed ap Nefydd Roberts, the new Principal of the Presbyterian College; spent an hour with Cyril Williams and his colleague from the Department of Religion; spoke with Officers of Coleg Coffa and members of staff of the Presbyterian College. Then the journey north to Bangor to meet Tudur Jones.

The visitation had been instigated by the General Assembly. John Rhys, a URC elder at Rhiwbina had been Director of the University of Wales Press; Michael Dunford was Assembly Church Life Secretary and Robert Way was minister in Leeds. We travelled first to Aberystwyth and met the staff and some students of the Annibynwyr College Coleg Coffa, the Presbyterian United College and the appropriate department at the University. We then proceeded to Bangor and met Tudur Jones, Principal of Bala-Bangor Independent College and a Welsh Church historian.

27th

What is Wales? An almost impossible question to answer. Bala Bangor College for a Welsh service at 8.45. The three students spoke in Welsh and John Rhys translated. It sounded reasonable in what was for our English friends, a foreign country. They were followed by the chairman and secretary of the College committee; then the Dean and a lecturer in the Biblical Studies department. Bala Bangor is in a far healthier position than Coleg Coffa. Tudur acted with great courtesy.

One of the critical issues was 'how to introduce students of the URC, and new ministers coming to Wales to the Welsh context?' These were the questions raised by Shoki Coe and the group on contextualization. These questions are even more critical today, now that most of those colleges have closed and there are very few ministers emerging from the churches in Wales.

1982

JANUARY

20th

Bettws is at the sharp end of grass roots ecumenism. The congregation is made up of three parties: Anglican and URC as official partners in the Shared Church, and a group of non-denominational Christians. Can these three 'ecclesiologies' cooperate to reveal God's reconciling action in Christ?

Bettws is a large housing estate outside Newport. The 'non denominational' Christians were basically one family of very energetic and committed people who 'knew' what it was to be Christians. They eventually withdrew from the Church because of its cooperation with the local Roman Catholic community.

21st

The 'church leaders' of the Covenanted Churches completed a draft scheme and shared it with the Pentwyn Sponsoring Body.

The leaders were the small group which had been meeting for several years either at the Bishops house in Llandaff or Newport. The Churches had no ecumenical officers at this time, and church leaders had to take many initiatives.

FEBRUARY

6th

The Nominations Committee representing all Districts and Committees filled every Synod vacancy.

A major achievement for a new committee to find the gifts and talents needed to serve the wider church.

18th

The churches in Mid Wales met for the first time: Montgomeryshire churches in the North Wales District; Aberystwyth from West Wales; Brecon and Radnor churches from East Wales. Fifty attended and represented 18 churches. In the past only 3 or 4 churches sent representatives to the East Wales District which stretched from Rhaeadr to Newport. A resolution was passed unanimously to ask Synod to set up the Mid Wales district.

20th

'Free Church' representatives sat towards the front of the nave in the beautiful cathedral of St David's for the installation of George Noakes as the new bishop.

George Noakes was Bishop of St David's from 1982-1991, and Archbishop of Wales from 1987 to 1991. He is described as the 'people's bishop, a patient man with a deep pastoral concern for his clergy and their parishes.' (Obituary by Barry Morgan in 'The Guardian'.) Norah and I maintained our friendship with George and Jean Noakes because of our mutual link with Trinity College, Carmarthen.

MARCH

1st

Malcolm Hill is to leave Penrhys. This is a tragedy because it will be difficult to find a replacement and could mark the end of ministry there.

10th

Cardiff elders and ministers met at City Church. Dafydd Jones spoke prophetically that the church reflects the same divisions in living standards as does the rest of society. What is an appropriate Christian life-style? Personally and communally? This raised serious issues for us personally and for the more wealthy city congregations.

Dafydd and his wife Daphne, both URC ministers lived on a large housing estate in Ely and Dafydd had every justification to ask tough questions.

16th

I read an article on vestments: until the 4th- 5th centuries, clergy wore the same clothes as the laity: then they were modelled on Roman civic uniform; the Reformed vestments are based on university dress. There seems to be a rationale behind my 'feelings' after all.

31st

The Moderators and their wives met at the Ecumenical Centre and enjoyed three splendid sessions with Sapsezian on 'Theological Education', C.S. Song on 'Faith and Order' and Emilio Castro on 'Mission and Evangelism'.
Fred Kaan, appointed Moderator of the West Midlands in 1978 had previously served the World Alliance of Reformed Churches and was eager to introduce the Moderators to the World Council of Churches. Therefore we all spent a few days of working holiday in Geneva. Emilio Castro became General Secretary of the WCC in 1985.

APRIL

1st

The morning was spent with Barkat (from Pakistan) who spoke on the Programme to Combat Racism; Koshy (from India) on International Affairs; Srisang (Thailand) on Participation in Development. We were greatly challenged. Members of the National Protestant Church of Geneva took us to their Conference Centre, 10 miles from Geneva. They have even more severe problems than the URC. When we returned to the Cathedral of St Pierre, I stood in Calvin's pulpit and later sat in his chair in the Consistory.
In 1968 the WCC had adopted the Programme to Combat Racism. Nelson Mandela expressed his gratitude to this programme for their tangible support in the South African struggle against apartheid.

2nd

We were privileged to have the company of Philip Potter, the General Secretary of the WCC. We had three sessions: von Wartenberg on 'Women and Men in the Church'; Brockway on 'Dialogue with Living Faiths and Ideologies' and Becker on 'Ecumenical Education'. Dr Potter arrived during the last session. I remember some of his words: 'the reconciliation which

Christ brings, comforts and through struggle makes peace WCC is a place of confrontation and not compromise'. Supper with Glen Garfield Williams, General Secretary of the 'Commission of European Churches'. Although he was formal and diplomatic, he has helped develop important relationships between East and West.

During the evening I was with Glen Williams, Norah was at a meeting with the 'Community of Women and Men' group. Norah had already been appointed to represent the URC in the next Assembly at Vancouver in 1983 and had been to a preparatory meeting for women in the Bahamas. The women were very impressed by the article Norah had written on the Bahamas meeting.

Sunday 4th

The American Episcopal Church was packed. Fred Kaan preached well. Norah and I walked to the pier and had a great conversation with six trade union leaders visiting the ILO from Black Africa.

The ILO = the International Labour Organisation.

Sunday 11th

At Maesyronnen we welcomed visitors from South Korea and Assam who are stopping at Trefeca, and I invited them to pray in their own languages. Communion with small glasses for the first time at Maesyronnen. The largest congregation they can remember: 80. We all stepped out to a glorious morning and remarkable view.

A memorable moment in the long story of Maesyronnen.

27th

On Caldey we had 15 year olds to over 70s, a variety of educational and social backgrounds and yet within 3 days, we are all challenged and comforted by God's presence and graciousness. For some it has been a highpoint in their Christian living. As this happens every time over many years, it is intimating the future shape of the church and the essential ingredients for Christian nurture: all ages, working with the Bible; living together; prayer; Eucharist; a sense of community.

MAY

1st

A full-scale battle is taking place above the Falklands. British planes are attacking Falklands airfields, Argentineans are attacking British ships. I refuse to use 'ours' and 'theirs': this war is absurd and tragic.

The Falklands' War was fought in 1982 between Argentina and the United Kingdom over the disputed Falkland Islands, South Georgia and the South Sandwich Islands. Their name and sovereignty over them had long been disputed. The war was triggered by the occupation of South Georgia by Argentina on 19 March 1982 followed by the occupation of the Falklands, and ended when Argentina surrendered on 14 June 1982. War was not actually declared by either side. The inability of the Churches to come to a mind on this tragedy had a profound effect upon my ministry. It taught me the crime of keeping silent when conscience spoke otherwise.

3rd

May Day. Labour Day. We celebrated by visiting the stones in memory to Aneurin Bevan on the mountain between Tredegar and Ebbw. However, to try and remember 'the people' has been impossible because of horrific news from the Falklands. A British submarine hit a cruiser outside the 200 mile 'protected zone'. What of the hundreds of sailors? I felt sickening futility and anger. British-ness can be disgusting. I would abandon this Land of Hope and Glory and retreat like Jeremiah to a hut in the wilderness.

4th

The tragedy deepens. This evening we heard of the sinking of a British destroyer with much loss of life. Now we must bomb the Argentinean mainland! God help us from stupidity, and preserve us from those whose livelihood is the war game. The church must speak vociferously against the jingoism of our political leadership.

Sunday 16th

An 88 year old elder at Berea, Blaina, John Jones a very fine Christian gentleman led the vestry prayer and after service quoted lines from James Russell Lowell's 'On the present Crisis'. He spoke them to me privately and I asked him to repeat them to the congregation. The people of Berea know him as Mr Greatheart, the man who led Christians to the Celestial City.
Lowell was an American poet of the Nineteenth Century.

18th

General Assembly revealed complete divisiveness over the Falklands' War and failed to offer a prophetic word to the nation. We succumbed to the drift towards war and were a mere reflection of the nation's confusion. We offered nothing in the name of the Gospel. I felt I should have spoken. Invasion is imminent.

19th
The Covenant resolution was proposed by Martin Cressey and David Marsden, and opposed by Caryl Micklem and Donald Hilton. 30 speeches (for and against) and prayers before the vote. 434 for and 196 against with 3 abstentions: 69%. We were asked to receive the result quietly.

21st
British Troops landed this morning on the Falklands. I do not feel British and have no sense of defending a righteous cause. Argentina is the aggressor but what were our actions before the Falklands invasion? God save us from Margaret Thatcher.

22nd
The war rages. 5000 British troops have landed, there are casualties but they are reported as statistics: 'we have lost less than the enemy, acceptable losses; this was expected; the highest qualities of British fighting men'. There is a new normality; escalation is acceptable in the struggle for freedom, justice and to defend our land and people. I watched the Papal Mass for Peace at St Peters with Argentinean and British cardinals con-celebrating.

24th
The tragedy continues with the British government hardening its attitude, rejecting the Pope's call for peace and asserting there can be no negotiations until the Argentineans leave the islands. Military logic has its inevitability. Are there any statesmen? I met Kirsty from Caerffili, an excellent prospective candidate for ministry.
Kirsty Thorpe is a minister of the United Reformed Church, will serve as minister at Wilmslow in 2008, and was elected joint Moderator Elect of the General Assembly.

25th
The nightmare continues in broad daylight, all eyes are open and we talk of casualties and death in cool, analytic style. We are immune to horror and our normality would have scandalized us a few weeks ago.

26th
A remarkable half-hour alone with a minister who knows he has terminal cancer and feels the end is near. He has great courage and proven faith: he heard Jesus speaking to him. 'I have gone to prepare a place for you'. His

funeral is to be one of praise and thanksgiving. I asked for his blessing and felt privileged to receive it.

29th

I have been awed by John Paul's ministry at Canterbury and Wembley Stadium. We were in the presence of a man of God: the lighting of candles to martyrs of our century; a scene of historic reconciliation.
The visit of John Paul II to the United Kingdom and Northern Ireland. The historic tour was the first - and until now, the only, - visit of the Pope to the United Kingdom.

JUNE

2nd

God bless John Paul. A man of God. I have been overwhelmed by his presence and grace, and am deeply grateful to Christ for raising up a saint. The church leaders walked to the castle and entered the Library where we met many cardinals. and were then taken to the old dining room. John Paul entered to applause; Bishop Vaughan (Council of Churches for Wales) spoke and presented a Welsh New Testament and a cheque for Poland; Frank Lee read the Beatitudes and 'prayed them'. The Pope responded - unity and world crisis - was introduced, shook hands with us all, said 'John Morgans, the same church as Mrs Evans (Mary Evans of Ely).' I wished him 'God bless you', he reciprocated and gave me a papal medal. A treasure. Home to hear Papal address from Ninian Park. Hugh returned later with great joy.
Hugh had been privileged to be at Ninian Park. Frank Lee had been minister at Pantygwydr Baptist in Swansea when I was a student. I remembered his sermon on Og's iron bedstead!

3rd

I sense personal growth. It began in February when I started to pray daily with the Taize Common Prayer, the Alternative Service Book of the Church of England and the lectionary. The prayers have deepened because of meeting Philip Potter at Geneva, and John Paul with his combination of holiness, compassion and justice for Gods creatures.

Sunday 6th

I spoke about the effects of Taize, the World Council of Churches and John Paul on (1) the need to develop holiness, prayer, spirituality, discipleship and

(2) the need to explore ways of sharing, loving our neighbours, especially the poor, and implementing ways of peace.

11th

The new URC District Council of Mid Wales was inaugurated with a full complement of District officers and committees, and with two-thirds of the churches represented. If there is stamina, we could see an effective unit for the life and mission of our churches in these scattered areas. It was first discussed in the 1930s and in the 1970s when I ministered at Llanidloes. The six District Councils are now operative.

19th

The new Pembrokeshire District Council has earned the respect of the churches and is the best attended Council. There is a growing sense of fellowship and loyalty.

22nd

A high-water mark in all the Summer Schools I have attended. There has been a transformation in numbers, mood and attitude and God willing, there could be growth during the years ahead. Gerry Hughes, a Jesuit from St Beuno's spoke on 'the devotional life'. He opened up a new world. Maitland Evans spoke on CWM's new role of partnership.
Gerard Hughes is now a member of the Lauriston Jesuit House in Edinburgh. He is a well known author and spiritual director. Maitland Evans was General Secretary of the United Church of Jamaica and Cayman and Moderator of the Council for World Mission. We had last met at the pit in Ynysybwl!

23rd

Fr Gerry spoke on 'hindrances to prayer' and 'practical ways of praying'. Maitland spoke on the perspective for mission: the Christ angle of vision. He was powerful and direct. 20 of us crossed the Gospel Pass to Llanthony Priory and Abbey: the Priory is the Augustinian ruin; the Abbey was formed by Fr Ignatius in the 19th century and continued by Eric Gill. It is a splendid retreat centre.
Father Ignatius had attempted to bring monasticism back to the Church of England. The monastery and lands were acquired in 1924 by Eric Gill, sculptor, engraver and typographer, who gave the site a new lease of life as a family home and workshop for himself and a loose community of colleagues.

JULY

3rd

Wales' first Synod Day, held at Llanidloes High School was memorable and overwhelming. The sun shone and the programmes went well: exhibitions, book stall, musical items, keep fit, sports and finally open-air communion at which I preached (journey, pilgrimage, race - being fed) and celebrated communion aided by 40 ministers and 40 elders. How many present? 34 full buses made 1700; 100 cars? And how many locals? About 2000 altogether. Just being together, enjoying and celebrating, and at Llanidloes.
What a miracle! To be able to organise such an event and to be able to encourage that number to attend. The United Reformed Church had truly arrived in Wales. The local arrangements had been made most efficiently by a group led by Richard Helmn, the URC minister in Llanidloes.

7th

Bernard came to Mods to tell us the Church of England had rejected the scheme for a covenant: bishops and laity had the sufficient majority but clergy had 61%. So disappointing. Some of us attended the 'Duke Ellington Sacred Concert' at St Paul's: Rod Steiger, Douglas Fairbanks, Tony Bennet, Phyllis Hyman, Jacques Lousier, Wayne Sleep, Swingle Singers and a good British band.

8th

Bernard is bitterly disappointed and feels the decision marks the end of this approach to visible unity.
Bernards premonition was only too right. In a sense it marked closure on the vision that had brought the URC into being in 1972. The vision of visible unity is no longer on the agenda of denominations or for most local Christian communities.

10th

The third occasion in recent weeks when key leaders in the Synod met: Ministers' Summer School, the first Synod Day and today our half-yearly Synod Committee Day which met at the Plough, Brecon. The three committees (Church Life, World Church and Mission, Church and Society) worked separately and then attempted to coordinate their programmes.
This was an attempt to coordinate the work of the various Synod committees and also an opportunity to develop relationships.

28th

The day has been spent with the Companions of Brother Lawrence, a movement founded by a dozen missionaries in 1960 serving in India, who were concerned about their personal spiritual life. I attended their annual meetings at Holland House, Copthorne: a beautiful diocesan house in glorious scenery. These were dedicated, sacrificial people. I led Morning Prayers and spoke of my personal spiritual heritage. Silence from 11 until 5. I started 'The Fed:' no more incongruous setting for such a reading. At 5, I spoke on where I am (theology, Bible, worship, Taize, Potter, JP II).

30th

Ken Morgan's 'Modern Wales' and 'The Fed' are providing an insight into my story.

Kenneth Morgan's 'Modern Wales', and 'The Fed' by Hywel Francis and Dai Smith opened up the story of Wales. The Fed is the South Wales Miners' Federation, founded after the defeat of the miners' strike of 1898.

SEPTEMBER

8th

I continue the search for ministers. I share with the local congregations and District Councils the shaping of pastorates, but the Moderator is responsible for introducing the ministerial candidate. Already I have introduced a large number of younger and more experienced ministers to Wales and we ought to fill the five vacant pastorates this year. It is ongoing work but a foundation has been laid.

15th

I met a cousin for the first time - Arfon Evans secretary of the National Union of Mineworkers' lodge at Maerdy. We talked about family, common social and political concerns and he warmed to my suggestion for a Christian / Marxist conversation.

This proved to be a pivotal meeting with far reaching repercussions. Arfon and I have later discovered we had the same great grand parents, the miner Thomas Morgans and his wife Sarah Davies.

22nd

The day of national support for health workers, called by the TUC. Although millions sympathize with low-paid workers, this hard government will not change its position. It does not know the difference between stubbornness and firmness, nor the meaning of flexibility and compromise. I wish I could be more active politically.

27th

The URC needs the mining valley churches which are nearer the thoughts and aspirations of the majority of people in this country. We are a church dominated by the conservative South East of England.

28th

The Synod Ministerial committee held its first Training Day for candidates for the ministry. Held at Beulah, Rhiwbina, its theme on 'Spirituality' was handled well by our own committee members. Glyndwr led with prayers; Edgar splendidly introduced 'Old Testament and prayer', and I continued with 'the Bible and devotional life'. Glyndwr spoke on 'Images of Spirituality'. Ken Graham presided at Communion.
This was an attempt to introduce contextualized training for our ministers. Dr Glyndwr Harris was a historian, Edgar Jones an Old Testament scholar recently retired from Northern College; Ken Graham the minister of Beulah was an ex-Presbyterian from Northumberland. Ken introduced the URC to Beulah.

OCTOBER

12th

Representatives of the Council of Churches for Wales met three visitors from the Chinese Christian Church at the Shire Hall Shrewsbury. Led by Bishop Ting, Principal of the Nanking Seminary, the others were a professor of religion from Shanghai and a theological student.
Born to a Christian family in Beijing in September 1915, Bishop Ting studied at Shanghai's St. John's University and was ordained an Anglican priest in 1942. He became principal of Nanjing Union Theological Seminary; in 1955 he was consecrated bishop. When the Cultural Revolution ended in 1976, he became head of the Three Self-Patriotic Movement and later, president of the China Christian Council, which worked to re-establish relationships with Christian churches around the world. Bishop Ting received an Honorary Doctorate at the University of Canterbury on the same day as our son Hugh graduated.

19th

There has been progress during the past five years: there is a younger, more concerned and competent ministry; more congregations have pastoral care; there are many candidates for ministry; Synod and its committees and District Councils are functioning; a financial base is being established; ecumenically the URC is playing a key role in the Covenant; we are discovering and training lay leadership; Wales feels as if it is becoming unified.

Sunday 24th

An amusing puzzle. Yesterday when Norah and I had tea with Fr Thaddeus, we reminded him that the clocks were to be put back. He laughed and said Wouldnt it be funny if he forgot, and the monks were to get up an hour early? We heard this morning that they were up at 2.15 instead of 3.15, but we have not ascertained from Thad whether it was an accident or not. A better story if we never find out.
A Caldey incident.

NOVEMBER

Sunday 7th

Abergavenny and Ystalyfera are very different communities: the former is an old market town, almost completely Anglicised and Tory/ Liberal: Ystalyfera is a decaying mining village towards the head of the Tawe valley, Welsh in language and culture; and politically Labour and Plaid Cymru. Yet in the Abergavenny chapel, the Welsh speaking community holds monthly worship; at Ystalyfera, ours is the only English speaking chapel. Abergavenny is in a ‘chapel’ tradition; Ystalyfera is more ‘church’. Life is never clear or simple.

8th

Mr T H Watson, church secretary, deacon, elder and good friend died quietly in his sleep in hospital at Llanidloes, the town in which he was born and where he spent his 90 years, except for the excruciating experience of the First World War. I received so much from his loyalty and friendship. He loved the church, was never narrow or parochial in his vision and always had great respect for the minister.

12th

I was privileged to participate in the funeral of a friend and helper whom I admired so much. Thomas Henry Watson was my first church secretary, took part in my ordination and latterly at my inductions at Manselton and as Moderator. Llanidloes will not be the same for us again.

30th

I am grasping the dynamism inherent in the advent-incarnation-epiphany shape. Taize provides a third pillar alongside 'theology' and 'the Bible'. Taize provides daily stability and a recognition of the rhythm of the Church Year. Theology, the Bible and the Liturgy cohere!

DECEMBER

7th

I am always glad to return to Wales; whether it be across the Severn Bridge, through the railway tunnel, down the M50 into Monmouth, or into Powys at Llanymynech. I rejoice when I return and am more vulnerable when I leave. I have spent my life in Wales, apart from Oxford and Hartford. Although I could have settled happily in both foreign countries I have never regretted the decision to minister to my own nation.

25th Christmas Day

Hugh was received into membership of the church at Roath Park. We were there as a family, including Dac. At lunch Hugh read from David Niccols' New Testament and Dac led in prayer.

David Niccols was great-grandfather to my father. He seems to have been converted in the 1859 Revival because the New Testament dates to that year. At the same time as the Revival began in New York, it also broke out in Ballymena, Northern Ireland. It is estimated that a million people were converted in the United Kingdom. Dylan was also received as a member at Roath Park, and Catherine affirmed her faith on the formation of the Penrhys Uniting Church in 1989.

31st

The year has been dominated by the Falklands crisis which has revived spurious English imperialistic nationalism and diverted us from the major problems of appalling unemployment with its attendant threats of social disorder. Nevertheless, there is now a more vocal community awareness of the needs of environment and especially the nuclear threat. Personally I have strengthened awareness of my roots in Wales and especially my mining working-class background.

1983

JANUARY

13th

During 1982 I was privileged to meet John Paul II and the Chinese Christians; today marked the visit from Christians in the USSR. Michael Kulakov, a young man studying for the ministry of the Seventh Day Adventist church is staying with us. I drove to the Church in Wales offices for a meeting of Church Leaders with the delegation: the Lutheran Archbishop of Latvia; Dr Alexei Stoyan of the Baptist church and Michael Kulakov.
Michael Kulakov was guest at our home.

14th

The public meeting at Ebeneser for the three delegates from the USSR surpassed expectation. There was the right blend for a public occasion with worship, greetings and an interview by the BBC. Geraint Tudur and I led worship: I spoke on Jesus' family; the Archbishop of Latvia and Michael spoke; interview with Stoyan; presentation of Welsh New Testaments before Geraint and I led closing worship. Michael is a fine Christian: his grandfather spent ten years in jail; his father 5 years there.
Geraint Tudur was minister of Ebeneser Welsh Congregational Chapel, Cardiff and is now General Secretary of the Undeb yr Annibynwyr Cymraeg.

19th

I anticipated an adventure as I drove to Pontypridd to meet George Rees, the General Secretary of the National Union of Mineworkers (NUM) for South Wales. The ice thawed as we recognized areas of common concern and he was glad to send the greetings of the NUM to their colleagues in Hungary and Czechoslovakia. Afterwards I discussed with the research and education

officer, Dr Kim Howells, how to develop a relationship between the URC and NUM.
The meeting had been arranged by Arfon Evans, my cousin from Ferndale. Kim Howells has been the Member of Parliament for Pontypridd since 1989.

21st

Today could transform a key aspect of my ministry. The day was spent at a conference at St David's Hall organized by the 'Medical Campaign against Nuclear Weapons' on 'The Human Cost of Nuclear War'. Three major sessions: medical consequences of nuclear weapons; health planning in relation to nuclear war; the threat and reality of nuclear war. There was also a seminar on 'The Church and the morality of nuclear weapons', chaired by Bob Morgan.
The Revd Bob Morgan, Vicar of Ely was leader of the Labour Group in Cardiff.

24th

We learned of the murder of John Williams of Brynambor outside Llanddewibrefi. As a family we spent an idyllic holiday in August 1975 in the remote, beautiful valley of Pysgotwr Fawr. While there we walked to Soar y Mynydd where we met John Brynambor, the church treasurer. He was shot at home by his own shotgun on Saturday night, discovered by neighbours yesterday and there is a major search for the murderer. He was a bachelor living alone; we remember his journey each Sunday to chapel at his beloved Soar, 30 miles each way by car. I also thought of the desperate man who shot him. Is he hiding in that wilderness of bare mountain and forest? I imagine John returning along that lonely, dark road on Saturday evening.

27th

Tracey Jones was accepted as a candidate for ministry. She is a first class young woman of 19, and is one of the best prospects I have seen. We have had a constant stream of candidates during the last five years.
Tracey Jones (now Lewis) from Fairwater is a minister of the United Reformed Church.

29th

Our Provincial Committees worked efficiently and responsibly with growing maturity and expertise. They discussed 'Christian Nurture'; unilateral nuclear disarmament; the appointment of an ecumenical officer.

FEBRUARY

Sunday 27th

Hugh, Dylan and Catherine led worship at Mount Zion, Troedyrhiw. Many family generations were grateful that the linear apostolic witness to the faith seems to be deepening, and will, hopefully, pass into the next century.
The URC suggested to all its churches that the major service of this Sunday should be prepared and led by young people.

MARCH

3rd

Wales is where I belong. Two aspects of Welshness press me in the same direction: Welsh Nonconformity with its radical Puritan commitment, and the Rhondda political and working-class tradition. I felt proud of the miners at Lewis Merthyr who are on strike to save their pit. Twenty eight of them sat down in the pit last week; they have convinced the South Wales miners to support them and are lobbying their fellow miners throughout the country. Next week there will be a national ballot of miners. They see the struggle as defending the coal mining industry in Britain. Where do I stand in this crisis? With the miners, but what will I do about it?

5th

The Cardiff Campaign for Nuclear Disarmament arranged a march from the City Hall to the Royal Ordnance Factory at Llanishen, a place where components for H bombs are manufactured. As a family we joined the two or three hundred assembled at the City Hall, marched into Queen St, up North Rd, across Gabalfa flyover and arrived at the ROF for speeches. It was peaceful, orderly and good-humoured; thousands pouring into the City for the match gave CND activists a chance to share their views in public. But there must be a broader base; how can I (we) get it across to the ordinary church member?

15th

The enthronement of the new Archbishop of Wales was well-ordered, dignified worship. Derek Childs greeted each of us in turn, and together we said prayers for unity.
The enthronement took place in St Woollos Cathedral Newport.

24th

The first battle for unilateralism is fought and won. The South Wales District meeting at City Church passed by a vote of 24-10 with 3 abstentions, a resolution calling for the UK's unilateral abandonment of nuclear weapons. There is a long road ahead before the church will accept these issues.

26th

To my delight and amazement, the Synod at Merthyr carried the motion for unilateral disarmament by 44 to 18 with 6 or 7 abstentions. This radical decision by Synod will have two consequences: the resolution is to be taken to General Assembly at Brighton; as a Synod we embark on a policy of peace-education. I vacated the chair for the first time in order to speak.

30th

Our Hungarian guide took us to the British Embassy to meet Mr Fisher, Cultural Attaché. He is from Rhymni and has a smattering of Welsh. He spoke of strengths and weaknesses of the system: very cultured society, liberal and open; bishops are political appointments; thought little of the peace Movement.

The official delegation of three from the URC had arrived in Budapest on the 29th March. The other two were the Revd István Kardos, a Hungarian minister serving the URC, and Helen Lidgett of the World Church and Mission Department of the URC. Throughout our visit there was the struggle to recognise the reality of the faith of the people, alongside the accusation that the leadership were compromising to the state. Discernment was not straightforward. What was the role of the church leaders? The visit raised questions of the Church being alongside a socialist and a capitalist system. There were no easy answers. In an attempt to share my experience with the churches in Wales, I produced a leaflet 'Hungary: A journey and a pilgrimage'. It was widely distributed and helped develop an interest in what was going on in the Churches 'behind the Iron Curtain.'

31st

At the General Synod office we met the Counsellor (General Secretary) Dr Zoltán Aranyos; and later spoke to Dr Kálmán Huszti minister of Pozsonyi ut. [ut = street] A pupil and friend of Hromadka of Prague, he spoke of the place of the church in a socialist society; the church of diakonia, servant of the community; we must work together for peace (nuclear threat as the issue

of today; Hungary as caught in the middle between the great power blocks). Pasareti ut congregation this evening was packed with all ages for a Passion Chorale. Talked to two students in a café. They have an amazing grasp of Gospel; they attend Bible study groups of young people at their church (40-50). These students talk freely of their faith to neighbours, workmates. What is this saying?
Hromadka had been one of the leading theologians in Eastern Europe. He and his family had escaped from Nazism and he lectured at Princeton before returning to Prague after the War. There he became Dean of the Comenius Faculty of Theology. He had always been committed to ecumenism and played a significant role in the World Council of Churches. Norah had received one of his books from one of his students, Mila Hradeçna when they were at a study group in the Bahamas.

APRIL

1st Good Friday
Holy Week is the Great Week in Hungary. We visited the new village of Dunavarsány where we joined the congregation of 20. We were asked questions about Northern Ireland. The local Catholic priest gave us a cross he made from nails. Visited the Albert Schweitzer Home, a 300 bed Reformed Church home; an impressive and caring witness to the Good News.

2nd
The church exerts pressure on the government through the pastors and laity who are members of 'Parliament'; Bishop Bartha is a member of the 'praesidium'; the government altered its policy on abortion because of church pressure. No food shortages in the well stocked market. At St Mátthiás we witnessed the Easter procession around the church when the host was carried under a canopy which during Holy Week covered the 'body of Jesus' in the church. To see 500 people following and singing was deeply impressive.
Bishop Tibor Bartha was the presiding bishop of the Hungarian Reformed Church.

Sunday 3rd Easter Day
Berti Tomás, a member of the foreign affairs department of the Reformed Church took me to the Scottish Mission for Hungarian service where I gave greetings and served at Communion. It was followed by the English service where I preached (35 and 20 present). Caught a train to Miskolc where Bishop

Kurti talked about in-service and ministerial training, socialism in Hungary. He read a poem of Arany János called 'A Walesi Bárdok' about the conquest of Wales.

The poem by János Arany has as its context the 'Massacre of the Welsh Bards' at Montgomery castle by King Edward. In fact the poem was a contemporary protest against the Austrian suppression of the Hungarians in the Nineteenth Century, but inspired by the Welsh legend.

4th

We met 20 men and women of all ages and backgrounds: a trade union leader, crane driver, trainee miner, chemical research worker, teacher, steel workers. We had an honest fresh encounter with alert, intelligent people of deep faith and concern.

5th

At the Old Age Home at Leányfalu, the elderly people talked about living in a Christian home which helped them prepare for death; it is 'a door into heaven' said one. Our final stop was the Home for Handicapped Children at Örbottyán which cares for 150 children. We met the ordained minister in charge, Zsófy who is a laughing energetic saint of 60. Her life is dedicated to the children - diakonia at its finest. Two dozen children shared a memorable service which included Kodály songs, a dance, hymns, Scripture passages, catechism - 6 are confirmed. This is the love of Jesus.

6th

I sat with Bishop Tóth on the three hour journey to Pécs in Baranya. What did I learn from this giant of a man? A world figure with WCC and CPC, he cares deeply about the church and his District. He has a great respect for Kádár and is grateful for the present mellowness; he works hard for his fellow Hungarians, especially in Transylvania; loves leading worship at Calvin Square; reads a chapter from the history, prophets and New Testament every morning. At Pécs we met the Dean and representatives of the deanery; saw an Exhibition of Csontváry. Called in Dunáujváros where a new church is being built in a socialist town.

Csontváry was one of the first Hungarian painters to be recognized throughout Europe. Dunáujváros was a new planned town where it was believed there would be no need for Christianity. The city was the 'trademark city' of socialism in Hungary, and was presented as such to foreign visitors. The fact that a church was being built there was a sign of great change.

7th

Bishop Bartha warmed as time proceeded; the church has adapted to a socialist system; socialism is here to stay; the Reformed church is becoming the church of the ordinary people; place of Word and Sacrament; the church's mission. We later met Dr Mihály Bocsay, the Director General at Ráday where there is a superb library and new college developments.
Bartha advocated weekly celebration of communion, very different from the Hungarian Reformed tradition of celebrating on 'high days'. Ráday was one of the two Reformed Colleges open at this time. The other was at Debrecen.

8th

We crossed the Great Plain of Hungary to the ancient Reformed College of Debrecen. After lunch with János Pásztor and his wife, we were shown around the College: Kossuth in 1849; 1944 parliament. Pásztor talked about diakónia, the political situation (Hungary will survive and can only be understood in the historic context of its suffering); World Council of Churches and Christian Peace Council balance one another in Eastern eyes; encouragement of exchanges of ministers and students.
Janos Pásztor was Dean and Professor of Theology at Debrecen. Later both he and his wife Judit visited Wales on separate occasions: Janos as an official delegate to the General Assembly, and Judit with the Debrecen Kántus Choir. Kossuth was the leader of the Hungarian Revolution of 1849. The Parliament of 1944 met in Debrecen because it had been liberated by the Russians from the Nazis.

9th

We all belong to a common humanity and differences enhance our life in the world. At Hójduhadház the pastor talked about his work with alcoholics, gypsies (2000 in the town) and suicides (20% of deaths in this small town). Drove to Sárospatak where we met Prof Újszaszy who showed us the magnificent library, museum and castle. A profound sense of Hungarian and Reformed history.
Sárospatak was another Reformed College. It had been closed by the Socialist government in 1952 but was re-opened in 1989.

12th

At the Miners Headquarters I had an appointment with General Secretary Mr Kovács. I read the greetings of George Rees and we talked about common issues: 'whatever our ideological, racial, national differences, we must move

from co-existence to cooperation; peace is more important; we are all human'.
I delivered the letter from the South Wales NUM.

13th
What a contrast in two days. Yesterday afternoon we had a relaxed meal in a restaurant overlooking the Danube in Budapest. The sun was warm and we were approaching the end of two weeks of hard rewarding work. We had taken time and energy to understand the Reformed Church. We arrived in Prague on a cool, grey, damp early morning to be met by Dr Otter, general secretary of the Evangelical Church of Czech Brethren. A much less relaxed situation; the State does not cooperate with the church.
The Czech Church was a union of Reformed and Lutheran Churches.

14th
I met the Deputy General Secretary of the Miners' Union: I read my letter; we talked of peace and mining.

15th
We are full of admiration for the Czech Brethren: difficult circumstances; a government official in most services; not allowed to publish for children (therefore mimeograph); discussions are not allowed but there is Bible study in every church; difficult for Christians to have higher education. Courageous, cultured and good humoured people. There is an awakening among young people; students for ministry; some churches full. We need each other.

18th
I gave Kim Howells the tokens from Hungary and Czechoslovakia and was invited to speak to the Executive.

MAY

5th
At the Council of Churches for Wales meeting at Aberystwyth I passed on the greetings from Hungary. Resolutions on disengagement from South Africa and on nuclear disarmament were passed unanimously.

11th
John Johannsen Berg, chairman of the Review Group asked about my 6 years as Moderator and what I believe should be the emphasis if I am asked to serve

another term: deepening faith and education; serving the poor and being with them; peace and working for greater West/ East understanding; the place of the URC in the Welsh nation. I asked him to raise these issues and if the Group felt they should not be pressed, I would be happy to stand down.

14th

Ann Clwyd, Ken Livingstone and two women from Greenham spoke in Penrhys at a Peace Festival organized by Rhondda CND. The URC Peace Resolutions were announced to applause.

25th

Our resolution for disarmament was passed overwhelmingly by the General Assembly. I am grateful for the privilege of playing a part in our Church's search to discover what is right from a Christian standpoint. The Southern/ Wales resolution was proposed by Tom Colvin and I seconded and we spoke 7½ minutes each. 25 speeches followed, 19 in favour. The vote was taken and to our joy it was 381 in favour and 180 against, 68% in favour. Over lunch I met the religious correspondents of 'The Guardian' and 'The Times'. They were delighted that 'the Nonconformist conscience is alive'.

The report of the debate from the July / August 1983 Reform (the URC Monthly magazine) records: 'URC members who were not there, may wonder how it was that Assembly, having declined in 1981 even to vote against Cruise and Trident, has now supported by a two-thirds majority a distinctly unilateralist motion brought jointly by the Southern and Wales Provinces... There was criticism from those (including the Church and Society department) who preferred to advocate a "freeze" movement because it was a politically practical way forward ... most of those who spoke in favour of the unilateral motion spoke of Christian values and obedience'.

26th

There was a reaction to yesterdays decision. Ron Williams and John ONeill spoke at length, disassociating themselves from yesterday. Kenneth Slack, supported by Newbigin stated we should accept the Church and Society resolution for a 'freeze' rather than yesterdays resolution on unilateralism. However the Moderator Alistair ruled that yesterday's decision could not be revoked. By this time John Jo-Berg and Michael Hubbard had proposed that HMG should receive yesterdays resolution. This was passed easily and was followed by the setting up of a 'peace group' in the URC.

JUNE

7th

I spoke to the Executive of the National Union of Mineworkers. Emlyn Williams was in the chair, received me politely but was cautious: 'suspicious of religious people; Moral Rearmament had taken them for a ride in the 50s'. It was agreed that a group should meet unofficially.
Frank Buchman founded the Oxford Group in the 1920s. It based its teachings on the 'Four Absolutes' (honesty, purity, unselfishness, love). Later, as the MRA (1938), it became more involved in political and social issues, particularly during the Cold War period when its anticommunist orientation found a receptive climate.

8th

Are Central Departments always to shape debates at Assembly? (Departmental resolutions are often compromises shaped by church professionals). What is the place of Synods? What of the movement of the Spirit during Assembly?
At the first Moderators' Meeting after the Assembly Disarmament Resolution, there were accusations that a Synod Resolution should not oppose a Departmental Resolution.

Sunday 19th

After service at Senghenydd, Norah and I walked with Mr Williams, an elder to the memorial of the Senghenydd explosion of 1913. The old gentleman described his hearing a 'thump' at 8.10 as he was reading his father's paper, and then walking with his friend to the scene. Gradually the hills filled with tens of thousands of people as the news spread.
On the 14th October 1913, 439 miners were killed. It was the worst mining disaster in British history. My grandfather, Dafydd Morgans, a miner, walked from Tylorstown to see if he could help.

20th

At Summer School at Trefeca, Will Roberts, an artist from Neath shared his passion for painting: scenes of people, strong backs of men working in the fields, large hands, scenes of crucifixion.
Will Roberts (1907-2000) was one of Wales' finest artists. His subject matter is focussed on his home area of Neath.

22nd

Philip Morgan lectured on the Vancouver themes: 'Life, a gift from God'; and 'Life in its Fullness'. He spoke with skill and passion with such an impressive use of poetry that my appetite for reading R S Thomas was awakened.

Philip Morgan was the General Secretary of the British Council of Churches and became Moderator of the URC General Assembly in 1984/5.

24th

The film 'Gandhi' celebrates the triumph of the human spirit, incarnational theology, the continuing perseverance, courage and love of a visionary who triumphed in the hard world of politics. I saw parallels in the anti-nuclear struggle. Is there a Gandhi to lead? What is the church's role in the struggle? The film also raises the issue of personal life style.

Richard Attenborough's film starred Ben Kingsley as Gandhi.

JULY

2nd

Committee Day at Llanidloes would have seemed miraculous 4 years ago: Church Life, Church and Society and World Church and Mission met with 34 people present: 2/3s lay and ½women with all Districts represented. Their work is of high quality and although there will always be untidy edges and blurred issues, there is a growing confidence. Major issues were Provincial Day at Llanidloes next year; peace-education, Hungary; the Welsh context in education programmes.

9th

Nigel Goodfellow was ordained to the joint pastorate of Buckley URC and Ewloe Green PCW. God willing, he will be an excellent minister. He is kind, generous, willing, energetic and of mature conviction.

16th

The ordination of Peter Noble and his induction to the pastorate of Brecon, Libanus and Cwmcamlais. The first ordination for Mid Wales Council proved distinctive: two anthems (one in Welsh); two sermons; a folk singing student from Manchester. Two hours but with the windows wide open it was not oppressive.

Sunday 17th

The URC service was held at the Friends' Meeting House at Llandrindod. Coffee with Mrs Powell-Jones, a faithful worker who was expecting her regular Sunday midday phone call from friends in the States, during which they sing 'All Things Bright and Beautiful'.

18th

Norah is on the eve of her great adventure. We first heard 3 years ago she was to be invited to attend the Sixth Assembly of the World Council of Churches at Vancouver.

21st

The Diamond Jubilee of the Brecon and Swansea Diocese was attended by the Queen, civic and ecclesiastical dignitaries.

AUGUST

6th

I spoke at a CND rally at Port Talbot to remember Hiroshima. The marchers, led by a jazz band, walked through the town to the Afan Lido. Speeches from: Dafydd Elis Tomos; 'the lady from the Rhondda' (on behalf of the Welsh Communist Party); a youth CND; a NUPE organizer, me and Joan Ruddock.
Lord Elis Tomos is now Presiding Officer of the Cynulliad, the Welsh Assembly. Joan Ruddock was chairperson of CND and is now a Labour MP. NUPE = National Union of Public Employees.

12th

The great day has arrived and Norah is home again. The expression on our faces when we saw her at Heathrow must have meant the world to her.
Norah arrived home after three weeks, as a URC delegate at the WCC Assembly in Vancouver. Preparations began two years ago when she was invited to attend a Women's Preparatory meeting in the Bahamas (28 women from 24 different countries). As a result of that meeting she was asked to be one of the 65 small-group leaders in the Assembly, meeting almost every day with a group which included the Archbishop of Finland, the Bishop of Dresden, several theologians including M M Thomas from India, Philip Morgan, politicians, musicians, Lynda Katsuno who became WCC advocate for people with disabilities. All shared their impressions and thoughts in this 'trusting' small group. It was a challenging but very affirming experience,

one from which we all as a family benefited. 'The plenary sessions were equally stimulating. Issues of peace, justice and the integrity of creation were the priorities. It was the worship of the Assembly which was the highlight with a magnetic quality which drew people towards the huge yellow and white tent with its music, prayers and liturgies from all traditions and every continent'. She was inspired and so were we as a family! We met Norah in Heathrow where she saw four beaming faces from afar as she pushed her trolley towards us.

20th

The annual pilgrimage to the grave of Fr Ignatius at Capel y Ffin, or more precisely, to Llanthony Tertia. The procession was led by swinging censor, candles and crucifix, the singing of a Lourdes processional and 150 followed up the hill; a reading at the crucifix; prayers at the statue to Mary, and Sung Evensong in the ruined church. I preached the sermon (on pilgrimage/ mission) after Cath and Hugh had read the first chapter of Acts in Welsh and English. Tea and cake in the cloisters.
I was the first 'non-conformist' to preach at the pilgrimage.

SEPTEMBER

3rd

The final ordination of the year. Howard Sharp was ordained and inducted to the United Church, Pontypridd. This completes the arrival of five young men this summer: David Fox, Nigel Goodfellow, Peter Noble and Patrick Taylor. There has been a transformation in ministry in Wales during the last six years. Our task is to keep up the standard of ministers: we can hardly improve on it.
Howard Sharp is Moderator for Mersey Province of the URC.

23rd

The delegation from the General Assembly crossed the hills to Painscastle to be greeted by the 4 members: Mr and Mrs Lloyd and the latter's two sisters. We tried to persuade them to stop within the URC, pointed out we could provide them with ministry, help them financially and enable them to feel part of the wider church. To no avail. 'I won't change my mind now': Mr Lloyd. All most sad and a long way from a trust and open-ness grounded in the Gospel. A well prepared tea before we left.
Painscastle is a chapel in the Radnor hills not far from Hay on Wye.

OCTOBER

19th

Penrhys for the induction of Pat Parrish. 150 present; Archdeacon presided and David Reece preached.

Gordon James presided and David Reece was assistant Bishop of Llandaff. Pat had served as a deaconess in the Presbyterian Church of England since 1962, and was ordained in 1979. She had served at Gorton since 1969.

NOVEMBER

2nd

My father died quietly and peacefully this evening. Norah and I had the privilege of spending this last day with him, and were with him at the point of death.

3rd

We went this evening to Tylorstown where we were surrounded by the warmth and generosity of the street which gives great strength. I woke many times during the night and experienced that gnawing emptiness: my father was dead, there was no-one like him to whom I could turn. What will I do without him as father, inspirer and above all, as great friend? How we had come to understand and respect each other; how much we loved our common roots in the valley; how we both loved Mam.

5th

One of the benefits of the past 2½ years was the way I came to appreciate Dad as a person in his own right. I saw and applauded the courage of his convictions in the way he lived: his Christian faith, his passionate concern for justice, his love for the underprivileged, his quiet generosity and the way these principles affected his day to day life.

DECEMBER

3rd

A strenuous and exhilarating witness for peace. I found it arduous because of the pain in my back, but supported by the trusty stick Dad used during the last couple of years (and which Dac, Church Tce also used), the rhythmic music and a large crowd of fellow protestors, I completed the 4 hour march which began on waste ground at the rear gate of the Royal Ordnance Factory. As a family we enjoyed the assembling of this great gathering of many shades of concern from all parts of Wales: Penlleyn, Holywell, Aberystwyth, Brecon, throughout South Wales; Marxist/Leninists, Trade Unionists, Christians of all descriptions, lawyers, medical people. To the sound of so much music we made our way around the base, down to Gabalfa roundabout, into Crwys Road and City Road, along Newport Road, through Cathays and back into the Centre, down the Hayes and up St Mary St to return to the Civic Centre. 4000 to hear speeches from so many: notably Dafydd Elis Tomos, Ann Clwyd, the Caerphilly MEP.

Ann Clwyd was MEP for Mid and West Wales from 1979 to 1984 and has been MP for Cynon Valley since 1984.

31st

I recognize the disappearance of that central pivot of mother, father and home. There will be no replacement. I know there is final reunion but the remainder of my earthly pilgrimage will be much greyer without them. It is also the year of Hungary, the Peace Movement and the continuing strengthening of the URC in Wales. Norah has been to Vancouver and there is her deepening involvement with many important issues. New Year again reminds me of parents and home: the colliery hooter sounding midnight; on a few occasions, the chapel party and the Watch Night service in Ebenezer. Days long gone and evoking a sweet sadness. However tomorrow is easier to face because of those good yesterdays.

1984

JANUARY

Sunday 15th

Bethesda Tongwynlais works hard to be faithful to its calling. The original chapel has been replaced by a smaller and more comfortable building. There was a warm welcome; a prayer in the minister's vestry and the minister is led to the lectern; children share in family worship; the organ leads and the small congregation sings. It is the kind of church I would join if I were a newcomer to the community.

Tongwynlais is between Cardiff and the Valleys and is often described as the gateway to the Valleys.

31st
Mrs Annie (John Griff) Davies who was my Sunday School teacher is 93 and has all her faculties: a remarkable old lady, and a privilege to see her.
Mrs Davies was in care in Llwynypia Hospital. It proved to be the last time we met.

FEBRUARY

25th
We joined friends and colleagues in the Peace Movement to celebrate the second anniversary of 'Nuclear Free Wales'. This is a declaration of intent rather than a reality. Brecon Cathedral was packed, and many Welsh church leaders took part. I read a piece entitled 'The last day of creation'.

MARCH

4th
Watched Dai Smith's programme on 'Wales? Wales!' where he describes the three Wales of the 1920s: Welsh Wales, English Wales (the Tory, Anglican, Anglicised areas), and American Wales (the valleys).
Dai Smith was Professor of History at Cardiff University. He is currently the Raymond Williams Chair in Cultural History at Swansea University.

APRIL

5th
Hywel Francis 'Miners against Fascism' is an account of the Welsh miners and the Spanish Civil War. There are parallels with the present crisis for our pits and communities.
Hywel Francis was Professor of Continuing Education at Swansea and founder of the South Wales Miners' Library and a prime-mover in the creation of the Community University of the Valleys. He is MP for Aberavon.

6th

Norah and I went to the TUC building in Cathedral Rd to a meeting in 'Defence of the Miners'. 150 present to hear Tyrone O'Sullivan, lodge secretary of Tower, Hirwaun; other speakers were Ann Clwyd, David Jenkins, union leaders and a dozen speakers from the floor.

Tyrone O' Sullivan became the chairman of Tower colliery in Hirwaun. He led the team of miners that fought to buy the pit from British Coal after it was due to close in 1994/95. David Jenkins was General Secretary of TUC Wales.

7th

We listened to speeches by Anti-Apartheid leaders and joined the march of 600 through the centre of town (flash point outside Crest Hotel when the Presidents XV walked past) to Sophia Gardens.

A South African team were playing the Welsh Rugby Union President XV.

Sunday 22nd, Easter Day

I led worship at Ebenezer on the third anniversary of my mother's death. I tried not to be too conscious of the day but it surfaced when Arthur Hughes, speaking in the second-meeting, reminded me that I was one of a group of older boys singing 'There is a balm in Gilead' many years ago at a Gymanfa.

Arthur Hughes, an Ebenezer deacon was an old family friend.

MAY

8th

We arrived at the Miners' Library for the Christian/ Marxist dialogue (exploration? encounter?). Hywel Francis brought Gareth Miles (dramatist and Communist Party), a NUM official from Gorseinon, an American working in miners' education, Harry Stratton (a Brigadier in Spain) and another young man. We included Roger Tomes, Dafydd, Kim, John H, Glyndwr Harris and Kirsty. So much to learn: their ignorance of contemporary Christian development; the NUM official coming to life as we showed concern; the invaluable contribution of the Hungarians, István Mészaros and János Pásztor.

Gareth Miles is a novelist and playwright. Harry Stratton was a member of the International Brigade in the Spanish Civil War. The URC group included Roger Tomes, tutor in New College London; Dafydd Jones, Kim Fabricius of Swansea, John Humphreys, Glyndwr Harris, Head of the Religious Education Department at Caerleon and Kirsty. The two Hungarians were on an official delegation from the Reformed Church of Hungary and I had met them both when I was in Hungary in 1983. István Mészaros was assistant bishop at Miskolc.

16th

District Council at Penarth responded to two major problems: the Miners' Strike and Apartheid in South Africa. The NUM representative, Keith Langley of Celynen South pit, Newbridge, spoke for 15 minutes and answered questions. He was honest, straight and courageous: he has refused redundancy pay of £14,000 and £75 per week! Doug Bale proposed a resolution to support the compassionate funds of the NUM and it was passed with 1 against, but several abstentions. Later a resolution relating to Welsh Rugby Union and South Africa was passed unanimously.
The District meeting was dealing with radical issues, on the cutting edge of church and society. They show the church was growing in confidence. The WRU was encouraging teams to play with South Africans.

18th

At the West Wales District at Parkmill, Eric Davies spoke on behalf of the NUM and by concentrating on social aspects, he won the respect of Council. After he left, we had the debate on apartheid which provoked a good discussion and a resolution deploring WRU proposal to tour South Africa. We must not shirk controversial issues.

23rd

Risca for Gwent District Council. Carl Browning, chairman of South Celynen lodge spoke effectively and had a good response. Also passed apartheid resolution.

30th

Paul Quilter, Norah and I led the way into Christchurch for the family. The service developed into worship: the singing was meaningful; the young people sang; Paul Quilter and I spoke. There were as many people outside the church as inside. Everyone touched by Dafydd and the family's great courage.
Daphne Jones and her young daughter Bethan had been killed in a head on car crash as they were returning from Christchurch, Fairwater on Sunday morning. It was such a profound tragedy. Norah and I knew the family intimately because Dafydd was from Manselton and was now minister in Ely. His sister Mary, and parents, John and Betty, were devout members at Manselton. The experience shook the whole of the Church. In many ways youth work in Wales never fully recovered. Daphne had initiated so much by

her faith, enthusiasm and hard work. Paul was URC Youth Secretary and a personal friend of Daphne and Dafydd.

JUNE

1st

The conclusion of the first stage of the tragedy which demolished so much of Dafydd's life. How fragile are our lives and all we build. For Dafydd a split second ended so much. I went with the family to the Western Cemetery for the committal. A quiet reassuring act: the two wooden caskets were placed side by side; the family each read a verse; I said the committal and we said the Lord's Prayer and Grace together. The sun shone, the air was warm, the trees were full and a bird sang.

22nd

A stimulating beginning to our annual Ministers' Summer School. Dai Smith spoke on 'Wales: Fracture and Unity.' Both his facts and interpretation were new to most of us.

23rd

Dafydd Elis-Thomas spoke with remarkable lucidity and was well informed, providing a fascinating view of the Welsh nationalist and wider political scene. He described himself as Welsh-British.
Dafydd Elis-Thomas was Plaid Cymru MP for Meirionydd Nant Conwy. He is now Presiding Officer at the National Assembly.

24th

Dai Smith and Dafydd Elis Thomas have described how Wales emerged during the last century and a half. Dai emphasized that we are now witnessing the destruction, almost the death knell, of industrialized Wales; also that we are a multi-cultural people. Dafydd's argument was very similar: seeking respect for the various traditions in Welsh life and emphasizing Wales' contribution to Britain and Europe. The issues of 'defence' of, or new life for, the community were crucial, as are the international issues of peace and justice in a nuclear age.

29th

Norah and I arrived at Mansfield, Oxford for the Commemoration Service at which I preached. John Marsh, John Huxtable as well as the staff were present. I preached on Luke 5 and related it to miners and community. I hope there was a good response. Several stated they felt challenged. Dinner was excellent but expensive with every sign of luxury. The young Student President was off to the Christchurch Ball, costing £84 (for two)! A revolution is needed: public repentance.

JULY

7th

Our Second Synod Day was again held at Llanidloes. Kirsty [Thorpe] has pulled all the strands into shape. Everything worked well; the crowds were dispersed throughout the campus; there was a varied programme, good exhibitions and key periods when we came together: notably the final Eucharistic celebration with a fine sermon by Philip Morgan. Very hot sun; people sat in the shade; I recognized people from 80 congregations. 25 buses and a full car park: 1500?

10th

The Commission of Covenanted Churches met in Shrewsbury. A resolution from the General Assembly of the PCW insisted on immediate 'recognition of ministry' with the 'threat' that Free Church unity should be pursued rather than the wider unity promised through the Covenant. The Anglicans were accused of not taking seriously the search for unity. I responded with 'to what extent are we implementing what is already possible? Are we breaking down traditional pastoral patterns in the search of a pattern relevant to mission? Are we seeking ecumenical pastorates? These things can be done now!'
I suspect this tension lay at the heart of the dilemma in the search for Church Unity. It has not been resolved and the decline of traditional denominations in Wales has continued.

16th

We have greeted Kántus from Debrecen and acknowledge them as sisters and brothers in Christ. We are creating the bridge between our two churches and nations; there can be no turning back and our oneness in Christ will be discovered, revealed and lived. Our peoples will together celebrate their common humanity.
The Choir was formed in 1737 in the Reformed Church College in Debrecen, Eastern Hungary, and is the only institution in Hungary which has survived both the Austrian occupation and the Soviet occupation. The singers are made

up of young people at the Reformed College, the secondary school and former students. The Choir Director was Dr Sandor Berkesi.

18th

If my earthly life were to end now, at least it has been an instrument for this magnificent expression of the Gospel. Kántus sang for the first time in the United Kingdom, and they have sung here in Cardiff as guests of the URC in Wales. We took the choir to the National Stadium where they sang to the manager of the field; and St David's Hall where they sang in the auditorium. The concert was at St Andrew's: I led with prayers, and Kántus shared an hour and 20 minutes of ecstasy: human and divine touched. We were presented with a pastor's embroidery. An audience of 500.

AUGUST

11th

I spoke for a second year at the CND march organized by the Port Talbot branch. An excellent platform: Dafydd Elis Thomas, me (I referred to the building of bridges and gave our Hungarian experience as an example), Illtud Harrington (the chairman of Greater London Council), Terry Thomas, (vice president of NUM in South Wales), Hilary from Greenham and Bruce Kent. This year has been hard for CND: difficult to keep up the momentum and discover new strategies. I believe we have discovered one with our bridge building with Hungary.

Bruce Kent was a Catholic priest and General Secretary of CND. He resigned from the priesthood in 1987 in order to be actively involved in the General Election.

OCTOBER

10th

I arrived at Transport House for the steering committee of the 'Congress for the Defence of Mining Communities'. The officers were elected: Hywel Francis in the chair, secretary Kim Howells, treasurer Ann Clwyd. We prepared a press statement and presented it to the media conference. To my consternation the first question was directed to the 'silence of the Free Church leaders' compared with the Church of England. I was in at the deep end and spoke on the nature of community. Consequently I was interviewed by 4-5-6 on Radio Wales, BBC News; and later at 4 for ITV News (Wales) with Ann Clwyd. I hope I expressed the Gospel dimension.

The day changed my involvement in the dispute from sympathetic concern to active support. I needed to be asked 'whose side are you on?' and until this point, I could avoid any decision which might affect my public profile. When the question was asked about the non-involvement of the Free Church leaders, I had to answer the question and had to decide (almost thinking on my feet) what was my personal position. I was tossed into the public arena. The Congress was officially launched and mobilized considerable support from the general public.

11th

I listened to the Welsh News and was astonished and petrified to hear the headline that a Welsh Nonconformist Church Leader had spoken in support of the striking miners. While at the office I was interviewed by a Sunday Times reporter. What is happening?

13th

At Synod, Cedric Mayson addressed us on his experience in South Africa. He lived there 26 years, was imprisoned for 14 months as he awaited trial, and was interrogated for 4 days. He portrayed the heresy of apartheid, emphasized the economic oppression and responded superbly to questions. Doris brought a resolution relating to the Miners' strike. The extremes were expressed, but a resolution was passed. I had to use my casting vote on an amendment for identify with rather than 'recognize'.

Cedric Mayson, former Methodist Minister, was banned for five years in 1977 and detained on 27 November 1981. He appeared before the Pretoria Supreme Court on charges including treason and being a member or an active supporter of the ANC. He was released on bail, fled the country. and arrived in Britain the day before his case was due to resume on 18 April 1983. Doris Leyshon's resolution asked Synod to 'identify with the mining communities' fears about the future: (a) calls on churches to be involved in the work of relief (b) to be involved in the work of reconciliation and reconstruction of the communities after the strike is over.'

Sunday 21st

Our eucharistic celebration at St Illtud's witnessed the penetrating of the Holy Spirit who gives peace. The Lima liturgy was magnificent; unaccompanied singing; everyone read; a short homily based on readings by the three Peters (Bunker, Trow, Noble); using the cup and plate given today by Carol; candles; baby Bethan put in my arms for blessing; silence. Howling gale.

On Caldey, another remarkable experience. Bethan was the daughter of Peter and Val Noble.

24th
A most unusual journey to Paddington in an older train with compartments. I sat with two dock officials/ directors in South Wales, living in the Vale; friends and holidays in the West Indies and Madeira, freemasons. I thought of class collision.

NOVEMBER

10th
Brian Wren's 'Education for Justice' is the book I needed to read because of my vulnerability which is a result of my stance on the miners' strike. Brian encourages the church to struggle for justice.

13th
We are witnessing the end of our mining communities and the defeat of the NUM which played a critical role in the creation of South Wales community life. Bitterness, disillusionment and anger will be the legacies of the strike.

14th
A personal crisis in ministry: how do I relate my faith in crucifixion/ resurrection/ Pentecost power to what is happening in the terrifying social and political issues facing our society and world? I am disturbed by world famine, the nuclear crisis and arms race, apartheid in South Africa, the deepening division in the United Kingdom and particularly the coal dispute. I know where I stand theologically on these issues, but what is my practise? What am I to say and do? How do I balance my 'moderating' and 'leadership roles' in the church: there is a real tension.

15th
The National Executive of the NUM met, decided to continue the strike and broaden its appeal to the churches and other organizations. Many churchmen have spoken courageously in England on behalf of the miners, but in Wales the major support has come from the URC. Has our support given the NUM confidence that churches actually share the NUM's concern about community, divisions in the nation and the nature of work?
Arthur Scargill appealed to churches and other organisations for support. I was contacted by Gronw ap Islwyn, a Welsh Independent minister and friend, to ask if we could respond. I phoned Noel Davies of the Council of Churches for Wales and Douglas Bale, the URC Urban Chaplain. I then arranged for the

four of us to meet George Rees of the NUM, and Doug phoned Philip Weekes, Director of the South Wales coalfield.

Sunday 18th

I felt both at the centre and on the edges. Geographically I travelled west to lead worship in a small and isolated church, and I returned to the heart of the coalfield. Theologically I had been sharing the centrality of the Gospel in worship, and on my return I found myself in the centre of this critical dispute tearing the heart out of our South Wales communities. I met Hywel's family at Crynant where Hywel was taking some women to a 'Tupperware' party (sit-in at Cynheidre).

Hywel and Mair Francis lived in Crynant. Because of the fear of telephone bugging, the arrangements for the sit-in had been disguised as a meeting for women to sell Tupperware.

19th

A tough exhausting day. Doug Bale, Noel Davies, Gronw and I spent an hour with Emlyn Williams, George Rees and Emlyn Jenkins (area organizer for Mid Glamorgan coalfield) at the NUM headquarters. At first Emlyn Williams seemed nonplussed by our visit but slowly 'thawed': 'We must act in accordance with national instructions, important for South Wales to remain solid and give an example; would be glad of a negotiated settlement but we are not hopeful.' Lunch in a pub on Caerffili mountain before we arrived at the NCB headquarters at 3 and spent 2 hours with Philip Weekes and Arthur ? Again a fruitful experience: They want a negotiated settlement but London will not have it. They would welcome good relationships with NUM in South Wales because we respect each other, there is a disciplined workforce, crucial to relate again. What happens next? We are held in high regard by both parties.

The Arthur was Arthur Shambrook, Deputy to Philip Weekes.

20th

I wrote my impressions of yesterday's meetings and discovered common attitudes with Union and management. To the reasonable mind it would seem that negotiation and a settlement were possible.

22nd

I shared my paper with Kim who saw it as a possible basis for creating the climate for negotiation. I shall prepare a second draft and share it with George Rees and Philip Weekes.

29th

I arrived at the Gwyn Hall for the Congress Meeting: Ystradgynlais choir; Kim Howells; Donald Coleman; two local speakers. The choir were singing at 8.40 when I was called out to meet the police; a bomb scare and the bomb was to go off at 9.15. I returned and told Hywel: Dai Smith and I spoke briefly; I gave a cheque from Congress to local support fund and we had all left by 9.12.

The Gwyn Hall was in Neath. Donald Coleman was the local MP.

30th

A frightening day. I woke at 7.15, switched on the radio and heard the sickening news that a taxi driver taking a miner to work at Merthyr Vale had been killed by a piece of concrete thrown from a bridge near Rhymney. I felt as disturbed and sickened as did all from our mining communities. Two miners, aged 20 and 21, have been arrested and charged with murder.

The day was the reaping of the whirlwind and reflected the bitter frustration. The incident forced a response from the sensitive; the ruthless used the incident ruthlessly.

DECEMBER

10th

A phone call from Dafydd L about our initiative on the miners' strike. He feels it has mileage.

13th

Norah and I found the NUM club without difficulty. At the Press Conference, Hywel gave introductions; Arfon stated that the Rhondda Congress had been established; I spoke on the churches' initiative; a sociologist spoke; then Dafydd L, Arthur True, a woman peacemaker. I was questioned and taped for radio. The Review Body or Royal Commission seems an acceptable solution. I drafted a letter for church leaders to sign.

The launching of the Rhondda section of the Congress for the Defence of Mining Communities. The sociologist was Gareth Rees who is now Professor within the School of Social Sciences at Cardiff University. Arthur True belonged to a well-known Rhondda Communist family. The letter which I drafted to the church leaders called on the government to set up an 'independent review body.' At the meeting was Donald McIntyre, the Labour Editor of the Sunday Times. He reported: 'the most significant development politically, not matched in any other coalfield, is a Wales Congress .. It includes senior churchmen.'

14th

My call for a Royal Commission and my interview were repeated several times on the Welsh News. What have I learnt from this process? Because I 'got alongside' the NUM and listened carefully to management, I was able to record a careful appraisal with 'suggestions for negotiation'. Now that I have discovered what seems a reasonable way ahead I need to convince others of the validity of the approach. Each task is difficult but this last one is the hardest.

Sunday 23rd

Tea 'in aid of the miners'. Cath took invitations to every house (100) in our area and to our delight 20 people came and brought tea and coffee.
A Sunday tea at home.

28th

Several years ago I felt that defence based on nuclear weapons was morally wrong; I committed myself to the unilateralist cause, met people, studied issues of defence and consequently learned how to argue the case reasonably. At first it was intuitive: rationality followed. The same is true of the mining dispute. My intuition was to support the miners because of my background and the need to defend mining communities. Then I met people who supported the miners, especially through the Congress. My reading has deepened and now I hope to argue the case rationally.

31st

I felt tonight the sound of the pit hooter and the church bell at midnight long ago in Tylorstown and I was melancholy.

1985

JANUARY

3rd

The Congress held an emergency meeting at NUM Pontypridd to discuss the 'Letter from the Welsh Church Leaders to the Prime Minister'.

4th

I drove apprehensively to the ex-mining village of Deri, north of Bargoed on a bitterly cold morning. Karl Francis arrived and the service began at 10.30: 100 present; the Sirhowy choir; women from the Cynon valley; miners. I preached on 'the word coming to John the Baptist'; an elder read, we sang two hymns and there were prayers. Crossed the mountain to Bedlinog for filming at the War Memorial.

'The outstanding film of the festival and the finest single documentary made in Britain last year was Karl Francis' "Ms Rhymney Valley 1985." It was a work of art, a personal and partial view of the 1984-5 miners' strike from the vantage point of Francis' native valley.' (The Daily Telegraph). 'If Karl Francis ever transcribes the 100 minutes of "Ms Rhymney Valley 1985" he will find among his heap of paper something approaching perfect historical drama.' (The Sunday Times)

8th

The Western Mail had a huge front page headline: 'Mine leaders back Church peace bid'. There followed a page of accurate detail and a very supportive editorial. The four of us went to Llanishen to meet Philip Weekes and Arthur Shambrook. Both feel our initiative is correct and Philip was prepared to welcome it publicly. He will work for it privately but must walk carefully because of the big three (Thatcher, McGregor, Walker) who make the decisions. I phoned the NUM and Arfon reported that support for the initiative had been passed unanimously by the South Wales Executive and would be taken to the Sheffield National Executive Council on Thursday. Phone calls from the Catholic Herald, Labour Weekly, Acas. Kim on 'Newsnight'; good reports on Welsh news.

The support of the 'Western Mail' became an important catalyst for further action by the media during the following weeks and for bringing the issues to the attention of the general public. 'South Wales miners' leaders are today planning an independent bid to end the pit strike by throwing their weight behind a peace formula drawn up by the Welsh Churches. The area executive meeting this morning in Pontypridd will discuss a resolution endorsed by all nine members of the Council of Churches for Wales and the Roman Catholic Church in the Principality.'

9th

I caught the 11.02 to Paddington and happened to meet Ann Clwyd on the station. We travelled up together. She hopes to table a question tomorrow in the Commons about the Churches Initiative. She shared important insights into the Congress and the Labour Party in Wales: a reluctance by the latter to get too identified because of Plaid's involvement.
An Early Day motion was endorsed by Ann Clwyd, Allan Rogers, Geraint Howells, Denzil Davies, Ted Rowlands and Alan Williams.

10th

The National Executive Council (NEC) of the NUM has unanimously welcomed the Welsh approach but George and Emlyn insisted there be no public statement so that the Churches could press on.

12th

The crucial aspects of this struggle are the future of coal and energy policy? do trade unions have the right to organize and take industrial action? the nature of community life? and the future of Wales?

14th

Doug Bale, Derek Evans, Noel and I travelled to London to meet Pat Lowry, head of ACAS and two senior colleagues - Dennis Boyd and Mick Melluish. I presented my paper; we considered a possible solution (an Independent Review Body combined with the ACAS proposals of October 31st) and then the strategy (is NUM prepared to negotiate? ACAS would press NCB to return to the table; possibly both parties press the government for IRB).
ACAS = Advisory Conciliation and Arbitration Service. Derek Evans was a member of Beulah Rhiwbina and I had met him a few days previously. It was he who arranged this meeting in London. Dennis Boyd succeeded Pat Lowry as head of Acas.

15th

What a struggle to find a way in this dense jungle. Gronw, Doug and I met Emlyn Williams, George Rees, Terry Thomas, Kim and Emlyn Jenkins. They could not accept the ACAS document of October 31st because it had been rejected by a delegate conference. They supported our original document and when pressed, suggested a moratorium during the period of an Independent Review. I met the Church leaders at Llanedeyrn and shared our position: all press for negotiated settlement, endorsed IRB; Church Leaders will travel to London next week to lobby MPs; we had full support and encouragement.

16th

The Western Mail's front page headline was 'Churches Peace Bid Boosted by Secret Talks.' I drafted the three-point plan for settlement: Independent Review Body; moratorium on closure during the period it sits; the parties to decide on the closing date for the Report of the Review Body. I was at NUM where the 4 of us presented the new points and had full acceptance of George, Terry and Kim. Many phone calls: Keith Harper of the Guardian; Steve Brown of Observer.

Virgin Trains in 2002 named one of its trains in memory of Keith Harper.

17th

Another supportive editorial from the 'Western Mail' which referred to the latest NACODS position who were insisting that talks should resume between the NUM and NCB. Doug and I saw Philip Weekes who was very supportive, grateful for our persistence, examined and accepted fully our new proposals and said he would try and arrange a meeting with McGregor. He told us the government wanted a slow trickling back, and knew they would win a war of attrition. Drove to NACODS office and met the secretary (Glyn Jones from Ynysybwl) and president (Bob Willis from Abercynon). They looked carefully at our proposals, accepted them and will take them to a delegate conference tomorrow. Ann Clwyd phoned: we meet Peter Walker next week.

NACODS = National Association of Colliery Overmen, Deputies and Shot-firemen. They did not take part in the strike.

19th

Noel, Dafydd and I met Melvyn Rosser (a member of the NCB Board of Directors) at the Council of Churches' office in Swansea. I presented the background and he expressed the NCB policy: profit and loss as critical, but gradually we talked about social consequences; he acknowledged the need

for a long term energy policy; suggested an approach to Walker (begin with Independent Review Body re pit closures with their social consequences; and then move on to IRB for coal within an energy policy); talked about the need for compromise and for the NCB to shift its position. He was sufficiently impressed to suggest we met McGregor. We gained a friend, rather than alerted an enemy. Took our papers to Ann Clwyd's before going to hear Gwyn Alf and poets in support of miners at Chapter.
Sir Melvyn Rosser, an accountant by profession, was an elder of the Presbyterian church of Wales and became President of the University of Wales, Aberystwyth. Professor Gwyn Alf Williams was the author of hen was Wales? Dafydd Owen, General Secretary of the Presbyterian Church of Wales.

21st

Met the secretary, Arnold Draper and president, Bill Davies of BACM. Gronw and I introduced our proposals and had their full support - it was unqualified and could be made public. They will take it to regional and national executives. Afterwards we saw David Jenkins of Wales TUC and again had full support. Home at 6.30: Trevor Barnes was waiting and he interviewed me in the garden for a more authentic sound! South Wales Executive gave full support for our proposals today.
BACM = British Association of Colliery Management. The Colliery managers also gave their support to the Churches' initiative. David Jenkins was General Secretary of the Wales TUC from 1984 to 2004. Trevor Barnes became an award winning journalist and reporter for the BBC's Religion and Ethics Department.

22nd

NACODS gave unanimous support to the Church proposal at a delegates conference yesterday. Noel and I were in the Commons at 7p.m. Ann Clwyd took us to Barry Jones who introduced us to Neil Kinnock, Stan Orme and Kinnock's aide. He shared his insight into the character of the protagonists. 'You could do it, but it will be hard'.
Barry Jones was MP for Alun and Deeside. Stan Orme was Shadow Energy Secretary.

23rd

A day filled with high drama left numbness. I walked to the Department of Energy where at 4, Noel, Derek Childs, John Ward, Dafydd Owen and I met

Peter Walker, Nicholas Edwards, David Hunt and others. A strange encounter in that it wasn't a conversation: Peter Walker repeated his confidence in the future of the coal industry; the impossibility of an 'independent body;' rejected a moratorium. He didn't listen to anything anyone of us said. It lasted an hour and 45 minutes. Derek Childs fumed, 'It was like being back in school and lectured by the headmaster'.

The climax of the public profile of the Churches' attempt to prepare the way for a just, negotiated settlement. Superficially it failed. It did not alter the governments or the NCB's positions. We were greeted by a half-hour lecture on the future of the coal industry and after we had been deigned to present our case, it was swiftly and ruthlessly demolished: 'I don't care whether the Unions now support the proposal for an Independent Review Body. .. there is no such thing as an Independent Body... the future basis of British energy policy is nuclear... look at our friends, the French who now have such cheap electricity.' We argued and failed, not because our case was invalid but because we were not listened to. Government policy was not for turning.

30th

Noel, Doug, Gronw and I went to Hobart House to meet Ian McGregor, Jimmy Cowans, Merrick Proton, Melvyn Rosser and Mr McPherson (and secretary). Noel introduced background; I spoke about our proposals; McGregor responded that the UK energy 'plan' is free enterprise; we seemed to be drifting away but got on course with my reference to Scargill as martyr-leader if NCB is not careful at this point. The Board could appear intransigent and extremist.

The meeting with the Board of the NCB. McGregor's approach to turning the NCB into a profitable concern was similar to the line he had taken at British Steel: cut jobs and close unprofitable pits. Despite many meetings between the two opposing sides, no agreement was ever reached, and the UK coal industry continued its decline when the strike finished. Against the 170 collieries operational in 1984, there are eight deep mines operating in the UK. McGregor's parents were members of the United Free Church of Scotland and he received a devoutly Christian upbringing. McGregor began by asking 'what is this United Reformed Church? There are three card-carrying Presbyterians this side of the table.'

31st

At 12.15 Kim phoned: could I catch the 1 train to meet the National Executive Council at Congress House. Doug and I were with the NEC for 2 hours

although Scargill, Heathfield and McGahey made entrances and exits. Norman Willis spoke at one time, and it looks as if he is trying to mediate. Doug and I had a good hearing; many questions and comments; but they were adamant there could be no preconditions.
This was a meeting with the opposite end of the spectrum. Peter Heathfield was the General Secretary of the NUM. Mick McGahey was a Vice President of the Union and a life-long Communist. Norman Willis was General Secretary of the TUC.

FEBRUARY

4th

If this were a 'normal' industrial dispute, our formulation would enable the partners to negotiate. However this is no 'normal' dispute and Mrs Thatcher's extremism will not allow her to mellow or move; she will budge only if her political safety depends on it. Congress meeting at Ebenezer: 70 present to hear Llew Smith (MEP), Gareth Rees (Communist Party), Peace Movement, Women's Support, local miners, Mattie Collins, JM.
A Rhondda Congress meeting was held in my home chapel Ebenezer. Its tradition had much in common with its 1920s support of the mining community. Llew Smith became MP for Blaenau Gwent. Mattie Collins represented the Tylorstown Ward on Rhondda Borough Council.

11th

I was interviewed for Channel 4 by Michael Crick, the author of a new book on Arthur Scargill.
Michael Crick had spent most of his time in Yorkshire researching his book. He stated how 'he felt it was a totally different atmosphere in South Wales. There was a sense of community solidarity and a more reasoned and questioning attitude towards the dispute. There was no blind following of any leader and no being swayed by demagogues. He wondered whether this was the result of the Welsh heritage.'

26th

We are approaching the end of the strike. Terry Thomas feels the crucial issue is to hold the Union together in South Wales and go back to work without a settlement. He is convinced that neither the government nor the NCB are interested in a settlement without the prerequisite of the NUM's acceptance (before negotiation) of the closure of uneconomic pits. What is the purpose

of a Union that signs away the jobs of its members? The timetable seems to be NEC on Thursday, South Wales delegate conference on Friday and National Conference early next week. To go back without a settlement seems disastrous.
Terry Thomas was the Vice President of the South Wales NUM.

MARCH

1st
The strike ends next week. The Executive and the Delegates of the South Wales miners met in Porthcawl and recommend to the National Delegates Conference on Sunday that they return to work without a settlement. This is a bitter blow for all who have struggled and sacrificed for a year, but there can be no compromise with the ruthless Thatcherite view of society. The Church must identify itself with a view of a just and compassionate society, and discover allies in the long struggle ahead.

Sunday 3rd
The miners return to work on Tuesday and the strike is over. The NEC split 11-11 and the Delegates Conference voted 98-91 in favour of the South Wales resolution for an orderly return on Tuesday - with the cries of betrayal at the South Wales leadership.

5th
As a family we left at 5.40 on a cold, clear, bright morning and travelled north guided by an almost full moon. It was like a pilgrimage to drive through Tylorstown to arrive in Maerdy by 6.30. We parked in a side street, walked down to the Hall and were amazed by the crowds. We joined in the procession as it wound its way up to the pit, led by Tylorstown Band and the advancing dawn. Remarkable experience as the miners stopped to line the road and applaud us the supporters, and then for the supporters to do the same for the miners of this pit where not one has returned to work. Met so many friends: Kim and family, Dai Smith, Geraint and Meryl (Treherbert), colleagues on the Congress. Media everywhere. Arfon and others spoke from the roof of the baths: not the end, not defeat.
Geraint Davies was a Plaid Cymru councillor in Rhondda and became Assembly Member for Rhondda in 1989. He is a deacon and secretary of Blaencwm Baptist Church and visited Caldey several times with our groups. He is the son of the late John Haydn Davies, conductor of Treorci Male Voice Choir.

11th

The half yearly Church Leaders Meeting at the Shire Hall, Shrewsbury. The major issue was whether to encourage the Covenant Commission's proposal to seek mutual recognition of ministry by 1990 or the Archbishop's suggestions about cooperation at ground level. A useful encounter.
Once again the dilemma is expressed. It is not an either/or but a both/and.

Sunday 24th

Elim Cwmbran had its buildings rededicated after considerable reconstruction. The main visual change was slight but basic: the removal of two pews from the front and the replacement of a central pulpit and side choir stalls with a central table, removal of 'clutter' and the fitting of a carpet. The building looked different and had a different atmosphere for worship. There was open-ness, a sense of space and a feeling it belonged to the family of the church.

APRIL

2nd

I have been invited to serve on the Religious Advisory Group for Harlech TV. Several years ago I was a BBC Religious Advisor but it served only to rubber-stamp what had been done. This group could influence policy makers. Chaired by Gwyn Erfyl, the three advisors were Edwin Reagan (RC), the retired headmaster of the Bishop of Llandaff School (Anglican) and me. This is a critical juncture because HTV are only starting to produce religious programmes in English for its Welsh audience.
Gwyn Erfyl was a television producer and executive who was amongst the best known person in Welsh language television in the 1970s. 'He had an interviewing style all his own, a mixture of penetrating analysis, philosophical reflection and sardonic humour that gave his programmes a quality that was much appreciated by viewers wanting intellectual stimulus rather than mere entertainment.' (Obituary by Meic Stephens). Edwin Reagan was priest at Bridgend and became Bishop of Wrexham. Norah also served on the BBC Religious Advisory Committee.

29th

Westcliffe on Sea, Southend for General Assembly. I am not at my best in the 'religious crowd,' particularly with pomp and circumstance, and the first day of Assembly has these elements

30th

I presented the Moderators' Report and because I had done most of the drafting, I presented it in the way I know best by sharing 'stories' of the Kingdom.

Each year a different Moderator presents the Report on behalf of the twelve Moderators. It therefore happened to me just once!

MAY

19th

I watched 'The Mimosa Boys', a play about four young Welsh guardsmen, three of whom were killed at Bluff Cove in the Falklands. Thatcherite militarism and jingoism makes me so angry but we must not be disheartened. Our young people must not be captivated by the idol of specious patriotism.

The Mimosa was the ship in which the Welsh settlers sailed to Patagonia in 1865.

JUNE

26th

Brian Wren has stimulated, provoked, challenged and at the same time reassured with the centrality of the Gospel. 'Dives and Lazarus' was studied very effectively through role play and comment. Brian's next session on justice and conflict was led in a quiet, unassuming manner that provoked our own self-searching. We later sang Brian's excellent hymns. A fresh exhilarating experience.

Ministers' Summer School.

27th

Brian Wren through his ideas and innovating presentation taught both content and method, but for me the challenge was in terms of personal life style. I have been discontented for a long time by the size of our house and the place it is situated. We should not live in this wealthy area but I also realize we only just manage to live on my salary. Our children do not have what others of their peer group get. A real dilemma.

JULY

2nd

I wrote to the two churches in which I haven't yet led worship: Maesmynis and Tretower, neither of which reply to letters. I believe they exist but there is little evidence to prove it!

Maesmynis is in the Epynt mountains and Tretower near Crickhowell.

9th

The 'public independent inquiry' into the closure of St John's Colliery, Maesteg is being held in the Glamorgan Council Chamber. It is not 'independent' because it has been organized by the NUM Lodge, but it should provide open discussion. Alan Fisher of NUPE (now retired) is in the chair; Gareth Rees is the sociologist; there is an Oxford economist and me! Evidence was given by 4 workmen from St John's - Charlie White (chairman), followed by a presentation by a geologist who had worked for the NCB. Andrew Glyn, the economist and Dr Tudor Hart of Glyncorrwg gave evidence.

This was an attempt by the Miners' Lodge at Maesteg to show the reasons for the survival of their pit. The attempt was inevitably abortive. 'Andrew Glyn was a fellow of Corpus Christi College, Oxford, from 1969, and an economist with an international reputation. His skills were put to particularly useful effect during the miners' strike of 1984-85. He backed up his instinctive solidarity with the miners by writing a series of articles and pamphlets unmasking falsehoods about the financial situation of the mines which were being purveyed by the Coal Board and the Thatcher government to justify their policy of massive pit closures. This was a signal example of rigorous academic work being used to support working-class struggle.' (Obituary by Nick Hall). Charlie White died suddenly in 1985. His enthusiasm and commitment were an inspiration to the panel. Dr Julian Hart dedicated his life and work to the community of Glyncorrwg. 'I feel my clinical work has always been political. Anybody who insists on high standards of care for poor communities... is involved in progressive politics, helping people to stand up for themselves.' (The New Generalist, Spring 2007),

10th

The second morning was spent with Bert Pearce (CP), the Chairman of Llynfi Community Council and the Planning Officer for Ogwr. The Chairman had a spark and love for his community - he had worked for 29 years at Coegnant.

This afternoon saw the Union's case presented by Ian Isaac, Terry Thomas and Kim Howells. Although it was a powerful, impressive presentation, we realized how heavily the cards are stacked against the Union.

Bert Pearce was a life-long member of the Communist Party. In 1998, when Nelson Mandela received the freedom of the city of Cardiff, he was singled out for praise, in the anti-apartheid struggle. Coegnant Colliery was in Caerau, Maesteg. It closed in 1981. Ian Isaac was Lodge Secretary.

11th

The three day enquiry was followed by a 4 hour meeting of the panel when we agreed how to prepare the Report, our conclusions and how it should be handled afterwards. This morning we had evidence from the County Council - planning, social care, industrial planner. Then Idwal Isaac spoke on behalf of Maesteg Support groups. After lunch a report by the Congress and finally questioning of Ian Isaac and Charlie White. We worked honestly and dispassionately to arrive at the conclusion that the pit should remain open for economic reasons.

Idwal Isaac was father of Ian Isaac.

AUGUST

31st

My 8th year as Moderator saw me drawn into that area of sharp edges where religion and the 'wider aspects of life' touch. The developing issues of the nuclear threat and my support for CND; the East West gulf and my commitment to our Hungarian relationship; polarization in this country and support for the miners; my pledges to the anti-apartheid movement and the Nicaraguan Solidarity group. My foundation is the Gospel and I am grateful for my deepening in Scripture (how thankful I am to Alan Dale), prayer life (Caldey and Taize) and the ecumenical support.

SEPTEMBER

18th

I worked on the Reformed/Anglican Report: 'God's Reign and Our Unity.' It presents critical insights into our search for unity and defines an urgent context. I am engaged in ortho-praxis as I struggle with major social issues. *This was the Report of the Anglican-Reformed International commission 1981-1984, which had been appointed by the Anglican Consultative Council and the World Alliance of Reformed Churches. One of its emphases was 'the plea of our members from the Third World was to make 'orthopraxis' the significant issue between divided Churches... This sense of urgency was presented as the first priority in bringing Churches together.' (page 14)*

NOVEMBER

1st

The consecration of the new Bishop of Llandaff at St Woolos Newport. As always I have an ambivalence: it is a spectacle with high drama and great sensitivity, and because there is Word, Sacrament and Commitment, there is the wholeness of the liturgy. Yet is this the way of the carpenter's son and the fishermen of Galilee? We walked to the Westgate Hotel and noted the bullet holes of Chartist times.

Roy Davies served as bishop from 1985 to 1999.

13th

Our future pastorates should be ecumenical and community-based. We will still need as many ministers but the 'ecumenical pastorates' should be able to sustain them. This Province may have turned a corner from the inexorable, long decline that has been accelerating since the War. Historic Nonconformity is rapidly declining, but the URC in Wales has at least held ground during the last eight years.

29th

A beautiful marriage. Norah and I acted as witnesses of the wedding of Dafydd and Jo. It included Communion. From the house we went to Grand Avenue for the exchanging of vows and signing registers: Mary officiated. Home for excellent reception: the 5 of us plus Catherine.

After the tragedy of the death of Daphne and Bethan, came this sign of hope and tenderness. The marriage took place in Dafydd's home. The minister was our mutual friend the Revd Mary Evans of Ely.

1986

JANUARY

3rd

I enjoyed 'Persuasion'. I compared Jane Austen's approach with the passionate storms of last year's mining dispute. The society she describes was genteel, had protocol and style but beneath the surface was the ruthlessness and guile which defeated the mining leaders and destroyed their communities.

Sunday 12th

A bracing walk through Blaina. A minister must love people to be happy living in this stark environment. I enjoyed the day because I belong to the valleys. Human qualities are palpable: the family with whom I spent the day, and the people with whom I worshipped were warm and receptive.

13th

Emlyn Williams presented me with a lamp with a 'thank you' for what I had done during the strike. Kim and Emlyn Jenkins were also there and I felt grateful they felt I had done something of value.
Emlyn Williams was President of the South Wales NUM. Emlyn Jenkins was also an official of the NUM.

FEBRUARY

6th

My 47th birthday. I thank God I was born in Tylorstown and I regret I have done little for it. I still have the feeling that one day I will help my home town in a tangible way.

26th

At the Penrhys Sponsoring Body, Pat gave a depressing account of vandalism and threats to the church; they are plagued by a dozen teenagers who interrupt worship, harass and frighten the members. How can we help?

MARCH

11th

I have fulfilled a life ambition. I visited the face of Maerdy colliery when it is breaking all records of productivity and profit. If a miracle has happened, it is because of human determination against all odds. I was kitted out and descended with Andrew Morton (Maerdy vicar). We were guided by Eric Price (Lodge Secretary from Tylorstown), safety and chief ventilation officer (Norman Hadfield, nephew of Doris Benbow, Llanidloes); rode along the main road for a mile and walked to the tail gate of the new face (6ft coal: 4' 6" high). We walked 'into' the face, saw it pass, the belt slide under and take the coal away, and the hydraulic shocks push over a further two feet. A fantastic half hour at B1 face. We looked at the start of the new development, came round to the main gate and saw the conveyor belt move the coal out towards the shaft. We walked out of the face and rode back to the shaft to reach open air. Showered before coffee with the manager: We cut 60½ inches last week (a record); this face should last until November when another face is ready; good market and possibly Maerdy is safe for 15 years. Everybody wanted to close the pit last November; the men nearly gave up because of loss of morale, but at a mass meeting, an older man persuaded them to try again.

Maerdy Colliery closed on the 22nd of December 1990. Andrew Morton is now an incumbent in the Monmouth Diocese. Norman Hadfield was training for the priesthood of the Church in Wales.

12th

Yesterday was spent in the strange world of a Welsh pit, a completely secular world, and yet both Andrew and I were at ease, accepted and fulfilled by the experience. I re-learnt dimensions of the good news of God's world: the thrill of working at a new face of coal hidden since its creation from human eye, and now released in its power and beauty by human skill; comradeship which enables a pit to work as a team, a family, a fellowship, a body which cannot function effectively if any part is hurt; the trigger experience of a miner who spoke in Maerdy Workmen's Hall last autumn so that these men should fight to save the community's pit; humility, awe and care in the face of the danger and threat of nature's challenge. Who are you to come and search out my treasures, hidden in earth's depths?

13th

As always I am glad to return to Wales. I am attached to my country and people, and increasingly convinced of my call to serve the Gospel in this small nation. I am entranced by the variety of our countryside. As Moderator I have travelled to every part of Wales and am intrigued by our people and particularly my own valley people.

22nd

How important has been our thinking today? It may come to nothing, but it raised a critical issue. Dylan brought the Western Mail with a full page on the problems of Penrhys, including a photograph of Pat. It was all rather foreboding. Norah and I discussed the possibility of living on the estate for my final three years as Moderator. There are many imponderables, especially the decision of the five of us as a family. It would mean going to Penrhys during the summer, after Dylan and Catherine have finished exams. I phoned Geraint Davies, Treherbert, to ask his advice about how to apply and whether permission would be granted. What a difference this will make to all our lives, but we don't want it to be seen as a gesture.
At this time we watched a scurrilous BBC Wales documentary in its 'Week in, Week Out' series. A few residents of Penrhys were interviewed and Penrhys was described in a lurid and damning fashion. Our experience over many years convinced us that this was a most unjust description of a whole community. Combined with the Western Mail report, it was enough to goad us into action.

26th

It is 3 years since I was a member of the official delegation to the Reformed Church of Hungary. It proved a pivotal moment in life, and we have developed strong links between the two churches and nations. Tomorrow, 53 of us from Wales travel to Hungary. Our people will see for themselves, ask questions and their attitude to East/ West relations will never be the same again. From tomorrow, they will have experienced.
This was one of the largest groups to travel from the URC on any overseas visit. The Welsh side was organised by a Hungarian Committee, centred on Bridgend but having representatives in every District Council. The Hungarian side was organised by John Humphreys and a group from the Reformed Church. The visit anchored the Wales-Hungarian link into the life of the Welsh Synod. John Pritchard created an excellent collection of slides, and a document was edited by Christine and Clifford Othen, entitled 'Bridge

Building in Hungary.' The Othens wrote: 'The party of 53 represented more than 20 United Reformed Churches from north, south and mid-Wales. Most of us had never been behind the so-called 'Iron Curtain' before. The visit we had been privileged to make has, we believe, made a small contribution to the on-going work of rebuilding in the realms of mind, heart and spirit. Our hope was that it represented the forging of another link in the chain.'

30th

A great Easter celebration of the power of the Risen Christ who has and is creating a community which exists for the redemption of the world. I sat with János in the front pew and conveyed the greetings of our party before the sermon was preached. János and I served the wine in Communion: two cups handed to the worshippers. 350 communicated and 1000 in worship. I served an old woman half-carried by her son, and a younger blind woman. Lunch was given in our honour by Elemér Kocsis, President of the College. I responded and presented a book on Wales. After a tour of the College we proceeded to Martin Luther King Church for worship which included music by Dezsö Karazon and our people singing

Easter at Nagytemplom Debrecen I first met János Pásztor in 1983. Dezsö Karazon was the accompanist for Kántus and had visited Wales.

31st, Easter Monday

As we arrived at the beautifully whitewashed church in the centre of the town square of Hajdböszörmény on a glorious Spring morning, the church bell began ringing and we saw the weather-beaten, black clothed peasants making their way to church. A splendid sermon on the Emmaus Road; the baptism of 4 children; I gave greetings. Out to the Hortobágy for a marvellous hour in carts on the puszta; the horsemen showing their skill with horses (sitting and lying down); and driving them around our three carts. Official reception at Ráday, Budapest where Bishop Tóth spoke and answered questions, I responded and it helped our people feel their visit is a significant historical event.

APRIL

4th

A family conference. The children spoke carefully and positively, realizing the implications of our move especially for Catherine.

Hugh was a student at the University of Canterbury but our move to Penrhys was particularly significant for Dylan and Catherine because they were both

studying at Ysgol Gyfun Glantâf. When we moved to Penrhys, Dylan studied for a year at the Further Education College at Rhydfelin before proceeding to Trinity College, Carmarthen. Cath studied for her A levels at Glantâf and this meant her catching a bus to Ystrad and train to Llandaff North from where she walked to school every day. She went on to study at Lampeter University. All three children state categorically that they benefited from living on Penrhys because it enabled them to learn alongside many who face some of the greatest challenges of contemporary Britain. In their early years on Penrhys they were of a very small minority of students. The situation slowly changed over the years.

5th

Is Europe more than a geographical fact? In 48 hours I have travelled from eastern to far western Europe, from Budapest to Cork. Last Sunday I was in Debrecen on the Hungary/ USSR/ Romania/ Czechoslovak border; tomorrow I shall be in the parish of Ballinsen in South West Cork in the Republic of Ireland. A very different world and yet both have a Christian heritage and witness today.

I was a member of the Assembly of the British Council of Churches meeting at Cork.

Sunday 6th

The heart of rural West Cork with many similarities economically and socially with rural Wales although the predominance of Catholicism makes it so different: 97% are Catholic, and the Protestant community has declined from 5% to 3% in the last 20 years because of mixed marriages and emigration. Six parishes are being amalgamated and three church buildings closed. The parishes worshipped together at Desert Serges with 100 for Morning Prayer. I spoke to the young people about Hungary. The response was quiet but sincere. Afterwards there was an open meeting at the Methodist Chapel. I spoke for 15 minutes (Caldey, Miners, Hungary) before discussion.

8th

We had an introduction to Ireland by George Birmingham (Minister of State for Foreign Affairs) who spoke on the Irish view of international affairs, and nearly committed me to Plaid Cymru. How sane, just and compassionate! A tour of Church-related social projects: care for mentally handicapped, shelter for women, housing for elderly. Most impressive. Eucharist at Anglican Cathedral: such triumphalism but a good sermon by Runcie. Coffee at the

Episcopal Palace! 'Jesus, where can we find you in our world today?' [a hymn by Doreen Potter.]

Sunday 13th

As I presided at communion I remembered celebrating with God's people with the Church of Ireland in Cork; Hungarian Reformed at Debrecen; Catholic Mass at St David's Caldey and the Covenanted rite at St Illtud's: the same presence and action of the Living God each time in each place.

18th

It becomes increasingly probable we shall move to Penrhys. This is what we ought to do for the church and the Kingdom. I phoned the Borough Treasurer who spoke openly about the horrific social problems on Penrhys: glue-sniffing, drugs, vandalism, criminality.

MAY

8th

The Ascended Lord who is the Crucified One spoke through Dr Kao at the Assembly. He referred to his 4 years in prison, his testimony to the grace of the living Christ and the hope and prospects for the Taiwanese Church. A disclosure incident when you know the presence of God.

The General Assembly of the URC. We first met Dr Kao when we lived in Manselton.

23rd

Bishop Desmond Tutu received the freedom of the Borough of Merthyr. There in the Rhydycar Leisure Centre, in the heart of the South Wales valleys, long secularised and devoid of Christian or economic hope, was a touching of God's finger. It was a combination of the expected: Bill Morgan, Vicar of Penydarren moving the motion, gave Christian reasons for giving the honour; Bishop Tutu spoke from deep Christian resources and experience; and the unexpected? The powerful, articulate and challenging singing of Côr Cochion Caerdydd, a quartet of Welsh children who saluted Tutu and Mandela (Tutu descending at once from the podium to embrace them) and our standing to sing the anthem of the ANC. God in Christian and socialist resources called us to struggle for justice, liberty and an egalitarian society. This afternoon I had been at Llandaff's Palace with other church leaders and officers, waiting to meet Tutu. The clinking of tea cups, the polite conversation and the genteel polish were a million miles away from Rhydycar and South Africa. Thank God that palaces, temples and fortresses will fall to dust.

24th

History at Llanelwedd where the Council of Churches celebrated their 30th Anniversary and the Covenanted Churches their 10 years with a great Festival, entitled Teulu Duw. It was hoped that 10,000 people would attend; 20,000 came. There have been exhibitions and seminars, many showing the cutting edge of church and society: Women and Men, social and industrial change and deprivation, ecumenical endeavour; but the key and climax has been the presence of Desmond Tutu who spoke and later preached at the closing worship. He called us to impose sanctions as the last pressure which might prevent South Africa tumbling over the precipice. Will you help us? Will you help me? One of Wales' greatest days. Realism of our faith. As Norah said, 'celebration in the midst'. Norah felt privileged to read a prayer in the service.

26th

At the Irish School of Ecumenics in Dublin, Robin Boyd spoke about the Anglo-Irish Agreement; a colleague spoke about peacemaking and a third on re-working and re-interpreting history. Then to the Department of Foreign Affairs where officials spoke on the Anglo-Irish Agreement.
A meeting of Moderators and their wives in Ireland. Norah was unable to attend because of the children's O and A levels. Robin Boyd was Director of the Irish School of Ecumenics.

27th

A journey into despair? I have experienced political boundaries: I smile and blow my car-horn gently as I return from England; I cannot forget the crossing from Hegyshalom into Hungary. Late this afternoon we crossed the border into Northern Ireland. When some of the elders of Clarkesbridge Presbyterian church spoke to us, their bitterness and sense of betrayal by the English government made us realize we were in a different world from Dublin. Drove to Maynooth, the Catholic Seminary and University: met Cardinal Tomas O'Fiachach before being shown around; the chapel and its organ; the Cork Principal and his humour. We were in civilized company. Then the long drive to Castelblaney where we met the Revd Maurice Barr. I talked to a young man, tired of the terrible situation, before the sad but understandable open session.

28th

The Ireland experience is difficult to 'understand'. How can one absorb without being led into despair because of the intractability? At Church House we met the Inter Church Relations Board whose leaders did not want their church to be isolated from the World Church or be hijacked by narrow fundamentalists entering the ministry. Stormont for 2½ hours for an excellent briefing by three civil servants on the political, security (Head of Security) and social/economic issues. The pattern is falling into shape: it does not make the issues easier to solve, but easier to understand. Drove up the Falls Road and down the Shankhill Road: graffiti, barbed wire, blockades, poverty. Tea at Fitzroy Church (chatted with a Brazilian minister) before an evening with members of staff of Union Theological Seminary: traditional pattern of ministry, ample candidates but a shift towards fundamentalism.

29th

Another day has drained our experience. The Moderators met the 'government committee' of the Church which makes representation to the government. At the Shankhill Mission and the drop in centre, we met the minister and deaconess who told us about unemployment, drinking clubs, paramilitaries. Then across to the Falls Road and Clonard Monastery: a most helpful encounter with priests and lay people: long feelings of being a minority community with no power; unemployment, nationalist aspirations. I felt more at home here than on Shankhill. Tea at Hillsborough with 5 representatives of the Presbyterian Church of Ireland again reflecting the toughness and intransigence of the issues. They will not go away but we must stand alongside our brothers and sisters.

31st

Ireland makes us realize it is impossible to escape from history; but it is critical we understand our history and inject it with the cross and resurrection history. That alone can penetrate the depths of the past and make new today and tomorrow.

JUNE

6th

The 'Church' can be opposed to the purposes of God. On June 21st an attempt will be made to drive away the evil spirits on Penrhys. An extreme Christian group has arranged for prayers on Penrhys in the open air at 5 in the morning.

It is depicted as an exorcism because 'there is Satan worship on Penrhys!' The community gets sucked further into a maelstrom of publicity. Penrhys has enough problems without the church creating them.

10th

'Faith in the City' provides a critical agenda for the Churches for the next decade. It is well researched and raises questions we should all be asking, and also points towards answers.

'Faith in the City' was a report published in the UK in Autumn 1985 by the Archbishop of Canterbury's Commission on Urban Priority Areas. The report created a large amount of controversy when it was published, as one of its conclusions was that much of the blame for growing spiritual and economic poverty in British inner cities was due to Thatcherite policies.

13th

We were guests at the pre-Gala dinner of the South Wales NUM. I was invited by Des Dutfield, the Area president, to offer grace for the meal. After everyone stood, I asked our brothers and sisters 'to remember South Africa and to ask that our wealth should not be based on injustice, through Jesus Christ.' There was an audible response and several thanked me. I felt my work with the miners had borne fruit. We were friends and comrades in the search and struggle for a fuller life for our people in Wales and elsewhere, - and we had been invited because they wanted to say 'thank' you and accept us as trusted colleagues. It was the first time that grace had been offered at the NUM dinner. We sat on the high table, chatting to Anita Gale, George Rees, Terry Thomas, Alan Rogers, Arfon, Donald Anderson, Barry Jones.

Anita Gale, who at one time lived on Penrhys, worked full time for the Labour Party, first as the Women's Officer for Wales from 1976, and from 1984 as the General Secretary for Wales - retiring from the post in 1999. Now as Baroness Gale she is a member of the House of Lords.

14th

The guests sat in the stand at St Helens and Des Dutfield introduced his guests to the crowd in the field: 'It may seem strange to have invited a minister as our guest but I want to thank the Revd John Morgans as a friend and helper especially during the strike.' There followed applause and I felt grateful to God that we were involved in the same struggle for a more just, peaceful society and world. Kinnock spoke of the future of mining, South Africa and the need for sanctions.

Sunday 15th

The eve of the Tenth Anniversary of Soweto. I led worship at St David's Newtown at an annual deanery service. In response to the request of the South African Council of Churches, I put white flowers on the pulpit and referred to Beyers Naude, Alan Boesak and Desmond Tutu - and their oppressors. After the service the only person who mentioned South Africa was a family from Kerry whose son is a miner in the Republic and has a different story from the one we hear. What saddened me was that no-one made any mention of the South African situation, and I was bound to compare the difference when my 'grace' at the Miners' Dinner created supportive response. What is that saying about justice and the struggle against apartheid? On whose side is the Church?

27th

Charles Street (Ebenezer Chapel) for a Celebration at which Jim Wallis preached: an evangelical call for justice and peace. A most powerful, moving experience, especially our singing together 'We shall overcome'. It endorses our move to Penrhys.
Jim Wallis is an author, theologian, speaker, preacher, and international commentator on religion and public life, faith and politics. He is President and Chief Executive Officer of Sojourners;

28th

A great demonstration in South Wales against apartheid. The Anti Apartheid movement estimated 7/8000; I thought 4000; Radio Wales News announced 2000. We walked to the Law Courts where the demonstration was gathering. Chris Short chaired and I was asked to speak first (they begin with the least famous and move up) and decided to start with 'God is always on the side of the oppressed.' I had thought to begin with 'Sisters and brothers,' but when asked to speak first, I began with 'God.' 'God is at the centre of the anti-apartheid struggle. I used Psalm 103, Exodus, Exile, Magnificat and Jesus' manifesto before referring to what we must do now for the struggle. Walked through Queen Street, Hayes, Saint Mary Street to Sophia Gardens for more speeches (notably Dafydd Iwan).

JULY

7th

Erzsébet said The God has no (she looked up her dictionary and added) obstacles. Here we were, a motley crew of 14 to 70 year olds, none wealthy, of influence or highborn, from Eastern and Western Europe, and we knew that the future of God's humankind is being expressed here and now on Caldey.

12th

'I was there'. We attended the dinner honouring the men from Wales who had fought for the International Brigade during the Spanish Civil War: it was the 50th Anniversary and most survivors were present. A remarkable parallel was Spain 50 years ago and Nicaragua today. There were links with the past with the old brigadiers, and the present with a speaker from the Nicaraguan Embassy and young people from Wales in the Nicaraguan Solidarity Campaign. Tonight saw the formation of the Wales/ Nicaraguan Solidarity Campaign. 200 at the Ystrad Leisure Centre; we sat by Morien and Elaine Morgan, Arfon and Eirlys a TV producer.

Dr Elaine Morgan, is the author of books on human evolution including: The Descent of Woman (1972), The Aquatic Ape (1982), The Scars of Evolution (1990), The Descent of the Child (1994), and The Aquatic Ape Hypothesis (1997). Her husband Morien was an old brigadier of the Spanish Civil War.

30th

Bob Blair and Pentecostalists have started a Sunday School in the Community Centre and have attracted three quarters of the United Church's Sunday School.

The Revd Robert Blair was pastor in Porth.

OCTOBER

6th

My ministry has taken on different shapes: exploring Christian Nurture in house groups and worship; discovering exciting approaches to theology and ecclesiology; struggling as Moderator to develop unity and hope amongst our churches; my commitment to the church's unity as a sign of God's purpose for humankind; in latter years that sharp edge where the Gospel and the life of God's people touch the life of humankind.

11th

Synod is the gathering together of a family who care for each other and seek calmly, carefully and resolutely to discover how to work for Christ in his world.

Sunday 19th

On Caldey most stated that their highlight had been the way Scripture opened to them. They had never read the Bible so deeply; had thought the Old Testament unimportant; never read the Servant passages in the context of the Exile and as pointing towards the community of faith. They wanted to share the Scriptures with their church communities and the wider community.

20th

One of our Caldey participants posed the question of whether 'reality' was Caldey or when we reach home. I remember the same question 15 years ago from Jimmy Vaughan of Llanidloes as we approached Tenby in the boat. It is the wrong question. There is one reality, one world in which we seek to live well; Caldey gives time and space for us to gain a better perspective, receive strength and peace, and live more strenuously for God and the fulfilment of his purposes.

Sunday 26th

Our last night at 16 Llwynygrant Road and tomorrow our first night at 12 Heol Dyfed. We move from Penylan to Penrhys. There can be no greater contrast within Wales. Although there are expectations, we have memories of 9 happy years in this house and in Cardiff, and for the children this is home. Yet it is right to move to Penrhys and if I used Biblical language, the Lord's hand is involved.

27th

Despite our chaotic arrival at Penrhys on a wild, wet day, it is right to be here. As we entered the house, problems stared at us: planks on the stairs; how to get the piano and wardrobe up two sets of twisting stairs. Almost as soon as we arrived, coal was delivered, the water cut off because of a leak in the shower unit, shelves came off the wall with the weight of books. Quite an afternoon.

28th

We are not here to 'help' the 'people of Penrhys'; we are here because God wants us to be here. Why? To support the minister in her struggle in this community? To learn from people on the margins of British society? To reflect church leadership as servanthood?

29th

This is the right place. We have enjoyed the houses the church has provided, and Llanidloes, Manselton and Penylan were a progress in living standards and status. Now, for the first time, we have made the decision about the kind of house in which we believe we should live. We have always accepted gratefully the houses owned by the church and have enjoyed them all, but 12 Heol Dyfed seems different. Is it because we have chosen to live in the same kind of house as the people of this community? Of course we are different because I am earning, we can afford to heat the house and we have chosen to come to be part of a Christian community.

30th

I am not returning to 'my roots' because the Penrhys of 1986 is not the Tylorstown of 1956, and yet for many years, I have felt a call to the valleys. This developed from the Gospel prerogative to preach 'good news to the poor' and the call to defend communities stricken by the destruction of the coal industry. Today Norah and Catherine saw two women discussing how they could share a piece of meat between their two families, and in youth club this evening Cath was asked if she was a proper Christian - she was told there were no 'proper' Christians in her church.

NOVEMBER

1st

Life is a privilege, especially when shaped by the Gospel. I sat at the desk in our study/ bedroom in our new home. The subdued lamp light gives a sense of peace and security. As I draw the curtains, I look at a beautiful autumnal night and see the light at the golf-course and down in the valleys, Llwynypia, Tonypandy and a glimpse of Wattstown. I am seated close to Penrhys Uchaf farm where as a boy I came on Saturday to fetch eggs. Now I am struggling to become a part of this deprived but lively community. Here is the challenge of the local. Will I learn from, and be of help to this community? Will the Gospel be made real? I have spent the day at Aberystwyth at the Council of Churches where I was welcomed as the new President of the Council of Churches of Wales. The challenge of the 'local' and the national.

I began a two year ministry as President of the Council of Churches. At the close of the two years I was asked to continue for a further two. This was to help create a smooth transition to the proposed Churches Together in Wales

(Cytun) which came into being in 1990 and replaced the Council. The major difference was that it would include the Roman Catholic Church as a full member.

6th

As we were leaving Llwynygrant for the last time, I looked out at the beautiful view of the city, Severn estuary, England across the Channel and a sun slowly setting. Why are we leaving this fine substantial house, convenient to office, station and motorway? It is right to leave this house of high ceilings, fine hall and landing because of the need of the Penrhys community and because of the inappropriateness of such a commodious place for servants of the carpenter.

8th

The new church at Llandrindod has light, warmth and ease of maintenance. I remember the impotence years ago when they were served with a demolition order.
My first visit to the new chapel built within the sheltered accommodation.

Sunday 9th

A miracle of grace. I officiated at the baptism of Jo and Dafydd's 10 day old baby girl, Cate. She has arrived safe and sound and was received into God's family at Saintwell. Today was an expression of healing and God's graciousness. Dafydd articulated that quietly with total assurance.

17th

A struggle getting out of the garage because stray dogs had ripped open the bags and strewed rubbish all over the entrance; one of the physical problems of our estate - I wrote 'ours' consciously and deliberately.

20th

A tremendous thunder storm somewhere to the south. After two loud, long rolls of thunder, the sky turned white and the storm was preceded by a violent rush of wind and heavy rain. To be up high in this house facing directly south gives a sense of being in the heart of the storm. A few months ago at the Council Offices, Councillor Mattie Collins said that 'if the problems of Penrhys were solved, we would at the same time be solving the nation's problems.' That is also to be at the heart of the storm.
Mattie Collins who represented the Tylorstown ward was the Leader of the Labour Group in Rhondda.

27th

Emilio Castro, General Secretary of the World Council of Churches, spent the day in Wales. I presided at two meetings arranged by the Council of Churches of Wales. At Cathedral Road I presided at a meeting between Dr Castro and church leaders, and this evening at Tabernacle for worship: a choir sang a beautiful Cerdd Dant and Emilio preached from Acts 1 with realism and hope. *I had first met Emilio Castro during the Moderators' visit to Geneva in 1982.*

DECEMBER

6th

Dylan and I went to Treorchy to watch Tylorstown lose 20-0. It was good being in the crowd: one elderly man arrived late, sat in the stand, took out his teeth, proceeded to unwrap and eat a round black German sausage to the delight of all who knew him.

Sunday 21st

Worship at Maesyronnen. 15 of us sat around the table for communion; women on the left, men on the right; the cloth was 100 years old; wine poured from the jug into two pewter cups and passed along - one for men and one for women.

22nd

Visitors see our situation through other eyes. M M Thomas (Mar Thomist from Kerala), spent the night here with his family. Good to listen to MM: Christian/ Marxist dialogue in an Indian context.
Norah and MM had been in correspondence since the Vancouver Assembly when M M was in the group at which Norah chaired. M M Thomas was a product of the Mar Thomist Church of Kerala South India and was one of the most creative thinkers in the post War ecumenical movement. He was appointed Governor of Nagaland between 1990 and 1992.

24th

The eve of Christmas: the celebration of God with us as Saviour. Despite the apparent meaninglessness of the universe and humankind, God is here in the midst, liberating from within. No situation or person is devoid of God's grace and power.

Sunday 28th

Holy Innocents. A few under 11 boys on the bus shelter are cursing with every other word. They are also innocents, led into unholiness as day succeeds day. What chance do these children have?

30th

What would life be but for God's graciousness and power discovered - no revealed! - in the Cross and Resurrection? What would life be but for our experience of the community which exists to celebrate and share the Gospel? What would my life be if I had not been born into the family of humankind in this land called Wales, and particularly for that community of Rhondda in which I find myself again? My family has been in Tylorstown since the 1870s and have been miners since 1840. Will the rest of my life be spent discovering the relationship between the Gospel of God and the Christian community in this peculiar context of Rhondda and Wales?

31st

I am residing in Penrhys, Tylorstown where my ancestors came for work and a better life 120 years ago! I am grasped by the Gospel and eager to share its love and power with my communities of Penrhys, Wales and Humankind. What has been 'achieved' during the years as Moderator? A sense of unity and purpose for the URC in Wales; that our future lies within the unity of Christ's Church within our nation; a growing commitment to standing alongside the marginalized in our national and international community. I am committed to the Welsh Covenant, Caldey, Hungary, the mining community and the search for allies in the struggle for justice and peace.

1987

JANUARY

14th

I should have read the Epistle at the Consecration of George Noakes as Archbishop of Wales at the historic site of St David's. Instead I was serving a community struggling during a major crisis caused by fierce winds and icy snow at the historic site of Penrhys. I was in the right place. Norah and I walked up to the Centre and volunteered our help to the Community Association. Stew was made and taken to 60 families. Volunteers systematically visited the 1000 houses. Reports were brought of no heating, no water, no food; doors, windows and roofs needing repair.

15th

Penrhys is a collection of houses perched on top of a mountain, in which lives a community. It is a community unlike any other I have experienced, but it struggles to live. Many people care for the most vulnerable in a marginalized society. There has been generosity of time and energy - there isn't much money to share. I have neither gold nor silver, but what I have, I give. We have been accepted for what we are; whatever skills we have are recognized without animosity. Although we have been here only months we are accepted as useful members of the community. I see hope in Penrhys. Volunteers came to the school and delivered 40 meals and fed 30 in the Centre. 16 are sleeping in the Centre.

16th

Classic formative experience. These days parallel the months of the mining dispute when I discovered and received so much. Then it was struggling in macrocosm to understand the critical issues of energy policy, its relationship to community, the place of persons alongside economic systems, the dereliction of valley communities which produced the wealth of the nation, and the place of the church in such social issues. These days have seen us struggling in microcosm with the same critical issues of the impossibility of heating your house adequately, the heartlessness of its consequences upon people, the overriding call of economic priorities and the scandal of a society oblivious to the needs of the vulnerable. Marginalize and forget them, and refrain from asking 'why' are people the way they are.

17th

A neighbour suffers from arthritis and is depressive. She lives on £38 a week and the house takes 3 cwt (£22-20) a week to warm. Because of the freeze, she has pipe bursts and there is no water in the house. She is typical of many on Penrhys and elsewhere.

Sunday 18th

I led worship in border country, the border between the Valleys and the Vale, between deprivation and relative affluence, between small, tight, traditional mining communities and the City which grew up as a consequence and used the wealth of the valleys; between Mid and South Glamorgan; between socialist/ nationalist/Welsh Wales and English Wales. Is there a difference in church life?

FEBRUARY

16th

William Morris of Hanover Chapel, Llanover was a minister of another generation, spending time at preparing and thoroughly enjoying the gift and craft of preaching. From all accounts, he did it very well. The chapel and vestry were packed for his funeral, and the family asked me to take the service which would include 'One Solitary Life' (Bill's reading at Christmas) and an emphasis on the value of preaching.

MARCH

8th

I have been exploring the passages beginning 'Love your enemies... do good pray... bless.' The words are self-authenticating: this is how the follower of Jesus must live because Jesus lived like that; Jesus knew that God, his Father, who is always working in the world, also lived like that. There is no other way. The foolishness of the world shows it is the only way left.

Sunday 15th

I try to help the URC in Wales discover its mission to the nation. It is difficult because of geography, a poor transport system, the contrasting nature of language and culture in various parts of Wales; but also because our Church has little understanding of the national dimension. Some feel Christians transcend nationality. Many unconsciously correlate Englishness and its way of life, as being the heart of religion.

18th

Derek Childs was a good leader of the Church in Wales, thoughtful, caring, resolute and determined. We agreed on a holy pragmatism: get on now within the areas of agreement, particularly in terms of the Covenant; and at the same time work towards future unity.
Derek Childs had recently retired as Archbishop of Wales.

19th

The Diocese of Menevia is established, based on the new cathedral of St Joseph's in Swansea. We processed into the cathedral across snow. A fascinating service: the reading of the Papal decree; greetings; a homily by the new bishop in Welsh; good singing with lay elements; Mass; a strong emphasis on the Church's mission to the nation of Wales. We are only beginning to grasp that emphasis within the URC, and I find it a struggle to convince my fellow church members of our mission field.
By a decree of 12 February 1987, the whole of the Catholic Church in Wales was restructured. The area known as the Welsh Province contains three dioceses; the Metropolitan Archdiocese of Cardiff and the suffragan sees of Menevia and Wrexham. The present Diocese of Menevia was restored to what is almost entirely its ancient Catholic Diocese of St David.

20th

I chaired the meeting of Covenanted Church leaders at Shrewsbury. An important item was the shape of the ecumenical instrument for these islands, a major theme for Bangor and other national conferences. Cledan Mears, Alwyn Rice, Bini Vaughan [three Welsh Bishops] and I favoured developing the CCW and a stronger relationship with BCC and WCC - an acknowledgment of the Welsh as a nation with special relations with British nations, but very much part of a world family of churches and nations. The Anglican bishops and I also favoured an instrument which includes the RCs in Wales.
The church representatives chaired in turn. Discussion focussed on the widening of the Council to include the Roman Catholic Church. The process was called 'Not Strangers but Pilgrims'. It was providential that the meeting should have taken place the day after the celebration in St Joseph's. How much more enriched Welsh church life would be when it became more

inclusive. The major Welsh meeting would be held in Bangor within two weeks.

30th

I glanced at the list of participants, the agenda and its supporting papers and realized the history behind the 'Not Strangers but Pilgrims' process. I feel enthusiastic about the Conference beginning tomorrow. What possibilities if we discover confidence in each other, and that means, confidence in Christ, and ingenuity to create the appropriate instrument for our common pilgrimage towards God and his Kingdom. Then I looked at the top of the agenda and it dawned on me that the Chairperson is the President of the Council of Churches of Wales - I felt awed and humbled by the challenge.
The Inter - Church process had been launched on the 8th of November 1985 when the thirty two churches committed themselves to discuss, pray and work together until the completion of the process in the autumn of 1987. The meeting at Bangor on these few days would determine the approach of the Churches in Wales to the whole programme.

31st

My inclination is not to dominate but to create an atmosphere which enables people have confidence to seek together. I hope this has begun at Bangor. I welcomed delegates and spoke about the purpose and context of our 'meeting'. Admirable worship by Graham Chadwick and excellent Bible Study on John 17 by Margaret Thrall. Noel sketched the Welsh context before group work. After tea a good session with Alastair Haggart, Colin Davey and Mgr Nichols. Excellent floor participation.
The Right Reverend Graham Chadwick was Bishop of Kimberley and Kuruman, in Cape Province, South Africa, from 1976 to 1982. As an outspoken critic of apartheid and the policies of the then government of South Africa, Chadwick was exiled from his diocese at the end of 1981 and was arrested and deported. On his enforced return to Britain, Chadwick became adviser on spirituality in the diocese of St Asaph. Noel Davies was General Secretary of the Covenanted Churches and the Council of Churches for Wales. Dr Margaret Thrall taught New Testament in the University of Wales, Bangor from 1962 to 1996. Alastair Haggart had been the Primus of the Scottish Episcopal Church until 1985. He had been a member of the small group at which Norah chaired during the Vancouver Assembly. Colin Davey had a long ecumenical experience working especially with Anglican and Roman Catholic cooperation. Vincent Nichols became Roman Catholic Archbishop of Birmingham.

APRIL

2nd

Is it an important turning point in history, or will this weekend be forgotten in a year or two? I cannot answer that question but I helped bring our work to fruition. The groups and six workshops had produced material shaped by four drafters: Clyde Johnson on 'the nature of the church'; Rodney Matthews on 'the mission'; Huw Jones on 'the unity'; and Bill Sewell on 'ecumenical instruments'. In two plenary sessions I needed to reflect that this was a kairos moment and at the same time help the Conference feel that the finished document was their production. Covenanted Eucharist at 7.30: George Noakes and I celebrated together, and Daniel Mullins preached. We completed the document in good spirit, humour, concern and open debate. A resolution endorsing the statement was accepted almost unanimously (no one against; one abstention - date of 1989 accepted while he wanted 1988).
Clyde Johnson is Chancellor of the Diocese of Menevia; Rodney Matthews was a Baptist minister; Huw Jones became Bishop of St David's; Bill Sewell was the URC Ecumenical Officer. George Noakes was the Archbishop of Wales, and Daniel Mullins was the recently appointed Bishop of Menevia.

MAY

4th

A joy to hear the cuckoo for the first time. We were returning from the top reservoir above Maerdy and were opposite a wood of conifers halfway between the two lakes. It was beginning to dusk and Louisa (aged 7) and Barry John (aged 6) heard the call coming out of the wood. Barry has a cuckoo living in his bedroom and from that point kept looking for this cuckoo's house. He eventually found it near the colliery. The washery is being demolished and the railway torn up between the pit and Maerdy.
Barry John had a cuckoo clock in his bedroom, and was certain that one of the colliery buildings was the home of the cuckoo.

5th

On this warm evening I am sitting in bed, the window is open and I see half a dozen young men sitting and talking on the wall by the bus stop. The sound is clear; dogs are barking and a car crosses the hill. There is a new quantity of sound on the estate: when I drove home at 9.45, there were a dozen young people on the roof of the bus shelter, and another dozen on the wall by the garage. Their language is limited, colourful, explicit, but not menacing nor deliberately blasphemous. It is natural; they have received it, and will pass it on to the next generation. Yet there is also a new quality of silence on this estate. There are moments when it seems there is no sound whatsoever. I thank God for all we have received these past six months: it will influence the rest of our lives.

13th

The most important day for the URC in Wales. The General Assembly meeting in St David's Hall, Cardiff experienced a powerful expression of the church's mission in the light of its context. The Celebration captured the confidence of 2000 people with no contrived manipulating of emotions but with a triumphant acclamation of the presence, grace and power of God who is bringing in a world of justice and peace. I thank God for the hard work by so many people over many months, for this night of celebration which emerged from the germ of an idea last summer, through months of hammering out a script, to the controlled and exuberant act tonight of proclamation

This was the first occasion for the General Assembly to meet in Wales and it provided the opportunity for the Synod to reflect its mission statement in the form of a Celebration. The Celebration had been a year in preparation: a group met to discuss the theme, others to write the script and then different Districts 'performed' different scenes. There had been only two full rehearsals: one in Manselton and the other at St David's Hall. Norah and I also had the privilege of sharing the Bible studies on the four mornings of the Assembly.

15th

1100 members of the URC from all over Wales were in St David's Hall on Wednesday -a large proportion of our 8000 members. A choir of 400 and a cast of 100 captivated the audience of Assembly attendees with a profound expression of a theology for our day, grounded in the Gospel and expressing mission in terms of unity, justice and peace. This was a remarkable 'form' for contemporary mission with the theatre as substitute for the 'temple'; dramatic liturgy replacing the great preacher, all demanding careful preparation by a group of imaginative, sensitive, dedicated people.

16th

A wonderful experience to preside at the induction of Kevin Watson at Manselton. People were still reeling from the impact of Wednesday: 'one of the greatest of all experiences.' Will it mark a transformation or a transitory experience? It depends on how it will continue to affect us - as in all 'religious disclosures?'

20th

Today began very early: youngsters were talking on the wall by the bus stop until well after midnight; girls and boys with limited, sad language. Soon after 1am, a car was driven around the roundabout at tremendous sped, a tyre burst, the car went out of control and ended on the grass. The boys ran out of the car and hid before police arrived.

22nd

A moment of poignancy. I had left Penrhys for Mid Wales and was driving down the hill towards Tylwch when I saw a flock of sheep being driven by a dog and a teenage girl, a shepherdess! She apologized for the delay, smiled and when I eventually passed, waited at the gate, waved and said 'thank you'. All that seems trite to record, but came as a great refreshment after listening to teenagers sitting on the wall by the bus shelter during the last few nights: foul language and sad behaviour until 1.30 in the morning. My feeling was of great sorrow: why should teenagers of the same age be so different? Tragedy seems imminent for the Penrhys teenager; hope and gaiety for the Tylwch teenager. Both are children of God, loved in Christ and have divine potential. How can the Christian community reflect God's generosity in a credible way?

29th

What caused the miracle of the Assembly Celebration? Many small things developing during ten years: new ministers; fostering gifts and skills; strengthening the sinews of the wider church to enable these gifts to be fostered and channelled; the traditional legacies of District Councils and Synod Committees, but also house groups, Bible and prayer circles, retreats at places like Caldey and Trefeca; the strengthening of our links with Hungary - many, small, unassuming things.

JUNE

13th

Fascinating to spend last night and today with politicians at the NUM dinner and rally. I talked with Arthur Scargill for over half an hour: he can be compared with fundamentalist Christians, 'full blooded Socialism is what is needed; it can't be compromised; if it is really pursued, its integrity will ultimately convince and be victorious; it demands whole hearted support; this election campaign was a compromise; savings from nuclear defence should be spent on social benefit and not on militarism.' At the Rally he called on the party to be united behind socialist principles. Then Michael Foot spoke powerfully about the need to win back the Social Democratic Party supporters, (he made a comparison between the NUM and the Union of Democratic Miners). Which choice will the Labour Party make?
The UDM was the 'Nottinghamshire' Union which did not support the strike.

20th

The sun was calculated to set at 21.21: from Bristol Tump it set 5 minutes later. A privilege to watch the sun disappear and be certain (almost certain) it will rise again early tomorrow. The song of the skylarks on the mountain was a clear tribute to divine hope.

JULY

11th

Here we are on Caldey, young people (except me) from Eastern and Western Europe, Marxist and Capitalist ideological systems, from two small countries with deep Christian traditions. We have been searching our common heritage in the Bible, especially as the Reformed branch of Christian people. It was beautiful to watch these young men and women learning how to laugh, play, study, praise and pray together. When I see the hatred created by militarization and ideology, I realize how powerful is God's grace who turns all our false values upside.
A group of young Hungarians had been brought by the Welsh Synod to Wales for three weeks. This was the first of many exchanges during the following years. Part of the programme was spent on Caldey with half Hungarian and the other half Welsh young people. It was a wonderful by-product of the Hungarian relationship. It seemed like a dream come true. Here were young

people striding across the barrier of the Iron Curtain and discovering their one-ness in Christ.

Sunday 12th

One of the young Hungarians stated 'This truly was for us all a kairos; we are all children of the same Abba and we are all to be disciples, apostles and martyrs.' Another reflected that 'We needed to come here as Hungarians to be introduced to Wales in order to understand Hungary better.'

20th

A nightmare. A minibus accident in North Wales and three of our Hungarian friends are in hospital, one seriously ill. I drove at once to Ysbyty Glan Clwyd. Sandor is seriously ill with head injuries and is in intensive care. God, how small we are, and how totally dependent on you.
A dreadful but ultimately formative experience. In later years Sandor Kereskenyi became a minister of the Reformed Church, and officiated at the wedding of our son Hugh with Barbara in Budapest.

22nd

A day of grace; a miracle of response to need, and we have witnessed the hand of God. Sandor had a stable night and although deeply sedated and remaining on the ventilator, the doctors seem pleased he has passed through the first 48 hours.

25th

God's presence and grace were focussed at the funeral of Chris Thomas, the 24 year old son of Terry and Vi Thomas of Gowerton. My challenge was to respect Terry and Chris' deep socialist principles and also present the Gospel in undiluted form. By God's grace, I believe I did this.
Chris was the son of Vi and Terry Thomas, the miner's leader. The parents asked me to officiate at the funeral service in Morriston because of the relationship and mutual respect which had developed during the Miners' Strike.

29th

A letter from Hywel Francis with an article for 'Marxism Today'. He had been inspired by the funeral and the reference to the fist and the open hand symbolizing justice and generosity. He regarded these as the primary virtues of the miner, and the need for reconciliation between the NUM and UDM.

AUGUST

14th

Last night the noise by the bus shelter wasn't the usual one of teenagers with cassettes and radios. It was a drunken ugly sound. Cath said someone had thrown something at her window. I put out our lights, carefully looked outside and saw a dozen men in their early 20s lurching around, and pulling up and throwing stones. A police car arrived, two policemen came out and the young men moved menacingly towards them. I phoned 999 and soon 3 police cars and a van arrived, and the young men fled into the estate. A stone had been thrown through the police car window and a policeman punched.
I was asked to give evidence at Crown Court in January 1988. It proved unnecessary because the young men pleaded guilty.

31st

The final conference of the 'Not Strangers but Pilgrims' process; I am one of 350 people from the three nations with Irish observers. I chair the three national sessions for Wales, and two plenary sessions when the whole conference debates the thorny, complex issues of ecumenical instruments. Who does God think I am? More than I can comprehend. I wouldn't dare give myself such responsibility.
The Conference at Swanwick, Derbyshire.

SEPTEMBER

2nd

I think, feel, suspect, guess, believe there might have been an important development in the relations between the Christian bodies within Wales. My words are as tentative as my experience, but there is hope. I chaired three sessions with the widest representation of Christian people we have known in Wales, tackling important and intricate issues. We discussed how as Christians we should live and act together at local, regional, national, British and Irish levels. On what kind of 'instrument' could we agree? Our major achievement was a total agreement, including Catholics, to create an appropriate instrument reflecting our Christian commitment.

3rd

Today marked a note in the history of the Christian community in Britain. We are witnessing a major breakthrough in the life of our people. At 9.30 the

Plenary at which I presided looked at ecumenical instruments at local and intermediate level. I began and ended my two sessions with Scripture and prayer, and many stated how helpful they found it. Second plenary from 11.15 to 12.30. Remarkable to preside and to give permission to David Sheppard, Archbishop Warlock and others to speak! I chaired the Welsh group from 3 to 4: great statement by Daniel Mullins that we are in on this process. Plenary this evening chaired by Bernard. That is when history was made with a statement by Hume: 'Our official policy will be to move from cooperation to commitment because of the Gospel imperative; confident that the right Instrument will be found; unity is God's gift - he has been giving it to us all this week. Then Runcie: 'Perhaps the greatest spectrum of Christian people, a historic moment, God is calling to us to do something for these islands!'

4th

I have returned from one end of the world to another and certain they belong together. Penrhys and Swanwick belong, and perhaps the key lies with the statue standing quietly in the darkness opposite my window. What is Jesus saying to us in his love for his mother, her love for him and their love for us all, especially the least of his sisters and brothers? The Declaration was received with acclamation. At worship we were presented with a shell for the pilgrimage. Lord, I pray you will help me always to be open to the moving of your Spirit and the warming of my heart.

16th

Trevor Griffiths the playwright came to lunch. We talked about the mining dispute and the place of the church in the issue. I found him sensitive and perceptive.

Trevor Griffiths has been writing for the theatre, television and cinema since the late 60s. His work has been seen throughout the world and he has won numerous awards. For his film 'Reds,' written with Warren Beatty, he received an Oscar nomination. He was researching for a play on the Miners Strike.

19th

I looked at new books on Welsh History by David Egan and Gareth Jones. How different from the historical method and material we were taught in school: the Welsh Bible, the Act of Union, Griffith Jones and the Methodist Revival. These two books are 'Coal Society', and 'People, Protest and Politics in 20th century'. This material will change our Welsh attitude towards Wales.

Our thinking in the Province is becoming contextualized and radicalised.
Gareth Jones and I were students living in Neuadd Gilbertson in 1957-8. Gareth became Archivist for the Welsh Synod of the URC and Professor of History at Aberystwyth.

OCTOBER

9th

This afternoon as I sat in the big-seat, behind the communion table and read the Biblical passage about Ebenezer - 'Thus far has the Lord helped us,' I felt I was responsible to the community which nurtured me into faith, and especially to my grandfather and father, deacons of the chapel. They, we, are in a most difficult situation, but I helped them to a healing position, and they decided to go forward together to seek the disposal of the building. We had prayers and discussed our future. A most responsible gathering without acrimony.
Reaching the end of the story of Ebenezer? Or does the story continue as long as Ebenezer is in the mind and spirit of those who were nurtured there?

13th

Who would have thought that David Morgan's grandson should have the dubious privilege of drafting the resolution by which the people of Ebenezer should give evidence that they did not need the building any longer. The positive thing is to claim that the building has lasted 105 years and the worshipping community 109 years.

21st

Two young South Africans arrived: William and Mandla. They attended the Tenants' Association and spoke with frankness, Christian commitment and courage. A remarkable moment when the Community policeman arrived: our guests showed fear. They looked at the Police Station and we went to United Church, Pontypridd where William and Mandla spoke and sang the African National Anthem.
This was a traumatic experience for the two South Africans. At the entry of the policeman, they subconsciously returned to South Africa where they would have been arrested for being in a meeting where whites and blacks were participating. The policeman then invited them to visit the Police Station on Penrhys.

26th
Caldey provides stability and encouragement. At Compline, as I sat in the corner seat in the stalls and sang gently reassuring psalms and music, I was carried along by a gentle swell of the sea, and had faith that ultimately we would be carried safely towards the haven.

NOVEMBER

28th
I took Sigmar Krause (German Democratic Republic foreign correspondent for radio) to meet Chris Yeates and John Phillips, both unemployed ex miners. Both were completely uninhibited by the tape recorder, and spoke intelligently and passionately about the injustice of our society. It was very humorous and deeply moving. We all had a great empathy with this Communist Party member.
An eye-opening experience for us all. What common ground we share as humans! Chris Yeates was the Chairperson of the Penrhys Tenants and Residents Association. John was his brother in law.

DECEMBER

Sunday 6th
Is this the last Sunday worship I shall lead at Ebenezer? I took a bilingual service: Philemon was read (9 verses) in Welsh and English and I used Welsh verses in the sermon and in Communion. The hymns were Welsh. 15 of us met in the vestry. How pleased they were to see Catherine.
Norah was teaching in Sunday school on Penrhys.

22nd
I have watched the sun set on the longest day, and rise on the shortest day this year. It was a calculated decision and awesome on both occasions: a kind of death and birth of light and life; a form of death and resurrection. I stood in our bedroom and looked at the sun coming up behind the half dozen trees above Wattstown; I watched it climb and in my imagination I saw it light up Mary and child, while when I looked through the back window, the windows had turned to gold and the whole estate was alight. It was Magnificat Now! In the bleak midwinter we witness the triumph of the light.
A kind of epiphany.

1988

JANUARY

8th

High wind swept heavy rain across the roundabout, but Mary and Child won't be frightened away from Penrhys by wind, weather or discouragement. As I walked up to Spar through thick drizzle and deep white mist, I thought this a great place to live.

19th

Miss Katy Starr, 91 years old, listened carefully to an hour's discussion about the future of Ebenezer; then spoke quietly and effectively that it should be sold to the Housing Association for the sake of the community and as a tribute to the past. She calmly proposed this as a resolution. There was a unanimous vote. She is Treasurer of Cancer Research, collects for Christian Aid, and is a great niece of Mary Jones of Bala (her grandmother's sister).

30th

The ordination of Julian Thomas and his induction to Gilwern and Llangynidr was so joyous. I first knew Julian 10 years ago as a History Student at Cardiff, and we kept in touch during his candidature and training.

Sunday 31st

Small churches can produce mature relationships and genuine meeting between people, and with God, as long as we practise styles of nurture appropriate for a small congregation. They must not perpetuate styles which evolved in large, crowded chapels.

FEBRUARY

1st

God has a delicate sense of humour and I smiled with him today. For months I had feared the possible repercussions of today. I drove to Crown Court, near Bute St as a witness for the prosecution relating to the incident of last August. I sat in the long corridor and waited, suspecting that the dozen others present were on the side of the defence. Three women sat opposite and when I spoke to them, I discovered they were mother, wife and mother in law of one of the accused. They knew my position but to my surprise supported me. The Penrhys people present respected what I was doing, and there were many conversations about 'deep issues'. When we heard they had pleaded guilty and I would not be summoned, we went into Court to hear the judge sum up and pass sentence. I took the family home: we were friends.

3rd

Some candidates are not suitable for ministry: the arrogant conservative who, on his introduction to a congregation, told them they were not a Christian community; the student who would not allow his children to live on a council estate because of its limitations of opportunity; the student who refuses to baptize babies but is prepared to stay in the URC until the church comes round to his way of thinking.

24th

At Porth we attended the first meeting of Rhondda people concerned about a Welsh Assembly. It was convened by John Osmond and Siân Edwards. 16 present.

John Osmond (born 1946) is the director of the independent Welsh think-tank, the Institute of Welsh Affairs. He has contributed to numerous books on the subjects of Welsh politics, culture and devolution, and is also a former journalist and television producer. Siân Edwards is a writer and translator. John Osmond visited Llanfair in 1993 and wrote an article entitled. 'When Dignity Can Grow from Despair... John Osmond on developments at Penrhys in the Rhondda' published in Planet December 93/January 1994.

25th

The huge chapel 'bod rhwng yr allt' (Bodringallt) is demolished; but on the river behind it, two swans live happily. Is this the changing Rhondda? Who would have believed a century ago that this vast cathedral (with six large windows on each floor and on both sides) would be pulled down. Who would have thought a century ago when there were 50 pits in the Rhondda that one day swans would eat and drink happily in the river?

Bodringallt Chapel belonged to the Union of Welsh Independents.

26th

Miss Katie Starr was interviewed for 'Wales on Sunday'. I sat in Miss Starr's

front room and listened to Rian Evans talking with this 91 year old who has lived in the same house in East Rd for 86 years and whose mind is sharp, and her heart full of concern. She had been filmed walking through Tylorstown and stopping at Ebenezer, the Welfare Hall and at the Post Office. Good for the community.
Rian Evans at the time working for the BBC, is a writer and critic specializing in music and the arts.

MARCH

1st
The love of God in Christ is articulated in Scripture and, in a very special way, in the language of the ancient People of Wales. I was glad I was Welsh, at worship with men and women from all over Wales, remembering our heritage, determined to live the Good News today, and preparing for mission in Christ's Way to our people. It was expressed in glorious worship at Tabernacl, The Hayes to celebrate the publication of Y Beibl Cymraeg Newydd. I gave thanks for the scholars present who had worked for many years by daylight and lamplight, to share with us this most wonderful gift. I was privileged to receive a Bible on behalf of the Council of Churches for Wales and to offer thanksgiving, and delighted that Catherine James, a 17 year old Welsh speaker from Beulah, should receive the Bible on behalf of the URC. The URC belongs to Wales.
This was the first major 'authorized' translation since the Bishop Morgan Bible of 1588.

2nd
Nonconformity is the production of Scripture in the language of today, and it is the creation of a community which offers respect and friendship. These are some of the reasons for struggling with one's nation.

9th
It is right to stand down as Moderator after 12 years. I also recognized that the Penrhys ministry will be re-appraised in May and possibly, the search for ministry begins in June. Am I being led to offer myself for ministry in this community?
The Revd Pat Parrish had left Penrhys and was serving the United Reformed Church in Paignton.

Sunday 13th

A 12 year old girl from Bettws saw something in the passage about the healing of the demoniac which had escaped me. I asked 'How did the sick man recognize that Jesus was "son of the most High God"?' Her answer came simply: 'because he realized that someone cared enough about him to come and love him; when this lonely man saw the one coming to him, he recognized it was God.' What insight. No need ever to say in whose name we come; just go ahead, do the right thing and leave the rest to the 'demoniac' and God.
Bettws was the large housing area on the outskirts of Newport.

21st

At the BCC Assembly at Llandudno, I gave a talk on the Welsh context.
As President of the Council of Churches for Wales, I gave the welcoming address to the British Council of Churches. The talk was printed under the title 'An Angle of Vision' and attempted to reflect the historical and contemporary context to our visitors from the other British nations.

22nd

Hands were outstretched to receive bread. The Cathedral at Llanelwy was packed. How inspiring for faithful church members touched by the ecumenical vision, to see the Church acting as One. I presided at this joint celebration alongside Alwyn St Asaph, Methodist and Presbyterian colleagues.

23rd

At breakfast, Philip Morgan stated how hard the waiters had worked; I pointed out there was probably no Union to support them; a colleague quickly broke in stating her pleasure that this was non-Union labour because Unions would make them unemployable.

24th

Cath and I walked in to Ebenezer where almost everything has been stripped and removed. The pulpit is ready to be transported to Ireland. We had a good look around for the last time. We brought away two old wooden footstools, one might have been from 'our seat', two jugs and a teapot.

30th

I led worship this evening for the people of Ebenezer. Norah came with me

to Ashfield House for a church meeting so that everyone might be informed about the sale of contents. To conclude, I led worship (Jesus at Bethany) which included communion. They were all pleased: possibly the only time the congregation has worshipped outside the Ebenezer building since 1877!
This proved the final service of the people of Ebenezer. Ashfield House was a Day Centre next-door to the chapel.

APRIL

21st
I worked hard at understanding 'To Strengthen the Poor' which has similarities to both poetry and a railway timetable. I had to read and summarize it several times before grasping it. Was I out of touch with theological language? Today I discovered that everyone, even the Christian Aid professionals found it difficult to grasp.
In July 1987 Christian Aid agreed, with the help of many partners at home and overseas, a statement of commitment for action and reflection called 'To Strengthen the Poor.' It became a document of considerable influence.

26th
I am to serve as President of the Council of Churches for Wales for a further two years, until the beginning of the new Ecumenical Instrument in September 1990.

MAY

21st
An important Synod committee-day. When I began as Moderator, one committee was responsible for the work of the Province. Today a cohesive strategy arose out of the agenda and work of the URC in Wales: One World Week (World Church and Mission), To Strengthen the Poor, and Faith in Wales (Church and Society); Justice, Peace and Integrity of Creation as the theme for Provincial Day in 1989 (Faith and Life). All shape into mission which is compassionate and unambiguous. Our contribution as a church to the mission of Christ's Body is radical, Biblically centred and claims shalom as the centre of God's reign.
'Faith in Wales' was a follow-up by the Church in Wales to the groundbreaking 'Faith in the City' Report of the Church of England.

JUNE

10th

When the convenor of the Review Group asked whether I would re-apply to stand as Moderator, I realized the finality of what I was about to say. I made the right decision.

28th

The Council for World Mission Executive came to Penrhys. I spoke about the background and Norah described the life of the local church. This visit was of historic significance.
CWM were now aware at first hand of the life of the church and the community of Penrhys. They were to become prime allies in the struggle to create a strategy of mission and service.

JULY

8th

Hendrefadog Infants School celebrated its 75th Anniversary. I walked up the outside steps and into a school I first entered at 3 years old, and left at the age of 7. I could hear the children leaving the hall to 'English Country gardens', see my father standing on a table changing a gas mantle. I spoke of Tylorstown past by showing a milking stool, candlestick, miner's lamp, picture of 6 and 7 pits, Dac's piece of coal cut in 1913; and Tylorstown present with a trout caught in the river. I looked around class 3's classroom and had tea with the staff. Dad would have been proud and pleased. I saw my name on the register.
The School closed in 1999.

SEPTEMBER

14th

When the train pulled out of Püsöpkladány, our passports were stamped and our multiple Hungarian visas taken - we assumed for checking. 40 minutes later, when we crossed the border, I wondered if something was wrong. The Romanians arrived, checked passports very carefully, changed money, searched for drugs with a muzzled dog and emptied out all our contents. That was frightening because of the food we were carrying and the addresses

written on the map. We pulled in at Rasboeini at 4.15. A shock to see crowds waiting in almost complete darkness in the waiting room. The train for Tirgu Mures (Marosvásárhély) left at 6.30 and was slow, packed and fascinating. A lovely peasant woman beamed when she discovered we spoke a little Hungarian. Arrived at 8 and booked in at Transylvania Hotel (medium price at 400 lei - the exchange rate is horrific, about 15 lei to £1). At the Reformed Church we found three pastors in the office and were escorted around this ancient, beautiful church; they talked about their work. Looked at a magnificent Orthodox Church before evening worship at Castle Church. A new church started to be built today.
For three months from the end of July, I had my one experience of a sabbatical. Norah and I resided in the Theological College at Debrecen where I attended the one month Language School at the University. Our intention had been to attend the school together but because of the illness of Norah's mother, Norah joined me at the end of August. Norah attended the Language School several years later. During the sabbatical, I was able as President of the Council of Churches for Wales, to present copies of the New Welsh Bible to some of the Churches in Eastern Europe. Our first opportunity was to present a Bible to a Reformed minister in Marosvásárhély. At the time, Hungarians in Transylvania (Erdélyi) suffered severe restrictions under the tyrannical Ceaucescu government.

15th

Today seemed like fiction. We both felt guilty eating eggs and bacon for breakfast. A Scotsman sitting at the next table (Free Presbyterian) asked if I was John Morgans, and stated he had met Árpád Penték, Rector of Kolosvár Theological College who was expecting us! How could he because we had received no response to my letter of last June? At the Roman Catholic church, two young children entered, crossed themselves with water, knelt and prayed and when they heard our English, spoke politely to us. Caught the 12.25 slow train to Rasboieni and another to Kolosvár / Cluj Napoca. We travelled up a beautiful valley in which the farms looked pre-industrial. A man and his son whom we met on the train, took us to the Hotel Continental - 1st class because foreign tourists must stay there. No choice but a room with a bath because nothing else available! Student demonstration outside as they queued to buy books. We visited an old professor and his wife, before meeting the Rector (Árpád Péntek) at the College. He had arranged a week's visit but I had not received his invitation. There were photographs of Barth and Ceaucescu in his room. He took us to the glorious Second Church, modelled on Nagytemplom, Debrecen and to the First Church which had the same architect as Nyírbátor. He took us opposite the hotel and left. We walked the very dark streets of this unreal city. We watched TV closure for the night with the President's speech and ecstatic applause.

Nyirbator is in eastern Hungary. Built between 1488 and 1511, it is one of the most beautiful Gothic structures in Hungary. Ceaucescu stared at us from every shop window and public building.

16th

We left the hotel at 5 in darkness and had a strange walk through dimly lit streets to the station. We caught the Baltic/Orient Express at 5.45. It dawned as we climbed the Transylvanian hills, whose green-ness reminded us of Wales, but the villages and scattered houses were not like Wales at all. The four other travellers were Hungarian: a lady from Budapest and three from Kolosvár. A young man was trying to leave, and a young couple hoped to spend a holiday in Budapest and be out of Romania for the first time. They had been recently turned back twice at the border. To their astonishment they weren't troubled this time and put it down to our presence. A joyous journey in Hungary because we felt at home and they sensed freedom.

20th

Prague is a most intriguing city. Norah and I crossed the river and climbed the hill to the castle/ palace/ ancient cathedral of the Bohemian kings. It has one of the most wonderful collections of buildings in central Europe. A strange highlight was the arrival of the President of India at the Presidential Palace with army band, salutes, black cars. Down the hill to the vast Wenceslas Cathedral and across the Charles Bridge to the Town Hall clock. Then to the Jewish ghetto, where we spent some time in the cemetery and the museum, looking at the children's paintings from the concentration camp. Words elude me. A lovely walk through Prague at night through Wenceslas Square to the museum and back to the Town Hall and the old city. Stylish lighting and tasteful restoration.

The second opportunity to present the Bible in Prague. We were cared for by a friend of Norah, Mila Hradeçna who was a secretary at the Christian Peace Conference. They had met at the Women's Workshop in the Bahamas in 1981. CPC ended in 2000 after forty years of ministry. The experience at the Jewish cemetery and synagogue was traumatic, particularly because of the 'exhibition' of the drawings and poems of the 'children of Terezin,' a Nazi concentration camp.

21st

We visited two contrasting churches: the Bethlehem church in which Huss and Thomas Muntzer preached and which is associated with Comenius; the

Church of Our Lady of the Snows which is majestic and still used for worship. Took Mila to lunch: a courageous, caring person, sharing our vision of the church as a sign of the kingdom. 'To be converted to Christ is to be converted to justice.'

OCTOBER

4th

A knock on the door woke us at 5.15. You are not far from Moscow. What expectations for a Rhondda boy. We arrived exactly on time at 6.27, stepped off the giant train on to Russian soil, looked for a bearded priest but were greeted by a long dark coated Tatyana. She took us by taxi to the huge Ukraine hotel. We would be meeting Philaret at 10 and would leave tonight for Leningrad. At 8.30 a black car took us to the Danilov Monastery where for half an hour, we met Metropolitan Philaret, and two Archbishops of the Foreign Department. The meeting was formal, kind, courteous and included the giving of the Welsh Bible and receiving Millennium gifts. Wales was being noted. After an hour in the monastery and lunch in hotel, we walked in Red Square where we saw the changing of the guard at 5. Visited a convent on the banks of the river and spent an hour in the rhythm of the evening liturgy. Great beauty.

The third journey was to present the Bible to the Russian Orthodox Church. Because of the illness of Patriarch Pimen, Metropolitan Philaret received the Welsh Bible. In return we received a book celebrating the Millennium of the Russian Church. We were told that I was the third President to receive the book. The other two Presidents were Gorbachov and Reagan. Some company! Philaret asked to take greetings to Father Deiniol in Manod, North Wales. It marked the beginning of a long friendship with Deiniol.

5th

Norah, Tatyana and I were met at the Leningrad station by Yuri, a lecturer at the Orthodox Theological College. A car was at our disposal and we were taken to the huge, Moscow Hotel on the banks of the Neva. Joined the liturgy of the old monastery church before going to the theological college. We were shown the library and chapel before meeting the new rector who was most disappointing. He seemed tired, cynical and too sure of himself. In the monastery cemetery we saw the graves of Dostoevsky, Tchaikovsky, Nikodim and many others. Sight-seeing included the magnificent Hermitage. The most wonderful setting coupled with a remarkable collection of buildings

and paintings. Evening worship at St Nicholas Cathedral: a rich sound of great strength and piety. Babushkas rule the world.
Of the very few English books in the Library of the Theological College, one was by Peter Anson who had been a monk on Caldey. Peter F. Anson was born in 1889. From 1910 to 1924 he was a member of the Benedictine brotherhood on Caldey Island, and one of the twenty monks who followed Abbot Aelred Carlyle over to Rome in 1913.

6th

From the sixth floor in the Moskva Hotel, the Neva is dark but promenaded by lights. The sun rose across the river and welcomed another wonderful day. Tatyana is enigmatic, intelligent and careful. We were taken to the Winter Palace of Peter the Great. It is at the seas edge, 30 kilometres from Leningrad. Beautiful crisp morning: the visit to the little palace, the fountains which included the 'joke umbrella' and 'bench' fountains. It was fun in this magnificent relic of aristocracy. We visited the superb St Isaac cathedral with the third highest dome in the world and now a museum; the island fortress with the tombs of Peter and other Czars. Finally to the mass cemetery of 700,000 who died during the 3 year siege of Leningrad: the most moving moment of our visit to Russia helping us understand the 'liberation monuments' in Hungary and elsewhere. They cannot let it happen again. Worshipped at Trinity where the rhythmic power and dancing light created an atmosphere of great devotion.

7th

At Kalinin we met Archimandrite Victor. Breakfast with a Japanese Orthodox group. We were taken to the banks of the Volga: an old merchant town from the Middle Ages but rebuilt in the 18th century after a fire. Taken to two merchants' houses and the beautiful cathedral; joined the reception at the church hall. Sumptuous meal with long speeches celebrating the absent Metropolitan. Great fun, especially with Tatyana translating. I also gave a speech. Called at a beautiful village church on the Volga.

8th

Today I began to feel what the emissaries experienced when they worshipped with the Orthodox in Constantinople, and saw heaven and earth joined. Nothing could be more splendid and reflective of the holiness and grandeur of God. Zagorsk for the Festival of St Sergei the founder of the monastery. Despite a dull overcast morning, the cathedral and monastery are breathtaking. We were squeezed into one of the churches near the iconostasis and part of a huge crowd. After 45 minutes of worship, we were taken into a second church and literally pushed and squeezed towards the iconostasis. Another vast crowd. What sound and colour. After the service we followed the procession of the Patriarch and Metropolitans out into the square for 'blessing the icon'. It was like a football match crowd. An electrifying moment when all the bells pealed after a long note by a bass voice. That was heaven. After worship we were part of a reception at the Academy - 500 students for priesthood. Two exhibitions: for the Millennium and the permanent magnificent Museum.

Standing near us was Andrei Sakharov (died 1989) the eminent nuclear physicist, dissident and human rights activist. He was awarded the Nobel Peace Prize in 1975.

Sunday 9th

We were taken to the Cathedral Church of Moscow, the Epiphany Church. The gate in front of the iconostasis was opened and we joined 4 others to participate in the service from this wonderful position. We were able to stand, without discomfort, from 9.50 to 12.20. It was a spectacle of colour and sound; the devotion and patience of the congregation; the choirs and soloists were heavenly; the nun invited us to kiss the relic of the 14th century patriarch and drink holy water. The Moscow Circus this evening was at fast pace with humour and thrills. I laughed so much. Wonderful to watch the children.

10th

We must not forget the kindness and respect given to the President of the Council of Churches of Wales, and his wife. Tatyana took us around the Kremlin. Magnificent but sad that these cathedrals and icons are now a museum. Then the most difficult task: we had been given 200 roubles by the Russian Church and we had to spend it. We bought a carpet piece for a very reluctant Tatyana.

14th

The 450th anniversary of the Reformed College was remembered at a service at Nagytemplom. We were placed in the front seat of honour with the chaired guests. A very wordy service was lightened by items from Kantus. A major prize was won by Lászlő Gonda.

Lászlő Gonda had been one of the students to come on exchange to Wales.

Sunday 15th

I gave a Welsh Bible to Botond and received gifts relating to the 450th anniversary of the College.

Dr Botond Gaal was President of the Theological University. He is now Professor of Christian Dogmatics and Systematic Theology at the University of Reformed Theology.

NOVEMBER

1st

A magnificent celebration of All Saints: I met the Queen at Westminster Abbey and presented New Welsh Bibles to the Archbishop of Canterbury and the representatives of the churches and ecumenical councils in the United Kingdom and Ireland. As I walked through the nave at the close of worship, I felt it right to candidate for the vacancy at Penrhys. What a day! I walked to Ystrad station and caught the 6.24 to Cardiff. A privilege to shake hands with the Queen before processing to the sacrarium. We sang Welsh hymns, heard an excellent sermon by G. O. Williams and then I presented the 8 Bibles: the Queen had just received her Bible from Owen Evans and Brynley Roberts. As we processed out, singly, I felt I should minister at Penrhys. Was that the call for which I had been waiting?

Owen E. Evans was a Minister of the Methodist Church, and until his retirement was Senior Lecturer in the Department of Theology and Religious Studies, Bangor University. He was formerly Director of the New Welsh Bible and editor of the Concordance. Brynley F Roberts was the Chief Librarian at the National Library of Wales. The Most Revd G O Williams was Archbishop emeritus.

2nd

Yesterday I made the decision. It was the internal stage in the process of the 'call'. I have felt for many years, before we went to live at Penrhys, that God was leading me towards Penrhys. Yesterday as I walked down that very long nave in Westminster Abbey, I felt it right to offer myself to the service of the church and the wider community of Penrhys. This morning at Moderators' meeting, when it came to my list of ministers and vacant churches and saw that for the first time ever, Penrhys was on my list and I was available to candidate, I offered my name. My fellow Moderators unanimously endorsed my candidacy. I have now offered myself to the church and it is for the church to make its decision.

This was our normal Moderators' meeting on the first Wednesday and Thursday of each month. I have no doubt that my sense of call was equally shared by Norah who had always felt comfortable on Penrhys and that there was a ministry for her there.

3rd

I feel at ease with myself. I sense there is a long personal history, perhaps from the days when I walked to the farm as a boy when there were no houses there; seeing the establishment of the community and since becoming Moderator, taking the initiative to ensure the continuation of ministry. Latter years saw our move to Penrhys, our increasing involvement and finally yesterday's decision. I am aware of the enormity of the task but all I can do is offer myself and seek the blessing of God.

29th

'He must be ready to make a fool of himself in other people's eyes, if he wants to be really wise.' (I Cor 3.18). As I prepared for the interview by the Penrhys Sponsoring Body, my prayers included that text. In a sense it is madness: why should someone with my experience serve in a community with a congregation of a dozen? Am I failing to utilize skills entrusted me? There is no emotional feel about 'coming home.' It is a quiet certitude that this is what I must do. I entered the meeting apprehensively because I haven' t been interviewed since Manselton days. After sharing my hopes, I was amazed and humbled by the overwhelming response: all saw the need for community, a place of worship, collegiality and the bringing together of spirituality and justice. There was an immediate confirmation of my call, before the more formal invitation which is the responsibility of the congregation.

At the very start of the process, we felt certain that a new form of ministry was necessary for Penrhys. There had been four successive Christian leaders in the seventeen years' existence of the Christian Fellowship. All leaders had worked faithfully but I suspect worked within a received pattern. The question which was posed to us, the congregation and the Sponsoring Body was 'is there a different way, and if so, what is it?'

DECEMBER

2nd

I led worship and shared hopes with the congregation, and was formally invited to join with them in the ministry of the church. It confirmed the call of God to service here. I begin in September. I called to see the Estate Manger and shared thoughts about a Christian Centre in one of the maisonettes. He promised full support. This evening all were present (14 including Donald and Edwina Owen) except Mrs Perkins.

Sunday 11th

Norah and I walked the circumference road of our site/ estate/ community. We noticed: (1) the hard work and expense given to redevelopment. This is the first stage of the renewal of the site which will be a much more comfortable place when the work is completed. (2) There is the continuing rundown of houses with graffiti, vandalism, litter, houses smashed as soon as they are empty. What will happen to the renewed houses? It confirmed the need for a church community, but was a warning of the challenge.

20th

The key to God's mission for this community lies in a theology and ecclesiology with the Magnificat at its heart. If we work hard, do not lose nerve and pursue every opportunity, we could experience a breakthrough in the unity and mission of the church. I have served the wider church for 12 years and been committed for much longer to a vision of unity and mission, but it is possible that here on Penrhys we will see a living embodiment of Christ's vision for the church. Is it because there is commitment to, and concentration on the very local and the very deprived?

1989

JANUARY

20th

At the Junior School we met Mr Morse, recently appointed as headmaster but who taught at the school for 11 years. We spoke about Russia to the school assembly of 300 children who behaved in exemplary fashion with a relaxed, attentive atmosphere. I was introduced to staff and children as the next minister on Penrhys.

Cerri Morse had previously taught at the Junior School, and was now returning as head teacher, a position he maintained until his retirement in 2003. Norah and I enjoyed a close friendship and colleagueship with Cerri and the staff at the school. This also applied to the head teacher of the Infants School, Pat Price, and with Bethan Williams, head teacher at the Nursery School. Relationship and trust are at the heart of community development. In our talk about Russia, we played a tape of Russian Orthodox bells, and in reply to Norah's question to the children, 'Would you like to have a bell on Penrhys?' came a thundering answer, 'Yes.' That provided the impetus for the receiving of a bell from Caldey.

MARCH

16th

Two splendid candidates: Sarah Bevan, an 18 year old from Llanelli and Alison Upham, eligible for a call to the Baptist Union of Wales. Her husband, Marc Dummer, a Baptist minister is applying for URC ministry. With Ruth Whitehead of Merthyr accepted last December, here are four potentially first class ministers.

All are ministers in the United Reformed Church. Marc Dummer is minister at Canton Uniting, the church where our family worship. Alison Upham is minister of Minster Road and Roath Park where we had worshipped until leaving for Penrhys. The two churches have recently united to become Roathminster URC.

Sunday 19th

Caldey will be remembered for Estelle and Louisa. They have contributed so much to the freshness and depth of our common experience in the way of young, uninhibited children. It is too easy to fall into the trap of thinking that Penrhys children are illiterate, maladjusted, abused, scarred by personal and environmental deprivation, but these 9 and 10 year olds are all one can hope from children of their age. They have been attentive, courteous and a credit to their families and schools. We joined the Palm Procession to the Abbey chapel and I was the crowd in reading the Passion Narrative.

21st

There was pride and joy on the parents' faces as they heard how well their children had behaved, and the contribution they had made on Caldey. The girls had met the Abbot!

Estelle came from a committed Catholic family. Louisa was baptised with her brother and sisters in a service televised from Penrhys in the following June.

31st

It feels like a summer night. It is warm, windows are open and although it is 10.15, there are the sounds of small children playing outside. The area immediately behind our terrace is a combination of rubbish tip, builder's yard and playground. The obstacles present splendid challenges: planks, scaffolding, containers, skips. The children range from 3 years old to early teens. What fun in this dangerous world of darkness! What is to happen to them? A break-in in chapel but not much missing.

The chapel was burgled on a regular basis.

APRIL

26th

Ebenezer is being demolished. We took photographs, one from the vestry door looking up to the sky; the ceiling of both vestry and chapel have been removed. What were my feelings? Sad to think of 111 years of witness to the community; that my family had been members from the beginning, and yet the end came with dignity, and a new building will bring homes for the elderly of Tylorstown.

Sunday 30th

The HTV profile of my ministry was professional and sensitive, reflecting my 12 years as Moderator and our preparing for ministry on Penrhys. The programme, produced by David Hammond-Williams and presented by Rian Evans, included interviews with Norah, Bernard Thorogood, George Noakes, Noel Davies and Kim Howells.

MAY

1st

May Day celebrates life as a journey together, a common pilgrimage, a living mission for humanity. Will the visit of our churches at Gowerton, Mumbles and Parkmill be the first of many to come on pilgrimage to Penrhys? One of our 12 year old girls was excited to exchange addresses with an elderly member from Parkmill: 'I've got a pen pal!' People here give thanks for the simplest things. The more sophisticated and comparatively wealthy, have much to learn. It is giving a new insight into the ministry of Jesus.

The visit proved the precursor of hundreds of visits and thousands of visitors during the next fifteen years. The welcoming of visitors proved an important element in the ministry of the church and helped change the image of Penrhys from being a 'no-go' area to a place of hospitality.

JULY

Sunday 4th

Tabernacle Llanfaches celebrates 350 years. When I discovered Welsh Puritanism in 1962, little did I think I would lead worship today in 1989. Erbery's dedicated life and open spirit were at the heart of my sermon. Now I have reached the age when he died, I recognise his courageous, adventurous mind.

14th

A very large 'Penrhys New Perspective' (PNP) hoarding was attached prominently on the Block. The Prince arrived at the Community Centre, signed Jonathan's leg in plaster and entered the hall. He talked with Norah and me for a few minutes and we shared our concerns and proposals for the church.

The visit of the Prince of Wales to Penrhys had been organised by Business in the Community. His coming was important symbolically and practically as it drew attention to the condition of Penrhys, and the need for both an internal change from residents and a different approach from 'outsiders.' Could there be cooperation to help develop long-term change? How was it to happen? What kind of vision and strategy were necessary? Jonathan was about six years old and our next door neighbour. PNP or Penrhys Golwg Newydd was the title of the Church's new programme and it was placed on a redundant block of flats. At the time it was a statement of hope and intention, but hardly grounded in reality.

17th

The house has new windows and doors; cladding, coating, a new roof, drainpipes and gutters. The house is warmer, quieter and more secure. It is comfortable. We enjoy living in our terrace and are good friends with our neighbours. If you share love quietly and persistently, relationships develop in the most unlikely situation.

Our house in Heol Dyfed was part of the first phase of property refurbishment which was initiated as a consequence of the Government's Priority Estates Programme. It was to be a four stage programme stretching over many years: three stages of property refurbishment and finally environmental enhancement. This development provided a key context for the development of the church programme during the next few years.

21st

We face an adventure into the unknown. Do we have the skills to pioneer the way? Ahead lie obstacles and hidden perils, but the journey is in the company of the author and sustainer of the mystery that is the universe.

24th

The script reflects what God is doing in this community and articulates it for a wide audience. The wider church needs to discover what Penrhys has to offer, and also help Penrhys discover self-respect.

At the time ITV scheduled a 'live service of worship' on television every Sunday morning. The service came from the different regions of the Independent Television Service. HTV broadcast two or three each year, and the Welsh producers thought it worth taking the risk of showing one from Penrhys on a Sunday morning. It was fraught with difficulties. The congregation comprised only ten adults and a large number of small children who were not used to the discipline of an hour's service. The regular Sunday service was often disrupted by teenagers who could well seek to vandalise the service. Although Norah worshipped regularly, I was an infrequent worshipper and had to learn the strengths and weaknesses of the few adults. There was also the challenge of trying to reflect something new. Could Penrhys be seen in a new light? Most people in Wales thought they knew that Penrhys was a place without hope and no future. I created a script which included recorded material reflecting signs of hope on the estate, and at its heart were the baptisms of four young children, symbolizing that there was hope and dignity.

Sunday 25th

The 'live HTV' service reflected this community and was faithful to the Gospel. I introduced the service from the Statue and the water carriers entered the chapel during the singing of 'Tell out my soul.' Everything went superbly: the pre-recorded reading in the coffee bar; my extempore interview with Beryl, Mary and Muriel; Beverley's singing; Bradley and Scott, two eleven year olds who sang 'Sing we a song of high revolt;' beautiful intercessions which included the 'cut-ins' of life on the estate; the baptisms of Louisa, Paul, Andrew, Laura. We came off the air to spontaneous applause and thankfulness.

JULY

12th

At one point in the Moderators' meeting I found myself looking round the room at familiar faces and realized I was doing it for the last time. Our meeting at Solihull was chaired by John Waller. He made a farewell speech, and at the close came solemn hand-shakes before we all left in different directions. Something precious has come to an end. When I meet the Moderators again, it will be different.

The Moderators' Meeting was held in Solihull and not in Church House in London because of a rail strike. John Waller was Moderator of Southern Province.

14th

Twenty young people between the ages of 14 and 24 ran across the beach to paddle in Priory Bay. The majority had never seen the sea before, especially this sea which runs out to the great Atlantic. Caldey is again the island of adventure. The hallmark of the day has been developing trust and resultant joy. The 8 from the Welsh Western Seaboard of Europe have met 12 guests from Central Europe who are encircled by the Carpathian ring which separates them from the steppes leading to Asia.

Another visit of Hungarian and Welsh young people on Caldey.

15th

A day of light. This evening in a mellow, tranquil Compline with its gentleness of sound and delicacy of colour, sunlight from a westerly window shone brightly and strongly. I gazed and asked God for a sign of his presence; the response was immediate: look around at your sisters and brothers worshipping - that is the sign of my presence. For what else do you look? Later many of us sat on the cliff-side near Nana's cave and realized that for 20,000 years women and men had lived on this island, Christianised for 1600 years, but divinised from the beginning until the end. In him we live and move and have our being: Christ is the centre of the universe.

19th

The reception for Brian and Rachel Griffiths was chaired by Idwal Symonds at the HTV flat in Dawn St, Mayfair. Brian is an advisor to Margaret Thatcher! Our speaker was Bill Milliken who pioneers 'Cities in Schools' in the US. He spoke simply, powerfully and compassionately about the need for an integrated approach to teenage drop-outs. I feel we are entering the front-line with our work on Penrhys.

Born in 1941 in Wales and educated at the London School of Economics, Brian Griffiths was a lecturer in economics at LSE from 1965-76. He served as a director of the Bank of England from 1985-1986. He also served as head of the Prime Minister's Policy Unit and as Special Adviser to Margaret Thatcher from 1985 to 1990. He is now Lord Griffiths of Fforestfach. Idwal Symonds was the Chair of the Directors of HTV. Bill Milliken was the President of 'Cities In Schools,' an organization working with young people who had dropped out of the normal education system. It is now known as 'Communities in Schools.'

Sunday 23rd

A personal achievement. I led worship at Salem Maesmynis, one of our churches tucked into Mynydd Epynt. This was my first visit. Now that I have been to Maesmynis, I have led worship in every one of our churches in Wales. I have preached in most many times, and I know many URC people throughout Wales, but my ambition was to lead worship in this last one. Probably it is the last time for me to preside at communion before Penrhys. 15 of us at Maesmynis.

31st

After the meal prepared by the Hungarians at Beulah Assembly Hall came the formal, tender goodbye characteristic of Hungarians. If I see them again it will not be as the Welsh Moderator who spent 6½ years developing an effective relationship between our churches and an eastern Europe church. Our work has gone on quietly and carefully, and is now an integral and critical part of our church. From September, I release this work to John as our Moderator and Hungarian speaker. He will lead the work very well, but I have regrets at no longer being involved in work I initiated.

The Assembly Room at Beulah Rhiwbina.

AUGUST

Sunday 20th

The Cathedral at Brecon was packed to capacity for the Sixth Annual Jazz Festival service. It began with the Adamant Jazz Band from Cardiff marching

down the central aisle. My sermon lasted 25 minutes and received an amazing response. I have never before been applauded.
This was like a dream come true for the teenager who had once listened to Willis Conover on 'Voice of America,' now to be sharing my love for jazz and passion for the Gospel. Conover was a legend amongst jazz lovers primarily due to the hour-long programme every evening on the Voice of America.

29th

A young woman of sensitivity and integrity wishes to have her sick child baptized. The baptism of children and families could be an important service and mission.
Never was a truer word written.

31st

My last words as Moderator of the Welsh Province of the URC. The 12 year ministry has been enriching and I am grateful for the privilege. I hope I faithfully served the community of the church and the wider community. When I look back on those first fearful days of great challenge, I realize I have changed, and the condition and morale of the church has also changed.
My final service was presiding at the ordination and induction of Simon Copley at Cwmbran. It is strange that my first and last public commitments as Moderator were ordination services.

PENRHYS

1989 - 2004

INTRODUCTION

Our decision to move to Penrhys was made on April 4th 1986 and we moved into 12 Heol Dyfed on October 27th of that year. However, there is a long history leading up to the decision and the move. For Norah, it might have begun at Easter worship in 1966 at East Harlem Protestant Mission, New York, and later that year when she heard George Webber (one of the founders of the church in East Harlem) saying that in order to understand and support, 'you must live there.' For me, the first overt signs were on visits to Penrhys on July 11th 1970 and September 15th 1973. In retrospect our move to Penrhys was as inevitable as was my decision to join Norah in her 'ministry,' and be inducted as minister of the Penrhys Uniting Church in October 1989.

From the day we arrived on Penrhys, we immediately felt at ease in our new environment. Although Penrhys is very different from any other community in which we had lived, we knew that it was where we should be - and we lived and worked there until our retirement in 2004. The period must count amongst the happiest and most fulfilling period of our lives, and from the vantage point of retirement, it amazes us how much was achieved by working with others in the community. We learned so much and received so much in those 18 years, that we always consider ourselves deeply indebted to the community of Penrhys.

Naturally it was a steep learning curve because we were soon aware we were novices in the new world of recognizing and developing community. How did we begin? By enjoying the experience of our neighbours, the small congregation with its minister Pat Parrish, community groups, the schools, and of the whole community of the city 'above the Star' (the pub in Ystrad at the bottom of Penrhys hill.) We learned by receiving.

One of the reasons for our moving to Penrhys was because we did not believe its scurrilous reputation which was depicted by the majority of the media. There was a particularly infamous documentary in 1986. It was obvious that the media were not reflecting a fair picture of the community. They looked for the sensational 'bad news.

Norah and I had of course grown a great deal from our experience of the wider church and community during the previous thirty years, and this helped us begin to understand what was going on beneath the surface and behind the headlines. We had much to learn before we could even begin to understand, and it was obvious that without understanding, we would not be able to support the community. We tried to discover the 'real story' of Penrhys and of one thing we are now certain, the real story comes only as a result of living in and entering fully into community life. On Penrhys we discovered R S Thomas' 'bright field' and we will remain the beneficiaries for the rest of our lives.

1. MODERN PENRHYS

Modern Penrhys has an unusual background. Its context is a combination of (a) *A 'Redundant' Coal-Mining Community.* Rhondda comprises thirty Nineteenth Century villages, all centred on a pit or pits. There was an explosion of immigration during the last fifty years of the Nineteenth Century and there has been an almost equally rapid and inexorable decline since 1924. Each village has experienced the collapse of its raison d'etre and is struggling to discover a life after the pit.

(b) *A Creation of 1960s 'Utopian Planning.'* When the estate was designed, there were long waiting lists of applicants for Council housing, in addition to a request from the National Coal Board for 250 dwellings to attract miners from the North of England. There was a lack of space in the valley floor because of the dereliction caused by many of the 53 collieries (some still operational in the 1960s). Although Glamorgan County Council favoured development along the coastal belt, Rhondda was concerned with maintaining its population, and its strategy was to halt the deterioration of the Valleys. Approval for the building of Penrhys would not have been given but for the influence of the Secretary of State for Wales, the late Lord Tonypandy. Before building began, the NCB withdrew its request because of the contraction of the mining industry which accentuated Rhondda's decline. Trends towards private home improvement, which included enveloping schemes, resulted in a reduced demand for Council provision. Demand for accommodation in peripheral areas like Penrhys slumped because of the rapid expansion of Housing Association programmes and the increase in properties for sale or rent.

(c) *Geographical Isolation.* Penrhys is built on a high mountain ridge between the Rhondda Fawr and the Rhondda Fach. It averages 1170' and gradients are 1:7. Weather conditions can be ferocious and the area suffers winds of Hebridean velocity. Work commenced in 1966 and 951 properties were constructed. Romantically inspired by an Italian hill-village, Penrhys is in direct contrast to traditional terraced houses. Penrhys' architecture militated against community spirit!

In the terraces of the Valleys, neighbours met as they hung clothes in the garden and walked to the shops along the same pavements. Neighbours met each other at the front door. On Penrhys, front-doors face in opposite directions so that it is very easy not to know even your next door neighbour, an almost unknown phenomenon for Valley people whose first question on meeting is not *'Where do you work?'* but *'Where do you come from?'* Roots and relationships are at the heart of Valley life - and of community. The estate was opened on Friday, the 13th September 1968. A district heating scheme provided warmth to every household, and pipes under pathways kept them free from ice in winter. Penrhys included a Community Centre with shopping arcade, Licensed premises, Junior, Infant and Nursery Schools. The Estate was the first phase of development with further schemes planned: additional dwellings (some privately built), a petrol station, additional nursery units, a branch library, medical facilities, and a building to be used by all churches. This second phase never materialised.

2. BACKGROUND TO 1986

Social Studies in the 1970s revealed serious problems: high rents, poor workmanship, inadequate heating, noise, rubbish, crime and vandalism. The heating system broke down (those living near the Boiler House lived in the Tropics and those farthest away in the Tundra!), and in 1982 individual central heating systems were installed. The increased cost of heating resulted in people having to economize on heating bills, but this caused dampness and condensation. Community spirit was never engendered and residents felt isolated from friends and family due to the Estate's location. Housing demand became non-existent and dwellings were allocated to families and individuals with 'problems'. The area developed a poor reputation and applications from potentially good tenants diminished. All these factors developed a downward spiral.

By the time we arrived in 1986 Penrhys was living with its third generation of unemployed. Many of the people living on Penrhys were unemployed when they arrived on the estate. Many had been marginalized in the traditional mining villages. Others were moved to Penrhys through compulsory purchase of their homes, and their bitterness at being evicted from their long-established homes remained with them as long as they lived. One of the consequences of life on Penrhys was the acceptance of a dependency culture.

Because of its high turn-over rate, Penrhys was depicted as a place for 'people with problems' who moved from one marginalized estate to another. People rarely move far, and then only into a similar kind of community. Penrhys had to live with the effects of a negative media image. If anything adverse happened in society at large, interview someone on Penrhys! Locals rarely wanted to admit they lived on Penrhys and would not use the address or post code if looking for work. Rhondda locals rarely visited Penrhys unless they had relatives there. Penrhys was targeted as the butt for cruel jokes.

There were very positive aspects of community life. As the estate grew older, strong support structures began to exist within the family network. Many young grandmothers were in their mid 30s and acted with great responsibility because they had been through similar experiences as their children. Most people had an accepting, open and forgiving nature. There was the capacity for enjoyment on limited means. People enjoy themselves on little money. Children play outdoors completely safely. Older brothers and sisters and friends looked after each other. Parties were common with people sitting outside chatting, playing, listening to music. Partly because of the pressure of stigmatisation, people developed a fierce loyalty to their community. There are remarkable human resources of resilience and compassion. Suffering often produces courage and determination: the mothers of young people with addictions; women who have been abused; children who have been neglected; many struggling against the demons of alcohol and drugs. There is a reservoir of life-experience in communities like Penrhys. This experience should be valued and listened to, and people encouraged to participate in the formulation of public policy. They understand through experience.

3. COMMUNITY DEVELOPMENT 1986 - 1989

We arrived on Penrhys in 1986 with optimism that the community was at a critical turning-point with the developments of the Priority Estates Project. For three years we listened and learned from the people of the Estate and were soon counted as fellow neighbours and tenants. Norah played an energetic role in the community. She was initiator and editor of *Penrhys Voice*, the community newspaper which was enthusiastically received by Penrhys residents and highly praised by the Welsh Office. Working on the newspaper gave Norah access to all groups on Penrhys, such as Gingerbread and the Boxing Club. She was asked by the Welsh Office to give workshops on community newspapers. Norah also served as an occasional supply teacher for the Primary School and this proved invaluable for later developments.

Through PEP, £15 million was earmarked to physically refurbish the estate. All houses and several maisonette blocks were refurbished. Environmental work followed. The quality of the houses was improved to the extent that Penrhys houses were superior to all other Council houses in Rhondda. However attention was not paid either to the declining population of Rhondda and its shift towards the south, or the housing developments of the 1980s. Consequently two blocks of houses (16 properties) refurbished on Penrhys in Spring 1990 were vandalized that Summer, and demolished in the Autumn. This caused a shock wave throughout the Estate, and this erosion of confidence continued for many years. Urban planners, skilled in demography should have known that the refurbishment of all houses on Penrhys was nonsense. The waste of the public purse had long-term repercussions, and the consequences on human lives was disastrous. A generation of children grew up on a building- and demolishing-site!

A brave attempt was made to develop the participation of the community in its own future. The programme encouraged the Tenants and Residents' Association, provided it with the necessary funds for developing community life, supported its agenda and provided training through the Priority Estates Programme (PEP). During the mid and late 1980s, the Tenants' Association employed a full-time Secretary, Community Worker, three workers for a Garden Project, two full-time and one part-time worker for a Craft Workshop, funding for a Community newspaper (Voluntary worker), a Credit Union and Community Cooperative (part-time workers with ample funding).

Many local volunteers worked faithfully and for many long hours, but like many similar community projects, it eventually ran out of steam. Capital development is comparatively straightforward, but sustainability in terms of funding and maintaining the interest and morale of members of the community are much more difficult challenges.

4. THE PENRHYS FELLOWSHIP 1971- 1989

The Church at Penrhys was formed by its Rhondda background. In 1914 there were 151 Nonconformist chapels in Rhondda; today there are less than a quarter of that number. In Tylorstown (the nearest village) there were nine chapels with two thousand members; today all that remains is a small faithful English speaking Methodist Church.

The Penrhys cause was founded in 1971 as an Interdenominational Fellowship in which all eight churches of the Council of Churches of Wales participated. This was, and remains a unique act of cooperation and commitment. It was a brave experiment in ecumenism and mission. At that time, the Churches in Wales - and elsewhere - could not agree on what constitutes a church and the experiment was called a Christian Fellowship. It was hoped that a lay-worker rather than a priest or minister would be closer to the people - there was also a suspicion that a minister/priest might develop a church of his own denomination! Probably the main pressure shaping ecumenism was the decision of the Local Authority, in response to an application by the Baptists for a new church site, that there should be only one site for a Christian community in Penrhys. Finally, a decision was made not to build a Church - the reason? It was economically impossible. The consequence was that the life of the Fellowship took place in a redundant shop in the Community Centre. The first two ministries were a Church Army Officer (1971-4) and a Baptist Lay-worker (1974-6); since 1980, the ministers have been provided by the United Reformed Church: the first from 1980-2; the second from 1983-8; I served from 1989 to 2004.

The life of the congregation reflected the life of the community. It was perceived that it would always be dependent, never able to stand on its own feet and always 'less than a proper church,' just as Penrhys was depicted as 'less than a proper community.' By 1989 a handful of adults and children belonged to the fellowship which attempted to reflect nonconformist patterns in the Valleys. The worshippers, brought up in a traditional church pattern, performed these functions with exemplary faithfulness, but often felt threatened and always extremely vulnerable. Were other patterns more suitable for today and for Penrhys?

5. PENRHYS NEW PERSPECTIVE

We began to consider a new approach to the Church's serving the community. Although we had learned issues of development from our experience of church and community life during the previous 20 years, the seminal experience was our living for two years on Penrhys.

A key issue involved the Penrhys Uniting Church re-thinking her role in the community. Was the church an ark to save the perishing from the community, or was her mission to assist the community discover self-respect and discover potential? Was the church a sectarian gathering of the faithful singing happy songs, or had the church received the blessing of unity as a sign of what God wishes and demands for the unity of humankind? This demanded a fundamental shift in attitude and life-style. The Church now attempted to create a relationship between Statutory Authorities, Private Business, Charities, the Churches and the Penrhys residents themselves. The aim of the Project was to:

(i) Provide a Team to Live and Work on Penrhys.
(ii) Re-furbish a Block of Maisonettes.
(iii) Develop a Programme which included
(a) Projects for Community Purposes
(b) Living accommodation
(c) a Small Chapel
(iv) Financial Provision in terms of capital expenditure and revenue.

The idea/vision/proposals of Penrhys New Perspective (Penrhys Golwg Newydd) was first suggested in December 1988 and by the Spring of 1989, it had been shaped into a blue-print with the architects. A derelict block was gifted by the Rhondda Borough Council, a Trust Deed created and accepted by the eight denominations, and miraculously by the close of 1990, £700,000 had been raised. 80% of the funding came from the private sector (Churches, dozens of individuals, Charitable Bodies, the Business Community). The work of refurbishment began in April 1991, Llanfair was opened on February 29th 1992 and all costs were met. Even more amazing was the fact that for the next twelve years, Llanfair was financially viable, generating sufficient income from rents and projects to maintain the building as a viable financial unit. This gave Llanfair an independence from the necessity of raising funds for three year projects which is so often the problem facing many community voluntary programmes. The new model which was Llanfair was a story of communal endeavour and laid the foundations for the continuing life of Penrhys. It helped transform a housing estate into a village.

6. LLANFAIR IS A NURTURING CHURCH

A. SHARING GRACE

Penrhys people are no different from the majority of people in Wales, except that in this community of gross disadvantage, there is often more open-ness and fewer inhibitions. It is common for people to reflect on life/religious questions. Nevertheless, as is common throughout Britain, there is a gap between the 'religious context' and the Church. Connections need to be made before people arrive at the conclusion that births need to be celebrated by baptisms; relationships by weddings; deaths by funerals; 'needs and thanks and forgiveness' by the lighting of candles and the saying of prayers. How are these connections to be made? How are the seeds to be sown?

This religious need is the fertile context for the sharing of the heart of the Gospel: the critical and startling message that God is gracious, kind, merciful, loving; and God expects his children, partners, colleagues to be similarly gracious, kind, merciful, loving. That is how God is and will transform the world. This unrealistic and simple message is exhilarating for individuals and a community which has experienced restriction, demands, prejudice and harassment. '*You are accepted for who you are; what potential you have as God's daughter or son. Reflect this kindness of God in the way you live.*' Although it may dawn suddenly that there is a loving God at the heart of the universe, that wondrous clarity brings with it a lifetime's privilege and responsibility. Grasping the divine resources available for transforming personhood, relationships and community demands constant patience. It is the work of maturing. It cannot be slick and is always costly.

The glory of the Resurrection and the presence of the Risen Christ with his people is at the heart of the Gospel and is celebrated in the life and work of Llanfair. The Eucharistic Liturgy places the list of resurrection appearances alongside the traditional remembering of the Last Night. However, day by day, life on Penrhys reawakened the need to emphasize the suffering of Jesus and the power of the Cross. God identifies himself with his world. God miraculously appears at the time and in the place where one would least expect to see the divine presence and grace. God is in the birth of a child in a stable. God is in the death of a young man on a hill on a Friday afternoon. God is found in a community described as God-forsaken. That is where one sees God! In our weakness we find God's strength; in our foolishness we find God's wisdom. God is found in the agony of his suffering people; the poor and marginalized in our affluent, aggressive society have been pushed to the corners by those who forget God and regard him as irrelevant. Yet, it is in this space that God reveals and liberates his people. Deliverance from Egypt; the creation of community through Covenant; the role of the people as Suffering Servant, living courageously in Exile, are living Biblical and contextual themes for the poor of Penrhys. No triumphalist God blasts his way into individual lives or into circles of community. God, by example, changes people and forms community from within.

In 1989, when the small congregation dared to explore the need for a new Church-Centre, at its heart was the vision of celebrating both the liturgy and the liturgy after the liturgy: how worship and work flow into each other. The hope of Llanfair was to integrate the offering of worth to God in worship, with the offering of life in service to the world in work. Wholeness for the person, the community and the world demands an integration of sacred and secular. The chapel communion cup and the café coffee cup both reflect God's People at work.

B. SHAPING LLANFAIR

Norah and I, the congregation and Sponsoring Body (representing the denominations and the congregation) saw that a new beginning was necessary. Could a new building be created which could reflect the vision? Llanfair, in the structure of its building, integrates work and worship. The reshaping of the derelict maisonette block was from theological principles. Llanfair is at the geographical centre of the estate; literally on the cross-roads of the north-south and east-west paths. As the estate has diminished, the majority of houses and the new infrastructure have encircled Llanfair.

Could there be Communal Ministry? The previous twenty years had shown that the leader/minister had experienced loneliness and frustration. As the only professional living in the community and with little support from the worshippers (there was no diaconate/eldership), every minister suffered some form of burn-out. Was it possible to create a new style of communal ministry? Residential spaces were therefore critical. At the top of the Maisonette Block are four flats: a manse, a flat for an education worker and two double flats for student volunteers. This means that the live-in community provides mutual support, protects the building, and is also accessible to the wider community of Penrhys.

Could there be a Serving Church? Could the Christian community offer something of value to the wider community? The Community area lies immediately underneath the flats, occupies several floors and includes a Café, Créche, Launderette, Nearly-New Shop, Music Room, Homework Club and an Education Room.

Could there be a relevant style of spirituality? Could the Church meet the needs of both the residential community and the wider community of Penrhys? Could the gap be bridged between the religious need and the perception people have of the Church? The Chapel and its ancillary rooms are found on the Ground Floor and extend outwards onto what was waste ground. The building forms a whole, reflecting that to be church is to integrate holiness into the wholeness of life. The sounding of the bell and the lighting of the candle initiate that service which ushers in the stability and dynamism of God who gives wholeness to the community of Penrhys. That service flows from the breaking of bread and sharing of wine to service in the projects which are as much the expression of being the church as is the service of worship. Llanfair's hope is that it also flows out of the building and reaches every part of the community of Penrhys.

C. CREATING UNITY

In October 1989 the Penrhys Fellowship was recognized as 'The Penrhys Uniting Church' by the Baptist Union of Great Britain, the Baptist Union of Wales, the Church in Wales, the Congregational Federation, the Methodist Church, the Presbyterian Church of Wales, the Union of Welsh Independents and the United Reformed Church. This recognition was the culmination of a long journey. In 1971 the Free Churches in Rhondda and the Anglican Rural deanery established the Penrhys Christian Fellowship to serve the new housing estate of Penrhys. The Local Authority, which owned all property had insisted that any building should house some form of united church. An uncertainty about the meaning of 'fellowship' and 'church' eventually resulted in work on a new Constitution which came into being in 1984 but was not fulfilled until October 1989 when the Uniting Church was inaugurated. That Constitution was created 'in the spirit of the Covenant for Unity in Wales' and consequently held together within the same Church, those churches which were in Covenant and those outside the Welsh Covenant. Because the Uniting Church had such a wide foundation of support and recognition, it was able to present a united front to the community and reflect a coherent expression of the Gospel. This unity was symbolized by placing a stone from a redundant chapel of each of the supporting denominations in the neighbouring villages, as foundation stones of Llanfair. Llanfair's Church Bell and Crucifix were gifts from the Cistercian Monks of Caldey Island and the Icons came from the Russian Orthodox Church in Blaenau Ffestiniog and the Greek Orthodox in Llanelli.

More important than these symbols were the everyday opportunities for mission provided by the church's unity. Because Llanfair is the Church of Jesus Christ on Penrhys - and because that 'name' has also been earned by action, Llanfair serves as our church for the schools, council officers and workers, for the commercial life of Penrhys, voluntary organizations, for local and central government, for the business community and most important of all, for the majority of Penrhys people. The mission of the church is a day by day presence and action.

D. SHARING THE GIFTS OF THE CHURCH

Between 1992 and 2004, Llanfair invited and enjoyed annually the company of a thousand visitors from all over the world: through the church world-wide, from secular agencies, schools and colleges studying 'church in community,' churches on pilgrimage, communities looking for renewal. Many members of the Llanfair congregation travelled widely, sometimes at the invitation of other congregations (there were long-term relationships with the Wilmslow-Manchester Partners group of United Reformed Churches, and with Highbury Congregational Church, Cheltenham) and hundreds of people visited and stopped for many days at the Cistercian Abbey at Caldey, Canolfan Rhyd Ddu in Snowdonia (the birthplace of T.H. Parry Williams), Trinity College Carmarthen, the home of Renice and William Castell, the Selby Wright Centre on Skye and many young people were guests of the Reformed congregation at Monor, Hungary.

This travelling and exposure to different life- and church-styles, as well as the receiving of visitors to Penrhys had a major impact on Llanfair's life. The most important source of visitors was through the Council for World Mission. This world-wide family of more than thirty churches provided a remarkable channel of communication between Penrhys and the wider world. From 1990 until the programme changed its venues in 1998 the Training in Mission Team visited Penrhys annually for a weekend. These were young people who take a gap-year to explore Mission values. In 1992 the Youth in Mission Work camp came to Penrhys for three weeks. Thirty young people lived, worked and prayed in Penrhys for three weeks.

These temporary visits laid the foundations for a deeper long-term relationship with the Council for World Mission. Aware that education included music and the arts, in 1993-4, Llanfair approached CWM to find a musician. Hope Evans came from Jamaica and spent 18 months on Penrhys establishing a music programme. That programme expanded beyond all recognition with the continuation of Llanfair's own teaching of music and the creation of Canolfan Rhys in 1997 by the Penrhys Partnership. Through CWM, Llanfair created a close relationship with the Church of Jesus Christ in Madagascar (FJKM) and each year since 1996 there has been a volunteer living in Llanfair. The Malagasy volunteer was joined by a second from 2001 as a result of Llanfair's new relationship with Akany Avoko, a Home for Girls in Antananarivo. Who would have thought that the seeds sown by David Jones and Thomas Bevan, Welshmen from Neuaddlwyd in Cardiganshire (the first missionaries to Madagascar in 1818), should have borne fruit nearly two centuries later?

Another member of Llanfair's core residential group came from Hungary. Each year Llanfair was served by a theological student from the Reformed Church of Hungary. This continued without fail from 1993, the majority coming from the Theological University of Debrecen. This too reflects the fruition of an ancient connection between Wales and Hungary through the protest ballad by Arany Janos, *A Walesi*

Bardok, which connects the persecution of Hungary by the Austrians with that of the Welsh bards by King Edward of England. These Debrecen students are the 'children of Kossuth,' the Hungarian revolutionary of 1848. This has not been a completely one-way relationship for in 2000, two Penrhys young people spent 6 months as English -conversationalists at Debrecen.

The fourth volunteer was a music specialist, continuing the work initiated by Hope Evans. Funded by the Presbyterian Church of Wales, a volunteer was found and supported by Time For God. This interdenominational agency enables young people to enjoy a year's experience serving the Church. One, a German was the grand-daughter of one of Nelson Mandela's chaplains at Robben Island; another from Denmark went on to work with Aids patients in Tanzania; a third, an English woman was the grand-daughter of a Jewish refugee from Hitler.

Alongside the support of the overseas volunteers was Llanfair's commitment to local and international justice and peace. This reflects an unswerving commitment to Christian Aid. Llanfair raised in the region of £2000 pounds for Christian Aid each year, was committed to Fair Trade in all its policies and had a strong nucleus of committed local volunteers. It is noteworthy that it was through Llanfair that many of the overseas volunteers were introduced to trade justice issues.

E. EXPLORING FAITH

Llanfair attempted to be faithful to the Gospel by serving the community of Penrhys. Work and Worship were at the heart of Llanfair's action. A pattern of Christian Nurture was developed, shaped by two basic principles: *faithfulness to the Text of the Gospel and faithfulness to the Context of Contemporary Community.* Llanfair struggled to develop a theological framework which reflected the Faith of the People of God. Llanfair was particularly blessed in this exploration because of the nature of her ecumenical foundation. Llanfair exists as a Uniting Church, supported and recognized by eight of the historic Churches in Wales. At the same time, the very nature of Llanfair's address - Penrhys, Rhondda - determined that nurture and mission are one, and at the heart of the Church's existence. Not only is Llanfair geographically in the centre of the Estate/Village of Penrhys but Llanfair is at the centre of the life of the community.

Although Llanfair has a specific text/context approach, the theological foundations originated in Ecumenical House Groups in Llanidloes and Manselton from 1967 to 1977, and developed during our wider ministry with the United Reformed Church in Wales between 1977 and 1989. This Gospel experience became focused and localised in the life of the congregation of Llanfair and the community of Penrhys.

Each year, the attempt is made to introduce the 'wholeness' of the Christian Faith. Although this may seem a demanding programme, it becomes a way of life and a way of nurture. The close of each year serves as a springboard for a deeper intensity, a continuing exploration until we meet God face to face. The journey-pilgrimage continues until we are released from this mortal coil and receive the new body in Christ's fuller presence. '*The whole of life is to be transformed by the action of God. The Christian's conviction directs the whole of life towards praise of God. By embarking upon the theological adventure, we are enabled to worship and serve in thought, word and deed the God who is Father, Son and Holy Spirit. Thanks be to God.*' (J. M. 'What we Believe' Volume 2, 2002)

F. EXPLORING WORSHIP

The tradition of worship we inherited were of large-scale forms for a small congregation. The liturgy was identical to that for a nonconformist church anywhere in the country. The forms had emerged from, and were appropriate for larger congregations. In the little chapel, it was difficult to maintain concentration because of interruption by children entering the place of worship, or banging on the reinforced, metallic windows. The congregation must be admired for their patience and determination to continue their worshipping life, but it was hard work!

Worship was remote for the outsider. A newcomer to worship would find the exercise almost incomprehensible. The Bible is foreign and unknown for most people; they have no experience of the history, the relationship between the Testaments, the books and events and characters. The Bible is a closed book. Many approach the Bible as though it were a collection of fairy tales with no relevance to the modern world.

Sitting quietly for a long period is a rare practice in contemporary Britain. Younger generations are influenced by the short concentration span induced by mass media and popular culture. There was the temptation to move towards worship which emphasized only the emotions and sought for response without content. How could one discover a wholeness to an act of worship which would be composed of elements which could be brief and complete in themselves? If newcomers were to be encouraged to worship, there was the need to discover a framework in which there was real participation, and yet there had to be boundaries for such participation. A liturgy was needed which would hold in balance, movement and stability, freedom and order, participation and discipline.

How could people be helped to pray? Most people living on the estate wanted to pray privately, to say 'Please ... forgive ... help ... thank you.' They would often also ask a worshipper: 'say a prayer for me.' And yet at the same time there was the danger of prayer becoming only a 'shopping list.' How could the boundaries of prayer be pressed back to include the glory of God's grace and the universe of God's concern?

(i) FOUNDATIONS FOR DEVELOPMENT.

Brought up in a classical Welsh Nonconformist background, as a student at the Congregational Memorial College, Swansea, I experienced that tradition in dozens of chapels in Wales; learned new insights in the Catholic and Reformed worship of Mansfield College Oxford, Lutheran Worship at Mansfield and Anglican Evensong at New College; experienced Orthodoxy and other church traditions at Hartford Seminary, Connecticut. Later in my pastoral ministries I experienced Catholic Liturgies (including Plainsong) at the Cistercian Abbey at Caldey and was deeply moved by the Orthodox Liturgy at Moscow, Leningrad and Zagorsk during the Millennium Celebration in 1988.

For twenty years from the early 1970s, I served on various working-parties with the Commission of Covenanted Churches (now Enfys) and the Council of Churches for Wales (now Cytun). This was a period of the study of 'Baptism, Eucharist and Ministry.' I knew the documents well but they came alive with the worship of the 'Lima Liturgy' which Norah brought back from the World Council Assembly at Vancouver. It provided a magnificent (if verbose) framework for the Church's Tradition (historical and international). I believe that the first time the Liturgy was celebrated in Wales was on a Caldey retreat in 1983. That experience was soon enhanced by the Prayer Books of the W.C.C.: 'Together with all God's People.'

Another seminal influence was the worship of Taize and Iona. Taize's form of celebration had shaped our devotional life for many years and its music became deeply embedded into our lives as a family. Iona was another positive experience and I craved for - and still do - an indigenous and contemporary Welsh sound, in the way it has been provided for the Scots by Iona.

The catalyst came soon after beginning to minister on Penrhys. Norah and I were asked to take part in a BBC Morning Service called 'This is the Day.' This service was shaped for a television audience, lasted half an hour and spoke to an audience which is religious but may not be Church-going. Its prayers were dignified, simple and very accessible. Working with radio and television convinced me that there was need to tap into the discoveries of worship on the media.

(ii) THE DESIGN OF THE CHAPEL
A new Chapel was designed and built, appropriate to Penrhys - and faithful to Tradition. It was a challenge for the architects: to build on the limited space of what were the washing lines of a redundant maisonette block; to create a place of dignity and silence on the crossroads at the centre of an estate full of life - and children and noise; a building which might be attacked and vandalized; a space faithful to eight Christian traditions - and yet welcoming to those who had never entered a place of worship, including children. It also had to be hard-wearing because the hope was that it would be used most days of the week. The architects conversed long and hard with the congregation; all were prepared to change their minds and went through many designs which included the shape of the building and the lay-out and design of the furniture.

The Chapel has plain, undecorated white walls - reminiscent of the Puritan and Cistercian traditions? Large Banners, created at Llanfair, are changed to celebrate the differing Seasons. One Banner, reflecting the history of Penrhys from Celtic to Modern times is a permanent hanging. It enables the community to discover and celebrate its heritage. The colour of the Chapel is a combination of a natural light-wood floor, ceiling and furnishings, white walls and green upholstered chairs. The natural atmosphere is always one of silence and tranquillity. The natural light from a roof lantern and discreet lighting brings a quality of light which can change the mood dramatically. The Lantern when lit at night serves as a beacon of hope.

Because the chapel has eighty interlocking chairs, the interior can have a variety of shapes (with an aisle for weddings; a stage for Nativity and Easter Plays) but normally the chairs form three-quarters of a square. The image is that of the people gathering around a village camp-fire to share the stories of the Gospel. In the centre is a round communion table. On the Table stands the plate and the cup, signs of our dependence on God's grace and our oneness in Christ. In front of the communion table is a large candle. Its lighting marks the beginning of worship, helps bring silence and aids concentration. Next to the table is the font and the lectern on which are placed copies of Welsh and English Bibles. Behind the lectern is the Icon of the Virgin of Vladimir which for Henri Nouwen is 'an invitation to belong to God.' The first icon and icon lamp were gifts from Father Deiniol of the Russian Orthodox Church. Another icon, Rublev's 'The Trinity,' was a gift from Father Luke of Llanelli. We rejoice in the Catholic bell and these Orthodox icons. At one of the three clear-glass windows, two of which look out onto the main path of the estate is a candle-holder which holds twenty-five candles. They are used for communal and personal prayer. When a candle is lit, the community knows that prayers are being offered. At the main door into the chapel is a Bible stand on which is placed an open Bible. It is open at the Reading of the week and is usually used for personal devotion.

(iii) LITURGIES

The first Llanfair Liturgy, the basis for worship on 'Ordinary Sundays,' was shaped by the Church's Catholic and Reformed Tradition. It combined a sense of history and universality with a response to the local context. Its roots lay in *the Lima Liturgy* (of the World Council of Churches) and the prayers of *This is the Day* (a BBC morning devotional service). There was no attempt to 'whip up emotion' or 'play on guilt complexes.' Worship is communal with genuine participation. Worship begins with the calling of the people by the ringing of the Bell - itself an ecumenical statement in that it was the gift of the Cistercian monks of Caldey and at one time hung on the Parish Church of St David's. The congregation enters the chapel when the Bell has stopped ringing, and worship begins when the Central Candle has been lit. This is followed by Silence as the people settle themselves to worship. This liturgy adheres to the traditional triple division of Preparation, Word and Communion and seeks to be dignified, ordered, flexible and responsive to the immediate. Music comes from the world church. The Sunday Service brings together the Last Supper and the Resurrection narratives in the Communion Service. This helps us recognize that the Liturgy remembers, celebrates and anticipates. The One Loaf is broken and the Wine is poured from a Jug into a Common Cup and both are passed from hand to hand. The Presiding Minister is served last.

The stamina and inspiration which lie behind Llanfair residents and congregation is the result of regular communal worship. In 1989 there was one act of worship each week. Llanfair's liturgical life developed carefully and systematically. Prayer took place six times each week, on four different days. Unity is established through the clarity of the liturgical form; the variety is established through a careful programme of nurture. Central to the stability of the programme of nurture is the rhythm of the Church Year. The Christian Year is not the secular pattern beginning in January, nor the academic year which starts in September. The Year begins Nine Weeks before Christmas with the Church looking towards the celebration of God's great acts centred on Jesus Christ. The discipline of the Church Calendar united the congregation with the history of the Church and with the life of the world-wide community of faith. We knew where we were in time and space. We are not alone, but together with God's People we are engaged in a life-long pilgrimage with an annual programme. This order ensures there is a stable rhythm and that each new year sees the re-launch for further development. There is an annual circular rhythm within a linear pattern leading from birth to death and to life beyond death. There is the provision for the maturing of the pilgrim by the guidance of God through a programme which has a clarity of direction and which leads towards a sense of wholeness.

When in 1972, the Rhondda Mains Committee established the Christian Fellowship, it concentrated not on erecting a church building but on introducing a Church Worker to the estate. However, the combination of not having 'a proper church' and not having 'a proper minister' meant that the sacramental life of the church suffered. The tendency was for baptisms and funerals to be celebrated in Valley Churches. Even Holy Communion was celebrated by Valley Ministers coming to visit the mountain top mission. This was the situation right through the 1970s and adversely affected the ministries during the following decade. Sadly it was not possible for marriages to be held on the estate because the chapel was part of a Community Centre. Therefore when I began my ministry in 1989, there were very few precedents for 'special liturgies.' I felt certain that these services needed to take place on Penrhys - and should be officiated with a combination of simplicity of language and form, but with beauty and dignity. It was also a challenge to recognize the reality of the Penrhys context. The community was marginalized and it was often felt that anything was good enough for the people of Penrhys. It was critical that Penrhys people should have the most appropriate worship: that every service should emphasis the uniqueness of the person or family involved, but also should reflect the catholicity of the church and the wonder of the Gospel.

7. LLANFAIR IS A SERVING CHURCH

In February 1992, Llanfair was opened and for twelve years, twenty volunteers, residents of the Penrhys estate enabled community projects to operate: day after day, and year after year. There was regular, open consultation and decision-making on all issues of the work of Llanfair. Volunteers experienced a sense of ownership of property and work. Because of the Projects, a large number of Penrhys residents found their lives enhanced, and most volunteers grew in confidence and skill. They provided the backbone to the service and leadership which Llanfair offered Penrhys. Llanfair was financially viable throughout those years because of the small profit from the Projects (of which the volunteers are extremely proud), the rents from the paid workers who lived in flats in Llanfair and the freewill contributions of congregation and friends.

Some of the projects proved temporary. They played an important role as long as they were helpful to the community or were financially feasible. When their usefulness came to an end, that particular project was terminated. *A Knitting Workshop* opened in 1992 but survived only a year when it was realised that it had become a burden on the three women who had begun the project, and that their products could not compete with goods sold in the local market. *A Créche* was open for 2 mornings and 2 afternoons each week until the Local Authority altered its Play School provision to include younger children. *A Minibus* was used for many years for weekly Shopping, Swimming Lessons, Local Library, special excursions for nature walks, holidays during Easter, Summer and Half-terms. It has been important to learn the art of flexibility. So often the Church can become burdened by programmes which have long-outlived their usefulness. We have to learn to discard as well as to create. Often there can be no creativity and development without leaving behind programmes which once were helpful but are no longer appropriate to the mission of the Church or the needs of the community. However, certain Projects remained throughout the twelve years and others were developed.

For many Penrhys residents, the Café was not only the centre of Llanfair but the centre of Penrhys. It was open four days and three evenings each week. Monday was a day for buying, stocking and preparation. Adults used the cafe during the daytime, and children and young people during the evenings. During the daytime, adults enjoyed good food at reasonable prices - many coming to breakfast. It was a place of lively conversation where local and world affairs were often discussed. Because it was a fair-trade café, key issues of justice and sharing were often discussed. The café, open three evenings each week for children and young people encouraged adults to play games with the children (reading, drawing, connect-four, frustration, cards, dominoes, draughts, solitaire, chess). Norah spent a great deal of time in the café serving, working alongside the volunteers and getting to know so many in the community. There was no day that the café failed to open for lack of volunteers. It was 'a touching place'.

A Boutique, dealing with nearly-new clothes donated from all parts of England and Wales was open four days each week. Monday was the day for pricing and preparing the shop. A Launderette was also open four days each week. Like the café and the creche, these projects were all run by volunteers. There was also a weekly Video, and two weekly Discos organised by the young people of Llanfair.

Educational work developed over a period of seventeen years. Between 1986 and 1988, Norah was often approached by parents to give support to their children, especially in reading. Early in 1989, the Laura Ashley Trust was approached for a grant. Discussions took place with the Nursery, Infants and Junior Schools and it was agreed to look for a Support Worker who would live on Penrhys and work in the schools and in the community. Norah did not apply for this salaried post and instead worked in a voluntary capacity, enabling us to have a larger team. In June 1992, Sharon Rees was appointed as the Educational Support Worker and the Homework Centre opened in September 1992. Progress was carefully maintained and developed. At first numbers were small and tended to be of Primary age. However as the Homework Centre became a normal part of Community Life, numbers gradually increased and the age range widened. From 1996, each week there were two evening sessions for Primary children and three evening sessions for High School students. For three years (from 1994-7) two Education Workers, Paul Sass and Cas Smith developed a most valuable relationship between Penrhys and Secondary Education. Paul was succeeded for a further two years by Joy Garfitt, who like Paul, was introduced to Llanfair by Trinity College, Carmarthen. After ten years of sustained work, Llanfair was recognised by the appropriate Assembly Department as a centre of excellence, and Sharon Rees work has since been funded by a Government Research Programme, entitled *On Track,* working within the Upper Rhondda Fach.

Llanfair became an important Centre for Adult Education. Courses were held in Life Skills, Literacy, Computer Skills, Video-making and Welsh. This cooperation, initiated by a relationship with the University College of Swansea, developed in a particularly fertile way with Trinity College, Carmarthen who established a Distance Learning Centre at Llanfair. Courses held from 2000 to 2004 were 'Understanding, Celebrating and Developing Penrhys... The Story of Penrhys.... The Story of Rhondda... The Story of Wales... The Story of Christianity in Wales... Reading the Bible What Christians Believe Christian Nurture at Llanfair.'

Courses appealed to Llanfair's overseas volunteers, local residents and those involved professionally on Penrhys. Some of these courses were validated and accredited at Trinity. Many Schools and Colleges visited Llanfair on a regular basis for studying Courses in Religious Education, Community and Health Studies. Llanfair created a local community programme with Penrhys Primary School and the Penrhys Partnership.

Community Development, Education and Art were critical aspects in nurture and development. The Music Programme, with free lessons for various instruments was maintained by a residential volunteer. Three other resident student voluntary workers, funded by church organisations were a Hungarian and two Malagasies. All were involved in the life of the schools and the wider work of Llanfair. They gave a critical international dimension to the nurture of the community. Their work led to the creation of Canolfan Rhys, the Arts and Education Centre.

The central element in the life of Llanfair was the religious dimension. Every child on Penrhys worshipped three times each term at Llanfair. Llanfair organized Sunday School and all-age worship which encouraged the participation of children and young people in regular worship. I also held discussion groups every week for those in the Secondary School. Between 1995-8, there were five such groups each week for 42 weeks with an average attendance of 35 each week. They discussed all sorts of issues: Bible Study tends to provide the foundation, but included issues like employment, human dignity, drugs and alcohol, relationships, history, Christian values. Even with the lower population of Penrhys, in 2003-4, there were three groups where 20 young people met each week for discussion.

All Llanfair teenagers, many younger children and all adult volunteers had a holiday led by Llanfair leaders. This began in 1990 and during each of the 14 years more than one hundred went on holiday. This was all part of an integrated set of programmes which were founded on what went on each day and each week in Llanfair's life.

8. LLANFAIR AND THE PENRHYS PARTNERSHIP

In 1989, The Prince of Wales visited Penrhys through the invitation of *Business in the Community*, and in 1991, BITC organised a *Seeing is Believing Visit.* One of the key figures of the visit was Bill Castell, Chief Executive of Amersham International. During the same year, a group from Penrhys attended a *BITC Conference in Manchester* which pointed out the value of *Partnerships* in High Priority Areas. In July 1991 I was asked to meet David Hunt, Secretary of State for Wales, who complimented the Church on its work, asked for further suggestions and responded to the concept of a Village Centre which would utilize two further Maisonette Blocks on the same model of Llanfair. With the help of Business in the Community, Norah and I, residents of Penrhys, Cerri Morse the head teacher and several business men formed the Penrhys Partnership in the summer of 1991. We became Directors and I served as Chairperson until 2003. The funding was granted during the summer of 1991. During the autumn a meeting of the Estate Liaison Group (chaired by Terry Winters, the Estate Coordinator) invited Michael Jenkins, Administrator of Mid Glamorgan Health Authority to visit Penrhys. We were surprised and delighted by his response to the proposal that there be a Doctor's Practice on Penrhys. Proposals for the new building were therefore complete: funding, plans for the building, architects. A Project Director, Paul Rowson, was appointed and his work began on April 1 1992 to oversee the work and completion of the Village Centre (Y Ffynnon).

The amphitheatre was created in the summer of 1992 by an international work-camp (Youth In Mission) organized by the Council for World Mission (an international community of partner churches) and Penrhys young people. Situated on the hillside between the two Rhondda valleys, it provides stunning views, requires little maintenance and has been used by rock groups, choirs, carnivals, the local schools and church activities.

The Village Centre, Y Ffynnon, is situated in the centre of Penrhys and consists of two linked Maisonette Blocks. It provides space for seven residential flats, a Doctor's Surgery, Post Office and Food Shop, Fish and Chip Shop, home for the Community Action Group and a department of the Social Services. The Partnership also has an administrative base in Y Ffynnon. The complex, opened in 1993 is surrounded by substantial landscaping. Y Ffynnon has been self-sustaining through rents from the residential and commercial units.

The Church was gifted a substantial sum from Bob and Ethel Huggard to provide accommodation for the vulnerable. Llanfair handed this sum over to the Partnership which inherited a derelict housing block, again gifted by Rhondda Borough Council. It was converted into high-quality, secure accommodation comprising four flats and two houses. There is one entrance leading to a carpeted communal area and has proved invaluable for Penrhys residents who felt vulnerable in the community. The accommodation has been fully occupied since it was opened in 1996 by William Hague, Secretary of State for Wales.

Because of the success of the Education, Music and Art Programmes of Llanfair, the Partnership was approached to encourage the development of an Arts Centre. Canolfan Rhys was opened on March 1st 1997 and provides a range of community arts programmes which seek to be relevant to the lives of the people of Penrhys and the Rhondda. Both the Art and Drama programmes which originated in Llanfair were transferred to Canolfan Rhys. Thanks to a generous grant from the Arts Council of Wales Lottery Unit the Partnership converted, refurbished and extended a previously derelict housing block to provide a recording studio, a performance area, art and music workshops, a dark room, a computer suite, and accommodation of three bed sits and two flats. Additionally there is an Education for Employment Suite.

Much of the educational side of the work has since been transferred into Y Ffynnon. The specific aim is to enable conscious and positive choices to be made in the areas of work, training and further education.

The new millennium was marked by the erection of a Beacon which lies between the Well and the Amphitheatre. It is dedicated to the eradication of world poverty, the cancellation of world debt and to a world of justice and peace.

9. LLANFAIR AND THE PENRHYS COMMUNITY ACTION GROUP

A. BACKGROUND TO THE CRISIS OF 1998

During the Spring of 1997, many Penrhys residents read in the local press (*The Rhondda Leader)* that their houses were to be demolished. Rumours had circulated for about a year but the news broke when people read in the press that their homes were to be destroyed. This proved the trigger for Penrhys residents to ensure that their voice was heard. What were the issues of housing policy? Was there a ecret plan for total demolition? Were private developers waiting in the wings for a prime brown-field site? At the time Dr Rukmini Rao, an Indian specialist in development, was residing on Penrhys as a guest of Llanfair and Christian Aid. Her pertinent question was 'even if Penrhys has an excellent infrastructure, what is its use if the estate is demolished?' The consequence of her challenge was the formation of the Penrhys Community Action Group.

During the summer of 1997, Llanfair initiated a programme by which Penrhys organized itself through surveys, a Public Meeting, the creation of the Penrhys Community Action Group and its recognition by Rhondda Cynon Taf. At a Meeting of the Action Group in September, attended by Officers of the Housing Department, it was agreed that a Joint Working Party be created to develop a Feasibility Study for the future of Penrhys. However by the end of October it became clear that the Action Group and the Housing Department had different ideas about Penrhys' future, and the Action Group was advised to produce its own suggestions and submit them to the Council. During the Winter of 1997/8 the Action Group developed a programme in consultation with various professional bodies.

B. LOCAL AUTHORITY STRATEGY

The general framework which created the long term nature of the Penrhys community - and communities like Penrhys throughout the country - was shaped not by those who live in the community, but by political and social influences controlled by outside powers. This happened in the creation of Penrhys in the 1960s, when the Estate was refurbished in the mid-1980s and it happened once more in the late 1990s. These ill-conceived ideas had tragic consequences for the Community.

The years leading up to the crisis of 1997 saw the wholesale demolition of block after block with no guarantee to the displaced tenants that they could have any security of tenure elsewhere on Penrhys. Residents felt unable to plan the most basic things: shall I paint the kitchen? Shall I lay a new carpet? Perhaps my house will be demolished this year! Many long-established residents left the estate. The Action Group was certain that if the Council continued with this *'laissez faire* policy,' 'even if it was termed a rationalization programme, or 'a drawing of residents towards the centre of the estate,' it would result in the extinction of Penrhys in the very near future. The community realised that the extinction of Penrhys would give considerable pleasure to many people not living on Penrhys: those who have despised Penrhys and enjoyed 'Penrhys jokes.' Those now living on Penrhys had very different proposals.

C. PROPOSALS OF THE ACTION GROUP

The critical issue was that of stability. Could there be some guarantee against imminent demolition? The Action Group's Surveys ascertained that 300 families wished to live on Penrhys if there was stability. The Community Action Group began its consultation with a Ten Point Plan. However the Local Authority was not prepared to enter into any serious negotiation. The Action Group knew the debate needed to be widened to more than 'housing issues.' If the debate was limited to 'concrete,' (bricks and mortar) the deeper problems would be ignored. To encourage a wider debate, the Action Group urged the Housing Department to widen the forum to include other departments responsible for Penrhys: Education, Leisure, Property Services, Highways. This was anathema to the Housing Officers. Their stance was to wear out the volunteers in the Action Group by attrition.

Then came the 'Long March' on March 5th 1998. Penrhys decided to celebrate its new life by marching from Penrhys to the Council Offices in Clydach Vale. It was not a protest but a celebration. The consequence was an instruction from the Housing Committee to its Officers to initiate a Multi-Departmental Forum to ensure there was a long-term strategy for Penrhys. Chaired by Professor Kevin Morgan, the Forum eventually succeeded in convincing the Local Authority that the people of Penrhys must be treated seriously. The future must depend on the cooperation, consultation and a strategy agreed by the community and the Council. Planners may create or demolish houses but they cannot create community. Penrhys lived through a bitter history before Rhondda learned that lesson.

CONCLUSION

Living on Penrhys was a most challenging and enriching experience: as tenant and resident; working with the Tenants Association and the Priority Estates Project in the 1980s; exploring with Penrhys New Perspective and enjoying Llanfair's ministry with community; initiating and developing alongside the Penrhys Partnership; helping to create and sustain the Action Group.

Llanfair has been incarnate in the life of community. Her life is in community but does not necessarily accept all of community's values. Llanfair belongs to God and then to Penrhys. The Church's ministry will last as long as people live on Penrhys. Llanfair is aware that it takes generations to create community, but it needs only the decision of a Housing Officer to destroy community. It has grown along with the community, shared its experience and rejoices that some qualities of community have emerged: Penrhys shows vibrancy and love and although there remain enormous challenges (many of which are typical of much of contemporary Wales), Penrhys has the courage and ability to face those challenges. There is much to be learned from the Penrhys story.

A residential group served as a catalyst for change. The group needed to cooperate with, and respect long-term residents. Long-term residents are the key to community. The community is shaped by those who feel it is their place. The core group must learn from them and discover their ways of doing things; but there is also the need for mutual motivation. It is critical to concentrate on long-term issues. There is always the danger of seeking the quick-fix, of believing there is a sticking-plaster solution. They cannot work unless we take people and relationships seriously. This leads to the critical value of relationships. Community development demands mutual respect, trust, sharing, learning from each other, discovering new problems and new solutions together. There is a need to discover new forms of communicating, and discovering mechanisms for this to happen. These may have to be 'invented' in these contexts. They may not just happen naturally. Programmes also must be based on relationships. Programmes introduced from outside may have short-term success, but they will have only short-term popularity. People will be loyal if the programme entertains but they can drop it like a hot-potato. Long-term solutions lie in a change of cultural attitude which depends on the quality of education. This demands a relationship between the young person, schools, parents and community forms of education.

Impoverished communities feel marginalized and rootless. On Penrhys, history was re-examined and re-interpreted. Since the 1970s Penrhys was scandalously depicted as 'an aberration and a place of failure.' A new name was important*: Llanfair, Penrhys, Rhondda.* Thirty years ago a fellowship was founded on a housing estate. This small congregation with 'no name,' worshipping in a redundant shop, opened its new chapel/community buildings in 1992, giving itself the name 'Llanfair:' recapturing the story of its own particular context. *Llan* reminds us of our Celtic inheritance. '*Mair*' recalls both Medieval Cistercian spirituality and Reformation zeal, but particularly celebrates *Mair* of the Magnificat, the Mother of our Lord who thirsted for peace and justice, and who knew the Way of God demanded a world where the poor would be lifted up and the rich brought down from their thrones. Llanfair is founded on the demand for God's shalom. The name *Penrhys* reminds us of our Medieval history, couched in legend, the burial place of Rhys the last prince of Dyfed. *Rhondda* serves as a symbol of the great coal era, the age of Chapel and Pit. The name Rhondda serves as an indictment on the scandal of unbridled capitalism but also applauds the courage and vision of the working people who created a new, vibrant coal community. That community died with King Coal, and the Valleys have to recreate themselves. What is their future in a post-industrial era? Rhondda raises questions of the future not only of the Valleys but also of Wales.

And the contemporary church? What is its role? To be alongside community, as church and community together discover their place in the Twenty-First Century. We have much to receive from the past. The gifts offered by the witnesses of the centuries are here for all of us in Wales to share and celebrate. In Llanfair we used the water of the pre-Christian and Celtic Well for baptisms and healing; we walked the Medieval pilgrimage route, demanding world equality and justice; we rang the Angelus with our Cistercian Caldey Bell; we meditated with Greek and Russian Icons; we celebrated our local inheritance by laying foundation stones from chapels demolished in the Rhondda Fach; we sang the hymns of Pantycelyn, Ann Griffiths, Alan Gaunt, Fred Kaan and Brian Wren; we intoned the plainsong of Caldey, the melodious rhythms of Taize and Iona, and the international music of the World Church. Llanfair created a small vibrant community from Penrhys residents, and guests from Hungary, Germany, Scandinavia and Madagascar. Christians continued to worship on this high mountain ridge.

The congregation began in 1971 with a tiny group of worshippers meeting in a small multi-purpose room in the Community Centre. This congregation was the seed which resulted in the opening of Llanfair on February 29th 1992. During the twelve years of Llanfair's ministry, the church provided a genuine service to the community. Because of Llanfair, the Penrhys Partnership came into existence, and Llanfair was formative of the Action Group which led the struggle against demolition. For the twelve years, Llanfair was open for service most days of the year: through the service of worship, and the service of work. Llanfair served the community through café, launderette, boutique, homework and music clubs. 143 were baptized, there were 20 marriages and 120 had Christian funerals. Tragically of that number, 8 were babies, a further 5 were under 20; there were 9 men between 20 and 30 and a further 17 adults between 30 and 50. Penrhys experienced and understood suffering.

In light of this context, it was imperative that the Gospel be lived and shared. Every child on Penrhys was introduced to the Christian faith through Llanfair directly, and through the work of the schools. Nearly 50 young people from many parts of the world lived in Llanfair for a year at a time; special connections were forged with Madagascar and Hungary. Hundreds of people went on retreat to Caldey, climbed Snowdon, enjoyed the Quiraing in Skye, holidays in Carmarthen and Hungary. Llanfair reflects an inclusive and loving Gospel ministry to Penrhys and Rhondda.

But we were not only worshipping. We were serving and working with the community in programmes which enabled a community to feel a pride of people and place. As a community caring for one another, and feeling a responsibility for all our fellow human beings in this increasingly precarious planet, we were grateful for all God has done through the story of his people and all God continues to do today.

The mission of Llanfair during her twelve years of ministry was to be alongside a community in the midst of her pain and to share the Good News of Jesus Christ. The work of Llanfair was open to the whole community and no-one saw Llanfair as the 'preserve of the religious.' For the people of Penrhys it was 'our church,' a people and a place dedicated to improving the quality of everyone's life. It would be difficult to over-estimate the value of this long-term programme for the community of Penrhys. However the Church is not in the business of evaluating and monitoring. It is in the business of serving. Its work is in sowing seeds and encouraging life in all its fullness.

1989

SEPTEMBER

1st

My first words as minister of the Penrhys Uniting Church although it is still a fellowship and I have not been inducted. I begin the fourth sphere of ordained ministry: Llanidloes, Manselton, Moderator for Wales and now where I began: a mile from my place of birth, home chapel and school, and a few hundred yards from where my family are buried. We have been here since the early 1870s when Tylorstown came into existence.

Sunday 3rd

My first Sunday as minister at Penrhys. What a superficial contrast from two weeks ago when I preached at Brecon before 1200. This afternoon we were 10 in worship including Norah, Cath and me. This is where we begin. Norah, Sybil and I went to the young couple's house for the baptism of their three children; the baby is very ill.

September proved to be a traumatic month for the family. On the 2nd, the day I preached at the Induction of my successor, John Humphreys as Moderator, Norah's mother became seriously ill and was taken into hospital. Her death on the 22nd of the month marked the end of a decade in which we had experienced the deaths of all our parents - and with it came the realization that Norah and I were now the senior generation.

5th

Norah and I met John Sheppard of Business in the Community and a group of Methodists including a businessman (Bob?) who wishes to invest £100,000 on starting ten private businesses on Penrhys. I could not help because I do not know ten righteous people and I would not want him to waste his money. *This was our first meeting with Robert Huggard who, with his wife Ethel, played such an important part in the raising of funds for Penrhys New Perspective. Bob and Ethel had watched the HTV service from Penrhys on June 25th. They were not very impressed by the minister (me!) but felt they would like to help the community of Penrhys. They certainly did, and at the same time helped initiate the work of the Revd Douglas Bale in the formation of the Huggard Centre in Cardiff which cares for the homeless, and the work of John Stacey Marks in the creation of the Amelia Trust Farm with its many facilities which include support for disaffected young people and adults.*

9th

I felt humbled and grateful to God, Lord of the Church. At the Synod Day at Llanelwedd, Glanville spoke carefully and movingly, and presented Norah and me with the gifts of the Church: the applause went on and on, and there was a standing ovation from the congregation of a thousand. It was humbling to feel such genuine affection. Twelve years of hard work created a wonderful response. In my reply I read the letter received yesterday from 99 year old Mrs Cheadle who wished she could be present and wished us God's blessing. It was a fare-well, a fare-forward and a moment to treasure. So ended in wonderful climax my ministry as Welsh Moderator.
Glanville Jones, retired minister at Barry, was Synod Clerk. Mrs Cheadle was an elder at Colwyn Bay and had been a friend since Llanidloes days.

Sunday 10th

Bob Huggard and his wife called and, to our amazement handed a cheque for £5000 to use as we thought best. I was speechless. They gave it because of our courage in refusing £100,000. They remember their working class origins.

29th

I represent the first Christian encounter for many people. I met the mother of two Sunday School children and was amazed to find four other women, half a dozen children and a few young men all in the kitchen. I was there an hour, was accepted as minister and was questioned on many issues.

OCTOBER

Sunday 1st

Patience is always a key virtue, but even more in a community where most people know little about punctuality and dependability. Greater gifts like compassion, determination and forgiveness all exist but it will be tough to see how these gifts should be cultivated and channelled. We need good liturgical material to maintain attention and develop participation.

7th

As Moderator, I presided at 80 inductions but today was different because it included the formation of 'The Uniting Church of Penrhys in the spirit of the

Covenant for Unity in Wales,' my induction and the commissioning of Huw Rhydderch. This is the first time in Wales for the recognition of such a congregation. A profoundly ecumenical experience: Gordon James presided; the Bishop preached; John Humphreys was Moderator; the highlights were the participation of Penrhys people when 40 responded with promises to the Church, and the greetings, especially by Fr Deiniol who presented a magnificent icon. Great singing. Beverley sang superbly. Offertory of £376; congregation of over 400.
Huw Rhydderch was Vicar of the parish of Ystrad; Gordon James was Archdeacon of Margam; the Bishop of Llandaff was Roy Davies; Fr Deiniol was Orthodox priest at Manod; Beverley Humphreys, the professional singer from Pontypridd, was an elder in the United Church there, and a friend of the family.

Sunday 15th

Norah and I participated in 'This is the Day,' a live service broadcast from our lounge. We were ready in our seats at 9.20 and at 9.26, little Jonathan, who lived next door, arrived with a note from his mother, relating to the afternoon harvest service. Norah signed and he scampered away.
This BBC service was designed to take place in people's homes in order to empathize with people watching in their own homes. It was very carefully designed and targeted an audience sometimes unfamiliar with public worship.

17th

We are with the parents in a terrifying tragedy: The baby died this morning at East Glamorgan Hospital: 3 months old with a sad, wise face. Mother and father nursed their son during the final hours of his short life. We woke to the phone at 2.15: the Sister asking us to come to the hospital. We were all privileged to share nursing the baby. When we returned to Penrhys we, including the godparents, had prayers in the chapel.
The child who had been baptized on September 3rd.

18th

Norah, with her experience of Primary education, helped me prepare, and I walked to school carrying a large cardboard box, inside of which was an inflatable globe to use in the Harvest. Everyone was intrigued by this mysterious parcel and there was great excitement as the children guessed wrongly. What was inside? One used the scissors to cut the string, and another pulled out the wrapping paper. Later I walked across the estate to the home of the grieving parents: they had asked me to speak to the children about the death of their baby brother. At Sponsoring Body we learned that one of our members had been accosted by a neighbour, who was Jehovah's Witness, and told that 'the baby had been taken by the devil to hell.'

19th

I completely rewrote the traditional funeral service because the family is unchurched, and because of the aggression of the Jehovah's Witness. A new church has to be born here with its own life and shape. We are discerning some signs for growing. The traditional approach of developing suburban patterns has failed: mid-week Guild, Bible Study, Sunday worship spoke to only half a dozen on the estate.

20th

A miracle of grace. The dignified funeral provided such support. Fifty people crammed into the lounge, kitchen and hall. Most were young, poor and had experienced much in short lives. Although faces seemed hard, there was love in that house. Norah and I called to see the family this evening: 'You are the right minister for Penrhys; perhaps youll marry me next year; we'll raise money for the church; my father was an atheist until today; come out for a meal next week.'

22nd

At Mass this morning, Laura (aged 12) was annoyed because 'a monk elbowed Fr Thaddeus out of the way.' The Penrhys Uniting Church Monk Protection Society was founded with Laura as the first president.
Another visit to Caldey.

NOVEMBER

18th

Ebenezer Tylorstown has sent a cheque for £3000 for ministry on Penrhys. Here is a legacy from the past: the congregation which nurtured me is helping the future mission to their own community.

21st

I re-presented Penrhys to a wider audience. Introduced by Herbert Hughes, whom I remembered as friend of Alwyn Charles, I addressed 60 first year students in the Humanities Course at Trinity College Carmarthen. I was asked

to speak on The Church and Contemporary Society and I introduced Disarmament, Hungary, Penrhys and the theological motivation.
The Revd Herbert Hughes was the Head of the Religious Department at Trinity. This was the beginning of such a fruitful relationship with Trinity which continued throughout our period on Penrhys.

29th

The Training in Mission team from CWM arrived. When one asked 'Is there any way in which the church can grow on Penrhys?' one of our young mothers answered: 'Of course it can grow. It has begun already.' This was endorsed by three other young mothers, all of whom are gratified by ministry which includes friendship, open-ness and new ideas.
Training in Mission was a programme of the Council for World Mission whereby a dozen young people from the different CWM regions spent a year together in exploring the nature and method of mission. The first six months were spent at Selly Oak, Birmingham and the next period in Jamaica. The Revd Ernest Cruchley was responsible for coordinating the programme in the United Kingdom and he led the group to Penrhys until 1998.

DECEMBER

2nd

Gwynfor Evans spoke well at the Chaplaincy at Swansea University on 'Religion and Culture in Wales.' I spoke about the Valleys, particularly Penrhys.

9th

Mandy Smallridge and Tony Underwood were married at Tonypandy Methodist Church. That is the most important fact: a man and a woman decided that their relationship should be blessed by God and recognized in law. What was also important? They are living on Penrhys and it is not usual for a couple to seek Christian marriage. Penrhys people have got married in other Rhondda churches but today was different. The minister of Penrhys officiated at the wedding of a couple from Penrhys and if there was an appropriate church building on Penrhys, the service would have taken place there.
The first wedding.

20th

The Welsh Office has rejected our Urban Aid application. Where do we turn now?

It seemed like the end of the road. We had been led to expect that our application would be successful because it had been endorsed by the Rhondda Borough Council. What we did not know was that the Rhondda was the only local authority to endorse all its applications, and did not place those applications in any kind of priority. They were sent to the Welsh Office in alphabetical order. Those reading the forms would be tired by the time they arrived at 'P' and would probably say 'not Penrhys again!' We were not given any advice on why the application had been refused.

Sunday 24th

Communion in chapel at 11.30: to my amazement 30 worshipped. One family saw the light in the window, decided to come and had their first communion. A blessing and an encouragement.

28th

Tragedy constantly punctuates the life of this community. I heard that a young mother had lost a baby. By checking the electoral list and the map, I was at the house within a few minutes and recognized the young woman. The baby had been born two months prematurely on the 23rd and died yesterday when the ventilator was switched off. That is tragic in itself but the background is intolerable. The parents were glad to see me and when we had prayer, there were tears in the mothers eyes, and the young father knelt, holding her hand. The unguarded gesture reveals hidden tenderness.

1990

JANUARY

5th

The stigma of poverty is not just a matter of money but it affects every aspect of everyday life.

11th

I must spend my time on Penrhys: the world is different off the estate. I must feel this community: to stop, listen carefully, watch actions and understand why people act the way they do. It will be a long process. I must ask how can there be change in the community? It lies partly in the vision of Penrhys New Perspective, but that vision is far from becoming reality.
Norah refers to this careful being alongside, as the theology of loitering.

12th

The baby's funeral, the first in the chapel in its twenty year history was an occasion of dignity, compassion and family solidarity. When the father placed the baby on the communion table, a sigh of caring came from us all. The church was serving the most vulnerable.

18th

At 12 promptly Brian Griffiths phoned. 'Will you write a personal letter to me about PNP? I will share its contents with Peter Walker. This deserves government assistance; this is the kind of development in which we believe.'
I had telephoned Brian Griffiths the previous day for advice at the behest of Huw Davies, the Chief Executive of HTV . We had both been at the meeting the previous July, in London with Bill Milliken, and apparently Brian Griffiths often asked Huw 'How is the minister getting on in Penrhys?' This was the chance to let him know. I was given a phone number. When I rang, the answer came '10 Downing Street. How can I help you?' Brian Griffiths, on receiving my message promised to phone the next day at 12. He kept his promise. Peter Walker was Secretary of State for Wales. We had met only once - during the Miners' Strike!

20th

I completed a 4½ page paper summarizing Penrhys New Perspective. It was challenging because it involved a theological basis, a strategy to include a team and a place, the work we feel called to do, architectural skill, costing and marketing. The project feels right because its agenda is set by the community. This community is asking for the leadership and service expressed in PNP.

Sunday 21st

At Llanidloes and Manselton I ministered to people who by birth, accident or conviction, are Congregationalists or United Reformed. That gives identity, but it is a limited and limiting identity. I could not be minister to the whole Christian community in either of those geographical/ historical areas. It is very different on Penrhys. The Uniting Church and its ordained minister is to serve the whole community of Penrhys. The Jehovah's Witness and Pentecostalists would find this impossible to accept.

23rd

I must restrict my ministry to this community. The pattern of ministry shaped at Penrhys could be modelled elsewhere in Wales. We have one 'ordained leader' for the one Christian community which exists to praise God and serve the wider community

26th

Like the Pied Piper, I walked ahead of mother, her sons, daughters, partners and 17 grandchildren to the Penrhys Chapel of Rest. Armed with flowers, cards and messages, they were to say goodbye to their grandfather. They sat in the Chapel and I stood at the front with the casket on the altar. I had to forget about the Service Book and enter into a conversation about life, death, eternal life, the importance of love, example and remembrance. We walked to the cemetery plot, the remains were buried and the children lovingly placed their flowers. I showed them where my parents were buried and we all returned home for a party. This is how to deal with bereavement. Brian Griffiths phoned enthusiastically about PNP and will discuss it with Peter (Walker).

FEBRUARY

6th

An old fashioned matriarch died today. She held her family together and is typical of a past generation. I feel privileged to be discovering the love which is the pulse of this family. I am a learner in the greatest human qualities.

PENRHYS

Entrance to the 'little chapel' in the Community Centre. The door has the letter box.

Sunday worshippers in the little chapel. None now live on Penrhys, and Sybil Smith (second row, far left) is the only one still worshipping in Llanfair.

The redundant block of maisonettes, 404-411 Heol y Waun.

Llanfair.

Laying the Foundation Stones. May 14th 1991.

The foundation stones from redundant churches, mostly from Tylorstown, representing the eight churches in the Sponsoring Body.

The Bell arrives from Caldey.

Opening Day: Fathers Barnabas, Robert and Deiniol with new friends, February 29th 1992.

Inside the chapel, showing banners created by people of Penrhys

Sunday School Infants share their theme in worship.

The Nursery School enjoy their monthly worship.

Children in Infants Sunday School prepare to share in worship.

1\. God made all these wonderful creatures
wonderful, special, different
full of surprises
And God said it was Good

God made all these wonderful creatures

But, most wonderful are....

Junior School classes in worship.

Shepherds wait.

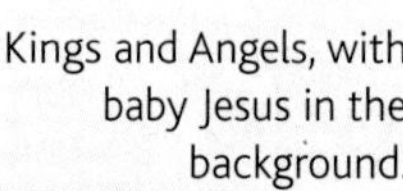

Kings and Angels, with baby Jesus in the background.

Good Friday.

Early Easter Sunday morning on Twyn Disgwylfa.

Easter Sunday afternoon service

Piano lessons were popular.

Local talent give a concert.

Welsh National Opera String Quartet.

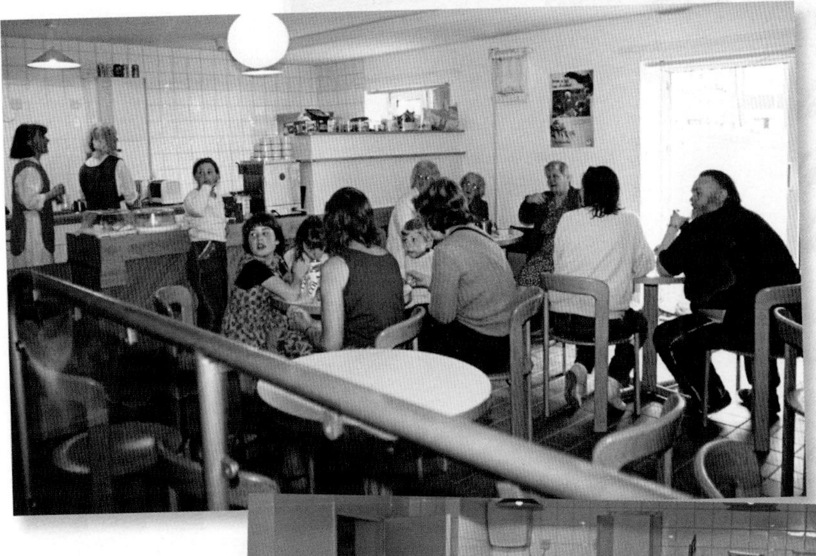

Daytime Café.

Evening Café.

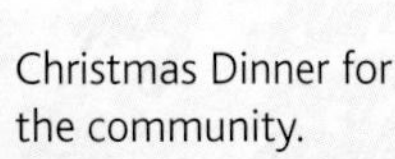

Christmas Dinner for the community.

Creche

Boutique or 'New for You.'

Launderette.

Sharon in Junior Homework Club.

Success in A Levels, August 19th 1999.

Adult Education Group Autumn, 2000.

A patchwork quilt for Christian Aid Week.

Ready to go on the Annual 'Fun Walk.'

'Drop the Debt' Action in London.

Our Monday meal.

John meets past volunteers in Madagascar September 20th 2000.

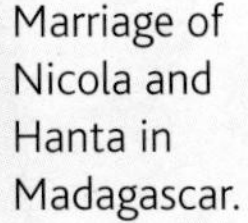
Marriage of Nicola and Hanta in Madagascar.

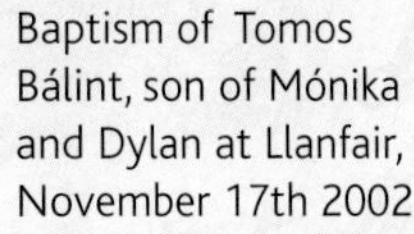
Baptism of Tomos Bálint, son of Mónika and Dylan at Llanfair, November 17th 2002

A day out at the Trehafod Sidings, July 2nd 2002

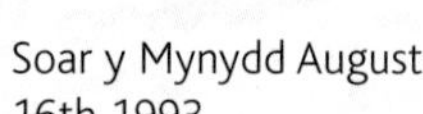

Soar y Mynydd August 16th 1993.

Norah photographs the group under the photograph of T H Parry Williams, one of her favourite poets, August 2nd 1995.

LYT returning from Hungary, August 23rd 1999

Reaching the summit of Snowdon

Youth in Mission
July 1992.

Training in Mission
Team 1995.

Rukmini Rao in
Sunday School.

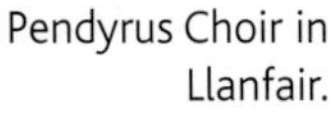

Pendyrus Choir in
Llanfair.

First concert at the amphitheatre, July 28th 1992.

Y Ffynnon, opened in 1994.

The Opening of Cartref by William Hague, June 24th 1996.

A Clean up Day outside Canolfan Rhys, opened March 1st 1997.

8th

Nearly everyone we meet on Penrhys is eager to talk about religious matters; quite different from the embarrassing silence often encountered in church circles.

Sunday 11th

Nelson Mandela is free: he walked through the gates of his prison at 2.16 this afternoon. I never believed it possible. For us on Penrhys it was unforgettable because joining us in worship was Idah Motha who lives in the next street to Mandela in Soweto. Our congregation stood to sing the African National Anthem with our fists clenched. The chapel was full and we will never forget that within 45 minutes of the release of this great man, we were to celebrate his freedom with one of his neighbours. The police woke us at 1 this morning to tell us the chapel had been burgled again.

12th

That death can be creative is a key discovery of the Gospel. The dying and funeral of the 'matriarch' has been a powerful, tender experience for the large family and the wider community. This has been the case in all seven funerals I have conducted since September. How does one go on to relate the God who comforts during bereavement with the God available at all times? The house was packed: front room, passage way, stairs, kitchen and outside the house. Fine services at home and at the cemetery in Tonyrefail where the sun shone for a brief period. Returned to the house.

14th

Should I focus my energy on this creative ministry on Penrhys or should I also exercise a wider ministry? Recently I have turned down nominations to stand as President of the Free Church Council, Moderator of the URC General Assembly, nomination for Vice President of Cytun, and Convenor of the URC Assembly Ministries Department. I have to be single-minded. If we fail here, it must not be because I have not given time and energy.
I don't think I made myself very popular with church 'authorities' - of course until recently I had been exercising that kind of role.

19th

We held our first Morning Prayers directed towards Penrhys New Perspective. We will hold it each week until ? the concept dies? until we open? as long as there is a church serving Penrhys?
The last question is answered in the affirmative.

22nd

Trust letters invite us to fill in forms and transfer material. I have written our leaflet and letter into their specific format. It is very time-consuming and although we have had hints and half-promises, our PNP Fund remains at £200 out of £375,000!

23rd

Is it an impossible dream? How can a congregation of 10 sustain such a vision? At other moments I feel we will achieve the goal of a new vision of church in community.

24th

The wedding of the year. During the autumn Betty Derrick asked me to 'marry' her 16 year old grand-daughter, Suzanne. Sadly, Mrs Derrick died this month. Who could forget Suzanne entering the chapel on her father's arm and followed by 7 bridesmaids and 1 pageboy? They were all under 10 and four were either 2 or 3 years old. The wedding was at Zion Methodist, Tonypandy.

MARCH

2nd

The breakthrough! I took Roger Northcott of Tudor Trust to the PNP block and for a walk around the estate. He knew our material and what to ask. He supports the programme and will recommend a grant. How much do you need from us? I didn't know what to say, and so his response was 'You still need £90,000 from the Voluntary Sector. I'll recommend £45,000 and if you need it, a loan of the same amount.' I was staggered.
Roger Northcott was the Assistant Director of the Tudor Trust. 'Tudor is an independent grant-making trust which supports organisations working across the UK. We aim to support work which addresses the social, emotional and financial needs of people at the margins of our society, and are particularly interesting in helping smaller, under-resourced organisations which offer direct services and which involve the people they work with in their planning.'

Sunday 4th

A Sunday in which we remembered those who died during the past month. The chapel was full to overflowing and children sat on the floor. An exciting service: Communion, elements of chaos when a chair snapped, the pageboy strolled around; one of the brothers asked for the wedding hymn 'One more step.' It felt good, positive and happy.

7th

Anne Power, consultant on the Priority Estates Programme [PEP] to the Welsh Office informs us that The Welsh Office will not support the project because it is 'too religious.' I felt angry. We are seeking the development of community and the religious component is the initiative behind it. What does this mean? If we can't do it, then it won't be done.
Anne Power is Professor of Social Policy at the London School of Economics and Political Science; Sustainable Development Commissioner responsible for regeneration and sustainable communities; member of the Government's Urban Task Force; author of books on cities, communities and marginal housing areas in the UK and abroad.

13th

Ideology is less important than persons. I never dreamt that an avowed Thatcherite would completely support anything I believed important. Brian Griffiths regards PNP as one of the most significant experiments in the country. He phoned to say he had spoken to Peter [Walker, Secretary of State for Wales] as they came out of Cabinet, was delighted we had raised so much money and that the church was growing.

15th

Penrhys New Perspective becomes reality. The URC Church Buildings Committee promises the cost of the manse - £40,000. Brian Griffith's Private Secretary phoned to read Peter Walker's letter to Brian: it sounded very supportive and suggested ways of applying for funding. We took Ethel to the BUPA hospital to see Bob, and to our astonishment they gave £60,000 to build the chapel.
The URC agreed to notionally purchase the manse, a flat in the refurbished block. Bob Huggard was receiving treatment for cancer which sadly proved terminal.

24th

I took a large stone from the ruins of Ebenezer to put underneath the new chapel.

Eventually we placed eight stones from redundant local chapels and churches belonging to the eight denominations of the Sponsoring Body. The chapels were Beulah, Bethany, Dewi Sant, Ebenezer, Libanus and Moriah, all from Tylorstown; North Street, Ferndale and Salem, Porth.

APRIL

9th

For some, 'holiness;' means separation from the world. Our Holy Week worship reflects that holiness is to be involved in the world, to affirm the secular as the sphere in which God is at work. John Shepherd of BIC brought 5 men from AMEC International, including David Taylor. We later met David Ashley to discuss our Literacy Worker. All learnt a good deal from Penrhys. *David Taylor was the founding Chief Executive of English Partnerships and founding Managing Director of AMEC Developments. David Ashley was son of Bernard and Laura Ashley. The Laura Ashley Foundation was prepared to fund a 'Literacy Worker' on Penrhys.*

12th

Beautiful worship in the little chapel on the corner of the Penrhys Community Centre. It could not be more meaningful wherever it had been celebrated. Twenty sat around long tables covered in white cloths; the Passion Narrative for Holy Thursday was read by 5 readers, none of whom had attended such a service before, and we all received bread and wine from the Lords Table. There is a maturity reflected in the silence, the intelligence in which the passages were read and the togetherness.

13th Good Friday

Easter is being alongside, in fact within, a worshipping congregation. 17 of us started, a week ago on Caldey, to read Mark's Gospel; and from last Sunday we have met each day to follow the Passion. This afternoon we arrived at that most solemn moment of the death of Jesus, and then together with Joseph of Arimathea and the women, we witnessed the burial. That must be the end of it all! Since then it has been silent and will be silent tomorrow. Will we be startled on Sunday?

15th, Easter Sunday

Resurrection was expressed in our growing congregation's quality of worship. To our delight and surprise, 37 met at 8 to walk to Bristol Tump. A strong cold wind helped give a sense of achievement. Prayers on the top and at the forestry gate before we returned for breakfast. There followed Communion services this morning and this afternoon, with 60 in each service.

20th

Penrhys becomes the universe. I have a ministry to a well-defined community of 951 dwellings and 3000 people.

Sunday 29th

A 6 year old boy is the first to be baptized into the Penrhys Uniting Church. We must work hard at baptism, confirmation, membership, belonging. I am not sure what direction to take but I am certain we did the right thing for this boy and his mother. To see her pride, thankfulness, dignity and resolution.

MAY

15th

The Welsh Office has agreed to Rhondda Borough Council's release of the Maisonette Block. The negotiations between PNP's and the Borough's solicitors can begin. John Sheppard arrived to discuss my proposals for 'Penrhys Village' which emerged from the afternoon AMEC visited.

17th

Norah organized a Rich/Poor Supper for Christian Aid. Of the 35 present, 6 had a 3 course meal and the rest a bowl of rice. An evening of humour and parabolic learning.

Sunday 20th

We held our first Sunday morning service to answer the request of a man who has always spent Sunday at the Club. He can now proceed to the Club after morning worship.

23rd

Is there a breakthrough with the Welsh Office? After a year of probing, applying, lobbying, despairing, we met those responsible for making recommendations to the Minister. I arrived at the Welsh Office in Cardiff, was joined by Mike Bradley (Rhondda Treasurer) and we were led to meet Charles Coombes, Freny Rees and John Mooney (a Southern Irishman) who took charge of the meeting. Suggestions were made on how to improve the application for Urban Aid and I was encouraged to apply for all we are seeking - £160,000 (25% from RBC - Bradley warmly concurred).

26th

I preached at 'Teulu Duw' in Llanelwedd, where 4 years ago the preacher was Desmond Tutu. I stood in the shoes of a prophet-saint and found it an awesome responsibility. I prepared well, tried my best and hope God's word was a blessing. Our Penrhys people were delighted.
This was the first time for Penrhys people to be part of the wider church. For them it was an amazing experience.

28th

The Telethon 27 hours has been a wonderful interrelation for church and community. Everything took place in the Hall, beginning at 7 last night and ending at 10 this evening. The church had a Sponsored Bible Reading, Fast, and a Disco with 50 participating. A natural and powerful witness.

JUNE

Sunday 3rd

I visited a woman worshipper who had been disturbed by an intruder during the night. She had woken to the sound of a masked young man in her bedroom.

6th

Another member was burgled this afternoon. So upsetting for this lovely family.

Sunday 10th

Our first 'child baptism' took place in the forecourt of St Mary's Well. When did this last happen? Before the Reformation? Perhaps never? The Penrhys congregation deserved the beautiful weather, 80 sitting on the low wall, marvellous worship, a belonging which can be magnificent in this community; commitment by the 9 year old girl, her parents, God-parents and the congregation. This unity, worship and mission reflects the deepening of our people and the widening of the circle.
It was a challenge to create a service for 'child baptism' - 'halfway' between infant and believer's baptisms.

12th

The relationship between the Churches, Trusts and the Statutory Authorities is deepening. The Welsh Office party arrived at 9.40 (20 minutes early): Freny Rees, John Mooney and Alison Jackson (David Hunt's advisor on the Valleys). After an hour, Norah and I took them to Norma's (knitting), Ann's (clothes, launderette), Michaela's (café); to Terry Winter (Estate Coordinator), Peter and Chris (Tenants) and Cerri Morse in the school. They had an hour with us before leaving at 3. They want us to work at management and accountability, but it is looking very hopeful. We seek £160,000.

A critical encounter in the development of the Church Project. Alison Jackson became Permanent Head of the Welsh Office.

13th

People must see for themselves. One of our visitors today told us 'If I hadn't visited, I would never have believed Penrhys could have existed.' It is the combination of long-term poverty, strange town pattern and isolation on this high ridge which creates this startling effect.

25th

More guests. The congregation's ministry includes introducing Christians and non-Christians to life for people marginalized by Mrs Thatcher's prosperous Britain. We also reflect a church life appropriate for our community and suggesting a possible model for other communities. We welcomed 19 from Wilmslow, led by Fred and Christine Noden.

The Revd Fred Noden and Christine had been in Manselton before Norah and I moved there in 1974, and we had kept in touch over the years. Fred had offered the help of the URC in Wilmslow to our struggling cause on Penrhys. The contact was maintained throughout the years and included exchanges of people, and the provision of excellent 'nearly new' clothes for the church boutique.

JULY

7th

My last engagement as President of the Council of Churches for Wales. I served four years because although the normal term is two, I continued until the end of the Council and the start of Cytun.

This proved the end of my work for the wider church in a formal and official capacity. It was of course replaced by the fact that the church on Penrhys became a sign of mission to the churches and enjoyed a very close relationship with many national and international bodies.

10th

Compline focuses on the gentleness of spirit which the rhythm of worship, simple beauty of the building and quiet dignity of music helps nurture night by night, year by year in the monastic chapel. As worship was beginning, our recently baptised 6 year old with his usual inquisitiveness, started to count aloud the number of monks, and consequently his mother thumped him so hard he could hardly hold back his cries of pain. Our community has so much violence. Give us, O Lord, a quiet heart.
Another visit to Caldey.

12th

Four delightful children helped us experience the miracle of Jesus' teaching. One of their mothers summed it up aptly in her reading in St Illtud's 'I praise you Father, Lord of the world - very clever people have missed the secret of your heart, simple people have found it. Yes, Father, I give glory to you; this is your way.' The angry mother of last night's Compline burst out 'I've found a new family.'

AUGUST

2nd

Penrhys was introduced to two special places: Trefeca and Maesyronnen, from the traditions of Welsh Calvinistic Methodism and Independency, both converging in the Penrhys Uniting Church. We saw the new beautiful little chapel at Trefeca, the late 19th Century Memorial chapel and the humble wonder of Maesyronnen. What is to be the design of the new chapel on Penrhys for the 21st century?
Trefeca was the home of Howell Harris, one of the leaders of the Eighteenth Century Methodist revival. Maesyronnen is the oldest Nonconformist place of worship in Wales. Two minibuses of Penrhys people were introduced to these places and their story.

16th

A day with older children on one of the great beaches of Wales: Rhossili is spectacular. The sea was like lace, a strong wind drove the tide in rapidly and in our five hours we saw a huge deserted beach transformed into an arc of sand and vast ocean. None of our party (28 of us) had been there before. They have been force-fed on a diet of Barry and Porthcawl, crowded beaches and the necessity to spend money on the fair. Today saw another outing when they need not spend anything. Later in the day we saw the memorial tablet to Petty Officer Evans who died on the Scott expedition to the South Pole. He died on February 17, 1912 - my fathers 10th birthday.

20th

Penrhys Uniting Church made a daring expedition by visiting a Sikh Gudwara in Southall. Our people were enthralled by the simple beauty of the place of worship, and the courtesy and hospitality of our new friends. We were given tea and a lovely vegetable savoury. There was a oneness in God.

21st

Yesterday marked another stage in our pilgrimage to become a compassionate, tolerant community. Penrhys people can become narrow and intolerant because we are not exposed to catholic experiences. However the rich culture of Southall and the kindness and generosity of the Sikh Gudwara warmed our hearts. We have much to receive from such a community. They received us, potentially their aggressors, not as strangers but as fellow pilgrims.

SEPTEMBER

12th

Lindsay Rice stopped overnight. She begins a course in Edinburgh next month. Those selected to explore the possibility of a CWM Youth Camp on Penrhys arrived. They represent the British Churches in CWM and were led by Roderick Hewitt.

Roderick Hewitt, a minister of the United Church of Jamaica and Grand Cayman became Moderator of CWM. The Revd Lindsay Sanderson works for Churches Together in Scotland.

26th

Andras' day. He has been here for a month and has won the hearts of many Penrhys people. He has lived with a 'typical Penrhys family' (whatever that means) and has entered fully into the life of the church and the community.

Andras Zambo a Hungarian Reformed Church student spent a month on Penrhys.

OCTOBER

2nd

A major event will pass into oblivion. Maitland Evans (Chairperson of CWM) invited me to stand for the post of General Secretary of CWM. I felt overwhelmed by the thought that the little boy awed by the visit of missionaries from the LMS to Ebenezer, could be considered capable of leading an organization which has inspired me throughout my life. It is with deep regret that I turn it down, but I know Penrhys is my calling.

10th

Of the sixteen on Caldey, twelve are from Penrhys - 6 are teenage girls with no experience of the church. On the surface they seem very raw material but by the close of our second day, we have experienced a deepening of relationships. The companionship develops naturally through the study of Scripture and all our activities.
A most significant visit to Caldey. It proved that in the right environment six Penrhys girls could relate well to adult strangers. Norah and I remained good friends of all the girls throughout the Penrhys years. None of them had straightforward lives.

11th

Was it possible for six girls on Penrhys to get on with 3 deacons/ elders/leaders from Maesteg? God surprises us and brought harmony and fun beyond expectation. The relationships worked because there is a power greater than human potential.

12th

These days present fresh opportunities to recognise each other in a new light and see the potential of community in a new way. The ten older ones were aware that the 6 teenagers were the most important people on Caldey. It raises issues of mission: bringing together 'mature, liberal, open-hearted Christians' with young people full of energy but not enquiring by nature. The theological approach must be open and inquisitive.

18th

Why did the young man take his own life? I listened to the tragic family story. His final note to his mother said there would no longer be problems; he was finishing it. I am skirting the edge but there seems to have been terrible

loneliness and emptiness. Dark, dark dark, we all go into the dark. No!
Sadly, this was the first of several tragedies. Some were the result of road accidents; others the result of a combination of common factors such as a sense of rejection and loneliness which often resulted in alcohol and drug dependency. Norah and I became friends with a very wide circle of young men and women and their families who experienced the traumas of tragedies of this kind. For whatever reason, the number of tragedies reached a peak in in the early 90s, and then gradually became less frequent on Penrhys.

Sunday 21st
This terrible experience teaches us never to judge by appearance or reputation but to take the risk of personal encounter with the possibility of rejection. Try and seek relationship.

23rd
The funeral included high drama and excruciating sadness. What could I say to comfort and challenge; to succour and warn? My careful preparation enabled me to speak almost extempore because people were silent and listened expectantly.

NOVEMBER

10th
Bob and Ethel have already given £85,000 to Penrhys and they intend the Penrhys total to be £250,000 (£65,000 further for the chapel and £100,000 for care of the elderly - a residential home?).
All the wishes of Bob and Ethel were fulfilled in the building of the Chapel, and several years later in the opening of Cartref, a home for the more vulnerable on Penrhys.

21st
The church representatives and solicitors met at Cathedral Road to discuss the Trust Deed, the dispersal of assets, and the nature of the Church Council. Another hurdle has been crossed because there is no similar Trust Deed in Wales, perhaps in the UK.
It was critical to have all the representatives and the legal advisors of the eight churches together in the same room. Only in this way could agreement be arrived at. It could have taken years by mail or telephone. They knew they were pushing back the boundaries and creating a precedent for the church in legal and financial matters.

DECEMBER

1st

Young people from America, Europe, Africa, Asia and Australasia are spending a weekend at the homes of the people of Penrhys and we trust the experience will be of mutual benefit.

Another visit from Training in Mission of CWM.

2nd

This community was touched by the universal church. It happened because the Penrhys congregation embraced our visitors with generosity and openness. Our visitors from the 'Third World' were at home in the 'Fourth World'. Fascinating service when Eric from Nigeria preached on the woman touching the hem of Jesus garment. His movements expressed the story's progress. 90 present.

10th

We have been successful in our Urban Aid Grant of £160,000. We have crossed the £½ million and are within a few thousands of the refurbishment of the block, and building and furnishing the chapel. Our first stage is almost complete but much work lies ahead.

Costs had continued to escalate from the earliest estimates given to us of £360,000. This had not taken into consideration VAT, architects' fees and the costs of furnishing the building.

12th

The Welsh Office Report on the Valleys singled out Penrhys New Perspective as a good example of cooperation between local initiative, Trusts, Business and Statutory Support.

Sunday 23rd

The Penrhys Uniting Church produced its first Nativity Play. It was particularly effective for all who rehearsed and prepared. It was not as effective for all the audience because some of the most disruptive children on the estate got into the hall and were determined to spoil as much as possible. Despite that, the play worked and the 40-50 participants learned a great deal from the experience. 120 present. The Christmas Story was told.

The importance of 'telling the story traditionally' proved critical. It was a way of sharing the 'true meaning of Christmas' for the first time to some residents of Penrhys. A key element of mission is sharing the story. Only when they know the story can people make decisions about it.

24th
A beautiful Christmas Eve Communion by candlelight. All experienced God's goodness to us and the whole of creation. There was a quiet firmness about worship accompanied by miraculous moments of reconciliation.

1991

JANUARY

15th
Iraq and the allied troops on the Saudi Arabia Front are on a war-footing; a million people are deployed with the most sophisticated, horrific weapons. 42 of us met for prayers for peace in the chapel at 11.30: candlelight, readings and prayers.
The war was similar but different from the Falklands War. One of the differences was that we were now living in a community which habitually produced young men for the armed forces. One of our neighbours had a young son in Kuwait and her presence altered everyone's feelings. One of the amazing features of Penrhys was the way people responded to crisis. It seemed natural for many to want to pray together, and the church was able to respond with a midnight vigil throughout the period of conflict.

16th
An ominous foreboding: nothing seems to have happened and we wait the inevitable. One million men watch each other across sand and above oil. The rhetoric has ceased, there is quiet paralysis before action begins. Lord of heaven, earth and beneath the earth, what will we experience? The War has begun. Bombing and missile attacks have started. Earlier in the day we saw children sitting exams and men drinking in café: now planes, bombs, anti-aircraft weapons, words like 'taking out,' 'intense, heavy pounding,' 'targeting' and 'unnerving.' The next 24 hours could see the most ferocious use of weaponry in the history of humanity. What a cruel madness is humankind! Commentators are ignoring that girls and boys are being killed.

FEBRUARY

6th

On a night with a biting cold east wind from behind the tip and deep in Europe, the ground ice is hard, polished like glass and very dangerous. We gathered by candlelight in a dark, cold, still Penrhys. I read a letter from Ian to his mother and father, and all were moved to tears, aware that a 21 year old Penrhys man is out there in the deserts of Saudi Arabia. He and a million other young men and women wait for an elderly, tired man in Washington to order a ground attack which will end many lives and which could change the history of the world. We met to pray that the Lord would have mercy on us, to whom is entrusted this beautiful, fragile earth.

22nd

At 12 prompt, on a day of high wind and sheeting rain, I greeted six business men from BIC: Stephen Walls (Wiggins Teape), Robert Montague (Tiphook), Gerald Ratner (Ratners), Bill Castell (Amersham), Peter Rawlins (Chief Executive of Stock Exchange), David Taylor (Amec). After introducing them to Penrhys, we crossed the mountain to Aberdare Historic Park where I spent 9 minutes with Prince Charles. The model of PNP proved an excellent talking point. He was supportive. 'You haven't had a breakdown yet?'
Who would have expected that some of the most influential business men should have spent time on 'our forgotten estate?' The event had been organised by Business in the Community and the Penrhys visit was led by David Taylor. What proved fascinating was the way the Prince remembered his previous visit and was to keep Penrhys 'on his agenda' for many years. This proved also to be the case with some, but not all, of the businessmen. Our chief ally proved to be Bill Castell. He was Chief Executive of Amersham International from 1989 until it was acquired by General Electric in April 2004. Alongside his business career he has been involved for many years in not-for-profit activities, including being a council member of the Medical Research Council (2001-2004) and Chairman of the Prince's Trust (1998-2003).

MARCH

1st

For Britain, Spring symbolically begins with the Equinox; for Wales it begins on a warm sunny day, with daffodils worn by girls, leeks half-eaten by boys, and eisteddfodau. I adjudicated the Junior School Eisteddfod. I sat on a burnished throne, the children performed and I delivered marks for red, yellow, green and blue houses.

2nd

This congregation is like the Early Church. Three quarters have been worshipping less than a year. Christian maturity is a rare gift, takes a lifetime to develop and is always centred on grace. We have been aware of quarrelling amongst members, but we must remember that belonging to the church is helping to mellow, moderate and sharpen conscience. We are all only beginning.

9th

Is the URC part of denominationalism which has to die for the Church to embark on universal reconciliation? Historic denominationalism had much to offer but are we experiencing the conclusion of the Nineteenth Century shape of the church? We are demanding more and more from the less and less in our congregations, and failing to grasp that God's Spirit is pressing us into a church whose mission is ecumenical. As long as we remain divided, ministry fails.

11th

Norah and I instructed Burgess Partnership on behalf of Penrhys New Perspective, to invite Laings to fulfil their tender of £413,000. In three weeks time the building of the Penrhys Church begins.

29th, Good Friday

Penrhys could again be a place of pilgrimage and mission. Peter Scotland invited members of the South Wales URC District, and 80 gathered at the Well, Shrine and at the site of the new chapel. We entered the hall and the play began at 2.50. Audience and players were awed. God was in this: 200 in the audience and 60 in the play.

Peter Scotland was minister of City URC in Cardiff. 'Jesus' was played most movingly by our son, Dylan and he did so for several years. This proved the first time for the Passion play to be performed/ celebrated/ worshipped. On Friday, the play ended with the death of Jesus, and on Easter Sunday the play was performed again, and this time included the Resurrection scenes. Just like the Nativity at Christmas, the play was written 'straight' so that the story could be introduced to the community. Very few of the residents knew of the resurrection appearances. It was genuine mission. A photographer arrived and asked if he could take photographs of us at the Well. Later we discovered it was Philip Jones Griffiths, the eminent Welsh photographer.

30th

'Were you there when they crucified my Lord?' echoed through the hall yesterday and brought many to tears. Penrhys Uniting Church and our visitors experienced Good Friday.

31st

Easter Day is resurrection hope and life. We began our walk to Twyn Disgwylfa (Bristol Trump) at 8 on a glorious spring morning with a light warm breeze and blue hazy sky full of skylarks. Thirty walked to the top where worship began, continued at the forestry gate and after a breakfast of boiled eggs, concluded in the chapel with Easter Communion: 45 for a lovely family service. Returned to chapel by 4.45 where the children and adults were being dressed. An audience of 100, mostly Penrhys people. It was very different from Friday's captive, responsive, mature audience but it is even more important to reach our own community. The play was greeted at the end with genuine, fulsome applause. 70 on stage with 10 helping. A wonderful achievement.

APRIL

10th

It is important to be walking about, enjoying and entering the life of the community, and revealing this is where we want to be, this is where we are happy, this is where we believe God wants us to be working together. This is a new beginning for Penrhys and God wants the church to be involved. We must have confidence to say this is why we are here; it is not a desperate last attempt to survive; it is being confident in God's future.

12th

The Ecclesiastical Insurance Company visited the block and declared it uninsurable.

The small chapel in the Community Centre had been insured for many years by the Ecclesiastical Insurance Company. They were quite happy to insure the new building when it was completed, but were not prepared to take the risk of insuring while it was being built. Because there had to be insurance by both Laings and the Church, we were in an impossible situation. Just one more problem for churches in high priority communities.

15th

Another day during which I did not leave Penrhys. Once my ministry stretched from Penmaenmawr to Llanfaches, from Dyserth to Milford Haven. Now it stretches from the roundabout at the bottom of the estate to the mountain and forest at the perimeters. It is from macrocosm to microcosm; from the whole of Wales to the square mile.

20th

I checked the income and expenditure of PNP. When we first envisaged the project, we guessed costs would be in the region of £100,000 (half for purchase of the maisonette block and half for its refurbishment). Then followed the architects' estimate of £360,000 for refurbishment and the chapel. This did not reflect architects' fees, VAT, nor furnishing. Now the cost is nearer £700,000. Would we have initiated the project if we had known the challenge? It would have been a wild dream.

24th

Penrhys interests a very wide audience, and is as foreign to the general public as my journey to Hungary in 1983. Then, few people went to the other side of 'the iron curtain' and hardly anyone spoke of the church there in a positive way. The only Christians belonged to the underground Church. The same ignorance applies to life within the high priority housing estate. The Telethon Trustees listened this afternoon as if I had returned from the dark side of the moon.

28th

As I prepared for Compline and felt the eternal silence; as the Salve Regina was intoned by this newer, younger community, I sensed the rhythm of God's purposes like the ebb and flow of that sea which has broken on this island since time immemorial. I asked Robert if he would preach at the opening of our new church, and if the community would present us with an ancient 'spare bell.'

Another visit to Caldey. During our talk on Russia to the school in 1989, we had played a tape of 'Russian Orthodox Bells.' Norah asked the children if they would like to have a bell on Penrhys - hence the request.

29th

To grow in Christ is a life long process. I saw the old friends (Robert, Joseph, Thaddeus, Stephen) who with Br John and Desiree are the only 6 monks left from when we first came to the island. Now there are 16 monks (fully professed and novices) with 5 enquiring seriously. I pray that the community of Caldey will out-live our 6 friends and that the church community of Penrhys will out-live my life. If it is grounded in the love of God, it will.

MAY

4th

The service for laying the foundation stones must include a continuity with the past (Celtic, Medieval, Nonconformist) and a radical discontinuity because of our ecumenism, social action and the establishment of a Church for the wider community of Penrhys.

14th

Several hundred were present on a gloriously warm, sunny day for laying the foundation stones. The service was simple but very moving, especially the laying of the 8 stones and the dedication by Ethel. After interviews with HTV and Elidir, I met Alan Titchmarsh for an interview at the Well.
The eight stones came from redundant chapels in the community of Tylorstown and Pontygwaith, from chapels of the eight denominations. Alan Titchmarsh was recording programmes on pilgrimages. We met at the Well, but he had no time to visit the estate.

19th, Pentecost Sunday

Michael Taylor, Jeff Williams and Elenid Jones, all of Christian Aid joined us and Michael spoke wisely and obviously enjoyed the children. We counted Christian Aid (£112) from the collecting boxes. Will Penrhys raise £250?
Michael Taylor was Director of Christian Aid for twelve years from 1985-97. He was President of the Jubilee 2000 Debt Campaign. Jeff Williams is Director of Christian Aid for Wales, and Elenid Jones served as the Education Officer for South Wales.

21st

A strange intersection of time and eternity, the sound of a great silence, the focussing of a great company of people into the life of an individual at the graveyard on Penrhys. The sky was blue, the grass trim and spring-fresh, a bird sang and a crowd looked down from the paths as the bereaved husband stood a solitary figure above the grave. He stood alone, perched on the edge for 5 minutes and the crowd was silent and motionless. We had witnessed tragedy but hope. A theme of the service was In my beginning is my end .. 'In my end is my beginning.' Everything was wrong about the young woman's death, and yet everything seemed right. The service was shaped by Christian humanism.

JUNE

7th

Norah and I drove to the Municipal General Office to pay insurance cover. Siarlys Evans, senior partner at Burgess, has no experience of an Insurance Company rejecting such a policy. Such are the problems of initiating projects in deprived communities.
A 'secular' insurance company was prepared to insure a church which an ecclesiastical insurance company had refused. Fools rush in where angels fear to tread.

12th

I met David Hunt, Secretary of State for Wales. In the company of Alison Jackson, we talked about Penrhys. He asked about PNP and what prospects I saw for our community. I had prepared carefully and shared the concepts of (1) the Village Centre, and (2) the Pilgrimage Route. He was delighted and instructed Alison to find ways in which the Welsh Office could be supportive of a long-term programme. Both he and Alison suggested that this was the opportune time before there are political changes! This miraculous opportunity will demand tough, skilful work during the coming months - before the end of August when Urban Aid applications are processed. What a challenge, but it could help change Penrhys.
Alison Jackson had phoned to 'invite?' me to meet the Secretary of State. David Hunt had last met me in Peter Walker's meeting during the Miners' Strike. I remembered him but did not remind him of our earlier encounter. This meeting was very different. There was a complete understanding of the needs of communities like Penrhys and the importance of 'faith bodies' who were in community and committed to genuine development.

20th

Norah, John Sheppard of BIC and I met Alison Jackson, Valleys Advisor to the Secretary of State. The meeting was a consequence of David Hunt's invitation to meet him last week. Alison encouraged us to apply for Urban Aid; showed us how to approach the Borough Council and Welsh Office; a cohesive plan with a 3-4 year rolling programme, and a suggestion of £300,000 total revenue.

21st

A teenager crashed a motorbike near the Youth Centre and in a split second, a very likeable young man of 18 has ended his life. We guessed for a long time that something like this would happen. The ring road and the internal paths and verges are racing tracks.

25th

The community mourns this tragic death. Penrhys, this fractured community expresses solidarity during crises. Many have talked about the enormity of their loss and are seeking for meaning to it and to their lives. If we could provide the right resources of people and the appropriate approach, the church could have an important impact for good on Penrhys.

27th

A sign of God's presence and action. The community of Penrhys (250 mostly young people) gathered in the Community Centre to give thanks for the life of their young friend, mourn his death, share their grief, affirm their oneness in sorrow and do all these things with sensitivity and gentleness. His sporting trophy stood alongside flowers and a central candle was surrounded by dozens of lit candles; even after the service had finished, there was prolonged silence because people did not wish to move. In the depths of this very human experience was the God who is the Father of Christ and shares the Spirit, who makes holy all human experience where love is expressed.

28th

Miracle in the midst of tragedy. As we walked out of the family home, we were surrounded by hundreds of people dressed in black and white. With a bright sun and sharply blue sky, it could have been Reformed Hungary. Minibuses and cars followed the hearse down Penrhys hill into Tylorstown, like a town on the move. We were a great tribe descending from the hills, evoking respect and fear.

JULY

11th

Norah and I met David Worrell of Amersham and John Sheppard before walking to school and joining the others to discuss the proposals for a Village Centre. A most productive meeting: positive and creative. We could be embarking upon a fresh chapter in the life of Penrhys.

This was the meeting which saw the formal establishment of the Penrhys Partnership. Previously it had been a Liaison Group meeting to discuss issues affecting the life of the community. After I had given a report of the meeting with the Secretary of State, it was agreed '1. To accept the main outlines of John Morgans' paper. 2. Developments would take place through the enrhys Partnership chaired by John Morgans, but consisting of the core group based around existing members.' The core group was Peter Bolger and Haydn Thomas of the Tenants and Residents Association, Norah Morgans and John Morgans from Penrhys New Perspective, Cerri Morse Head-teacher, Andrew Boucher and Geoff Summers of AMEC, John Sheppard, Director of BITC Wales and David Worrell of Amersham. [Minutes of meeting.] The formal application for the Welsh Office grant was made on behalf of the Partnership through PNP because the Partnership had not legally come into being by this time.

25th

A fairy tale was written at the Annual Conference of Business in the Community at Grey Coates Hospital, London. I spoke on the same platform as Neil Shaw, Chief Executive of Tate and Lyle and Chairman of BIC; Brandon Gough of Coopers and Lybrand Deloitte; Louise Ellman of Lancashire County Council; John Banham Confederation of British Industry, and the Prince of Wales. I sat next but one to the Prince throughout the Plenary - his aide sat between us. I had an unparalleled opportunity to speak about PNP and the Prince referred to Penrhys in his excellent speech. A dozen of us were introduced to the Prince. Question Time was chaired by Jeremy Paxman with Chris Patton, Tony Blair, Charles Kennedy, Louise DAccordia. Prime Minister called in from talks on Ireland.

AUGUST

2nd

A privilege and delight to climb Snowdon, the heart of Wales which has preserved us as a people with an identity. Seven of us reached the summit, feeling not conquerors but recipients of a gift.

We had taken two minibuses of people from Penrhys on our first week's holiday. We had slept on church floors in Rhyl and toured North Wales. For all the Penrhys people, it was their first visit to North Wales, and for most, their first holiday.

8th

We have enjoyed the company of Bill Castell, David Worrell and Wally Olins (the image maker). They met 8 from the church projects, had lunch at home and spoke with the Partnership group before meeting Council officials in the Mayor's Parlour: Gwyn Evans, Mattie Collins, the Deputy Mayor.

Wally Olins is a leading consultant in corporate identity and branding. He was responsible for the BT logo on telephone kiosks. At the Mayor's Parlour we were greeted by Gwyn Evans, Chief Executive and Mattie Collins, Labour leader. Wally Olins stated that 'Penrhys is not ready for a marketable image yet.' I wonder what he would say now?

9th

Bob Huggard died this morning. Here is a man larger than life, powerful in ideas and action, meticulous in detail, with a marvellous sense of humour but above all a kind man with a passion for helping life's failures. He is the man who asked us to dream about the future of Penrhys, and then willed himself to support those in the front line. He is a unique figure, the man who strode into our lives for two years and helped change the direction of the community of Penrhys.

31st

When I return after an absence of a few weeks, we see Penrhys as when we arrived 5 years ago. There are the superficial impressions of noise, squalor, violence of language, small children playing in and near a skip full of rubbish, a child riding a bike in total darkness behind the house at 11 o'clock, a young man driving a motorbike up the main path, a house covered with grills because it is vacant, young people talking on the bus stop roof, a car screeching around the roundabout. This is the only world the majority of young Penrhys people know. This is their square mile; this is their universe. Here the Gospel of hope and light needs to be preached and lived. It's good to be home.

SEPTEMBER

15th

Church Meeting decided to call the church complex: 'Llanfair.'

'Llan' after the Celtic church community or church complex; 'Mair' after Mary of Well, Statue and above all the Magnificat.

OCTOBER

Sunday 20th

The third annual visit from TIM has made a difference to our congregation and our visitors. As they were returning to Birmingham, a large crowd gathered on the balcony and steps leading from the Community Centre. There were tears from those who received them into their homes. Young Christians from all over the world were saying goodbye to people whose lives, until two years ago, had been totally confined to the circumference of this housing estate. The world church now comes to Penrhys.

22nd

Glenys Williams told Norah she felt for the first time the heritage of Ebenezer was continuing.

Glenys had been a deacon and Sunday School teacher in Ebenezer, Tylorstown. Her kind words meant the world to us.

27th

Scripture confronts us with the brutality of human experience. The Old Testament is the essential context for understanding the Gospel. This natural context enables us to grasp that the writers of the Good News in Christ knew what life was all about. There is no naiveté, no escapism; they lived in identical circumstances to ours and yet, out of this context, comes the discovery of God's action. As we read about Saul, David, Michel, Ahimelech, it was difficult to see God at work. And yet in our world of Yugoslavia, Northern Ireland, South Africa it is also difficult to see God at work. In just such a world, we profess Jesus is Lord.

As always the Bible came alive on Caldey. We were studying the Books of Samuel.

28th

Having been engrossed by the feuding and brutality, nobility and sensitivity of the people in the Books of Samuel, the crucified and risen Christ came as a tender, reassuring presence in the celebration of Holy Communion. After all, it is good: everything is alright; there is hope; love is the victor and we can have faith in God. In life, in death, in life beyond death, God is with us.

29th

What hope is there without the knowledge of God with us?: this God of David, Michal, Nabal, Abigail, Joab, Abner and Absalom. Today also witnessed the journey of the bell from St David's, (St Mary by the Sea) to St Mary, Mair o Benrhys. The bell has been brought to this place once holy to the Cistercians. Penrhys has received a gift from the same Order to this new Llanfair. Fr Robert, Norah and I fetched the bell from the carpenter's shop where it has been for 20 years.
Fr Robert was delighted that this historic Cistercian bell from St Mary's would soon be ringing in the new church at the ancient Cistercian pilgrimage site of Penrhys. Peter Cruchley-Jones, our intern student from Mansfield and I physically carried the bell to and from the boat with great pride - despite torrential rain. Peter is now URC minister in Beulah Rhiwbina.

31st

Penrhys is again a place of pilgrimage. Last year 900 visited; this year 1000; next year when Llanfair is opened? Receiving visitors, dealing with questions, providing hospitality makes us realize we are part of a wide world and a wide church.

NOVEMBER

7th

A small model of a table encapsulates what we believe. It is round; its front leg reclines to enable people to approach without hindrance; it is tasteful and welcoming; it invites people to stand around it; it is round, has no head or foot, has no corners. It is a table at which all can commune. That table is an expression of the Gospel. It is a creation of God for God's People on Penrhys.
'Wales and Wales' were commissioned to create all the interior furnishings for the chapel. They have been producing remarkable furniture since 1980 and are based in Lewes in Sussex. The Penrhys 'men' collected the furniture in the church minibus. The decision to have a round communion table was

partly because of Fred Kaan's hymn: 'The church is like a table, a table that is round./ it has no sides or corners, no first or last, no honours; / here people are in one-ness and love together bound.' Fred wrote it in 1984 when he was a URC Moderator. He acknowledges that the idea came from a poem by Chuck Lathrop, a Maryknoll Missioner in the Appalachians.

DECEMBER

6th

Will we provide Penrhys with the basic facilities for a healthy community? Three years ago, there was an impossible vision that refurbished maisonettes could become a home for a Christian community. Llanfair surpasses expectation. Now there is the possibility of a 'Penrhys Village' by refurbishing two further blocks in the centre of Penrhys. As the physical heart is transformed, we trust there will come a new confidence in the future of Penrhys. Yesterday brought the hope of supportive accommodation; today the hope for a surgery, dentist and pharmacy. Who would have believed?

7th

My three previous ministries are coalescing in what I imagine is my final pastorate.

11th

The Partnership application for Urban Aid is successful and we will receive £300,000 pa for 3 years for capital expenditure, and annual revenue of £83,000 for 3 years. This should see a major transformation in this community. No one could have dreamt the changes between 1990 and 1994. It was announced today in the Grand Committee of the House of Commons.

24th

The morning of Christmas. We have been confronted by a host of angels; we have seen a star rise and move towards the west; we have walked in the light and Penrhys Uniting Church has walked one more step along the world. Our worship began at 11.15 when 50 gathered in the old shop in the Community Centre. The place was packed and the service simple and direct; we walked along the main path into the New Chapel where by candlelight and under the star, worship was filled with silence and rhythm.

The first service in the still unfinished chapel in Llanfair.

1992

JANUARY

3rd

As I sat in a ground floor maisonette flat, a young bereaved mother and her mother taught me theology. On the day after we celebrate the birth of Jesus, she lost a 12 hour old baby. The two women questioned me searchingly: 'Why did she die? And why did Jesus live until his 30s? And why are you still living at the age of 52? What is God's will? Is the baby alive? If so, is she sleeping and waiting for her mother and the fulfilment of humankind? Or is she growing and maturing now? And, why do the children of neglectful and unloving parents survive?' This mother cares so deeply for her lost child. What love, pain, sense of loss, feeling of failure and hopelessness. I listened, shared, prayed.

6th

The funeral was strangely peaceful and beautiful. A lovely mild, sunny morning with signs of Spring. We held hands and stood around the graveside for the closing prayers.

11th

Hugh shared his experience of Romania. He was eloquent in his description and lucid in his analysis of the complex situation which is Transylvania. Tomorrow he travels to Nagyvarád.

Our son Hugh had spent a year as a English language assistant at the Reformed Theological University in Debrecen, Hungary, and during this second year was an English language assistant to László Tökés, an ethnic Hungarian politician in Romania, bishop of the Romanian Reformed Church in Transylvania. An effort to transfer him from his post as an assistant pastor in Timisoara (Hungarian: Temesvár) and to evict him from his church flat helped trigger the Romanian Revolution of 1989, which overthrew Ceaucescu and spelled the end of the communist era in Romania.

27th

Anarchic behaviour lies just beneath the surface in many societies and is sometimes overt and paramount on Penrhys. It saps strength and stretches patience. Three windows were smashed in the library yesterday afternoon and topsoil raked so carefully, thrown over pathways and against doors and windows. What was gratifying was the anger of many Penrhys people. Why do the mindless few engage in futile destruction?

29th

I chaired the meeting of the Partnership appointing Paul Rowson as Project Director for the 3 year programme.

The Partnership depended so much on the commitment, stamina and expertise of its directors, all of whom were unpaid. A core of directors served for many years, including Norah, Geoff Summers, David Worrell, Cerri Morse, Jan English, Andrew Edmunds, Maurice Padfield, Ann Lord and John Sheppard. Paul Rowson served the Penrhys Partnership until 1997 and supervised the major period of physical development of Y Ffynnon, Cartref and Canolfan Rhys. Since Paul Rowson moved from Penrhys, the work of the Partnership has been managed by Wayne Carter (Partnership Manager) and Beverley Chick (Finance Manager).

FEBRUARY

12th

Do not take miracles for granted - was this for Jesus, the unpardonable sin? For my father, cynicism was a grievous fault. Our first 'ordinary' weeknight service used Caldey Compline and managed the three psalms in plainsong. The congregation moved from a faltering, hesitant beginning to a resolve which was not afraid of silence. The sound touched the little lantern roof.

Young people who had visited Caldey and enjoyed Compline had asked if it could be introduced to Penrhys. It continued every Wednesday until we left in 2004. There was a variation after some years when a Taize service was introduced for the last Wednesday of each month.

13th

The young mother stood silently, looking at the candle she had lit in memory of her baby girl; the chapel was in darkness except for the central candle and the light in the lantern; the chapel was empty apart from mother and grandmother. The chapel was full of silence. When she stood back, the candle seemed to fill the sanctuary and penetrate the darkness of the street outside. There was a moment of calm, peace and gratitude. In the middle of tragedy, God was reaching out to this desperate young woman. The chapel had been built for her.

17th

A 4 year old from the Nursery School knelt on the floor and blew out the central candle. 25 Infants and 4 teachers arrived at 10, took off their coats and entered the chapel to sit quietly on the central chairs. Their eyes danced when we put on the lights, and sparkled when a candle was lit for each child as they stated their names. Then upstairs for pop and a biscuit. It showed how wonderful the relationship could be between church and school. The new chapel is coming into its own.
The first visit of Nursery and Infants children to 'see the new church.' Little did we think this was the beginning of a process which would continue throughout the years.

19th

The rhythm of plainsong is the ebb and flow of the eternal sea; it is the greenness of the Abbey Church of Caldey; it is the remembrance of family and friends on the island; it is the reality of music this evening in Llanfair; it is the expectation of the great weekend on Penrhys with Friday Compline with Robert, and Saturday Vespers with Deiniol and Barnabas. God is good and good to us. The Boutique opened for the first time. Great excitement with many customers who also wanted to see around Llanfair. A day of expectancy. £107 raised. The hard work is bearing fruit. At our flat, twenty of us watched Troeon's 'Launderette i Dduw.' This was followed by several enthusiastic phone-calls, including Dewi Eurig, Norah's Doctrine Professor at Coleg Coffa, and Farther Deiniol of Manod.
This was a remarkable documentary during which Norah had been interviewed and filmed throughout the previous year. It was shown to coincide with the opening of Llanfair. It became a film we often showed, especially to our Welsh speaking visitors.

21st

The Kingdom demands hard, patient, tiring work, day by day, and at last in my life, I am on the verge of touching the hem of the Master's garment. The gruelling, painstaking challenges of the past months are fulfilled by the worship of God's People on Penrhys. The work of the Children of God is to love, praise and serve him for ever. The chapel enables the heart to beat.

28th

The People of God meeting on Penrhys were led in Compline by Fr Robert, Abbot of Caldey. The plainsong, especially when Robert sang, brought Caldey into Penrhys. Llanfair is full of people preparing for tomorrow: men tidying the grounds; women making Welsh cakes and cleaning. There is a sense of expectancy. Elwyn Thomas hung some fine paintings.

Elwyn Thomas was a local painter who had recently retired as Senior Art Master at Ferndale Comprehensive School. He had been a close friend of my father.

29th

Glory to God in the highest, in the High Street, at 1200 feet on a priority housing estate. 600-700 people gathered on Penrhys to give thanks to God for his great work. The worship of the 8 churches, supported by the Roman Catholic and Orthodox churches pealed out in bell, book, candle and in a great hymn of praise. The Spirit lifted our spirits and there was a touch of glory. Glory was coupled with the method and organization of days and weeks of long, hard work; but above all God's love was expressed by the people of Penrhys, and the people of such a wide circle. The service began at 3 in the Centre: Beverley sang; Cath read; Dylan lit the candle; Steeler played; Robert preached. Ethel rang the bell; then 4 services in Llanfair; projects, tea. All left at 6.30. Orthodox Vespers at 8, led by Deiniol and Barnabas: 60 of us in the beauty and strangeness of Orthodoxy; incense and coughing. We were presented with a beautiful lamp from Kazan. Glory is due to God alone.

Many people had worked extremely hard to produce such an event. Our intern student, Peter Cruchley-Jones and his wife Rhiannon thought through many of the practicalities, but it was certainly a team effort of dozens of people. Deiniol and Barnabas were two Orthodox monks: Deiniol from Manod in North Wales, and Barnabas from New Mills in Mid Wales. Fred Kaan, who was present on the day, wrote a new hymn for the occasion, 'God among us, Sense of Life,' to the tune Llanfair.

MARCH

Sunday 1st

Hard daily work is the basis of the life of the Church week after week, century after century. Yesterday was created by innumerable todays. Stamina and perseverance are critical gifts of the Spirit. The bell rang for the first time to call people to the worship of God on the Lord's Day.

4th

Ash Wednesday was celebrated. We gathered on the forecourt and burnt the palms of last Palm Sunday. We moved into the chapel where our service included the signing of the cross with ashes on the forehead, and Holy Communion. It was an appropriate start of the pilgrimage towards Easter Day. It will be wonderful to hear the bell peal after we have climbed Bristol Tump on Easter morning.

5th

Llanfair is full of people. It is quickly establishing itself as a focal point for Penrhys. At its heart is the chapel but already the café and the 'New for You' clothes shop are places to visit in what can be seen as a dreary monotonous place. The café was busy during its four hours across midday, and presented an important place this evening when teenagers and adults met. Where else can they meet in our village?

Sunday 29th

The Good News is that at the heart of creativity is mercy. God, source, guide and goal of all that is, is the Father of Jesus. Our Lady of Tenderness gently led us into the centre of the universe. In the Christ/ child/ man is our light and life, and he waits for us; there is space between the Virgin's inviting hand and the body of her Son. Our worship has been centred on the icon of Our Lady of Vladimir and it spoke from 700 years ago in Constantinople.

'Our Lady of Tenderness' had been presented by Fr Deiniol to the church during the service of recognition in October 1989. It was used on this occasion for Mothering Sunday and became a feature of this service, with a special liturgy created for the day, inspired by the meditations of Henri Nouwen.

30th

It was good to look over the snow-covered roof of the chapel and into the community. We are in the centre of the village and at the crossways of the north-south and east-west pathways. Our lives would be quieter if we were on the edge of the estate, but this is where we should be.

APRIL

16th

Holy Thursday reflected tenderness and poignancy. Judas was the first to walk into the darkness; he was followed by the squabbling, ambitious James and John, the rest of the disciples, and then all of us. Yet we stood in a circle around the Table and shared bread and wine; baby Leon received wine from Maria's finger; the basin and towel were placed on the table; Caroline gently rocked baby Leon to sleep. Penrhys was touched by God's grace and presence.

Easter Sunday, 19th

The Lord is risen. His resurrection power was experienced at Llanfair in the Vigil and Celebration which reflected Good Friday darkness and Easter light; the Baptisms of Lee, Linda, Michelle, Michaela, Susan, Paul, Sheila, Hazel, Suzanne and Ann. The conviction and love of the candidates was the channel of God's grace. They had determination and happiness in their eyes. The chapel was filled with the prayers and praise of innumerable saints. Easter is celebrated.

24th

I have branded your names on my hand. I have tattooed your names on my hand. 'Its the names that did it,' the final words of the film, 'The Healing of the Nation' about the creation of the Vietnam War Memorial. It is the names that matter; individuals in a personhood centred universe. The Cross and the Resurrection stamp the cruciality of personality at the core of all being. Creating, liberating and consummating God, it is in Jesus of Nazareth that we know you as Father.

MAY

6th

150 people came to Llanfair today, the majority from Penrhys. This was a normal day. What does it augur for the future? There were 25 from the Infants class; café launderette, créche and boutique were so busy; the knitters were at work. This evening there was a Welsh class. 30 Welsh speakers from Pentyrch called; 25 of our people were at Compline. Llanfair is serving in ways beyond what we could imagine. Ahead lies work with literacy, craft and music!

This kind of day was 'the bread and butter day' of Llanfair. The church premises were open every day of the week and for almost every day of the year. A large number of people were involved in their regular work at Llanfair every day. It was its reliability and good organisation which ensured that the mission of Llanfair was recognized and appreciated by the community. The whole team of people, residents of Llanfair and residents of the wider community of Penrhys worked together for the sake of the community as a whole.

7th

As the project developed, a question under discussion was whether a residential community should be scattered in different houses in different areas of Penrhys. Living together could isolate the church from the community. The 'religious people' live together! After careful consideration, we decided to live in the same block of flats to provide mutual support, it was less expensive and we could together look after the building. What we hadn't bargained for was our availability to the community. We meet more people here in a week than we did in 5 years at 12 Heol Dyfed.

8th

A major, irrevocable decision about the future of Penrhys. All who care for our community must feel defeat and hope. The Borough Council proposes the demolition of 10 blocks of maisonettes: 5 near the pub; 4 on the west side of the estate; 1 in front of Llanfair. The Partnership has asked that 2 blocks be released for the health centre. Only 2 blocks will be maintained by the Council for residential use. What will these changes mean? the removal of potentially excellent housing, although for years many of these have been used by people with serious social problems. Will Penrhys be a better place in which to live?

11th

During the last months all the children and staff from the Nursery and Infants have seen the chapel, visited the café and have worshipped. 300 children have come to Llanfair. This is a wonderful opportunity to bind church, school and community, and we must try and develop it into a regular pattern in the life of Penrhys. If two classes visit every week, each class could come to Llanfair 3 or 4 times a year. That could make a profound difference. I must put it to the church and the schools.

JUNE

6th

Norah focussed the chapel lights on the new Pentecost banner. The effect was startling. Penrhys people have created a work of art. The tapestry portrays the power of living flames and the tenderness of the hovering dove. This is new creation, from the knitting workshop. It is our first piece of art.

23rd

Enfys Hâf was born at 2.30 this morning. Daughter of Rhiannon and Peter, she is the first born in Llanfair Penrhys. There was joy for those who live in this house, and when the Church bell was rung at 8 am, the happiness was shared by those who came out to discover what had happened.
Enfys was the only baby born at Llanfair during the twelve years, 1992 - 2004.

JULY

10th

Two years ago the Penrhys Uniting Church was invited by CWM to serve as hosts for Youth in Mission, an international work camp. Today the participants arrived from Tuvalu, Guyana, Mozambique, Romania, Taiwan, North India, Scotland, England, Holland and Wales.
The Youth in Mission Work-camp was a highlight in the twelve year story of Llanfair. Forty young people spent three weeks at this residential event centred in Llanfair but using the facilities of the community. The young people slept in the Community Centre and had all their meals in Llanfair. The theme was 'Growing in Community.' They studied, worshipped and engaged in practical activities for the benefit of the community. This included a play scheme for the children of Penrhys, and the creation of the amphitheatre. Residents of the estate and the YIM volunteers created this permanent mark on the future of the community. Their theme was to study mission in context and this demanded an understanding of how 'God works as recorded in different periods of Biblical history' and an introduction to 'the story of Rhondda and Wales.' In their reflections, 'CWM Together, July 1992' they recorded 'Questions of community are very real in Penrhys as people struggle for dignity and liberation. For three short weeks we shared in that struggle and we have been enriched by what we have seen and heard.'

15th
Hywel Francis introduced the coal history of Rhondda.

16th
Gwynfor Evans, one of the heroes of Wales in this century, spoke to YIM.

17th
Jorge of Mozambique touched the depths of the human spirit in the power of gentleness. Cennard Davies spoke on 'Rhondda Religion' by taking us to the Statue, Well, Ton Pentre where we worshipped in the ancient church of St John's (was St Tyfodwg) before lunch at Hermon Treorci.
Cennard Davies is a pioneer in the renaissance of the teaching of Welsh, especially in the Valleys.

21st
The day reflected the struggle between civilizing pressures and barbaric forces. Children set fire to two empty maisonette blocks and someone destroyed our beautiful tree. This was a day when YIM pulled out weeds, cut grass, and worked on the amphitheatre and in the schools. We took a busload to the top of the tip and to St Gwynno's where we felt the total stillness.

22nd
The cutting down of the beautiful tree has increased the determination not to give in. The young people worked hard, played sensitively and fervently, discussed acutely and looked for God's Way for them. YIM is a beautiful expression of growing in community. Andrew Prasad spoke about CWM.

24th
Sankuma, a minister of the Presbyterian Church of India, led worship. Mysterious moments were his singing Psalm 51 with a gentle sound and movement which expressed each word; intercessory prayers accompanied on the drum by Jorge of Mozambique; praying in several languages, in which his voice was strong and with hwyl; the singing of the final mantra. He was a channel of grace.

28th
A small amphitheatre has been built in a week by the unskilled labour of young people from all over the world, including Penrhys. It is in a most beautiful setting overlooking the Rhondda Fawr; and on a glorious summer

evening without a breath of wind, 600 people gathered and enjoyed themselves without problems. The two groups were our local Steeler and a Christian Rock Group, Rhythm Works. It was a great joy for Youth in Mission who have worked hard, long and lovingly.

30th

Christian Community slowly developed. YIM and the Penrhys congregation and community have enjoyed a rich fellowship and we have all glimpsed a church living, worshipping and serving community. We have witnessed the indispensable connection between unity and mission, grasped that religious experience and worship is deeper than theological expression and have rejoiced in the diversity of culture, worship and personality.

31st

At the 9.15 service in the chapel, Sankuma gave a vote of thanks, Jason presented a beautiful banner, Rachel played the harp. There were short scriptures in Dutch, English and Welsh before each participant shared a Scripture sentence and a snapshot to share at home. After candles were lit, we walked to the Statue to sing 'Magnificat Now!', and to the amphitheatre for Communion where 100 met in glorious sunshine. Later Lesley and Graham were the first to leave from the Centre. As the car pulled away, the Angelus rang, they stopped and we all sang there in the centre of Penrhys.

SEPTEMBER

3rd

Violence has broken out: flooding a maisonette block; breaking into the Estate Office stores and office; heavy graffiti; shooting at workers with pellets has resulted in the withdrawal of the workforce.

14th

Penrhys at its best and worst. Penrhys is close to a 'riot' and there is an ominous feeling that something will happen tonight. 20-30 youths with several older men are encouraging children to set fire to derelict maisonette blocks, wait for firemen to arrive, instigate fetching the police and then throw stones. The rumour is they will use petrol bombs tonight. The trigger incident was an accusation that a policeman had beaten up a local young man because of a stolen car incident; the deeper causes are boredom, wanting to taunt and challenge the police, a pride in being notorious. Yet today Bill and Renice

Castell spent the day with us and were thrilled, encouraged us to keep up the struggle and promised support of time and energy. Bill is a remarkable ally and has proved his stamina over the past 18 months.

23rd

I listened to Radio Wales News at 7.30. I half expected the worst and was right: 'Arson attacks on Penrhys... the stoning of fire officers... riot police... a fire crew being told by police to let a maisonette burn because of a rioting crowd'.At 7.50 the Echo phoned and was soon followed by the BBC. I was interviewed by the Western Mail and Independent.

28th

I am recording the story of Llanfair. It is important to be accurate: there is despair, exhilaration, perseverance, single-mindedness, doubt and ultimately a victory against the odds. The story must not be forgotten. It is a record of how God works in his world. We can learn from the experience; it should strengthen faith and encourage us and others to seek God's will and persevere.
The booklet was Penrhys: The Story of Llanfair, published in June 1994

OCTOBER

3rd

Thirty-five of us went for the first Project meal in Ted's in Treherbert.
The Project Meal became an annual fixture in the calendar. It was always an expression of gratitude that a year of hard work had been accomplished, and an encouragement to fare forward a further year.

19th

Twenty properties became vacant last week.
The demolition of the maisonettes was inevitable but caused a repercussion. If the blocks are demolished, will any houses be safe?

21st

Our first Weekday Communion. I used a traditional rite, different from the styles of the last few years, but because we have learned 'the shape of the liturgy' and are not tied to a language form, this was most effective for adult worship.
One of our residential team, a young member of the Church of England, reflected on the need for a weekly Communion service. It was not always

possible during the Sunday All Age worship. It often happened that developments were an answer to a specific need.

NOVEMBER

6th

An evening of beauty, delicacy and courtesy. It was a risk to invite a small choir from Atlantic College. Would anyone turn up to listen to high-brow music? What kind of music would be sung? Would people walk out, eat, drink or talk during the performance? Would there be interruptions from outside? Would their buses be damaged? Everything was beyond expectation. The chapel was full and the listening as attentive as at the Reardon Smith; the applause was genuine and enthusiastic, and there developed an affection and relationship.

The Reardon Smith was the Lecture room at the University of Cardiff.

11th

Shelagh, Kirsty and Jenny arrived. All are training for URC ministry, are linked with Mansfield and I serve as a support.

Mansfield asked me and Llanfair to provide a resource to the three young women all studying by extension. They were Shelagh Pollard, Kirsty Thorpe and Jenny Davies. We met monthly for two years and it provided mutual stimulus. We had started meeting the previous summer.

13th

When one dares in the name of the Gospel, the Church encourages. The arrival of the Training in Mission team has lifted the community and congregation. Just being here is a statement of mission. The world has come to Penrhys because of Jesus Christ: England, Guyana, Jamaica, Central African Republic, Madagascar, Hungary, South India, South Korea, Kiribati, Papua New Guinea, Western Samoa and Myanmar. I shall call this place a house of prayer for all nations.

17th

The Infants arrived, eager, expectant, exuberant, polite. The bell was ringing to welcome; we were waiting to greet them and help them with their coats; each child participated in worship and was applauded for their contribution; one little boy celebrated his birthday by lighting and blowing out the candle; another rang the bell 20 times, once for each child; all had squash and biscuits.

The children were treated with dignity and were seen to be important - they responded to this. Will ten years of this help the development of the individual child and the creation of a new generation of young people?

DECEMBER

2nd

Tom Evans brought students from Carmarthen. I took them to school and the clinic. A good lunch before meeting Terry Winters in the estate office. I presented the church's position and we celebrated Communion.
The first visit of the Trinity students. A day's programme was shaped, involving the Llanfair team and the wider community. Naturally a great deal of practical work went on, especially in the provision of meals for the visitors. Tom Evans is Director of Student Services at Trinity. He and his wife Marilyn had been our friends for many years. Terry Winters was Estate Manager employed by RCT.

3rd

Lunch in the café with Phil George and Rowan Williams, Bishop of Monmouth. Rowan was intrigued by the Llanfair story.
Rowan Williams gave a paper (later published) on 'Catholic and Reformed' on the 3rd July 1993 at Gloucester Cathedral. He stated: 'Llanfair Penrhys is a Church which has asked itself very searching and serious questions about what needs to be criticized and worked out in order for the Gospel to be preached. The corporate life and witness of John and Nora and the people who live with them in the little church complex seems to me to be a very remarkable illustration of what it might be to be Catholic and Reformed.' Phil George, a producer and director, is Founder and Creative Director, Green Bay Media.

Sunday 20th

The Nativity Play was miraculous. The chapel was packed with dozens sitting on the floor. Some of the toughest families were introduced to the Gospel story.

24th

Christmas Communion combines popularity and spirituality. Seventy worshippers enjoyed a devout, simple and beautiful atmosphere. The chapel looked its best: candles on the stand, advent candles, the icon lamp and the Christmas tree. It was a festival of light.

1993

JANUARY

13th

Karl Francis and his film crew arrived to work on a series entitled Harvey and the Gimp; they are working on the estate, eating at Llanfair and today they filmed in the chapel. Church people took part in several scenes, especially those related to the Passion Play.

When the series was completed, it was shown as 'Judas and the Gimp.' We had first met Karl during the filming of 'Ms Rhymney Valley' during the Miners' Strike. He is one of Wales' premier film makers. During the work on Penrhys, his religious feelings were re-awakened and he was baptised with others at the Easter Vigil. Of the many acting in the film, Rhys Ifans is probably the most well known. He signed the visitors' book with the word 'Powerhouse!'

18th

Hope Evans left Kingston Jamaica yesterday and arrived in triumph. She heard of Penrhys in the Caribbean and offered to serve here.

The Council for World Mission searched for a musician and Hope came to us after working on Grand Cayman. Llanfair was privileged to share her ability, enthusiasm and stamina because she built up a most successful music programme.

25th

What should have been another creative day was soured by unpleasant, vindictive graffiti on the chapel door: 'Hang the Blacks' greeted Norah and Sharon as they investigated a banging noise. How sickening if Hope had seen this at the end of her first week. This is the work of a very small minority but is a dangerous sign for a young woman who has travelled from home, friends and a lovely climate to bring music and the Gospel to this barren land.

Llanfair never again experienced graffiti of this kind. Our overseas volunteers, simply by their presence, but also because of their friendliness and hard work, were instrumental in breaking down a great deal of racist prejudice.

26th

A most creative day. Llanfair fulfilled its mission by doing nothing spectacular. It was a wonderfully ordinary day.

27th

Wednesday is a heart-day, central to the week. It is an adult day for those seeking more contemplation and a eucharistic and theological search. Morning Holy Communion was quiet and compassionate. Compline reached the depths of history and our inner being. Bible Study enabled Jesus to speak in our context: 'Pick up your bed and walk; those who listen to the voice of Christ will no longer live "half-dead" lives but will begin to live life in all its fullness.'

30th

The last day of Karl Francis' 'Judas and the Gimp.' Many locals worked hard and well, and enjoyed this once in a lifetime experience. Penrhys was the location and Penrhys people served as extras. Llanfair proved a hospitable base. I went to the Ystrad side of the mountain for a final scene which included four large crosses.

Sunday 31st

In the filming of the Penrhys Calvary, Linda and Beryl were asked to 'hang on crosses.' Today, Beryl said that as she looked at Mary Magdalene, she felt she had come home; Linda as her head rested against the wood, experienced 'the completion of my baptism.'

FEBRUARY

15th

Father Deiniol arrived with Bishop Alexander of Riga who was accompanied by a young priest and a translator. We had prayers in the chapel and a talk to 15 people. A very moving story. School assembled for greetings and singing. To our delight the guests took clothes home.
The Orthodox Bishop who described the boutique as 'Aladdin's cave.'

Sunday 28th

The television service celebrated Llanfair's First Anniversary by thanking God for his work from Celtic Saints to Llanfair.
HTV televised a service live from Llanfair. There were not the apprehensions

of June 1989, and the contrast between the location and congregation of 1989 was startling.

MARCH

2nd

Of the 17 letters from people who watched the service, 15 were very positive, including one from an 86 year old lady who has had a stroke and sent £200. One letter accused me of betraying the principles of my father and grandfather. We have had more than 600 visitors since July.

3rd

Llanfair welcomed David Hunt, Secretary of State for Wales. He was brought by Bill Castell. Norah and I took him around the projects; there was a short service in the chapel with the Infants School before he met the Partnership. Finally Bill and I took him to admire the amphitheatre.

David Hunt questioned Norah on the decision not to buy British washing machines. We had spent many tens of thousands of pounds on equipment and furnishings, most of which was British but with exceptions like the washing machines and the excellent and tasteful church, café and dining room furniture which came from Germany. They had offered a very generous discount for churches. Norah and the local volunteers had visited innumerable cafes, launderettes, créches and charity shops to explore lay-outs and furnishings before making decisions. Preparations had been thorough.

10th

In Bible Study, we have explored John's Gospel. This evening three groups worked at the classic themes of the Person and Work of Christ. We enjoy a vigorous, faithful searching of Scripture.

20th

Llanfair has visitors from all over the world. Elenid of Christian Aid brought Daniel from Burkina Faso who is working in community development in the rapidly expanding urban areas. He never imagined Western European poverty until he came to Penrhys. He recognised the same problems in our community as he does at home.

Elenid, a great friend of Llanfair, brought Daniel Thieba from Ougadougou, Burkina Faso. He remains involved in his country's development.

26th

I enjoyed key duty today because I spent an hour outside in the sun. As I cleaned outside doors, I was helped by Liam (aged 3). He repeated every sentence I made; Its cleaner now; its hard work; naughty boys are riding motorbikes on the pavement. He proceeded to tell the naughty boys that they were naughty, and why they were naughty. It was Liam's first lesson to the community.

For me, key duty did not become a regular task, particularly after my attack of Bell's palsy. Key Duty developed into an important service taken in turn by the overseas volunteers. It was an easy and natural way for relationships to develop between them and the local people. Norah fulfilled the task of co-ordinating and supporting activities until we left in 2004. By the time of our retirement the 'Communities First' programme had come into existence. After a careful appraisal it recognised the value of Norah's voluntary work and provided funding for a full time worker.

APRIL

1st

Barbarism and Beethoven. I rejoiced this evening in the 'Agnus Dei' from the Missa Solemnis. It is when we are confronted by unruly behaviour that we also glimpse the wonder of grace. The Passion comes alive on Penrhys. Children can become amoral when they join the mob. They become the crowd on Good Friday. Jesus must have been the Son of God: who else could have lived with such faith?

Palm Sunday 4th

God has been very kind. The live broadcast of 'People on the Way' began at 9.30, halfway down the main path and, led by a French horn we made our pilgrimage with hymns, readings and prayers to the chapel. Hope, Norah and I were interviewed on 'our call to Penrhys;' Bishop Holloway preached.

Richard Holloway was Bishop of Edinburgh and was elected Primus of the Scottish Episcopal Church in 1992. He spoke from Edinburgh.

10th

Fourteen teenagers and adults, including Karl Francis were baptized or confirmed. There was clarity in the eyes of young people and they made their affirmations with dignity.

Easter Sunday 11th

Resurrection began last night as 90 streamed out of Llanfair at 1 in the morning. Fourteen had entered the committed community striving to reflect God's Way. At 8 this morning, 25 brave people left on a wet, cloudy, windy morning for Twyn Disgwylfa. The cross appeared through the mist.

13th

Euros Lyn started a course on video making organized by the University College of Swansea.

Euros Lyn led a Course from the University of Wales, Swansea. Euros has since directed episodes of 'Casualty' and 'Dr Who.' The relationship had been initiated by Hywel Francis, Professor of Adult Education and one of the founders of the University of the Valleys. The film made was 'Rhys ap Tewdwr and the Last Crusade' and was produced by, and 'starred' locals, including our son Dylan, who played the ill-fated Rhys.

15th

Locals are cleaning a public building! Llanfair is 'owned' by the community. Llanfair could have been just another building owned by 'someone or other,' some 'anonymous body' and as such be ignored, neglected, or even worse, abused and attacked. The building is respected and loved.

MAY

21st

A Fun Day. People of Penrhys, supported by four visitors from Myanmar, dressed as nurses and pushing wheel chairs (with patients) descended upon Llwynypia, Tonypandy and Penygraig and raised £326 for Christian Aid. Exuberance and vitality were channelled towards sharing human and natural resources, pulsated by the powerful dynamic of the Gospel. This evening Llanfair was packed with 70 people for a Dutch Auction at which a further £106 was raised. This is a remarkable token of generosity by the poorest in Britain for the poorest in the world. Much of the credit lies with Norah who has placed Christian Aid in the church's liturgical framework.

Four young men visited from the Presbyterian Church of Myanmar (Burma), which is a member church of CWM.

29th

The chapel door was opened wide, the organ played and in walked the proud Lance, his daughter Sharon, followed by the flower girl Camilla, the pageboys Anthony and Duane and six bridesmaids. It was a moment of dignity and beauty. All worked well: the singing of 'One Heart' by the children's choir; lighting candles; the procession leaving to the sound of organ and bell. The crowd from inside the chapel merged with the crowd waiting outside, and there was such communal happiness.

JUNE

14th

We met the BITC delegation of the 'Seeing is Believing programme' led by Bill Castell. They walked through the precinct, worshipped with the Nursery and our Youth choir; Norah and I showed the projects; plenty of questions. They included Robert Ayling (British Airways), Richard Dykes (Post Office), Peter Kellner (Sunday Times), and Julia Cleverdon (BITC).
Robert Ayling later served with the New Millennium Experience Company. Peter Kellner is now a Labour member of the House of Lords. Julia Cleverdon remained Chief Executive of BITC until March 1st 2008. Also present were Dominic Proctor of J Walter Thomson; Chris Hughes of Whitbread and Julian Knott of Electra. Post Office Counters developed a very successful two year mentoring scheme with Llanfair.

15th

Peter Roberts of BITC and Bill Castell emphasized the influence Penrhys had on our visitors. They saw that change is possible when there is leadership and management. This mountain top village exercises a wide ministry.

21st

Penrhys will have its first doctor. After 25 years, the housing estate is having key facilities of a community: surgery and doctor. The interviewing panel met at the Mid Glamorgan FHSA and appointed Chris Shaw. That he wants the Church to be part of a holistic approach is such a bonus. We could now have integration of education, health and Church. Racist graffiti on the Community Centre.
The struggle to have a doctor for Penrhys had been long and hard fought. Before the creation of this local practice, the residents of Penrhys were served by the doctors from the communities in which the residents lived before moving to Penrhys. This meant that no one practice had any sense of responsibility or care for Penrhys. Because of the creation of the Penrhys Partnership and the provision of facilities in the recently opened 'Y Ffynnon' the situation was transformed.

Sunday 27th

Elenid Jones presented Christian Aid certificates. £1026 had been collected. Thank you God.

JULY

13th

Norah and I attended a Garden Party at Buckingham Palace. We entered the Palace by the Grand Entrance, walked through the Reception Rooms to the gardens and joined thousands in the rain. The band struck up and the Queen arrived. We happened to meet Tony and Val Burnham and enjoyed two hours strolling, having tea, walking the lawns, recognizing the famous, looking at fashions.

Val and Tony were long-standing friends. Tony had been a Provincial Moderator and was General Secretary of the United Reformed Church from 1992 to 2001.

16th

Hope is contented. Llanfair's music programme presented an hour and a half of entertainment. The chapel was full, the audience behaved and 35 participated. Each young person introduced their item, was dressed impeccably and the audience responded warmly. An evening of wholesome entertainment created by the people of Llanfair for the people of Penrhys.

21st

Ironic to speak about Penrhys tomorrow and spend the night at the Holiday Inn in Berkeley Street, Mayfair. I am uncomfortable in this world of expensive hotels and first class rail travel. Probably everyone at the seminar at St James' Palace is accustomed to this life style. Their luxurious living would put my day in the shade. How is it possible to bring the world of Penrhys close to the world of these business leaders? A start was made by bringing them to Penrhys. Can our nation become more egalitarian without a revolution?

22nd

I was the main speaker at the 'Seeing is Believing' Seminar at St James Palace. Eighty influential people were present: business leaders, politicians, newspaper editors. I spoke first and was followed by Bill Castell and two men from BP. I was introduced to the Prince of Wales and we walked together down the Grand Staircase to the group photograph. Home by 8.15 to play games in the café.

The two men were John Browne Chief Executive of BP Exploration and John Leggate, Asset Manager. John Browne was appointed Group Chief Executive in 1997 and resigned in 2007. Since 2001 he has been a member of the House of Lords. Leggate is Chief Information Officer for BP.

24th

The struggle to create a sense of community is colossal. Many teenagers are grandchildren of the unemployed and victims of dependency; some live from different facets of criminality. Today I saw young men just out of prison who will soon return to prison; all ages from mid teens to early thirties. Today many of us were with 40 children and teenagers who played in and around the café, made music, played cards and did the sorts of things good ordinary children enjoy. Here on a Saturday night. If we can engage these for five years, there will be the chance of a new community. It is the best opportunity in 25 years.

28th

As a student, my energy was focussed on the sermon, preaching the Word of God. The liturgy was a framework for the sermon. On Penrhys I have prepared 98 different liturgies: the liturgy is the vehicle of God's Word; the sermon is an integral part of the liturgy but the whole service has a shape, rhythm and direction which finds its climax in the liturgy after the liturgy.

AUGUST

2nd

I am sleeping on the floor of an old church school at Cwmdauddwr. I am sharing the room with 6 boys, aged 8 to 17. It is 25 years since Norah and I took young people to Rhossili where Alwyn Charles spoke so effectively. I never thought that a quarter of a century later I should be doing the same work with the same enthusiasm and hope.

14th

Trinity College, Carmarthen is providing an 8 roomed flat on campus, each room with its own toilet/shower; there is a dining room and a lounge.

This gave the opportunity to take the local volunteers on holiday - for some, it was their only holiday of the year. For some it was their first ever holiday.

Sunday 15th
Some beautiful moments: laughing in the kitchen as two women told stories of hiding from debt collectors; standing at the castle at Llanstephan, and above the Boat House at Laugharne. The world is opening up.

16th
We climbed into the mountains of the Upper Tywi valley and were awed by its grandeur and wildness. We returned to the Lyric in Carmarthen for the breathtaking 'West Side Story' which felt uncomfortably close to home in its vitality and cruelty, and delicacy and hope against the odds. Will the cycle of violence be snapped? The group picnicked at the river Tywi at Dinas; then along the spectacular road to Soar y Mynydd which awed in its holiness.
As a family we had first visited Soar y Mynydd and met John Williams, Brynambor, during our camping holiday of 1975. We visited several times over the years with our Carmarthen group. The visit to the Lyric had been arranged by Christine Drake, a Trinity student who had visited Penrhys with Tom Evans and Vaughan Salisbury.

25th
Monteverdi from the Proms: the delicacy and control; beauty and dignity of the performance were matched by the restraint and enthusiasm of the audience: these things reflect civilization. Last night saw demolished houses brutally vandalized at the top of the estate. The housing estate can breed contempt for property and people. Our task is impossible but for the grace and strength of God. The day, like every Wednesday at Llanfair, is encircled by prayer: Communion hallows; Compline reassures.

30th
Caldey gives a sense of well-being; God opened our eyes to see him at work. Amos reached from the Middle East of Jeroboam II to speak on this island to a generous, open, friendly company of people - the majority young people from Penrhys, beginning to discover the Church. At the guesthouse we had the privilege of meeting Br Senan with Fr Joseph. He has to be fed and dressed, but was so pleased to see us.

31st
Two worlds are impinging: Penrhys and Caldey, Rhaeadr, Trinity Carmarthen. All are touching. I noticed Lynsey looking up at the face of Jesus at the Calvary. It was a moment of purity.
Lynsey later passed her A levels and proceeded to University.

SEPTEMBER

1st

Eight Llanfair young people shared the pool with the Castell family. There is no greater contrast of backgrounds than that between the children of Penrhys and the children of this large house near Oxted. Bill and Renice have risked so much inviting our children to their home for the next few days; we take a risk because we cannot be certain all will work well.
Of the many kindnesses of the Castell family, this was surely the least assuming and the greatest.

6th

I am so impressed by the love and method by which the Castells have given time, energy and money in such unstinted fashion. They have provided an exciting introduction to one of the great cities of the world, a beautiful open house and garden, and a very caring family.

18th

For two hours we played and worked with children in the café: outside they enjoyed being noisy, running, chasing; inside were games and I played solitaire with 10 children. So tired when we returned to the flat at 10.15. I listened to the 16 minutes of the Agnus Dei from Missa Solemnis: Donna Nobis Pacem. Peace is always and everywhere the gift of God. Yes we can and will go on whatever comes. The world belongs to God; the earth is the Lord's; Penrhys with all its violence, neglect and selfishness belongs to the Lord.

Sunday 19th

Today, in Llanfair, our people celebrated with our visitors from Manselton: the chapel was full (150); the theme was Amos. The words, music, dancing, costumes and vitality captured the congregation. The festival emerged from the liturgical and study framework of the church, and became an effective instrument of teaching and celebration.
'Amos' was written by Hope Evans. Much of the scenery was created by David Coleman, an internship student from Mansfield College, Oxford. David is now a URC minister. The music and words included rap and involved at least two dozen teenagers. How faithful Manselton had been to Penrhys from the first visit when we were meeting in the little chapel. It is good to know that Christwell when it created its new premises, during the ministry of Kevin Watson, was partly inspired by what was experienced at Llanfair.

22nd

A Compline of strength, beauty and vitality shaped by simplicity and silence. There was a natural rhythm of affirmation and confirmation as one side of the chapel echoed the other. The sound flowed gently to and fro, and the young voices climbed softly into the lanterned roof. Thirty affirmed faith in God with psalm and prayer.

28th

When I offered for ministry, my 'trial services' were held at Ebenezer (demolished), Tabernacle Ferndale (demolished), Trerhondda (vandalized) and Ramah (demolished). Not only buildings but people! As a society we reap because there has been no Gospel-ethic-sowing for 40 years. But a lot else has been sown during those years!
Trerhondda is now a centre for the Arts Factory, a community programme based in Ferndale.

OCTOBER

8th

The General Secretary of the Council of Churches of New South Wales had a remarkable insight into the life of Llanfair: Paul was reading from 'One World' on Equatorial Guinea; Ivor, practising piano was playing the melody from Beethovens 9th; the little choir was singing a modern hymn by DT Niles; the boutique led prayers which included a reading from Wordsworth's Tintern Abbey: all happening at the same time in a church on a high priority housing estate in Rhondda.
The Revd Ray Williamson is a noted Australian ecumenist.

22nd

The Spectacle Theatre Co presented 'The Shakespeare Factory' by Dic Edwards. The chapel was packed (half adults; young people, a few Juniors); the play lasted 1½ hours, with a short interval and there was rapt attention. Llanfair introduced people to Shakespeare. Llanfair has developed a programme of theatre and music and now links it with visiting live drama and music.
'The Spectacle Theatre' was created in 1979 to bring theatre to a wider audience.

NOVEMBER

2nd

I met an eccentric Welsh-American photographer on his way home from China (he said).

Here was a meeting with the foremost Welsh photographer, Philip Jones Griffiths. He had actually visited Penrhys on the previous Good Friday and asked permission to take a photograph of prayers at the Well. He returned to present a copy of the original. His work in Vietnam is a classic of photojournalism. Norah and I were later invited to the Opening of an Exhibition of his work in the National Museum of Wales. On this day, I had no idea who he was nor of his contribution to art and to humanism.

9th

On a wet cloudy November afternoon, I walked 100 yards from the church to enter the waiting room and surgery of the new health practice. I asked the young receptionist (a Penrhys girl) if I could join the practice and was informed that my initial interview would be in two weeks time. 100 have joined the practice in the first two days. Chris Shaw was a happy man when I saw him. I'll see you tomorrow in Compline! What a blessing for Penrhys.

Chris' wife, Adrienne was to be a practice nurse at the surgery.

DECEMBER

6th

Cinderella is a tale of happiness and goodness triumphing over sadness and badness; lovely to see good-natured laughter and participation by the audience who became actors in the pantomime. The narrow restricted hall of the Beulah Assembly Room becomes an extension of the stage. We were all actors and actresses in this pantomime. Thank you Beulah for our fourth annual visit. 110 made the trip and all were so pleased.

11th

I saw violence in broken windows and heavy stones lying on the kitchen floor in Hazel's house. It is her third break-in in 6 weeks. I was going to bed at 11.30 when Hazel phoned. Norah and I rushed down and were joined by the policeman and council workers. A familiar story I fear.

Hazel reluctantly left Penrhys a few months later. She had enjoyed her life on Penrhys and participated fully in the life of Llanfair. She was one of the organisers of the adult evening dances in the café and had become a faithful worshipper.

18th

More gale force winds and driving rain. I walked Tammy and Leanne home from the café at 8.30. As soon as street lights are repaired in their area, they are vandalized. And so we walked in almost total darkness. Many steps are broken, and roads and pavements pitted with large holes. The wind and rain were so fierce that, at one stage, we three had to walk backwards. It would have been a nightmare but for the fact that the girls laughed all the time and enjoyed the challenge. The postman arrived with a Christmas card, handwritten from Charles! It was a lovely sad photograph of him with two young princes.

The girls and I left a very busy café with all activities in full swing. The whole of the Llanfair house was fully engaged in the Friday evenings in Llanfair. It became the place to be on Friday nights for children and teenagers.

Sunday 19th

The Christmas play has been performed/ worshipped. It was our best production, very satisfying because the young people worked well, tried hard and were most conscientious. Between 40 and 50 children and young people took part and more than half are in the Comprehensive School. We are still holding on to this group and we must continue to work hard year after year.

24th

A great celebration of the coming of the Saviour, the Christ, the Lord, coming to shepherds watching flocks in the fields. We greeted the coming of the Day with ringing the bell by one of the youngest, and lighting the candle by one of the oldest, and nature lightly bestowing a delicate gift of gentle falling snow. As we walked out of chapel, we entered a white Christmas. It all seemed like magic. 50 of us together tonight.

1994

JANUARY

8th

I am enjoying reading War and Peace and yet despite its magnificence, it is not the 'Word of God.' What is the difference? It is inspired, reflects experience and wisdom and is deeply religious. The Word centres on Christ, the man of Nazareth who never wrote a book!

11th

The name Llanfair runs off the tongue! Yet it was not an easy decision as Church Meeting discussed several approaches to the choice of a name - English or Welsh? Biblical Nonconformist or Anglican Saint? our locality or theological stance? Llanfair!

13th

This evening was beyond our wildest dreams. A String Quartet from the Welsh National Orchestra played Corelli, Bártok, Haydn, Beethoven, Britten and Mozart to a packed Llanfair. The music, silence and applause were miraculous. Pru, Kay, Dawn and others ecstatically claimed they had never heard such music before, and how they loved it. I had asked Hilary Minto if they would play music to introduce classical music, but when they arrived they told me they could not play lighter music; they were unable to compromise. They wanted Penrhys to hear the real thing. They were right. Ordinary people can discover and enjoy the greatest music of the world. Why should they suffer less?
Norah was largely responsible for encouraging an audience to attend what was a totally new experience. The next ten years saw dozens of such concerts and the constant search for an audience. Hilary Minto was a member of the URC.

Sunday 16th

One of our neighbours was found dead at home. He had a severe stroke in his 20s, and thirty years later lived alone. He came to the café and drew clowns for the children. He was always well-spoken, courteous, did not make much of his disability and got on with life. After worship I was called by the police and went to say prayers.

FEBRUARY

3rd

I felt anger and guilt at being human. We saw a Penrhys resident in East Glamorgan hospital. On Saturday morning he was attacked in his own home by two men with a mandrel shaft and a crow bar. He heard a window smash at 3.15 and listened to the shouts 'We will knock the s- out of you' - they said it about 50 times and, when he tried to get out of the house, they beat him many times, broke his arm and rained blows on his head while he lay on the floor. They left, and minutes later returned as he was phoning the police. 'Next time we'll kill you.' He is 64, a bachelor living alone, having treatment for cancer. Human beings cannot descend lower. Sheltered Housing is an urgent need.

4th

Last night had a profound effect upon Norah and me, and could result in a major change for the community. Older residents are frightened by this apparently unprovoked, indiscriminate attack, and are fearful in their own homes. A protected/ supported/ sheltered housing scheme is necessary. Llanfair should commission the Partnership to supervise the work.

5th

I sat in the café playing whist with Carrie (11) Diane (13) Michelle (11) Leanne (11) and Lisa (11). There were 42 in the café and 60 used it during the two hours it was open. An evening of good humour and excellent behaviour. The volunteers were Pru, Kay and Dawn; the takings £30 and everyone felt it had been worthwhile. Relationships are deepening and extending, and the church's place recognized in the community. The last two years have been hard work, but they are bearing fruit.

All the Llanfair residential team would be present in the evening café. Each would look after a table and converse with and play games with a group of children. We also encouraged parents to come and play and talk with the children.

MARCH

4th

The church is tolerated when it is ineffective. People sympathize with a failing church. When the church is an active, effective instrument for change, it becomes a threat. Some are hostile because Llanfair has suggested that youth work should be focussed in the ailing Community Centre. It could rejuvenate the Centre and help integrate young people and the wider community. Others are determined to focus youth work in the derelict Boiler House on the edge of the estate in the belief that young people wish to be alone. I fear the battle for quality leisure facilities is lost because Penrhys cannot sustain the Boiler House and the Community Centre.

8th

I hardly dare write the words: Chris Shaw has leukaemia. This evening was a frightening shock. Thirty of us met to read and sing the Easter Play. Nicky read 'Believe me, you'll be with me in heaven itself - today. Father, I put my whole life in your hands.' Jonathan responded with 'This man was innocent. He was the Son of God.' Chris and I smiled gratefully to each other. Half an hour later, Adrienne took Norah and me into chapel where we heard the news they had only just received.

21st

Steve Williams' special needs class came to Llanfair: nine 11 year olds. I used the palm cross, taking it apart and asking the children to feel it. They recited poems. We all grasped the glory of human potential when it is touched by concern, patience, skill and grace. Steve, a searching agnostic epitomises these gifts and we all shared them this morning.

23rd

I spent the afternoon with Nan Todd's class of 8 and 9 year olds, exploring the Industrial and Nonconformist periods - Chapel and Pit. We have spent the past month on the Celtic, Medieval and Nonconformist history of Penrhys and it has been a discovery for me, children and teachers. This exploration of roots is a deliberate attempt to look at history from a Penrhys and Christian perspective. When we look at the construction of Penrhys in the 1960s, we might see it in a new light, as part of the continuing history of God's purposes focused on this piece of earth (this corner of the vineyard), and as the church seeks to be faithful to this time (these kairos moments).
This marked the beginning of the development of local historical awareness which was expressed beautifully in the banner made by the knitting group and which hangs permanently in the chapel.

30th

There are no short cuts on the road of mission if we reflect the Gospel value of persons - each individual is of intrinsic worth, needing time and attention.

APRIL

1st, Good Friday

This afternoon's presentation of the Gospel expressed true grit, triumph against the odds, the church having stamina not to give in. Last Monday I thought there was little chance of presenting the play. Our rehearsal had been a disaster and our young people are only learning to play 'adult' roles.

2nd

The Easter Vigil is the greatest act of worship in the Christian Year. It has the ingredients of miracle: darkness to light, death to life; lighting candles and ringing the Easter bell; the powerful re-telling of the Good Friday and Easter Morning story; the dedicated lives of young people seeking a better way; sharing the body and blood of our Saviour, followed by blessing the newly baptized, all of us as members of the Body of Christ and above all, almighty God. Gareth, Lisa, Lynsey, Michelle and Carrie were baptized/ confirmed. God continues to work miracles.

3rd Easter Sunday

As the church presented the Easter Play, it told the story for the world; it makes sense of history. The boys left with the Cross at 7; thirty of us left at 8 to walk through snow to Twyn Disgwylfa. A mild quiet morning with birds singing. We worshipped on the top, at the edge of the estate and in the courtyard.

21st

We appointed two Education Workers to create links between Penrhys and the Comprehensive School at Maerdy, and provide support and guidance for young people moving between the Schools.

The appointment of Cas Smith and Paul Sass marked a break-through in the educational work. Cas developed the art and craft, and soon children and young people were producing work of high quality. Paul concentrated on the humanities and helped lift the academic aspirations of the High School young people. Both were of course fully committed to the whole of Llanfair's life in its daily, weekly and yearly cycles. We were fortunate to have three year funding from the Tudor Trust for the programme. There is no doubt that the emergence of Canolfan Rhys and the educational programmes of the Partnership were built on the foundation of Llanfair's work.

22nd

There is a madness about humanity. This evening I played cards with one of the boys; at closing time his brother was violent and I spoke to him reasonably. Minutes later, a large stone was thrown through the study window. The police were informed; the culprit was not one of the brothers but had been encouraged by the violent one. I went to the father of the brothers who disclaimed any responsibility for his sons; the stone thrower was stupid to listen. Why spend time with the three boys? I know why, but it is hard at times.

In later years we took the stone-thrower on holiday to Rhyd Ddu when he climbed Snowdon, Caldey and to the home of Bill and Renice Castell.

23rd

A sign of hope after last night's stupidity. An 11 year old, expelled from school, saved a penalty while playing for Llanfair against Caersalem Welsh Baptist Chapel at the Morriston Leisure Centre.

27th

Norah arranged for the distribution of the Trevor Huddleston 'Prayer for Africa.' Are we the only community in Europe where every public building has a copy of the prayer in its window?

MAY

7th

It would be good to have two lives: one to pursue the academic, enjoy reading and have time to write. The other life would be to work and live in tough, uncompromising places, and help the underprivileged discover potential. But the worlds belong together and if there is anything to share about God and people, it must be a result of the daily pressure to strive for a new world. What is important is not what we write: it is what we do. We must not turn flesh into words.

JUNE

3rd

Mónika Dávid will be our Hungarian student next year.

Mónika came to visit Péter, our Hungarian volunteer and asked if she could join us for six months, beginning in September. She did and during the period met our son Dylan. Later they married and we have three Welsh Hungarian grandsons.

16th

Prince Charles was interviewed on HTV and stated his pleasure with the positive developments on Penrhys. The heir to the throne was talking about this small marginalized estate!

17th

Prince Charles was interviewed on BBC and made similar remarks about Penrhys.

20th

A member of the church at Gwaelod y Garth organized our first 'Live Music Now' concert. It was given by the Trio Sirocco - three young musicians: Jonathan (flute), Craig (guitar) and Peryn (clarinet) playing Bach, Stravinsky, Gershwin. They had expertise and fun and our audience responded well. Could we create a small, consistent audience and sustain 3 or 4 concerts, theatrical productions and an art exhibition each year?

Gillian Green is the Wales Director of 'Live Music Now,' the movement founded by Yehudi Menuhin to bring music into the community. Llanfair enjoyed many such concerts during the coming years. Gillian had made the suggestion to Norah during a visit she made to the Congregational Chapel at Gwaelod y Garth where Gillian is a member. Norah had been invited by the minister, Dr T J Davies to speak on the work of Llanfair. Jonathan Rimmer, Peryn Clement Evans and Craig Ogden are members of the Ensemble Cymru, based at Bangor.

24th

The Second Annual Concert of the 'Music Department' as Hope calls it. 30 children, young people and adults sang, played guitar, drums, recorders, clarinet, keyboards. Most have improved considerably since last year. The chapel was packed with families and friends.

29th

I was interviewed for Radio 4's Good Morning. I had been invited to talk about the Prince's concern for Penrhys, but virtually with her final question of a half hour recorded interview, Sarah Cullen raised the breakdown of his marriage. I was not happy.

30th

I was up at 7 to listen to the interview with Sarah Cullen. It was innocuous but concentrated on the breakdown of the marriage. It was repeated on Radio Wales. One of our colleagues believes we do not challenge for personal salvation and would like our young people to go to 'March for Jesus.'
Llanfair experienced a constant pressure to be more direct in its evangelism. However our ethos was centred on a long-term being alongside the community and reflecting, by the quality of our relationships and service, that there was a faith content. No-one using Llanfair had any doubt that we served in the name of the Church and many were attracted to the life of the Church.

JULY

Sunday 3rd

The Prince of Wales arriving by helicopter at Powis Castle, walked into the garden. Hope was one of four people to be introduced, and she had a couple of children with her. The Prince came to chat with the Llanfair children. They sang for fifteen minutes and sang better than I have ever heard them. Charles was close at hand and they had a good response.
Hope and the Llanfair Choir had been invited to sing before the Prince at the Garden Party in Powis Castle.

4th

A joy to read in the Western Mail that the highlight of yesterday's Garden Party at Powis Castle was the youth choir from Penrhys, conducted by Hope Evans who had come from Jamaica to help develop music. As a guest from Treorci said to one of our children yesterday, 'Are you from Penrhys in the Rhondda?' It was too much to believe after our 25 year history of failure.

5th

Last Wednesday, members of a Pentecostalist church looked around Llanfair; last Saturday they leafleted the village centre; on Thursday I had been urged to adopt a more aggressive approach towards personal commitment; on Saturday, at Welshpool, Hope and I were attacked for not doing 'real Christian work for children.'

AUGUST

1st

24 went on holiday to Aberpedwar. Some had never been on holiday; some were experienced Llanfair travellers. We must develop a world in which it is more fun to belong to the church than to the anarchic, tragic, short-lived world of drugs, alcohol and car thefts. Are we creating a counter-culture?
Aberpedwar was a school converted into a small residential centre not far from Trecastle.

8th

This evening's 'house' meeting had a good easy atmosphere, humour, recognition of different functions, a sense of team and family. We are beginning a fourth year of colleagueship with Norah, Sharon and I providing the base. Each year we are joined by two or three others and on the whole, we work effectively and consistently. We have a system for managing the building, the team works well with other volunteers and the public and we share a common purpose.

12th

The story of Llanfair is remarkable. Because I am so close to its life, I forget its significance until I share it with someone who has experienced similar projects and is also a sympathetic listener. Such a listener was Matthew Butler, assistant chief advisor to the Prince of Wales. He arrived promptly at 10, intended leaving at 12 but stopped until 2, having lunch in the café. He was shocked by the enormity of Penrhys problems, but moved and humbled by the laying of foundations.

29th

We have been accompanied and comforted by the Suffering Servant, and although we have recognized him in the unknown prophet, in the people of Israel, Nelson Mandela, Gandhi and Martin Luther King, it is Jesus who has been the key to us.
A visit to Caldey.

SEPTEMBER

21st

Another crisis: in its 26 years Penrhys has faced many difficult issues but this is possibly irrevocable. It is not a crisis of housing, criminality, unemployment, poor health, or education, although all are serious issues on this estate. The crisis is caused by external factors: there is excess housing in the valleys, some privately rented and others through housing associations. Five people have come this week for references to leave Penrhys. There are 120 empty properties.

30th

Strangers to Penrhys were standing on the main path and in the village centre, handing out leaflets and inviting Penrhys to experience miracles this afternoon in the Community Centre. They cannot see that having a Village Centre with the facilities of Y Ffynnon and Llanfair is a miracle created by those who seek to be faithful to God every day.

OCTOBER

6th

Nurture and worship must be modelled on mission. How is the Gospel communicated in a community with no background of faith? Central to our strategy is the three fold programme we embraced six years ago: (a) build up a team of committed, concerned, skilled, residential people who would work with the community of Penrhys; (b) meet the needs of the community; (c) provide a place of peace.

8th

What was it like for medieval pilgrims making their way to the Shrine and Well at Penrhys? Sixteen of us walked from the bridge on the Tâf north of Pontypridd, crossed the mountains past the monastic grange at Mynachlog, Llanwynno and crossed Cefn Gwyngul to the spot where you could look down on the two Rhondda valleys. The statue of Mary was clearly visible on the saddle with the housing estate stretching to the north. We were pilgrims ready for the steep descent into the Rhondda, to cross the Afon Rhondda Fach at Pontygwaith and climb the steep hill. We washed in the well, had tea at Llanfair and worshipped. The walk had been organized by a group interested in Celtic/ Orthodox links, led by Maddy Gray and Anthony Packer. They had walked two other stages from Llantarnam.

Dr Madeleine Gray was developing her research into what was to become The Cistercian Way. Anthony Packer lectured at the School of Education at Cardiff University.

14th

God is always good. Year after year we are reminded of his goodness by the arrival of the young people of the Training in Mission programme. Late this evening saw a wonderful example of God's graciousness. Thirty years ago I went to a Ceilidh in Ballinskelligs and just before it finished in the early hours of the morning, a priest arrived and everyone went on their knees to say prayers before leaving into the night. Here in the café after a riotous evening of great fun which had concluded with a disco, I asked everyone to get on their knees and say the Lords Prayer in their own language. 40 people, everyone in the room, did so and it was like Pentecost.

21st

On Tuesday a new altar was dedicated at St David's Church on Caldey. It was a gift from the Prinknash community celebrating their centenary, a period of which had been spent on Caldey. This evening we worshipped and celebrated communion at the same altar. When the Prinknash monks were here, a bell hung at St David's and today it hangs and rings on Penrhys. The Gospel creates a world of providences which stretch into eternity.
This Roman Catholic Benedictine community began life in the Church of England when their founder, Abbot Aelred Carlyle set up a small community in the Isle of Dogs, London, a place now covered by Canary Wharf. After many wanderings, that community eventually settled permanently on Caldey Island and became Roman Catholic in 1913. Financial pressure forced them to leave Caldey and come to Prinknash Park in December 1928, where they have been ever since.

NOVEMBER

2nd

I read the second half of John's Gospel as if I had never read it before. Last night at an excellent confirmation group, we explored examples of religious experience. In comparison with the Hindu, Muslim and Isaiah Visions, John's account of Jesus was miraculous in its naturalness. This is how the mysterious God shares life with humankind; love and power are expressed in the words, deeds, death and resurrection of Jesus. God's revelation reached this culmination in First Century Palestine, and reaches through space and time into our lives today.

The weekly 'confirmation class' was for young people. They were discussion groups held almost every week of the year. The term confirmation class stuck in the terminology of the young people throughout our period. If young people wished to enter the church, they did so during the Easter Vigil, but in fact the discussions were eventually organised into three or four groups meeting each week for many years. They varied considerably in personnel and the content of the material, but they proved a foundation to youth work throughout the years.

7th

This morning I felt something was wrong with my mouth. I have Bell's Palsy and probably it will last 6 weeks. It is a blow but at least it isn't a stroke. I cannot read because I cannot blink with my right eye. The twist in my mouth makes eating a bit of a problem. Writing is not easy.

In fact I never fully recovered from this attack, and had it not been for therapy arranged through a member of Wilmslow URC, there would have been no improvement. I had a second attack in 2006 (on the other side of the face) but because of receiving steroids within a few hours, the recovery was complete.

15th

Norah and I received letters from the Prime Minister stating we are recommended for OBEs in the New Years Honours Lists. This is confidential until December 31st but we told Cath, Hugh and Dylan: a delight to witness their joy.

We received the OBEs on behalf of our work in the community of Penrhys. Both of us saw these honours as a tribute to the work of Llanfair. The work of churches within community does not receive enough recognition.

21st

Another wonderful 'Live Music Now' concert. A percussionist, Simone Rebello and pianist, Stewart Death performed with skill and enthusiasm, and the response of the 60 people (half adults) was spontaneous delight.

Simone graduated from the Royal Northern College of Music with Distinction and a collection of awards including a major scholarship and The Phillip Jones Prize. She began a solo career which has taken her around the world with concerto appearances, solo recitals, master classes and appearances on national and international TV and radio.

DECEMBER

8th

I completed the Cambridge Annotated Bible (the New Revised Standard Version.) I started 3 months ago, but because of the debilitating illness of the last 5 weeks I have had time to read in sustained fashion. It has been memorable, particularly as earlier this year I had spent 8 months reading the Authorized Version. Reading through the Bible twice in a short period of time has brought me very close to Scriptures. The careful, scholarly reading of the Bible brings the truth of God. Reading the Gospel comes as a wonderful revelation after the long hard road of the Old Testament.

17th

The last six weeks of illness have passed like a dream. The church prepares to celebrate the incarnation and everything progresses smoothly. My contribution was to lay foundations: writing the liturgy and the Christmas Play, and organizing the shape of the final weeks. These emerged during the last five years and now proceed with only a very gentle hand on the tiller.

Sunday 18th

The Christmas Play opens 'the story' to a wider audience. Today it was done with flair and dignity. It was the best performed of all our Christmas plays. Our young people and children proved faithful and enthusiastic and the Llanfair leaders have considerable talent.

24th

Midnight Christmas Communion is a highlight. The liturgy was identical last year, but it was new, refreshing and a climax to this month of Advent waiting. Will the Saviour come? What kind of person will he be? Where will he be born? He came as a baby born in a stable, laid in a manger and surrounded by a host of angels. As I grow older, I am not growing further from 'trailing clouds of glory' but am growing nearer to that heavenly host which praises God and announces peace to God's people. Fifty people met in Llanfair and 6 young people (Suzanne, Diane, Hayley, Donna, Lynsey, Natalie) served bread and wine; Norah, Cath, Donna and Erika read. We are surrounded by a cloud of witnesses.

31st

The year has closed dramatically because it was announced that Norah and I are to receive the OBE in the New Year's Honours list. We hadn't anticipated the response in the media and with our friends and colleagues.

1995

JANUARY

18th

Chris Shaw's coming to Penrhys was a new beginning. Penrhys had a doctor for the community, someone with skill, dedication, personality, compassion and Christian commitment. The surgery, staff and first patients, followed by the pharmacy were tangible signs that there would be a coherent programme of medical care. In March came the terrible blow of Chris' illness and although his struggle was courageous and filled with Christian hope, I was filled with foreboding. I regret (?) that my conviction is not in a God who intervenes to upset the natural order to bring about miracles. We see God at work in the 'ordinary' world. The miracle is that God has come in Jesus, crucified and risen. We must hold on to him.
Chris Shaw died on the 17th of January.

31st

Terry Winters, the Estate Coordinator shared his concerns. When we arrived on Penrhys, there were 951 dwellings and a population of 3½ thousand. The unemployment level was 90% and there were frightening problems of poor housing, crime, violence, drugs and no choice of shops. There have been dramatic changes: the quality of housing stock has improved dramatically; there is a good infra-structure; Llanfair and Y Ffynnon are establishing themselves. However Rhondda's population is decreasing rapidly, there is a marked increase in housing stock in the Valleys and many Penrhys residents are opting to live in rented accommodation on the valley bottom. Penrhys has seen rapid decline: 176 dwellings have been demolished, there are 120 empty proprieties and a further 50 giro-drops. Terry estimates the population to be less than 1500. We need a strategy which responds to this new situation.

FEBRUARY

2nd

I stood on the staircase of the Rhondda Borough Council Offices at Pentre and received the Borough shield from Brian Rowland, Mayor of Rhondda. Our two little choirs had sung well (20 children and young people; 20 women) from the staircase to the Mayor and his guests who sat on the balcony. Our people were so excited: Stacey aged 9, asked 'Am I dreaming? It's like "Beauty and the Beast"' as she gazed at the glittering chandelier and the sweeping staircase.

The children's choir had continued from the days of Hope Evans, but the Women's Choir had been formed by our new resident musician, Sian Pearce who had begun her work in the autumn of 1994. Sian became the first female Musical Director of the Morriston Orpheus Choir from 2004 to 2007. She then helped form the Morriston Phoenix Choir and became its Musical Director.

11th

'Schindler's List' has made my heart full but my mind blank. Its enormity is too much to take in; a film like this must be made every decade. It must influence a whole generation, in case we forget, and also rein in our latest barbarism. The film also expressed the possibility of redemption of a hardened, corrupt materialist like Schindler. There is wickedness in us all - and there is virtue.

Sunday 12th

Kelly and Luke (both aged 4) blew out the candle and gazed into each other's eyes for an eternity. Both are involved in the church's ministry and mission.

13th

At the Whitbread headquarters in London, twenty businessmen discussed how their companies should be involved in community development. Chaired by Bill Castell, they included Richard Dykes, Robert Ayling and Dominic Proctor, all having visited Penrhys two years ago. That visit marked the beginning of their community involvement.

Dominic Proctor was chief executive of J Walter Thompson. In September 1997, he launched MindShare Worldwide, the first media investment management agency.

15th

Alwyn, Bishop of St Asaph, Archbishop of Wales spent 4½ hours with us. He caught the vision of Llanfair. If we ever wanted confirmation of our life, here it was.

The Archbishop signed the visitors' book with 'A very thrilling experience, with gratitude.'

Sunday 19th

A church member has been burgled a second time; another one earlier this week; a Penrhys resident talked about her son in prison and dreads his release in two weeks. What did my sermon on 'ascension' have to do with these issues? By the close of worship I was aware that God is stamped in the image of the crucified and risen Christ, and that God is with us and in us at all times and in every situation.

20th

I enjoy visiting people in their homes, the place where the person is confident because she is on home ground and can set the agenda. I visited two families and we had time to talk gently. These are the normal, decent, ordinary people of Penrhys; people who rarely come to the surface but are the basis of community life. They have lived on Penrhys since it was built.

21st

The key to long-term ministry is visiting. I went to the north-east edge of the estate, met two families whose houses are to be demolished and are moving from Penrhys. We have worked with their children for years and will be sad to see them leave. What kind of place will Penrhys be in five years?

23rd

For our first 3 years we lived as residents. I commuted to work, knew my neighbours, but my impressions were often immediate, volatile and had stark contrasts. During the two years of ministry in the old chapel, we made many new contacts but it is as a result of the past three years at Llanfair that the church has touched so many in the community: all children under 11, the schools, our daily programmes.

This was of course not true for Norah because during those first three years, Norah's life was confined to and committed to the community. A foundation of relationships was being established.

MARCH

14th

This is old fashioned pastoral ministry with a radical difference. I am minister to the community and can visit indiscriminately. Because Llanfair and Y Ffynnon serve the whole of Penrhys; because Norah and I have lived here eight years; because we have never indulged in evangelical campaigns; because we understand the community and are accepted as long term residents; because our theology is one of acceptance and service, I find respect and affection for what the church is doing. It is a great miracle of grace and has happened imperceptibly and gradually.

21st

Our family entered Buckingham Palace. Norah and I went to the gallery to be briefed and were taken to the Music Room. Norah and I walked in together to be welcomed and invested by the Prince of Wales. 'It's excellent you have been honoured together. John, thank you for your letter; how is the work progressing? Bill Castell keeps prompting me about Penrhys; I really must visit again.' Musicians played from the gallery. After leaving the Palace, we were greeted at the House of Lords by Lords Hooson and Tonypandy. A splendid occasion as the 10 of us sat at the round table. Lots of humorous anecdotes from Lord Tonypandy who is now 86 and so proud of Rhondda.
Apparently this was the first double-act of a husband and wife. We were referred to as 'Torvill and Dean.' Emlyn Hooson had invited our family to lunch and asked George Thomas to join us. George Thomas admitted that one of the greatest mistakes of his life was to bend to pressure and agree to the creation of Penrhys in the 1960s. He was now delighted by the signs of development.

24th

A service of thanksgiving for a young man, aged 26 and a good friend. It was a service of compassion and strength; personal and communal. Because the chapel is small and people were standing round the walls, everyone seemed to be sustaining each other. The service spoke poignantly but with reassurance through singing the Nunc Dimittis, reading the affirmation of hope, prayers together and the reading of a poem by his closest friends. Everything was dignified and reflected Penrhys at its best.
Penrhys was sadly familiar to tragedy, but at last there was the opportunity for an assertion of the significance of all human life, especially in the light of the

Christian Gospel. There was also the gentle opportunity for the congregation to reflect on the value of their own lives, and the care in which we need to live our daily lives. During the following years there were a series of tragedies, mostly completely unconnected. As the years passed, they thankfully became less and less.

APRIL

3rd

I am able to visit a complete community. Is this possible anywhere else in Wales? It can only happen if there is a defined community, if there is one church at work there and if that work is accepted. I enter most homes and work with the institutions on the estate - the Buffs Club, Pub, Tenants, Schools, Social Workers.
The Buffs = The Royal Antediluvian Order of Buffaloes.

13th

Thirty people gathered in the upper room. As the bread dipped in wine was passed from hand to hand, we knew we had been accepted by the Son of God at infinite cost. It was a core moment, rare in most people's lives, but which arise regularly in Llanfair. A people estranged from roots are in fact close to the presence of God. Is it because this people gladly welcomes the grace which accepts?

14th, Good Friday

150 people met at Llanfair, and more than 110 of them live on Penrhys. The remembrance was disciplined and joyous, and the majority understood this day. How different from the reception of our first Christmas Nativity. Llanfair is coming of age.

15th

The young woman's face shone as she professed faith and determination to be faithful in public and private worship. There was a transparent illumination of God's generosity - she was a living icon.

19th

Caldey creates diamonds from raw material, however rough-hewn. Three years ago the story of Rena making an impromptu collection at a rock concert in the amphitheatre, went around the world in TIM reports. As we were

reading Paul 'I am what I am,' Rena reminded us that those words paralleled God's words at Sinai. It was a moment of illumination.
During the opening of the amphitheatre, Rena had organized a collection for 'our church.' Some of the YIM participants had been very suspicious when they witnessed this unofficial collection. Later they realized that we all need at times to be far more trusting.

26th
We have had more visitors this week than we had in 7 years in Llanidloes, Manselton or the Synod office, and Penrhys never had any until we cultivated them. Receiving guests is a most important ministry. A delight to share bread, wine and stories of our pilgrimage with Gwen Cashmore and Joan Puls. They knew what we were about, were enthralled by the liturgy and stated its importance in a world setting. It was a great lift to the spirit.
Gwen Cashmore and John Puls wrote many books on spirituality and ecumenism: 'Every bush is burning: a spirituality for our times.' (1985). 'Seek treasures in small fields: everyday holiness.' (1993); 'Clearing the way: en route to an ecumenical spirituality.' (1990)

MAY

1st
Downstairs to wait the Nursery. The alarm was raised. They have reached the Community Centre but Miss Williams has stopped to talk; the bell rings, children arrive, coming down the path and enter the narthex; they are helped to take off their coats; the bell stops and they quietly enter the chapel; the talk is on 'thank you' and the children talk well. Kelly lights the candle; prayers are offered to God who gives us sausages, beef burgers, chips; the children sing two songs; Luke blows out the candle. Squash and biscuits and the last thank you before they put on coats and return to school.

Sunday 14th
Christian Aid Sunday expresses our commitment to justice. We were joined by Michael Taylor who introduced us to great themes, touching us deeply by stories from his experience. John and Ann Nockels joined us. John came for the YIM work camp of 1992 when he found the experience life-transforming.
Michael Taylor, Director of Christian Aid, spoke most appropriately to the children about the monster of world debt. He was very moved by the children's response and naturalness.

25th

It is miraculous to look through the window and see, in the light of our street lamp, rain on the leaves of the tree. Surely that is ordinary and natural? We have had a tree for months and it hasn't been destroyed; we have a lamp and it hasn't been smashed. In our first three months we lost our six trees and our three external lamps were all smashed.

27th

The third and last day of the pilgrimage from Llantarnam to Llanfair Penrhys. 40 people began the walk on Thursday and it ended with 60 making the final stage; at the Shrine we were joined by 30 from the 'Faith and Light' group from Swansea. Led in prayer by Fr Liam of St Cuthbert's Butetown, we started the track up the incline, made our way to Ynysybwl, and across moorland and forest to arrive at Llanwynno at 12.30. Lunch in the graveyard, tea provided by parishioners and prayers by Paul Bennet, vicar of the parish. We retraced our steps before making our way west through the forest to arrive at the old parish road with its stupendous view of Rhondda; Penrhys and the shrine standing out strongly. We walked to the Bridgend Inn and up the hundreds of steps to the shrine where Luke (Greek Orthodox) led us in prayers, and Faith and Light in songs. At Llanfair our liturgy led us with readings and prayers by the congregation. We were presented with an icon of Rublev's Trinity by Luke. Tea throughout the building before they left at 7. Is this the first pilgrimage of many?

The first full pilgrimage from Llantarnam to Penrhys. Led by Maddy Gray, it included Father Luke of the Orthodox Church at Llanelli. We were regularly welcomed by the generous congregation at Llanwynno, which included Father Paul Bennet who tragically died at St Fagan's Church in Trecynon in 2007. The pilgrimage continued every year we were at Llanfair.

JUNE

3rd

The Angelus was ringing midday as I walked into the house. The son had been killed in a motorbike accident on Thursday. The father sat by the French windows, waiting for his son to return. They are a nice family devastated by horrific tragedy. They showed photographs of him with his little daughter - she looks so like him, and he looked so much like his mother. He had been out of the house only an hour when they heard the news of his accident, but it wasn't until they were shown into the side-room at the Casualty Department of Church Village that it dawned upon them that he was dead. What can be said about a further tragedy for this small community? They live on the edge of the estate and I had to walk through the total dereliction of many blocks around the Nursery School. When is this senseless vandalism to end?

Sunday 4th

Jesus appeared to the disciples meeting behind locked doors, for fear of the Jews. When we began to design this church/ community building, our proposal was that the chapel would be on the first floor because we never anticipated a congregation larger than 30, and because it would be far from the harassment the congregation had endured in the Community Centre. Today on Pentecost, Erika read this passage and Paul opened the large chapel door. It remained open for the service. Some walked in to worship; others showed interest as they passed; and there was not the slightest antagonism or abuse. Never take miracles for granted.

Erika Cerna was a volunteer from the Theological University at Debrecen, Eastern Hungary. She is now a minister of the Reformed Church. Paul Sass was our Education Worker and also played piano in worship.

8th

The bereaved father helped me as he talked about his and his son's respect and love of nature. This proved the key to our service today: it was a worship of God the creative spirit, God's sharing of creativity and care of the universe with humankind. The flight of the owl and the cry of the vixen were the signs of care for God's world. But despite the hope of the Gospel, there is no escape from the brutality of a young life ended, and of parents who have lost their only son. The service progressed with dignity and tenderness; the burial was poignant, and the gathering for hospitality in the dining room therapeutic.

15th

We welcomed the Chapter of St Woolos Cathedral at Newport for their Quiet Day. St Woolos comes to Penrhys for inspiration! This evening we received a Brass Quartet from the BBC National Orchestra of Wales: 60 for a delightful evening. Llanfair is a place of high class performance.

23rd

Prayers were led by the Creche. It was marvellous because Erica had invited the babies and their parents. We were also joined by six young women studying for their Masters degrees in Nursing at Swansea.

A journalist joined us for prayers and chatted with us during part of the morning. None of us knew it was Nick Danziger researching for his book 'Danziger's Britain.' 'A Journey to the Edge.' It includes a chapter on Penrhys and some of his photographs of Penrhys in that book are included in his later 'The British.'

29th

£1300 has been collected for Christian Aid: a small congregation on a housing estate.

JULY

20th

The weather remains heavy and close. It is 11.30 but I cannot open the window because of hard, loud music which has been played non stop all evening. It is coming from the garage under a flat and young men have been there all evening. Impossible to protest. Powerful influences are dragging young people downwards into lives of monotony and emptiness. They experience immediate gratification and are, or choose to be, unaware of the consequences. Llanfair is a fragile plant in face of this exotic flourishing.

27th

Last night the music stopped at 12.15 - it had started soon after 6; it has been like this for weeks. With the sound of music come loud voices hour after hour. Tonight it nearly erupted into violence because a large number of young boys (13+) had drunk too much and were ready to fight the world. What will happen during the summer if the weather remains hot and humid? The struggle for the soul of our young people is hard fought. We take 18 teenagers to Snowdonia on Monday and this evening I have been visiting parents who have no money for the £10 we charge for a 5 day holiday. At times I feel our marginalized society is on the edge of disintegration. The hot weather drives what is happening indoors outdoors. We can hear it, see it, touch it, feel it: it permeates the fabric of all that exists. Anything could happen on a night like this.

28th

The hot weather, open windows and loud banal music and raucous, uncouth and aggressive language continues night after night. There is a fatal combination of cheap alcohol, the availability of any kind of drug, hot nights and young people with nothing to do. They can sleep as long as they like during the day, and during the evenings out they come. Here we are again at 12.30. What is so distressing is to see young men who were hanging on to the life of the church descend within weeks into this life-style. We feel impotent and deeply disappointed after years of hard work with them. The pattern of Penrhys, and many places like it, is deeply set. The vandalism at the top of the estate is a frightening consequence of society which does not know how to deal with the range of problems in places like Penrhys: we destroy our own community and environment and no-one will pick up the pieces. Llanfair held its weekly disco at 9. A full, pleasant evening. What a struggle it all is. We have to keep our nerve, persevere and not give up hope.

29th

The choir of the Orthodox Seminary of Baie Mare in Northern Transylvania sang Vespers in the courtyard of Llanfair. Lining the railings were dozens and dozens of Penrhys people: old, teenagers, children. When they had concluded, our choir sang three numbers, followed by more Romanian singing. It was worship in the midst, in the midst of a typical Saturday evening café. Resting on the ledge were Rublev's Trinity and an Orthodox Cross, incense hallowed the atmosphere and strong music filled the air and carried its prayer throughout the estate. Our visitors had been introduced for the first time to the depths of Western poverty and the generosity and openness of Llanfair's gracious hospitality. They were shocked at the gaunt, skeleton-like faces of some teenage boys - as if they lived in a concentration camp, stated the bus driver.

31st

I wonder what TH Parry-Williams makes of it all. Twenty young people from Penrhys are spending a week in Ty'r Ysgol, Rhyd-ddu.
Sir Thomas Herbert Parry-Williams 1887-1975 was a Welsh poet, author and academic. He was born at Ty'r Ysgol, Rhyd Ddu. He was the first to win the double of Chair and Crown at the National Eisteddfod.

AUGUST

1st

I share a room with Lee, Barry John and Michael. There are ghosts in Ty'r Ysgol - the ghost of T H Parry Williams who died in the shower room and his body lies in the Museum. Paul shares a room with Geraint, Nathan and

Matthew (16-17 year olds). They were even more frightened. They heard me listening to Radio 4 News this morning and were convinced it was a ghost. However they are equally fearful of eating sandwiches! We all ate well at breakfast except one of the girls who cannot eat crusts, and I suppose never will. Drove to Black Rock Sands where the sea was clean. Some of our young people had never been in the sea because they say it is so dirty.
The girls were in the large dorm in the school building.

2nd

The young people of Llanfair achieved the impossible. 15 young people and 5 adults climbed to the top of Snowdon. Jubilation when we eventually reached the top, especially for Nathan. To him it was a monumental achievement. We all had drinks in the wonderful café where everything tastes marvellous.

7th

Matthew Butler (one of Charles' advisors) called. He has read my book and said Charles has it on his book-shelves (he usually returns books to Matthew).

19th

We worshipped at the Presbyterian chapel in Brynsiencin, Sir Fôn; in Sir Gaernarfon at the Annibynwyr chapel at Drws y Coed; and in Meirionydd at the Orthodox chapel at Manod. We joined the Cistercians on Caldey in Sir Benfro, and this week we are in Sir Gaerfyrddin and Ceredigion where we visited Ystrad Fflur with its Cistercian and literary tradition; Llanddewibrefi with its roots in the Celtic church, and Elfed Lewis at Cynwil Elfet. This morning, on this VJ weekend, I led worship for Peace and Justice in Trinity Carmarthen where 55 years ago, Uncle Noel left his studies and joined the army to defend his nation. He found himself in the Fall of Singapore and a prisoner of the Japanese for 3½ years.
VJ = Victory over Japan day from the Second World War.

SEPTEMBER

2nd

Several years ago a large number of Penrhys people saw an amateur production of 'Oliver' at Beulah Rhiwbina. I remember feeling uncomfortable because of its parallels with our community. It was even more explicit tonight at a wonderful performance at 'The Palladium.' Lionel Bart and Charles

Dickens put their finger on social issues. Is the remnant of the Victorian urban underclass still alive and well?
One of the many entertainments arranged for the group during their stay with the Castells.

8th

A young Oxford geography student came to ask questions about urban planning. Penrhys has been subject to two major planning blunders: (1) the creation of the estate in the 1960s. This has been articulated many times - the wrong place, the wrong style; (2) the refurbishment in the late 1980s: (a) Rhondda's declining and increasing number of available houses makes it inevitable that people living on peripheral estates will exercise their choice and move away; (b) by refurbishing in three stages, followed by landscaping means the estate is always a building site. This continues now that houses are being demolished. The bold decision would have been to concentrate on an estate of 300 houses. What is the future? Community buildings must have a life for a small estate and reach a wider public. Llanfair is a model for this.

9th

Why are we particularly aware of drug taking ? Is it because we have lived here long enough to know who deals and who takes drugs? Is it because as the population decreases, the proportion of drug-users increases? Is it that the arrival of the surgery and pharmacy has made the users more noticeable? Is it that the drug culture is growing in extent and deepening its hold? Is it because there does not seem to be law-enforcement and therefore dealers and users become more blatant? It is the way of life. Alongside the taking of drugs are break-ins and car thefts (by boys), shop lifting (by girls); fences receiving stolen goods; purchasers of bargains; those who know what is going on but do nothing about it because someone in their family, or friends, or neighbours or someone whom they fear, is involved. So much of the estate is enmeshed in the web of the drug culture and industry. Will it ever stop? This is the world to which we woke this morning and went to bed this evening!
The majority of Penrhys people were equally concerned and deeply affected by these issues. We all felt a sense of helplessness.

13th

Menja arrived at Heathrow: We looked expectantly at every passenger as they turned the corner and walked along the passageway into the concourse. We expected to see him pushing a trolley. I felt shamed when I saw a young man

smiling and carrying a small suitcase, a briefcase and a small bag in which was a lampshade. He was wearing a suit, a shirt and tie. He was coming from his island for the first time. We felt privileged to be receiving this brother in Christ.
Menja was the first volunteer to serve us from the Church of Jesus Christ in Madagascar, a member of the Council for World Mission. The relationship was particularly important because the founders of Protestant Christianity in Madagascar, Thomas Bevan and David Jones came from Neuaddlwyd in Cardiganshire.

14th
It is easier for a Malagasy to grasp the Penrhys culture than it would be for someone from the Vale of Glamorgan. Another 90 houses are to be demolished. We will be reduced to 580 properties (1300 people). We looked at the place of the church in this context and I laid out a programme for discussion.

15th
Menja and I walked through the estate: 'It is the wealthy in Madagascar who have beautiful, comfortable houses like these on Penrhys. Why this destruction? Man cannot live by bread alone.' It was a salutary experience. Café and disco. A good night: lively and friendly. No tension or aggression; 50 children and young people used Llanfair. It is consistent work that matters and helps young people have rhythm to their lives.

Sunday 17th
We received certificates for the Christian Aid collection of £1450: more than £1 per head of Penrhys population. Norah's hard work ensures that we make a tangible effort for the support of the poor.

19th
Menja and Uzonka met me for our first weekly session: we agreed on subjects to work on together. Now we are eight residents working together, the ministry is conciliar rather than individualistic. That makes it predictable that we will have problems, but it is much easier to deal with.
Uzonka was a Hungarian student from Debrecen.

29th
The Western Mail published a dreadful account of the demolition of the 88 houses: the beginning of the end of the estate in which no-one wants to live.

OCTOBER

16th
A faithful member of the Llanfair family died this morning in the boutique. She has been a tower of strength throughout the years and her loss is immeasurable. She started coming to church five years ago, never asserted herself but was a natural leader: she was wise, compassionate, got things done and had the gift of being loved and respected. She was a clear thinker and excellent judge of character, who always looked deeply for the causes which lie behind human behaviour. She was totally reliable and always ready to help. She became a regular worshipper, a methodical, caring worker in the church, and above all a good, loyal friend. She never let you down. Her death was a terrifying shock.

23rd
The funeral expressed in the evening there will be light. This faithful servant never seemed old and grew in stature. Her family emphasized that her final years were her happiest and most fulfilling because of her second home, the church. The chapel was filled with dignity, hope and respect. People were present because it was their duty and delight: her death was a diminishing of our spirits, but a confirming of growth in maturity as we grow in Christ.

28th
The twelve young people from TIM are from Tuvalu, New Zealand, Taiwan, Korea, Hong Kong, India, Malawi, Mozambique, Botswana, Scotland, Jamaica and Canada.

Sunday 29th
The World Church responded to the particularity of the Gospel within a local community. The solo singing of the women from Korea, Taiwan and Tuvalu had strength and gentleness. Words and music were vehicles for their deep Christian experience.

NOVEMBER

7th

I have never known anything like it. At the crematorium, the youngest daughter read a poem of her mother's entitled 'To a child who inquires.' That was remarkable but nothing compared with the closing music, Barbra Streisand singing 'Memories' from 'The Way They Were.' To everyone's amazement, including their own, the three daughters started to sing quietly and then with strength and passion. Everyone else wept.

14th

Norah saw Dr Camilleri, consultant in rheumatology at East Glamorgan Hospital. Norah is suffering from acute arthritis but he does not know what kind, how it originated or why it developed so quickly. Norah received courtesy and efficiency: we have high praise. But what of the future? Is this a periodic attack or the start of permanent disability?
We were fortunate that after a long period of treatment with the searching for the appropriate medication, the arthritis was stabilized. At this point we had the frightening uncertainty of permanent disability. Of course this would have resulted in our leaving Penrhys.

18th

The University College of Swansea has invited us to become 'Honorary Fellows' of the University College. I have a clear recollection of my first journey to Swansea as a student 38 years ago.

20th

A 7 year old stated that 'When I hear the bell, "God is waking me up to a new morning."'

DECEMBER

4th

The bell welcomed the Infants as they walked along the path; their coats were taken off and hung; the big chapel door was opened and there before them was the great tree touching the roof with its coloured lights, golden and silver balls and angel on the top; by its side was the crib with hay and nearby the donkey which had come clip-clopping all the way to Bethlehem; the cow and sheep. Mary and Joseph placed baby Jesus tenderly in the crib. They stood there for the rest of the service with Mary tapping the child, making sure his clothes kept him comfortable and warm. A timeless moment, a highpoint of Christmas.

6th

Five 'older' girls (Years 9-11) worked with 11 'younger girls' (Years 7-9) with conviction, skill and a sense of achievement. This group has grown in the church during four years and is capable of leadership.
Here were signs of emerging leadership. Despite an occasional hiatus, young leaders helped in developing children's and youth work throughout the years. They also served the worshipping life of the congregation.

7th

What would we expect at a reception given by the Prime Minister and Mrs Major at 10 Downing Street? John Major said he had invited people he wanted to bring together. We were a wonderfully motley group. Hard to believe going through the gates and into Number 10. We were announced as we entered the banqueting rooms and were introduced to John and Norma Major. He welcomed us by name. During the next couple of hours we met a writer of children's books on sport; an Indian couple from Belfast; the Director of 'Pride and Prejudice;' Norman Wisdom; Donald and Wendy Woods (Cry Freedom); Chairman of Texaco from North Dakota - the size of Great Britain; also there were Nick Faldo, Jane of 'Pride and Prejudice;' Michael Buerk.

23rd

It is difficult to distinguish between work and leisure, enjoyment and responsibility. This is because of our delight in people, seeing neighbours as friends. Penrhys can create community because we have similar houses and backgrounds, attend the same schools, buy in the same shops and share the same village community. The permeating influence of the church is certain to have a long term effect on the lives of this community.

Sunday 24th

God surprises earth with heaven, coming down on Christmas Day. No, he wasn't found in the palace, temple, or inn, but was found in a stable and laid in a manger. The mother had nowhere to lay her head. Christmas is a miracle each year.

Sunday 31st

An evening of disco and karaoke for 40 young people. They enjoyed it, behaved well, there were no problems and the older group exercised leadership. New Year Service at 11.30. It was right to be in chapel and receive Communion as the bell rang twelve times to greet the New Year.

1996

JANUARY

18th

Another Discussion/ Confirmation group. Today there were 12 boys between 12 and 16; yesterday there were 16 girls the same age. We have enjoyed this number since September and there has been growing attention and concentration. We are with the girls for an hour, working on the same theme as the church. The boys meet for 45 minutes and have started looking at Mark in 'New World.'

22nd

The Penrhys Sponsoring Body had many struggles bringing the fellowship into existence, trying to reflect the church style of the valley. It was only when we searched for a new pattern, faithful to the One, Holy, Catholic and Apostolic Church, and faithful to the context of Penrhys, that Llanfair reached into this community.

FEBRUARY

2nd

For fun and exuberance, it would be hard to beat 30 young teenagers in tonight's disco in the dining room. Especially lively is the line formation, a contemporary dance from Pride and Prejudice! The young people are happy without drugs, alcohol, tobacco. We do not know how long this will succeed, but it has worked for 5 months during a critical year in their lives. They will always say with a smile - I remember when I was young that we had good, simple fun in church.

5th

Once more the enormity of the death of a young man. When I completed comforting the family, the tragedy surfaced in my mind. A young, mentally ill man had died alone on Penrhys. While at the funeral, I was told, 'None of us know where he is gone Penrhys is in the hands of the devil; perhaps God is preparing for a great victory.'

What an indictment of religious values.

6th

The funeral of the baby girl was unforgettable. The snow began falling yesterday until it was feet deep throughout the estate. Would the funeral take place? Members of the Church and the community cleared the snow and cut a path. The father carried the baby along the path cut through thick snow as far as the school. The parents' walk through the snow will last a lifetime.

7th

We walked up the snow-covered path with the close family carrying flowers. It was bitingly cold, especially when we reached the top and saw the snow-filled mountains stretching from Cefn Gwyngul, Cefn y Rhondda and the Rhondda Fawr ridge. It felt primeval; a pioneering family surviving in a wilderness. The only certainty was each other's presence, struggling in the face of the enormity of the death of a two day old. They needed each other, not understanding but being alongside.

19th

This afternoon I was looking through our kitchen window and saw a neighbour trying to cut with a hacksaw the handcuffs off the wrists of a young man. After a while the young man walked down the main path, one hand free and links dangling from the other. It was like watching someone repairing a car, painting the house or digging a hole. What is the story behind this incident in the everyday life of Penrhys folk?

21st, Ash Wednesday

We sat in the café and placed our palm crosses on the little fire which swiftly turned the palms into ash. I added water to make paste. In the chapel we prepared for our public repentance by sitting opposite each other, responsively reading Psalm 51 and passages narrating the healing and inclusiveness of Jesus, praying the Kyries and Lamb of God. We marked our hands with the sign of the cross and sat together in a circle on the floor. We need to start again and move forward.

MARCH

27th

A student from the University of Glamorgan is writing a paper on urban theology. She had prepared well, but? Was I influenced by South American Liberation theology? Not directly. What British experiments in Urban Theology influenced you? Again none directly!

Both Norah and I had experienced many years of living, worshipping and reading about the need for the Church to respond to the community, and had gradually worked out a text and context approach to the mission of the Church. We had both been influenced directly by ecumenical experience, and the way in which the Churches had responded and failed to respond to the social and economic crises of the 1980s. However, it was by living on Penrhys and witnessing how the Church could meet some of the needs of our community which led us to help shape the ministry and mission of Llanfair.

APRIL

6th

A poignant but expectant day of waiting, and a glorious entry to the day of resurrection. 125 were in church on Good Friday, and 54 this evening, the majority teenagers. This evening Tammy, Samantha, Charlene and Marilyn were baptised; Rena affirmed her faith. Our recently baptised young people presented Bibles, certificates and candles.

Easter Sunday 7th

The greatest day. Llanfair celebrated the resurrection. Alex, the 9 year old playing the centurion in the play, told me afterwards that he had spoken the most important line: 'Truly this man was the son of God.' Luke and Kelly, our 5 year olds sang 'Feel like shouting, Shout for Joy.' Our afternoon play was worship, not a performance. This morning we gathered outside Llanfair on the sweetest Easter morning: the air was warm, skylarks and sheep joining in praise. Bristol Tump was the centre of the universe, a Mount of Transfiguration.

23rd

A registered letter from Buckingham Palace and Prince Charles. 'I can see I shall have to revisit you before too long to catch up on your progress! I could not be more grateful for all the love and dedication which you and Norah have shown toward the people of Penrhys for ten years now. You are very much in my thoughts and prayers. Yours most sincerely, Charles.' Having read of dozens of kings of Israel and Judah, Charles ranks highly, despite or because of his tragic life.

27th

The Third Rhondda Eisteddfod was held at the new Leisure Centre in Tylorstown. It is on the site of Numbers 6 and 7 collieries in which 100 years ago 50 men and boys were killed. It is the pit in which John Davies, my great-grandfather was killed in 1883. We gathered outside the school where my grandmother was amongst the first pupils, our family educated and Dad was head-teacher. We walked with our church banner with 300 others with their Miners' banners along Edmund St and East St (where John Davies and family had lived) to the Leisure Centre. I introduced the Mayor of R.C.T. whose first engagement was to unveil a memorial to the miners lost in 1896. Llanfair led opening prayers. Later the choir (under 15s) sang and the rock band played. All groups and winners were presented with a prize. We were the only church taking part.

MAY

9th

Andrew Prasad and his dozen colleagues stated that Penrhys is mission in action. They were thrilled with the service to the community, long-term education, quality of worship and the growing maturity of children and young people. It was thrilling to have the work confirmed by discerning Christian leaders.

A consultation for missionaries serving in the URC took place at Llanfair.

Sunday 12th

Christian Aid Sunday falls between Easter and Pentecost; it is haunted by Good Friday contemporary realities but charged with Easter Day hope. Waiting for Pentecost, we pray to be empowered as workers and livers of peace and justice. As Christians it is not difficult to believe in 'life after death' but it takes true resolution to believe in 'life before death.'

14th

Fred Redwood writes in The Sunday Times: 'A church inspired project is bringing hope to a community where education is beset by social ills perhaps the Penrhys Partnership should be taken as a model for the remotivation of children in more of our deprived areas.'

Two months previously Lynne Wallis had written a similar article for The Guardian.

JUNE

15th

Cas prepared a Fashion Show, using clothes from the Nearly New shop. 20 young people acted as models; Diane was in charge of lights and music, Paul as compere, the staging set up in the dining room and boutique and there was an audience of 50. The young people displayed confidence and charm, and it was a thoroughly happy professional evening.

Cas Smith and Paul Sass were two full-time workers, specializing in Secondary Education. Diane was one of our faithful young people.

17th

At the graveside were fellow students. The young mother had lost her baby prematurely. As I stood at the grave with the family, on the roadside above were 40 young people, who when invited came down to stand around the grave. It was a glorious morning and the air was still: it was appropriate to ask these young men and women to look after each other and recognize the responsibility of having children. Drove to London where Bill Castell invited a dozen to the Athenaeum to discuss Business' responsibility for Community: Richard Dykes, Dominic Proctor, Chris Hughes. Jonathon Porritt shared his views. Rather esoteric after the earlier part of the day.

Jonathon Porritt is the leading ecologist. Needless to say, I was not comfortable in the Athenaeum. My only previous visit was to meet Dr Daniel Jenkins when I served as Moderator.

21st

A miracle of grace when the little daughter walked with me across the floor of Llanfair to light a candle for her 23 year old father. The funeral was drawing to a close, I pronounced the blessing, the chapel door opened, the bell tolled and the music 'Simply the Best' started to play. The familiar popular song created a sobbing of anguish which would lead to the breakdown of many deeply hurt and caring people. Was God prompting me? Was my experience telling me to channel the grief? The little girl started to sob and I fetched her to light the candle; other children came, followed by adults, and hope began to shine. A crowd gathered at the graveside on a warm afternoon. Many knew it could be them next.

24th

Ethel and Bob Huggard were recognised for their generosity and faithfulness. Cartref was opened, a housing scheme enabling half a dozen families to live in a secure, pleasant environment. William Hague, Secretary of State, opened Cartref and unveiled a plaque in thanksgiving to Bob and Ethel. The morning began with worship in Llanfair with Nursery, top Infants and top Juniors singing. We walked to Cartref in brilliant sunshine, the unveiling took place, there were photographs and Hague left at 11.45. Ethel knew her work was accomplished.

William Hague was Secretary of State for Wales from 1995 to 1997. He was most impressed by his visit to Penrhys and publicly referred to the Church's work on several occasions.

JULY

8th

Sharon was in the Junior School Assembly when the pastor of a church in Ystrad addressed the children: How many of you go to Sunday school? Half the children raised their hands! How many of you go to church? Every hand went up. He was dumbfounded. What about his programme to bring the Gospel to Penrhys? All he could now do is attract children from a second rate brand of Christianity to the pure faith.

9th

At the Dinner for Honorary Fellows at Swansea, Emrys Evans spoke about each Fellow and Lord Howe responded on our behalf. Also honoured was Ernest Zobole from Ystrad, one of Wales' premier painters. As we chatted before the meal, he commented that when he saw the parents and children graduating, he thought of young people gathering at the bottom of Penrhys hill day after day. He cannot accept this unjust world.

Geoffrey Howe was Margaret Thatcher's longest-serving cabinet minister, ultimately serving as Deputy Prime Minister. Ernest Zobole is regarded as one of Wales's 'most important artists...one of the visionary artists of Wales. His subject was often singular: the night-time Rhondda Valley in South Wales and his home and family in it. However, the way in which he used his chosen subject shows that his paintings illustrated his "vision of the way in which we sense the world."' Peter Wakelin.

10th

What an honour bestowed by the University of Wales Swansea. As Norah and I stood on the platform of the Brangwyn Hall, facing a crowd of a thousand and listened in turn to the citations by Emrys Evans and Hywel Francis, it was clear the University had granted their highest gift. Many years ago my father introduced me to Ivor Owen, the organist of the Brangwyn and I sat with him on the organ stool.

Emrys Evans was the public face of the Midland Bank in Wales. He was one of Wales' great philanthropists and a dedicated worshipper at Ebenezer, Cardiff. Hywel Francis was a long established friend and colleague.

Sunday 21st

I shared worship with Norman Drummond today. This morning Norman and I led the service at Stenschell Parish Church. Our young people sang most effectively. This afternoon we were at Kilmuir, and again this evening in Stenschell.

Norman Drummond had visited Llanfair several months previously and had invited us to bring a group of young people to stop at the small Selby Wright residential centre near his Staffin home. He had been Headmaster at the Loretto School and was soon to be minister of the parish of Stenschell and Kilmuir. He is the founder of the Columba 1400 Project in Staffin, Skye. This was the first of several visits by Penrhys young people to Skye. They did not only worship! They climbed the Quiraing and reached the Old Man of Storr, visited the island of Raasay and were courageous enough to swim in the not so mild water of Staffin Bay.

AUGUST

Sunday 4th

The wedding of Rena and Hugh was the first where wife and husband worship at Llanfair. It was formal, relaxed, serious and had humour. A celebration of the best of Penrhys. It would have been difficult to get more into Llanfair (130), many watched outside, the weather was beautiful; Rena and Hugh repeated their vows honestly and clearly; Cy sang 'Myfanwy' with charm; a small group sang 'A New Commandment' and the dozen infants sang 'All things bright and beautiful,' repeated the blessing and we all sang 'Happy Birthday' to Rena.

17th

Halfway through the summer holiday and most children have not been far from the estate. It is a warm night, windows are open and I listen to the familiar sounds of children playing. When, 10 years ago I first heard the children playing in the darkness I was shocked and wondered what would be the future of those children. Llanfair came into being in an attempt to break the cycle of poverty, poor health, devaluing education and unemployment which continues its inexorable, ruthless erosion. There follow the attendant problems of cigarettes, alcohol, gambling, drugs, crime, impoverished and short-term relationships. The deaths of eight young men in the past year is the tip of the iceberg threatening our society as well as bringing personal tragedy. Will it change? Only God's grace can provide empowering which will bring newness of life and reconciliation.

SEPTEMBER

2nd

Today marked the close of summer holidays for the people of Penrhys. One hundred have visited Caldey, Carmarthen, Limpsfield Chart, Snowdon and Skye. We learn from the negative and positive; we see potential for good and ill; leadership ability; bullies and bullied; those who help and those who avoid work at all costs.

9th

Jonathan Skaw, 'Deputy Chief Secretary' to the Prince of Wales arrived. He was eager to learn.

14th

'Pride and Prejudice Revised' was performed at the Community Centre by the Llanfair Drama Group directed by Rachel Mann.

Rachel Mann, a young woman from Pontypridd had inspired a Llanfair youth drama group throughout the year and this was their highlight: a play written and directed by Rachel. It was a great success and such a delight to see our teenagers immersed in such a classic.

OCTOBER

24th

The secret of ministry with young people is to be consistent. A pattern must be created which is faithful to the Gospel and appropriate to their life style; this pattern must be maintained until it becomes part of their lives. This happened in Llanidloes where I created appropriate material and met young people every Sunday evening in the cottage at Glanhafren. We now have the right theological material for Penrhys and have developed a pattern of weekly meetings and an annual programme. We must maintain this programme because young people will break away if the pattern is not fulfilled.

NOVEMBER

4th

The Nemo Brass Quintet presented an excellent concert through the Live Music Now Programme.

The Nemo Brass Quintet, formed in 1991 has won many international chamber music competitions and continues to tour throughout Britain and Europe.

7th

Young people read Exodus 3. As Beca said, 'This call of Moses was the only way in which God could help the Hebrews. He has to use human beings.' Kerry added, 'Just like us. God needs us.'

20th

Another young man has died. There was a tragic inevitability and all know this is not the end of this community's pain. It will go on again and again until there is a new generation.

21st

Everyone says 'No one will learn; who is going to be next?' This is the life cycle of many Penrhys young people living beyond the bounds of society. Is it hopeless for them? It convinces me of the rightness of Llanfair's approach to create new structures and opportunities for children at the earliest age so they will grow with different norms and expectations from their older sisters and brothers.

Sunday 24th

Phil Cuddy (the last manager of Maerdy colliery), on behalf of Rhondda Rotary, presented me with the Paul Harris Award, apparently the Rotary's highest award.

27th

We welcomed the Bishop of Stockholm and six Swedish people guided by Huw Jones, Bishop of St David's, Anthony Crocker and Gethin Abraham-Williams. They arrived at the same time as the Juniors and Infants classes, accompanied by teachers and Head teachers. The children sang in English and Welsh and the Bishop presented a glass snowball, lit by a candle. Our guests were most perceptive, able to make connections and so enthusiastic. *The Church in Wales had entered into a special relationship with the Lutheran Church in Sweden through the Porvoo Agreement. Llanfair was later to receive Maria Lindgren, a Lutheran Deacon who lived and worked on Penrhys for six months. Anthony Crocker was Bishop of Bangor until his untimely death in 2008, and Gethin Abraham-Williams became secretary of Cytun, Churches Together in Wales.*

DECEMBER

6th

This evening I led discussions with two groups of young people, most in their mid-teens (14-16), half of them boys, several dropped out of school. They live on a perilous edge and in 5 years some could be dead. Today I helped them explore the abrupt end of Mark's Gospel. 'Why did Nero want him dead? Because he was writing about Jesus who was crucified and raised from the dead, and therefore exercised the greatest power in the universe.' The 20 young people began to grasp they were exploring the key to history. I pray they begin to grasp that Jesus is the key to all our lives. How many ministers in Wales are able to share the Gospel every week with 40 teenagers, none brought up in a Christian tradition? This morning I shared the story with the 3 year olds as they came for the Christmas service.

11th

The National Museum hosted an Exhibition of the work of Philip Jones Griffiths, 'Dark Odyssey.' It emphasized the futility and barbarism of war, especially in Vietnam. He remembered meeting us on Penrhys in 1993 and signed his new book for us.

We were pleased to meet Ivor, our friend and postman, at the Exhibition. He had also met Philip Jones Griffiths on his visit to Penrhys.

16th

He had stipulated that his grandchildren should not attend his funeral. As a child, he had been scarred by a similar experience. When I began to share the service with the family, the two grandchildren sat on the settee and started to read the service, singing 'Away in a manger,' reading prayers, asking the parents to put their hands together and close their eyes. It was gentle, noble, genuine, where the extraordinary reaches through the ordinary. It reinforced Llanfair's identifying with the community and giving people the opportunity to recognise God at work in the midst. 'Whether we are in life, in death, or in life beyond death, God is with us' read the two children.
Before every funeral, the family helped me create the service. After shaping it, I shared it with them before producing a final draft for the actual service.

1997

JANUARY

10th

Dr Pennar Davies has died. Pennar was a great influence during my training at Coleg Coffa. I remember his course on Puritanism and his encouragement to study William Erbery at Mansfield. He was a humane, gentle Christian man of powerful intellect and renaissance experience.
Pennar influenced generations of theological students, many linked with Llanidloes, and of course Norah during her year at Coleg Coffa when we lived at Manselton.

FEBRUARY

5th

Lisa has attended 123 discussion groups without fail. It means I have attended that number and hundreds of other groups. That says something about us both.

9th

After my father died, I thought it would be rare to visit Rhondda. How close I have come to my place of birth! A strange discovery this evening. I have known for years that my father's grandfather, John Davies, had been killed in No 7 pit in 1883. Today I looked at the map of the 1896 explosion and found that my mother's grandfather, David Davies, was also killed in No 7 pit. A strange legacy.

14th

Apart from family, who would I like to meet in heaven? Those who influenced me directly - Mrs John Griff Davies my Sunday School teacher when, as twelve little boys we sat with her under the clock in Ebenezer vestry; Alwyn Charles, minister when I was 12 and a profound influence until his early death in the 1970s; those who taught in theological colleges - Dr Pennar Davies, Dr S L Greenslade, Dr Ford Battles and Dr Robert Paul. And other heroes? Shakespeare and drama, T S Eliot and poetry, Beethoven, especially his quartets. We all share this chain of receiving and giving, and we are all redeemed by the divine spark which is the gift of God.

MARCH

1st

Nicola Heywood Thomas formally opened Canolfan Rhys. The infrastructure exists for quality community life.

Canolfan Rhys was to provide a range of arts and education programmes for the community. Its first two professionals were Liz Gardiner to develop relationships between education and employment, and Ruth Garnault who concentrated on the Arts and also managed Canolfan Rhys. Nicola Heywood Thomas was a major BBC broadcaster. Canolfan Rhys was awarded Welsh Community Enterprise of the Year, 1998 ' in recognition of the excellence of provision, degree of community involvement, and sustainability of the whole project.'

6th

A few weeks ago I thought a particular teenager impossible to work with. She was arrogant, rude and we confronted each other in discussion group. Today she proudly introduced me to her sister's baby and was pleased to talk about his baptism. She came to discussion this evening and talked about serious, long standing family problems. At that point we realised the four other girls in the group knew similar trauma and had experienced broken parental relationships. How could I judge her who has been through so much in her short life?

8th

In a house group in Llanidloes in 1969, a participant asked 'What is community?' I could not answer then and still find no answer. It is possible to recognise when community has broken down and describe the consequences: the erosion of law and order; low esteem; powerlessness; poverty of spirit. I rediscovered papers on the 'Priority Estates Project, Faith in Wales, To Strengthen the Poor' and I re-examined my paper on Penrhys New Perspective, the creation of the Partnership and reports on the work of Llanfair. It has been critical to listen to community and to God, to combine vision and stamina, be faithful to priorities and above all remember that people matter.

27th

Another young man was buried today. It was charged with foreboding as dozens of young men kept coming into the chapel. There was total silence during the 30 minute service as we focussed on the coffin draped with a Welsh flag, and by its side two large wreaths with his name and 'son.' Here was a generation of young men, out of work, having been in prison, most on hard drugs, saying goodbye to one of their number, and acutely aware that one of them could be next. I tried to reflect on the Christian hope and the need to work together to struggle with this 'no exit' drug scene. The chapel was crammed with a hundred standing; there was no spare space in the vestibule, and more outside. Most streamed down through mist and wind to the committal at the cemetery. I returned to the pub where I spoke to dozens of young men almost pleading for help - a petition? Will you help us?

Good Friday, 28th

When the story of Jesus is told and when Almighty God is worshipped, there are resources for healing. In yesterday's tragedy, we came face to face with the desperate, haunted faces of young men and women who daily dice with death, and do not know how to be released from the ecstasy which kills. Today the story was told, God was worshipped and the faces of young people participating in this drama were full of commitment and hope. Lisa, as Jesus had internal luminosity which made her face reflect the Gospel, like an icon. She was the central figure, 'knowing' her words without script, and knowing the words. The drama was told with simplicity and competence, and the music expressed the story. A strong core of people, young and old are seeking to live the Gospel.

29th

Many young people baptized during the last few years supported those baptized today. More than 14 are loyal to their commitment and 8 made vows this morning. Four have older brothers and sisters baptized during the last few years. There is the feeling of a growing 'family' of church. The majority of the 70 in worship were under 30. Seeds are being sown and will grow in God's Kingdom in the next century.

30th, Easter Sunday

The most significant 24 hours in the Year. The glory and wonder of the Nativity Celebration pale to insignificance compared with the events since yesterday evening. We gathered outside Llanfair on the mildest, gentlest Spring Easter morning. We greeted the Risen Christ on the summit of Twyn Disgwylfa and faced north, west, south and east to give thanks to the God of resurrection who brings fulfilment to creation. Larks and sheep joined in praise. Prayers at the black gate and outside Llanfair before 40 enjoyed two boiled eggs each. The Easter Play was impressive: Lisa is so mature, having learned her words and speaking with distinction; the singing was a joy; the children a delight; the response tremendous. 1000 worshipped this week.

APRIL

16th

An illuminating day. We enjoyed the company of Dr Rukmini Rao, a development worker on the Deccan plateau in South India. As we stood around the table to receive the bread of life and vowed to live the sacrificial life, we were Hindu, Christian, Asian, African, European in unity. We walked through the estate, gossiping with many in the warm sunshine. After Compline, Rukmini spoke to 30 about her work in the villages. There are many points in common.

Dr. V. Rukmini Rao is the Director of the Centre for World Solidarity in Hyderabad, and the Gramya Resource Centre for Women. Rukmini was invited to Wales by Christian Aid and we were privileged to offer hospitality. She came at what proved a most opportune time. In 2002, Norah with Elenid Jones visited Rukmini in Hyderabad on a Christian Aid visitation.

Sunday 20th

Rukmini Rao's development work on the Deccan plateau is based on the village and the need for self-sufficiency within the village or group of villages, and concentrates on work with women. Her themes of economic development, food production, education and health all relate to our work here; but our work has challenges caused by the person and community not needing to struggle for development because of our very adequate social care system. Because housing is provided and financial support expected, there is no determination to see change. How do we raise expectations of a new future and develop the determination to bring it about?

22nd

Playing harp and piano, Sian Williams' programme of popular music appealed to an audience of adults and teenagers. There now exists a stable audience of 40 adults and 'older' young people.

Siân Williams is a Welsh born Harpist who trained at the Royal Welsh School of Music and Drama.

Sunday 27th

We have a regular worshipping congregation of 40 adults and teenagers; an educational programme for all ages; the church has a caring, vibrant, versatile ministry with the community; the church is respected and valued; we have creative relationships with the schools; excellent premises; we are creating financial security; above all we seek the mind of Christ as the dynamic of life. And yet this is a volatile society. What if half a dozen church families moved elsewhere? What will happen if Penrhys continues to decline? Whatever happens this has been a good day and Christ is Lord of tomorrow.

30th

By focussing on the marginal seats of Middle England, the political parties have forgotten millions on the margins of society. What control do we have over our future? How can we engage with the resources necessary for development? How can we draw education, health care, work, leisure into our communities? And where is the church in these critical issues?

MAY

1st

A historical footnote. Llanfair serves as polling station. In Wales there is an apprehension of the combination of a Welsh Office and Local Government both controlled by the Labour party. We may see 'New Labour' at Westminster but the cosy old guard remain in the Valleys. My little footnote was that I was the first to vote in Llanfair and my address is the same as the polling station. 364 voted on Penrhys, possibly 60% and a record.

21st

What is the future of our community? I prepared a paper in readiness for meeting Terry Winters. My theme was to encourage confidence by tackling the questions of housing, infra-structure, responding to community initiatives and developing good publicity. The Llanfair group met Terry to discuss the future of the estate. The Council are drifting with the tide - 170 empty properties out of 590. Unless residents are active, there is no future. I must think through our programme and strategy. How do we struggle to make something of our community? Where are our allies?

Although I was unaware of the significance of the day, this was the beginning of the struggle to enable Penrhys to speak with a communal voice about its future. Up to this point we were all consulted as individuals or separate groups, and there was no sense of a common identity.

24th

Of the 50 on the annual pilgrimage/ sponsored walk, 36 were from Penrhys. A light cool east wind made the walk very pleasant. At Llanwynno we enjoyed eating in the graveyard before a good service led by Paul Bennet. Then falling head-over-heels to Stanleytown and up the hundreds of steps through the parks to Penrhys where we were joined by Faith and Light. Prayers and singing at the Shrine, and Llanfair for an ecumenical service: Roman Catholic, Orthodox, Greek Catholic, Protestants, Quakers, Salvation Army, Evangelical Brethren, Romanians, Hungarians, imbued by the spirit of Faith and Light.

Faith and Light was initiated by Jean Vanier and Marie-Helene Mathieu, in response to the call of a couple with two children with learning disabilities. Today 1500 communities of different Christian traditions, rooted in their parish or their local church are developing in 78 countries.

26th

We, residents of Penrhys have no influence on our future. External forces determine the programme and Penrhys people are at the mercy of decision makers. This is 'socialism' in the heartland of the Labour movement. We must do something! During the day, I realised I must use the opportunity presented by the Christian Aid Consultation at Llanfair. The key question which needs to be put to the community is: 'If you were guaranteed 5 year tenure on your house, would you stay on Penrhys?'

28th

The paper I wrote last night was the basis of today's discussion with the 'football supporters.' At 12 precisely, into Llanfair walked Sammy, Timmy, Gacchi, Ivor, Cavill, 'the Scotsman,' Wayne, Andrew, Kay, Jack, Dave, Norah and Graham. We want the estate to survive and need to talk with those who make decisions. The key question is the issue of guaranteed tenure.

30th

Our visitors arrived for the Christian Aid Consultation on 'Global Poverty and Community Development.' When I got up to speak, the dozen who gathered on Wednesday walked in. There could not have been a greater contrast with our visitors, most of whom were middle class professionals. I spoke on our future as a community and then invited the 'two kinds of people' to talk. It was an electrifying half hour. I have never experienced a contrast so fertile with hope.

JUNE

9th

I have been challenged by Hamlet and the Grosse Fugue: a play and a string quartet, a book and a compact disc. These gifts are available at the close of the Twentieth Century in the Northern Hemisphere. We read Shakespeare and listen to Beethoven at home. I am grateful for words and notes.

18th

Young men ran down the path, a car screeched in Pen Tyntyla, rooks cawed and in the distance, one bird sang. That was Penrhys's dawn chorus. But the God of creation is the God of redemption and morning communion reassured us with grace.

26th

My 'spirit' returned to the vibrant communal days of the Miners' Strike of 1984 and 1985. That ended in defeat but was a battle fought with courage, dignity and skill. I remember the social togetherness as we struggled for a cause. The Penrhys Community Centre was packed with 156 adults. I

addressed the meeting, responded to queries and an hour later, we unanimously decided to set up the Penrhys Action Group and agreed on representation (1 per block). We have advanced dramatically in a month and have communal backing for action. The real struggle begins.
On Penrhys each 'block' constitutes eight properties. At this time 40 blocks had survived out of almost 120 blocks when the estate was opened.

JULY

7th

The 40 representatives are creating a democratic process for Penrhys. The results of the house meetings were that 211 wish to stop; 41 to leave; 13 don't know (265 out of 400 homes). Our aim could be an estate of 300 properties - there are now 597 with 170 vacancies. Officers were elected - myself as chair, Ian as secretary, Wayne as treasurer. Five working groups were established: Housing, Finance, Environment, Publicity, Protection.
Ian was soon to be replaced by Idris Hemming, and the three of us served many years until Idris' death. Idris was then succeeded as Secretary by Robert Poole.

9th

Penrhys is treated with contempt. As we walked from Communion, The Rhondda Leader was thrust into our hands. The front page read that 88 houses will be demolished, of which 25 are still occupied, and the number of each house was listed. Rita read that her house was one; Donna read it in school; others were told in the shop or on the street. That is how they learned of the proposal to destroy their homes, some having lived there for 25 years. Everyone felt humiliated, angry, determined that justice should be done. It could not happen to any other community in Wales. It could be the catalyst for determined action.

19th

Most reached The Table on the Quiraing. A spectacular triumph which helped bind the group together. Everyone made the attempt and all reached 'The Prison' where Leanne and Lisa stopped. The rest made our way around 'The Needle' and over the steep lip into the gully leading to 'The Table.' The boys burst out with 'Mae Hen Wlad fy Nhadau.' We had just finished when a group from Brittany and Pau asked us to sing it again. They sang their anthems and we parted in mutual admiration.

The young people are on holiday in Staffin, Skye as the guests of Norman and Lady Elizabeth Drummond. One of the highlights of this visit was to see the young people eating and enjoying fresh mackerel for the first time. It had been given to us by a fisherman in Staffin Bay and the Penrhys youngsters looked at the fish with distaste. After Norah had cooked it, they were encouraged to 'extend their taste buds' and they thoroughly enjoyed the meal. Another much used phrase on the holiday was 'absorb the atmosphere' and they did!

AUGUST

4th

The work of community regeneration begins. When the Estate Manager informed us in May that consultation would be only with individuals or select groups, it looked as if there was no future for Penrhys. Only 140 families wished to remain and demolition would continue until the estate ceased to exist. Today the Action Group met the Deputy Director of Housing and was encouraged to adopt a Constitution, seek funding, and have consultations to work out a future. The hard work will continue for many years.

5th

The Skye young people formed the Llanfair Youth Team (LYT) for weekly discussion, a monthly service, a social programme, and have its own officers. If this mature group work together for a couple of years, they will provide leadership in the church and community.

18th

The Penrhys Community Action Group is formally established. At a public meeting, a Constitution was adopted, officers elected and a committee of 14 appointed. This completes the first stage but more difficult issues lie ahead. Will the Action Group develop in confidence and maturity? Will it create an appropriate and achievable agenda? Will it hold the confidence of community and Council?

19th

I completed RS Thomas' fascinating and puzzling 'Autobiographies.' RS seems closer to nature than he is to people; conveys no sense of forgiveness; refuses communion under the revised liturgy. Yet his search for truth makes us all ask questions, and his language is clear and beautiful. What a contrast from my life and ministry. He moved from Anglesey to Manafon, Eglwysfach, Lleyn and returned to Sir Fôn. I moved from Tylorstown to Llanidloes, Manselton, Cardiff and now to Penrhys. Our contexts have shaped our lives.

20th

The undertaker mentioned that the facilities at Llanfair were the best in the valleys. The Tonypandy florist who used to refuse to deliver to Penrhys told Norah he was amazed by the progress in the community. We are winning the confidence of many in the Rhondda.

22nd

I am writing at 11.30 and can hear men speaking outside on the path. They are closer than our dining room; and because the window is open, their voices are clearer than anyone speaking in the next room. There is no anonymity on Penrhys; most know each other well and know what is going on. Penrhys can be Llaregyb, the community of 'Under Milk Wood' with its humour, tolerance and easy going nature. People know what others do and why they do it; they know action and motive, and this gives a deeper understanding of human nature. We need never have superficial judgments and this makes prayer life more valid.

30th

A perfect day. The first Penrhys Carnival 'celebrated' Rhys ap Tewdwr, beheaded on Penrhys in 1097. It was a high risk exercise. Would the Penrhys Action Group have stalls on the statue field? Could this group, not used to organizing, pull it off? And the weather? Well, it all worked. Stalls, bouncy castle, hot dog stall, music, plenty of people. Many joined the Carnival and Samba band through the estate and back to the amphitheatre for rock groups and fireworks. It will boost morale, pull the estate together and help the community realize it has much to struggle for.

SEPTEMBER

4th

I put a book of condolence in the chapel. Today at 9 the first people came to sign, and for 5 hours they came quietly and with dignity into the vestibule, waited their turn and spent many minutes in the chapel. Almost all wrote sentiments of sincerity and deep emotion. It continued this evening from 7 to

9.15. People feel they have lost a member of the family. The messages reflect that people had a love and respect for Diana because she had suffered and seemed warm and caring. Almost all have a passionate conviction she is now with God.
Responses to the tragic death of Princess Diana.

11th

The new year of work starts well. There are new ideas and fresh energy. Our three young volunteers (Aiky from Madagascar, Bethany from England and Eszter from Hungary) are energetic, enthusiastic, eager to learn and serve, and each has an attractive personality. They have brightness of eye and openness of face. We (Norah, Sharon and I) too have a continuing enthusiasm.

18th

The polling station at Llanfair closed an hour ago. It is the day of the National Referendum for a Welsh Assembly. No one predicts the result. Although the major parties (except the Conservative) and Wales' major institutions have advocated a 'Yes vote,' will the ancient ghosts of language, distance between North and South, surface and prevent a sensible democratic shape to our government? It is also an issue of national dignity. We will see. It is just before 4, Carmarthenshire was last to declare and the majority for 'Yes' was 559,419 to 552,698.

19th

I hadn't expected the 18th of September, 1997, to be a historic day. Is it that I remembered the 4-1 vote against the 1979 Referendum and did not believe it could happen? The people of Wales agree to listen to each other as people from all parts of Wales, and learn to act together. Is there a growing maturity and confidence? What a night it was! The first two results from the North East were emphatically No; Anglesey scraped Yes; hope from Merthyr; then Newport, Cardiff and Barry - No. Holding on because of Neath, RCT, Caerffili. Three to go - Powys No. That seemed to be that! 30,000 behind. Then Gwynedd and finally Carmarthen and it was Yes with a 5000 majority.

OCTOBER

2nd

Mission is based on relationships. I had the joy of being with 10 young people at 7, and 7 young people at 8. In the first more mature group, we discussed

Jesus talking of his followers as his true family. Norah, Sharon and I have discussed, prayed, shared meals, played games, been on holiday, discussed homework, celebrated baptisms, weddings and funerals with these young people for 4 years. Some have attended 150 Bible studies. We are growing together. The second group is more 'rough and tumble' - at times concentrating, then disruptive but we have been together for 2 years. We shared the account of a healing by Jesus. We must not fail our young people.

Sunday 5th

Worship was led by the Llanfair Youth Team for the first time. They chose and discussed the theme and developed it according to the liturgy. Gavin presided, and Tammy, Lisa, Donna, Michael and Lee played important parts.

6th

The boutique is not selling as many clothes because a small Christian group have opened a clothes shop. They wish to be in direct competition.

23rd

We worshipped at the Calvary, listening to the powerful sound of the sea and a lovely bird singing the holy liturgy of Dafydd ap Gwilym. At the harbour I enjoyed my annual conversation with Brother Paul the hermit: I came here for silence and those seals keep making their noise, sometimes in the middle of the night. Perhaps God is teaching me something.
Caldey again.

NOVEMBER

18th

I completed the Collected Poems of R S Thomas (to 1990). It has been a glorious adventure and compares with my rediscovery of Shakespeare earlier this year. He provokes me to pray more earnestly and give time to silence; he has opened my eyes to nature and God's epiphanies.

19th

I did not expect to be a teacher on Penrhys. I preached to a dozen this morning; gave a talk to ten on the poetry of R S Thomas this afternoon; this evening helped 6 young people read Mark; and later had an hour's study of the Bible with 20, mostly young people. This is not untypical and helps create a people who will understand 'the faith of the church' and will have the opportunity to live it.

25th

We expected a quiet funeral because this single man had lived here only 6 years. He has recently been in touch once more with his children in Australia, after a gap of 35 years. His son had flown over from Brisbane and when he arrived at Llanfair, he was amazed that 50 people from Penrhys had arrived. It was so loving and courteous. In the service the son spoke to thank all who had helped his father, said goodbye to Dad, touched the coffin and said 'I'll be seeing you in the long paddock.' I gave him water from our well to pour on his parents' fields.

27th

Horeb, the last Welsh chapel in Tylorstown is to be demolished. No more hymns, prayers, reading the Bible and preaching the Word of God in our native tongue, for the first time since the community was shaped in the 1870s.

28th

I am being led into the roots of faith as it emerged in Wales. My ministry has always been within Wales but I am barely conscious of our Welsh language inheritance. I am reading magnificent contemporary poetry and prose, so different from that created in English.

DECEMBER

8th

Lisa and Michael started work experience. Both worked hard, have been enquiring, polite and cheerful. Michael has ambitions to be a chef, while Lisa has set her sights on being a teacher of religious education.

24th

Christmas never fails. Many years ago in Llanidloes as I walked to Zion on a perfectly ordinary, grey, damp, mid-winter, Christmas morning, I realized the coming of Christ was to an ordinary place on an ordinary day. However on Penrhys it is important to emphasise the mystery of the coming of Christ. We look forward with expectation throughout Advent, and during Epiphany we will emphasize the in-breaking of the divine through the life and ministry of Christ. And yet because of the incarnation, Christ comes to a world we experience. Today I spoke of the Archangel Gabriel (Michael) who wore trainers and spoke in an earthed way. A good Midnight communion - 49 for a devout, intelligent, sensitive celebration. We knew why we were there, and that there was no other place to be at the start of the Christmas season.

31st
The year ended with bread broken and wine poured. The new year began with darkness except for a few candles, silence apart from twelve strokes of the bell, and sharing bread and wine. It was followed by a quiet, firm resolve to seek Gods will.

1998

JANUARY

13th
For generations the chapel door is closed all week and children do not enter when it is open on Sunday. Because Llanfair is open every day, and open for different activities, the church welcomes all ages, including children. This begins for every Penrhys child starting in the Nursery and continues throughout Primary education.

20th
The shyest little girl rang the bell. She never speaks in school but showed delight at pressing the red button the correct number for the bell to ring for 23 children and 3 adults. The class applauded when she returned, a child whose father died two years ago.

22nd
Another tragedy. It is tragic we are accustomed to tragedy. It is part of our way of life. Hugh Jones arrived with a police sergeant to tell me one of his friends had been found dead in his flat, and would I come to say a blessing before the arrival of the undertaker. We walked thought the mist to the flat. The window had been broken for Hugh to gain entry an hour previously. I knelt and prayed, managing 'Lord have mercy, Christ have mercy, Lord have mercy. Lord into your hands I commit the spirit of our brother. Now Lord let your servant depart in peace. Our Father who art in heaven.' Here died a man of 49 alone surrounded by emblems of Welsh and Pontypridd rugby: scarves, shirts, programmes, tickets. Life should not end like this.

23rd

I am collecting music we have been using during the last eight years. We began with the music of the World Council of Churches, Taize and Iona and have since introduced the music of Caldey, the Catholic Mass, Orthodox music and the new URC hymnbook.

24th

Statistics for discussion groups during the last 4½ years make fascinating and encouraging reading: with 40 meetings each year, we averaged 15 in 1993/4, 9 in 1994/5, 25 in 1995/6, 28 in 1996/7 and 31 this year.
Our year began at the beginning of September and closed at the end of July. Most of those young people would go on holiday in August with Llanfair.

FEBRUARY

9th

Steve (Williams) came to prayers with the Special Needs Class. We looked at pictures of terraces from Tylorstown, and blocks from Penrhys, recognized them as houses and tried to distinguish a house from a home. One of the children saw its simplicity: 'a home is where you go when your parents don't want you any more.' Norah helped by reminding them of the song 'I'm going home.'

24th

The Infants provide fun. Before they arrived, I put a table into the church and turned it upside down. The 30 children trooped in to the chapel and had hardly sat when they started laughing - look at the table! It's upside down! They thought it the funniest thing, and so did the adults as a consequence. The story of Jesus getting into a boat was told, and two disciples rowed to the shore to pick up Jesus. The table was of course a boat.

28th

An envelope with a royal sign. The Prince would like to see our young people at Highgrove and will visit Penrhys this year. The letter was written by his Welsh advisor, Manon Williams, sister to the wife of William Hague. A wonderful boost to LYT. What effect will the visit of the prince have on the plans for the estate?

MARCH

Sunday, 1st

The first Welsh language service on Penrhys.

The trigger for the decision to have a monthly Communion Service in Welsh was the closure of Horeb, the last Welsh speaking chapel in Tylorstown. The deeper reasons were that Welsh is the first language of Norah and Sharon, and many Penrhys children now attend Ysgol Llyn y Forwyn, a Ferndale school teaching through the medium of Welsh. Our son Hugh teaches there.

10th

Worship with a class of 4 year olds with a few having reached 5 and being ever so grown up. The youngest Humphreys boy played the shepherd (wearing a scarf and cap, and carrying a stick); he had ten sheep, one of which was lost, and two dogs. The children burst into spontaneous jubilation when the good shepherd found the lost sheep. They chose as their hymn the appropriate 'Baa baa Black Sheep.'

APRIL

9th

Dozens stood around the walls for the funeral of the young man. The congregation was dignified, attentive, worshipful with 'amens of agreement' responding to prayers and address. I know these young people with sad eyes and gaunt faces. Who will be next? I pray there will be no more. The Union Jack was draped on the coffin, but his brother insisted it be covered by the Welsh Dragon

10th, Good Friday

Yesterday was Penrhys' tragedy in the burial of the young man without faith, and a family without hope. Love will take them into heaven. Today was full of thankfulness. 30 formed a pilgrimage at Well, Amphitheatre, Statue and Courtyard on a very cold, sleety day. 120 present.

11th

The baptism of 7 fine young people during the Easter Vigil. As we crossed from the darkness of Good Friday and the disillusionment and emptiness of Holy Saturday to the dawn of new life on Easter Sunday, Gavin (19), Jason (17), Laura (14), the two Leannes (16 and 15), Michael (16) and Ryan (14)

were baptized. All attend Confirmation Class regularly and are members of the Llanfair Youth Team. They have reached commitment and must now be supported in their growth in faith.

12th, Easter Sunday

Thirty reached Twyn Disgwylfa and took in the breathtaking view of God's creation: the glistening snow clad mountains to the north at the edge of South Wales, and to the south the snow covered hills of Somerset.

14th

Half a dozen times each year, Norah organizes the Llanfair cleaning day. It is a chore or a pleasure, depending upon who turns up and the mood of the participants. One factor is invariable: work is never completed. Today was a pleasure: 20 worked from 9.30 for 5 hours and as it included communal chips, everyone felt valued. There is a sense of ownership. The people of Llanfair clean, paint and maintain the building.

23rd

The baby was buried with his brother who died only weeks ago; their 19 year old cousin had been laid there a year ago and it is only two years since their grandmother had been buried in the same area. Around me in the cold, very heavy rain were the family dropping roses of love and grief.

MAY

5th

One of the most important days in the story of Penrhys. The community walked with drums beating, whistles blowing and girls singing behind colourful, celebratory banners. We walked from the Community Centre down the hill towards the Star, turned left to Llwynypia Hospital, right to Tonypandy Square and up the steep hill to Clydach Vale. We gathered at the Headquarters of Rhondda Cynon Taf and greeted councillors as they arrived for Housing Committee. Over 200 Penrhys people were present and 30 went inside to the public area. Daniel and Kelly presented the children's work, Sybil presented the 450 signatures petition and Wayne and I showed slides for 15 minutes. The Committee decided unanimously that 6 representatives of the Penrhys community be part of a working group seeking a strategy to be presented to Committee in October. The community felt proud of this culmination of a years work. Now the next hurdle!

This 'Long Walk' was a critical turning point in the struggle.

15th

Fun Walk in Tonypandy raised £217: Norah was unrecognisable in a baggy tartan suit and ginger wig.

20th

Thirty from Llanfair sat in the choir stalls at Llandaff Cathedral to sing Caldey Compline. Electrifying to hear the first sounds echoing in the distance. Laura read I Corinthians 13, such a privilege for a girl of 14.

JUNE

6th

One of the happiest family days. Dylan and Mónika married this afternoon at Llanfair. The wedding in three languages felt absolutely right. The couple looked good and spoke clearly. John H preached bilingually. Canolfan Rhys for photographs and a perfect reception. Norah and Llanfair friends catered, and Hugh was the best man.

Mónika had been a volunteer from Ráday Reformed Theological University at Llanfair. John Humphreys was Moderator for Wales of the URC and had spent four years in Hungary during the period of close relationship between the Synod of Wales and the Reformed Church of Hungary.

16th

Nelson Mandela received the freedom of Cardiff. The hero thanked those who had supported the fight against Apartheid and mentioned Bert Pearce, the 84 year old communist who kept the struggle in the forefront of people's minds. My memory returned to the days when it was not a popular cause, when the church was warned to 'keep out of politics... stop interfering with sport... when men like Hanif Bhanjee and Peter Hain were seen as interfering immigrants and troublemakers... when Côr Cochion Caerdydd were part of the lunatic fringe.' Norah, Cath and I were glad to see Hywel and Mair Francis, Hanif Bhanjee, Dafydd Elis Thomas, but not so pleased to see some Cardiff dignitaries playing politics.

18th

Gombrichs 'The Story of Art' extended the boundaries of my world.

Ernst Gombrich's work has had a seminal popularising influence on the appreciation of art. It has been one of Norah's favourite books since teenage days.

27th

MRA organized a conference on 'seeking the unity' of Wales in light of devolution.' Delegates came from all over Wales and many walks of life. Llanfair's hospitality and facilities were excellent.

Moral Rearmament is an international movement calling for oral and spiritual renewal founded by the Christian evangelist F N D Buchman in the 1920s as the Oxford Group. It based its teachings on the our Absolutes (honesty, purity, unselfishness, love).

JULY

Sunday 5th

The Llanfair Youth Team prepared worship. Michael's sermon was based on the theological material, and Donna and Laura used Pauline material from the discussion group. They integrated the material with the liturgy and spoke with feeling and humour. They have grown since their first service last October.

16th

Yvette Rabemila and Zo from Madagascar, and Sheila Maxey from the URC are experienced in mission and unity, and came to Llanfair to evaluate the Llanfair/ Madagascar relationship. They were surprised, delighted and saw Llanfair as an important example of world mission. They want to encourage similar ministries and opportunities for young people.

Yvette Rabemila was a Vice-President of the Church of Jesus Christ of Madagascar and its ecumenical communications officer. Sheila Maxey was Secretary for Ecumenical affairs in the URC and became the Moderator of the URC General Assembly in 2004/5. Zo was an administrator in Yvette's department.

25th

Ten young people are working in different rooms at this house in Staffin. They are discussing and writing about four themes in readiness for worship at Kilmuir and Stenschol. They have been struggling with (1) the formation and key principles of LYT (2) the functions of LYT each week (3) our faith (4) how we have been helped by the holiday mission on Skye. Seeds are sown in their lives and for the Christian community.

Holidays in Skye.

Sunday 26th

A momentous day for Llanfair took place 700 miles away on the Isle of Skye. Our 10 young people participated in services at Kilmuir and Staffin. Last night they prepared talks and songs, and today they shared them with sincerity and clarity. It was difficult to have a dry eye and both congregations were deeply moved. Jason and Michael shared their faith openly and with flair. They are born evangelists.

27th

All 13 reached 'The Table' on the top of Quiraing. The section from 'The Prison' to 'The Table' is steep and demanding and although not dangerous it demands care and working as a group rather than as individuals. When we tried to climb two years ago, a half reached the Table; last year most reached the top, and this year when all 13 accomplished the goal, there was a sense of corporate achievement. Songs, silence and prayer on the top.

31st

The group enthusiastically climbed Quiraing, enjoyed the Outer Hebrides and centred their holiday on worship. Several churches graciously help our people: Kilmuir, Staffin, Balloch, Wilmslow, individuals and families who have influenced our young people. It should remain with them for the rest of their lives.

AUGUST

5th

What are the reasons behind the 'success' of Llanfair? The sense of 'wholeness and holiness' with the integration of work and worship, strategy, determination, single-mindedness to the exclusion of extraneous distractions, listening to the voices of the community, creating a team of colleagues from Penrhys and Llanfair residents, developing sound finances which are transparent, honest and compassionate, worship and prayer under-girding all action, working hard day after day, satisfaction from the effects of Llanfair's ministry over a wide area and in deepening lives.

18th

I receive so much from this stark, subtle, fierce, delicate land. We have enjoyed Carmarthen, the area which won for us the Assembly. Wales is growing in confidence and on this holiday we have heard the language in

shop, mart and street. Penrhys needs this story to stand alongside the local and valley stories. Valley people can be bewildered and embittered by Welsh nationhood, language and culture.
Holidays with adults in Trinity College Carmarthen.

28th
In our journeys to Skye, Snowdon, Carmarthen and Caldey, we have encountered men and women of faith. Llanfair also needs to express its vision of a community of faith living in unity and service, being inclusive, open and rejecting intolerance and fundamentalism.

SEPTEMBER

4th
Lynsey and Rhian asked for help to study Matthew's Gospel for A Level RE.
It was most gratifying to see Penrhys young people achieving in the world of education.

5th
Having spent 8 months reading the Old Testament, arriving at Matthew's Gospel is discovering a New World. Jesus strides out of the Old Testament world. There is no-one like him and nothing like his teaching with his uniqueness, freshness, fulfilment, expectation. I have been challenged by the Old Testament, but Matthew presents a new dimension. God is amongst us. I have to restrain myself from reading too much too quickly.

12th
All weddings are beautiful, and the marriage of Nicola and Paul was prepared meticulously. The entry of the bride, six bridesmaids and two pageboys deserved the main aisle of Westminster Abbey rather than the circuitous entry of Llanfair. It had dignity, friendliness and humour. Nicola expected 140 guests and all arrived at Llanfair. How well everyone looked and responded.

28th
Julia and Nan's class is classified as special needs but only to the extent that we all have special needs. 15 arrived with teachers and helpers; the main door was opened for the little boy in a wheel-chair; another who sings like Pavarotti rang the bell; a kind boy held the door open and in walked the children with sounds of delight as they saw the table, banner, fruits and flowers. Young

Pavarotti sang 'New York, New York.' Fruit salad in the café before the children left.

OCTOBER

10th

Christ Well, the church-community premises for the URC at Manselton is the fruit of hard work for Kevin as minister, the leaders and members of the congregation. We have good memories of our ministry there 20 years ago and it was a delight to be welcomed home today.

The minister was Kevin Watson who had been inducted in Manselton in 1987.

20th

Ten of us met Robert Bevan in Clydach and discussed the Officers' Report. We then sat in the back row of the Chamber as the Housing Committee presented its report on Penrhys. Robert proposed the amendment, seconded by Geraint: 'no demolition without consultation with the Action Group; a multidisciplinary group to be established and to include the Welsh Office, Ward Councillors and an independent chairperson.' The resolution, passed unanimously was a shock to the Officers. Phoned Kevin Morgan who is prepared to act as chair.

Robert Bevan was the Ward Labour Councillor for Penrhys and Geraint Davies the Plaid Cymru Councillor in Treherbert and a good friend of Llanfair. Both were prepared to cooperate for the sake of the community of Penrhys. Professor Kevin Morgan was teaching at the Department of City and Regional Planning at Cardiff University and was passionately supportive of communities like Penrhys.

NOVEMBER

Sunday, 1st

The service incorporating All Saints and All Souls was created for the nine Penrhys families bereaved during the last year. Llanfair needed to exist for them.

13th

The phone went at 8 am from St James Palace. 'Are you coming today to the Prince's birthday? Will you be one of a group presented to the Royal party?' I entered the palace (Buckingham) at 5.30, asked for Emma and was taken to the front of the Art Gallery to join Tony Blair, the Secretary General of the Commonwealth and five others (including a cellist from the National Orchestra of Wales, and a young soldier). The great doors opened and the Queen, Queen Mother, Prince of Wales and Duke of Edinburgh appeared and greeted us! I mentioned to the Queen Mother that the King had died on my birthday - 1952 she said, and seemed pleased. The Queen talked of 'it's like coming onto a stage;' the Prince remembered Penrhys and stated he would visit again. Later I chatted with Spike Milligan (talked of tackling a Springbok!), William Hague (referring Penrhys to Conservative Christian MPs next week), a bassist from Maerdy.

Sunday 15th

Worship was led by the Overseas Volunteers: Maria, Mamy, Ildiko and Rosina. The intention is that LYT should lead on the first Sunday of the month, and the Volunteers on the third Sunday. What with different leaders at Friday prayers, a dozen preside at worship. This is the result of (1) a well structured, flexible liturgy (2) the theological sweep to the year (3) Bible Study on Wednesday. Our worship, shape of building and open-ness of heart encourages those beginning to lead.

Maria Lindgren was a Deacon of the Lutheran Church of Sweden, Mamy from Madagascar, Ildiko from Hungary and Rosina a musician from Germany. Llanfair had grown into a truly international and ecumenical community.

17th

David Lawrence, editor of Reform, phoned to say that William Hague had addressed Conservative Christian MPs yesterday and his one specific example was Llanfair. He asked MPs to listen to the church's work. Remarkable after the Thatcher days. I do not forget the Coal Dispute of the 1980s.

19th

The love revealed at the funeral of Jan English was a tribute to humankind. The chapel, vestibule and lounge were packed and there were many outside. As I drove to the cemetery, dozens were walking down the main path. It was an awesome sight. Here was a woman who attracted by the quality of her love, and had translated love into action for the last fifteen years on Penrhys. The family arrived; we started with 'The Nun's Chorus,' a song which meant so much for the family. The congregation responded magnificently, following attentively each line written, singing with care, saying the prayers. The interment was on Penrhys and family and friends returned to the dining room for hospitality.

29th

The last day of 9 years of relationship with the Training in Mission teams. As the years progressed, we became more and more aware that the need for each other was mutual. This afternoon's service included the baptism of Taylor Leigh, Joshua and Luke. The family were seated before the children entered to sit on the floor - there were 123 present. One from each continent extended greetings, all prayed and lit candles; the 3 children responded well to their baptism. TIMs final words were 'I felt my spirit had left until I came to Penrhys... God has blessed us through you ... Friendliest people we have met church and community are one.' They brought a sign that we have been blessed.

The location of training for the TIM team was changed from Birmingham to the Church of South India. Their move was an impoverishment of our life on Penrhys.

DECEMBER

1st

The Multi-disciplinary Group met at the Action Group Office. There were representatives of the appropriate departments because an instruction had been sent out by the Chief Executive. I could not believe the change in tone. Our agenda and choice of Chair (Kevin Morgan) were accepted.

This was the first meeting of the Multi-Disciplinary group. It had been an almighty battle to move decision making out of the hands of the Housing Department so that any future proposals could take in the social costs of community. The attempt was to develop an independent and objective analysis of the life of Penrhys, and to acknowledge the many changes which had taken place during the previous decade. Some members of the Housing Committee would be oblivious to these changes because they had not been implemented as a result of their policy.

16th

A young teenager died this morning. She was part of a family which was very much involved in the life of the church. She belonged to a group of young people who frequent Llanfair, and also spent many holidays with the church.

23rd

There have been many tragedies in Penrhys' short history but today was the vehicle for the family and community to express grief. We all sensed we would experience something unique, but no one was prepared for the size, dignity and compassion of the congregation. The grace of God worked through many people in such different ways - Paul spent hours preparing the chapel; Myra and friends were immaculate with their catering in the dining room; Sharon and Norah looked after the flowers; Simon and Lee organised the external sound system. There were 250 people in the chapel and vestibule, and at least 100 outside; when we arrived at the cemetery and I looked for the grave, the road held hundreds of people. Everything went with courage, compassion and dignity. We all felt proud of our community.

Sunday 27th

Seven year old Kelly was knocking at 9.15 - is there church? She had a Lidl carrier bag and inside was her doll for Christmas. It laughed, cried and she was such a happy girl. It was right to worship because of Kelly and Luke: they read the scriptures with verve and volume and led the carol singing.

31st

A privilege to worship God the Father of Jesus Christ. As the Caldey bell was ringing the midnight which separates the Old from the New Year, we were reading 'the heart of the Good News is that Jesus is not dead but alive.' With that proclamation in our hearts, we greeted each other with Happy New Year and read 'this is the meaning of the words of the Bible. Death has been totally defeated, for the fact is Jesus was raised to life. God be thanked - we can now live victoriously because of what he has done.' With that conviction 20 people at Llanfair Penrhys celebrated the first communion of this final year of the century and millennium. There could be no better way. We had gone downstairs at 9 for a disco and party organised by LYT (30 present). Communion followed at 11.30.

1999

JANUARY

Sunday 31st

The preparation for the sermon began in Bible Study on Wednesday, continued during three discussion groups and yesterday morning, I struggled with text and context to discover a new angle on the passage. Today I delivered the message in quiet, concise, clear form and shared it as the heart of the Gospel and the centre of God's purposes for us in Llanfair, and for the whole universe. What was the response to the sermon and the worship? I don't know. I hope it helped people on their pilgrimage, but I do not know. That is often the burden of the preacher.

FEBRUARY

Sunday 7th

If yesterday was the privilege of our family celebrating my 60th birthday, today was the opportunity for Llanfair to join in. I had anticipated that sometime during the day there would be a 'secret party' but had no idea it would give me and everyone else so much pleasure, and reflect such mutual affection.

17th

Norah and I were with a large family of 40 children, grandchildren and great-grandchildren surrounding the bed of the invalid. This morning the grandparents had re-married and the marriage was now blessed. In reality the couple were blessing their family, and their family blessing them.

18th

Kevin Morgan brings hope to the Penrhys Community Action Group. However, if I feel too optimistic, I look at the remains of the Hendrefadog Estate. I saw it built and demolished. We have lived through 9 years of the physical erosion of Penrhys, at the same time as we enjoy its mini-renaissance.

MARCH

Sunday 7th

A memorable ordinary Sunday with worship and Sunday School. The church witnesses as it has every Sunday since the Resurrection. Today Llanfair ministered in this little acre, corner of the vineyard, blessed spot, area for which we are responsible - as the church meets this challenge everyday throughout God's world.

17th

A month ago we had been at the 'blessing' of the newly married couple. Today, as warm as a summer's day, I took the husband's funeral and was asked to stand at the door of the house so that those inside and those in the garden could participate. Afterwards we walked across the road to the graveside. It was so appropriate.

APRIL

4th, Easter Sunday

One of our happiest Easters. Thirty walked through low cloud and drizzle to Bristol Tump. The chapel was full of Penrhys people for the Easter Play. The hard work paid off and the greatest story was reflected with clarity, humour and sincerity.

29th

Daleep Mukarji was appointed Director of Christian Aid a year ago and is visiting South Wales. He arrived with Jeff Williams and Elenid Jones of Christian Aid, ate in the café was shown around the building by Norah and met the residential team. This inspiring leader worked as a doctor in Indian villages, and affirmed our work.

Daleep Mukarji trained as a doctor in Vellore, India, before working in a leprosy hospital in Andhra Pradesh. In 1994 he was appointed executive secretary for health, community and justice at the World Council of Churches in Geneva. He joined Christian Aid in 1998.

30th

The residential team enjoy each other's company and work well together. It had been another long day and we all came home at the same time, tired and satisfied that good work had been accomplished. There is no alternative to

hard work but it is fulfilling when people work together, there is unity of purpose, equality of effort and a shared sense of achievement.
It often took 20 minutes on a Friday evening for the residential team to enter our flats off the central staircase. There would be a sharing of the fun and challenges of the evening as we began to wind down after another hectic evening which began at 6.45 and closed at 10.30 when the last disco-dancer had left, the equipment carried and locked away for another week and the staircase mopped. The sound would still be ringing in our ears. On the Monday evening at the shared meal we would talk about the issues more formally.

MAY

5th

The Blessing of Father Daniel as Abbot took place on Caldey. The brothers of Caldey and the Cistercian Order celebrated; Daniel's own brothers and sisters from the Netherlands rejoiced in the happiness of one they loved dearly; the Islanders were glad to see this friendly, devout man as leader for their community; others from the wider Catholic Church included Daniel Mullins, Bishop of Menevia; and there were those like Norah and me who respect and love this community because it has been a sign of faith, hope and love throughout our ministry. The service was followed by a superb party in the refectory. Daniel's sister and husband danced, and the monks and nuns sang and tapped their feet to the music.

7th

The Welsh political scene witnessed its most dramatic change since radical Liberalism gave way to the new radical Labour Party. Now the tired old Labour party of Wales has almost lost its position to Plaid Cymru. The results came as a shock to politicians and media because the secret lay with the electorate. It is hard to believe that Islwyn, Rhondda, Llanelli and Conway fell to Plaid; the state of the parties has provided a splendid hung Assembly - 28 Labour/ 17 Plaid Cymru with Tory and Liberal Democrat. In the local elections, Rhondda Cynon Taf had gone to Plaid Cymru. Will there be a different attitude towards Penrhys?

11th

We took Lisa, Donna, Michael and Gavin to Trinity College, Carmarthen. Our link with Trinity began ten years ago when I was invited to speak about

Penrhys. Our programme developed slowly, carefully and naturally: two groups of students visit each year; students live here for 6 weeks for Teaching Practice; two of our teacher/workers have come from Trinity; sixteen volunteers come to Trinity annually for holiday. Today the young people met the Deputy Principal, Head of Religious Education, Careers, and it was agreed to establish a link for education at Llanfair.

14th

The Fun Walk in Tonypandy was a great success and Norah and 9 others collected £298 in 4 hours. This shows the determination of Llanfair volunteers and the generosity of the Rhondda community. Will we reach the target of £2000 which is £2 per head of Penrhys population. If only this could happen in affluent areas!
All the other activities took place over a period of a month.

26th

Wales' greatest day since Owain Glyndwr held his parliament at Machynlleth: the official opening of the Welsh National Assembly. It is a new beginning, a celebration that we are Welsh. There was an overwhelming sense of being one. I entered the castle with 9 young people, introduced them to Tom Shebbeare and to the Prince. They also met the Queen and I met Gareth Jones (Blaenau now Assembly Member for Conwy) and Geraint Davies (A.M. for Rhondda).
Tom Shebbeare was the Director of The Prince's Trust. Gareth was my student friend from Swansea University days.

28th

The four young people (Michael, Gavin, Donna, Lisa) met Medwin Hughes (Vice Principal), Tom Evans (Director of Project 2000) and the Head of Religious Studies. Medwin articulated the mission statement of the College: Church in Wales, bilingual, pledged to sustainable community development. If we substituted the word 'ecumenical' for 'Church in Wales,' it expresses Llanfair's mission statement.

JUNE

4th

In discussion with this group of boys, I am aware of deep seated problems: three excluded from school, another about to be excluded, the uncontrollable temper of the fifth, another very confused, three in the lowest sets about to leave school. We struggle for an hour's discussion every week. I know them well and like them very much. I believe there is mutual affection and respect.

Sunday 6th

Just before 9.15, I could hear voices outside Llanfair and I went down to let the two little sisters into chapel. They came to light candles for their father who died at home yesterday. After service they had squash and biscuits and made drawings: One drew a large coffin covered in flowers.

7th

Our first film night. 'Now Voyager' with Bette Davies. Fifteen enjoyed it.
A new development in Llanfair's social life. The 'black and white' movies brought fond memories to many older residents and new delight to younger people.

30th

A consultation at the Council Chamber in Trinity, chaired by Bishop Huw Jones included Principal Clive Lloyd Davies, Deputy Principal Medwin Hughes, Head of Religious Studies Will Strange and representatives of the denominations (many on the Penrhys Sponsoring Body). The young people impressed and the decision was made to develop a Diploma of Church and Community Development.

JULY

15th

I attended the BITC presentation at Whitbreads to industries committed to Community Development. I was a guest at Bill Castell's table which included Philip Lader, the American Ambassador (related to Peter Marshall and Norman Vincent Peale). The Prime Minister made the presentations.
Philip Lader was Ambassador from 1997 to 2001.

16th

'Patience and time; time and patience' was the advice of the old wise Russian general. Napoleon will be defeated. That is the heart of our work. It needs imagination, foresight, understanding, skill, but above all it needs stamina, determination and keeping going.

AUGUST

12th

Ten young people flew to Budapest to stop with different families in Monor. *This was the first time for a group from Llanfair to travel to Europe. They were led by Hugh, Dylan and Mónika and spent their time with Mónika's home congregation at Monor, near Budapest. The following summer saw the visit of the Monor young people to Penrhys.*

19th

Three Penrhys young women have passed A levels. Lynsey and Rhian called to express joy and thanks, and Tammy spoke with me in Woody's. I had helped Lynsey and Rhian with weekly meetings in their Religious Studies course.

23rd

We saw the happy faces of the young people, heard their joyous, excited stories and realized that God worked a great act of reconciliation in drawing together young people from Penrhys and Monor. Hugh told us it was their common commitment to Christ which united them. The strangeness of culture and language was overcome and at the heart of the change was God in Christ.

26th

We welcomed Bill Castell who first came to Penrhys in 1991 as member of a 'Seeing is Believing' visit, and has remained loyal to our work ever since. He is able to evaluate the changes.

30th

The community celebrated near the Statue and the Amphitheatre, and enjoyed stalls made by Penrhys people and activities organised by the community. LYT sold cakes; LYTeen sold toys, Norah had a Jubilee 2000 exhibition and petition, the shop sold clothes, the football team organised games and food. The great Tip had the words 'Tidy' visible for miles. This evening there were rock groups and fireworks. It was such a success, prepared and organized by the community and not by outsiders paid to do it for us.
The young people's group (LYT) had created a younger group which they called LYTeen.

SEPTEMBER

6th

A good start. I am under no illusions and neither are the young people, but they begin the exacting, demanding task of being students of the Opportunity 2000 programme of Trinity College Carmarthen.

This was an important experiment in learning by extension. Three of our young people began a Course on 'An Introduction to Christianity,' a course of 16 modules which would be accredited. All three passed the course, and one successfully passed a further Course. It was however too demanding to be seen as a way of achieving sufficient accreditation for them to eventually enter College full-time. In that I was their local tutor, I did not find it easy to differentiate between my role as 'minister' and my role as 'teacher' seeking their entry into the academic world.

15th

When I began work on Penrhys, the key was the ministry of service, diakonia, being alongside, entering the lives of people who have suffered and been marginalized. The minority who exercise authority ignore, whilst the majority of people are oblivious to what goes on in the great urban wildernesses of the modern housing estate. Llanfair does exercise that ministry of servant-hood. I did not however anticipate a ministry of teaching, presbyterate. That ministry is also at the heart of what goes on daily. Today I administered morning Communion, helped the students read the Old Testament, led a discussion group on John the Baptist, presided at Compline and participated in Bible Study. All in one day and for 50 people.

22nd

This day could not have been invented. Our students were engrossed by the doctrine of creation, the double procession of the Holy Spirit and its expression in the Nicene-Constantinopolitan Creed, when Norah looked through the window and saw Father Deiniol trying to attract our attention. We asked Deiniol to explain the filioque clause. He was astounded, came in and talked to the students.

Father Deiniol of the Orthodox Tradition did not accept 'the double procession of the Holy Spirit.' The filioque controversy has to do with the Latin phrase, translated 'and the son,' which was accepted as an addition to the Nicene Creed by the Western churches and subsequently opposed by the Eastern churches. The theological dispute was a continuing source of friction between the east and the west and was eventually elevated to become one of the 'official' causes of the Great Schism in 1054 A.D.

NOVEMBER

1st

Each person's loss diminishes us all. All Saints/ All Souls is a sensitive service. Fourteen families were bereaved this year and most came to light a candle and say prayers

12th

The six boys provided a stimulating discussion. Our friendship has built up over the years and this evening Scripture opened us to the action of God. We had been discussing Peter's denial, and contrasted it with his courage when facing martyrdom. What changed this man? Barry John burst out with 'the resurrection of Jesus of course, that's why he wasn't afraid any more. He knew there was life after death.' I shook Barry's hand and we all applauded. Hard work will pay off, but in the long run!

Barry John had been the 6 year old who heard the cuckoo near Maerdy reservoir in May 1987.

23rd

The infants entered the chapel and noticed the model round table with a plate, biscuit, jug, four glasses and a candle ready for lighting. Who had a birthday? Adam, nearly 7, invited three children to share, everyone sang, he blew out the candle and shared the biscuit and juice. The large table was also prepared and I pointed out that we celebrate the birthday of Jesus just as we celebrate Adam's birthday.

27th

Every day for 48 years I have written the diary and said prayers. As the book is closed, the passing day and the night which falls is placed in the hands of God. I am conscious of One who looks at what is written and offers forgiveness. Donna phoned to say she had 64% for her first assignment; Gavin had 62% and Michael 64%.

DECEMBER

13th

Forty people were enthralled by the Beethoven Razumovsky String Quartet No 1 and Ravel's Quartet, performed by members of the Welsh National Opera Company. The performers were delighted by the acoustics, the welcome and concentration, especially of the children.
The WNO Quartet were friends of Simon Preston, the Music Coordinator at Canolfan Rhys. Simon Preston has been musical director of Samba Galez, the Cardiff Samba Band from 1991 to the present.

14th

God weaves a pattern in which we have freedom, but our distinctiveness is carefully shaped into the overall picture. Nothing is wasted. The Junior School performed 'Oliver.' We knew all taking part and most in the audience - Mattie was Oliver, Keira Fagin, Nikita the Artful Dodger, Cory Mr Bumble.

24th

On a wild wet night 40 gathered to pray at the last Christmas of the Millennium. At 11.20 there were 5 of us and because of the weather, I did not expect many more. And yet they came, those worshipping weekly and those who attend once a year. The chapel was filled with the mellow, warm, comforting light of a hundred candles opening the beauty of the icons of Our Lady of Tenderness and the Trinity; the snowball candle threw light into the open stable; there were lights on the window sills, piano and the candle-stand which stood between the table with bread and wine, and the banner of star and stable. Scripture, sermon, prayers, silence, hymns, greetings, bread, wine and above all people with God.

25th Christmas Day

Jean Noel and Csaba joined us for our Christmas dinner and we enjoyed our evening together.
Our pattern for Christmas day was to have a short act of worship at 9.30 am and to spend the day with our family at home. The residential volunteers who had not returned home for Christmas joined us for dinner and for the evening. Jean Noel was from Madagascar and Csaba from Hungary. Sarah, our English volunteer had joined her family in the Midlands.

27th

A nostalgic walk along the river to Ferndale. We passed the Memorial for Nos 8 and 9 pits, (Wayne's and Pendyrus collieries) which were open for 100 years. My grandfather took my father when he was aged 7, on a Sunday morning after chapel and pointed down to where the new pit was to be sunk (1909); as we walked along the river a large heron rose up beside us and flapped its way up the mountain towards the site of the old Powder House. Hugh and I put sticks in the river and watched them travel swiftly in the turbulent water. Our ancestors walked that same path 130 years ago, in the mid 19th century. And in a few days we enter the 21st century.

28th

Norah and I walked through the non-existent Hendrefadog estate to the derelict school which the last children left in July. Although boarded up, the main door had been prized open and we walked in to total devastation. The roof, floorboards, doors had all been stripped, but I could see Miss Davies playing 'Country Gardens' as infants marched out of the hall to our classrooms. It felt not just the end of an era but the close of civilization which would be followed by the onset of barbarism. I had a sense of foreboding as we returned to half derelict Penrhys. What will become of us?

31st

The end and the beginning. Llanfair at the stroke of midnight was a blessing. I would not wish to be elsewhere at this moment in the measurement of time. We crossed from the past into the future.

We shared the Millennium Prayer which had been written by Peter Trow, URC minister. It was the centre of the BBC's televised New Year celebrations.

2000

JANUARY

1st
I looked out on a night sky with a single bright star and a crescent moon, and knew we should greet the dawn of the new millennium from Twyn Disgwylfa, Bristol Tump, a hill I have always climbed, especially on auspicious occasions. Norah and I left at 7.20 and were thrilled by streaks of snow on the Beacons, Channel, and English coast.

17th
Four children have been orphaned by the sudden death of their mother. How could I channel hope and comfort? I thought of the Gospel's ambiguity of the Cross. I looked at the valley hidden in an ocean of mist. The theme shaped. A delicate service, with attention and love focussed on the children.

18th
In the funeral yesterday I asked us to put children first, not giving material things, but time, space, energy, educational and moral guidance.

20th
The Christian Fellowship have started serving breakfasts in the old chapel. They have tried all ways to undermine our work. It is difficult never to respond.
They were obviously unaware of the stringent health and safety and hygiene regulations adhered to in the Llanfair Café. All the volunteers in Llanfair earned the appropriate certificates and they proudly hung on the café walls. Often the Food Inspector would call unannounced and always the café received high praise.

FEBRUARY

2nd
For 2½ years the Community Action Group tried to converse with the Housing Officers and Housing Committee, and believed in a multi-disciplinary approach with an independent chairperson. The process included public

meetings, exhibitions, demonstrations, countless meetings and conversations. Ultimately the multi-disciplinary group, chaired by Kevin Morgan, agreed that there be an independent review to which we would all subscribe. The 'Independent Review' began its work.

29th

The Nursery helped us celebrate our Llanfair's 8th birthday. Three School Inspectors were present. We all felt nervous but the children were as wonderful as always. Dafydd Jones (Manselton, now of L'Arche) came to meet Gavin to encourage him to join them in Brecon.
Gavin was delighted by the opportunity to serve in L'Arche and lived in the community for a year. In L'Arche Communities people with learning disabilities and their assistants live and work together. L'Arche means 'The Ark' in French. It was founded by Jean Vanier.

MARCH

15th

As I presided at Communion the Spring sun focussed on bread being broken and wine as it was poured, on the centre of the round table at the heart of Penrhys.

23rd

Once the Church was accused of working only with 'the better kind' of young people. Llanfair is at the centre of Penrhys' problems. This evening seven 11-14 year olds talked about how they got hold of drink, how one collapsed, another was violent and suicidal, a third (who had not drunk) cried himself to sleep because he was afraid his friends would die. What can we do when we are surrounded by drinks and drugs? A cry for help!

27th

The Independent Review Group presented its preliminary report to 200 people in the Community Centre. The audience questioned passionately and judiciously. Applause at the close because people felt there was hope and a strategy.

APRIL

20th

The abyss. At the Supper, Judas went out into the night. Having sung the Hallel psalms, (Psalms 113-118), Jesus walked into the garden with weary friends and waited for the betrayer. There was a moment of stillness and darkness before lights, swords, shouts, and a frenetic night of speeches, silence, shrieks for vengeance, cowardly denial, abrogation of responsibility, scourging, spitting, and in the daylight, the painful walk to the Cross. From the day of palm waving and Hosannas, we are on the path to Calvary.

21st

A most meaningful Good Friday. Paul and I walked in torrential driving rain and were the only ones to make the pilgrimage to the Well, Amphitheatre, Shrine and Vestibule where we were joined by Mónika and the Newport congregation. Then the play: 30 children and young people and a full chapel.
Paul Harrison was one of our most faithful worshippers. He had been first introduced to church when he was in his 20s, just before the opening of Llanfair. Mónika (our daughter in law) was serving at Community House, an important Church Project in East Newport.

22nd

Easter arrived. As we crossed midnight we were drawn together by the love of the Cross and the power that made the Tomb empty. We shared with joy as the community gathered for repentance, celebration and commitment. The night had been dreadful because at 1, we were woken by a pellet hitting the bedroom window. A dozen were fired from a teenagers flat opposite; I put on lights and it stopped. At 3 it restarted, I called the police who went to the house to discover three of 'our' teenagers. Their gun was confiscated and they promised to apologize and pay. They came at midday and apologized. At the core of the Vigil was the baptism of Amy, Natalie and Nicola.

Sunday 23rd, Easter Sunday

After a short night, we gathered outside Llanfair on a misty mild morning. 28 walked to Bristol Tump with the Cross, carried (at first) by Keira, the blind man in the Easter play. 50 at the play, plus a cast of 30.
Before entering the chapel, I went upstairs to the dining room which was full of eager and excited children who had been dressed in their costumes in readiness for the play. We had prayers before celebrating the Easter story to a packed chapel.

24th

Easter brought the unexpectedness of the walk in the Garden, forgiveness and nurture when sharing breakfast at the sea's edge, the call to serve and share the Good News with the final meeting with Peter. Easter reassures because of its ordinariness: daily worship in Holy Week, the Easter Play, the Vigil with its baptisms are all part of a pattern of daily labour, and the people who came on these special occasions are parents of children, friends and neighbours, all using Llanfair as a home. 120 residents came this week (some many times): over 15% of our population.

MAY

1st

I read the preface to the Oxford Book of English Verse, edited by Christopher Ricks. I bought my first edition (Quiller Couch) 40 years go, and the Gardner edition in the 70s. Poetry has always exercised a profound influence from the Romantic Poets (Wordsworth, Keats and Shelley) in Form VI with my teacher at Porth County, Mr Burnell; T S Eliot as a young minister, and at the moment R S Thomas.

6th

Penrhys went to Ton Pentre to support Penrhys Athletic in the final of a local cup. The weather was like mid-summer and one of the stands was filled with Blue Army supporters. Midway through the second half a Penrhys defender scored and towards the end came the final goal. Penrhys proudly received a shield; they had won their third trophy of the season. All except two live on Penrhys and 5 of the 6 teenagers playing have been members of confirmation classes.

22nd

A concert by a Sudanese Duo with 50 present.
Another successful concert.

23rd

Every Infants child is introduced to the Christian Aid children, and pictures of two Indian children hang in every class. These small Indian children are world figures and for many British children are partners in changing the world community.
Norah had distributed these posters to every class in the Infants and Junior Schools. When the children came to the Café they were delighted to see the

same posters on the wall. Norah often spoke to the school-children on the Christian Aid themes.

27th

Norah had encouraged eight Blue Army supporters (Penrhys Athletic) to walk for Christian Aid. They walked up the main path having completed the 30 mile walk along the old pilgrimage route from Llantarnam. As they reached the estate, the church bell welcomed them home, pilgrims for a fairer world. At the café they drank water and tea, and as I thanked them on behalf of the poorest of the world, one had tears in his eyes. Hold on to this moment in our cynical, materialistic society.

JUNE

5th

The Nursery said thank you for the big bright yellow sun and the many trees they passed on their walk from school. When we came to Penrhys there were only 2 trees in this area of the estate (and only a few elsewhere) but now there are 60 around Llanfair and Y Ffynnon. The Inspectors' Report stated that the school was 'unequalled for moral and spiritual standards.' They had attended when the children worshipped in Llanfair. At 7.30, Tubalaté from LMN.
Another successful concert from Live Music Now. 'Tubalaté' is one of the country's leading professional brass ensembles.

14th

The Nursery presented Llanfair with a Millennium candle. Bethan Williams lit the candle; the children sang 'Jesus loves me' and the parents joined in; Csaba sang a Hungarian version of 'Winnie the Pooh,' Jean sang a Malagasy hymn and Sarah played variations on 'Baa, Baa, Black Sheep' on cello. It was a celebration of the unity of school and church: the consequence of 8 years trusted relationship.
Bethan Williams was Headmistress of the Nursery School. Our three volunteers were Hungarian, Malagasy and English. Sarah Adam was our musician. All worked together with flair and conscientiousness.

JULY

3rd

Tylorstown school is burned to the ground. The school has been deliberately set on fire and the school has been destroyed. The school served the community since Tylorstown came into existence and has now been destroyed by one of its own community.

11th

Norah and I were received as Honorary Fellows of Trinity College, Carmarthen, because of our work with the community of Penrhys. Does this reflect 'there is a divinity which shapes our ends?' That was the theme of my address to the graduands, words shared by my father a week before he died. My great great grandfather made his journey from Carmarthenshire to Aberdare 160 years ago, my father was educated in Carmarthen 80 years ago and Norah and I were there today. On the way home we called in Aberdare to say thank you at the grave of David and Letitia Nicols, my great great grandparents.

My Uncle Noel and our son Dylan had also been educated at Carmarthen.

14th

At the Millennium Beacon, Councillors from Rhondda Cynon Tâf signed the Jubilee Petition to remove international debt: Geraint Davies AM, Pauline Jarman AM the Leader of RCT, the chairperson of RCT from Rhigos and our two local councillors, Mike Britain and Robert Bevan. We showed them round Llanfair. They were surprised and impressed.

The Jubilee Debt Campaign demanded an end to the scandal of poor countries paying money to the rich world. It called for 100% cancellation of unpayable and unfair poor country debts.

17th

The last class for this term arrived for worship. For eight years, classes from the three schools have made their way from school to Llanfair to worship. This has been a key factor in drawing school and church into community. It has made a difference to hundreds of children. This year Nursery came 12 times, Infants and Juniors came 30 times each, the highest number throughout the years.

22nd
Geraint Davies unveiled the beacon. Jeff Williams, Christian Aid, Martin Stagles, a member of Llanfair and serving as our local doctor, and Ben Gregory, Jubilee 2000 all spoke.

31st
Michael completed Module 2: 'What is religion?' We read different Christian approaches to other religions: exclusive, inclusive, one seeing all religions as equal paths. Most satisfying to see Michael grasping the issues and reaching his own position of tolerance and open-ness.

AUGUST

3rd
Geraint arranged for us to meet John Griffiths, the new Director of Housing for RCT. He has been in post only 4 weeks but already has been fed the line that Penrhys is unsustainable. We had a 'good frank exchange' and he learned that we seek a genuine interchange of views and hope for the community. He did not know about the existence of the Consultative Group and will recall it.
There can be little doubt that if this meeting had not taken place, the new Director would have accepted the Report from his Officers, agreed to massive and immediate demolition and to the virtual extinction of Penrhys.

9th
I remember the shock while we lived in Penylan, of seeing members of Kántus coming down our stairs. They were dressed in black and white and looked young people of integrity. The same was true today when eleven Hungarians arrived in black and white for Communion. There was a sense of being 'one people' as Hungarian and Welsh stood next to each other in a circle, receiving and passing the bread and wine.
The return visit of the young people from Monor in Hungary.

21st
The sun and heat draws 'villains' into the open. Far more young men are around at the moment and many are strangers. Some live behind Llanfair, others in the flat opposite. Some look dangerous; some are dangerous, especially when alcohol and drugs are involved. I fear violence might erupt!

23rd

Jean Noel stood at Neuaddlwyd and reminded us that from there the light of the Gospel began to shine on the island of Madagascar. It was hard to believe looking at the green rolling garden of the Aeron Valley that 200 years ago, young men on fire with the Spirit took the Gospel across oceans to the great island. In 3 weeks I shall make the same journey.

David Jones and Thomas Bevan were members of the congregation at Neuaddlwyd and had been inspired by a Report on the need for missionaries for Madagascar. All our Malagasy volunteers were taken to this 'shrine' for them.

30th

Bishop Barry of Llandaff arrived for Communion. We had tea in the café before I took him to meet the project people. His visit was affirmative and encouraging.

Barry Morgan had been Bishop of Bangor from 1992 to 1999 and had recently been appointed Bishop of Llandaff. He became Archbishop of Wales in 2003. In the Visitors' Book, he wrote 'Thank you so much for showing me what goes on. I wish we could replicate this across the diocese.'

31st

John Griffiths the new Housing Director, reported to Wayne, Robert and me as members of the community and to Geraint Davies, Robert Bevan and Mike Britain as our political representatives. His recommendations reflect a way forward for us as a community.

Wayne Carter was Treasurer and Robert Poole the Secretary of the Community Action Group.

SEPTEMBER

5th

Kiady arrived from Antananarivo and Jean Noël returned this evening. This is the cross-over period when mature volunteers leave to be replaced by apprehensive, adventurous searchers. These young people are full of courage to spend a year in a high priority housing estate on the western edge of Britain. István and I met Kiady at Cardiff. What would he look like? It was not difficult to recognize a Malagasy walking towards us. A bright smile, a slight figure and a brisk way of walking. We chatted all the way home. He is intelligent and articulate with good English.

The volunteers this year were István from Hungary, Kiady from Madagascar and Hanna from Germany who had visited Taize and delighted in playing the music at Llanfair.

6th

Jean spoke about poverty in his home village which has just had a well with clean water (a tap for every five houses), has no electricity, uses candles for light. The villagers walk miles to market and carrying is on backs and heads; medical care is very expensive; secondary schools out of range. This evening Kiady spoke in Bible study about similar issues; backed it up with statistics, added political issues and the place of FJKM in the struggle for justice. What an articulate, passionate young man.
FJKM = The Church of Jesus Christ in Madagascar.

8th

Next week I fly to Madagascar. I am excited and fearful but I need this experience. All my life I have tried to be on the side of the poor, from my earliest days when I learned about the London Missionary Society, the John Williams ships, exploring Africa; I was soon supporting the West Indies as my favourite cricket team because they were black and poor. But I have never been to a Third World country, a developing country, a country changed irrevocably by imperial powers.
I had been invited to participate in a Workshop on Community Projects organized by the Council for World Mission.

9th

Soon I will focus on my first journey outside Europe and the United States. My ministry has been in Wales; apart from 4 years at Oxford and Hartford, my life has been in Wales; I travelled to Rotterdam as a student in 1962; as Moderator I visited Geneva and Hungary. I am not a travelling man. I have been rooted in local communities - Llanidloes, Manselton, Wales, Penrhys. This new journey/ pilgrimage presents a great challenge. I do not live in a comfortable community, but this journey will stretch me physically, mentally, emotionally, spiritually.

11th

Is today the sign of a new future? At a public meeting in the community centre, I introduced the meeting chaired by Kevin Morgan and addressed by John Griffiths, new Director of Resources, Geraint Davies AM and Mike

Brittain, local councillor. The community trusts that change will come quickly, that the new people in authority support our community, responsibility will be shared with residents, and money and resources are available to create change.

15th

A world of which I know nothing. We flew in to Antananarivo at 10.30 this evening and immediately it felt different, even at the airport, the main contact with the outside world. Everyone was a different colour to the few whites; £1500 for Steve Wilkinson was exchanged into millions of Malagasy franks; Yvette and Zo drove us to the hotel. On the short journey I felt poverty in unmade roads, little light, clusters of young people everywhere, dogs in streets, people walking to market from villages, carrying on head or back, tiny infants begging in the airport. I had the feeling of underlying menace and I remembered how Norah and I felt crossing the border from Hungary to Romania in 1988.

Steve Wilkinson was a CWM missionary who had served in Madagascar since 1972. He and his wife Hardy were leaders at Akany Avoko, a remarkable project working with children and young people in Antananarivo. I had acted as a carrier of the money from Steve's father for the purchase of a minibus to replace one which was past its use. I had last met Yvette and Zo at Llanfair several years previously.

16th

When I woke at the hotel just outside the city, I wondered what would be the other side of the door. The hotel is on the river bank; in the grounds are large exotic trees and birds of bright colours make harsh sounds; flat fields stretch to red hills on which are small villages with red wells and red roofs. Many worked in the fields until sunset. Aiky, Mamy and Jean Noel arrived. A glorious reunion. Penrhys was a wonderful experience for them.

Sunday 17th

Poverty is all around. I see Antananarivo with the eyes I first saw Penrhys. I see, hear, touch, smell, taste with an acute sensitivity which has become mellowed, or blunted, within my own community. This is my first exposure to absolute poverty - I respect and fear. We were taken to the Martyrs Church in the centre of the city - narrow streets, crowded especially with the young (60% are under 15); everything is hectic; the funeral of a dignitary with a line of soldiers; what singing at worship; a splendid sermon translated by an official; the Memorial Tomb to the Welsh missionaries, David Jones, Thomas Bevan, David Johns and others.

18th

A privilege to be introduced to Madagascar by Malagasy people. We learn about the context (history, geography, colonialism, social and economic problems - the island of Madagascar is rich; it is the people who are poor) and the text (towards a theology of development; the God who encounters us in Christ; the Christ who is in, and with humankind; the People of God must live God's Gospel in social, political and economic issues). How humbling it was to hear the names of David Jones, Thomas Bevan, David Johns, David Griffiths

19th

Because the gifts of race, colour, culture, language are so varied, we have discovered the unity in diversity at the heart of the Trinity. God shares many gifts with the people of Madagascar, ranging from the vision, determination and business acumen of development programmes, to the exuberance, commitment and professionalism of the Scripture Union musicians and dancers. Although there is great poverty in this green island turned red, faith, hope and love will make the island green again.

The green island had turned red because of the exposure of the red soil through erosion.

20th

Aiky, Mamy and Jean Noel helped present Penrhys. Delegates recognized Llanfair as being 'at the heart of community.' In their experience, few projects are initiated by the local church. There is a separation between mission, worship and development. A project may be the initiative of an individual Christian, but not the initiative or normal work of the local congregation.

It is rare to find a congregation, like Llanfair, totally engaged in mission projects. In the experience of the CWM delegates, projects were the concern of individuals and enthusiasts, not the work of the whole local congregation. This was the experience of all the delegates who came from varied backgrounds like Namibia, Zimbabwe, Bangladesh and Singapore.

21st

In Majunga in the far west of the country, we visited a project making tiles and wells, and spoke to puss puss pullers who have a short cruel life.
A puss puss is a rickshaw pulled by an individual.

22nd

Another shock. We walked into the centre of a shanty town where we were greeted by a 60 year old white woman and two black men on a veranda of an old house - there were rabbits, birds, a small lemur. What a lesson in community struggle. Her (their) struggle was against all odds, including government corruption, to have a water pump, save erosion, develop work and education for young people. She lobbied, protested, petitioned, was defeated again and again but never gave up. Why does she do it? her love of people, especially the poor. At midday she strode off to show us the pump. It was a walk amongst the poorest of the world. Inspiring and humbling. After lunch we visited the Secondary School Year 12 English class (18s) - 50 in rows, courteous, alert, inspiring. I spoke of Wales and David Jones. They deserve much and receive little, and our waste at home! God forgive us.

23rd

Yesterday exposed the urban poor of Madagascar, but I was not prepared for the rural poverty of the rice areas around Marvoay. Here was abject destitution in communities recently ravaged by cholera and who live daily with malaria. As we journeyed across the wilderness, huts of grass and leaves huddled near the roads; an FJKM primary school had a few rows of ancient desks; we reached the rice growing villages, a world where people grimly survive. The mayor asked for a bicycle to make his work easier; the village shop had rice, sugar, salt and a few dusty tins; peasant farmers with feet hard and disfigured; the dispensary in a broken down college from colonial days. Hundreds walked 8 kilometres each way to market. All smiled and waved. At Marvoay we ate with the minister, were shown the medical practice of a remarkable young doctor at a broken down LMS station; were entertained by wonderfully enthusiastic Dorcassi and children.
The Dorcassi is a women's organisation within the Church.

Sunday 24th

We worshipped in one of five FJKM congregations in Majunga: Sunday School for 286 began at 7.15; worship at 8.30 for 600, led by lay leaders. I spoke for 8 minutes (another 8 for translation). At the beach we paddled and collected drift objects. Because I wrote the names of David Jones and Thomas Bevan in the sand, this led to a long conversation with a lovely family. When we returned to the hotel, 70 men from Sion FJKM entertained with Malagasy dance and songs. Here is wealth: young people with talent, exuberance, courtesy, Christian commitment, love of country. One day it will be released.

25th

What are the necessities of life? Water, food, basic education, health care. Every human deserves these rights. We have witnessed such urban and rural destitution that it would be natural just to weep. I have seen poverty on Penrhys, saw that word plummet new depths in Romania in 1988 and 1991, but the Madagascar experience has been traumatic. Here the vast majority are desperately poor.

26th

God broke into my experience of Madagascar. I have been given when I had not asked, I have received from the unexpected - No, No, No - I have received from the expected, the poorest of the poor of our world. The children of the rubbish dumps of Antananarivo, spending their days scouring in waste thrown away by others, have given the pearl beyond all price, the field worth all my possessions. I have met Pere Pedro of Akamasoa, the hill of hope. We were guided around the village of 15½ thousand people: houses, toilets, primary and secondary schools, playing field, market, employment and then we met Pere Pedro surrounded by children. Vespers were led by children (150 in the congregation) with devotion and such a sound. Pere gave the blessing; we all spoke, the children sang inside and outside. They made our hearts dance.
'AKAMASOA was founded by Pere Pedro Opeka. A South American priest, Pere Pedro is committed to helping the poor of Madagascar escape the ills of drug and alcohol abuse, violence, and prostitution. In 1989 he started a village outside Antananarivo (Madagascar's capital) that offers temporary housing and rehabilitation for people living in extreme poverty. Thus far, over 17,500 people have been served, including 9000 children who are currently being educated through AKAMASOA. Pere Pedro's village is renowned as a model for urban third world development. The village helps sustain itself through workshops producing traditional handicrafts, construction and agriculture.

27th

I'll lead you all in the dance, said he. Sometimes there are no rational answers to questions, but Gods response is in the rhythm of the universe as it moves from creation to consummation, dancing to the music of cross, resurrection and sharing the Spirit. Last evening that rhythm was lived by the children of Akamasoa as they sang evening prayer, and this evening it was lived by the children of Akany Avoko as they danced a Malagasy response to the God of creativity, liberation and fulfilment. The kingdom was shared with us by the poorest of the poor. They were the donors. Please Madagascar, teach Europe how to dance, praise, pray and say thank you.

29th

I woke with a 'project.' I have been deeply affected by the poverty of this beautiful, tragic island, and have been given hope by Pere Pedro and Steve Wilkinson. Could Llanfair receive girls from Akany Avoko? During prayers, as I was remembering the project, Steve walked into the room. He was delighted but can it be funded? A life-transforming experience.

OCTOBER

9th

We prepared the study room for the new Course on 'The Story of Penrhys.' 13 met for a good, happy session, using cuttings from the Rhondda Leader. *This was a development of the 'learning by extension' programme with Trinity College Carmarthen. This proved to be a most important element in Llanfair's ministry during the following years. The education courses began with an attempt to understand our community, and eventually included four further courses on introductions to Rhondda, Wales, an approach to community development, and an understanding of the Bible. More than 50 different people were involved in various courses between 2000 and 2004. The courses were recognised and accredited at Trinity College.*

12th

I completed the leaflet 'Madagascar; a Journey and a Pilgrimage' based on my diary accounts. 17 years ago I wrote a leaflet 'Hungary: A Journey and a Pilgrimage,' and that journey introduced countless people in Wales to Hungary and has resulted in long term relationships. Will something similar emerge from this journey?

20th

We posted 135 Akany Avoko letters to friends whom we knew would empathize with this new project.

The letters were accompanied with the new leaflet, and within four months more than £16,000 was raised to create a Scholarship Fund. It enables a young person from Akany Avoko to come to Penrhys for a year. The first arrived in September 2001 and the project has continued ever since. It, of course, means that Llanfair receives two young people from Madagascar every year, usually one from the Church Office of FJKM and one from Akany Avoko.

Sunday 29th

One of our young men in the Army has been part of the church since he was very young, attended discussion groups, was baptized at 14, went to discos and holidays every year. While I was in Madagascar he brought a dozen young men from Fiji to worship and sing at Llanfair. They were again on Penrhys this weekend. One came to church this morning and stated they would all come this afternoon. A party in the Club was too strong an attraction for these tee-total Methodist Fijians. Once we helped root the Gospel in Fiji; now we help erode that faith and practice when they visit Wales.

NOVEMBER

3rd

For 7 years Llanfair has integrated discussion groups, discos and holidays within a coherent programme. This week 30 came to discussions and disco. The young people expect a stable programme and we must provide it every week. Once the pattern is snapped, they find something else to do.

7th

Jane Asher and Gerald Scarfe arrived on behalf of Christian Aid. There was filming, photography and interviewing for the On the Line project - linking our café and the restaurant at Banfora in Burkina. The key domestic people were Pru from the Café and Sharon.

The 'On the Line' Project was an idea of John Snow to link communities on the same longitudinal line. Christian Aid linked Llanfairs Café with a restaurant in Banfora. Norah and the café volunteers had been corresponding - exchanging community and family news, exchanging recipes - with the women of Banfora. Pru, one of our local volunteers and Sharon, our education worker spent several days in Burkina. Pru taught them how to make Welsh-cakes. Madame Laurence, President of a Women's Association in Banfora visited Llanfair the following January. Jane Asher visited both Llanfair and

Banfora. Her comments on Llanfair were 'A delight to visit such a wonderful project - and the soup's terrific.' Gerald Scarfe added, 'I agree with my wife.' The soup was home-made by Norah. Jane Asher first appeared as a child actor in the 1952 film 'Mandy' and continues in high profile roles. Gerald Scarfe is one of the most influential cartoonists in the United Kingdom.

16th

We reached the target for the Akany Avoko Scholarship. We have raised £8100 and the first young woman should be here in September. There has been a gracious response. People respond because they have confidence in a programme which will change lives and has no wasted expenditure.

Sunday 26th

Our three overseas volunteers led worship. Kiady presided with sensitivity, well chosen words and also spoke extempore; Istvan preached well; Hannah read, played and taught a new German response. A privilege to worship with young people who want us all to deepen in faith.

27th

The study group looking at local history met for the 8th time. Interest deepens as each participant learns the background to this community. They enjoy themselves and contribute according to their experience: Linda makes us laugh because of her stories - today how on a Christmas morning, as she walked from the bake house with the cooked turkey, grease ruined her new dress; Ann discovers new information which she eagerly shares - today about housing clubs during the development of Tylorstown and Stanleytown; Ivor by his radicalism and enthusiasm. He was introduced to Socialism by Ernest Zobole.

DECEMBER

4th

The Nursery looked with wonder at the beautiful green tree, decked with gold, silver and red balls, and marvelled at the angel looking down on us. They were thrilled by the banner with star beams reaching the stable; they participated in the drama of stable, crib, donkey, cow, lamb, shepherds, wise men, and in the centre Joseph, Mary and baby Jesus. The candles, central, advent and millennium and the lamp were lit; they sang 'Away in a manger'

twice, once from their chairs and once sitting around the tree; they said prayers and had squash and biscuits in the café.
I remember how important our little Nativity Scene was in the house in 12 Heol Dyfed. Norah used to encourage the two little girls living next-door to act out and sing the story of Christmas and they invited their parents to join us to hear the story. After hearing the story, the father commented, 'I think I've heard the story before. Has it been on television?'

Sunday 10th
Worship at Glyndwr, a home for the elderly at Ystrad, brought Christmas home to us. The residents enjoyed familiar carols, applauded when the Bible text was read in English, Welsh, Hungarian, German, French, Dutch and Malagasy; the children sang; they said their prayers and were so cheerful. One elderly man, a friend of Stanley Baker sang 'Pennies from Heaven' and many joined in. How we need the elderly! They too cannot defend themselves and know they are vulnerable. Our problem is we try to hide our weakness. We had a similarly beautiful moment during afternoon service when Shayla, sitting on the floor near Hannah, closed her eyes and put her hands together for prayer. Such wonder.
Stanley Baker, the famous Welsh actor, had been born in Ferndale, a neighbouring village.

11th
A string quartet from the National Opera played Debussy; Penrhys Quartet No 1 by Simon - including marimbas and Mozart.
Simon Preston had written a piece of music played by the Quartet and the Penrhys children who played on marimbas

13th
Yesterday at the Infants party, 30 children looked forward to the coming of Father Christmas; this evening we had an equal number of Juniors. There are also 30 of secondary age in discussion group. Together they are a good proportion of children and young people on Penrhys.

16th
Carols around the estate is not singing by lantern light, with holly and ivy over doors, and a welcome inside with mince pies and sherry. Ours is a hard sing in darkness with broken, overgrown steps, derelict properties and, at times, disruptive children. The challenge gives such pleasure. 25 went around

this evening. Singing began with George and Myra, the only occupants in their block, Myra an invalid for many years; for Lil to whom we sang from outside her door; and Danny who had had a severe stroke; to the pub where everything stopped, everyone joined in and where a collection was taken (one put two crumpled £20 notes in my hand), Spar, Fish Shop, Woody's; outside Margaret's, Sue's mother, Mrs Jones, Ngaire and Rita. A cold, starlit, frosty night. Returned to the café for hot chocolate and toast, quickly prepared by Norah, Sharon and the volunteers.

Sunday 17th

Our loveliest Nativity. The chapel was packed (104), 30 children and a dozen adults took part: Becky a perfect Mary; Jenna a fine Joseph; Karli (whose drawing was on the front of the programme), Sadie and Shayla were angels and baby brother Brad a wonderful Jesus, the first time a baby had played Jesus. Taize music gave a real edge. A most perfect expression of Christmas. Our happiest Christmas on Penrhys? We went to 'Buy as you View' Carols where I read Ann Lord's poem; Cory Band.

'Buy as You View' is a local company founded in 1972 and a supporter of the Penrhys Partnership. I had been asked to offer prayers at this their first Annual Carol Service. The chief attraction was of course the world famous Cory band which at the time was sponsored by Buy as You View. I read a poem which Ann Lord, a Penrhys resident, had written for our Local History Course.

19th

Llanfair's most successful Christmas dinner, as usual organized by Norah: 50 had a first class four course meal plus coffee/tea for £3-50; those who were served and those who served met happily together; Penrhys residents; staff of the Nursery School; council workers and Partnership staff. Eleven helped prepare the meal, serve, clear up afterwards and the place was left spotless at the end of the day. Our overseas volunteers were brilliant and worked hard and cheerfully. How blessed we are in having them.

20th

While we sang Carols by candlelight, Martin's car was stolen.

Martin and Annet Stagles were one of two families who lived in the valley and worshipped regularly at Llanfair. Martin, an eye specialist, was our GP after the death of Chris Shaw and served the community with great faithfulness and compassion until the Penrhys Health Centre became part of the Ferndale Practice. Martin and Annet, who was a qualified nurse, had served in Africa with the Baptist Missionary Society, and they and their three children Tom, Ellen and Charlene were a great blessing to the congregation. The other faithful valley person was Sheila Hollins who with her husband Ted, exercised a ministry of foster care. We had a special connection because I had blessed their marriage (before Llanfair was built), and they lived in my parents' family home in Brynbedw. Several families who moved from Penrhys kept close links with Llanfair and were faithful worshippers.

Sunday 24th

Christmas arrives and always surprises me as it surprised the shepherds going about their daily work. Much of my work is to help people recognize the extraordinary presence and grace of God in the ordinary. Morning service centred on the baptism of Suzanne and three of her children - Laura, Ryan and Jessica. Also present were her mother and Suzanne's three older daughters and families. It was right for them to enter the church on Christmas Eve. Fine Communion at 11.30: 43 present. Most were young people and many were not expected.

25th

It is a story worth telling throughout the world and throughout the ages. A story about a young, poor couple, whose baby is born in a stable and whose first visitors were despised, poor workers. It is a story where evil is met by good, and where the spiritual and material intertwine. And behind and through the story is Immanuel, God with us on a dark Monday morning, indeed every day and throughout our lives.

29th

A father was buried next to his son who died a few months ago. At the graveside were another son escorted by prison wardens and a police guard. I had been entrusted not to have hymns and asked to note he was not a religious man. What this means is that he was not a hymn singing chapel goer. I tried to communicate an inclusive, redemptive, compassionate God. From the chapel we went to the white cemetery with a fierce blue sky.

2001

JANUARY

11th

A strong east wind drove horizontally past the great tip onto Penrhys and aimed directly at the east wall of Llanfair. This wind brought the icy waters of the Baltic (Hanna denies that), the ferocity of the Carpathians and the puszta (a theory rejected by István) but everyone agrees it is a gift from Russia.

Hannah was from Eastern Germany and István from Hungary.

FEBRUARY

Sunday 4th

Norah is very excited as she crosses South Asia and approaches India. A great event in her life. After years of commitment and stamina, Norah, Sharon and I have been stretched by our visits to Hyderabad, Burkina Faso and Madagascar. These pilgrimages confirm that Llanfair is where the worship and work of the People of God are one; and also at the sharp end of Welsh contemporary society.

5th

Our Second Course on 'Penrhys' explores questions of development. We enjoy a rich variety of international and socio-economic-political experience especially because of the residential group who have all lived under different forms of communism.

8th

The Akany Avoko Project is supported as a joint Llanfair/CWM project. We hope the work can continue for 5 years. This is a wonderful endorsement of a vision which caught fire last autumn.

13th

Norah found her experience enriching and challenging. She visited community projects in villages and city, and has been affirmed by the exuberance and determination of many she met. Because the challenges are great, those who struggle must work with the little they have. She visited a nursery whose sole furnishing was a mat, where the teacher created paints out of spices; a school where they made their own books and produced excellent craft work. One of the problems we have, having visited Madagascar, Burkina and India is to remember the challenges in our community.

In the company of Rukmini Rao and Elenid Jones of Christian Aid, Norah visited many projects in villages of the Deccan plateau and in the city of Hyderabad. They visited day and night schools - the night schools were crammed with bright eyed children who had to work during day time to support their families, often in tied labour to pay off family debts. These children left a great impression on Norah.

14th

I thought of many, good, ordinary Penrhys people making the most of their lives, I applauded them and realised I need to learn once more from them. I say 'once more' because this is where Norah and I began 15 years ago. I must return to grassroots. Because of the work we have done and the relationships we have made, I should be able to visit many Penrhys homes. I started again today.

16th

I embarked on the privilege of visiting the whole of the estate twice previously during my time on Penrhys. In Llanidloes and Manselton I was expected to visit only 'Congregational/URC people.' To visit those of other churches was a cardinal sin and many claimed a connection, however tenuous, with chapel or church. On Penrhys, I visited a list inherited from my predecessor. It was a short list, even when it included the families of Sunday School children. In 1995, I visited many homes during a period of several months. Now I begin a third systematic approach.

MARCH

12th

The annual Llanfair Project Dinner. 24 gathered in the Ynys Cynon in Trealaw, enjoying the meal, the company and the remarkable fact that this event has taken place for 9 years. When we were raising funds for the creation of Llanfair, we were constantly challenged on whether business skills existed. That Llanfair continues its work with stability and gets through its crises is proof of the necessary managerial skills. Our study group had another stimulating session as we explored Porto Alegre, Rhondda mining and Penrhys issues. There were 15 of us and conversation was lively.

Although neither Norah nor I had received any specific business training, the work of Llanfair continued day after day. The café never failed to open due to the lack of volunteers. Every morning (Tuesday to Friday) at 9.00 am prompt, the café was ready to welcome the mothers on their way home from taking their children to school. They were always ready for their coffee, and some regularly had breakfast. At the same time the launderette and the boutique were also opening and ready to serve the public. Norah was downstairs every morning preparing the café with the resident volunteer who was on key duty. The overseas volunteer served as a facilitator, ready for any problems and to welcome visitors. Key duty gave the volunteers a great opportunity to meet local people. This was done in turn and each of the Llanfair resident volunteers had their day each week. Porto Alegre in Brazil explores alternate forms of democratic government. It was introduced to us by Ann Lord, a Penrhys resident and a member of the study group.

14th

Bishop Saunders of Bangor arrived with four working on the Maesgeirchen estate in Bangor. We visited the Schools, there were 40 in Compline and afterwards Saunders and Vicar Emyr spoke about their lives. It did us good to hear new voices with new stories. We all need to be stretched.

Saunders Davies was Bishop of Bangor from 2000 to 2004. Penrhys and Maesgeirchen have much in common.

24th

This evening the café was full of children but when they heard there was a police raid for drugs in properties behind the church, away the children went in great excitement. What entertainment - police vans, dogs, violence, noise, children crying.

Sunday 25th

Yesterday we were on the verge of a serious community incident. I noticed late afternoon that several young men were hanging around drug dealers' houses. Normally the young men arrive, collect drugs and leave quickly. Yesterday they seemed unsure, they were hanging around. Then came the raid at 7.30. This morning we learned that five Penrhys residents had been arrested for possession of heroin. Two had been arrested in Cardiff and of course the minor dealers had been waiting in vain behind Llanfair. That news dominated today, a Sunday, Mothering Sunday, a day for celebrating the Gospel. This is a tangled web.

30th

After 12 years, Llanfair's ministry is recognised as honest, stable, faithful, consistent. It keeps on doing its work without seeking praise or reward. It keeps on in word, sacrament and service. It has taken 5 years for political leaders to recognise that Penrhys is maturing into a community, and has grown the infrastructure of a Village Centre.

APRIL

13th, Good Friday

A good Good Friday. Against high odds, many in this community heard and saw the story of the death of Jesus acted before their eyes. István who played Jesus, believed the story. He had learned the text so well he was able to deal with the lapses of others. Today gave as genuine and realistic a performance as we have had throughout the years. The struggle and hard work was blessed. *Lisa, who had played the part of Jesus for the last few years, was with Leanne, serving as English conversationalists at the Theological University at Debrecen. The majority of the Hungarian volunteers at Llanfair came from Debrecen.*

14th

A few months ago I stated I should try to understand more deeply an element of Penrhys life, namely the world of drugs, crime and prison. After stating the ought-ness, I prayed personally and in public in Llanfair. Soon afterwards I began my visiting, journey, pilgrimage and I am approaching a heart of darkness which could become light.

Easter Sunday 15th

Gospel in the midst of life. As I was going to bed I noticed an ambulance and police cars behind our house. One young man had attacked another with a jagged pint glass. One was taken to hospital and the other to the police station. I went to see the victim's mother and the house was full of young men involved in hard drugs. I confronted them with the issue of heroin; it must stop before someone dies or is killed. All listened with respect. Something must be done. This is Easter Day. A dozen met at 8 and because of foot and mouth, we walked the ring road, with prayers at Black Rock and the Shrine. This is Easter, the centre of life at its hardest.

16th

During the past months, Norah and my awareness of the drug scene has intensified by what has been happening around us and what we see from the windows of our flat. Drug dealers are all round us.

19th

'Raging Bull' expresses the inarticulate rage behind violence. La Motta lived in desperate loneliness and fear of betrayal. I thought of my Sunday night conversation with one young man: 'My father says "If you have one friend, you're lucky; if you say you have two, you're a liar." Why am I so violent? I want to love everybody but I can't.' 'This is a film all young men should watch.

'Raging Bull,' directed by Martin Scorsese stars Robert de Niro.

21st

At 9 this evening, eight of us were seated around our table enjoying a meal Norah had made - Hanna, her parents (both pastors in Germany), Sharon, Norah, myself, when there was a bang from the rear of the house. I ran from room to room and discovered a huge hole in the window of the spare bedroom. I went outside, saw children playing and they told me it was two teenage boys. I went to the Club and spoke with their families who were as shocked as we were. Was it the two boys? And if so, why did they do it? It is many years since we had a deliberate, malicious attack. It is disturbing.

23rd

I am visiting quietly, carefully, sensitively, methodically. It is a central facet of ministry. How old fashioned! What a waste of time and energy for the contemporary professional minister! Many homes are surprised to see me, but all give a welcome. I learn many personal stories, but also take the communal pain of the scourge of drugs. Today a young man who spoke openly in front of me, his mother and neighbour. There was a similar story from a young woman about her partner. One young man promises to see me tomorrow with another young man. I wonder and hope.

24th

I waited anxiously in the café. Would he turn up? A historic conversation took place and Norah and I are on a steep learning curve. Two desperate young men (28 and 26) appeared. They have been taking and selling drugs for years, struggle to come off injecting, but need a fix every day and their day relates to that event. There are 40 young people on hard drugs on Penrhys.

They want a new life because their present existence is being destroyed. It was a moving encounter. Something must be done.

30th

Our Community Development Course sees Penrhys within a historic and geographic context. We focus on the past 30 years but we also learn from areas with similar problems within the United Kingdom and many parts of the world. We are discovering objectivity and commitment to our own community. We balance 'scholarly information' with our personal experience and observation. There were 15 of us.

MAY

1st

May Day, Spring Day, Day of the Workers, Day of the People. In Oxford, at Magdalen Tower the privileged sing to the privileged of the wonder and beauty of May Morning with all the hope and joy of new opportunities. At 2 oclock, five struggling with heroin arrived at church. What can one say about their sense of degradation, failure and impotence against their enemy? Their partners repeated the story from the other side of the coin.

3rd

We are all God's children, born into a world to reflect God's image. But we do not have the same opportunities and many children are deeply scarred. How can we help each other recognise our image, develop potential and be offered opportunities for growing?

10th

There are lovely people in our community and the more I meet, the more convinced I become that we must maintain and deepen Penrhys' distinctive life. Penrhys is now a size when we can all know each other, and if we have sufficient ingenuity, courage and compassion, we can help people overcome their problems. No one need feel alone any more; there is a place for everyone.

22nd

Several years ago on Boxing Day, we went to the car park to discover that the car belonging to Cath's [our daughter] friend had been stolen. We found it wrecked in the forest and soon heard who was the culprit. He had stolen the car on Christmas Day. Nothing could be proven but I found it difficult to be courteous towards him. This afternoon I spent two hours with him and his brother in law, and they spoke openly about the horror of heroin addiction.

26th

The last months have helped me rediscover the centrality of the ministry of visitation within pastoral care, the third element alongside Word and Sacrament. On Penrhys I never neglected the first two, but in place of visiting homes, my energies were drawn towards creating a community infrastructure through Llanfair, the Partnership and Community Action Group. Without that infrastructure, Penrhys would not now exist. In pastoral work, I serve 'the central moments of life' with baptisms, marriages and funerals but had insufficient time for 'visiting the neighbour.'

JUNE

4th

During the past months we have been meeting regularly a group of young people trapped by addiction. Last week, two of them prepared a programme for rehabilitation. Today they spoke and presented it to Ieuan Wyn Jones (President of Plaid Cymru), Gill Evans MEP, Geraint Davies AM and Leanne Wood, candidate for Rhondda. They appeared on HTV and S4C News. Along with their document went Ivor's essay on the effect of addiction on community life.
Ivor Williams had prepared the paper as part of his Penrhys Community Course.

5th

Several weeks ago I arranged for the manager of TEDS (Taf Ely Drugs Support) to come to Llanfair. Ten young and older men arrived. We went into the lounge where two made tea and where all these drug users talked openly and passionately about their need to be free of drugs. As they left they were succeeded by 5 of the partners/ family, and later followed by a dozen community leaders. The manager stated that in her 16 years of drug work she had never met a group of drug users prepared to articulate their struggle.

9th

The church is an integral part of community. Chloe was baptized last Sunday, 100 attended and most were from Penrhys; 100 were present at a funeral on

Monday; 30 visited from Maerdy School on Tuesday, the same day we had the meeting on heroin problem; on Monday the Plaid Cymru leaders attended our education class; Wednesday saw Communion and Compline; 180 voted on Thursday; 30 young people came to discussion groups; 30 arrived from the Nursery on Friday; and the week saw a record number in the café, more than any week since opening. A thousand attended in one week. Remember this week when despondent.

29th

This afternoon my day changed completely and I am fortunate it was not more serious. I had gone to visit, aware the family had a dangerous Alsatian. I went up the path, tapped the glass door and asked if the dog was in the room. They answered 'no' but as I opened the door, the lounge door opened and the dog leapt the length of the room. I held up my arm to defend myself and the dog's mouth encompassed my arm. I shouted for help, somehow tore my arm out of his mouth and scrambled down the bank. I lurched along Pentyntyla shouting for help, but there was no one in sight. I managed to get to Kay's, an ambulance arrived quickly and took me to the Royal Glamorgan Hospital. I was examined, wounds dressed - 16 serious bites - and allowed to go home.

JULY

11th

Thirty years ago the Rhondda Mains Committee established the Penrhys Christian Fellowship; it remained a Fellowship until 1989 when the Penrhys Uniting Church came into being. Its Constitution shaped by experiments in church cooperation in the 1970s and 80s, was cumbersome and did not reflect the emerging vitality of Llanfair. Two years ago work began on a new Constitution which came into existence this evening. The core committee is made up of 16 named representatives, 8 from the denominations and 8 from Llanfair.

21st

I officiated at the weddings of Sarah and Tanya who married Malcolm and Michael - two sisters married two brothers. The family had prepared carefully to make it a good occasion! There were 8 bridesmaids, 6 pageboys and 2 ushers, all looking good.

24th

A Live Music Now evening - Quartz - for saxophonists; classical, jazz and dance. Great entertainment.

The Quartz Saxophone Quartet is a young British group dedicated to presenting contemporary music.

28th

Hugh and Barbara married today. It was officiated with dignity and friendliness, and both spoke their vows with clarity and love for each other. The wedding took place at Cardiff Registry Office. Everything went perfectly on one of the hottest, sunniest days of summer.

Was the meeting of Hugh and Barbara providential or fortuitous? Barbara is a Hungarian who moved with her family to Cologne in the 1980s, and came for a year's study in Cardiff in 1999. Hugh met Barbara's uncle when leading the Llanfair young people to Monor in 1999. Why the visit to Monor? Because Mónika, Dylan's wife, had been a volunteer to Llanfair in 1993. Why the Hungarian link with Llanfair? Because of the URC delegation to Hungary in 1983? Why was I chosen to be a member of that delegation? And so the questions continue? The official church wedding took place in August in Budapest.

SEPTEMBER

6th

A miracle of grace as Hanta and Nicolas came off the bus in Cardiff. What a wonder is the Church of Jesus Christ! The story is long and complex, but my small part began when children and young people from Akany Avoko sang and danced to the rhythm of God's goodness. The following day Steve Wilkinson and I conceived of a proposal to bring one of the girls to Penrhys. A year later and after pamphlets, letters, raising £16,000, the backing of CWM, altering our lounge to create a new bedroom, the kindness of CWM and URC, here at last is Hanta. God acted through many to make this happen.

Nicolas came from the Central Office of the FJKM and Hanta from Akany Avoko. Apart from one previous introduction, they met on the plane. They are now happily married with daughter Kezia, and living in Antananarivo.

11th

Horror. Terrifying acts of terrorism took place in the United States. Four passenger jets were hijacked, two piloted into the World Trade Centre in New

York, one to the Pentagon and one in Pittsburgh. The first two were at 8am Eastern Standard Time, the third an hour later. The twin towers of the Trade Centre subsequently collapsed to rubble, and fires are still blazing in Washington. No one knows the death toll but it is certain to be massive. The US and the world is in a state of shock. At first it seemed like a disaster movie. The horror dawns, and as for implications! Everything else pales to insignificance.

12th

The day after the eleventh of September. Not only is the Unites States in shock, but gradually the whole world begins to be aware it is on the edge of international nightmare. Horror and evil, led by fanaticism, stalk the world. Unreality bred by video game violence is replaced by reality.

18th

I am privileged to minister to a man ministering to me with his strong convictions, love for family and his judicious words. We worked together on the Action Group. He worked hard for his Union and his community.

20th

I have completed material for various Courses. 'Wales Today' introduces geography, history, literature, art, music and religion. We begin using it next Monday. It will be one of four booklets: introduction to Penrhys; Penrhys and Rhondda; Community Development; Christianity in Wales.

25th

The funeral reflects a community responding to a man who shared his life. People came because they admired and respected his integrity and selflessness. I emphasized his work and Union, his community of Browntown and Penrhys, and his family. The atmosphere was loving and strong. People deserved a message of confidence and hope. The congregation was responsive, grateful and encouraged. This kind of day justifies Llanfair's inclusive ministry.

19th

I am regularly confronted by crises because Llanfair touches almost everything that happens in this community. Throughout 15 years, half of Penrhys life, we have been close to most people's lives. There have been 120 baptisms, 100 funerals and 20 weddings; every Penrhys child worships at

Llanfair 6 times each year from the age of 3 to 11; there are countless activities week after week. And as a founder of the Partnership and Action Group, I am deeply involved in community life.

OCTOBER

Sunday 4th

Llanfair seeks to be inclusive and aware that creativity, goodness and love reflect God's purposes. We are challenged to respond by using our talents and tongues. We looked at material from Jacob Bronowski (comparing artistic and scientific open-ness through a drawing), Kenneth Clark, T. S. Eliot and Pennar Davies. Humankind can respond to God's goodness. Our first Welsh Communion for the overseas volunteers. The winter world is dark but the chapel is warm and full of light. The evening bell rings and the world knows people are turning to God.

23rd

A week ago a young man of 19 was killed in a car crash. The family have no church background and do not wish for hymns. The Bible is a foreign book. I related their chosen music to a Biblical message and the congregation listened intently. This evening twenty young people in three groups all looked with care at the service. Disco went well.

30th

Wayne is completing the bid for European funding from the Assembly Communities First Programme. Penrhys is described as having the best practise in RCT.

Wayne Carter, Partnership Manager was brought up on Penrhys and was now responsible with Bev Chick, (Finance Manager and also a local woman), the Directors and Staff for formulating and developing policy. The Communities First Programme was just coming into being and the Partnership was ideally placed to take advantage of the new opportunities. It already had ten years of experience.

NOVEMBER

5th

Trystan Hughes and Peter Jones, the new Chaplain at Trinity came to validate our Courses on Penrhys, Rhondda and Wales. I showed them the Nurture programme. They were astounded by its thoroughness, wish to 'convert' it into accredited modules and offer it for distance learning options.
Dr Trystan Hughes was Senior Lecturer at the School of Theology and Religious Studies at Trinity.

7th

As a teenager, my Friday evenings were spent in Ebenezer vestry. Twenty of us, between the ages of 13 and 17, had a regular programme of talks, discussions, followed by table tennis and dancing. Our Friday programme with young people is not very different. We have maintained this programme since 1993.

DECEMBER

Sunday 9th

Signs of charm, delicacy and courtesy: Sadie and Carley speaking earnestly and with pride in the Nativity Play; Charlene and Tracey singing at the Glyndwr Nursing Home; Keira, Katy and Laura meeting the elderly at Glyndwr. These are signs of the kingdom of God. Whatever happens tomorrow, today's events have their effect on eternity. Remember this at all times and do this in memory of me.

13th

Christmas demands energy, time, skill and leaves us close to exhaustion, but they are central to the presentation of the Gospel in the natural rhythm of the seasons. Llanfair's pattern relates to the school, and together they enable Penrhys to experience the essentials of faith. I visited the Junior School for the celebration of Christmas; particularly poignant and celebratory were the presentations of the special needs classes. Persons are unique and share community.

Sunday 16th

These moments of beauty were the result of hard work, being uncompromising with ourselves and performing small things well. Great delicacy during the Nativity Play when Laura passed her tiny baby Keenan into the hands of Kelly - Mary was receiving the gift of the Son of God, and she joyously shared him with Keira - Joseph. At that moment of mystery, the squabbling shepherds and quarrelsome angels fell silent as did the audience which turned into a congregation. The hard graft of the past week had been fulfilled. The other powerful incident was in the Buy As You View Christmas Concert where Nicolas and Hanta sang two carols. The large audience were amazed that such a gift should have come from the community/ village of Penrhys. Their applause was unstinted and generous. They recognized the wonder of it all.

17th

For the first time the whole Infants school came to Llanfair, prepared in its finery to celebrate Christmas. The tiny Nursery children were the first to walk into chapel. We could hear their gasp of disbelief when they saw a gigantic tree touching the ceiling. The room filled and we looked at the banner, Christmas scene and spotted the angel perched on the font. All the classes sang, candles were lit, prayers said, lights extinguished and they marched excitedly through the big door down the path.

18th

The top classes arrived from the Junior School and Llanfair was filled with cheerful children. Every child on Penrhys is aware of the story of Christmas, and has heard and seen the meaning of the coming of Christ. The seed sown will bear fruit. It is God in Christ who harvests.

19th

The younger Juniors arrived. It is a blessing to laugh, sing and pray with children. This is the first time in ten years that all the children from the schools have seen the chapel decorated for Christmas.

21st

The Confirmation group of young people had a wonderful party which marked a happy conclusion to four months of consistent work.

22nd

Early this morning, at sunrise, the body of one of our elderly neighbours was brought along the fifty yards separating her house from Llanfair. Her family walked with her and entered a chapel lit by Christmas tree, candles, lamp burning and a welcome from the community who had arrived for this 8.10 funeral service. Just before 10 there was a loud explosion (there had been one a few hours earlier) and Llanfair shook. We saw flames near the derelict buildings near the club. Ominously, five teenagers were around, denied involvement but knew all about it. A car had been set on fire and canisters exploded deliberately. Someone could have been killed. The violence on the surface of this community contrasts with this morning's dignity.

24th

Communion on Christmas Eve/Morning is a central element in our liturgy. Christ is at the heart of this holy time. During the past dozen years we have joined with the Holy Church in its celebration of the Eucharist, welcoming the Christ child into our dark world. 60 worshipped, including many teenagers. The chapel was beautifully lit and the worship combined seriousness and joy. A central act was the baptism of Kelly aged 10. You just knew it was a key experience in her life. Her sister gave the certificate, her brother the candle and Aunty Rena the Bible. At the close, young Fijians arrived to pray, light candles and sing. Nicolas and Hanta sang for them. It will be difficult to imagine Christmas without the Llanfair mystery.

31st

The day and year ended and began in the warmth and light of Llanfair. Outside was a dark, icily cold world. Inside and outside are both the House of God, but inside we were deliberately remembering. How far into the past we remembered - patriarchs, kings, prophets, Jesus the shaper and fulfiller of faith, and onwards and across the desert wildernesses to the ocean-edge wilderness of Wales where we remembered Illtud, Gwynno, Tyfodwg, Meilir, Latimer, the pioneers of Nonconformity - I recollected my grandparents and parents - to the founders and worker/worshippers of Llanfair. Twenty met this night to bring the story up to date and tip-toe into the new world of a new year. We have ended and begun again.

2002

JANUARY

11th

Each week for nine years, I meet young people to discuss the world, the community, themselves, the church. Often I am 'holding on;' at other times there is insight and quality sharing. With how many have I done consistent work? Probably a hundred, and in-depth relationships with half that number. During the last four months I have consistently met 15 young people.

28th

Our history class met for the 13th time to mark the close of the semester, and to introduce the work of R S Thomas, an unknown name for most. We were challenged by his poems, and watched the lovely documentary showing his love of birds. This evening we enjoyed the annual visit of a string quartet from the Welsh National Opera. 40 present for a stimulating programme of early Mozart and late Janacek. Beryl Rubens (of Cardiff) complimented the children.

The quartet were accompanied by a few friends, including Beryl Rubens, a past member of the orchestra. At the end of the concert, Norah spoke to her and said she hoped that the children (some of whom had been quite lively) had not been too much of a distraction. She replied with 'Distraction! - where else would you get such children listening to such music? It's wonderful.'

31st

Ivor and I enjoyed reading the 'The Miners' Next Step.' Ivor had been to the PDSA in Cardiff with two cats his family had saved - Thomas saved one from a teenager about to throw it to a pit bull; another was saved from the house of a fierce dog; they kept a third rescued from the mountainside.

Ivor was a member of the Penrhys Study Group and was thrilled by this radical approach to the future of the coal industry, written by Rhondda miners and published in Tonypandy in 1912. The People's Dispensary for Sick Animals (PDSA) is a veterinary charity founded in 1917.

FEBRUARY

2nd

The Community Action Group organised an Open Day for the Penrhys Village. For the first time all the commercial and community spaces in Y Ffynnon were open, and hosted On Track, Credit Union, SWALEC, Action Group, an art exhibition and activities, Action for Jobs, aromatherapy, créche, a cooking competition, computers; Llanfair provided tea, coffee and Welsh cakes. There were two music workshops in the lounge and vestibule, and a concert at 2 in the chapel. Would anyone come? Several hundred came and there was appreciation, excitement and happiness. The concert was home made: singers from First Year Juniors; drumming group; guitar group; Taizé; Hanta and Nicolas sang; Jim Bayliss sang. Local politicians were present - Gill Evans MEP, Geraint Davies AM, the chairperson of RCT, local councillors. A highlight in the life of our community. There lies the potential.

14th

The younger infants arrived on a cold, crisp morning. James had his 5th birthday yesterday and was thrilled to ring the bell; two kind boys held the chapel door open. In they walked proudly. My first question: what gives light during the day? We can see it on the floor now; it was our first sunshine for weeks. Such fun as the pool of light appeared and disappeared. What about the night? Moon and stars. They all sang 'Twinkle, twinkle.' Kurt sang alone and then taught the grown ups. The lamp being lit led to Anita playing 'God is forgiveness.' [Taizé] Shayla recognised the music and brought the volunteers out to sing. She lit a candle for her new brother. Anita and James blew out the candles. The liturgy after the liturgy was another delight. They left happily and so did we.

Anita, from Germany, was our musician for the year.

15th

The two year old sat in the café drinking pop from a bottle, eating a sandwich and surrounded by his immaculately dressed sisters. Their little baby brother of a few days old was at home. Another two year old sat in discussion group with Rebecca. He has come faithfully for weeks and behaves impeccably. Trailing clouds of glory do we come

18th

Our history class/study group shared their essays. Anita began with the status of women in Wales in the 20th century; Hanta compared the Maes yr Haf settlement with Akany Avoko; Tünde spoke on The Treaty of Rhuddlan; Nicolas concluded with the life of David Davies, Llandinam. Ivor spoke about The Miners' Next Step; Ann on the origins of Urdd Gobaith Cymru; Suzanne on the struggle for Welsh Independence, and Siân on the story of her great grandfather who came as a refugee from China in 1912 and the racial discrimination faced by her family. All were surprised by how much we had learned during the past few months. There could not be a better style of learning.

Anita from Germany, Tünde from Hungary, Hanta and Nicolas from Madagascar were studying with Ivor, Ann, Suzanne and Siân from Penrhys. All were to receive certificates for their work at Trinity.

20th

We welcomed three lecturers and twenty four students from Trinity Carmarthen. The students were graduates in religious studies working for the PGCE. When they arrived and saw the dereliction around the ring road, their thoughts were 'How can any one live in such a place? There's nothing to get up for in the morning.' Six hours later they described the work as inspirational, a reflection of the Gospel, what the church should be about. What caused the transformation? The welcome tea in the pleasant lounge; the new Course in Community Development; an excellent home prepared lunch; a tour of Llanfair with an account of its activities with Norah and Sharon; visit to the Partnership and a final get together in the chapel.

PGCE = Post Graduate Certificate in Education.

MARCH

11th

Simon organised an evening of jazz performed by students of the Welsh School of Music and Drama in Cardiff. They were supported by Penrhys young people in two pieces. Dylan and his colleagues brought a group from the Residential Care Home in Llantrisant.

Simon Preston was the music co-ordinator at Canolfan Rhys. He worked with Lee Williams, the arts coordinator.

29th, Good Friday

The Gospel is miracle: the extraordinary in-breaking of God into the world of humankind. Jesus! What a human being! What a man, this son of Mary who is love in a world which contains violence and hatred, and yet which can evoke the most beautiful generosity. The poor blind beggar, the rich lonely tax collector, the old widow giving all, the centurion falling on his knees in faith, the courage of Joseph Arimathea. What Gospel! Jesus who died, living God's love to the uttermost. The Gospel is miracle. Today I was aware again that the telling and living of the Gospel on Penrhys (as it is everywhere) is miracle. Once more the story has been told: Charlene, the blind beggar, struggling to find her words; Kelly speaking earnestly; Shayla (aged 5) walking as an old woman; Jordan saying 'Surely this is the Son of God' and sinking to his knees; Nicolas, from one of the poorest, troubled nations in the world, being a most moving Jesus for us.

APRIL

4th

Grace arrives unexpectedly to share the gift of being surprised by joy. Our Cistercian hosts rejoiced in that grace this evening. They share that gift to others throughout their lives. Tonight they received it unexpectedly, from the community of Llanfair Penrhys. We celebrated our Easter Play for the monks in the monastic guesthouse. It was received with delight because it was presented with flair, discipline and careful preparation. The story was told because it is being lived. After the service, we had the privilege, men and women, of walking through the cloisters to the Abbey Chapel for Compline and afterwards for a beautiful Communion at St Illtud's.

Some of those who had participated in the Llanfair Easter play now performed it on Caldey.

5th

Earlier this morning Norah and I walked to St David's to pay respect to many we have loved and who have died - Aelred, Z, Thaddeus, Joseph - and met the Abbot on the path: 'Thank you for last night. The highlight of Easter... the genuine nature of the presentation... I was in tears, and so were many of my brothers... you should come more often... I'll fetch you bread I have made.'

MAY

8th

How does the Holy Spirit work? At Compline I listened to Sadie (aged 8) singing the psalms, reading the Biblical text, reciting the Salve Regina. Afterwards she read the Children's Bible (her favourite book) for half an hour. There was the Spirit making whole.

11th

Yesterday I started the New Testament, having completed Malachi on Thursday. I received so much from the Old Testament: reading Job in a morning, and I did the same with Ecclesiastes, Second and Third Isaiah. Today I felt a thirst for the Gospel. I read Matthew and to my amazement, three hours later I had completed the Gospel in a single reading. I read aloud everything which was speech - half of Matthew. Anyone reading it with an open, critical mind would be challenged by the life style, ethic, courage, wisdom, compassion of Jesus and be puzzled and moved by the Cross, and the wonder of the Resurrection. The Bible is old and new as I received it with understanding and challenge.

14th

Hanta is 21 and celebrated her birthday for the first time. She has so much pleasure on Penrhys. How right we were to invite a young person from Akany Avoko. She lost her parents when young and has lived in the Children's Home since she was 9. We have seen such a change in the shy young girl who arrived eight months ago. She reflects charm, energy and a sense of fun.

17th

The Fun Walk to Tonypandy raised £324, higher than the last few years and everyone was delighted.

Sunday 19th Pentecost

Jordan and his sister Riana described the Honduras cross and carried it so that each worshipper could acknowledge 'Nuevo Creation.' The Holy Spirit given by the crucified and risen Christ was shared with us as we listened for the Word of God and received the bread and wine.

Jordan was aged about 6 and his sister two years younger.

JULY

15th

The four young people living with us in this house are like family. They reflect a family of faith, hope and love. Blood is thicker than water is an expression of biological affinity which has little of eternal significance compared with the gifts of the Spirit. Sharon, Norah and I have prayed, worked, eaten and played with Anita, Hanta, Nicolas and Tünde for nearly a year. The year has been a miracle of grace.

16th

At Llanfair Joint Council, the four overseas volunteers read their Reports. Each communicated the Gospel with a profound understanding of this community. They were the finest testimonies I have heard from young people. As we listened, a silence fell and nothing could be said but acknowledge we had been touched by the Spirit of God. They presented with honesty, compassion and eloquence.

22nd

Sharon arranged for 28 children from Homework Club to be taken to the Trehafod Sidings' Park. What made the day successful? Not money! They travelled 5 miles, fed domestic animals, had fun in an adventure playground and played soccer. They were together and a dozen adults supervised and played with them.

27th

I shared with professionals from Communities First the need to see life and work as a seamless cloth. My father, a school teacher, and many like him lived in the community where they were employed, spent their 'out of work' time unconsciously developing community, and consciously served community through conviction. Rhondda was served by a variety of people: some of religious faith, others with political principles based on socialism or nationalism; many combined faith, politics and altruism. If Communities First is to work, it will need a motivation other than stipend.

AUGUST

Sunday 4th

Hugh was baptized on this final Sunday for the four volunteers. Hugh responded positively with the affirmations, the baptism was deeply moving as were the gifts of a Caldey stone (with a text) and the singing of the volunteers. Hugh and Rena served the congregation with bread and wine.
Hugh had been worshipping for several years and was now in his 50s. His wife, Rena, had been received into membership several years previously, and they had married in Llanfair.

5th

A land of rare beauty. The sun shone, grass was multicoated green and we crossed hills, valleys and mountains before reaching the precipitous awe-inspiring range. Added to natural beauty was a sense of ownership, stewardship, trusteeship. We have possession and responsibility for this garden of Eden. We own nothing and everything; it costs nothing and everything - this wonderland. Our party of 20 were partaking of an adventure holiday, journey, pilgrimage in our home land of Wales.
Beginning another Llanfair holiday in Rhyd Ddu.

14th

After ten years with 40 residential volunteers of varied gifts and experience, Llanfair is developing an open, inclusive ethos where work and worship are the two hands of the Christian person. Stamina and skill are shaped by love and there is special care for the vulnerable. We seek a life style shaped by the Gospel and conformable to living with the materially poor.

16th

We arrived at Soar y Mynydd, the goal of our pilgrimage. While looking at the pulpit chair dedicated to John Williams Brynambor, someone asked me about him. I mentioned his terrible death at the hands of Richard Gambrel and no sooner had I mentioned his name when one of our number told us he had been threatened by him in prison. All we could do was to say prayers and read Psalm 23.
A group on holiday at Trinity Carmarthen.

19th

I have completed 'What we believe.' It began in ecumenical house groups in Llanidloes, was reshaped in Manselton and revised when I was Moderator. It has been refined once more to become the theological foundation for Llanfair's programme of Nurture.

21st

As late summer approaches, I become more conscious of the problems facing this community and innumerable places like it. Something happens at the close of long summer evenings when doors and windows are open and sounds carry. This awareness is also because we have been in beautiful, less stressful communities like Lampeter, Llandovery, Tregaron, Aberaeron, Carmarthen.

SEPTEMBER

2nd

Nine young adults came out of the flat next to the church. All had received their daily fix. Their life is such a transparent part of Penrhys' life.

20th

A horror story. The Angelus was ringing midday and I heard the normal shouting at the next door flat - the usual clients were entering for the daily fix. That is the norm, but 10 minutes later something had gone wrong - girls ran shouting and screaming. Someone had overdosed. I phoned 999 - ambulance and police were on the way. We waited outside the flat, the usual suspects fled before the authorities arrived. A middle aged woman had gone under and nearly died twice. I was angry and told the boys they were all responsible - one got so angry with me. The flat tenant was taken in handcuffs. I eventually got through to the Local Housing Office and through Community Services to his mentor. Death was close, but it could have been any one of a dozen.

21st

Love is a many splendoured thing. Many years ago when I first knew the Yeates family, I was introduced to these words and the film with William Holden and Jennifer Jones. I visited the Yeates in their 4 bedder: Chris, Denise, Denise's mother Ada and her single brother John, the children still at home - Joanna, Emma and Carrie. A full house, but not untypical of Penrhys. Since those days I have buried John and Ada, and married Emma - and today

Carrie married Neil. A lovely wedding - simple, dignified and genuine. Here were good people doing the right thing.

26th

Tomos Bálint Morgans was born at 1.34am weighing 9lb 7oz. He has brown hair, long fingers, clear skin and his father's ears! What joy and miracle. There is the sense of providential guidance. Dafydd Morgans (son of Thomas Morgans) born in 1866 held his grandson John, born in 1939 who now holds his grandson Tomos in 2002. Our hands stretch across centuries. The three looked a lovely family. A wonderful beginning to his life. Let us pray he will have a happy life. What a privilege for Norah and me to be grandparents.

OCTOBER

1st

Llanfair hosted the first Assembly Communities First Conference to be held in a community. I introduced Kevin Morgan who acted as chairperson, and keynote addresses were given by Norma Barry (Assembly) and Pauline Jarman (RCT Leader). Then the people of Penrhys presented themselves with variety, flair and conviction. Working groups before a final plenary. 85 present. People were surprised by the story, professionalism and conviction of the day. A small community has done this.

4th

Twenty young people attended four different groups yesterday and today. We are looking at the mystery of the universe, its formation and development, the Earth and evolution. They enjoyed shaping a pattern and several pointed out they study this in school. Will there be fruit from our labour? This is an art rather than a science and we must be satisfied with 'sowing the seed.'
Discussion Groups continued with their habitual momentum.

21st

The white coffin was placed in the hands of the father. The parents are young, vulnerable, unprepared for the sudden unfairness of the death of their first-born child. They are surrounded by family and friends whose love is focussed upon the three of them. Little can be said except that we are loved within the womb of the mother; and that here we have a physical body, and there is a spiritual body. Without Gospel we have nothing; with Gospel nothing can separate us from the love of God. People do care.

23rd
A Live Music Now concert. Four women saxophonists entertained superbly. *Kintamarni are one of the UK's leading saxophone quartets.*

NOVEMBER

9th
Three in the morning and the door of our neighbour's flat was being kicked; through the mist I saw half a dozen local young men shouting and cursing. About midday we were returning from Lidl's and saw a fire near the derelict blocks above Pen Tyntyla. A fire engine pulled up. A few days ago an emergency ambulance arrived for another suspected overdose of drugs. This is part of normality.

Sunday 17th
Tomos Bálint Morgans was baptised this afternoon at Llanfair Penrhys. His Uncle Hugh, his grandfather and great grandparents were all baptised in the community of Tylorstown/Pontygwaith. The chapel was so full that children sat on the floor. Our hymns were 'Now thank we all, our God' and 'Dros Gymrun gwlad' to Finlandia - music on radio when Tomos was born.

DECEMBER

12th
A young man [from a neighbouring community] follows his two brothers who died in the same way twelve and six years ago. The congregation was made up of 'older young men and women who had lived on the edge. I knew many, and we all knew I could be officiating at their funerals. Many of the old friends were not there. Perhaps many are dead; others may not attend because of their drug habit. Did I say anything to help? I tried to find the right words; at least I was there.

Sunday 15th
Beauty, delicacy and refinement. From the moment 40 children walked into chapel, I knew the story would not only be told but also lived. There were a hundred present including many adults and families. The children walked to their chairs: Brad (aged 2 and Jesus 2 years ago) lit the Nursery candle; between the prayers there was silence; the children knew when and where to move; most said their lines clearly; such love when Mónika passed Tomos to

Mary (Kirsten) who in turn passed him to Joseph (Keira). Shayla sang the first verse of 'Away in a manger.' This evening I spoke and the three overseas women sang at the Buy as You View Concert given by the Cory Band.
The volunteers were Tiana and Estine from Madagascar and Trine from Denmark.

16th
58 had melon, turkey dinner, gateaux, cheese and biscuits, tea or coffee. The cost - £3-50p. Why so inexpensive? Norah's hard work, organization and 10 volunteers. A pleasure to see the Staff of the Nursery, Infants, Partnership, local workmen and residents of the community. We were especially pleased to see Mrs Ann Jones, 90 years old and the oldest resident of Penrhys.

17th
For the first time in the 11 year history of Llanfair, the whole Junior School came to worship. One of the reasons is that the school is much smaller. The chapel was packed with 100 children and teachers. I showed them the Nativity; Tiana and Trine sang, Endre played the piano, and Estine danced. All were given home made cards.
Endre was a volunteer from Debrecen, Hungary.

18th
We worshipped with the Nursery and Infants School. I introduced the tree, angels, Nativity, Advent candles. The School and Llanfair sang and entertained alternately. The climax was the presentation of Christmas cards and the singing of 'We wish you a merry Christmas.' The next time we meet they will be Penrhys Primary School. We have had 400 people in 4 days out of a community of 700.

24th
My expectations were not high for Christmas Eve Communion. Our volunteers are away; a large faithful family have left the area, but I was determined not to be disappointed. I went downstairs and lit the candles and lamp: the chapel looked beautiful but no worshippers. At a minute before 11.30 we were only nine, but within minutes we were 25 and all worshipped. I had not expected such a blessing.
Tiana and Estine spent Christmas with Eleri Edwards in Liverpool. She had been a missionary in Madagascar. Trine and Endre had returned home for Christmas.

2003

JANUARY

11th

Tomos Bálint brings light and love and doesn't have to do anything to give joy. He simply has to be. Isn't that a parable? Do we expect people to do things, rather than just be? What does this mean? I chatted with two girls who can be very difficult. They prattled on about school, what they liked, disliked, problems at home. I enjoyed their company because I accepted their being and that is enough.

13th

A day of quiet consistent work, fulfilling little things. No grand gestures, flamboyant images, extravagant claims. It is doing little things faithfully and consistently.

17th

I am a parish priest of an age fast disappearing. I have tried to focus ministry. In Llanidloes it was the community viewed from the Gorn; the parallel streets of Manselton from the racecourse; my third parish was Wales; now it is a diminishing community within the ring road.

24th

Some in Joint Council have the impression that Llanfair is seeking the continuation of ministry and doing nothing to help itself, reinforcing the stereotype of a dependency culture. It is important to remember that (1) in building Llanfair, the churches contributed less than 20% of the total of £700,000; (2) of the annual revenue, the cost of a minister is £20,000, just 20% of the total income when revenue 'in kind' is considered (including voluntary work). Year by year, Llanfair paid 80% of its expenditure.

When the final bill for the building of Llanfair had been paid in 1995, £40,000 was invested for future contingencies. It was invested wisely and remained untouched. Every year from 1992 until 2004, Llanfair had been financially self-sustaining apart from the cost of the ordained minister.

FEBRUARY

6th

I presided at the funeral of a good friend. I prepared by careful listening. 200 worshippers participated with compassion. I knew of whom I was speaking, and I was speaking to people whom I knew and who knew me. Love, faith and hope were tangible.

7th

The funeral rites lasted several days: 'viewing the body,' receiving the deceased into the church, the service at Llanfair, the committal at Glyntaf, finally the burial of the remains this morning. I had been with the family 13 years ago when the mother was buried, and 4 years ago with one of the brothers. We held hands and repeated prayers, the practice at Llanfair and at school. We returned home for sandwiches and to watch family videos. Much laughter and relief. Our normal Friday evening with two discussion groups in which we read my notes on the funeral. They listened with care because they knew the family well. The bereaved was speaking or better still, living a lesson for these young people.

21st

Almost since the opening of Llanfair, discussions for teenagers have been followed by a disco. Several hundred teenagers have participated in this programme. I have been working for two years with a group which, at first, found it impossible to concentrate. They are settling, and today in three groups of 40 minutes each, we looked at maps of the Middle East, compared routes and dates of Biblical stories with what is going on today. I worked with 17 young people, a fair proportion of that age group on Penrhys. The number has been consistent for six months.

22nd

The café is open Thursday, Friday and Saturday evening. It is the only place for children on Penrhys. Alternatives are to hang out around the pub and the club. This evening 50 children used the premises, some for two hours, the majority for an hour. The youngest was 3 and the oldest 19. We three, Trine served behind the counter, Norah played with younger children and kept a watching brief, I played dominoes and draughts and kept an eye on what was going on. Llanfair has served with perseverance, patience and (usually) pleasure for ten years. A generation of Penrhys children have grown up in

the church. Tonight the total takings were £29, a good night. What was the cost of keeping it open?
This was Saturday evening when half of us were on duty. On Thursday and Friday, all seven residents were serving.

MARCH

1st
A celebration of Dydd Gwyl Dewi. Last year Penrhys celebrated 02-02-02. The highlight of today was a concert divided (like Gaul) into three parts. It began with 50 members of Pendyrus. What a sound in the packed chapel. There were a couple of hundred in the chapel, vestibule and lounge. They were followed by music from Llanfair: Estine, Sadie and Kirsten danced; Hugh and Dylan sang folk songs; Trine sang a Danish song, Chris Fisher arranged a Welsh folk dance. Norah and I were surprised to receive flowers and cards from the Action Group.

3rd
Our 'Community Development' Course began with eight participants.

4th
I welcomed half a dozen to the new 'Understanding the Bible' Course.

5th
The Ash Wednesday prayer is: 'Loving God, I haven't always tried to be good. Today, help me to be kind and forgiving and to help others, just as you help me.' 25 sat in a circle in the café and burnt our palm crosses before going into chapel. After a liturgy of penitence and affirming the healing hands of Jesus, we each said the prayer and marked crosses on our hands. The sign will be remembered.

Sunday 16th
How well Estine led worship. She presided with understanding, flexibility and flair. Her English was excellent and above all she was genuine in sharing her experience and understanding of being a Christian, and a Christian from Madagascar. 'I am grateful that I am poor because in my country it is the poor who attend church. The rich are so satisfied with things that they do not feel need for God.'
Estine was our second volunteer from Akany Avoko.

21st

The pictures of Baghdad were apocalyptic. The Americans used the terms 'shock and awe', believing that Iraq will be beaten into submission by destructive power. It might cause fear, even surrender but it will never produce respect and love. I felt ashamed. This was not a conflict. It was a bully destroying an enemy it describes as sub-human. Ultimate force demands an ultimate enemy, and by creating the 'monster' Saddam Hussein, a force is unleashed which will have monstrous consequences. Bush has captivated Tony Blair. How duped we become when we have power. This evening four discussion groups of 20 young people looked at militarism and war.

Sunday 23rd

The baptism of Jessica Soweri Michelle Coburn, daughter of Donna and Nathan. Llanfair was comfortably full and the service a delight. All the Coburn family were there; Nathan had three of his Fijian friends. Plenty of music including a song in Fijian by four young soldiers.
Donna, one of the most faithful of Llanfair's young people, had a partner, Nathan a Fijian serving in the British Army.

31st

Penrhys Primary School has appointed its first Head-teacher. When the Governing Bodies of the Junior and Infants schools were dissolved at the end of the year, Norah and I planned not to serve again. However, when the governors failed to appoint a Head and Deputy, we agreed to serve for this final year. A delight to see Chris appointed unanimously.
Chris Fisher had been Deputy-Head for several years, and her appointment ensured that good practice would be maintained, but also that there would be fresh initiatives in the 'new school.'

APRIL

3rd

As Penrhys shrinks, the diminishing numbers include a larger proportion of disruptive children and young people. Llanfair knows their backgrounds, and has seen them develop over the years. I compare the list of young people during 10 years: the number has diminished but the proportion of disruptive individuals has increased.

4th

Nick Danziger's 'The British' contains portraits of the British Establishment, the Duke of Westminster, the House of Lords, Trinity College and halfway through the book, you realise there is a second half. The book has two beginnings and you turn the book upside down to start again. The other half contains portraits of poverty and there are pictures from Penrhys. It reveals disastrous divisions within contemporary British society.

17th

As we gathered around the table in the Upper Room, Kelly (aged 11) asked the question, 'Why is this night different from other nights?' I, who am 64 years old, and a son, grandson and descendant of people of faith, answered in Hebrew Tradition, 'Because this night is when we remember that your forefathers were delivered from Egypt, and you were delivered from Egypt; tell it to your children and grandchildren.' This is no result of evolutionary processes! This is no human attempt to make sense of our world! This is our human response to the action of God. Therefore we praise God with our Hallelujah. This is what Jesus did on Passover night before going on to his death, experiencing the betrayal, denial and running away of his friends, and facing the political and religious powers. He died on a Roman cross. An extraordinary evening then and now.

29th

I have been reading the New Testament in Welsh. There is the affirmation page after page, that Jesus Christ was raised from the dead, the event which changed the living story of humankind. We are born to live, die and live in him, with him and for him for eternity. Death has been defeated. The last enemy has been conquered. If there is one difference between the Old and New Testaments it is that fact - the God of Patriarchs, Moses, kings, priests, prophets, people has come in Jesus and through his life, death and resurrection, he never leaves nor forsakes us. I trust I live in the light of that conviction.

30th

The 'jewel in the crown' were the three schools: Nursery at Tir Gwaidd, the Infants and Juniors. Their heads were Bethan Williams, Pat Price and Cerri Morse. Today marked a significant moment in the story. Pat retired 18 months ago. Today Cerri Morse said goodbye, as did Mrs Collins and Mrs Trembeth from the Nursery, Mrs Jones from the Infants and Mrs Lewis, a school secretary. Between them, they had served 100 years on Penrhys and all finished the same day. There is now one school and Chris Fisher will prove a first class head. The deputy is Bethan Williams and there is an experienced, loyal staff. They will maintain a high quality of education, but the situation is so different with 90 local children compared with 600 at its peak.

MAY

12th

At the close of yesterday's delightful baptism, one of the visitors asked,'How long have you been on Penrhys?' I began to answer with 'I was born in Tylorstown, have been a minister 36 years, was instrumental in creating Llanfair in 1992,' when she broke in and asked 'Are you born again?' 'We are born-again Christians.' We live with different agendas. She cannot understand God's mission of care, service and inclusiveness.

JUNE

14th

Perched high on this ridge our flat looks down on the fields beyond the statue, where the isolation hospital used to be, to the golf course and on to the horizon. On both west and east of the ridge are the vestiges of two old coal tips, both completely greened. Also on the ridge is Penrhys Isaf farm, one of the remaining farms of the pre-industrial period. To the east are parts of the Rhondda Fach and to the west a magnificent view of the Rhondda Fawr stretching down from Llwynypia, Tonypandy and Penygraig. Why did I notice the view today? Because of the demolition of the block of flats opposite, flats which have been derelict many years. Behind the flat, the removal of two derelict blocks and good landscaping has improved our views towards Twyn Disgwylfa. We have lived here for 11½ years and at least we have views for our final months!

25th

Norah and I went to the Exhibition at Pontypridd College, specifically to see Rebecca's work. She is enjoying college life and her tutor spoke very well of her. As Beca took us around the exhibition, we felt a little like her parents who are so supportive.

Norah had taken careful interest for many years in Rebecca and had responded to her interest in art and design. It was a delight to see her proceed to further education and to learn later that she graduated.

JULY

8th

Visitors often affirm our work. We work so quietly and patiently that we regard our work as normal: in what other way should Christians live? Isn't Llanfair's life style the norm of Christian people? Eleri Edwards who was a missionary in Madagascar enjoys and admires the work here. Having lived in community in Antananarivo she is aware of the difficulty of creating community at Llanfair and is amazed by its stability. Tom Evans brought 15 religious education advisors in conference in Cardiff. We met at school where Chris spoke and I walked them to Llanfair where Norah and I spoke, and Norah took them around Llanfair, sharing the work of each project in turn. They were pleased with what they saw as 'a perfect example of a church/school relationship.'

AUGUST

5th

It seems to go on all day and every day. From the window I face the world of drugs. The flat on our right has been used for injecting for over a year. The customers come hour after hour, normally in groups of half a dozen who enter the flat and come out half an hour later. Then once a day a car arrives bringing supplies. Two dozen hang around, most well known to us, ranging from mid teens to the 40s. Using the same outside space are children playing games. They regard the gathering of the drug users as a normal part of life.

6th

A blessing to begin the day with Holy Communion and complete the day with Compline and Bible study. I am making all things new. It is accomplished. How critical to receive reassurance in light of yesterday's and today's and tomorrow's despair. I see what is happening in those young faces, haunted by the poison of drugs. Most have been through deep waters of neglect, some from their earliest days. I see those who will follow them, the young neglected today. I wish I could share the Gospel in word and action, so that they might believe and begin the new life. God knows I have tried, but I am aware of personal failure. Have I tried hard enough? Faithfully enough? Imaginatively and sensitively enough?

7th

The relationship between text and context is critical. Text relates to the Faith of the One, Holy, Catholic and Apostolic Church, centred on Scripture. The context relates to our address of Penrhys, Rhondda, Wales. Llanfair must be faithful to both principles. If we are, God will bless the seeds sown.

20th

Breaking bread and pouring wine brings us to the crucified and risen Christ. The Gospel is the heart of life. The Eucharist is complete: prayers, reading and meditating about the Bible, sharing bread and wine. There is a combination of words and music, of sitting, walking, standing - facing each other when seated and when standing around the table. There is the passing of bread and cup, the movement of hand and eye, and speech - all of us speaking in turn and serving each other.

30th

As Mars rose in the south-east above Wattstown, the slim crescent moon disappeared across the western horizon in the direction of Gelli. The fireworks at the Beacon marked the close of the Festival. Penrhys had been entertained by Pendyrus, a group who sang from Godspell and Jesus Christ Superstar, a rock and roll band - all at the amphitheatre created eleven years ago. Penrhys was at its best and every visitor was full of praise. The venue is one of the most symbolic and scenic in Wales. Norah was delighted by an excellent response to the exhibition on Fair Trade.

SEPTEMBER

4th

I completed serving as Chairman of the Penrhys Partnership. I handed over to Professor Kevin Morgan. I feel as relaxed about relinquishing my responsibilities as I did last November when I handed over the Chair of the Penrhys Action Group to Robert Poole. I will feel the same when I complete my ministry at Llanfair. I have done my best to introduce life in its fullness to individuals and the community.

15th

Years 5 and 6 arrived with Cliff and his class of 24 children. There are now only two mainstream classes in the Junior section of the school, but the advantage is that we know them by name. The children taught our overseas volunteers the pattern of the morning, and they responded in song and music. Later I met the volunteers for the first time. We begin studying 'God's People have two hands' and this evening we met at Sharon's for our weekly common meal.

The volunteers for our final six months were Elyse and Naomi from Madagascar, and Ilona from Hungary. A fourth volunteer, Dorothea came from Germany but soon realized Penrhys was not for her. She was the only volunteer during the 12 years to leave prematurely.

19th

Four discussion groups with 20 young people was followed by an excellent disco.

23rd

I am to give the BBC Regeneration Lecture at Cardiff University. My experience of community development is a result of working in and with community. I am not a theoretician and have had little time to study the subject. All I will do is tell a story, a story centred on Penrhys. That story is based on the motivation of the Gospel and, without that, the story has no drive.

29th

A most creative house meeting. We met in Ilona's flat. She had prepared meticulously. Elyse shared reflections with thoroughness and initiated an excellent discussion on key issues: how to work with children in Sunday school; the beginning of craft work. Three mature young people are concerned and share new ideas. It could be a most productive year.

30th

The Bible Reading class met: Ivor, Kelly, Bev, Sam, (who have never read the Bible) our three volunteers and Norah. We began in the Old Testament with Amos, Jeremiah and the Servant Songs which they found amazing, a shock to the system.

OCTOBER

6th

Fred and Christine Noden are loyal friends. Our ministerial lives have criss-crossed, beginning when I succeeded him at Manselton. Fifteen years later he

invited Penrhys into the Partners Group of Churches and ever since, a van load of clothes comes twice each year to Llanfair.
It was good to see the Nodens for the first time since Fred had retired. They arrived with the six monthly delivery of high quality clothes for the boutique.

7th

Mattie Collins, leader of the Labour Group in Rhondda, said to me that 'if we could solve the problems of Penrhys, we could solve the toughest social problems in the country.' Penrhys is a focus of what happens to the marginalized, and reflects what takes place in hundreds of similar communities. We struggle to find an appropriate ministry in work and worship, the two sides of Llanfair's life.
Mrs Collins, the local member for Tylorstown had shared this with me in my early years on Penrhys.

14th

Penrhys always surprises by its compassion, friendship, loyalty and shared grief. A middle aged man living alone was buried and the chapel was full to overflowing. People listened with great care. It felt like Jesus' first sermon in Nazareth when all eyes were fixed on him. Rena read from the Beatitudes in front of her friends from the pub. I returned to the pub. Everyone was grateful for the dignity of the day.

18th

Early this morning as we left Penrhys, a large fox darted across the road towards the disused quarry. This evening as we descended the steps from the Monastery Chapel, Beca, Norah and I were mesmerised by a star shooting out of the heavens. Both were signs of beauty gifted to us on our final visit to Caldey with the people of Penrhys.
Our final visit to Caldey.

NOVEMBER

13th

Last February a small group began exploring the Bible. They were suspicious and some thought it mythological and therefore untrue; they feared the Bible created fanatics. Because this group trusted Llanfair, and knew me through community events, secular courses I had led, they wondered why I trusted the Bible. Last week we finished the Old Testament. The OT Scriptures were complete in themselves, had created the Hebrew people and were the foundation of three religions. I ended with: 'Why should Jewish people create the New Testament which would undermine the Old?' We began with passages from the Pauline Letters and I asked them to choose a sentence: all found it new, radical, challenging and questioning. 'How could Paul claim he saw the creative light of God shining from the face of Jesus? Do we have to wait until next week for an answer?'

29th

Forty children, including a dozen teenagers, spent two hours in the café or as a base for the evening. Nothing unusual happened. I sat in my corner and played dominoes with a dozen different children, from Jodie and Thomas who are 8, to Liam and Keira who are 14. Norah played games at another table, as did Rena, while Ilona was fully stretched behind the counter where she took £43, a lot of different items in an evening. We four returned home at 9.30 feeling a job had been well done.

DECEMBER

12th

The three Christmas Dinner turkeys had been cooked by Myra, Pru and Norah; a dozen others served, washed, dried, gave the sweets and coffee in the café. 60 meals were served, including the helpers. Hard work but fun.

Sunday 14th

The Nativity was amongst our most effective and best attended. The children performed very well; the chapel was so full we brought in extra chairs. More than a hundred in service. The atmosphere was relaxed because Penrhys is like one big family, and attentive because the adults were listening for their children. Everyone seemed proud and pleased. The only sadness was that baby Ieuan is in hospital again and Jesus was played by a doll for the first time for four years. Many highlights: five of LYT came; Tomos Bálint was shepherd No 6. He sat with me most of the time. Café was full for an hour afterwards and the atmosphere was perfect. This evening we went to the Buy as you View Christmas Carol Concert. I spoke towards the end.

16th

We greeted the older Primary children. The chapel was full of our friends: Chris (head teacher), staff and children. We all know and care for each other. Our half hour was sheer delight: the tree and its light, the crib, banner, lighting candles, children singing, prayers. As they returned to school the bell rang to thank them for coming.

17th

A beautiful morning: cold, sharp, blue skied with a warm sun. The infants and nursery children were full of expectancy as they looked for a big tree, but were surprised that it reached the ceiling. They liked the silver, gold and red balls; the candles were lit and later blown out: three red advent candles, Nursery Millennium candle, lamp, central candle, candle by the icon, the triple candle on the piano; and finally the snowball behind the stable. They were delighted by angels on the font and on the banner. Everything gave pleasure. We sang and prayed and as they returned to school, the bell rang them on their way. What a privilege it had been for us - and for them.

19th

At 4.30, Keira came to the back door.'I hope the party is still on. I'll prepare the food. I'll let everyone know,' and so at 8, twenty young people arrived. They ate, danced, played games and were happy with each other, leaving contentedly at 10.15 and we gave thanks. And so ended the week of the dinner with 60 people, the infants party with 17 children, the junior party with 18 children and this evening more than 20 teenagers.

24th

I did not anticipated a queue waiting to come to church. Within 10 minutes, more arrived and Norah had to duplicate extra services. 60 were in service, a large congregation for Christmas Eve.

25th, Christmas Day

Such a happy Christmas because of a most positive Advent. Since lighting the first Advent candle and singing the 'Seven O's' the whole sequence of events has been fulfilled. We have organized good social events, worship has been fulfilling and Llanfair is respected and cared for by the community. Llanfair has touched 400 people this Christmas in a community of 700.
'The seven antiphons consist of prayers addressed to God, or Christ, in the person of each of these word-pictures; they all begin with 'O' and thus were known collectively as the 'great O's.

2004

JANUARY

1st

A day in which we experienced much genuine affection. For almost all our years here, we have gone to Myra's for a meal on New Year's Day. She prepares with great thoroughness and it is always delightful. This evening Myra had been helped by Mitch, the three young people - Lissie, Emma and Courtney, and we were joined by Aisha, Pru and Paul; at the close of the evening Griff set off fireworks. The evening could not have been more pleasant and showed Penrhys at its most friendly and hospitable.

20th

At the final Joint Council I gave my 51st Report to a full complement which included David Cornick, the General Secretary of the URC, Peter Noble, Presbyterian visitors and Hugh Jones who came for the first time. Ifor and Hugh presented a splendid reflection of Llanfair's mission: Hugh's thanksgiving that he had become a Christian, and Ivor's honest assertion that 'I am not a Christian, but my life has changed because of the church, and one day I could become a Christian.' A kairos moment as they spoke.
Peter Noble is Moderator for Wales of the URC.

21st

A new relationship and a fresh programme in the life of Llanfair. The new Genesis project which started in the redundant Infants School provides a service for babies and children under the age of three, so that parents can embark on further education or training programmes. Two helpers are Sarah and Jessica who spent a lot of time in Llanfair when they were younger. They felt it would be good for the children to experience the church. The five helpers and five children looked at the bell ringing, liked the lights in the chapel, put their hands together for prayers and blew the candle out together. This was the first excursion for the children. They enjoyed squash and biscuits in the lounge. They intend to come once a month.

FEBRUARY

3rd

Our first fare-well. A few years ago we had a group of young people who seemed designed for leadership. They had been members of the youth group, sung in choirs, been on holidays to Caldey, Skye, London, Hungary. They shaped themselves into the Llanfair Youth Team (LYT) and led worship once a month. As they approached mid and late teens they drifted away; most no longer live on Penrhys but naturally share common memories, and speak so positively of their experience of the Church. Their time at Llanfair was so important to them. Six of them invited us to a meal at the Bertie in Trehafod. It was a pleasure to see they are making something of their lives: four in steady employment, one a second year university student and one a young mother. Two not present are also in employment.

4th

A stimulating day with visitors from Carmarthen. Peter Jones, Chaplain at Trinity, brought 16 students from the theology department who have begun a model on 'understanding community.'

13th

Twenty young people have been attending discussion groups for the last 18 months, a considerable proportion of that age group on Penrhys. This evening I met three groups of eight. Each was so different: the first with potential leaders of youth work; the second involved my listening and trying to make contact; the third listened intently to Naomi talking about Akany Avoko. Then all came to an excellent disco.

Sunday 15th

A remarkable occasion for Rena's family: the baptism of Kelly's three children, Zoe's son, Claire's son, and Gary and Donna's little boy. The baptism of the six, marks the culmination of a significant element of ministry: preparing the soil for the sowing of seeds.

21st

Our last normal Saturday. There have been more than a thousand like this! They are an example of the faithfulness the Gospel demands. Saturday evening provides a dependable rhythm in an unreliable community. More than 60 people used the café. I played dominoes and chess and enjoyed the company of the children. I sat in my usual spot with my eyes roving the whole of the café.

23rd

Norah and I are fulfilling our commitments with enthusiasm and thoroughness. We are not ending our world here with a whimper. We welcomed Nan, Julia and the special needs children. Llanfair is greatly blessed by the ministry with children. Our Annual Church/ Projects Dinner. 29 of us enjoyed a most pleasant evening together.

24th

Hilary arrived with Years 1 and 2, and Diane with special needs. The class is being introduced to baptism and had brought their pet bear, Spencer Bear, for baptism, with parents and God parents. A party followed.

25th

I prepared carefully for a new, challenging congregation which met this morning for Ash Wednesday. Five helpers in the new Genesis Project brought four children between 2 and 3 years old. Seventeen met for confession, forgiveness, marking the hands with the cross and sharing communion - all received bread and water. By 11, Norah and I were in school and to our surprise, children and staff were out in the southern facing yard. We each planted a rowan tree and were presented with a lovely bench from the community. Later, Ash Wednesday service began in the café and ended in the chapel: 20 present for an act of devotion which felt very right.

27th

The last weekend at Llanfair, Penrhys, Rhondda. Despite trauma and farewells, it is the right decision for us and we trust for Llanfair and Penrhys. It is reassuring that we have no choice and that I continue to the end of the month of my 65th birthday. Our last Friday night: dominoes in the café; discussions interrupted by someone breaking the fire glass. All out for ten minutes. Then a good disco. Our last evening with 60 children, including 20 young people.

28th

Such warmth, affection, respect and understanding. Although neither Norah nor I wished or anticipated such a fare-well, and although at the end of the day, we feel physically and emotionally drained, we are deeply grateful for the effort, skill and passion which shaped this day. A large number in this community have grasped what we have attempted to fulfil during the past 18 years. The concert began at 1. The bench was in the centre of the chapel floor and we were the chief guests. The chapel was packed and there were many in the vestibule. Chris Fisher conducted and Cerri Morse played for the children to sing (including Jackson), Ilona led a Hungarian dance, a young friend of Gerwyn's sang, as did Amy and the Malagasies. A short break for children to leave. During the short break, Norah was interviewed for S4C. Beverley, Hugh, Dylan and Amy then sang before finally we were taken to Canolfan Rhys for a superb 'thank you' film in the form of a CD carefully prepared for our leaving.

Sunday 29th

The day has come and almost gone. In 20 minutes, I retire after 36 years in pastoral charge and 7 years of training. Thirty in chapel this morning. As always we read the Bible in turn; I had written my sermon, read it and each member of the congregation commented. We completed the service by singing 'Put Peace into each others hands' and celebrated Communion by standing in a circle. This afternoon more than 100 present, including Doris Leyshon. I had written my sermon, but felt quite relaxed. The caring for us was very clear. After the service, chatting, presents and tea. And so retirement has come.

It was so appropriate to sing Fred Kaan's hymn in the morning service, and it was such a joy to welcome Doris Leyshon, our long-standing friend and colleague in the afternoon.

POSTLUDE

There is a time for the evening under starlight,
A time for the evening under lamplight
(the evening with the photograph album).

T S Eliot, East Coker

Our final days at Llanfair ended not with a whimper but with a bang. Norah and I worked until the last day of February (the 29th), the day of retirement which also happened to be the twelfth anniversary of the opening of Llanfair in 1992. Our final celebrations were local, and as centred on Penrhys as had been our lives for 18 years. The days were full of laughter and tears and we knew we loved and were loved.

We were reluctant to say fare-well to Llanfair and Penrhys which had provided light and shade for so many years, but we knew two things. It is important to say good-bye. As a minister I knew I must not interfere in the life Llanfair would now be forging. This would not be easy because Norah and I had served as 'midwives' in this new birth. Yet strangely it did not prove difficult because we had learned the lesson of saying goodbye at Llanidloes, Manselton and as Moderator. A minister must have grace to move on. It was also important for Norah and me to fare-forward. We needed time, space and silence to rediscover that our relationship was not dependent upon common action and shared ministry. What would we discover in the time God would give us in retirement?

As Norah and I celebrated the 40th anniversary of our marriage in August 2004, and the 40th anniversary of my ordination in December 2007, I felt the need to ask 'What has made me who I am?'

I am the son of Tylorstown, the village between the Giant Tip and Bristol Tump, between the sound of trams climbing the incline and skylarks hovering over the mountain. Home, street, school, chapel and Welfare Hall helped shape me. Amongst a myriad of formative personal influences, Mrs John Griff Davies of Sunday School, Alwyn Charles minister of Ebenezer, Pennar Davies of Coleg Coffa, Stanley Greenslade of Christchurch, Robert Paul and Ford Battles of Hartford stand out as beacons of faith. I am who I am because of them.

I am the son of my parents, my extended family, and more recently I have grasped the unconscious shaping influence of my ancestors: Carmarthen farm labourers, Pembrokeshire farmers, seamen from Cei Newydd and Cricieth and particularly, colliers from Tylorstown. All have exerted a gentle pressure. I am who I am because of them.

I lived from 1939 to 1964 in Tylorstown, between the Great Tip and Bristol Tump. Norah and our family lived from 1986 to 2004 on Penrhys between the Great Tip and Bristol Tump. I had no choice in my first residence, but many decisions coalesced for us to choose to live on Penrhys.

In the journey I have been blessed by the love and companionship of Norah, also the child of a mining community and a Nonconformist family, but privileged by a truly bilingual upbringing and education. In our journey together we have learned from each other, and we have also learned from our children, Hugh, Dylan and Catherine. They are now adults and we are grateful that we, and their families, share a common pilgrimage.

Through it all, but in retrospect, is it possible to discern the gentle but firm hand of a 'divinity that shapes our ends, rough-hew them how we will?' (Words by Hamlet, almost my father's final words to me.) Throughout life there has been the Jesus who has kind hands, the crucified and risen Lord to whom I responded in faith in 1960, and needed daily to guard and guide. Here in Newchapel, and now in 2008, beneath the starlight and the lamplight and in the sunlight, I resolve with Eliot, that 'old men ought to be explorers (and to) fare forward.'